FAITH IN JESUS

FAITH IN JESUS

WHAT DOES IT MEAN TO BELIEVE IN HIM?

EDWIN AARON EDIGER

WestBow Press books may be ordered through booksellers or by contacting:

WestBow Press
A Division of Thomas Nelson
1663 Liberty Drive
Bloomington, IN 47403
www.westbowpress.com
1-(866) 928-1240

ISBN: 978-1-4497-6867-6 (e)
ISBN: 978-1-4497-6865-2 (sc)
ISBN: 978-1-4497-6866-9 (hc)

Library of Congress Control Number: 2012918118

Printed in the United States of America

WestBow Press rev. date: 8/26/2013

DEDICATION

Dedicated to those who promote the gospel of the grace of God without compromise, warriors all, who, "earnestly contend for the faith which was once delivered unto the saints," Amen.

TABLE OF CONTENTS

ACKNOWLEDGEMENTS

The custom of expressing gratitude to those who have contributed to the production of a book offers an author the opportunity to reflect on the process that he has undertaken. While this writer will express gratitude to those who have selflessly and sacrificially been part of the final product, there is a feeling that I would be remiss if I did not express the debt owed to two essential ingredients without which this book would have been impossible. The first of them is the gospel presented in the Bible with magnificent clarity. This book is an attempt to reflect what God has made abundantly clear.

With apologies for what is not meant to be self-commendation, this writer is grateful for his own salvation that occurred more than a half century ago at five years of age. Thank you, Jesus. Reflecting on what happened to me when my mother, who is now in heaven, presented the gospel to my sister and me has been a source of indispensable inspiration. Thank you, Mom. The faith of a child that I exercised so long ago has served as a model that can only be fully understood by those who have likewise similarly put their trust in Jesus for their eternal destiny, whether they did so as a child or as an adult.

Walking in the footsteps of ancient travelers is not always easy for interpreters who attempt to do so in the 21st century. This writer's appreciation for and understanding of those who trod the dusty roads in biblical times has been immeasurably enhanced by the experience of accompanying my father on numerous missionary journeys without the convenience of modern transportation. I recall many afternoons during my childhood spent lying on a church bench listening as my father counseled indigenous pastors as they discussed church matters. Recalling those days brings back memories of witnessing events literally not that dissimilar to those experienced by companions of the apostle Paul. Thank you, Dad.

I wish to especially thank my wife Joy who lives up to her name and has been that for me for more than 40 years of my life. She has been an enabler, in a positive sense, of every endeavor that has been meaningful to me. She has put up with a person whose intense focus and attention has many times been difficult to engage. Her gentle spirit and tenderness have influenced countless kindergartners whose educational pursuits she has positively launched and will be remembered by them their whole lives. I envy them. Joy has read every word (in English) of the manuscript and given her valuable input, both technical and personal. The depth of her love for Jesus, her Savior, has been an inspiration to me. Her patience with me during the writing of this book has been invaluable. I love you. Thank you, sweetheart.

In this digital age computer skills are indispensable. My skills are woefully lacking, matched only by a utilitarian stubbornness that refuses to learn any more than I have to know about computers. Without the assistance of my brother-in-law, Jon, this endeavor would have been impossible, or perhaps taken longer than I may have left to live.

Thanks to Jon the complexity of the computer component of writing a book, which continues to bewilder me, has actually come to pass. Not only has Jon been of technical assistance, he has also served as a trusted and confidential focus group of one, on whom ideas have been tested. I may well rue those rare occasions when I have ignored his valuable suggestions. The voices one could listen to are many but singular trusted opinions are worth their weight in gold and are the greatest of timesavers. For doing and being all of the above, thank you, Jon.

I am particularly grateful for the editorial assistance of Dr. Roy B. Zuck. His corrective and supportive hand is apparent, especially to me, on every page written. I have benefited not only from Dr. Zuck's editorial ability but also his lifelong walk with Jesus. The editing was done while Dr. Zuck was undergoing serious medical issues. This extraordinary man brings to mind another exemplary octogenarian, the biblical Caleb, who at eighty-five said, "Give me this mountain" (Joshua 14:12), by which he meant, "Let me, with God's help conquer these Canaanites." A life well lived is one worth imitating and a beautiful thing to behold. Dr. Zuck's editing was always done graciously, and although I have tried not to, if I have failed to follow his advice, this book is poorer for not having done so. Thank you, Dr. Zuck.

I am thankful for friends and other members in my immediate and extended family that I have not mentioned by name who knowingly and unknowingly, have played a part in the writing of this book. I am grateful for their prayer and support. In addition to them there have been teachers, professors, and pastors who have had a positive influence on me. I alone am responsible for any shortcomings in this book.

Chapter 1

The Soteriological Paradigm

When James Harrison, an Australian man, was fourteen years of age, he underwent major chest surgery and was given thirteen liters of blood. At the time it was discovered that Harrison had an extremely rare and life-saving antibody in his blood. Since then his blood has been used to save the lives of more than two million babies. These babies had blood plasma that was either Rh-negative or Rh-positive while their mothers were the opposite. The blood type incompatibility results in either death or permanent brain damage. Amazingly, Harrison's blood has the ability to treat this condition, so that lives have been saved and brain damage prevented.

The story of James Harrison was posted online and received many responses. One of them said this of Harrison: "in this day and age, heaven bound he is for sure" ("'Man with the golden arm' saves 2 million babies in half a century of donating rare type of blood," http://www.dailymail.co.uk, accessed 7/6/2012). Contrary to many people's belief, including that of the writer of that well-intentioned e-mail, whether or not James Harrison is headed for heaven, is not because of his generosity in giving of his own blood that has granted physical life and mental health to millions. While his blood, undeniably, has the ability to save and improve the quality of human lives, it has no power to prevent his or anyone else's spiritual death.

What can prevent spiritual death and provide eternal life? Or in the words of the Philippian jailer in Acts 16:30: "Sirs, what must I do to be saved?" The answer Paul gave that inquirer seems simple enough (Acts 16:31): "Believe on the Lord Jesus Christ, and thou shalt be saved, and thy house." Simple, yet profound and far-reaching as these words may be, they have been the subject of almost endless theologizing. Given the foundational nature of eternal salvation, one would expect that Scripture would be clear and unambiguous in its presentation of the gospel. While such is indeed the case, diverse interpretations of the gospel abound and continue to be propagated. Since there are so many opinions about the nature of the gospel message, why is another one needed? This is because an impasse seems to have been reached. The theological logjam needs a breakthrough.

Why has a subject of such significance and magnitude not been settled long ago? Early on, the church dealt with a controversy about Gentile conversion at the Jerusalem Council and issued its decision in the form of a letter that is preserved for us in Acts 15:23-29. Later in church history councils dealt with other theological questions as they came up. Why is the church, which is approaching the five-hundredth anniversary of the Protestant Reformation, still engaged in theological tinkering when it comes to the subject of salvation? Is there no definitive biblical answer? The present writer believes that there is, and while this book is not intended to be a presentation of something new, its desired purpose is to provide a route for a theological return, to reclaim biblical ground.

How is it that what should be the ultimate unifying message of the church has become a focal point for doctrinal divisiveness? Conservative evangelical opinion on the nature of salvation seems to divide and multiply. Why is this happening? While the causes are no doubt multiple and complex, with nearly two thousand years of practice and indefatigable persistence, the enemy of men's souls has found strategic, many times institutional, means to prevent the clear interpretation, articulation, and dissemination of the gospel.

One of Satan's strategies that has met with considerable success in other areas of doctrine has been the pitting of Scripture against itself. This is seen in the Wellhausen view of a multiple authorship of the Pentateuch, the first five books of the Old Testament. Another is the theory of a dual authorship of Isaiah. The biblical text has been subjected to this strategy; and even God Himself has not been spared by those who see a different God in the Old Testament and the New. The unending search for sources of the New Testament Gospels demonstrates, among other things, the need for a unifying principle. While it has long been in vogue to emphasize differences in the Gospel accounts, this present work seeks to demonstrate the unity of the biblical record.

This is particularly important for soteriology. Many scholars, while acknowledging divine authorship, observe and emphasize divergence rather than congruence. This work, while not denying differences, will show that they are far outweighed by a unity of purpose, and a hermeneutical paradigm shared by all of Scripture. To be useful, a paradigm must not only explain all the details, but it also must not be of such a general nature, that, while accounting for everything, is of little or no practical interpretational value. Hopefully the evidence that is provided will be that. The paradigm, which will be explained and demonstrated, comes directly from the biblical text. Hopefully, it will become apparent that the proposed paradigm is not a framework superimposed on the text by the interpreter, but one that is shared by the original authors, both human and divine.

This idea is offered with trepidation and humility, yet boldness. The reader is not being asked to accept this as *the* paradigm, unless it is supported by all the biblical evidence. To be pointing out something so obvious is almost embarrassing and yet this paradigm is often unrecognized and ignored. One would expect something as basic as the gospel message to be simple to understand, and it is; and it is hoped that this explanation will also be that. While that seems obvious enough, Satan seeks to complicate and cloud the clear message of the gospel; the simple has become complex, the concise has become convoluted.

The intent of this work is not simply intellectual, so that we can love God better with our minds. The primary purpose is that it be implemented in the propagation of the gospel message. Indeed, such was the desire and example of the biblical authors, whose united proclamation we would do well to imitate. The hope and prayer is that the saving message, which is already biblically clear, will be clearly understood so that it will be communicated effectively.

The value of looking at the text with a correct biblical lens will become apparent when it is applied to the requirement for salvation. Interpretational detours have resulted from a failure to use the biblical paradigm. Entire soteriological systems have been birthed from and driven by a reliance on mistaken notions. In the intense search for biblical answers to basic soteriological questions, many times wrong questions are being asked of the text. The answer to these questions may be logical and coherent, albeit less than biblically comprehensive or satisfactory. Two basic components are necessary for a correct understanding of the biblical text in soteriological contexts. One is structural, the other is semantic.

The Structural Paradigm

The 20th century was an important one in human history. Change took place at an almost dizzying pace. The church in America was not immune to change. Waves of theological liberalism that had swept over from Europe in the previous century came to a head. Intense debates took place between theological liberals and conservatives in academic circles as well as in churches throughout the country. Theological conservatives reacted to what they perceived as the subjectivity of liberal positions. Basic to the debate was the issue of propositional truth. Does the Bible have objective statements that are true, or is it a subjective account of people and their encounters with God? Churches split, denominations splintered—some were convinced by liberal arguments, others by conservative ones.

Prominent theologians and scholars with expertise in various academic specialties contributed to the debates. Notable in the conservative camp were the Princetonian theologians such as Benjamin B. Warfield and J. Gresham Machen. As they passed from the scene, they were replaced by other theologians and scholars, one of whom was Gordon H. Clark (1902-1985), a Reformed philosopher, logician, and prolific writer. Without a doubt, he is a formidable intellect. His contributions to the theological and philosophical wars with liberalism and modernism are legendary, and his influence on soteriology continues to the present day.

The contention of this present book is that Gordon Clark and conservatives with similar views, many of whom were influenced by him, unwittingly perhaps, have affected the direction of the soteriological debate in a detrimental way. This should in no way be construed as an attack on either the man Gordon Clark nor diminish the enormous value of his contributions to the debate over propositional truth. Clark was at his best when he brought his talents and erudition in philosophy and logic to bear on the subject of truth. But he must be viewed in light of the theological context in which he lived. Not only did he face the challenge of liberalism and modernism, but he also encountered the inherent subjectivity of neo-orthodoxy. His ideas were forged in the crucible of theological controversy. Clark himself provides a window into that world:

> By and large, twentieth century religion is irrational and anti-intellectual. The earlier modernism was covertly so; the later humanism, neo-orthodoxy or existentialism are violently so. Anti-intellectualism has no place for Biblical and Calvinistic faith. . .

.Karl Barth, for example, ridicules the empty tomb and talks vaguely about "the Easter event." Instead of preaching propositions, these men recommend an irrational experience, an encounter, a wager, a confrontation. If anything is to be believed, it is that authentic Christianity is self-contradictory (Gordon Clark, *Faith and Saving Faith* [Jefferson, MD: Trinity Foundation, 1983], 111).

With his opposition to neo-orthodoxy Clark's emphasis on theological objectivity as opposed to experiential subjectivity reached its peak.

In examining Clark's views the present writer is aware of the high esteem in which he is held. The late John Robbins, who made it his mission to keep the memory of Clark alive, wrote the following about his mentor:

> . . .few seminary students hear his name even mentioned in their classes, much less are required to read his books. If I might draw a comparison, it is as though theological students in the mid-sixteenth century never heard their teachers mention Martin Luther or John Calvin. . . .you ought not consider yourself well educated until you are familiar with the philosophy of Gordon Haddon Clark (John W. Robbins, *The Trinity Review*, "An Introduction to Gordon H. Clark," www.trinityfoundation.org).

Certainly a debt of gratitude is owed to Gordon Clark and all who labored to articulate and defend the concept of propositional truth. This present work is not against propositional truth. Propositional truth is fundamental to biblical orthodoxy. However, the crucial question is this: "Given the existence of propositional truth in the Bible, in what way is it employed when it comes to salvation and what response to it does God require?" That is where the present writer believes a theological wrong turn has been taken.

The Case for Maximum Content

For Gordon Clark, in a sense propositional truth was an end in itself. Given the existence of propositional truth, the only possible response to it, according to Clark, was either to believe the declarative statements made to be true or believe them to be false. Being a philosopher and logician, for Clark it was entirely an epistemological (the study of knowledge) matter; propositional truth comes under the epistemological category of philosophy, of which he was a practitioner.

Propositional statements or declarative sentences are viewed in the conceptual framework of "content." Fundamentally content is what fits into a container, either literally or figuratively. The epistemological content in the container or box can be expanded or contracted to include a greater or lesser number of propositional statements. Clark himself recognized this characteristic of his model when he used it for understanding soteriology. Logically content is what is to be believed.

Clark recognized that the question that needed to be answered if one employed the concept of content in relation to salvation, was, "What goes in the container?" Or "What must a person believe in order to be saved?" Giving the example of the early church father, Justin Martyr, Clark notes that, in his opinion (Clark's), Justin Martyr's beliefs raised the issue of content: "He must have been regenerated and justified, must he not? But it is doubtful that any strong Lutheran or Calvinistic church would have admitted him even to communicant membership. His view of the Atonement was abysmal" (*Faith and Saving Faith*, 109). Clark then writes, "Now, Justin Martyr was not a moron. Morons have doubtless been regenerated and justified. . . Is there any passage in Scripture that identifies, in a scale of decreasing knowledge, the very minimum by which someone can still be justified?" (ibid.).

Clark thought that soteriologically there are only two logical possibilities: to believe a minimum number of propositions or to believe a maximum number of them. He did not like the alternative of a minimum number of propositions that would fit into the content box. "Even if a minimum of propositions could be listed. . .it would still be the wrong question with a perverted outlook. This is the basic weakness contributing to the low spiritual level of most so-called fundamentalist congregations" (ibid.). Conversely, after commenting positively on the thirty-three chapters of the Westminster Confession, consisting of propositional statements, Clark concluded, "The Bible commands the maximum, not the minimum. Jesus said, Matthew 28:19, 20 Teach all nations. . .instructing them to observe *all whatever* I command you" (ibid., 109-10, italics Clark's). Being a logician, Clark's propositional content box led him to write the following:

> There seems to be no other conclusion but that God justifies sinners by means of many combinations of propositions believed. For which reason a minister should not confine himself to topics popularly thought to be "evangelistic," but should preach the whole counsel of God, trusting that God will give someone the gift of faith through sermons on the Trinity, eschatology, or the doctrine of immediate imputation (ibid., 110).

With Clark's maximum content model it would be pointless to do any kind of "exit interview" with a recent convert, to determine what had resulted in the giving of the gift of faith, because, as Clark believed, God gives faith as He sees fit without any specific, identifiable, content, consisting of a propositional statement, or combination of them, that would apply to everyone. A new convert would probably be unable to answer the question anyway, since for Clark the working of God in salvation seems to be shrouded in mystery. This sounds strangely similar to the Roman Catholic view of "implicit faith" in which faith need not have explicit content. However, in Clark's propositional soteriological construct everything needs to be explicit and has the entire biblical canon as its content. Since man is not privy to the divine working, evangelistic methodology amounts to throwing out biblical statements with the hope that something will stick and result in salvation.

With such a view, if you were told you had only five minutes to present the gospel to someone, and you knew it would be the last and only opportunity you would have, you could say anything so long as it was biblical, and that would be the gospel, and God would save the individual. To be fair, a person using that method would probably be guided by a set of priorities so that, given a time limitation, they would not immediately engage in a recitation of biblical genealogies or Levitical instructions, for example, but rather material that was recognizable as soteriological. Nevertheless the logic of the choice of minimum versus maximum, the latter which was Clark's preferred evangelistic method, is problematic. Surely something is awry. The example of evangelistic preaching in the book of Acts did not follow either of those patterns, minimum or maximum. Clark presents a false choice because his conceptual structural framework is unbiblical.

The Case for Minimum Content

While Clark was comfortable with the "maximum" alternative, in which the gospel consists of many propositional statements, that cannot be specifically defined or enumerated, the "minimum" route has been taken by other conservatives. A prime example of the latter is the position of the Grace Evangelical Society (GES). They employ Clark's conceptual framework that there is a content to the gospel, but they are driven logically to the "minimum" portion of the epistemological continuum. Their statement of faith includes the following: "Faith is the conviction that something is true. To believe in Jesus ("he who believes in Me has everlasting life") is to be convinced that He guarantees everlasting life to all who simply believe in Him for it (John 4:14; 5:24; 6:47; 11:26; 1 Tim. 1:16)" (www.faithalone.org, accessed 8/11/12). According to GES, the content of the propositional truth, what must be believed to be true to acquire eternal life, is the statement, "He guarantees everlasting life to all who simply believe in Him for it."

One widely held assumption by those of the minimalist camp is that the Gospel of John is the only New Testament book whose purpose is evangelistic. While some may be careful to say that it is the only book whose *stated* purpose is evangelistic, the practical result is that the Johannine Gospel is given evangelistic exclusivity. This is usually taken from John 20:31: "But these are written, that ye might believe that Jesus is the Christ, the Son of God; and that believing ye might have life through his name." The first difficulty encountered is that "these" (ταῦτα–plural, neuter, pronoun) most likely has as its antecedent "signs" (σημεῖα–plural, neuter, noun) in verse 30, rather than being a purpose statement for the entire Gospel of John. "Signs" (σημεῖα) are found in John's Gospel, but other material is found there as well.

For instance, John's famous first eighteen verses, his prologue, do not fit the category of a "sign" (σημεῖον). The account of Jesus recruiting His first disciples in John 1:35-51 is another example, as is the Upper Room discourse. Examples could be multiplied. The point is that the proof text (John 20:31) used to establish the point that John's Gospel is the only New Testament book with an evangelistic purpose, does not necessarily say what its proponents say it does. One still might argue that the overall purpose of the book is evangelistic, given the importance that the author places on "signs" (σημεῖα). Detailed proof is needed if the Johannine Gospel's uniquely evangelistic status relative to the four Gospels, as well as the rest of the New Testament, is to be maintained.

The other Gospel writers, as well as all the other New Testament writers, must be allowed to speak for themselves. The problem with some who hold the assumption that John's Gospel is the only book with an evangelistic purpose is that they use it to restrict to that book the data for their interpretation of what the gospel message is. They predetermine the parameters of the outcome of their inquiry by ruling other evidence inadmissible. But the basis for their ruling of the inadmissibility of evidence is suspect at best. Often this minimalist approach involves a search of John's Gospel for something on which to base a synthesis sentence (a proposition), which (according to those holding the view) is to be believed. The synthesis propositional statement from the GES website is an example of this. The difficulty of agreement on what specific synthetic proposition is to be believed militates against that being what the Gospel writers had in mind when they presented something as important as the requirement for eternal salvation. As will be demonstrated from the text, the four Gospels, each in perfect harmony, contribute to the single salvific message.

The Case for Medium Content

Some within the GES movement felt uncomfortable, to say the least, with content minimalism, because it fails to mention Jesus' death and resurrection, among other omissions. Some have pejoratively called the gospel of GES the "crossless gospel." The "medium" position is exemplified by J. B. Hixson in his book, *Getting the Gospel Wrong*. That Hixson holds to the content construct is seen in the following:

> Saving faith is the belief in Jesus Christ as the Son of God who died and rose again to pay one's personal penalty for sin and the one who gives eternal life to all who trust Him and Him alone for it. There is nothing magical about these particular English words; nor is it suggested that saving faith necessitates the articulation of a particular formula, verbiage or incantation. What is important to recognize is that the gospel has a particular, non-negotiable content (*Getting the Gospel Wrong* [Longwood, FL: Xulon Press, 2008], 332-33).

Hixson has a five-point rubric by which he believes the content of the biblical gospel is to be judged:

> The case studies in this present work were evaluated based upon the biblical standard of the gospel. This standard was expressed in terms of five non-negotiable components: (1) Jesus Christ, (2) the Son of God who died and rose again, (3) to pay one's personal penalty for sin, (4) gives eternal life to those who trust Him and (5) Him alone for it. These five essentials, however they may be expressed or articulated, must be included in the gospel and the gospel must *not* include anything that contradicts these five essentials (ibid., italics in original).

The above quotation brings up the definition of "faith," which Hixson holds, that is a bit confusing. He uses the term "trust," which it seems, is the equivalent for believing the truth of a proposition. Hixson expresses his view in the following:

A significant aspect of the present work was a focus on the nature of saving faith. It is not enough to establish the biblical standard of the gospel if one does not understand what it means to *believe it*. It was suggested that there is a difference between *generic* faith and *saving* faith. Generic faith may be defined as *the assurance of confidence in a stated or implied truth*. This truth may be in the form of a simple *proposition*, or it may be in the form of a *person* with one or more propositions inseparably wrapped up in that person. . . . To *believe, have faith*, and *trust* are all ways of expressing the same thing: assurance or confidence in a stated or implied truth (ibid., 333, italics in original).

For Hixson, the difference between generic and saving faith is not in the nature of faith itself, but in the object of faith: "Saving faith occurs when *faith meets the right object*—the gospel" (ibid., italics in original). According to him both types of faith are believing that propositions are true, the only difference being what comprises the proposition, or the thing or person the content is about. Hixson writes, "Though one can and does believe many things in life, saving faith occurs when one believes in Jesus Christ as the Son of God who died and rose again to pay his personal penalty for sin and the one who gives eternal life to all who trust Him and Him alone for it" (ibid.). For Hixson the word "trust" means "to believe propositions to be true."

Semantics, with its attention to the meaning of "believe," is needed to arrive at the paradigm the biblical authors used when they wrote about eternal salvation.

The Semantic Paradigm

The meaning of the word "believe" is crucial to understanding the gospel. Given advances in lexicography and semantics, beginning more than fifty years ago with the text of James Barr, *The Semantics of Biblical Language* (London: Oxford University Press, 1961), there should be little doubt as to the meaning of many theological words, and particularly this key soteriological term "believe." Nevertheless in 1983, Moisés Silva lamented, "We may agree that the past two decades have seen considerable progress in the proper use of language for biblical interpretation, but we must not fall under any delusion that linguistics and exegesis have been genuinely integrated in modern scholarship" (*Biblical Words & Their Meaning: An Introduction to Lexical Semantics* [Grand Rapids: Zondervan, 1983], 21-22). The intervening years between Silva's words and the present, have seen little improvement in the implementation of Barr's conclusions, especially in popular theological writings and in the pulpit.

The meanings of words have limits. Each term has a semantic range that cannot be expanded and contracted, stretched at the will and whim of the interpreter. One is reminded of the quote attributed to Martin Luther who complained that those he opposed in the Roman Catholic Church "treat the Scriptures and make out of them what they like, as if they were a nose of wax to be pulled around at will" (Martin Luther, quoted in A. Skevington Wood, www.biblicalstudies.org.uk/article_luther_s-wood.html, p. 6, accessed 7/6/2012). We are living in the day of spandex semantics and elastic exegesis. Words without parameters make communication difficult if not impossible. As will be shown, the direction of soteriological debate has been skewed by semantic misconceptions.

The Semantics of Subtraction

As already noted, Gordon Clark combated the subjectivity inherent in liberalism, modernism, and neo-orthodoxy. Being a philosopher and logician, he was at home with objectivity and he deplored subjectivity in any form. He was particularly opposed to psychology about which he wrote that "modern culture as a whole is impregnated with Freudian irrationalistic emotionalism" (*Faith and Saving Faith*, 111). Strangely Clark's obsession with objectivity led him to write the following: "One should not interpret, misinterpret, Scriptural love in terms of the secular psychology of the twentieth century. God has no emotions, and his image, man, in his unfallen state, may have been analyzed into intellect, and will, knowledge and righteousness. Emotion and disease came in with the fall" (ibid., 115-16). Without addressing the implications of his quote for theism, Christology, and anthropology, Clark's elimination of sinless emotion, provides a window into his mindset. Clark could not countenance any measure of what he considered subjectivity in the nature of saving faith.

Clark's definition of faith and his support for it is a scathing criticism of the Reformers' initial understanding, which he refers to as "the popular analysis." The Reformers described saving faith with the use of three Latin words, *notitia*, *assensus*, and *fiducia*. While biblical terminology, whether Hebrew, Aramaic, or Greek, rather than a Latin description is ultimately what counts, the astuteness of the Reformers' selection of the Latin terms they used will become apparent when we look at the relevant words in the original languages. Here is Clark's criticism of the Reformers' choices of the three Latin terms:

> The crux of the difficulty with the popular analysis of faith into notitia (understanding), assensus (assent), and fiducia (trust), is that fiducia comes from the same root as fides (faith). The Latin fide is not a good synonym for the Greek pisteuo ["to believe"]. Hence this popular analysis reduces to the obviously absurd definition that faith consists of understanding, assent, and faith. Something better than this tautology must be found (ibid., 52).

The statement "*fiducia* comes from the same root as *fides* (faith)" is problematic. Clark has committed the "etymological root fallacy," against which Barr spoke, that words continue to have the same meaning their linguistic ancestors did. Clark imports the meaning of the "root" into the terms *fiducia* and *fides*, rendering them virtually synonymous. The dismissal of the Reformers' formulation as "obviously absurd" and a "tautology" does not do justice to their expertise in Latin. In their use of the three Latin terms the Reformers were conveying what they understood the Greek term "believe" (πιστεύω) to involve. Clark disagreed with the use of *fiducia*, because its meaning ventured into what he considered the psychological realm, which for him was unacceptable because of its subjectivity.

Clark's disciple, the late John Robbins, who wrote the foreword to Clark's book *What Is Saving Faith?* and who was probably responsible for the marginal inscriptions in the 2004 edition, wrote this note in the margin: *"The term* fiducia, *which today is often confidently joined with knowledge and assent to make the definition of faith, has never been unambiguously explained"* (Gordon Clark, *What Is Saving Faith?* [Jefferson, MD: Trinity Foundation, 2004], 150, italics in original). While for Robbins, and probably Clark as well, the term *fiducia* had not been defined to their satisfaction, the Latin term suffers no such definitional deficiency. The Reformers were not using words they did not understand, but chose terms they viewed as the best descriptive translation of the original. Attempts to add to or subtract from their choices are a reflection of theological agendas.

The debate over the Latin terms, and whether the third term *fiducia* is to be included, is important only if it applies to the biblical words in the original languages. The semantics of subtraction is indeed relevant, and will be discussed when we discuss the Greek and the Hebrew terms. But first some words about semantic addition.

The Semantics of Addition

The Reformers' use of the three Latin words, *noticia, assensus,* and *fiducia,* which they said comprise what it means to "believe" (πιστεύω), are useful in understanding the attempt to add elements to the gospel. Some conservative evangelicals believe that the Latin word *fiducia* gives them license to include commitment, submission to Christ's lordship, dedication, and a host of other similarly articulated provisos as a part of what it means to "believe." The debate over the tripartite Latin definition of faith has centered on the term *fiducia.*

Because some have added these illegitimate extralinguistic elements to *fiducia,* other conservative evangelicals have abandoned its use altogether. Considering the Reformers' expertise in Latin, as well as the biblical languages, exclusion should not be taken lightly. The elimination of *fiducia* has been discussed in the preceding section, "The Semantics of Subtraction." As for "The Semantics of Addition," no Latin lexicon or dictionary includes "commitment" or "submission" or their synonyms in the meaning of *fiducia.* They all define *fiducia* in terms of "trust."

For instance *The Latin-English Lexicon* by E. A. Andrews, has "trust, confidence, reliance, assurance" (*The Latin-English Lexicon: Founded on the Latin-English Lexicon of Dr. William Freund* [New York: Harper & Brothers, 1877], "fiducia"). *The Englishman's Pocket Latin-English and English-Latin Dictionary* defines "fiducia" with "trust, confidence boldness, courage" (Sidney C. Woodhouse [London: Routledge & Degan Paul, 1913, 1982] "fiducia," 70). The *Medieval Latin Dictionary* has "reliance, expectation to be protected by a person" (Jan Frederik Neirmeyer and C. Van De Kieft, *Mediae Latinitatis Lexicon Minus (Medieval Latin Dictionary)* [Leiden: Brill, 1976, 2002], "fiducia," 557). The *Dictionary of Ecclesiastical Latin* defines *fiducia* as "boldness, trust, confidence" (Leo F. Stelten, [Peabody, MA: Hendrickson, 1995], "fiducia," 102). With the term *fiducia* the Reformers intended to convey the idea of "trust" and nothing more. They did so because "trust" is present in the meaning of the Hiphil form of the Hebrew verb "believe" or "trust" (אָמַן) and in the Greek verb "believe" or "trust" (πιστεύω). Attempts to employ *fiducia* to add "commitment" or "submission" are not legitimate.

Some Bible teachers who add commitment to the requirement for eternal salvation use as support the grammar book of H. E. Dana and Julius R. Mantey, *A Manual Grammar of the Greek New Testament*, where in a note they opine:

> ii. Deissmann in *Light From the Ancient East* [Adolph Deissmann, reprint, Toronto: The Macmillan Company, 1957] gives several convincing quotations from the papyri to prove that πιστεύειν εἰς αὐτὸν ["believe in him"] meant *surrender* or *submission to*. A slave was sold *into the name of the god of a temple*; i.e., to be a temple servant. G. Milligan [perhaps J. H. Moulton and G. Milligan *Vocabulary of the Greek Testament* (reprint, Peabody, MA: Hendrickson, 1997), 514] agrees with Deissmann that this papyri usage of εἰς αὐτὸν ["in him"], is also found regularly in the New Testament. Thus to believe on or to be baptized into the name of Jesus means to renounce self and to consider oneself the lifetime servant of Jesus" (*A Manual Grammar of the Greek New Testament*, [reprint, Toronto: Macmillan, 1957], 105), italics in original).

Dana and Mantey's words are baffling. Inexplicably they fail to cite the page in Deissmann's work that they appeal to. A thorough search of *Light From the Ancient East* reveals that pages 326 and 327 is likely what they refer to. There, rather than "to be a temple servant," as Dana and Mantey assert, Deissmann says the opposite: "not, however, a slave of the temple, but a protégé of the god" (*Light From the Ancient East*, 326). The context is that of "manumission" ("the act of freeing from slavery"). Deissmann quotes the Greek inscription to which he refers, but nowhere does he cite the Greek phrase πιστεύειν εἰς αὐτὸν ("believe in him") or εἰς αὐτὸν ("in him"). Deissmann does use the verb πιστεύω, and translates it "committed," on page 327 where he quotes the inscription: "Nicaea hath committed unto Apollo, *for freedom*" (italics Deissmann's). The context is the payment for the freedom of a slave. The payment was given to temple personnel who were "entrusted" with its proper disbursement. Dana and Mantey's grammar appears to use this as an example of the use of the preposition "in" (εἰς) with the verb "believe" (πιστεύω), something that is found nowhere in Deissman's entire work. Dana and Mantey's statement that Deissmann "gives several convincing quotations from the papyri to prove that πιστεύειν εἰς αὐτὸν ["believe in him"] meant *surrender* or *submission to*" is false, reflecting perhaps an *a priori* agenda and/or the result of theological inbreeding.

Milligan is also used by Dana and Mantey to bolster their argument. Again they not only do not cite where that evidence is to be found but fail to even name the title of the work. Milligan's name, and not that of both Moulton and Milligan, may have been used because Moulton had passed away by the time their work, *Vocabulary of the Greek Testament*, (J. H. Moulton and G. Milligan, *Vocabulary of the Greek Testament* [reprint, Peabody, MA: Hendrickson], 1997) was published. Moulton and Milligan do mention Deissmann and his work *Light From the Ancient East* in their entry on "believe" (πιστεύειν) and quote him (Deissmann) with these words: "the purchase, however, Nicaea hath committed unto Apollo, for freedom (see Deissmann *LAE*, p. 327)" (Moulton and Milligan, 514, italics and parenthesis in original). Moulton and Milligan say nothing about the preposition "in" (εἰς) in that citation, but rather see it as an example of the use of the dative case. Dana and Mantey's conclusion, "Thus to believe on or to be baptized into the name of Jesus means to renounce self and to consider oneself the lifetime servant of Jesus" (*A Manual Grammar of the Greek New Testament*, 105) finds no support either from Deissmann nor from Moulton and Milligan, unless the latter wrote something sometime somewhere of which the present writer is unaware. Dana and Mantey's attempt to add renouncing of self and servanthood to the salvation equation is grasping at nonexistent straws.

Sometimes the term "repentance" is used to introduce "commitment" or "submission" in addition to "faith" as requirements for salvation. Wayne Grudem says that there are two required elements "when true conversion takes place" (*Systematic Theology: An Introduction to Biblical Doctrine* [Grand Rapids: Zondervan, 1994], 709). According to Grudem, "The turning from sin is called *repentance*, and the turning to Christ is called *faith*" (ibid., italics in original). Grudem is essentially correct when he says the following about faith:

> There must be some basic knowledge or *understanding* [noticia] of the facts of the gospel. There must also be *approval* of, or agreement with, these facts [assensus]. Such agreement includes a conviction that the facts spoken of the gospel are true, especially the fact that I am a sinner in need of salvation and that Christ alone has paid the penalty for my sin and offers salvation to me. It also includes an awareness that I need to trust in Christ for salvation and that he is the only way to God, and the only means provided for my salvation. This approval of the facts of the gospel will also involve a desire to be saved through Christ. But all this still does not add up to true saving faith. That comes only when I make a decision of my will to depend on, or put my *trust* in [fiducia], Christ as *my* Savior (ibid., 712, italics in original).

The problem arises when Grudem adds his interpretation of "repentance" to "faith" for what he calls "true saving faith."

According to Grudem, "We may define repentance as follows: *Repentance is a heartfelt sorrow for sin, a renouncing of it, and a sincere commitment to forsake and walk in obedience to Christ*" (ibid., 713, italics in original). Further complicating his definition he says, "Repentance, like faith, is an intellectual *understanding* (that sin is wrong), an emotional *approval* of the teachings of Scripture regarding sin (a sorrow for sin and a hatred of it), and a personal decision to turn from it (a renouncing of sin and a decision of the will to forsake it and lead a life of obedience to Christ instead)" (ibid., 713, italics and parentheses in original). Perhaps recognizing that this comes perilously close to "works salvation," Grudem adds, "We cannot say that someone has to actually *live* that changed life over a period of time before repentance can be genuine, or else repentance would be turned into a kind of obedience that we could *do* to merit salvation for ourselves" (ibid., italics in original). For Grudem a willingness and commitment to works is sufficient.

Grudem's primary concern appears to be the time element involved rather than a problem with the nature of his added requirement for salvation. He recognizes the implications for assurance of salvation when he says, "But we should never attempt to require that there be a period of time in which a person actually lives a changed life before we give assurance of forgiveness" (ibid.). Assurance, for Grudem, is nevertheless based on faith plus repentance.

The Gospel of John, that Grudem quotes for the "faith" part of his "faith-repentance tandem" never uses the Greek verb "repent" (μετανοέω) or the noun "repentance" (μετάνοια), even though at least one of the author's purposes for writing was "that believing you might have life in His name" (John 20:31). In the book of Revelation the Apostle John uses the Greek verb "repent" (μετανοέω) a dozen times (Revelation 2:5 [twice], 16, 21 [twice], 22; 3:3, 19; 9:20, 21; 16:9, 11) and never once does John make it a requirement for salvation as Grudem does. Grudem counters the objection that many times faith alone is stated as the requirement for salvation by saying, "But what we do not often realize is the fact that there are many other passages where *only repentance* is named" (ibid., 716, italics in original). Among the examples Grudem uses to prove his point is that Jesus asked the rich young ruler to "give up his possessions" (ibid.) The passages where this appears in the New Testament will be discussed later on in this present work. However, it should be noted that Jesus was asking the young man to do something, not to be willing or committed to doing it.

To Grudem's credit he does not attempt to illegitimately extract the meaning "commitment" from the term "believe" (πιστεύω). That meaning is simply not there. Instead he adds "repentance" (μετάνοια) to introduce an additional element to the requirement for eternal salvation. However, "believe" (πιστεύω) can be understood in no other way than that intended by the biblical authors. In salvific contexts it means either "to believe something to be true" or "to put one's trust in someone or something."

Much debate has focused on the meaning of "repentance" (μετάνοια). Johannes P. Louw and Eugene A. Nida give the verb and noun the meaning: "to change one's way of life as the result of a complete change of thought and attitude with regard to sin and righteousness—'to repent, to change one's way, repentance'" (*Greek-English Lexicon of the New Testament: Based on Semantic Domain*, 2nd ed. [New York: United Bible Societies, 1989], 1:510). Louw and Nida do have a footnote for this entry that says, "Though it would be possible to classify μετανοέω [the verb "to repent"] and μετάνοια [the noun "repentance"] in Domain 30 *Think* the focal semantic feature of these terms is clearly behavioral rather than intellectual" (ibid., italics in original). Louw and Nida's dismissal of an intellectual aspect for a behavioral aspect reflects their interpretation of the intrusion of the contexts in which the terms (verb "repent" = μετανοέω and noun "repentance" = μετάνοια) are used and not the basic unaffected meaning of the terms. In doing so they have effectively eliminated a meaning of the words.

Grudem rejects the intellectual meanings of the terms, specifically that the terms can refer to a "change of mind." He takes issue with Lewis Sperry Chafer and quotes the latter's statement: "The New Testament does not impose repentance upon the unsaved as a condition of salvation" (Chafer, *Systematic Theology* [Dallas, TX: Dallas Seminary Press, 1948], 3:376, cited in Grudem, *Systematic Theology*, 714). Grudem says, "Chafer recognizes that many verses call upon people to repent, but he simply defines repentance away as a 'change of mind' that does not include sorrow for sin or turning from sin" (Grudem, *Systematic Theology*, 714). Grudem's dismissal of Chafer's position of repentance as "a change of mind" as well as its marginalization by Louw and Nida's lexicon invites closer inspection.

If to "repent" (μετανοέω) means "to be sorry for sin," why did the translators of the Old Testament from Hebrew and Aramaic into Greek, the Septuagint version (LXX), repeatedly apply that term to God? Two times in one verse, 1 Samuel 15:29, that verb "repent" (μετανοέω) is used. The NASB gives it the meaning "change of mind." It says that God will not "change His mind; for He is not man that He should change His mind." The KJV says that God will not "repent: for he *is* not a man, that he should repent" [italics in KJV]. Speaking in Jeremiah 4:28, God says, "because I have spoken *it*, I have purposed *it*, and will not repent, neither will I turn back from it" [italics in KJV]. The NASB has, "because I have spoken, I have purposed, and I will not change My mind, nor will I turn from it." Using the verb "repent" (μετανοέω), these verses say that God will not "change His mind," but other verses that will be mentioned seem to say that God does do so. The answer may lie in the conditional nature of some of God's statements and promises.

Jeremiah 18:8 says, "If that nation, against whom I have pronounced, turn from their evil, I will repent of the evil that I thought to do unto them." The NASB translates the verb "repent" (μετανοέω) as "relent." God says, "If that nation against which I have spoken turns from its evil, I will relent concerning the calamity I planned to bring on it." Two verses later God says, "If it do evil in my sight, that it obey not my voice, then I will repent of the good, wherewith I said I would benefit them" (Jeremiah 18:10). The NASB says, "if it does evil in My sight by not obeying My voice, then I will think better of the good with which I had promised to bless it." The words "think better" translate the Greek verb "repent" (μετανοέω). The one doing the "repenting" or "changing the mind" is not the one doing evil; it is God.

The prophet Joel says that God is "slow to anger, and of great kindness, and repenteth him of the evil" (Joel 2:13). The NASB says that God is "slow to anger, abounding in lovingkindness, and relenting of evil." In his use of "evil" the author is not conveying that God has "sorrow for sin" but that He has a "change of mind," however that is understood, in imposing judgment for sin. In the next verse Joel asks, "Who knoweth if he will return and repent, and leave a blessing behind him?" (Joel 2:14). The prophet Amos says, "The Lord repented for this: it shall not be, saith the Lord" (Amos 7:3). The NASB reads, "The Lord changed His mind about this. 'It shall not be,' said the Lord." Three verses later Amos again says, "The Lord repented for this: this also shall not be, saith the Lord God" (Amos 7:6). This brings up the issue of how the effectiveness of prayer is to be understood. Obviously, what God does in response to prayer is never "sorrow for sin" on His part.

Jonah asked, "Who can tell *if* God will turn and repent, and turn away from his fierce anger, that we perish not?" [italics in KJV] (Jonah 3:9). The NASB has, "Who knows, God may turn and relent, and withdraw His burning anger so that we shall not perish?" The NASB reverses the verbs "turn" (ἀποστρέφω) and "repent" (μετανοέω) from the Greek order. The KJV also reverses them. God's answer is in the following verse: "And God saw their works, that they turned from their evil way; and God repented of the evil, that he had said that he would do unto them; and he did *it* not" [italics in KJV] (Jonah 3:10). The NASB says, "When God saw their deeds, that they turned from their wicked way, then God relented concerning the calamity which He had declared He would bring upon them. And He did not do *it*" [italics in NASB]. Of course, as in all of these instances God's "repenting" or "relenting" (μετανοέω) had nothing to do with sin that God had committed. Jonah's use of the verb "relent" or "repent" (μετανοέω) may be an example of a conditional statement with the choice of the alternative option.

Zechariah 8:14-15 says, "For thus saith the Lord of hosts; as I thought to punish you, when your fathers provoked me to wrath, saith the Lord of hosts, and I repented not: so again have I thought in these days to do well unto Jerusalem and to the house of Judah: fear ye not." The NASB reads, "For thus says the Lord of hosts, 'Just as I purposed to do harm to you when your fathers provoked Me to wrath,' says the Lord of hosts, 'and I have not relented, so I have again purposed in these days to do good to Jerusalem and to the house of Judah. Do not fear!'"

The LXX does use the verb "repent" (μετανοέω) and the noun "repentance" (μετάνοια) of humans with the meaning "change of mind." The noun "repentance" (μετάνοια) is used in Proverbs 14:15: "The simple believeth every word: but the prudent *man* looketh well to his going" [italics in KJV]. The "prudent *man*" [italics in KJV] (πανοῦργος) in the LXX is one who is "crafty" or "sly." His being "worldly wise" is contrasted with the gullible who is easily taken in. Because he is not naïve he "thinks again" and is able to "change his mind" when he processes information. Nothing in the context implies that he has a "sorrow for sin."

An example of the LXX using the verb "repent" (μετανοέω) in reference to man is Proverbs 20:25 which warns about making a vow and then changing one's mind. "*It is* a snare to the man *who* devoureth *that which is* holy, And after vows to make inquiry" [italics in KJV]. The NASB has, "It is a snare for a man to say rashly, 'It is holy!' and after the vows to make inquiry." The LXX literally reads, "after making a vow to repent" (μετὰ. . .τὸ εὔξασθαι μετανοεῖν γίνεται). The meaning is a change of mind about the vow that was made and not "sorrow for sin."

In the New Testament the verb "repent" (μετανοέω) and the noun "repentance" (μετάνοια) do not in themselves include sin as something to be repented of. Grudem's summary dismissal of Lewis Sperry Chafer's "change of mind" position is unwarranted. In the New Testament each use of the terms "repent" (μετανοέω) and "repentance" (μετάνοια) must be individually assessed and not automatically assumed to refer to a "sorrow for sin." In many contexts the basic unaffected meaning of "a change of mind" about the evidence of the identity of Jesus as presented in the gospel is what the author intends to convey. Using these terms to add to the requirement of trust in Jesus for eternal life must be rejected.

The Semantics of the Old and New Testaments

One might ask, "What does the Old Testament have to do with it?" To begin with the Old Testament is quoted in the New Testament in passages directly related to salvation. Although the former was written in Hebrew and Aramaic, the LXX serves to connect it with the New Testament that was written in Greek. Even though the LXX was a translation worked on two to three hundred years before the New Testament was written, it was used by New Testament writers when they quoted the Old Testament. While semantic changes can occur over such a time period, the writers of the New Testament saw no need to qualify or explain terms related to salvation or other topics when they quoted the LXX. Consequently the meaning of the Greek term "believe" (πιστεύω) in both the LXX and the New Testament should be understood to have undergone no significant change in meaning.

The value of the LXX for establishing the meaning of the term "believe" (πιστεύω) must not be underestimated. Care must be given not to depreciate it because it was translated before the gospel appeared. Although Gordon Clark used the LXX in his discussion of the word "believe" (πιστεύω), he did write something that is a bit troubling. "The Biblical verses from the Septuagint are not chosen because they are Biblical, but, like the pagan sources, they show how the word was used in pre-christian times" (Clark, *Faith and Saving Faith*, 95). Although the LXX was written "in pre-christian times," the New Testament authors, by means of their quotations, give it a Christian imprimatur that pagan writings lack. That is not to say that the word "believe" (πιστεύω) meant something different in a secular versus a biblical setting, a fact that Clark reinforces. Instead one should resist the temptation to disparage the LXX as a legitimate source for understanding the meaning of that word πιστεύω.

The two examples of "believe" (πιστεύω) that Clark gives from the Old Testament are Psalm 78:22 and Isaiah 53:1. The meaning of "believe" (πιστεύω) in Isaiah 53:1 is clearly that of believing a proposition to be either true or false. The KJV has "Who hath believed our report?" The other Old Testament example chosen by Clark is Psalm 78:22: "Because they believed not in God, and trusted not in his salvation." The KJV "believed" is a translation of the Hiphil form of the Hebrew verb "believe" or "trust" (אמן), and in the LXX the verb is translated with πιστεύω. The second verb in the verse rendered "trust" in the KJV is the Hebrew word "trust" (בטח) and in the Greek LXX the verb is ἐλπίζω which means to "hope for," "look for," or "expect."

Clark insists that "believe" (πιστεύω) in this verse has the same meaning as it does in Isaiah 53:1, to believe in the truth of a proposition. While it cannot be stated with certainty that the two clauses in Psalm 78:22 form a synonymous parallelism, if they do, it would be difficult to reconcile "hope" (ἐλπίζω) with thinking that a proposition is true. On the other hand "hope" (ἐλπίζω) does fit well with the idea of "trust" (πιστεύω); one can have hope for a felicitous future if one is trusting in God for it. In some examples "trust" is unambiguously the intended meaning for the Hiphil of the Hebrew verb (אָמַן). These will be discussed in the chapter on Old Testament evidence.

Strangely Clark denies that there exists such a thing as trust in a person. His disciple Robbins, in the foreword he wrote for Clark's book, *Faith and Saving Faith*, states his and his mentor's position: "trust in a person is a meaningless phrase unless it means assenting to certain propositions about a person" (ibid., p. vi). After itemizing creedal propositions that for Robbins are the same as trust in the person of Christ he adds, "Trust in Christ, unless it means belief of these propositions, is totally without value. Christ *means* these propositions—and a lot more, to be sure, but at least these. No one who trusts in the Christs of Barth, Brunner, Renan or Tillich will be saved" (ibid., italics in original). The "and a lot more" that Christ means for Robbins would be more of the same; more propositions, not an ontological existence beyond them or in addition to them. In their battle against the vacuous faith of the theologians they rail against, Clark and Robbins threw out the "baby with the bathwater." In the effort to steer clear of a subjective "encounter with God," they swung the pendulum to an objective intellectualized extreme, arguing that faith logically had to be limited to the content of propositional truth and not a person.

Clark took issue with theologians who he thought mistakenly saw a distinction between belief in a proposition and trust in a person, and he used Louis Berkhof as an example:

> While Professor Berkhof serves as a good example, many other Protestant theologians also, both Lutheran and Reformed, tend to make a sharp distinction between "a confident resting on a person" and the "assent given to a testimony." "Confident reliance" is supposed to differ from "intellectual assent" (ibid., 106).

Clark attempted to deny the existence of "confident reliance" by stating, "The term *resting* or *reliance* is seldom if ever explained in theology books. One is left in the dark as to what it means" (ibid., italics in original).

One reason this argument over belief in a proposition rather than in a person has gone on as long as it has is that the debate has illogically been narrowed so that an impasse is all that is possible. Because Christ, the ultimate truth-teller, is the subject matter, the distinction between His person and propositions by Him and about Him become blurred. All one has to do to understand the difference between belief in the truthfulness of propositions and trust in a person is to change the positive referent to a negative one.

For example, one could speak with a convicted murderer and believe that everything he said is the absolute truth. But if one were asked if he trusted the murderer he might say, "Not as far as I can throw him!" The difference between believing that he is telling the truth and trusting or relying on him is obvious. The basic reason for the difference is that the former falls under epistemology, while the latter is in the realm of psychology. Psychology could play no part in Clark's philosophical (epistemological, intellectual) world.

Interdisciplinary phenomena are notoriously problematic. But that is exactly the semantic range in which the Greek verb "believe" (πιστεύω) resides. The range of meaning of the Greek verb "believe" (πιστεύω) occupies semantic territory in two academic disciplines: philosophy (and epistemology under that), "to believe something to be true or that someone is telling the truth," and psychology, specifically a state of mind, that of "relying on someone or something."

Louw and Nida attempted to faithfully follow the guidelines for linguistic investigation articulated in James Barr's book, *The Semantics of Biblical Language*. Of significance for the study of the verb "believe" (πιστεύω) is Louw and Nida's remark in the introduction to their lexicon where they note: "In general, the different meanings of a single word are relatively far apart in semantic space" (Johannes P. Louw and Eugene A. Nida, *Greek-English Lexicon of the New Testament Based on Semantic Domains*, 2nd ed. [New York: United Bible Societies, 2nd ed], 1989, 1:x). The methodology they use in their lexicon, as reflected in the examples given in the introduction, exhibit a measure of caution, and if in doubt they tend to combine rather than distinguish between meanings. This is significant because they find four distinct meanings for the verb "believe" (πιστεύω) identified by their usage in the Greek New Testament.

A single word having more than one meaning is a common phenomenon known in linguistics as *polysemy*, which derives from the Greek *poly* meaning "many" and *semy*, which contributes the idea of "meaning" from which comes the term "semantics." A word can have more than a singular meaning. English has many polysemic words. For example the word "bank" can mean the edge of a river and a financial institution. The noun "trunk" can refer to part of a tree, part of an elephant's anatomy, a compartment in an automobile, or an item of furniture used for storage. People do not confuse running in a "race" with "race" as a reference to someone's ethnicity. To ignore the presence of polysemy is to invite confusion and uncertainty in communication. This is no less true in Greek. The conflation of meanings of a word into a composite or contraction and elimination of inconvenient meanings to fit one's theological or philosophical agenda may simplify matters, but it will result in a distortion of the author's intended meaning.

When *polysemy* (more than one meaning) is present in a text, the method to employ for interpretation, for selecting the meaning in a particular usage, is to note the context. The failure to recognize and appreciate the *polysemic* nature of "believe" (πιστεύω), in both the Greek New Testament and the LXX has contributed to confusion. As mentioned, Louw and Nida's lexicon has four meanings for the verb "believe" (πιστεύω), the first of which is:

> 31.35 πιστεύω: to believe something to be true and, hence, worthy of being trusted—
> "to believe, to think to be true, to regard as trustworthy. ἀκούω σχίσματα ἐν ὑμῖν

ὑπάρχειν, καὶ μέρος τι πιστεύω 'I have been told that there are opposing groups among you, and this I believe is partly true" 1 Cor. 11:18; ἀνθ᾽ ὧν οὐκ ἐπίστευσας τοῖς λόγοις μου "but you have not believed my message" Lk. 1:20; ἐάν τις ὑμῖν εἴπῃ, Ἰδοὺ ὧδε ὁ Χριστός, ... μὴ πιστεύσητε "if anyone says to you, Here is the Christ, ... do not believe them" Mt. 24:23; σὺ πιστεύεις ὅτι εἷς ἐστιν ὁ θεός; "do you believe that there is only one God?" Jas. 2:19 (Johannes P. Louw and Eugene A. Nida, *Greek-English Lexicon of the New Testament Based on Semantic Domains*, 2nd ed. [New York: United Bible Societies, 2nd ed], 1989, 1:370).

This meaning, "to believe something to be true," is easily recognized when the English "that" is a translation of the Greek conjunction ὅτι which can introduce content, a proposition, or a truth to be believed. Gordon Clark and those who follow his reasoning have argued that this meaning of the verb "believe" is the only one that exists.

Another meaning of the verb "believe" (πιστεύω) is soteriologically significant. Louw and Nida's lexicon entry is placed under the domain of "trust, rely," for which they give the following meaning:

> 31.85 πιστεύω. . .: to believe to the extent of complete trust and reliance—"to believe in, to have confidence in, to have faith in, to trust, faith, trust." πιστεύω: ὃς δ᾽ ἂν σκανδαλίσῃ ἕνα τῶν μικρῶν τούτων τῶν πιστευόντων εἰς ἐμέ "if anyone should cause one of these little ones to turn away from his faith in me" Mt. 18:6; ἐπίστευσεν δὲ Ἀβραὰμ τῷ θεῷ "Abraham trusted in God' Rom. 4:3; ὁ πιστεύων ἐπ᾽ αὐτῷ οὐ μὴ καταισχυνθῇ 'whoever believes in him will not be disappointed" 1 Pet. 2:6 (ibid., 1:376-77).

Clark and Robbins do not think this meaning exists.

A third meaning for the verb "believe" (πιστεύω), found in Louw and Nida's lexicon, is "to be a believer, to be a Christian, Christian faith":

> 31.102 πιστεύω. . .: to believe in the good news about Jesus Christ and to become a follower—"to be a believer, to be a Christian, Christian faith." πιστεύω: τοῦ δὲ πλήθους τῶν πιστευσάντων ἦν καρδία καὶ ψυχὴ μία "the group of those who were believers was one in heart and mind" Acts 4:32; δύναμις γὰρ θεοῦ ἐστιν εἰς σωτηρίαν παντὶ τῷ πιστεύοντι "for it is God's power to save everyone who is a believer" Rom. 1:16 (ibid., 1:379).

This substantival (functioning as a noun) meaning of the verb in participial form refers to those who "believe." It could combine the two preceding meanings into one, a Christian is one who has believed propositional statements related to the gospel to be true, and they are those who have put their trust in Christ.

A fourth meaning, under the domain, "Entrust to the care of" is: "to entrust something to the care of someone—'to entrust to, to put into the care of.' ὅτι ἐπιστεύθησαν τὰ λόγια τοῦ θεοῦ 'because they were entrusted with God's message' or '... with God's promises' Rom. 3:2" (ibid., 464).

The two meanings of "believe" (πιστεύω), significant for soteriology, are "believe something to be true," and "to have confidence in, to have faith in, to trust." Both are possible meanings in the Greek New Testament as well as the LXX. The writers of the Old Testament chose a Hebrew verb, and a specific form of that verb, that also had both of these meanings. That Hebrew verb אָמַן in its Hiphil form also has those two meanings, one of which is used in the epistemological realm of philosophy, "to believe something to be true," and the other a psychological term, "a state of being, that of trusting in a person." The choice of the LXX translators of the Greek "believe/trust" (πιστεύω) for the Hebrew Hiphil form of the verb "believe/trust" (אָמַן) was appropriate; it met the two criteria. The Reformers recognized the presence of both and included *fiducia*, "trust," in their tripartite Latin formula.

The error made by Clark and Robbins appears in a nutshell in the statement that has come to epitomize Clark, "All truth is propositional." That sentence can mistakenly be taken to mean that all reality is propositional. However, such is not the case. Actions, mental states, emotions, objects, and people, all exist outside the realm of propositional truth. God exists, Jesus exists, outside of, and other than, any descriptive propositional statements that can be made about them. Propositional truth, by its very nature, is a linguistic phenomenon. God and Jesus would exist even if they had not been revealed to man in special revelation, in propositional statements, by means of language.

The psalmist David wrote about general revelation: "The heavens declare the glory of God; and the firmament sheweth his handywork" (Psalm 19:1). The Apostle Paul expressed similar thoughts in Romans 1:20: "For the invisible things of him from the creation of the world are clearly seen, being understood by the things that are made, even his eternal power and Godhead; so that they are without excuse." While propositional statements can be made about God by observing His creation, God chose, by means of general revelation, to communicate those truths in other than linguistic terms. Even though creation is not in the form of propositional truth, it nevertheless communicates truth. Perhaps one of the responses to creation that God expects from man is simply to stand in awe of His handiwork.

Clark recognized that many renowned theologians, even conservative ones, did not share his view that to "believe" is limited to belief in the truth of a proposition. After discussing their disagreements with him he wrote,

> It is necessary to remind the reader that these criticisms of Warfield and other Calvinistic theologians with reference to the nature of faith as assent do not derogate from the excellence of their exposition of Biblical faith. . . .The point of the criticism is that these spiritual qualities belong to an act of assent, rather than to a very vague something else (Gordon Clark, *Faith and Saving Faith*, 81-82).

Far from being vague Benjamin B. Warfield clearly states:

> The most common construction of הֶאֱמִין [Hiphil form of the verb אָמַן "believe" or "trust"] is with the preposition בְּ ["in"], and in this construction its fundamental meaning seems to be most fully expressed. It is probably never safe to represent this

phrase by the simple "believe;" the preposition rather introduces the person or thing in which one believes. This is true even when the object of the affection is a thing, whether divine words, commandments, or works (Ps. cvi. 12, cxix. 66, lxxvii. 32), or some earthly force or good (Job xxxix. 12, xv. 31, xxiv. 22, Deut. xxviii. 66). It is no less true when the object is a person, human (I Sam. Xxvii. 12, Prov. Xxvi. 25, Jer. Xii. 6, Mic. Vii. 5) or superhuman (Job iv. 18, xv. 15), or the representative of God, in whom therefore men should place their confidence (Ex. Xix. 9, II Chron. Xx. 20). It is above all true, however, when the object of the affection is God Himself, and that indifferently whether or not the special exercise of faith adverted to is rooted in a specific occasion (Gen. xv. 6, Ex. Xiv, 31, Num. xiv. 11, xx. 12, Deut. i. 32, II Kings xvii. 14, II Chron. Xx. 20, Ps. lxxviii. 22, Jon. iii. 5) (Benjamin B. Warfield, *Biblical Doctrines* [Carlisle, PA: The Banner of Truth Trust, 1929, 1988], 468-69).

Clark rejects Warfield's evidence by saying, "It is impossible for any honest student of the Old Testament to avoid the idea of promise, and this requires the object of faith to be a proposition." (Gordon Clark, *Faith and Saving Faith*, 81). However, even with a "promise," belief in its fulfillment can include reliance on the person responsible for its fulfillment. Warfield's words, "whether or not the special exercise of faith adverted to is rooted in a specific occasion" apply to trust in a person for any eventuality without the conscious need for a propositional statement. Regarding Abram's faith in Genesis 15:6, "And he believed in the Lord; and he counted it to him for righteousness," Warfield says, "The object of Abram's faith, as here set forth, was not the promise which appears as the occasion of its exercise; what it rested on was God Himself, and that not merely as the giver of the promise here recorded, but as His servant's shield and exceeding great reward (xv. 1)" (Warfield, *Biblical Doctrines*, 471). Warfield adds, "It is therefore not the assentive but the fiducial element of faith which is here emphasized; in a word, the faith which Abram gave Jehovah when he 'put his trust in God'" (ibid.). According to Warfield, "To believe in God, in the Old Testament sense, is thus not merely to assent to His word, but with firm and unwavering confidence to rest in security and trustfulness upon Him" (ibid.). What is true of the Old Testament verb (אָמַן) in the Hiphil form (הֶאֱמִן) is true of the verb "believe" (πιστεύω) in reference to Jesus in the New Testament as well. Both can mean "to believe a proposition to be true" or "to put trust in a person or thing."

J. Gresham Machen holds the same view of "trust in a person" as Benjamin B. Warfield. In Machen's defense of belief in propositional truth as integral to "faith" he does not dismiss the existence of "trust." He writes:

> faith in a person is more than acceptance of a creed, but the Bible is quite right in holding that it always involves acceptance of a creed. Confidence in a person is more than intellectual assent to a series of propositions about the person, but it always involves those propositions, and becomes impossible the moment they are denied (J. Gresham Machen, *What is Faith?* [Grand Rapids: Eerdmans, 1925], 48).

Clark unleashes his ultimate weapon against those who disagree with him on the existence of "trust in a person." The ally he summons is the highly respected James Barr. First, Clark succinctly laid out his thesis: "The mention of the person of Christ is pious language. Similar expressions are common today. One slogan is, 'No creed but

Christ.' Another expression, with variations from person to person, is 'Faith is not belief in a proposition, but trust in a person'" (*Faith and Saving Faith*, 49). It should be noted that Clark set it up as an either/or choice, rather than a both/and. The biblical word "believe" (πιστεύω), chosen to express the requirement for eternal salvation, provides for both. The supposed support from Barr is in a crucial footnote in Clark's book:

> In recent years the neo-orthodox and pseudo-evangelicals have propounded the pious nonsense that the Greek word for faith (pistis) should be understood by its use for a Hebrew term and not in its Greek meaning. The Hebrew term or terms mean trust or faithfulness and not belief. James Barr, who can in no sense be thought favorable to what Manton calls "the mistake of the former age" i.e., "the mistake" of the Protestant reformers, in his superbly scholarly volume, *The Semantics of Biblical Language* (Oxford University Press, 1961), reduces the pseudo-evangelical view to unscholarly ruins (ibid.).

Clark's footnote, however, provides no specific, verbatim quotation from Barr. And since Clark does not give a page number, one is left to scavenge Barr's text in hopes of at least finding words that support the gist of what he says. The opinion of "unscholarly ruins" to which Clark claims Barr reduced the "trust in a person," is not supported by a careful reading of the latter's seminal work. Chapter 7 of James Barr's book, *The Semantics of Biblical Language*, is titled, "'Faith' and 'Truth'—an Examination of some Linguistic Arguments" (161). In it there is a discussion of the Hebrew verb "believe" (אָמַן) in its Hiphil form. He writes:

> It is possible however perhaps to explain some of these usages as derivative from the sense of "trust." In any case it is clear that a general sense of "be firm" and "firmness" continued active in Hebrew only in certain formations. It is the sense of "feel secure," "trust," that remains active in others and productive, and its verbal expression in Hebrew is he'emin [Hiphil form of אָמַן] "trust, believe." Ultimately no doubt the senses can be united through a meaning "be sure," which can be used for the external sureness of some object and also the internal certainty of the mind. But the specific form he'emin [Hiphil form of אָמַן] "trust, believe" must with little doubt be traced to the latter (Barr, *The Semantics of Biblical Language*, 186-87).

Barr left open the possibility of "trust" or "belief in a person," as can be seen in his footnote related to the above passage. Barr's footnote reads, "For my purpose it is not necessary to differentiate between 'trust' and 'believe,' as is done by van Dorssen op. cit., pp. 98, 126" (ibid.). Barr does not here give his opinion on the distinction between the two meanings; and he does not dismiss what van Dorssen says. Barr's citation of van Dorssen is to a Dutch monograph from the Vrije Universiteit te Amsterdam (Free University in Amsterdam) with the title: "De Derivata van de Stam אָמַן in het Hebreeuwsch van het Oude Testament." The Dutch monograph includes a summary in English which includes the following:

> The Hiphil is probably to be regarded as a subjective causative, meaning "to make oneself firm, to exhibit firmness." This firmness is acquired by taking hold of something and in the majority of cases the person or the thing that is taken hold of is

introduced by the prepositions בְּ ["in"] or לְ. Of these two constructions the one with בְּ ["in"] has the stronger meaning and expresses that one confidingly [sic] leans on a person or thing. It may be rendered by "to believe in, to trust." The construction לְ has a weaker sense expressing the idea that one gives credence to a person or to his words. In this case we should render "to believe." It is true that it is often difficult to distinguish between these two meanings and that several passages are capable of an interpretation in either direction, but on the whole the evidence of the material is such that the distinction can be justified (Jan Christiaan Cornelis van Dorssen, De Derivata van de Stam אָמַן in Het Hebreeuwsch van Het Oude Testament (with a summary in English), [Amsterdam: Vrije Universiteit te Amsterdam, 1951], 125).

Clark's out-of-hand dismissal of the notion of "trust" is unwarranted and unsupported by James Barr, whose endorsement Clark claims to have. Barr did not vanquish to "unscholarly ruins" the position of "trust in a person."

Additional evidence for the presence of the meaning "trust" for the verb "believe" (πιστεύω) is found in the Egyptian papyri bracketing the time period when the New Testament was written. J. H. Moulton and G. Milligan in their *Vocabulary of the Greek Testament* (reprint, Peabody, MA: Hendrickson, 1997) compiled non-literary texts, consisting of written material ranging from official documents to scraps of papyri, that were discarded by the original writers and owners, uncovered by archaeologists in ancient rubbish heaps. A papyrus dated 164 B.C., says, "whom no one would trust, even if they were willing to do the work" (ibid., 514). Also from A.D. 123, "distrusting both her and my own youth" (ibid.), and from the third century A.D., "I have trusted no one to take it to her" (ibid.). The Koine Greek of the New Testament was the common everyday language of the people. Finding the meaning "trust" for πιστεύω in the garbage dumps of that day is significant. The existence of the meaning "trust," that is to have confidence in something or someone, for the verb "believe" (πιστεύω), cannot be denied.

The Biblical Paradigm

The writers of the Old and New Testaments did not have the mindset of content when it came to soteriology. They saw themselves as witnesses, who had received divine revelation, by which they wrote Scripture, through the inspiration of the Holy Spirit, and/or who had been eyewitnesses to the Incarnation. As witnesses they gave testimony. Their methodology was to provide evidence of many kinds, the more the better, which would prove the identity of God, beginning with God the Father in the Old Testament, and culminating with the identity of Jesus as the Son of God, so that trust would be placed in Him.

They presented evidence of Jesus' identity, which included who He is, what He came to earth to do, and for what purpose. Once an individual has sufficient evidence, which he or she is convinced is true, to correctly identify the Jesus of divine revelation, then trust can be placed in Him for one's eternal destiny.

Propositional truth is foundational to the gospel. The identity of God the Father and of Jesus Christ and the requirement to "believe" are all revealed by means of propositional statements. But the veracity of the statements and the belief that they are true is not intended to be the end. Man is to respond to the propositional statements in Scripture, about the identity of Jesus Christ, first believing them to be true and thereby identifying the One in whom trust is to be placed. Then one is to place trust in that person for his eternal destiny.

The God of Scripture is the one true God. No one else is the real God. And He calls for trust to be placed in Him. The uniqueness of God requires that trust in Him be exclusive. To trust in something or someone other than Him alone is to impugn His very identity. As Peter boldly preached in Acts 4:12, "Neither is there salvation in any other: for there is none other name under heaven given among men, whereby we must be saved." The Lord of the universe invites us to trust in Him.

The biblical paradigm is that of divine identity proven by means of evidence. In the Old Testament propositional truth and demonstrations of divine power reveal the one true God. The identity of God the Father is fully revealed and that of His divine Son is prophesied. In the New Testament all the messianic prophecies are fulfilled either in Jesus' first coming or will be when He returns. Jesus' death on the cross makes possible man's salvation. His resurrection is the ultimate proof of who He is and the demonstration of His divine power. Jesus' death and resurrection are part of His identity. The combined evidence of the works and words of Jesus unmistakably identify Him as God.

The purpose of propositional truth is to lead to trust in the Savior. Belief in the veracity of propositions that prove Jesus' identity do not in and of themselves result in salvation. The moment of transition from condemnation to eternal life occurs when trust is placed in Jesus for one's eternal destiny. Jesus Himself pictured that wonderful moment in time to a man named Saul who would be known as Paul with words that describe the effect of the gospel on the unsaved: "To open their eyes, *and* to turn *them from* darkness to light, and from the power of Satan unto God, that they may receive forgiveness of sins, and inheritance among them which are sanctified by faith that is in me" [italics in KJV] (Acts 26:18). The on-going mission of the church is to proclaim who Jesus is and to invite the whole world to receive eternal life by trusting in Him.

Chapter 2

Exegetical Eye-Openers

Perspective and Presuppositions

In the seventeenth century, Spanish author Miguel de Cervantes wrote the novel *Don Quixote*, in which the protagonist, Don Quixote, thinking that they were imposing giants, engaged windmills in battle. To some, soteriological doctrinal debates deal with the imaginary and the inconsequential, much like attacking windmills. It is this writer's belief that the battle over the requirement for salvation is not some Quixotic adventure, but that the issues are substantive and what is at stake is the eternal destiny of men's souls.

The paradigm of evidence for the identity of the one in whom trust is to be placed is crucial for biblical interpretation. However, having the proper lens for interpretation is useless if presuppositional blindness prevents one from properly applying the perspective of the biblical writers. In the theological realm, as in the anatomical world, there are degrees of blindness. Congenital and total spiritual blindness is the condition from which all humanity suffers, and is only cured by a spiritual new birth. Partial physical blindness, experienced later in life, sometimes requires the services of an ophthalmologist and perhaps surgery might be performed. Whatever the visual problem might be, identifying the cause of the impairment is indispensable. Soteriologically, there are some identifiable misinterpretations that either obscure a believer's doctrinal acuity and impede his or her daily walk, at best, or at worst prevent the salvation of the lost. From among these errors, espoused by both believers and unbelievers, four have been selected to discuss in detail.

Soteriological Grammar

Probably the most familiar verse in the entire Bible is John 3:16 that says, "For God so loved the world, that he gave his only begotten Son, that whosoever believeth in him should not perish, but have everlasting life." An issue of importance in John 3:16 is whether the present tense participle of the verb "believe" (πιστεύω) is to be translated "keeps on believing," or whether it refers to an event that has a beginning and an end. Does this verse, and others where the verb "believe" (πιστεύω) is in the present tense, mean that salvific faith must continue for it to be genuine?

Daniel Wallace uses John 3:16 as an example of a substantival participle (a verb functioning as a noun) in the present tense with the comment, "The idea seems to be both gnomic [timeless or universal] and continual: 'everyone who continually believes.' This is not due to the present tense only, but to the use of the present participle of πιστεύω, especially in soteriological contexts in the NT" (*Greek Grammar beyond the Basics* [Grand Rapids: Zondervan 1996], 620-21). Wallace gives evidence for his view in an extensive footnote that deserves to be quoted in its entirety:

The aspectual force of the present ὁ πιστεύων seems to be in contrast with ὁ πιστεύσας. The aorist is used only eight times (plus two in the longer ending of Mark). The aorist is sometimes used to describe believers as such and thus has a generic force (cf. for the clearest example the *v.l.* at Mark 16:16; cf. also 2 Thess 1:10; Heb 4:3; perhaps John 7:39; also, negatively, of those who did not [μὴ] believe: 2 Thess 2:12; Jude 5). The present occurs six times as often (43 times), most often in soteriological contexts (cf. , John 1:12; 3:15, 16, 18; 3:36; 6:35, 47, 64; 7:38; 11:25; 12:46; Acts 2:44; 10:43; 13:39; Rom. 1:16; 3:22; 4:11, 24; 9:33; 10:4, 11; 1 Cor 1:21; 14:22 [*bis*]; Gal 3:22; Eph 1:19; 1 Thess 1:7; 2:10, 13; 1 Pet 2:6, 7; 1 John 5:1, 5, 10, 13). Thus, it seems that since the aorist participle was a live option to describe a "believer," it is unlikely that when the present was used, it was aspectually flat. The present was the tense of choice most likely because the NT writers by and large saw *continual* belief as a necessary condition of salvation. Along these lines, it seems significant that the *promise* of salvation is almost always given to ὁ πιστεύων (cf. several of the above-cited texts), almost never to ὁ πιστεύσας (apart from Mark 16:16, John 7:39 and Heb. 4:3 [which] come the closest [the present tense of πιστεύω never occurs in Hebrews]) (ibid., 621).

Wallace's qualifiers "most likely" and "by and large" notwithstanding, his statement that "The present was the tense of choice most likely because the NT writers by and large saw continual belief as a necessary condition of salvation" (ibid.) does not hold up under scrutiny.

The reason the present tense participle of the verb "believe" (πιστεύω) is used is not to connote the idea of continual belief but instead reflects an evangelistic purpose. John's Gospel has evangelism as a stated purpose (John 20:31), and gives the requirement for becoming one of God's children. "But as many as received him, to them gave he power to become the sons of God, *even* to them that believe on his name" [italics in KJV] (John 1:12). The present participle of "believe" (πιστεύω) explains what it means to "receive" (λαμβάνω) Jesus. The writer's evangelistic emphasis explains why a present tense and not an aorist tense is used for "believe" (πιστεύω). The writer wanted his readers who had not done so to put their trust in Jesus in the present.

One example Wallace uses to support his view that belief is continual, is preceded by Paul's evangelistic invitation, "Be it known unto you therefore, men and brethren, that through this man is preached unto you the forgiveness of sins" (Acts 13:38). Paul then says that the benefits of the gospel are available for "everyone who believes" (Acts 13:39) (πᾶς ὁ πιστεύων). The present tense does not mean "all who continually believe." The same evangelistic purpose, or an explanation of the readers' conversion, is present in the book of Romans where Wallace argues for a continual nuance (Romans 1:16; 3:24; 4:11, 24; 9:33; 10:4, 11).

First Corinthians 1:21 says that "it pleased God by the foolishness of preaching to save them that believe." The words translated "them that believe" (τοὺς πιστεύοντας) are an articular present active participle. To require the author to use a tense other than the present tense, that is, the aorist tense, to communicate a punctiliar meaning for belief, as opposed to a continual nuance, is to impose on the author an unnecessary and arbitrary requirement.

In English, as well as in Greek, the present tense does "double-duty" because there are not separate tenses to communicate a continuous and a punctiliar event in the present. For instance, my wife might ask me what I am doing and I might reply, "I am getting dressed." She understands that I am only getting dressed once. It is not an activity that I will continually be doing. In Greek, as Wallace says, "In general, we can say that **aspect** *is the unaffected meaning while* **Aktionsart** *is aspect in combination with lexical, grammatical, or contextual features*" (ibid., 449, bold and italics in original). "Aktionsart" is the meaning of a term in a given linguistic situation. In salvific contexts, with the present tense of "believe" (πιστεύω), lexical and contextual matters govern whether the meaning is continuous or punctiliar. If one holds *a priori* (Latin for deductive reasoning formed or conceived beforehand) that the nature of salvific belief is that of an ongoing event, that meaning will intrude on one's understanding of the nature of the present tense. On the other hand, if one has the biblical perspective that salvific belief is punctiliar, the present tenses that express it will be understood as punctiliar rather than continuous.

The fact that the present tense is used when referring to Christians as "believers" does not mean continuous belief is a requirement for salvation. It is customary for titles to reflect a personal characteristic. Mark 1:4 calls the one who baptized Jesus, "John the Baptist" or literally, "John the Baptizer" (Ἰωάννης ὁ βαπτίζων) using a present active participle. Although there is a question whether the definite article "ὁ" was in the original manuscript, there is no question about Mark's use of the article in Mark 6:14. Herod put a stop to John's baptismal ministry by putting him in prison and then having him beheaded. After Herod imprisoned and executed John the Baptist, Herod heard that people were speculating about what Jesus was doing and saying, "John the Baptist [name with present active articular participle Ἰωάννης ὁ βαπτίζων] was risen from the dead, and therefore mighty works do shew forth themselves in him" (Mark 6:14). People mistakenly identified Jesus as John, the one known for his baptizing and not as one who was continually baptizing. John the Baptist was no longer baptizing in prison, a fact that Herod was all too aware of.

Likewise, when Christians are called "believers" they are known for having put their trust in Jesus. That is the way in which the present tense is to be understood in salvific contexts. Sometimes the present tense participle of "believe" (πιστεύω) is used in sanctification rather than salvation settings to refer to the fact that Jesus is the one in whom believers are presently believing and relying on. The epistle of 1 John was written to believers and uses the present tense participle in this way in 5:1, 5, 10, and 13. Contextual considerations, whether salvation or sanctification is in view, will dictate whether a punctiliar or continual nuance is intended by the author and/or what Jesus said. In a salvation context (a belief/trust/plus no works context) the former punctiliar meaning applies. In a sanctification (belief/trust/plus works) context the latter continual connotation is appropriate. The fact that the title "believer" is used in the present tense does not prove that continuous belief is a condition for becoming a child of God.

The use of other tenses, besides the present tense, for salvific belief, is significant. As mentioned, the present tense does "double-duty." It can refer to a continuous, ongoing event or a punctiliar occurrence in the present. The perfect tense in the indicative, while used to convey either a process or a punctiliar event in the past, cannot be used to refer to an event as having begun in the past and continuing into the present (from the point of view of the speaker). The results continue in the present, and those results may be emphasized, a phenomenon contextually influenced, but the event or occurrence itself does not continue. The pluperfect tense is similarly restricted to the past. The same can also be said of the aorist tense and the imperfect tense that refer to an ‚occurrence that ended in the past and does not continue into the present.

The flexibility of the present tense, with its ability to convey a continuous or punctiliar nuance in the present is a missing feature in these other tenses. The use of the present tense, and that of the other tenses, in the Greek New Testament are complementary and not contradictory. The issue is not one of numerical or statistical superiority, as Wallace seems to suggest, but a matter of harmonious expression.

Not only did the New Testament writers not see "continual belief as a necessary condition of salvation" (ibid.), Jesus Himself did not hold that view. In the soteriological context of Jesus' encounter with the Samaritan woman at the well He used the metaphor of "drinking" (πίνω) for believing. Jesus said, "Whosoever drinketh of this water shall thirst again" (John 4:13) (πᾶς ὁ πίνων ἐκ τοῦ ὕδατος τούτου διψήσει πάλιν). The substantival (functioning as a noun) articular participle with the inclusive adjective translated "whosoever drinketh" (πᾶς ὁ πίνων) is a present active participle, the same as in John 3:16, "whosoever believeth" (πᾶς ὁ πιστεύων).

In John 4:13 Jesus referred to physical water and was not saying that "everyone who continually drinks of this water shall thirst again." Jesus was saying that a single drink would not satisfy physical thirst indefinitely. Obviously continuous drinking would continue to slake one's physical thirst. In contrast to that water, what Jesus offered did not require continual drinking. Jesus' application moves the discussion to the spiritual realm. Jesus said, "But whosoever drinketh of the water that I shall give him shall never thirst" (John 4:14). If Jesus had meant continual believing was required to slake spiritual thirst, His metaphor and His explanation of it would not have made sense.

Jesus introduced His discussion with the woman with the words, "If thou knewest the gift of God, and who it is that saith to thee, Give me to drink; thou wouldest have asked of him, and he would have given thee living water" (John 4:10). If the woman knew Jesus' identity, "and who it is who says to you" (τίς ἐστιν ὁ λέγων σοι), she would have been able to put her trust in Him. If she knew about the gift and who the giver was she could trust in Him to give her the gift.

The apostle John recorded his inspired editorial evaluation of this encounter with the words, "And many of the Samaritans of that city believed [aorist active indicative] on him for the saying of the woman, which testified, He told me all that ever I did" (John 4:39). The Samaritans did what Jesus invited them to do and put their trust in Him. In turn, Jesus accepted their invitation to stay in their city and the result was, "And many more believed [aorist active indicative] because of His own word" (John 4:41).

In John 5:24 Jesus said, "Verily, verily, I say unto you, He that heareth my word, and believeth on him that sent me, hath everlasting life, and shall not come into condemnation; but is passed from death unto life." The two parallel participles translated "He that heareth" (ὁ. . . ἀκούων) and "believeth" (πιστεύων) are both present active participles. Jesus was not saying "he who continues to hear and he who continues to believe Him who sent Me has eternal life." The two parallel participles have the same aspectual force and it is not continual hearing and continual believing. The two cannot be separated. One cannot have one's grammatical cake and eat it too.

Jesus' soteriological discussion following His statement, "I am the bread of life" (John 6:35) sheds additional light on what Jesus meant when He said, "believe" (πιστεύω). Jesus then said, "he that cometh to me shall never hunger; and he that believeth on me shall never thirst" (John 6:35). The participles translated "he that cometh" (ὁ ἐρχόμενος) and "he that believeth" (ὁ πιστεύων) are both present participles. Jesus was not saying, "he who continually comes to Me shall not hunger, and he who continually believes in Me shall never thirst." In John 6:37 when Jesus said, "and him that cometh to me I will in no wise cast out," and used the present articular participle (τὸν ἐρχόμενον = "him that cometh"), he did not mean, "and the one who continually comes to Me I will certainly not cast out."

In John 6:40 Jesus said, "And this is the will of him that sent me, that every one which seeth the Son, and believeth on him, may have everlasting life: and I will raise him up at the last day." The participle with the inclusive adjective translated "every one which seeth" (πᾶς ὁ θεωρῶν) and the participle translated "believeth" (πιστεύων) are both present participles. Jesus was not saying that "everyone who continually beholds the Son and continues to believe in Him will have eternal life."

In addition to John 6:35 Wallace gives John 6:47 for support of his statistical analysis. Jesus said, "Verily, verily, I say unto you, He that believeth on me hath everlasting life" (John 6:47). Jesus then repeated the metaphor, "I am that bread of life" (John 6:48). In Jesus' discussion that follows, the metaphor of "the bread" (ὁ ἄρτος) is expanded. Jesus explained, "This is the bread which cometh down from heaven, that a man may eat thereof, and not die" (John 6:50). The present participle translated "which cometh down" (καταβαίνων) does not mean "this is the bread which continually comes down out of heaven." In the next verse Jesus makes that clear by saying, "I am the living bread which came down from heaven" (John 6:51). The aorist participle translated "came down" (καταβάς) shows that Jesus' "coming down" had already occurred and was over when Jesus spoke these words.

The extended metaphor for belief is further expanded by Jesus with the words, "Verily, verily, I say unto you, except ye eat the flesh of the Son of man, and drink his blood, ye have no life in you" (John 6:53). Jesus explained, "Whoso eateth my flesh, and drinketh my blood, hath eternal life; and I will raise him up at the last day" (John 6:54).

The two present participles translated "whoso eateth" (ὁ τρώγων) and "drinketh" (πίνων) do not mean "he who continually eats My flesh and continually drinks My blood has eternal life."

Not surprisingly, these words of Jesus caused consternation among His disciples. Knowing their thoughts, Jesus asked them, "Doth this offend you? *What* and if ye shall see the Son of man ascend up where he was before?" [italics in KJV] (John 6:61-62). The present participle translated "ascend up" (ἀναβαίνοντα) does not mean that the Son of Man would continually ascend where He was before. In John 6:64 Jesus said, "But there are some of you that believe not." To hold that the present participle and negative particle translated "that believe not" (οἳ οὐ πιστεύουσιν) has a continuous aspect and not to do so with other present participles in the passage carries its refutation on its face.

Wallace uses Acts 2:44 as another item in his numerical comparison. Acts 2:44 says, "And all that believed were together, and had all things common." The words "that believed" (οἱ πιστεύοντες) translate a present tense articular participle. If this present participle has a continuous nuance, so does another present tense participle in the immediate context. Acts 2:47 ends with the words, "And the Lord added to the church daily such as should be saved." The words translated "as should be saved" (τοὺς σῳζομένους) are a present tense articular participle. An individual is not continuously being saved, and yet consistency in one's exegesis requires that to be the case if the present tense participle in Acts 2:44 is to be understood as having a continuous nuance. The individuals in question believed and were saved; both were completed and not ongoing events.

In his list of biblical references to prove his point, Wallace contrasts the present tense with the use of the aorist: "The present occurs six times as often (43 times), most often in soteriological contexts." While frequency may increase the probability of a particular meaning, it is not determinative. Employing frequency as an exegetical axiom does not relieve the interpreter of explaining the presence of contrary evidence, particularly in the immediate context. Wallace concludes with the words, "Thus, it seems that since the aorist participle was a live option to describe a 'believer,' it is unlikely that when the present was used, it was aspectually flat. The present was the tense of choice most likely because the NT writers by and large saw *continual* belief as a necessary condition of salvation" (ibid., italics in original). Wallace qualifies his statement with the words "most likely" and "by and large." He further hedges saying, "The aspectual force of the present ὁ πιστεύων seems to be in contrast with [aorist] ὁ πιστεύσας" (ibid.). Wallace has selectively narrowed the biblical evidence, restricting his discussion to present and aorist tense participles. However, the biblical authors did not restrict the Greek choices available to them to these two grammatical alternatives.

A grammatical alternative that the author of the Gospel of John chose, in the immediate context of John 3:16, in the same soteriological context, and that other biblical authors regularly use, is the Greek perfect tense. Wallace defines the perfect tense: "The force of the perfect tense is simply that it describes an event that, completed in the past (we are speaking of the perfect indicative here), has results existing in the present time (i.e., in relation to the time of the speaker)" (ibid., 574, parentheses in original). Right after John 3:16, in John 3:18 Jesus said, "He that believeth [present active participle] on Him is not condemned; but he that believeth not [present active participle] is condemned already, because he hath not believed [perfect active indicative] in the name of the only begotten Son of God."

Three times in this verse (John 3:18) the verb "believe" (πιστεύω) is used, the first two as present participles and the third in the perfect indicative. The perfect active indicative found in the third occurrence in this verse of the verb "believe" (πιστεύω), means that man is not judged because he fails to "continue to believe," but because, as the text clearly states, "he has not believed," which is "an event that, completed in the past…has results existing in the present time" (ibid).

The third use of "believe" (πιστεύω) in the perfect tense of the indicative is determinative for interpreting the prior two present tense participles in the same verse. That is because the meaning of the participles can conform to the meaning of the indicative perfect tense, but the indicative perfect tense cannot have the meaning of an event continuing into the present, only ongoing results of a previous event. The Greek perfect tense conveys cause and effect. To extract present continuous belief from the perfect tense in John 3:18 requires running roughshod over it, obliterating any distinction between cause and effect. Because John 3:18 has a present tense participle that cannot be understood as continuous, to claim that in John 3:16, the same present tense participle is continuous flies in the face of the immediate context. Scripture is consistent in its portrayal of salvific belief as a punctiliar and not a continuous event.

A case in point is the Greek pluperfect, a relatively rare use, whose meaning is similar to that of the perfect, with a cause/effect nuance. As Wallace says,

> for the most part, these two tenses [perfect and pluperfect] are identical in aspect though different in time. That is, both speak of the state resulting from a previous event–the perfect speaking of existing results in the present (with reference to the speaker), the pluperfect speaking of existing results in the *past* (as this tense occurs only in the indicative mood). Thus, it may be said that *the pluperfect combines the aspects of the aorist (for the event) and the imperfect (for the results)* (ibid., 583, brackets added, parentheses and italics in original).

Luke, writing about Paul and Barnabas in Acts 14:23 says, "And when they had ordained them elders in every church, and had prayed with fasting, they commended them to the Lord, on whom they believed." With the use of the pluperfect active indicative, Luke described the salvation of the Christian brethren in these cities with "they believed" (πεπιστεύκεισαν). Their salvation had occurred at a time in the past, and it had results that existed in the past, from the point of view of Luke the author.

If the biblical authors had wanted to convey the necessity of "continuing to believe" as a requirement for eternal salvation, in order to unambiguously communicate the idea of continuous activity in the past, they could have used the Greek imperfect tense. An inspection of how the inspired writers used the imperfect tense is instructive. Wallace writes, "(Note that since the imperfect only occurs in the indicative mood [1682 times in the NT], this tense always grammaticalizes time)" (ibid., 541, parenthesis and brackets in original). There are some exceptions to the use of the imperfect to describe an event in the past. As Wallace says, "occasionally it portrays other than the past time (e.g., the connotative imperfect may have this force to it sometimes; also the imperfect in second class conditions connotes present time–but such is due more to the aspect than the time element of the tense)" (ibid., parenthesis in original). The imperfect normally has the meaning of past tense continuous action. However, the biblical writers were careful in their use of the imperfect tense in soteriological contexts.

The imperfect tense used with the verb "believe" (πιστεύω) in John 2:24, "But Jesus, on His part, was not entrusting [ἐπίστευεν] Himself to them" will be discussed in the chapter on John's Gospel. Ignoring the fact that what Jesus was doing (or more correctly was not doing) was not something related to His own salvation (that obviously would have been impossible), the aspect of the imperfect tense of the verb "believe" (here correctly translated "entrust") is continuous. The use of the imperfect tense in this verse says nothing about an individual's eternal salvation.

In John 5:46 and 47 the verb "believe" (πιστεύω) is used four times, two times with the imperfect indicative tense in John 5:46, and in verse 47 one time with the present indicative and once as a future indicative. "For had ye believed [imperfect active indicative] Moses, ye would have believed [imperfect active indicative] me: for he wrote of me. But if ye believe [present active indicative] not his writings, how shall ye believe [future active indicative] my words?" (John 5:46-47). Jesus' implied His identity by equating His words with those of the inspired words of Moses, and the significance of His divine Person as the subject of Old Testament Scripture.

The verb "believe" (πιστεύω) is probably to be understood as meaning "believe something to be true" within a context of the content of Jesus' words and those of Moses. The content is most likely related to who Jesus is. If it is a soteriological reference, it is significant that Jesus' use of the imperfect tense with the verb "believe" (πιστεύω) in John 5:46 is in the plural "you [plural] believed" (ἐπιστεύετε = imperfect active indicative second person plural) and the plural "you [plural] would believe" (ἐπιστεύετε = imperfect active indicative second person plural). The significance of the plural with the imperfect of the verb "believe" (πιστεύω) is as follows.

Wallace describes what he refers to as "Broad-Band Imperfects" (ibid., 546). Under this classification, in his definition of the "Iterative Imperfect" he says, "The imperfect is frequently used for *repeated* action in past time. It is similar to the customary imperfect, but it is not something that regularly recurs. Further, the iterative imperfect occurs over a shorter span of time" (ibid., italics in original). Wallace notes that under the category of the "Iterative Imperfect" is a further subdivision: "There are two types of iterative imperfect: (1) **Iterative** proper, in which the imperfect indicates *repeated action by the same agent*; and (2) **Distributive**, in which the imperfect is used for *individual acts of multiple agents*" (ibid., italics and bold in original). Wallace uses as an illustration of the latter iterative imperfect distributive, Matthew 3:6 (ibid., 547). "And they were being baptized by him in the Jordan River" (καὶ ἐβαπτίζοντο ἐν τῷ Ἰορδάνῃ ποταμῷ ὑπ' αὐτοῦ). Obviously, those who "were being baptized" (ἐβαπτίζοντο = imperfect, passive, indicative, third person, plural) were not each continually being baptized. They were each separately, individually (distributively) being baptized.

Another New Testament example of the iterative imperfect distributive that Wallace gives is Mark 12:41 (ibid.): "And Jesus sat over against the treasury, and beheld how the people cast money into the treasury: and many that were rich cast in much." There are two uses of the imperfect tense in this verse; the first translated, "beheld" (ἐθεώρει), and the second the last word, "cast in (much)" (ἔβαλλον). The first imperfect tense verb, used of Jesus, who "beheld" (ἐθεώρει) is translated in the NASB as an ingressive (also known as "inchoative" or "Inceptive," ibid., 544) imperfect, indicated with the italicized (in NASB) *"began* observing." The second imperfect tense verb in the verse is translated in the NASB "were putting in" (ἔβαλλον), referring to rich givers who were contributing substantial amounts. The imperfect tense does not mean that the wealthy contributors were each continually casting large sums into the offering containers, but that each was separately, individually (in a distributive sense) doing so.

What is of exegetical significance about the iterative imperfect distributive, is that by its nature this use of the imperfect requires that the verb be plural in number. If there is one individual, obviously, the action cannot be distributed among several. In the above examples those being baptized were plural, and so were those contributing money. An author can use an imperfect tense verb that is singular in number, but then the aspect or nuance of the verb is that of continuous action and is not appropriate to describe a single act or event.

The purpose of the above discussion is to lay the groundwork for seeing how the biblical writers carefully used the Greek imperfect tense, singular and plural, particularly with the verb "believe" (πιστεύω) in soteriological contexts, so that there would be no question that it referred to an event that happened at a point in time, and not something continuous or ongoing. The only time, in the entire New Testament, in which the verb "believe" (πιστεύω) is found in the imperfect tense, and is singular in number, and not plural, is John 2:24: "But Jesus did not commit himself unto them, because he knew all *men*" [italics in KJV]. Significantly, this is not a soteriological use, because Jesus had no need of salvation, and is translated by the KJV "commit" and the NASB "entrusting." The aspect of the imperfect in John 2:24 is continuous, but the meaning of the verb is neither "to believe something to be true," nor "to believe in a person," but "to entrust something to the care of someone." The imperfect tense in the singular is used of Jesus with a continuous meaning.

An examination of the instances when the verb "believe" (πιστεύω) is used in the imperfect tense, which are always plural in the New Testament when used in soteriological contexts, even when surrounded by imperfect tenses that are singular in number, confirms the perspicuity (precision or exactness) of the biblical record. The conviction of the early church, based on the carefully communicated words of the New Testament, was that the faith required for conversion happened in a glorious moment and point in time, and was not a process.

In Galilee Jesus' brothers were urging Him to go more public with His ministry by going to Judea, in spite of His life being threatened in Judea. John 7:1 says, "for He was unwilling to walk in Judea, because the Jews were seeking to kill Him" (NASB). Perhaps the disciples were somewhat embarrassed by being associated with Him. After their discussion with Jesus, John, the Gospel writer, comments, "For not even His brothers were believing in Him" (John 7:5 NASB). The verb translated "were believing" (ἐπίστευον) is the Greek imperfect tense that could be understood as "were continuing to believe," however, the verb is a plural, and in concord with the plural "brothers" (ἀδελφοὶ) the use is most likely an iterative imperfect distributive. If the brothers had believed in Him, they would not have done so simultaneously but individually. The verb does not necessarily indicate that they would have collectively continued in their belief. The expression of their unbelief cannot be used to support a "continuing belief" nuance if they had believed in Him.

Another example is found in John 12:11. John 12:10-11 says, "But the chief priests took counsel that they might put Lazarus to death also; because on account of him many of the Jews were going away, and were believing in Jesus" (NASB). Again the verb translated "were believing" (ἐπίστευον) is a plural imperfect tense, having an iterative, distributive meaning; those defecting were doing so individually and there is nothing grammatical that requires their belief to be understood as continuous. In this same chapter another use of the verb "believe" (πιστεύω) as a plural imperfect is employed negatively: "But though He had performed so many signs before them, yet they were not believing in Him" (John 12:37 NASB).

In Acts 18:8 the verb "believe" (πιστεύω) appears twice: "And Crispus, the leader of the synagogue, believed in the Lord with all his household, and many of the Corinthians when they heard were believing, and being baptized" (NASB). The first appearance of the verb tells of Chrispus's salvation, and naturally it is singular in number. Luke appropriately uses the aorist indicative "believed" (ἐπίστευσεν) to refer to his conversion, an event that had taken place in the past. When writing about the Corinthians' salvation, a plural is used, "were believing" (ἐπίστευον), and significantly the imperfect tense is a plural because it is an iterative imperfect distributive. Each of the Corinthian converts was saved, by individually believing. Their saving faith occurred at a point in time, and was not a continuous event.

The presence of an iterative imperfect distributive is clear because Luke has another imperfect at the end of the verse that says the Corinthians were "being baptized" (ἐβαπτίζοντο = plural imperfect passive indicative). This parallel verb is also a plural iterative imperfect distributive; they were not each continually being baptized. Their individual baptisms were not repeated and neither was their saving faith. The New

Testament never uses the imperfect tense in the singular to refer to anyone's saving faith. To do so would be to violate and contradict the New Testament's consistent presentation that conversion faith takes place in a point in time, and is not a continuous event.

A Soteriological Additive – Acts 2:38

Reading English versions of Acts 2:38 one could conclude, or at least question, whether one must believe and be baptized to be saved. Acts 2:38 says, "Then Peter said unto them, Repent, and be baptized every one of you in the name of Jesus Christ for the remission of sins, and ye shall receive the gift of the Holy Ghost." Much has been written about this verse, and many alternatives have been offered to the Campbellite "belief plus baptism for salvation" interpretation.

One proposed alternative to the Campbellite interpretation is that the Greek preposition translated "for" (εἰς), in the phrase, "for the remission of sins" (εἰς ἄφεσιν τῶν ἁμαρτιῶν ὑμῶν), should be translated with a "causal" nuance, "because your sins have been forgiven," rather than as a result; believe and be baptized with the result of having your sins forgiven. A problem with the "causal" interpretation is that the existence of that meaning for the Greek preposition translated "for" (εἰς) has been questioned. Without getting into a detailed analysis of the arguments for and against the existence of that meaning for the preposition, even if that alternative is a possibility, its rarity would militate against its presence in this text. Campbellites, and those who agree with them doctrinally, understandably question the theological motivation rather than exegetical evidence for that explanation. Wallace rejects the interpretation that resorts to the "causal εἰς" that was argued by Julius R. Mantey in his journal articles, "The Causal Use of Εἰς in the New Testament," and "On Causal Εἰς Again" (*Journal of Biblical Literature* 70 [1952]; 45-59, and JBL 70 [1952]; 129-30, in Daniel Wallace, (*Greek Grammar beyond the Basics* [Grand Rapids: Zondervan 1996], 370).

An interpretation that excludes baptism as a requirement for salvation in this verse holds that a parenthesis is present. Wallace mentions that possibility:

> *The text should be repunctuated* in light of the shift from second person plural to third person singular back to second person plural again. If so, it would read as follows: "Repent, and let each one of you be baptized at the name of Jesus Christ, for the forgiveness of your sins. . . ." If this is the correct understanding, then εἰς is subordinate to μετανοήσατε alone, rather than to βαπτισθήτω. The idea then would be, "Repent *for/with reference to* your sins, and let each one of you be baptized. . . ." Such a view is an acceptable way of handling εἰς, but its subtlety and awkwardness are against it (ibid., italics in original).

This interpretation that posits the presence of a parenthesis deserves a second look. What Wallace is referring to with "the shift from second person plural to third person singular back to second person plural again" can be understood and amplified with the following rendition of Acts 2:38: "Repent [**second person**, **plural**, aorist, active, **imperative**] (and he is commanded to be baptized) [**third person**, **singular**, passive,

imperative] each of you [**second person, plural**, pronoun] in the name of Jesus Christ for the forgiveness of your [**second person, plural**, pronoun] sins; and you shall receive [**second person, plural**, future, middle indicative] the gift of the Holy Spirit." As Wallace notes, the change within the proposed parenthesis is twofold: (1) the person, which is who is being addressed, is changed from second person to third person; and (2) the number switches, from plural to singular.

Wallace's first objection to the interpretation of the presence of a parenthesis is its "subtlety." However, it should be observed that the context of the verse in question is a sermon, audibly received by an audience. Additionally, the Acts of the Apostles, in written form, would have had the majority of its audience, hear it audibly, having it read to them. The presence or absence of subtlety must be decided on the basis of the audience's audible reception rather than analysis of a written text. Bible students today are understandably better at the latter than the former.

Having been born and raised in an environment of quadrilingualism, and having more than one first language, the present writer is sensitive to how a language sounds to a native speaker. What might appear to be a subtlety to a nonnative speaker may be obvious, elementary, and automatic to a native speaker. This is especially true audibly. Children, who initially learn a language, have a quite sophisticated automatic grasp of rather complex grammar even though they do not understand its particulars, nor are they able to give an explanation for it.

In English, if you put together the two words "had" and "went" and say "had went," even a child in the lower elementary grades can tell you that it should be "had gone." They cannot explain past participles or auxiliary verbs but that does not stop them from using them properly. Grammatical changes that might appear to be subtle to a nonnative speaker are audibly significant and substantial to a native speaker. The "awkwardness" that Wallace senses in interpreting the presence of a parenthesis in the verse in question is what he senses and is not what someone who had Greek as their first language would have experienced.

In fact, to understand the verse without a parenthesis, in spite of significant grammatical changes, in both person and number, would itself have seemed awkward to a native speaker. While the earliest extant manuscripts, and presumably the original autographs, do not have punctuation, and therefore no written clue signifying the existence of a parenthesis, anyone reading this verse aloud, unless they did so in a flat expressionless monotone, signaled the presence of parenthetical material with their cadence and either raising or lowering the pitch of their voice. Peter, as he preached, would have given audible signals that he was mentioning baptism within a parenthesis, and it would have easily been picked up by his audience for whom it would have sounded quite natural and neither subtle nor awkward.

Another grammatical issue needing attention in Acts 2:38 is the presence of the third person singular imperative. It is difficult for a nonnative speaker to grasp the nuances of a grammatical device not present in his or her native language. In English we have a second person imperative, but not a third person imperative that is present in Greek. The third person imperative in this verse has been translated by the NASB with "let [him] be baptized" (βαπτισθήτω) implying a permissive meaning. As Wallace observes, "the *third person* imperative is normally translated *Let him do*, etc. This is easily confused in English with a permissive idea. Its force is more akin to *he must*, however, or periphrastically, *I command him to.* . . (ibid., 486, italics in original)." In Acts 2:38 baptism is not mentioned as an option, but is commanded. As Wallace says, "A number of passages could be easily misunderstood as mere permission in most English translations. . . .The Greek is stronger than a mere option, engaging the volition and placing a requirement on the individual" (ibid.). As Wallace notes, "The imperative moves in the realm of *volition* (involving the imposition of one's will upon another) and *possibility*" (ibid., 485, italics and parenthesis in original).

The introduction of a third person singular imperative in the parenthesis, after having used a second person plural imperative, would have been audibly significant to Peter's audience. The third person imperative addresses a different audience than a second person imperative and is significant in Acts 2:38, because it separates "repent" (μετανοήσατε) from "be baptized" (βαπτισθήτω). Peter did not say that both are required for eternal salvation. Wallace's note showing the importance of the Greek third person imperative needs to be taken seriously. Wallace illustrates how English translations can contribute to misunderstanding and can

> involve the ambiguity of who is being addressed . . . For example, in 1 Tim 4:12 ["Let no one despise your youth"], does this mean "Don't *you* let anyone despise your youth" or "I command *others* not to despise your youth"? The first translation would have a second person verb; the second would have a third person, as it does in the Greek [καταφρονείτω] (ibid., 486, italics and brackets in original).

In 1Timothy 4:12 it makes a difference if Timothy is being told not to allow others to despise his youth or if those who would despise him are being commanded not to despise the youth of Timothy. With the presence of the third person imperative, a grammatical option available in Greek but not in English, Paul addresses other people and not Timothy with his command. Who is addressed makes a difference in interpretation and application.

Likewise it makes a difference in Acts 2:38 who is addressed and therefore what they are told to do, and with what purpose or result. Repentance and baptism are not two parallel requirements for the forgiveness of sins. To combine the addressees, and conflate their distinct individual commands, invites theological confusion and anxiety or angst at best, and doctrinal heresy at worst. The latter, the route chosen by the Campbellites and their heretical heirs, is to be rejected.

Another Soteriological Additive – Romans 10:9

The problem with soteriological additives is that they nullify the gospel of eternal salvation. The nature of grace, of which the gospel is its resplendent expression, was described by the apostle Paul with the words, "And if by grace, then is it no more of works: otherwise grace is no more grace" (Romans 11:6). One drop of works added to the requirement for eternal salvation, whether directly, or in diluted form, destroys the gospel of the grace of God.

The identity of Jesus has been hijacked by some Bible teachers who twist it so that it is transformed into works in disguise. The identifying term "Lord" (κύριος) has been used to blatantly infuse works, or has been watered down to wanting, being willing, or being committed to do works as a requirement for obtaining salvation. A contextual identifier has been converted into an imperative. In that soteriological system the verb "believe" (πιστεύω) is no longer sufficient for salvation. The biblical gospel is shored up to make it salvifically sufficient in their minds. Sadly their supposed sufficiency is in fact a fatal deficiency.

Jesus created the world. That is a part of His identity. But it is not to be employed as a characteristic that is to be addressed in a manner that adds an additional requirement for salvation. Jesus gave Himself on the cross as the all-sufficient sacrifice for the sins of men. Man's relationship to that sacrifice is not to imitate His death as a requirement for eternal life, but to trust in the one who suffered on man's behalf. God exists in a Trinity, and Jesus is a member of the Trinity. That is who Jesus is, but there is nothing that is to be taken from His Trinitarian identity and added to placing trust in Him for salvation. Taking something that identifies Jesus and using it to add another requirement for eternal life violates the biblical unity of His person.

Romans 10:9 has been the keystone verse used by many Bible teachers who add "lordship" to their soteriological formula. That verse needs to be removed from supporting such a position. As with the removal of a keystone from an architectural arch, the biblical removal of that illegitimately used buttressing element should rightfully result in the collapse of that unscriptural soteriological construct.

The meaning of the terms "believe" and "trust" are not to be twisted into a lexically indefensible definition such as "commit." The use of the adverb "as" to change an identifier such as "Lord" (κύριος) into something to be done, mentally, emotionally, psychologically, or physically is inappropriate when used soteriologically. The reason Jesus is identified as Lord is for trust to be placed in Him. To choose a part of His identity and change Him from the one in whom trust is to be placed into the one for whom anything is to be done for eternal salvation is to run afoul of the clear prohibition of Scripture (Ephesians 2:8). Works, by any other name, are still works. The biblical position is that only words that nullify works are legitimate in relation to salvation; words that qualify or modify works in an attempt to make it acceptable as a requirement for eternal life are never appropriate.

Romans 10:9 says, "that if thou shalt confess with thy mouth the Lord Jesus, and shalt believe in thine heart that God hath raised him from the dead, thou shalt be saved." To understand what Paul was saying his words need to be taken in context. In Romans chapters 9-11 Paul is speaking about and to his fellow Jews even though there are applications for Gentiles in the New Testament church. Paul says in Romans 10:4: "For Christ is the end of the law for righteousness to every one that believeth." The alternatives for obtaining righteousness are self-produced righteousness versus righteousness that results from faith in Jesus. About the former Paul says, "For Moses describeth the righteousness which is of the law, that the man which doeth those things shall live by them" (Romans 10:5). With this method there is no need for faith, although the entire history of Israel proves the futility of that approach. For fallen humanity perfection is not possible.

The other alternative is introduced with the words, "But the righteousness which is of faith speaketh on this wise" (Romans 10:6). The principle was true in the Old Testament when the Law was given and is true for the righteousness of faith in the present. This is not a mystery; it is a clearly communicated truth. In the context of Moses talking about obedience to the Law he also said, "And the Lord thy God will circumcise thine heart, and the heart of thy seed, to love the Lord thy God with all thine heart, and with all thy soul, that thou mayest live" (Deuteronomy 30:6). This was in contrast to physical circumcision. The spiritual, not the physical, is man's primary need. The faith/works dichotomy was alive and well in the Old Testament.

In Colossians 2:11 Paul uses the same metaphor for salvation, "In whom also ye are circumcised with the circumcision made without hands, in putting off the body of the sins of the flesh by the circumcision of Christ." Negatively Paul referred to the unsaved condition with, "And you, being dead in your sins and the uncircumcision of your flesh" (Colossians 2:13). The outward physical symbol of membership in the Abrahamic family was superseded by membership in the community of faith which constituted an inner transformation.

In Romans 10 Paul discusses the principle of God's forthright communication to man, first stated negatively, "Say not in thine heart, Who shall ascend into heaven? (that is, to bring Christ down from above:) Or, who shall descend into the deep? (that is, to bring up Christ again from the dead)" [parentheses in KJV] (Romans 10:6-7). Man does not have to go to extraordinary lengths to know what God has said; He has made it readily accessible.

Paul introduces the application of the principle positively with the words, "But what saith it?" (Romans 10:8). Paul answers the question, stating what Moses said about God's way of communicating, "The word is nigh thee, *even* in thy mouth, and in thy heart" [italics in KJV] (Romans 10:8). This is a quotation of Deuteronomy 30:14: "But the word *is* very nigh unto thee, in thy mouth, and in thy heart, that thou mayest do it" [italics in KJV]. The word about trusting in God was known and verbalized by Israel. Paul's application for his readers is, "that is, the word of faith, which we preach" (Romans 10:8). The clear manner in which God communicated in the Old Testament was matched in the way Paul preached; it was available and accessible.

The content preached is introduced with the conjunction "that" (Romans 10:9) (ὅτι). There has been considerable debate and controversy regarding Romans 10:9 and the verses that follow. It is ironic that in a context where Paul expresses the principle and the certainty of clear communication from God there would be such confusion. While there are numerous proposed interpretations to this passage, there are certain foci around which a correct interpretation must revolve. A crucial one is whether the two parts of verse 9 occur simultaneously or subsequent to each other. The first part Paul mentions is, "if thou shalt confess with thy mouth the Lord Jesus." The NASB says, "if you confess with your mouth Jesus *as* Lord" [italics in NASB] (Romans 10:9). The second part of the sentence is, "and shalt believe in thine heart that God hath raised him from the dead."

Some Bible teachers assume that they occur simultaneously, at the time of conversion, and are both requirements for salvation. Are they separate or simultaneous events? The fact that "confess" (ὁμολογέω) is mentioned before "believe" (πιστεύω) is sometimes used to argue that while later on in chapter 10 "call" (ἐπικαλέω), what is done with the mouth, is placed chronologically after "believe" (πιστεύω), since what is done with the mouth comes first in verse 9, the interpreter is free to go with that option. However, the order of both can be accounted for contextually.

The order in verse 9 reflects the order in which the Deuteronomy passage has them. Because of that, Paul's quotation about the "mouth" (στόμα) comes first, followed by "heart" (καρδία). However, in the following verse (Romans 10:10), where Paul introduces his explanation with the explanatory conjunction "for" (γὰρ), he reverses the order of the clauses: "For with the heart man believeth unto righteousness; and with the mouth confession is made unto salvation." If they are taken as simultaneous, the change in order would be inconsequential, perhaps a stylistic variation on Paul's part. But Paul does concern himself with chronological issues in this passage as his explanation demonstrates.

If the words "confess with thy mouth" (ὁμολογήσῃς ἐν τῷ στόματί) are a requirement for obtaining eternal life, it is curious that the apostle John, who wrote his Gospel with the express purpose that people might receive eternal life (John 20:31), used the verb "confess" (ὁμολογέω) only four times which is outnumbered by the verb "believe" (πιστεύω) that is used nearly one hundred times in the Gospel of John. One might argue that numerical considerations are not determinative. However, in none of the four times that John uses the verb "confess" (ὁμολογέω) does he associate it with the term "Lord" (κύριος).

In John's Gospel, John the Baptist was questioned about his (John the Baptist's) identity. John 1:20 says, "And he confessed, and denied not; but confessed, I am not the Christ." John the Baptist denied being the Messiah. In the confrontation between the blind man whom Jesus healed and the Jewish religious hierarchy, John, the writer, gives an editorial comment on the proceedings. He said this about the blind man's parent's hands-off approach: "These *words* spake his parents, because they feared the Jews: for the Jews had agreed already, that if any man did confess that he was Christ, he should be put out of the synagogue" [italics in NASB] (John 9:22). Excommunication was the consequence for identifying Jesus as the Messiah. The term

"Lord" (κύριος) is not mentioned. Similarly, John 12:42 says, "Nevertheless among the chief rulers also many believed on him; but because of the Pharisees they did not confess him, lest they should be put out of the synagogue." Again the title "Lord" (κύριος) is nowhere present in this context.

Surely the apostle John would not have left out an indispensable part of the gospel, would he? Is the biblical reader expected to go on a scriptural scavenger hunt to collect and assemble the pieces to the puzzle for the acquisition of eternal life? To ask such a question is to answer it. What did Paul mean when he used the term "confess" (ὁμολογέω) in the book of Romans?

Paul's concern for his people the Jews was not only evangelistic, but eschatological. Paul's evangelistic concern was for their individual conversion, His eschatological concern was for corporate national deliverance. The requirement for individual conversion was "believe in thine heart" (Romans 10:9) (πιστεύσῃς ἐν τῇ καρδίᾳ σου). Conversion was also a condition for corporate deliverance. After they had individually believed, they would be eligible to "call upon the name of the Lord" (ἐπικαλέσηται τὸ ὄνομα κυρίου) and be delivered.

The Old Testament quotation that Paul uses is Joel 2:32, an eschatological context of the "day of the Lord" (Joel 2:31). Romans 10:13 says, "For whosoever shall call upon the name of the Lord shall be saved." Joel 2:32 says, "And it shall come to pass, *that* whosoever shall call on the name of the Lord shall be delivered: for in mount Zion and in Jerusalem shall be deliverance, as the Lord hath said, and in the remnant whom the Lord shall call" [italics in KJV]. Paul confirms the chronological order of "believe" (πιστεύω) and "confess" (ὁμολογέω) or "call upon" (ἐπικαλέω) and what must precede them with the words, "How then shall they call on him in whom they have not believed? And how shall they believe in him of whom they have not heard? And how shall they hear without a preacher? And how shall they preach, except they be sent?" (Romans 10:14-15).

The context is clearly that of the nation of Israel. Romans 10:19 says, "But I say, did not Israel know? First Moses saith, I will provoke you to jealousy *by them that are* no people, *and* by a foolish nation I will anger you" [italics in KJV]. Israel had been forewarned and would face the consequences of captivity. But Israel has hope of a future deliverance. Romans 11:1 says, "I say then, hath God cast away his people? God forbid." Personal eternal salvation is available to individuals, and corporate deliverance is promised to the nation Israel.

Nothing in Romans 10:9 adds to "believe" (πιστεύω) as a requirement for obtaining eternal life. In Paul's explanation, the separation of the two terms "believe" (πιστεύω) and "confess" (ὁμολογέω) and linking them to different outcomes was intentional. "Believing" (πιστεύω) results in "righteousness" (δικαιοσύνη), that is, imputed righteousness that God gives. What is done with the "heart" (καρδία) differs from what is done with the "mouth" (στόμα). Anyone, Jew and Gentile alike, can receive eternal life on the basis of believing; national deliverance is offered to His chosen people, the nation of Israel by "confessing," that is, calling on Christ. However, just as Israel in the last days will call on God for deliverance, believers can call on Him today.

The theological controversy over Romans 10:9 and the phrase "confess with thy mouth the Lord Jesus" (ὁμολογήσῃς ἐν τῷ στόματί σου κύριον Ἰησοῦν), needs to stop. Romans 10:9 does not give an additional condition, in addition to "believing" (πιστεύω), for the reception of eternal life. To take Israel's postconversion truth and make it a personal requirement for eternal salvation, and employ it to inject submission to Christ's lordship into the conversion equation "gets the camel's nose in the tent." Works, whether it be a wish or willingness to do them, a promise to do them or actually perform them, as a requirement for the new birth, results instead in the second death rather than eternal life.

Soteriological Introspection – 2 Corinthians 13:5

At the end of Paul's second epistle to the Corinthian believers is a verse that has been used by some as a command to test oneself for the genuineness of one's personal salvation. Second Corinthians 13:5 states, "Examine yourselves, whether ye be in the faith; prove your own selves. Know ye not your own selves, how that Jesus Christ is in you, except ye be reprobate [NASB = "unless you fail the test"; Greek = εἰ μήτι ἀδόκιμοί ἐστε]." Some Bible teachers take being "in the faith" (ἐν τῇ πίστει) to mean whether one is in a believing or saved state or not.

The only other time in the New Testament when that exact Greek prepositional phrase "in the faith" (ἐν τῇ πίστει) is used is when Paul says, "rebuke them sharply, that they may be sound in the faith" (Titus 1:13). In that context "faith" (πίστις) is a reference to the body of Christian doctrine. There are two other Greek constructions where English translations have the same prepositional phrase, "in the faith." One is with the preposition "in" (ἐν) but without the definite article, the other is the noun "faith" (πίστις) in the dative case without the preposition or the definite article.

The context of 2 Corinthians 13:5 is believers' rejection of Paul's apostleship and his right to confront them about their sin. 2 Corinthians 13:3 says, "Since ye seek a proof of Christ speaking in me, which to you-ward is not weak, but is mighty in you." Paul himself did not doubt his spiritual authority to address their sin but was having to defend his right to do so. Perhaps Paul was making reference to the spiritual braggadocio of his opponents and speaking sarcastically when he says, "which to you-ward is not weak, but is mighty in you" (2 Corinthians 13:3).

Paul defends his "weakness" (ἀσθενέω), a reference to his lack of verbal forcefulness, by using Jesus as his model. Paul says, "For though he was crucified through weakness, yet he liveth by the power of God" (2 Corinthians 13:4). Jesus appeared powerless on the cross but the fact is that as God He is omnipotent. Paul applies Jesus' experience to his own situation with the words, "For we also are weak in him, but we shall live with him by the power of God toward you" (2 Corinthians 13:4). Paul's weakness was undergirded by divine power.

Paul had "proof of the Christ who speaks in me" (2 Corinthians 13:3 NASB) (δοκιμὴν. . . τοῦ ἐν ἐμοὶ λαλοῦντος Χριστοῦ), evidenced in Christ's power in his ministry. Paul said, "But I trust that you will realize that we ourselves do not fail the test" (2 Corinthians 13:6 NASB) (ἐλπίζω δὲ ὅτι γνώσεσθε ὅτι ἡμεῖς οὐκ ἐσμὲν ἀδόκιμοι). Paul's words were enabled and empowered by Christ. Paul's challenge was for his antagonists to prove whether their criticism of him passed the same test. Paul operated under the auspices and authority, privilege and power of Christ because he (Paul) and his associates were "in Him" (ἐν αὐτῷ). Paul's challenge to his opponents was not about his own salvation or theirs but whether they could say the same about their own "ministries" as he could about his. The bottom line was that their criticism of him did not have Christ's approval.

It could be questioned whether the personal controversy and problem that Paul was experiencing, and his exhortation to his antagonists, is to be elevated to the level of a universal principle for every believer. That aside, Paul was not exhorting believers to constantly scrutinize whether they were saved or not. He was not describing a process of spiritual introspection that he was engaged in to check His spiritual sonship. As Paul says in 2 Timothy 1:12, "for I know whom I have believed, and am persuaded that he is able to keep that which I have committed unto him against that day." The NASB renders the verb "committed" (πιστεύω) with "entrusted." Paul based his assurance on his belief, not his behavior.

Paul spoke confidently when he said, "He that spared not his own Son, but delivered him up for us all, how shall he not with him also freely give us all things? Who shall lay any thing to the charge of God's elect? *It is* God that justifieth. Who *is* he that condemneth?" (italics in KJV) (Romans 8:32-34). The answer to those questions is given in the words, "*It is* Christ that died, yea rather, that is risen again, who is even at the right hand of God, who also maketh intercession for us" (italics in KJV) (Romans 8:34). Paul asked, "Who shall separate us from the love of Christ? Shall tribulation, or distress, or persecution, or famine, or nakedness, or peril, or sword?" (Romans 8:35).

Paul spoke of his assurance with the words, "For I am confident that neither death, nor life, nor angels, nor principalities, nor things present, not things to come, nor powers, nor height, nor depth, nor any other created thing, shall be able to separate us from the love of God, which is in Christ Jesus our Lord" (Romans 8:38-39). These are not the words of a man who was constantly questioning whether or not he was saved, nor did he teach others to do so. Paul was not contradicting his confident assurance with his statement in 2 Corinthians 13:5 about examining one's doctrine.

Believers are not immune to doctrinal deviation. As a believer one is to make sure that his or her doctrinal beliefs are in line with what Jude called, "the faith which was once for all delivered to the saints" (Jude 3 NASB). Rather than promote constant personal introspection to see if one is saved, one is to diligently pay close attention to one's doctrine. Second Corinthians 13:5 was not intended to be used to hammer believers. Those who pervert the gospel of the grace of God need to follow Paul's exhortation and examine themselves to see if they are in the doctrine that has been delivered to us.

Chapter 3

Evidence for the Identity of God in the Old Testament

God Is Revealed

Beginning with the account of creation God initiates His self-revelation. His existence is assumed and his identity begins to be progressively revealed. He is introduced as the creator of all things, culminating in the creation of man. The first recorded verbal communication from the creator God to man are the words, "Be fruitful, and multiply, and replenish the earth, and subdue it: and have dominion over the fish of the sea, and over the fowl of the air, and over every living thing that moveth upon the earth" (Genesis 1:28). God delegated dominion over His earthly creation to man.

God is further revealed as the One to whom man is accountable. On a positive note God told man: "Of every tree of the garden thou mayest freely eat" (Genesis 2:16). God gave man one prohibition: "But of the tree of the knowledge of good and evil, thou shalt not eat of it: for in the day that thou eatest thereof thou shalt surely die" (Genesis 2:17). God is the divine command issuer and judge. This relationship with man was on God's terms and conditions. When man failed to comply with the divine prohibition, we get a glimpse of what his relationship with God had been, and what it would have continued to be had it not been for his disobedience. The sad aftermath of the first sin is described in these words: "And they heard the voice of the Lord God walking in the garden in the cool of the day: and Adam and his wife hid themselves from the presence of the Lord God amongst the trees of the garden" (Genesis 3:8).

We are not left to speculate, hypothesize, or infer God's existence and identity; the divine self-disclosure leaves no room for doubt. Progressive revelation is primarily the biblical unfolding of God's self-disclosure. The Trinity is progressively revealed from the Old Testament to the New Testament and the motif of divine identity and the expected human response to it are a unifying theme throughout Scripture.

In God's pronouncement of judgment on the serpent there appears a ray of hope for mankind: "And I will put enmity between thee and the woman, and between thy seed and her seed; it shall bruise thy head, and thou shalt bruise his heel" (Genesis 3:15). This prophecy, theologically known as the "protevangelium" (Latin = "first gospel"), the beginning of salvation history, gives the initial clue to the identity of the coming Messiah. The term "seed" (זֶרַע), indicating human descent, becomes an identifying characteristic that will be described with increasing detail as revelation about the Messiah progresses. Speaking to the serpent, God the Father in Genesis 3:15 identifies the Messiah as One who will be victorious, "it shall bruise thy head, and thou shalt bruise his heel" (Genesis 3:15). The Messiah would deal a fatal blow to the serpent whereas the serpent's wounding of the Messiah would prove to be temporary.

In the recently fallen world God continued to reveal Himself. A child was born to Adam and Eve, and the first couple wondered whether Cain was the promised seed. To their sorrow they found out that he was not. When Cain and Abel brought their offerings to the Lord, it is understood that God had given instructions as to the proper manner and means of sacrifice. When Cain murdered his brother Abel, Cain's moral responsibility and accountability to God whose justice he had violated is graphically described: "And he said, What hast thou done? the voice of thy brother's blood crieth unto me from the ground" (Genesis 4:10). Nothing that happens can be hidden from God.

As a consequence of the fall, Adam, Cain's father, found that God had "cursed" (אָרַר) the ground. This added difficulty and struggle to his agricultural efforts. God told Adam, "cursed *is* the ground for thy sake; in sorrow shalt thou eat *of* it all the days of thy life" (italics in KJV) (Genesis 3:17). Cain's punishment would be more severe. He was personally "cursed" (אָרַר), for he was banned from farming altogether: "And now *art* thou cursed from the earth, which hath opened her mouth to receive thy brother's blood from thy hand" (italics in KJV) (Genesis 4:11). Cain's association with the soil was severed; his labor would no longer be rewarded: "When thou tillest the ground, it shall not henceforth yield unto thee her strength" (Genesis 4:12). Ironically he would reap what he had sown by not being able to reap what he sowed. Cain polluted the ground by spilling his brother's blood on it, and in describing God's dealing with Cain the author communicated truth about God to whom man is accountable.

As God the Father, the first Person of the Trinity, is progressively revealed, the thread of identity of the second Person of the Trinity, Christ, the coming Messiah, continues. Why is a genealogy included in chapter 5 of Genesis? Ross summarizes the lesson to be learned with the words, *"Those who enjoy the blessing of the calling of God may anticipate victory over the curse as they walk with the Lord"* (Allen Ross, *Creation and Blessing*, [Grand Rapids: Baker, 1988], 176 italics his). That can certainly be learned from this chapter, but why use a genealogy to teach it? As is the case with other genealogies, their primary purpose is to provide proof of identity. Eve was promised that her seed (זֶרַע) would defeat Satan (Genesis 3:15), and although every human being would be Eve's progeny, the need to trace human lineage to the future Messiah would become indispensable in establishing His identity. The biblical authors give additional information of the Messiah's identity as His genealogical roots emerge. Genesis chapter 5 provides the genealogical link from Eve to Noah and his sons.

Some have suggested that in Genesis 6:1-4 "the Nephilim" (הַנְּפִלִים), offspring from the "daughters of men" (בְּנוֹת הָאָדָם) and the "sons of God" (בְּנֵי־הָאֱלֹהִים), were a satanic attempt to pollute the human gene pool and thereby preclude (or at least confuse) the possibility of a Messiah coming from the "seed" (זֶרַע) of Eve. Whatever one's view of the identity of the "sons of God" (בְּנֵי־הָאֱלֹהִים) in this account, man's wickedness had reached a breaking point: "And it repented the Lord that he had made man on the earth, and it grieved him at his heart" (Genesis 6:6). God reached a decision: "And the Lord said, I will destroy man whom I have created from the face of the earth; both man, and beast, and the creeping thing, and the fowls of the air; for it repenteth me that I have made them" (Genesis 6:7). Were it not for Noah, who was "a righteous man" (Genesis 6:9) (אִישׁ צַדִּיק), the human race would have been wiped out and God's plan for the Messiah would have been thwarted. The occurrence of the adjective "righteous" (צַדִּיק) is the first biblical appearance of this Hebrew root that is important for understanding salvation in the Old Testament as well as the New Testament. In the account of Abraham the biblical reader is told how a man becomes "righteous" (צַדִּיק) in the sight of God.

After the Flood God revealed Himself as one who establishes "covenant" (בְּרִית). God communicated a covenant with Noah and his sons: "And God spake unto Noah, and to his sons with him" (Genesis 9:8). The covenant included their posterity: "And I, behold, I establish my covenant with you, and with your seed after you" (Genesis 9:9). The Noahic covenant included more than man: "And with every living creature that *is* with you, of the fowl, of the cattle, and of every beast of the earth with you; from all that go out of the ark, to every beast of the earth" (italics in KJV) (Genesis 9:10).

As with Adam and Eve, with the shrinking of humanity to eight individuals, Noah, his wife, their three sons and their wives, a prospective genealogy follows. In Genesis 11, transitioning from the genealogy of Shem to that of Abram, is the account of the tower of Babel. God directly intervened, disrupting their united effort by linguistically and geographically dispersing the builders of Babel. The genealogical information that follows, from Shem to Abram, together with the previous one from Adam (and Eve) to Shem (Genesis 5:3-32), would be incorporated in the messianic line. The line of the messianic "seed" (זֶרַע) continues.

Abraham is significant, not only because of his place in Jewish history but also because of his place in the history of redemption. The apostle Paul's theological treatise on justification by faith identifies believers as those who have the "faith of Abraham" (Romans 4:16) (πίστεως Ἀβραάμ). Those under the Law were also included: "Therefore *it is* of faith, that *it might be* by grace; to the end the promise might be sure to all the seed; not to that only which is of the law, but to that also which is of the faith of Abraham; who is the father of us all" [italics in KJV] (Romans 4:16).

Before Abraham individuals were saved, but in Genesis 15:6 for the first time in the biblical text the requirement for someone to have "righteousness" (צְדָקָה) put to their account is stated: "Therefore *it is* of faith, that *it might be* by grace; to the end the promise might be sure to all the seed; not to that only which is of the law, but to that also which is of the faith of Abraham; who is the father of us all" (italics in KJV) (Romans 4:16). God emphasizes the significance of Abraham with His promise to "bless" (בֵּרַךְ) those who treat Abraham well and to "curse" (אָרַר) those who curse him: "And I will bless them that bless thee, and curse him that curseth thee" (Genesis 12:3). God includes the salvific effect that Abraham through the coming Messiah will have on mankind in the statement, "and in thee shall all families of the earth be blessed" (Genesis 12:3). The Messiah, through whom salvation is accomplished, will be identified as a descendant of Abraham.

The call of Abram is recorded in Genesis chapter 12. "Now the Lord had said unto Abram, Get thee out of thy country, and from thy kindred, and from thy father's house, unto a land that I will shew thee" (Genesis 12:1). Abraham obeyed God's command: "So Abram departed, as the Lord had spoken unto him" (Genesis 12:4). Bible students have debated the chronology of Abraham's obedience to God's call reported in chapter 12 and the pronouncement that Abram had "righteousness" (צְדָקָה) reckoned to him in Genesis 15:6. The question is whether Abram was saved prior to his call out of Ur, at the time when he was called, or when the pronouncement is made three chapters later.

The New Testament book of Hebrews says, "By faith Abraham, when he was called to go out into a place which he should after receive for an inheritance, obeyed; and he went out, not knowing whither he went" (Hebrews 11:8). This seems to suggest that he was saved before he received God's call to leave Ur. In Genesis 31:53, in Jacob's confrontation with his uncle Laban, when Laban referred to God, he said, "The God of Abraham, and the God of Nahor, the God of their father, judge betwixt us." Because Nahor is not mentioned as one of the family members who went from Ur to Haran (Genesis 11:31), it could be that this is a reference to Abram's belief in God before the journey began and before the call to leave.

Most likely God's pronouncement in Genesis 15:6 refers to a prior occurrence, a conclusion supported by the Hebrew construction. As Ross says:

> A close study of the Hebrew construction "and he believed" reveals that the writer did not intend this verb to be understood as a result of the preceding section. The construction is not the normal sequential construction ([וְהֶאֱמִן] is a perfect tense with the *wāw* [ו] prefixed; the *wāw* [ו] thus cannot be a *wāw* [ו] consecutive, otherwise the translation would have to be future); if the writer had wished to show that this verse followed in sequence the preceding, he would have used the normal structure for narrative sequence ([וַיַּאֲמֵן], "and [then] he believed"). We must conclude that the narrator did not want to show sequence in the order of the verses; rather, he wished to make a break with the narrative in order to supply this information about the faith of Abram (Allen Ross, *Creation and Blessing*, [Grand Rapids: Baker, 1988], 309).

Ross gives the exegetical implications:

> The verse may be a summary statement of Abram's faith, or a transitional note between sections. It could be translated parenthetically, as disjunctive clauses often are ("Now Abram believed. . ."). The verb could be explained as having a characteristic nuance ("now Abram believed," in the sense that he was a believer). In other words, the text does not necessarily mean that Abram came to faith here. Hebrews 11:8 asserts that he left Ur by faith. Genesis 15:6 simply reports at this point the fact that Abram believed, and for that belief God had credited him with righteousness (ibid., 309-10).

The statement about Abram in Genesis 15:6 is not placed at the beginning of Genesis 12, and one should not conclude that Abraham's faith plus his action of leaving resulted in his salvation. The "disjunctive clause," that Ross mentions, serves to isolate faith as the sole requirement for Abram receiving imputed righteousness. Paul's inspired quotation of this verse in Romans (Romans 4:3), as proof of salvation by faith alone apart from works, is consistent with the grammar employed in Genesis, and with its location in the biblical text. Neither Moses, the human author of Genesis, nor Paul in Romans, intended to convey that Abraham is an example of a synergism between faith and works as a requirement for the imputation of righteousness, forgiveness, and eternal life.

Those who hold to a "content" viewpoint of salvific faith sometimes associate Abram's faith with "a proposition to be believed as true" in the immediate context of Genesis 15:6. The search for such a proposition or statement is both misguided and unproductive. Abram put his trust in God on the basis of what he knew about Him. Abram's knowledge of God can be stated in propositional statements, and those statements serve to identify the one true God in whom Abram trusted. God addressed Abram right after the statement in Genesis about Abram's faith and identified Himself as the one who was speaking to him, the one who had previously spoken and led him out of Ur: "And he said unto him, I *am* the Lord that brought thee out of Ur of the Chaldees" [italics in KJV] (Genesis 15:7). He is the same God in whom Abraham had placed his trust.

The meaning of the verb "believe" (אָמַן) in the Hebrew Hiphil form הֶאֱמִן is important for a correct interpretation of Genesis 15:6. As Ross writes, "The central theological idea thus concerns Abram's faith in the Lord. A word study of believed ([אָמַן] > [הֶאֱמִן]) is essential to the exegesis of this chapter, especially since the New Testament makes use of the verse in the discussion of saving faith" (ibid., 305). The Hebrew Hiphil form of "believe" (הֶאֱמִן) that is used here can refer to either "belief in the truth of a proposition" or "trust in someone or something." Genesis 15:6 is an example of the latter, that is, trust in God. Keil and Delitzsch explain that

> in *Hiphil* to trust, believe (πιστεύειν), expresses "that state of mind which is sure of its object, and relies firmly upon it;" and as denoting conduct towards God, as "a firm, inward, personal, self-surrendering reliance upon a personal being, especially upon the source of all being," it is construed sometimes with לְ (*e.g.* Deut. ix. 23), but more frequently with בְּ ["in"] (Num. xiv. 11, xx. 12; Deut. i. 32), "to believe the Lord," and "to believe on the Lord," to trust in Him. . . .Faith is therefore not merely *assensus*, but *fiducia* also, unconditional trust in the Lord and His word, even where the natural course of events furnishes no ground for hope or expectation (C. F. Keil and F. Delitzsch, *Commentary on the Old Testament in Ten Volumes* [reprint, Grand Rapids: Eerdmans, 1981], 1:212-13).

In Genesis 15:6 faith is expressed with the preposition "on" or "in" (בְּ) and the explicit object of faith is "the Lord," "Yahweh," (יהוה) and not propositional statements about Him. God did reveal Himself to Abram in terms of propositions or statements about Himself, which Abram believed to be true, but Genesis 15:6 is referring to the culmination which was trust placed in the one who had identified Himself to Abram. As this present study will show, the Hiphil form of the verb "believe" (אָמַן) is used to convey either the acceptance of the veracity of a proposition or trust in a person. The latter does not preclude and in fact it includes the former. Trust in God is possible because propositional statements about Him are believed to be true. By means of divine revelation the one in whom trust is to be placed is identified.

Throughout the book of Genesis God is identified in reference to Abram, or Abraham, and his descendants. In his prayer Abraham's household servant addressed God, "O Lord God of my master Abraham" (Genesis 24:12). God identified Himself to Isaac with the words, "I *am* the God of Abraham thy father" [italics in KJV] (Genesis 26:24). When God identified Himself to Jacob he added, "And, behold, the Lord stood above it, and said, I *am* the Lord God of Abraham thy father, and the God of Isaac" [italics in KJV] (Genesis 28:13). Jacob identified God as the source of his blessings. Jacob told his wives that in spite of the actions of their father, "the God of my father has been with me" (Genesis 31:5).

Laban identified God when he confronted his son-in-law Jacob and said, "the God of your father spoke to me yesternight" (Genesis 31:29). Laban, inadvertently perhaps, contrasted the true God with his own gods, asking Jacob, "wherefore hast thou stolen my gods?" (Genesis 31:30). Jacob acknowledged that God had intervened on his behalf in his confrontation with Laban: "Except the God of my father, the God of Abraham, and the fear of Isaac, had been with me, surely thou hadst sent me away now empty. God hath seen mine affliction and the labour of my hands, and rebuked *thee* yesternight" [italics in KJV] (Genesis 31:42). Perhaps in tacit recognition of the superiority of Jacob's God over his idols, Laban suggested that the agreement between him and Jacob be sealed with an oath by the God of Jacob's ancestors. Laban said, "The God of Abraham, and the God of Nahor, the God of their father, judge betwixt us. And Jacob sware by the fear of his father Isaac" (Genesis 31:53).

Jacob identified God as the one worshiped by his ancestors in his desperate prayer before his encounter with Esau: "And Jacob said, O God of my father Abraham, and God of my father Isaac" (Genesis 32:9). After Jacob's name was changed to "Israel" (Genesis 32:28) (יִשְׂרָאֵל) and he returned to Shechem, Jacob built an altar and called it "El-Elohe-Israel" or "God, the God of Israel" (Genesis 33:20) (אֵל אֱלֹהֵי יִשְׂרָאֵל), reflecting the new name God had given to him.

Joseph in Egypt did not forget the God of his ancestors, and while his brothers were unaware that he was their brother, Joseph said to them, "your God, and the God of your father, hath given you treasure in your sacks" [italics in KJV] (Genesis 43:23). When Jacob, now known as Israel, was on his way to see his son Joseph in Egypt, he worshiped the same God his father Isaac had worshiped. "And Israel took his journey with all that he had, and came to Beer-sheba, and offered sacrifices unto the God of his father Isaac" (Genesis 46:1). God identified Himself when He reassured Jacob about his sojourn into Egypt with the words, "And he said, I *am* God, the God of thy father: fear not to go down into Egypt; for I will there make of thee a great nation" [italics in KJV] (Genesis 46:3).

When Jacob spoke to his son Joseph in his deathbed blessing, Jacob identified God with the words, "But his bow abode in strength, and the arms of his hands were made strong by the hands of the mighty *God* of Jacob; (From thence *is* the shepherd, the stone of Israel)" [parenthesis and italics in KJV] (Genesis 49:24). Jacob further identified God by saying, "*Even* by the God of thy father, who shall help thee; and by the Almighty, who shall bless thee with blessings of heaven above, blessings of the deep that lieth under, blessings of the breasts, and of the womb" [italics in KJV] (Genesis 49:25). Jacob's death aroused a deep-seated fear in Joseph's brothers, who thought that Joseph would now avenge their previous treachery. Their message to Joseph mentioned their father Jacob's God: "and now, we pray thee, forgive the trespass of the servants of the God of thy father" (Genesis 50:17).

The identification of God with reference to His relationship with one's ancestors continued after the days of the patriarchs. Ancestral continuity was used to identify the one true God. God spoke to Moses from the burning bush, He identified Himself: "I *am* the God of thy father, the God of Abraham, the God of Isaac, and the God of Jacob" [italics in KJV] (Exodus 3:6). Perhaps Moses, feeling insignificant in the company of his illustrious ancestors, told God his concern that no one would listen to him: "And Moses said unto God, Behold, *when* I come unto the children of Israel, and shall say unto them, The God of your fathers hath sent me unto you; and they shall say to me, What *is* his name? what shall I say unto them?" [italics in KJV] (Exodus 3:13).

The last news that his fellow Israelites had heard about Moses was that he was a fugitive from justice. Now this fugitive would arrive on the scene and claim that God had spoken to him from a fiery bush. Would Moses and his message be taken seriously? The Israelites were downtrodden and disheartened. They associated God with their ancestors and He had not spoken for four hundred years. God's name had become "the God of Abraham, Isaac, and Jacob." Perhaps the memory of the patriarchs and their names were beginning to fade from the collective memory of their descendants. Would the God of the distant past reveal Himself dynamically in the present? How could Moses prove that God had chosen him to lead them?

The name God revealed to Moses relieved some of those fears, for He said, "I am that I am" (Exodus 3:14) (אֶהְיֶה אֲשֶׁר אֶהְיֶה). Moses was to tell the Israelites that "I am hath sent me unto you" (Exodus 3:14) (אֶהְיֶה שְׁלָחַנִי אֲלֵיכֶם). George Bush (1796-1858) says that the name "I am" "denotes the underived, eternal and unchangeable existence of the great Being to whom it is applied, carrying in it also the implication that He, in distinction from all others, is the one only true God, the God who really *is*" [italics in original] (*Notes on Exodus* [New York: Newman and Ivison, 1852; reprint, Minneapolis: James & Klock, 1976], 50). The eternal implications of God's name associated Him with Israel's past, present, and future. God told Moses, "Thus shalt thou say unto the children of Israel, The Lord God of your fathers, the God of Abraham, the God of Isaac, and the God of Jacob, hath sent me unto you: this *is* my name for ever, and this *is* my memorial unto all generations" [italics in KJV] (Exodus 3:15).

Moses boldly addressed Pharaoh and identified the God who had sent him as "the Lord, the God of Israel" (Exodus 5:1) (יהוה אֱלֹהֵי יִשְׂרָאֵל). The God of the patriarchs would be known as the God of the nation Israel, who demanded that His people worship Him exclusively. When God enacted the Mosaic covenant with Israel, He told them that it excluded association with pagan peoples and their deities. God told Israel, "Thou shalt make no covenant with them, nor with their gods" (Exodus 23:32). The God of the covenant is identified as "the God of Israel" (Exodus 24:10) (אֱלֹהֵי יִשְׂרָאֵל).

Joshua led the Israelites into the Promised Land under the banner of their God. In victory or defeat the reputation of the one true God was at stake. Following the debacle at Ai Joshua told the people to prepare themselves for the process of identifying the person responsible for their defeat. Joshua told the people, "Sanctify yourselves against to morrow: for thus saith the Lord God of Israel" (Joshua 7:13). Achan, who was singled out as the cause of the defeat, was told by Joshua to "give, I pray thee, glory to the Lord God of Israel" (Joshua 7:19). Achan confessed what he had done and acknowledged against whom he had sinned. He said, "Indeed I have sinned against the Lord God of Israel" (Joshua 7:20). The name "Lord" or "Yahweh" (יהוה) was identified as "the God of Israel" (אֱלֹהֵי יִשְׂרָאֵל).

In addition, throughout the book of Joshua, God is identified as "the God of Israel" (אֱלֹהֵי יִשְׂרָאֵל) more than a dozen times. That description is used in Joshua 8:30; 9:18, 19; 10:40, 42; 13:14, 33; 14:14; 22:24; 24:2. In Joshua 22:16 the wording "the Lord, the God of Israel" (יהוה אֱלֹהֵי יִשְׂרָאֵל) is not used, but the descriptive phrase "the God of Israel" is used once with the title "Lord" "Yahweh" (יהוה) that is used three times in the verse: "Thus saith the whole congregation of the Lord [Yahweh יהוה], What trespass *is* this that ye have committed against the God of Israel, to turn away this day from following the Lord [Yahweh יהוה] in that ye have builded you an altar, that ye might rebel this day against the Lord [Yahweh יהוה]?" [italics in KJV].

The book of Judges repeatedly refers to God with the title and description, "God [Yahweh], the God of Israel" (יהוה אֱלֹהֵי יִשְׂרָאֵל). Deborah referred to God's command with the words, "the Lord God of Israel commanded" (Judges 4:6). The song of Deborah and Barak has the words, "The mountains melted from before the Lord, *even* that Sinai from before the Lord God of Israel" [italics in KJV] (Judges 5:5). A prophet spoke to the Israelites when they cried out to God under the oppression of Midian. His message began with the words, "Thus saith the Lord God of Israel" (Judges 6:8).

Israel's God is given credit for their victory over King Sihon and the Amorites. Judges 11:21 says, "And the Lord God of Israel delivered Sihon and all his people into the hand of Israel, and they smote them." The thought is repeated in Judges 11:23: "So now the Lord God of Israel hath dispossessed the Amorites from before his people Israel." When the tribe of Benjamin was almost annihilated, the rest of the nation of Israel asked, "O Lord God of Israel, why is this come to pass in Israel, that there should be to day one tribe lacking in Israel?" (Judges 21:3). Throughout the Old Testament the one true God is identified as "the God of Israel" (יהוה אֱלֹהֵי יִשְׂרָאֵל).

The identity of God is revealed as a unique existence that demands exclusive worship. The first of the Ten Commandments is, "Thou shalt have no other gods before me" (Exodus 20:3). Idolatry is a violation of that command and is expressly prohibited:

"Thou shalt not make unto thee any graven image, or any likeness *of any thing* that *is* in heaven above, or that *is* in the earth beneath, or that *is* in the water under the earth" [italics in KJV] (Exodus 20:4). Making idols is prohibited. Some may argue that they are just symbols that facilitate the worship of God. However, making them was prohibited. Perhaps the reason for the command against their construction is that inevitably the idol itself would become the object of worship. Usually the reason they are made is to be worshiped and served, which God expressly prohibited: "Thou shalt not bow down thyself to them, nor serve them" (Exodus 20:5).

The reason God gave for the first commandment is "for I, the Lord thy God *am* a jealous God" [italics in KJV] (Exodus 20:5). The Hebrew adjective "jealous" (קַנָּא) has been taken by some to refer to having "zeal" or being "zealous." In Exodus 20:5 it is better to understand it as Bullinger does, who uses it as an example of "Anthropopatheia; or Condescension: The Ascribing of Human Attributes, etc., to God" (Ethelbert Bullinger, *Figures of Speech used in the Bible* [reprint, Grand Rapids: Baker, 1975], 871 and 883).

The use of this figure of speech does not attribute the negative characteristics of human jealousy to God but instead emphasizes the exclusive nature of the relationship with man that God demands. God, whose identity is revealed in Scripture, is intolerant of idolatry, and so His reaction to it is described as jealousy. Man is to imitate God's intolerance of idolatry. Aaron's grandson Phinehas is a godly example of intolerance toward idolatry whom God singled out. God told Moses, "Phinehas, the son of Eleazar, the son of Aaron the priest, hath turned my wrath away from the children of Israel, while he was zealous for my sake among them, that I consumed not the children of Israel in my jealousy" (Numbers 25:11).

The Old Testament speaks of gods who are not God with the adjective "other" (אַחֵר): "other gods." Exodus 20:3 and Deuteronomy 5:7 say, "Thou shalt have no other gods before me." Brown, Driver, and Briggs' lexicon (BDB) says that "other" (אַחֵר) refers to "one coming behind" (Francis Brown, S. R. Driver, and Charles A. Briggs, *A Hebrew and English Lexicon of the Old Testament* [Oxford: Clarendon, 1907, reprint, Oxford: Oxford University Press, 1977], 29). All other gods are idols. They are counterfeits of the original. God is the only real God. Gods other than the God of Israel are to be rejected. In Deuteronomy 6:14 God commanded, "Ye shall not go after other gods, of the gods of the people which *are* round about you" [italics in KJV]. The Old Testament warns numerous times about not going after "other" (אַחֵר) gods (Deut. 7:4; 8:19; 11:16, 28; 13:2, 6; 17:3; 18:20; 28:14; 28:36, 64; 29:26, 28; 30:17; 31:18, 20; Joshua 23:16; 24:2; 24:16; Judges 2:12, 17, 19; 10:13, etc.). Not until after the Babylonian captivity was Israel cured of her incessant pursuit of idolatry.

When God is rejected, there is no one who can replace Him. Bleak days in Israel's history are described in 2 Chronicles 15:3 with the words, "Now for a long season Israel *hath been* without the true God, and without a teaching priest, and without law" [italics in KJV].When God's people abandon Him, they experience His absence. The Levitical prayer in Nehemiah 9:6 acknowledges the uniqueness of God: "Thou, *even* thou, *art* Lord alone; thou hast made heaven, the heaven of heavens, with all their host, the earth, and all *things* that *are* therein, the seas, and all that *is* therein, and thou preservest them all; and the host of heaven worshippeth thee" [italics in KJV]. The prophet Jeremiah says, "*there is* none like unto thee, O Lord" [italics in KJV] (Jeremiah 10:6). In comparison with God, Jeremiah describes the wisest of men with the words, "But they are altogether brutish and foolish" (Jeremiah 10:8). On the other hand "the Lord *is* the true God, He *is* the living God, and an everlasting king" [italics in KJV] (Jeremiah 10:10).

What Does God Require?

In the first chapter of this book it was seen that "believe" can include the thought of believing a proposition to be true and trusting in a person. An examination of Hebrew terms is in order to better understand the lexical choice the authors of the Old Testament (and the Holy Spirit) made. As mentioned earlier, in Hebrew a specific verb אָמַן, and a form of that verb, the Hiphil stem הֶאֱמִן, is used to refer to Abraham's faith. That verb form הֶאֱמִן is also the only one that is translated πιστεύω in the Greek Septuagint (LXX). Why was that Hebrew verb and Hiphil stem chosen, and what were the other options available to the writers?

Trusting Something or Someone

Other Hebrew terms can be used to mean "trust in a person." The verb "seek refuge" (חָסָה) is used in Deuteronomy 32:37 that asks, "And he shall say, Where *are* their gods, *their* rock in whom they trusted" [italics in KJV]. The psalmist David used the same verb when he said, "O Lord my God, in thee do I put my trust" (Psalm 7:1) and in Psalm 11:1: "In the Lord put I my trust: How say ye to my soul, Flee *as* a bird to your mountain?" [italics in KJV]. Psalm 16:1 says, "Preserve me, O God: for in thee do I put my trust." The verb "take refuge" or "trust" is used in many Old Testament passages (Judges 9:15; Ruth 2:12; 2 Samuel 22:3, 31; Psalms 2:12; 5:11; 17:7; 18:2, 30; 25:20; 31:1, 19; Proverbs 14:32; 30:5; Isaiah 14:32; 30:2; 57:13; Nahum 1:7; Zephaniah 3:12, etc.).

The noun meaning "refuge" or "shelter" (מַחְסֶה) can be used literally or figuratively. Job used the term for a physical "shelter." "They are wet with the showers of the mountains, and embrace the rock for want of a shelter" (Job 24:8). The psalmist also used it literally for physical protection in Psalm 104:18: "The high hills *are* a refuge for the wild goats; *and* the rocks for the conies [NASB = "badgers"]" [italics in KJV]. The KJV also translates the noun figuratively with the word "trust" in Psalm 73:28. "I have put my trust in the Lord God." A figurative meaning for this noun is the most common in the Old Testament and in addition to Psalm 73:28 it occurs in Psalms 14:6; 46:1; 61:3; 62:7, 8; 71:7; 91:2, 9; 94:22; 142:5; Proverbs 14:26; Isaiah 4:6; 25:4; 28:15, 17; Jeremiah 17:17; Joel 3:16.

Another Hebrew verb that can mean "trust" is בָּטַח. In the conflict between Abimelech and Shechem Judges 9:26 says, "And Gaal the son of Ebed came with his brethren, and went over to Shechem: and the men of Shechem put their confidence in him." Second Kings 18:5 says of king Hezekiah, "He trusted in the Lord God of Israel." The king of Assyria taunted Hezekiah about his alliance with Egypt with the words, "Now, behold, thou trustest upon the staff of this bruised reed, *even* upon Egypt, on which if a man lean, it will go into his hand, and pierce it: so *is* Pharaoh king of Egypt unto all that trust on him." [italics in KJV] (2 Kings 18:21). This verb meaning "rely" or "trust" (בָּטַח) is also used many times in the Old Testament (Deut. 28:52; 1 Chron. 5:20; Job 6:20; Psalms 13:5; 22:4; 25:2; 26:1; 28:7; 31:6, 14; Proverbs 31:11; Isaiah 36:4, 5, 6, 7; Jeremiah 39:18, etc.).

The Hebrew noun מִבְטָח means "trust" or "confidence." In Job 8:14 the word translated "trust" in the KJV is מִבְטָח: "Whose hope shall be cut off, and whose trust *shall be* a spider's web" [italics in KJV]. David wrote, "Blessed is the man that maketh the Lord his trust" (Psalm 40:4). Proverbs 22:19 says, "That thy trust may be in the Lord." The NASB translates this noun "security" in Job 18:14: "He is torn from the security of his tent." The KJV has "His confidence shall be rooted out of his tabernacle." The noun "trust" or "confidence" is also used in the Old Testament in Job 31:24; Psalms 65:5; 71:5; Proverbs 14:26; 21:22; 25:19; Isaiah 32:18; Jeremiah 2:37; 17:7; 48:13; and Ezekiel 29:16.

The reason these examples of "trust" are given is to show that the biblical writers had options available if they wanted to communicate the idea of "trust in a person" that excluded the notion of "believing a proposition to be true." The authors also did not choose the lexical option available if they had meant to convey that salvific faith was belief that a proposition is true to the exclusion of trust in a person. A verb that the writers could have chosen for that, is יָדַע.

Believing Propositions

The verb "know" (יָדַע) has several possible meanings. In the Hebrew Qal stem, to have knowledge or to learn can have the meaning of believing a proposition to be true. Job said, "For I know *that* my redeemer liveth, and *that* he shall stand at the latter *day* upon the earth" [italics in KJV] (Job 19:25). Job believed that to be true. God told Moses, "And I will take you to me for a people, and I will be to you a God: and ye shall know that I *am* the Lord your God, which bringeth you out from under the burdens of the Egyptians" [italics in KJV] (Exodus 6:7). It would be difficult to distinguish between "knowing" and "believing" in this context.

One of the purposes of the plagues inflicted on Egypt was to provide evidence for God's identity. The Israelites could point to the plagues as examples that show that God is the one and only true God: "And that thou mayest tell in the ears of thy son, and of thy son's son, what things I have wrought in Egypt, and my signs which I have done among them; that ye may know how that I *am* the Lord" [italics in KJV] (Exodus 10:2). "Knowing" and "believing" in this context are virtually indistinguishable. Exodus 7:5, 17; 8:22; 14:4, 18; 16:12; 29:46; 31:13 are some other occurrences of "knowing" (יָדַע) that God is the Lord, the one true God.

Rahab said to the two Israelite spies, "I know that the Lord hath given you the land" (Joshua 2:9). She was expressing her expectation, which she stated in the form of a proposition that she believed to be true. At the end of his life Joshua warned the Israelites that disobeying God would have calamitous consequences. Joshua said, "Know for a certainty that the Lord your God will no more drive out *any of* these nations from before you" [italics in KJV] (Joshua 23:13). The Israelites were to know/believe the warning. Frequently in Hebrew the conjunction "that" (כִּי) is used to introduce the proposition to be "known" (יָדַע). Similarly, Greek uses the conjunction "that" (ὅτι) before stating a proposition to be believed.

The point of giving examples of Hebrew words that can mean "trust in a person" without the idea of "believing a proposition to be true" and a common one that can have the latter connotation without the former is to show that the biblical writers had those options. Instead they chose a Hebrew verb that could be used to communicate both of those ideas when it came to saving faith. If they had meant to convey that either "trust in a person" or "belief that a proposition was true" were not to be included, they could easily have done so. The words they did use were deliberately chosen.

Believing That a Proposition Is True or Trusting in a Person or Thing

The Hebrew verb "believe" (אָמַן) occurs in the Hiphil stem (הֶאֱמִן) fifty-one times in the Old Testament. Eighteen of these are in the preterite (past tense), two in the imperative, twenty-nine in the future tense, and two times as a participle. The Hiphil stem of "believe" (אָמַן) is first used in Genesis 15:6 where it refers to Abram's salvation: "And he believed in the Lord; and he counted it to him for righteousness." Righteousness was imputed to Abram on the basis of faith alone. The preposition "in" (ב) is used by the writer to communicate trust in a person, that is, in God. The only other time the Hiphil stem of "believe" (הֶאֱמִין) occurs in Genesis is in the account of Jacob's sons telling him that Joseph was still living: "And told him, saying, Joseph *is* yet alive, and he *is* governor over all the land of Egypt. And Jacob's heart fainted, for he believed them not" [italics in KJV] (Genesis 45:26). Jacob did not believe that what his sons were telling him was true.

Moses resisted God's recruiting him to confront Pharaoh. Moses said to God, "But, behold, they will not believe me, nor hearken unto my voice: for they will say, The Lord hath not appeared unto thee" (Exodus 4:1). The context indicates that Moses feared that his words would not be accepted as being true. In the dialogue between God and Moses that ensued the Hiphil form is used four times in a similar manner (Exodus 4:5, 8 [twice]; Exodus 4:9). God would provide signs to prove that what Moses said was true. Because of Moses' reluctance to speak, Aaron took his place: "And Aaron spake all the words which the Lord had spoken unto Moses, and did the signs in the sight of the people" (Exodus 4:30). The result was, "And the people believed" (Exodus 4:31). The people believed Aaron's statements.

The success of the exodus from Egypt, and particularly the drowning of the Egyptian army in the Red Sea, resulted in the Israelites putting their trust in God and in Moses:

"And Israel saw that great work which the Lord did upon the Egyptians: and the people feared the Lord, and believed the Lord, and his servant Moses" (Exodus 14:31). The trust placed in God and Moses is indicated with the use of the preposition "in" (בְּ). God wanted to make sure that His people trusted in Moses as their leader. "And the Lord said unto Moses, Lo, I come unto thee in a thick cloud, that the people may hear when I speak with thee, and believe thee for ever" (Exodus 19:9). The preposition "in" (בְּ) is used with the second person singular pronominal suffix translated "thee" (בְּךָ) to indicate that God wanted His people to trust in Moses their leader. The NASB reads, "in you" signaling the presence of the preposition.

In Numbers 14:11 God expressed his displeasure over the Israelites' failure to put their trust in Him in spite of all He had done. "And the Lord said to Moses, 'How long will this people spurn Me? And how long will they not believe in Me, despite all the signs which I have performed in their midst?'" (NASB). The preposition "in" (בְּ) with the first person singular pronominal suffix translated "in Me" (בִּי) indicates that trust in God is the meaning.

The sin that would prevent Moses from entering the Promised Land is recorded in Numbers 20. Instead of speaking to the rock as God had commanded, Moses struck the rock two times. God responded. "And the Lord spake unto Moses and Aaron, Because ye believed me not, to sanctify me in the eyes of the children of Israel, therefore ye shall not bring this congregation into the land which I have given them" (Numbers 20:12). Moses disregarded God's words of instruction. Did Moses not believe to be true what God had said, or did he not trust that God would produce water by his speaking to the rock? The presence of the preposition "in" (בְּ) with the pronominal suffix, literally, "in me" (בִּי) indicates that trust in God is in view.

After referring to God's hand in delivering Israel from Egypt, and His care for them in the wilderness, Deuteronomy 1:32 uses the Hiphil participle of "believe" (אָמַן) in the statement, "Yet in this thing ye did not believe the Lord your God." Although untranslated in the KJV or the NASB, the Hebrew has the preposition "in" (בְּ) "in the Lord your God" (בַּיהוה אֱלֹהֵיכֶם), connoting trust in a person, that is, in God. Israel's failure at Kadesh-barnea is described with the words, "Likewise when the Lord sent you from Kadesh-barnea, saying, Go up and possess the land which I have given you; then ye rebelled against the commandment of the Lord your God, and ye believed him not, nor hearkened to his voice" (Deuteronomy 9:23). The untranslated preposition (לְ) with the pronominal suffix (לוֹ), translated "Him" in the phrase "you neither believed Him" (וְלֹא הֶאֱמַנְתֶּם לוֹ), is to be understood to mean "belief in the truth of a proposition," in this case not believing that God would do what he said. The synonymous parallel phrase is, "nor listened to His voice" (וְלֹא שְׁמַעְתֶּם בְּקֹלוֹ).

In Deuteronomy 28:66 is an enigmatic use of the Hiphil future that the KJV translates "assurance": "And thy life shall hang in doubt before thee; and thou shalt fear day and night, and shalt have none assurance of thy life." The preposition בְּ ("in") with the impersonal noun "life" (חַיִּים) can refer to the expectation expressed in the proposition that one will lose one's life. However, it could be understood as not trusting that one's life will continue. The latter seems to be what "assurance" refers to.

The conquest of Canaan included negotiations with its occupants as Israel advanced. Before entering the territory of the Amorites Israel sent emissaries to secure safe passage. "And Israel sent messengers unto Sihon king of the Amorites, the king of Heshbon; and Israel said unto him, Let us pass, we pray thee, through thy land into my place" (Judges 11:19). King Sihon's response: "But Sihon trusted not Israel to pass through his coast" (Judges 11:20). Sihon did not have confidence that Israel's intentions were peaceful: "but Sihon gathered all his people together, and pitched in Jahaz, and fought against Israel" (Judges 11:20).

Before David became king he had to flee for his life. At one point he pretended to ally himself with the Philistines. Instead he was attacking the Philistines' allies. David lied to Achish, the Philistine king of Gath, about which cities he was destroying. First Samuel 27:12 says, "And Achish believed David, saying, He hath made his people Israel utterly to abhor him." Achish believed that what David told him was the truth.

The queen of Sheba, who visited Solomon, said to him, "It was a true report that I heard in mine own land of thy acts and of thy wisdom" (1 Kings 10:6). The queen continued with the words, "Howbeit I believed not the words" (1 Kings 10:7). She did not believe the reports she had heard were true. In 2 Chronicles 9:6 the same incident is recorded with the Hiphil form of the verb "believe" (אָמַן) used identically to refer to believing what had been said about Solomon.

Second Kings 17 gives reasons for the captivity of the northern kingdom of Israel. Foremost among the failures was their disobedience to God's commands. Israel's response is expressed with the words, "Notwithstanding they would not hear, but hardened their necks, like to the neck of their fathers, that did not believe in the Lord their God" (2 Kings 17:14). The preposition translated "in" (בְ) indicates that their failure was not trusting in God. Contextually, it was primarily God's command about idolatry that was disobeyed. They replaced the true God with false gods in whom they trusted instead.

In 2 Chronicles 20:20 king Jehoshaphat said, "Hear me, O Judah, and ye inhabitants of Jerusalem; Believe in the Lord your God, so shall ye be established; believe his prophets, so shall ye prosper." The NASB says, "Listen to me, O Judah and inhabitants of Jerusalem, put your trust in the Lord your God, and you will be established; put your trust in His prophets and succeed." The preposition translated "in" (בְ) is used with "trust" (אָמַן) both times, to convey the idea of trusting in God and His prophets. Jehoshaphat was exhorting the southern kingdom of Judah to put their trust in God and in His messengers who were His spokesmen.

Sennacherib, king of Assyria, taunted Judah, saying, "Know ye not what I and my fathers have done unto all the people of *other* lands? were the gods of the nations of those lands any ways able to deliver their lands out of mine hand?" [italics in KJV] (2

Chron. 32:13). Hezekiah had exhorted Judah to trust the Lord for deliverance. Sennacherib advised Judah with the words, "Now therefore let not Hezekiah deceive you, nor persuade you on this manner, neither yet believe him" (2 Chron. 32:15). His advice was not to believe what Hezekiah had said to them.

Eliphaz, Job's erstwhile counselor, asked Job, "Shall mortal man be more just than God? Shall a man be more pure than his maker?" (Job 4:17). Eliphaz denied the possibility with the words, "Behold, he put no trust in his servants; and his angels he charged with folly" (Job 4:18). The preposition "in" (בְּ), used in the prepositional phrase "in His servants" (בַּעֲבָדָיו), indicates that the verb (אָמַן) in the Hiphil refers to "trust." God does not place confidence in people. Compared to God, even His angels are unreliable. When Job argued his case, he despaired that God would even listen to him. Job said, "If I had called, and he had answered me; *yet* would I not believe that he had hearkened unto my voice" [italics in KJV] (Job 9:16). The conjunction translated "that" (כִּי) introduces the content of what Job believed, that is, that God would not listen to him.

In Job 15 Eliphaz has some words to say to Job. Among other things Eliphaz says this about God, "Behold, he putteth no trust in his saints" (Job 15:15). The preposition translated "in" (בְּ) used in the prepositional phrase "in his saints" (בִּקְדֹשָׁיו) conveys trust in a person rather than belief that a proposition or statement is true. A proposition or statement to be believed is meant by Eliphaz's words about the wicked, "He believeth not that he shall return out of darkness, and he is waited for of the sword" (Job 15:22).

Another statement by Eliphaz using the same verb form means "trust." "Let not him that is deceived trust in vanity: For vanity shall be his recompence" (Job 15:31). Here the preposition "in" (בְּ) indicates trust in something or someone. The noun "vanity" or "emptiness" (שָׁוְא) is personified and refers metaphorically to what the wicked trust.

In Job 24:22 the Hiphil form of "believe" or "trust" has the meaning of "assurance." The author speaks of how God treats the wicked: "He draweth also the mighty with his power: He riseth up, and no *man* is sure of life" [italics in KJV]. Longevity is not assured or guaranteed to the wicked. In his distress Job reminisced about the past when people respected him and sought his advice. "Unto me *men* gave ear, and waited, And kept silence at my counsel" [italics in KJV] (Job 29:21). Job thought about the times when his advice was not accepted: "*If* I laughed on them, they believed *it* not; And the light of my countenance they cast not down" (Job 29:24). The NASB says, "I smiled on them when they did not believe and the light of my face they did not cast down." Perhaps they did not believe the wisdom of his counsel. Job's equanimity was unaffected by them.

God responded to Job's complaints with a series of rhetorical questions that put Job in his place. The questions highlighted Job's impotence compared to God's omnipotence. One of the questions was, "Can you bind the wild ox in a furrow with ropes?" (Job 39:10 NASB). God followed up that question: "Or will he harrow the valleys after you?" (Job 39:10 NASB). A third question followed: "Wilt thou trust him, because his strength *is* great? Or wilt thou leave thy labour to him?" (Job 39:11). The term translated "trust" is the Hebrew word בָּטַח that was discussed earlier. It means to trust in something or someone and not belief that a proposition is true. Here it is trust in the wild ox for agricultural purposes. God's final question in this series is, "Wilt thou believe him, that he will bring home thy seed, and gather *it into* thy barn?" [italics in KJV] (Job 39:12). There is a parallelism between verse 11 and verse 12. Both refer to reliance on the wild ox. In verse 12 "have faith" translates the Hiphil form of אָמַן followed by the object of belief in a prepositional phrase with the preposition "in" (בְ), in the prepositional phrase "in him" (בּוֹ), that is, the wild ox, that conveys the idea of "trust."

In Job 39 God asked Job a series of questions that contrast God as the mighty Creator with Job the mere creature. The questions in verses 19-25 relate to the creation of the awesome war horse. Verse 24 describes the war horse thundering across the field of battle. "He swalloweth the ground with fierceness and rage: neither believeth he that *it is* the sound of the trumpet" [italics in KJV]. The conjunction "that" (כִּי) introduces the content of the war horse's "belief"; a personification to express the fact that a war horse is unaffected by the noise of battle and is able to ignore all distractions.

In Psalms the Hiphil form of the verb "believe" (אָמַן) is used seven times. Psalm 27:13 says, "*I had fainted*, unless I had believed to see the goodness of the Lord in the land of the living" [italics in KJV]. What the psalmist David "believed" (אָמַן) he would see happen is expressed with the preposition "to" (לְ), with the transitive verb "see" (רָאָה) and its object "the goodness of the Lord" (טוּב־יְהוָה). David believed that it would occur. Psalm 78:22 uses a parallel structure to say why God was angry with the nation Israel. God was angry "Because they believed not in God, and trusted not in his salvation." The term translated "believe" is the Hiphil form of אָמַן, and the term translated "trust" is the verb בָּטַח. Both can mean to place trust in someone or something. The first verb translated "believe" (אָמַן) is followed by the prepositional phrase with the preposition "in" (בְ), "in God" (בֵּאלֹהִים), that is, trust in Him. Israel did not put her trust in God; another way of saying the same thing was that they rejected the salvation that He offered, a salvation given on the basis of their putting their trust in God.

Later in the same psalm David recounted God's miraculous provision of meat in the wilderness that resulted in death, and the fact that in spite of that Israel still rejected God. David said, "For all this they sinned still, and believed not for his wondrous works" (Psalm 78:32). To "believe in His wondrous works" would lead them to trust in the one who had performed them. But rather than seek God, they sought the gifts. They craved His provision, but did not care for His Person.

In Psalm 106 the theme is repeated. God saved Israel from the Egyptians and the psalmist wrote, "Then believed they his words; they sang his praise" (Psalm 106:12). They believed that what God said was true, but their faith was fickle. The next verse says that "They soon forgat his works; they waited not for his counsel" (Psalm 106:13). But they still wanted some of what God had to offer. Psalm 106:14 says that they "lusted exceedingly in the wilderness, and tempted God in the desert." Forgotten words and forgotten works led to falling dead in the wilderness. From craving to satisfy their physical hunger, they lowered themselves to crafting a graven image. Psalm 106:19 says that "They made a calf in Horeb, and worshipped the molten image."

The beautiful and expensive golden calf was worth far less than what they gave up for it. The psalmist says that "Thus they changed their glory into the similitude of an ox that eateth grass" (Psalm 106:20). They who were made in God's image traded Him for something far beneath them. The psalmist summed it up with the words, "They forgat God their saviour, which had done great things in Egypt" (Psalm 106:21). Psalm 106:24 recounts the golden calf incident in Israel's history with the description "Yea, they despised the pleasant land, they believed not his word." The preposition "in" (לְ) in the prepositional phrase translated "in His word" (לִדְבָרוֹ) in the NASB refers to belief in the truth of statements or propositions.

The psalmist in Psalm 116 recognized his helplessness and need for God. Psalm 116:10 says, "I believed, therefore have I spoken: I was greatly afflicted." The psalmist believed that he was in dire straits. He acknowledged that it was God who had sustained him: "What shall I render unto the Lord *for* all his benefits toward me?" [italics in KJV] (Psalm 116:12). The psalmist determined to continue to look to God in praise and prayer: "I will take the cup of salvation, and call upon the name of the Lord" (Psalm 116:13).

Psalm 119:66 says, "Teach me good judgment and knowledge: For I have believed thy commandments." This use with the preposition "in" (בְּ) in the prepositional phrase translated, "in Your commandments" (בְמִצְוֹתֶיךָ) in the NASB, seems to be more than a belief that God's commandments are true. The psalmist was relying on them for his physical and spiritual well-being. For deliverance he placed his trust in what God said and was eager to hear more: "My soul fainteth for thy salvation: *but* I hope in thy word" [italics in KJV] (Psalm 119:81). The emphasis is not only on knowing what God says, but also on obeying His word. The Psalmist said, "I have refrained my feet from every evil way, that I might keep thy word" (Psalm 119:101).

Proverbs uses the Hiphil form of "believe" twice with the idea of believing something to be true. Proverbs 14:15 says that "The simple believeth every word: but the prudent *man* looketh well to his going" [italics in KJV]. The object of belief uses the preposition לְ to introduce the content that is believed. Proverbs 26:25 also warns against believing what someone says: "When he speaketh fair, believe him not: for *there are* seven abominations in his heart" [italics in KJV]. The individual who is not to be believed is identified in the preceding verse: "He that hateth dissembleth with his lips, and layeth up deceit within him" (Proverbs 26:24). The reader is warned against deception. Everything someone says is not necessarily to be believed.

Isaiah 7 includes the prophetic messianic sign of the future arrival of Immanuel by means of the virgin birth (Isaiah 7:14). The context of the prophecy is the southern kingdom of Israel, that is, Judah, shaking in their sandals because of the Arameans. Uzziah, the king of Judah, was given the message that the Arameans were on the march. Isaiah 7:2 says that "it was told the house of David, saying, Syria is confederate with Ephraim. And his heart was moved, and the heart of his people, as the trees of the wood are moved with the wind." God sent Isaiah the prophet to Uzziah with a message. It said, "Take heed, and be quiet; fear not, neither be fainthearted for the two tails of these smoking firebrands" (Isaiah 7:4). Terrorism was on the agenda of Judah's enemies who said, "Let us go up against Judah and terrorize it, and make for ourselves a breach in its walls, and set up the son of Tabeel as king in the midst of it" (Isaiah 7:6 NASB).

Judah was not to fear the advance of the Arameans because, "Thus saith the Lord God, It shall not stand, neither shall it come to pass" (Isaiah 7:7). God would intervene, but there was a condition to His promise. "If ye will not believe, surely ye shall not be established" (Isaiah 7:9). In Hebrew there is a play on words with two forms of the verb אָמַן. The first verb, which is translated "believe" is the Hiphil form of אָמַן, and the second, rendered "last," is the Niphal (medio-passive meaning) form of the same verb אָמַן. The second use of the verb, the Niphal, refers to the lack of permanence, or the failure to be established, that will result if Judah does not fulfill the condition of the first verb, stated in the Hiphil. The first use of the verb, in the Hiphil form, can refer either to the failure to believe Isaiah's words or the failure to trust in God. The object is unstated, and there is no preposition to indicate the meaning of the Hiphil form of אָמַן. Perhaps the writer is conveying that fear of the Arameans is to be replaced with trust in God.

Isaiah 28:16 says, "Therefore thus saith the Lord God, Behold, I lay in Zion for a foundation a stone, a tried stone, a precious corner *stone*, a sure foundation: he that believeth shall not make haste" [italics in KJV]. The NASB says, "Therefore thus says the Lord God, 'Behold, I am laying in Zion a stone, a tested stone, a costly cornerstone *for* the foundation, firmly placed. He who believes *in it* will not be disturbed'" [italics in NASB]. The word translated "disturbed" (חוּשׁ) in the NASB should be understood as in the KJV "make haste."

The conjunction "therefore" or "thus" (לָכֵן) refers the reader to the prior context. Judah was in a rush and made a rash alliance. Instead of entering precipitously into an ill-advised alliance Judah should have waited on God. God described the alliance with the words, "Because ye have said, We have made a covenant with death, and with hell are we at agreement; when the overflowing scourge shall pass through, it shall not come unto us: for we have made lies our refuge, and under falsehood have we hid ourselves" (Isaiah 28:15). The presence of "lies" (כָּזָב) and "falsehood" (שֶׁקֶר) in the context (Isaiah 28:15) could indicate that the term "believe" (אָמַן) in Isaiah 28:16 means to believe that the message about the coming Messiah is true. On the other hand, the lack of a stated object of belief, and the mention of the Messiah in the context, leaves open the possibility that trust in the person of the Messiah is the intended meaning.

Isaiah 43 emphasizes the unique identity of God. The scene is that of witnesses bearing testimony to God's identity. Pagan nations are invited to present their witnesses. God says, "Let all the nations be gathered together, and let the people be assembled: who among them can declare this, and shew us former things? Let them bring forth their witnesses, that they may be justified: Or let them hear, and say, *It is* truth" [italics in KJV] (Isaiah 43:9). In Isaiah 43:10 God addresses His people: "Ye *are* my witnesses, saith the Lord, and my servant whom I have chosen: that ye may know and believe me, and understand that I *am* he: before me there was no God formed, neither shall there be after me" [italics in KJV]. The Hebrew preposition and pronominal suffix translated "believe Me" (תַאֲמִינוּ לִי) is לְ, which makes it more likely that the proposition about God's identity is to be believed.

God again spoke of His identity in verse 11: "I, *even* I, *am* the Lord; and beside me *there is* no saviour" [italics in KJV]. God continued with the words, "I have declared, and have saved, and I have shewed, when *there was* no strange *god* among you: therefore ye *are* my witnesses, saith the Lord, that I *am* God" [italics in KJV] (Isaiah 43:12). God then mentioned His eternality, "Yea, before the day *was* I *am* he" [italics in KJV] (Isaiah 43:13), and His relationship with Israel: "I *am* the Lord, your Holy One, the creator of Israel, your King" [italics in KJV] (Isaiah 43:15). God's uniqueness required Israel's exclusive worship.

Isaiah 53:1 asks, "Who hath believed our report? And to whom is the arm of the Lord revealed?" The message to be believed is about the Messiah. The immediate context of the statements about the Messiah are declarations of God's own identity. God the Father and Jesus His Son would provide the solution for the problem of man's sin. Isaiah declared, "For thy Maker *is* thine husband; the Lord of hosts *is* his name; and thy Redeemer the Holy One of Israel; the God of the whole earth shall he be called" [italics in KJV] (Isaiah 54:5). The writers of the Gospels in the New Testament use the evidence of the Messiah's identity in Isaiah 53 to prove that Jesus is the one whom Isaiah predicted.

Jeremiah 12:6 uses the Hiphil form of the verb "believe" (אָמַן) to convey the idea of belief in the truth of a statement or proposition. Included in God's response to Jeremiah's complaint are the words, "For even thy brethren, and the house of thy father, even they have dealt treacherously with thee; yea, they have called a multitude after thee: believe them not, though they speak fair words unto thee." Jeremiah was not to be fooled by their flattery.

In Jeremiah 40 Judah's army commanders met with Gedaliah, whom the king of Assyria had installed to rule over Judah as his proxy. They tried to warn Gedaliah. They said to him, "Dost thou certainly know that Baalis the king of the Ammonites hath sent Ishmael the son of Nethaniah to slay thee?" (Jeremiah 40:14). Gedaliah's response is described with the words, "But Gedaliah the son of Ahikam believed them not" (Jeremiah 40:14). The preposition לְ and the pronominal suffix translated as the object of belief, "believed them" (הֶאֱמִין לָהֶם), indicates that belief in a statement or proposition is the intended meaning. Gedaliah did not believe that they were telling him the truth. When Johanan offered to kill Ishmael instead, Gedaliah turned him down, saying, "But Gedaliah the son of Ahikam said unto Johanan the son of Kareah, Thou shalt not do this thing: for thou speakest falsely of Ishmael" (Jeremiah 40:16).

Gedaliah paid with his life for his failure to believe that his assassination was being plotted.

The defenses of Jerusalem were considered impregnable to military assault. Lamentations 4:12 says that "The kings of the earth, and all the inhabitants of the world, would not have believed that the adversary and the enemy should have entered into the gates of Jerusalem." The information that was believed is introduced with the conjunction "that" (כִּי). In spite of the universal consensus, because God had decreed the judgment of Jerusalem, she succumbed to a prolonged siege.

The result of Jonah's reluctant evangelistic crusade in the city of Nineveh is described with the words, "Then the people of Nineveh believed in God; and they called a fast and put on sackcloth from the greatest to the least of them" (Jonah 3:5 NASB). The object of the Hiphil form of the verb "believe" (אָמַן) is "in God" (בֵּאלֹהִים) in which the preposition translated "in" (ב) conveys the idea that belief in a person, that is, God is in view, rather than the fact that they believed the message of impending judgment. Whether one believes the Ninevites had eternal salvation, the verb "believe" (אָמַן) and its object conforms to the construction meaning trust in a person, as opposed to belief in a proposition.

In his prophecy of impending captivity Micah said, "Trust ye not in a friend, put ye not confidence in a guide: keep the doors of thy mouth from her that lieth in thy bosom" (Micah 7:5). A day was coming when suspicion would be the better part of wisdom. The term translated "trust" (תַּאֲמִינוּ) is the Hiphil form of the verb "believe" or "trust" (אָמַן) and has the preposition "in" (ב) in the prepositional phrase "in a friend" (בְרֵעַ). "Trust" is the preferred translation instead of "belief" that one is being told the truth. The parallel phrase "put ye not confidence" translates the verb (בָּטַח) that means "trust."

Habakkuk 1:5 says, "Behold ye among the heathen, and regard, and wonder marvellously: For *I* will work a work in your days, *which* ye will not believe, though it be told *you*" [italics in KJV]. Amazingly, God was going to use bad people, the Chaldeans, to judge God's chosen people, Israel. That was unbelievable. That proposition is expressed with the Hiphil form of the verb "believe" (אָמַן). The conjunction translated "if" (כִּי) introduces what would not be believed, the "telling" (סָפַר) of the hard-to-believe information about the source of divine judgment. An unexpected subject would carry out an unusual sentence.

Of the fifty-one uses of the Hiphil form of the verb "believe" or "trust" (אָמַן), twenty-eight of them have the meaning of belief that a statement or proposition is true. Twenty uses refer to trust in something or someone. Three uses are difficult to determine. Two of them, Isaiah 7:7 and 28:16, have neither a stated object nor a preposition. Psalm 78:32 has the preposition "in" (ב) that normally indicates trust in someone or something; however, it is difficult to understand the way in which trust in the object, "wonderful works" (נִפְלָאוֹת), is to be understood.

The two possible meanings that the Hiphil form of אָמַן can have are belief that a statement or proposition is true and trust in something or someone. Those are also two of the possible meanings that the Greek verb πιστεύω can convey. For that reason the translators of the Septuagint (LXX) used πιστεύω to translate the Hebrew Hiphil form of אָמַן.

The Old Testament identifies God as the one in whom trust is to be placed, and prepares for the coming of the Messiah, identifying Him by prophetic means. The first four of five questions that Proverbs 30:4 asks are, "Who hath ascended up into heaven, or descended? Who hath gathered the wind in his fists? Who hath bound the waters in a garment? Who hath established all the ends of the earth?" The writer then asks a fifth question that takes an unexpected turn: "What *is* his name, and what *is* his son's name, if thou canst tell?" [italics in KJV]. The NASB says, "What is His name or His son's name? Surely you know!" His Son's name is Jesus of Nazareth, as the New Testament writers will show.

Chapter 4

Evidence for the Identity of Jesus in the Gospel of Matthew

Proof from the Past

Foundational to the rest of the New Testament are the Gospel accounts. What follows them in the biblical text builds on what they establish and assumes a knowledge of their content. Early in the history of the church the Gospel of Matthew was recognized as the Jewish Gospel. While that characterization might be disputed, the presence of Old Testament quotations and allusions in Matthew is not up for debate. As the first Gospel in the canonical order, Matthew uniquely serves as a bridge between the Old and New Testaments.

Because Christianity was charged as being a heretical sect that spun off from Judaism, the movement that followed Jesus needed to establish its legitimacy. Was the New Testament church a continuation of what began in the Old Testament, or was it a cult? Was the God who was revealed in the Old Testament connected to Jesus whom New Testament believers worshiped? One of Matthew's goals was to connect the God of Judaism with Jesus the God/Man/Messiah. Matthew forges a link in the Gospel chain that unites faith in God the Father with faith in Jesus. Matthew's primary purpose is to provide credible, admissible evidence that Jesus is the One in whom man is to believe for salvation, which he does by authenticating Jesus' identity. Matthew makes sure there is no possibility of mistaken identity. Is Jesus, who lived in the first century, of whom Matthew had firsthand knowledge, the person in whom one is to believe for eternal life? The evidence of Jesus' identity that Matthew provides is irrefutable.

Matthew Chapter 1

Matthew begins with a "genealogy of Jesus Christ" (Matthew 1:1) (γενέσεως Ἰησοῦ Χριστοῦ), which provides evidence of Jesus' identity by means of family of origin. In order for Jesus to be the Messiah he had to fit Old Testament prophetic criteria. Matthew begins with a summary statement by mentioning the two most important ancestors of the Messiah. Abraham and David are both mentioned because the coming Messiah had been promised to each of them as being their descendant. Abraham had been told, "And in thee shall all families of the earth be blessed" (Genesis 12:3).

In his selective genealogy Matthew chose a triad of fourteen generations, perhaps doubling the number seven to indicate perfection. The Apostle Paul also describes the perfect timing of Christ's first coming in Galatians 4:4: "But when the fullness of the time was come." Matthew makes a point of identifying Jesus as the one "who is called Christ" (Matthew 1:16) (ὁ λεγόμενος χριστός), a reference to the promised Messiah of the Old Testament. In Matthew's summation of his genealogy he emphasizes whose identity he is concerned with by repeating the title Messiah (Χριστός) twice (Matthew 1:16-17).

One frequently noticed detail in Matthew's genealogy is the inclusion of women, particularly Gentile women who implicitly reveal the universal character of the Messiah's mission. This was something Jesus explicitly taught in the Sermon on the Mount: "Ye are the light of the world" (Matthew 5:14), and in His Parable of the Tares where He tells of the sphere in which the "good seed" (ὁ σπείρων τὸ καλὸν) of the gospel is proclaimed; "the field is the world" (Matthew 13:38) (ὁ δὲ ἀγρός ἐστιν ὁ κόσμος). Matthew also includes Jesus' universal soteriological and eschatological comment in Matthew 24:14: "And this gospel of the kingdom shall be preached in all the world." The idea is repeated in Jesus' commendation of Mary, who had just anointed His feet, when He said that word of her good deed would be spread to "wheresoever this gospel shall be preached in the whole world" (Matthew 26:13). The objective of the Great Commission is to "make disciples of all the nations" (Matthew 28:19 NASB). All of these identify Jesus as more than just a Jewish Messiah.

Matthew presents the identifying facts of the deity and humanity of Jesus. In the genealogy Matthew traces the paternal line of the Messiah but mentions Mary. He included her because although the genealogy is traced through Joseph, he wants to clarify that Joseph was not Jesus' earthly father. He indicates this by using the feminine singular relative pronoun "by whom" (ἧς) which agrees with the feminine "Mary" (Μαρίας) and not with the masculine "Joseph" (Ἰωσὴφ) at the end of the genealogy; "and to Jacob was born Joseph the husband of Mary, by whom was born Jesus, who is called Christ" (Matthew 1:16). Mary was physically related to Jesus while Joseph was not. It is reinforced that Mary and Joseph had not physically consummated their relationship by saying that her pregnancy was "before they came together" (Matthew 1:18), and the statement that "she was found to be with child by the Holy Spirit" (Matthew 1:18). This evidence of the virgin birth would be corroborated by Joseph, which shows the author's concern for plural witnesses.

Joseph is given collaborative testimony from "an angel of the Lord" (ἄγγελος κυρίου) that confirms the virgin birth; "for that which is conceived in her is of the Holy Ghost" (Matthew 1:20). One of Matthew's favorite ways of providing proof of Jesus' identity is the use of an Old Testament prophecy paired with a fulfillment event to conform to the Jewish legal requirement of two or three witness for acceptable testimony (Deuteronomy 17:6, et al). After the account of the virgin birth, and the angel's confirmation (Matthew 1:20-21), Matthew referred to an Old Testament prophecy from Isaiah 7:14, "Behold, a virgin shall be with child, and shall bring forth a son, and they shall call His name Emmanuel" (Matthew 1:23). The three witnesses who testify to Jesus' identity are; Joseph, the angel, and an Old Testament prophecy.

Names have significance for identity and this is especially true of the Messiah. Matthew records a name for Jesus which is not Greek, but is a transliteration from the Hebrew "Immanuel" (עִמָּנוּאֵל) from Isaiah 7:14. A translation of the transliteration is given, which is "God with us" (Matthew 1:23) (μεθ᾽ ἡμῶν ὁ θεός). This title contributes to the author's purpose to prove the Messiah's identity which is the primary paradigm for his gospel account.

Matthew Chapter 2

Matthew submitted testimony related to the manner of the Messiah's birth and offered the identifying evidence of Jesus' place of origin. The magi, who were looking for Jesus, arrived in Jerusalem expecting that a king would be born in the capital city. A supernatural star had led them and they asked, "Where is he that is born King of the Jews? for we have seen his star in the east, and are come to worship him" (Matthew 2:2).

The magi referred to Jesus as a king; "Where is he that is born King of the Jews?" (Matthew 2:2). This forms the first part of an *inclusio* (literary bracketing consisting of the same or similar material at the beginning and end of a text). The magi refer to Jesus as a king near the beginning of Matthew's Gospel and near the end at His crucifixion the placard placed on the cross read, "THIS IS JESUS THE KING OF THE JEWS" (Matthew 27:37) (οὗτός ἐστιν Ἰησοῦς ὁ βασιλεὺς τῶν Ἰουδαίων). The magi's use of the term "king" (Matthew 2:2) (βασιλεύς) piqued the interest of "Herod the king" (Matthew 2:3) (ὁ βασιλεὺς Ἡρῴδης), who felt his position was being threatened. One day Jesus will reign on the earth as its King, but He did not come to take Herod's place.

The magi and a supernatural star testified that Bethlehem was to be Jesus' birthplace. An additional witness was the Old Testament prophet Micah whom Matthew quoted, "And thou Beth-lehem, *in* the land of Juda[h], art not the least among the princes of Juda[h]: for out of thee shall come a Governor, that shall rule my people Israel" [italics in KJV] (Matthew 2:6). Matthew's quotation is from the prophet Micah, "But thou, Beth-lehem Ephratah, *though* thou be little among the thousands of Judah, *yet* out of thee shall he come forth unto me *that is* to be ruler in Israel" [italics in KJV] (Micah 5:2). Matthew's words, "that shall rule ["shepherd" NASB] my people Israel," coincide with words spoken about God as Israel's shepherd (Genesis 49:24) and the role which He delegated to the nation's kings (2 Samuel 5:2; 1 Chronicles 11:2). Jesus would shepherd Israel in His role as her King.

When the magi located the child, their actions served to identify Him. They "fell down and worshipped Him" (Matthew 2:11) which would have been recognized by his readers as blasphemy had He not been God. The supernatural warning the magi received, "And being warned of God in a dream that they should not return to Herod" (Matthew 2:12) and to avoid Jerusalem, adds to the evidence of the unique identity of the child.

The account of what has become known as the "Flight into Egypt" continues the motif of identity. Interestingly, there are parallels between the Old Testament prophet Moses, and the greater prophet, the Messiah. Both had an Egyptian connection, had their lives threatened at an early age, had wilderness experiences, and had the story of their lives told with a significant time gap between their early life and the account of their major adult life's work. Many of these similarities also exist between the Messiah, and God's chosen people Israel. Several differences between Moses and the Messiah may be noted. Not least among them is the fact that the latter is without sin. And while Moses was prevented from completing the journey to the promised land, at the end of the Messiah's labors He could conclude, "It is finished" (John 19:30) (τετέλεσται).

The Messiah's departure to Egypt was precipitated by the threat of Herod's infanticide and an angelic appearance; "the angel of the Lord appeareth to Joseph in a dream, saying, Arise, and take the young child and his mother, and flee into Egypt" (Matthew 2:13). The flight was divinely ordained and orchestrated to fulfill the identifying prophecy of Hosea 11:1; "When Israel *was* a child, then I loved him, and called my son out of Egypt" [italics in KJV]. The identity of the Messiah would be proved by the fulfillment of seemingly conflicting prophecies of origin.

While the Messiah escaped the infant massacre, many did not. In Matthew 2:18 is found another enigmatic Old Testament prophecy that required fulfillment, "In Rama was there a voice heard, lamentation, and weeping, and great mourning, Rachel weeping *for* her children, and would not be comforted, because they are not" [italics in KJV]. Matthew quotes Jeremiah 31:15: "A voice was heard in Ramah, Lamentation, *and* bitter weeping; Ra[c]hel weeping for her children refused to be comforted for her children, because they *were* not" [italics in KJV]. Without the specific fulfillment of the Old Testament prophecy of these fatalities the identification of Jesus as the Messiah would have been a case of mistaken identity.

How could the Messiah be born in Bethlehem and come out of Egypt, two distinct geographical locations, and have a Galilean/Nazareth connection? The return of Jesus and His family from Egypt is again marked by the message of an angel who directs Joseph, "behold, an angel of the Lord appeareth in a dream to Joseph in Egypt, saying, Arise, and take the young child and his mother, and go into the land of Israel" (Matthew 2:19-20). Supernatural protection is another witness to the identity of Jesus.

The family's return to Israel but not to the area of Judea, shows how God used Joseph's fear of the ruler Archelaus to orchestrate an unlikely fulfillment, "But when he heard that Archelaus did reign in Judaea in the room of his father Herod, he was afraid to go thither" (Matthew 2:22). No doubt Joseph's fears were relieved when he was instructed to avoid Archelaus, "Being warned of God in a dream, he turned aside into the parts of Galilee: and he came and dwelt in a city called Nazareth" (Matthew 2:22-23). The text says, "that it might be fulfilled which was spoken by the prophets, He shall be called a Nazarene" (Matthew 2:23).

It is beyond the scope of this work to explore the problem of there being no specific Old Testament quotation of which "Nazarene" (Ναζωραῖος) is a fulfillment. It should be noted that "the word" (τὸ ῥηθὲν) fulfilled is that of "the prophets" (τῶν προφητῶν), plural, indicating more than a single prophecy, although "the prophets" (τῶν προφητῶν) could be a reference to the prophetic writings of the Old Testament as a whole. It has been suggested that a solution might lie in the shared etymology of the name "Nazareth" (Ναζωραῖος) with the Hebrew stem (נֵצֶר) meaning "branch" or "shoot." Whatever the solution, Matthew used this as additional evidence of identification of Jesus as the Messiah. The evidence of identity that Matthew marshaled was intriguing. As McGee writes, "What seemed rather strange prophecies became very sane realities" (J. Vernon Mcgee, *Thru the Bible with J. Vernon Mcgee* [Nashville: Thomas Nelson, 1983], 4:17).

Matthew Chapter 3

John the Baptist was the supreme New Testament witness to the identity of Jesus as the Messiah. Matthew does not call him a witness per se but that was his role. The message he preached was, "Repent ye: for the kingdom of heaven is at hand" (Matthew 3:2). Every kingdom has a king and the presence of King Jesus signaled that the kingdom, in some fashion, had arrived. Just as a witness in a court of law may be asked to identify someone, John the Baptist points out who the Messiah is. With the demonstrative pronoun "This" (οὗτος), placed in the emphatic initial position in the sentence, the Gospel writer Matthew addresses the issue of identity with the words, "For this is he that was spoken of by the prophet Esaias [Isaiah]" (Matthew 3:3) (οὗτος γάρ ἐστιν ὁ ῥηθεὶς διὰ Ἠσαΐου τοῦ προφήτου). Although the quotation speaks of the mission of John the Baptist, his message is of great importance, "Prepare ye the way of the Lord, make his paths straight" (Matthew 3:3). What an astounding announcement he made. The one for whom he was preparing the way was none other than "the Lord" (κύριος).

A devout first century Jew hearing those words would immediately have been reminded of the Old Testament context in which they appear in Isaiah 40:3, "The voice of him that crieth in the wilderness, Prepare ye the way of the Lord, Make straight in the desert a highway for our God." In this verse "Lord" (κύριος) is the Greek translation for "Yahweh" (יְהוָה), and "God" is the translation for "Elohim" (אֱלֹהִים). The two witnesses Matthew provided, in keeping with the Jewish two or three witness legal requirement for acceptable testimony (Deuteronomy 17:6, et al), were John the Baptist, and the corroboration of his testimony by Isaiah's prophecy concerning John the Baptist himself, and his message that identifies Jesus as deity.

In John the Baptist's confrontation with the Pharisees and the Sadducees he contrasted who he was with the identity of the Messiah he was about to introduce. In Matthew 3:11 John the Baptist says, "I indeed baptize you with water unto repentance: but he that cometh after me is mightier than I, whose shoes I am not worthy to bear: he shall baptize you with the Holy Ghost, and *with* fire" [italics in KJV] (Matthew 3:11). John metaphorically described other divine activities of the coming Messiah; "Whose fan *is* in his hand, and he will throughly purge his floor, and gather his wheat into the garner ["barn" NASB]" [italics in KJV] (Matthew 3:12). The person is pictured as the owner of the world who exercises the prerogatives of ownership, cleaning it out, and sifting and separating and gathering humanity as He wills. The descriptive analogy culminates with the statement, "but he will burn up the chaff with unquenchable fire" (Matthew 3:12). The One about to be introduced will be the eschatological implementer of divine judgment.

The stage was superbly set for the Messiah to make His grand entrance. The baptism of Jesus rose to the same level as His transfiguration and resurrection as evidence of His identity as the divine person. True to the author's paradigm of giving acceptable evidence of identity, he presented two witnesses. They are (1) "the Spirit of God descending like a dove, and lighting upon him" (Matthew 3:16), and (2) "a voice from heaven, saying, This is My beloved Son, in whom I am well-pleased" (Matthew 3:17). The two witnesses are the Holy Spirit and God the Father. We are not told if everyone who was present saw and heard both witnesses but the evidence of Jesus' identity was not lost on Matthew's readers/listeners.

Even before the Messiah began his public ministry the issue of identity was foremost in the mind and message of the Gospel writer. And it is fitting that it be so, given the centrality of messianic identity for the proclamation of that gospel.

Matthew Chapter 4

In the encounter of Jesus with the devil in the wilderness, known as the Temptation of Jesus, the devil began with a question in the form of a conditional sentence related to His identity, "If thou be the Son of God" (Matthew 4:3) (εἰ υἱὸς εἶ τοῦ θεοῦ). Satan was aware of the importance of Jesus' divine identity for His earthly mission. And Jesus' identity is tied to His sinlessness. The Savior from sin cannot Himself be a sinner, so the devil was tempting Jesus to sin.

The first temptation seems harmless enough. Jesus would not have sinned by creating bread, but He would have sinned by doing the devil's bidding. Satan's strategy was simple enough—he asked for obedience before he requested worship. Jesus responded by quoting from the Old Testament (Deuteronomy 8:3), "Man shall not live by bread alone, but by every word that proceedeth out of the mouth of God" (Matthew 4:4). As God, Jesus is divinely self-sufficient; He is self-sustaining, in need of no earthly sustenance. However, as the God/Man Jesus submitted Himself to the needs and requirements of human beings for their survival, and the devil was tempting Him on that level.

Jesus answered the conditional sentence that the devil posed with its "if" (Matthew 4:3) (εἰ) with a sense of "since" or "because." Jesus' response was, in effect, "Since" or "because" I am the Son of God, God Himself, why would I need bread? Spiritual sustenance which the Son of God provides trumps physical provision. So Jesus answered, "It is written, Man shall not live by bread alone, but by every word that proceedeth out of the mouth of God" (Matthew 4:4). Jesus, the One answering the devil's question, is God Himself. In a sense, the word of God is all that man needs. While man needs food, all material things that man requires to survive were brought into creative existence by the word of His mouth and continue to exist because of Him.

In the second temptation the devil introduced his question with the same protasis (the part beginning with "if") in the conditional sentence as he did his first question: "If thou be the Son of God" (Matthew 4:6) (εἰ υἱὸς εἶ τοῦ θεοῦ). This question cast doubt on Jesus' identity. The devil knows that the issue of Jesus' identity is a crucial one. If Jesus is who He claims to be it is all over for the devil. The second temptation took place at a different location than the first: "Then the devil taketh him up into the holy city, and setteth him on a pinnacle of the temple, and saith unto him, If thou be the Son of God, cast thyself down" (Matthew 4:5-6). While the first temptation was about physical provision, the second was about physical protection.

The second temptation rises to the level of a taunt. The devil's response to Jesus' quotation of Scripture was a quote of his own from the Psalms. The devil challenged Jesus to apply Psalm 91, a psalm of deliverance for Old Testament believers, to Himself. If Jesus were to do that He would have done so at the behest of the devil. Furthermore the devil's suggestion would be tantamount to testing God. This would be attempting to manipulate God to act, a usurpation of divine initiative. Satan was tempting Jesus and thereby tempting God. Jesus asserted His rightful place as the Son of God, that is, God Himself, in His scriptural response, taken from Deuteronomy 6:16: "Thou shalt not tempt the Lord thy God" (Matthew 4:7). The quotation included "Yahweh" (יְהוָה), a name for God in the Old Testament. Jesus asserts his deity by calling Himself "Yahweh" (יְהוָה).

The devil's third and final temptation dropped all pretense and did not bother to quote Scripture. Blatantly the devil attempted to get Jesus to worship him: "All these things will I give thee, if thou wilt fall down and worship me" (Matthew 4:9). Jesus' quotation of Deuteronomy 6:13 was a claim to His divine identity and the role of everyone else in relation to Him: "Thou shalt worship the Lord thy God, and him only shalt thou serve" (Matthew 4:10). The devil refused to take Jesus up on His challenge to "serve" (λατρεύω) Him. Instead holy angels took up their rightful place to "minister" (διακονέω) to Him; "Then the devil left Him; and behold, angels came and *began* to minister to Him" (Matthew 4:11, italics in NASB).

King Herod heard of John the Baptist's growing movement and arrested him, and Jesus, not wanting to get swept up in the dragnet, left the area: "Now when Jesus had heard that John was cast into prison, he departed into Galilee" (Matthew 4:12). No doubt Jesus would have been perceived as an even greater threat to Herod's power and having His own timetable, He diffused the situation by leaving. He went and stayed in Capernaum, in the region of Galilee, to delay the inevitable confrontation. Galilee was more Gentile than Jewish. Matthew included the fact that it was called "Galilee of the Gentiles" (Γαλιλαία τῶν ἐθνῶν) (Matthew 4:15) in his quotation from Isaiah 9:1 (גְּלִיל הַגּוֹיִם). Having many immigrants in the area, the influence of the Jewish religious authorities would have been minimal.

Matthew quoted from Isaiah 9:1-2, which is part of the messianic passage which includes the familiar verse: "For unto us a child is born, unto us a son is given: and the government shall be upon his shoulder: and his name shall be called Wonderful, Counseller, the mighty God, the everlasting Father, the Prince of Peace" (Isaiah 9:6). The prophetic description of this ruler, whose government would have naturally centered in Jerusalem, was nevertheless to be associated with the backwater region of

Zebulon and Naphtali—another piece of the puzzle identifying Jesus as the predicted Messiah. Matthew adds, "From that time Jesus began to preach, and to say, Repent: for the kingdom of heaven is at hand" (Matthew 4:17). Jesus continued where John the Baptist left off—He was the King of that promised kingdom.

Jesus began His ministry by calling those who would be eyewitnesses, some of whom would give written testimony to what He would do and say. The authority with which Jesus' invitation was extended was not lost on Matthew who records Peter and Andrew's response; "And they straightway left their nets, and followed him" (Matthew 4:20). The absence of any hesitancy on the part of the recruits is noted again in the response of James and John; "And they immediately left the ship and their father, and followed Him" (Matthew 4:22).

Matthew uses the words, "the gospel of the kingdom" (τὸ εὐαγγέλιον τῆς βασιλείας) for the first time in Matthew 4:23. There has been much discussion about the term "gospel" (εὐαγγέλιον) and what it refers to. Thomas Stegall in his book, *The Gospel of the Christ*, has an excellent discussion of the textual (manuscript) evidence for the inclusion of the term "gospel" (εὐαγγέλιον), that means "good news" in the titles to the gospels: "The Gospel according to Matthew," "The Gospel according to Mark," etc. (*The Gospel of the Christ: A Biblical Response to the Crossless Gospel Regarding the Contents of Saving Faith* [Milwaukee: Grace Gospel Press, 2009], 240-60). While not agreeing with all the conclusions in other parts of the book, evidence of the manuscripts and writings of the early church fathers from the second and third centuries attests to the widespread use of the term "gospel" in all of the titles of the Gospels from a very early period. Significantly, the Gospel of John was not singled out as the only "Gospel." The evidence shows that early interpreters had no problem using the word "gospel" when referring to each and all of them.

Matthew describes Jesus' Galilean ministry as "teaching in their synagogues, and preaching the gospel of the kingdom" (Matthew 4:23). While some may want to make dispensational distinctions as to the nature of the kingdom, that does not change the identity of the King. The presence of eschatological matters in the Synoptic Gospels does not prevent them from legitimately being referred to as "Gospels." The "gospel" is about Jesus, and the paradigm of His identity as Messiah/King is found throughout all four Gospel accounts.

Jesus' words were accompanied by His works. Matthew expressed the extraordinary nature of the events he witnessed by use of inclusive adjectives. He describes Jesus as "healing all manner of sickness and all manner of disease" (Matthew 4:23). As a result people from all over followed Jesus: "And there followed him great multitudes of people from Galilee, and *from* Decapolis, and *from* Jerusalem, and *from* Judaea, and *from* beyond Jordan" [italics in KJV] (Matthew 4:25). From the amazing demonstration of works which attested to Jesus divine identity Matthew shifts to include His discourses.

Matthew Chapter 5

In Matthew chapters 5 and 6 and almost to the end of chapter 7 is found what has become known as the Sermon on the Mount. Exegesis of that material abounds and is outside the scope of this work. But relevant to the present work is how Jesus' ethical demands are to be taken. Following the Beatitudes Jesus made a statement about "good works" (Matthew 5:16) (τὰ καλὰ ἔργα). He said, "Let your light so shine before men, that they may see your good works, and glorify your Father which is in heaven" (Matthew 5:16). Good works glorify God.

Jesus did not come to do away with good works, nor nullify the Law which is an expression of good works and the holiness of God. Lest there be any misunderstanding Jesus said, "Think not that I am come to destroy the law, or the prophets: I am not come to destroy, but to fulfill" (Matthew 5:17). Jesus "fulfilled" (πληρόω) the Law by obeying it. He qualified to be the Savior because He perfectly met the demands of the Law. Biblical soteriology requires a robust Christology. God's perfect standard that Jesus met has not been lowered. Jesus' absolute obedience did not result in either the abolition of or a reduction in God's perfect standard and requirements. Jesus said so as sternly as He could; "For verily I say unto you, till heaven and earth pass, one jot or one tittle shall in no wise pass from the law, till all be fulfilled" (Matthew 5:18). God's holiness is absolute, not relative.

Some infractions may be considered major, others minor; "Whosoever therefore shall break one of these least commandments, and shall teach men so, he shall be called the least in the kingdom of heaven: but whosoever shall do and teach *them*, the same shall be called great in the kingdom of heaven" [italics in KJV] (Matthew 5:19). Bullinger explains Jesus' use of "least" (ἐλάχιστος) and "great" (μέγας) in Matthew 5:19 as an example of "Synœceiosis" or "Cohabitation" which involves the repetition of a word in the same sentence with a different or extended meaning. Bullinger explains:

> In the former place [breaking of the least of the commandments], the allusion is to the distinction which the Pharisees made between different commandments (just as Rome has since made the distinction between "venial" and "mortal" sins). There is no such distinction, and therefore, when in the latter place Christ says "he shall be called the least," He means that he will not be there at all, for there will be no such distinction there. There is no least in either case (*Figures of Speech Used in the Bible*, 294).

Lest one conclude that being called "least" (ἐλάχιστος) or being called "great" (μέγας) are both good because they guarantee presence in the kingdom, Jesus' explanation that follows precludes that interpretation. Jesus continued, "For I say unto you, that except your righteousness shall exceed *the righteousness* of the scribes and Pharisees, ye shall in no case enter into the kingdom of heaven" [italics in KJV] (Matthew 5:20).

Jesus did not explicitly say by how much the righteousness that grants access to the kingdom must exceed that of the scribes and Pharisees, but the implication is that it is not by just a little. Nor was Jesus introducing relative righteousness as a sufficient requirement for eternal life. Jesus opposed watering down God's holiness. In fact, the Law was not an exhaustive expression of it. Because Jesus is God He could not only explain the Law but reveal what lay behind it. God's holiness, and therefore the righteousness that guarantees entrance into the kingdom, is greater than the truncated version of the Law that the scribes and Pharisees created. More than that, the righteousness required to obtain eternal life is greater than the Law itself. Jesus said,

> Ye have heard that it was said by them of old time, Thou shalt not kill; and whosoever shall kill shall be in danger of the judgment: but I say unto you, that whosoever is angry with his brother without a cause shall be in danger of the judgment: and whosoever shall say to his brother, Raca, shall be in danger of the council: but whosoever shall say, thou fool, shall be in danger of hell fire (Matthew 5:21-22).

The requisite righteousness for entrance into the kingdom is rigid and unbending and every one of the Ten Commandments in the Decalogue could be expanded to include attitudinal and not just active elements. Jesus said about adultery, "Ye have heard that it was said by them of old time, Thou shalt not commit adultery: but I say unto you, that whosoever looketh on a woman to lust after her hath committed adultery with her already in his heart" (Matthew 5:27-28). And lest anyone think that the price is too high for such a prize as heaven, Jesus said,

> And if thy right eye offend thee, pluck it out, and cast *it* from thee: for it is profitable for thee that one of thy members should perish, and not *that* thy whole body should be cast into hell. And if thy right hand offend thee, cut it off, and cast *it* from thee: for it is profitable for thee that one of thy members should perish, and not *that* thy whole body should be cast into hell [italics in KJV] (Matthew 5:29-30).

To water down Jesus' requirement for entrance into the kingdom and avoidance of hell to a relative ethical standard to be achieved in the here-and-now does violence to the text. That is not to say that God's holiness is not the standard for Christlikeness in the realm of sanctification, but no percentage of performance short of perfection will do anything other than deliver one to eternal punishment.

After numerous other examples of God's standard of perfection, Jesus summed up what He was saying before adding many more. Jesus said, "Be ye therefore perfect, even as your Father which is in heaven is perfect" (Matthew 5:48). Jesus intended the adjective translated "perfect" (τέλειος) to be taken in an absolute and not a relative sense such as "mature," which it sometimes does. Anything short of perfection is insufficient to qualify as obedience to Jesus' command.

Matthew Chapter 6

Those who have acknowledged that the route of self-righteousness is impossible and have obtained from Jesus His imputed righteousness by trusting Him know that there is nothing to boast about. Pharisaical attitudes do not flourish among those who have undergone a regenerational reorientation. Jesus knew that His disciples, minus Judas Iscariot, were saved and gave instructions to them and those in His audience who were also saved. Jesus said, "Take heed that ye do not your alms before men, to be seen of them: otherwise ye have no reward of your Father which is in heaven" (Matthew 6:1) This was in direct contrast with what the Pharisees practiced.

Those whom Jesus was addressing were no longer on a performance-for-paradise track. They were on the road to reward. God wants His children to trust that He can see what they do in secret. The spiritual journey that began with trust in Jesus for salvation is to result in a life of reliance on Him. While those seeking to enter by their good works will find that the kingdom cannot be bought, those who have accepted Jesus' payment for them are to seek to follow in ways appropriate to kingdom living. Jesus said, "But seek ye first the kingdom of God, and his righteousness; and all these things shall be added unto you" (Matthew 6:33). The kingdom and the righteousness sought are not payment for what has already been given. They are not requirements which if not met will rescind what was previously granted. Nor is performance of them proof that the prior position was indeed acquired or that if not performed that the memory of the gift had been nothing more than a mirage. Eternal righteousness is granted, the experiential reality of righteousness is to be sought. Entrance into the kingdom is obtained by faith alone; life as a citizen is daily following the King.

Matthew Chapter 7

Near the conclusion of Jesus' Sermon on the Mount He said something related to His identity. In Matthew 7:21 He said, "Not every one that saith unto me, Lord, Lord, shall enter into the kingdom of heaven; but he that doeth the will of my Father which is in heaven." Jesus contrasted words, "Not everyone that saith unto me," with actions, "but he that doeth the will of my Father." Jesus is saying that in that final day of reckoning, claiming Jesus as one's "Lord" (κύριος) will not substitute for "doing" (ποιέω) His "will" (θέλημα). The desire, will, or willingness on the part of man is not being addressed. The human requirement is active obedience, the attitudinal state or "will" (θέλημα) is that of God the Father. In the context, specific items are mentioned that would not qualify one to be (Matthew 7:21) "he that doeth the will of my Father" (ὁ ποιῶν τὸ θέλημα τοῦ πατρός μου). Prophesying, exorcism, and performing miracles are mentioned: "Many will say to me in that day, Lord, Lord, have we not prophesied in thy name? And in thy name have cast out devils? And in thy name done many wonderful works?" (Matthew 7:22).

Jesus did not answer their question directly but the context assumes that He accepted that they had done the works they were claiming to have done and yet He scathingly replied, "And then will I profess unto them, I never knew you: depart from me, ye that work iniquity" (Matthew 7:23). Despite their performance of these works God will not acknowledge knowing them (Matthew 7:23): "I never knew you." "The will of the Father" (τὸ θέλημα τοῦ πατρός) was not synonymous with or to be equated with the performance of these works. The works were not proof of anything.

What was claimed were the greatest of works, thereby implying that lesser works could not result in a favorable response by God. Instead of characterizing them as those who did good deeds, Jesus referred to the performers of them as those "that work iniquity" [NASB = "practice lawlessness"] (Matthew 7:23) (οἱ ἐργαζόμενοι τὴν ἀνομίαν). The summary judgment Jesus leveled at them labeled the very works that they claimed as assets, to be liabilities.

The best interpretation is to view the Sermon on the Mount as presenting the path of perfection. This would fit with Jesus' words: "Be ye therefore perfect, even as your Father which is in heaven is perfect" (Matthew 5:48). Jesus came to fulfill the law, to obey it in every detail (Matthew 3:15; 5:17), and that is the way of salvation for those who refuse to have His perfect righteousness put to their account. Perfection, one's own or Christ's, is the price of entrance into the kingdom. Jesus "knows" (Matthew 7:23) those, has a relationship with those, who not only claim that He is their "Lord" (κύριος), but also are His by means of their own perfection, or because of His.

Matthew's editorial comments and appraisal of this sermon are important for his theme of Jesus' identity: "And it came to pass, when Jesus had ended these sayings, the people were astonished at his doctrine: for he taught them as *one* having authority, and not as the scribes" [italics in KJV] (Matthew 7:28-29). They were "astonished" (Matthew 7:28) (ἐξεπλήσσοντο) or astounded. From the beginning to the end of His message the Messiah had them mesmerized.

Matthew Chapter 8

In Matthew 8:1-4 a leper was cleansed. The act of healing itself was a witness to the identity of the One doing the healing. It says the leper "worshipped him." The NASB says that he "bowed down to Him" (Matthew 8:2) (προσεκύνει αὐτῷ). While we can't be sure that this was the act of a man consciously worshiping the Messiah, it would not have been lost on Matthew's later audience and on us who read his words. Likewise, the leper's words, "Lord, if thou wilt, thou canst make me clean" (Matthew 8:2), with the address "Lord" (κύριε), at the time they were spoken may not have signified an understanding of exactly who he was talking to, but Matthew's initial readers/listeners and we who follow in their footsteps appreciate its fuller significance. The leper did have faith in Jesus' ability to heal. "Thou canst make" (δύνασαί) expresses the leper's confidence, contingent only on Jesus' volition. Jesus could have healed him by speaking, but for a leper, who was considered an untouchable, it says, "Jesus put forth *his* hand, and touched him" [italics in KJV] (Matthew 8:3). One can almost hear the gasps of those who witnessed the cleansing.

Jesus told this leper two seemingly contradictory things, "See thou tell no man; but go thy way, shew thyself to the priest, and offer the gift that Moses commanded, for a testimony unto them" (Matthew 8:4). This is the first time Matthew uses the noun "testimony" (μαρτύριον) that can also mean "witness," both nouns referring to the testimony given. We are not told what the "testimony" (μαρτύριον) of the leper to the priests consisted of, but no doubt it would have been followed by questions about how the healing had taken place. Matthew did not intend for it to be overlooked that there were many witnesses to this event which is preceded by the words, "great multitudes followed Him" (Matthew 8:1). The miracles of the Messiah did not take place in private—Jesus made it a habit to select at least two followers to accompany Him so that even the most private of miracles were witnessed by more than one person.

The healing of the centurion's servant in Matthew 8:5-13 again provides intriguing testimony to Jesus' identity. Having just shown a literal personal touch with the cleansing of the leper, this miracle will show that the personal physical presence of the Great Physician was unnecessary. Knowing how the centurion would respond, Jesus said, "I will come and heal him" (Matthew 8:7). The centurion, who held a prestigious position in first century Palestine, recognized something of the grandeur of Jesus. He said, "Lord, I am not worthy that thou shouldest come under my roof" (Matthew 8:8) (κύριε, οὐκ εἰμὶ ἱκανὸς ἵνα μου ὑπὸ τὴν στέγην εἰσέλθῃς). The centurion also recognized Jesus' authority, which was inseparable from His identity, and he said, "For I am a man under authority, having soldiers under me: and I say to this *man*, go, and he goeth; and to another, come, and he cometh; and to my servant, do this, and he doeth *it*" [italics in KJV] (Matthew 8:9). Jesus' divine identity is emphasized because He healed from a distance; "And Jesus said unto the centurion, Go thy way; and as thou hast believed, *so* be it done unto thee. And his servant was healed in the selfsame hour" [italics in KJV] (Matthew 8:13).

Jesus healed the fever of Peter's mother-in-law when He "touched her hand" (Matthew 8:15). Following this healing, word spread so that "they brought unto him many that were possessed with devils" (Matthew 8:16). This is Matthew's first mention of demon possession and the fact that Jesus "cast out the spirits with *his* word" [italics in KJV] (Matthew 8:16). Jesus thus demonstrates His power over the devil's domain. On this occasion Jesus also "healed all that were sick" (Matthew 8:16), and Matthew says these miraculous works were done "in order that" or "that it might be" (ὅπως), indicating purpose, "That it might be fulfilled which was spoken by Esaias the prophet" (Matthew 8:17). The miracles served a prophetic purpose which was to identify Jesus, the One who performed them as the Messiah. Matthew wrote that Jesus "Himself took our infirmities, and bare *our* sicknesses" [italics in KJV] (Matthew 8:17). Isaiah 53:4-5 is not directly quoted but parts of it are paraphrased, showing that Jesus' healing ministry fulfilled the messianic prophecy. Matthew emphasizes that Isaiah was referring specifically to Jesus by placing the personal pronoun "himself" (αὐτὸς) at the beginning of the sentence. The healings themselves were not as important as the One whom they identified.

Matthew 8:18-22 is a break from the supernaturally miraculous to the comparatively mundane. There were times when Jesus wanted to get away from the crowds: "Now when Jesus saw great multitudes about him, he gave commandment to depart unto the other side" (Matthew 8:18). On this occasion, before they could leave, a scribe came up and wanted to join them. The scribe addressed Jesus as "teacher" (διδάσκαλος) and said, "Teacher, I will follow You wherever You go" (Matthew 8:19 NASB). The man did not know what he was getting himself into, so Jesus said, "The foxes have holes, and the birds of the air *have* nests; but the Son of man hath not where to lay *his* head" [italics in KJV] (Matthew 8:20).

The designation "the Son of Man" (ὁ υἱὸς τοῦ ἀνθρώπου) is found 94 times in the New Testament and most often, 32 times, in Matthew's Gospel where it is always used by Jesus, of Himself. The title emphasizes His humanity. The Old Testament prophet Ezekiel repeatedly used it in reference to a human being, a descendant of Adam. A Jewish audience would likely recognize it as something more than a human being. In the Davidic Psalm 8 the designation is found in a messianic context. While that may be challenged, its quotation in the New Testament by the author of Hebrews, leaves no doubt about the title's messianic character. The author of Hebrews introduces the quotation with: "But one in a certain place testified, saying" (Hebrews 2:6) without mentioning David but the source is clearly Psalm 8:4-6. The author of Hebrews quotes Psalm 8 in its argument for the superiority of Christ over angels:

> But one in a certain place testified, saying, What is man, that thou art mindful of him? or the son of man, that thou visitest him? Thou madest him a little lower than the angels; thou crownedst him with glory and honour, and didst set him over the works of thy hands: thou hast put all things in subjection under his feet. For in that he put all in subjection under him, he left nothing *that is* not put under him. But now we see not yet all things put under him [italics in KJV] (Hebrews 2:6-8).

The book of Hebrews characterizes the Old Testament messianic passage as "testimony" using the compound verb (preposition + verb) "testify" (διαμαρτύρομαι) from the preposition "through" or "by means of" (δια) + the verb "testify" (μαρτύρομαι). The meaning of the compound word "testify" (διαμαρτύρομαι) is virtually synonymous to the uncompounded term "testify" (μαρτύρομαι). The mindset of the New Testament writers was that they were providing evidence of Jesus' divine messianic identity.

Equally important for understanding the significance of the title "The Son of Man" (ὁ υἱὸς τοῦ ἀνθρώπου) and a reference that would be remembered by Jesus' audience is Daniel 7:13-14:

> I saw in the night visions, and, behold, *one* like the Son of man came with the clouds of heaven, and came to the Ancient of days, and they brought him near before him. And there was given him dominion, and glory, and a kingdom, that all people, nations, and languages, should serve him: his dominion *is* an everlasting dominion, which shall not pass away, and his kingdom *that* which shall not be destroyed [italics in KJV].

While it might be argued that the designation "the Son of Man" (ὁ υἱὸς τοῦ ἀνθρώπου– Hebrew = בַּר אֱנָשׁ) refers to a personified idealized Israel, the context is undoubtedly messianic and understood as such by the Jews in Jesus' day. Matthew is explicit with his application of Old Testament messianic quotations, while Jesus does so obliquely, but no less powerfully.

Jesus' interaction with the scribe is immediately followed by another encounter with a man whom Matthew describes as a "disciple" (μαθητής) who approached Him: "And another of his disciples said unto him, Lord, suffer me first to go and bury my father" (Matthew 8:21). With this man Jesus underlined the urgency of following Him: "But

Jesus said unto him, Follow me; and let the dead bury their dead" (Matthew 8:22). Whether the man's father had died was not in view. Jesus was communicating that following Him was more important than even the closest of human relationships and obligations. Dead people do not bury dead people. Jesus was saying that those who were dead spiritually should be left to bury their own kind.

The account of Jesus calming the storm is Matthew's second use of the single Greek compound word translated "ye of little faith" (Matthew 8:26) (ὀλιγόπιστοι) to describe the doubting disciples. The incredible calm, "and there was a great calm" (Matthew 8:26) describes a miracle that only God could perform. The disciples' reaction contributes to the emphasis on Jesus' identity which Matthew includes; "But the men marvelled, saying, What manner of man is this, that even the winds and the sea obey him!" (Matthew 8:27). A mere man could not perform what they had just witnessed.

The miraculous exorcism of demons and Jesus' casting them into swine provides yet another opportunity for evidence of His identity. These are hostile witnesses but they give valuable corroborating testimony. The presence of Jesus led to their asking, "What have we to do with thee, Jesus, thou Son of God? Art thou come hither to torment us before the time?" (Matthew 8:29). The witnesses present were the two men delivered from the demons, the pig herders who ran away, as well as Jesus' disciples who were probably there.

Matthew Chapter 9

In Matthew 9 the issue of Jesus' identity rises to a new level when He tells the paralytic, "thy sins be forgiven thee" (Matthew 9:2). The scribes who were present did not verbalize their opinion; "And, behold, certain of the scribes said within themselves, This *man* blasphemeth" [italics in KJV] (Matthew 9:3). Jesus read their minds: "And Jesus knowing their thoughts said, Wherefore think ye evil in your hearts?" (Matthew 9:4). Although mentioned almost incidentally, this obviously has implications for Jesus' identity. Mind reading and forgiveness of sins cannot be attributed to a human being. Because some of the scribes denied that Jesus had the authority to do the latter their conclusion was that He blasphemed. Jesus proceeded to prove that He did have the authority to forgive sins by healing the man. The participants in this exchange were multiple eyewitnesses and the author does not fail to mention, "But when the multitudes saw *it*" [italics in KJV] (Matthew 9:8).

Jesus inevitably aroused jealousy in the established religious community and the Pharisees started complaining to Him about His association with "publicans [tax gatherers NASB] and sinners" (Matthew 9:10) (τελῶναι καὶ ἁμαρτωλοί). Jesus defended His actions with the quotation, "I will have mercy, and not sacrifice" (Matthew 9:13) which was from Hosea 6:6, "For I desired mercy, and not sacrifice." The Hosea context makes it clear from the first verse of the chapter that "Yahweh" (Hosea 6:1) (יְהֹוָה) is the speaker and Jesus identifies Himself with Him by continuing to use the first person singular in His mission statement, "for I am not come to call the righteous, but sinners to repentance" (Matthew 9:13). Jesus linked God the Father's desire with His own redemptive mission. The implication of Jesus' words was that He did not come to call the righteous (sinners who falsely think they are righteous), but sinners (sinners who see themselves as sinners).

Not only did Jesus' ministry elicit professional jealousy on the part of the Pharisees, the disciples of John the Baptist felt He was a threat to their mentor. They saw a noticeable difference between the ministry of their leader and that of Jesus. In their defense of John the Baptist they even used the Pharisees for support; "Why do we and the Pharisees fast oft, but thy disciples fast not?" (Matthew 9:14). Matthew included this incident in his account to bring up the issue of identity where Jesus used the metaphor of a wedding and Himself as "the bridegroom" (Matthew 9:15) (ὁ νυμφίος) who introduces the new order ushered in by the Messiah, illustrated by two additional metaphors of garment patching and storing new wine. In His person Jesus supersedes the old order represented by the Pharisees and that of His introducer John the Baptist.

The raising from the dead of the daughter of the "official" or "ruler" (Matthew 9:18) (ἄρχων) is a high point in Matthew's account of the life of Christ as shown by the author's comment, "And the fame hereof went abroad into all that land" (Matthew 9:26). This is followed by the healing of two blind men who say, "*Thou* Son of David, have mercy on us" [italics in KJV] (Matthew 9:27). Jesus requested that they remain silent, which would have included who it was who had healed them, but they ignored His warning and "spread abroad his fame in all that country" (Matthew 9:31).

In the healing of a demon-possessed man the multitudes dared not say what they were thinking about Jesus' identity, no doubt for fear of the ever-present Pharisees. Instead they made the innocuous statement, "It was never so seen in Israel" (Matthew 9:33), which begged the question, "Who is this doing these things never seen before in Israel? Who has that kind of power and authority over demons?" The Pharisees recognized that the multitudes' comment was meant for them, and so they attributed Jesus' supernatural ability to perform exorcisms to "the prince of the devils" (Matthew 9:34) (τῷ ἄρχοντι τῶν δαιμονίων) that is, the devil himself. On this occasion Jesus did not counter the Pharisees' contention but does so in a similar subsequent incident recorded in Matthew chapter 12.

In Matthew 9:35 is a summary statement describing Jesus' ministry as: "And Jesus went about all the cities and villages, teaching in their synagogues, and preaching the gospel of the kingdom, and healing every sickness and every disease among the people." Seeing the spiritual need of the people, He exhorted the disciples to ask "the Lord of the harvest, that he will send forth labourers into his harvest" (Matthew 9:38). This is immediately followed by the commissioning and sending out of the twelve, because Jesus Himself is "the Lord of the harvest" (τοῦ κυρίου τοῦ θερισμοῦ) and it is "His harvest" (τὸν θερισμὸν αὐτοῦ), both of which provide evidence of His divine identity.

Matthew Chapter 10

Matthew indicates that Jesus was more than a teacher sending out students with an assignment: "And when he had called unto *him* his twelve disciples, he gave them power *against* unclean spirits, to cast them out, and to heal all manner of sickness and all manner of disease" (Matthew 10:1). The delegation and commissioning of the disciples had a prophetic significance beyond the immediate mission that would continue through their successors "till the Son of Man be come" (Matthew 10:23). The disciples' being brought before the authorities would give significance to Jesus' claim because it would be "for My sake" (Matthew 10:18) and the purpose given would be "for a testimony against them and the Gentiles" (Matthew 10:18). Jesus' prophecy would begin to unfold in the disciples' immediate mission, and their "testimony" (μαρτύριον) would continue in the history of the early church as recorded in the Acts of the Apostles.

Jesus made statements about having direct access to God the Father which were not true of any mere man: "Whosoever therefore shall confess me before men, him will I confess also before my Father which is in heaven. But whosoever shall deny me before men, him will I also deny before my Father which is in heaven" (Matthew 10:32-33). The assertion that men's response to the disciples as His representatives, and thereby to Him and to God the Father, went beyond what any man could claim; "He that receiveth you receiveth me, and he that receiveth me receiveth him that sent me" (Matthew 10:40).

Matthew Chapter 11

John the Baptist apparently had difficulty reconciling his incarceration with the arrival of the anticipated kingdom. So while in prison he relayed an identity question to Jesus, "Art thou he that should come, or do we look for another?" (Matthew 11:3). Jesus answered him with evidence of His identity in the form of Old Testament prophecies that were being fulfilled in Him. John the Baptist's disciples were to report back to him "Go and shew John again those things which ye do hear and see" (Matthew 11:4).

The message Jesus wanted John's disciples to return with was, "The blind receive their sight, and the lame walk, the lepers are cleansed, and the deaf hear, the dead are raised up, and the poor have the gospel preached to them" (Matthew 11:5). Isaiah's description of the coming kingdom was similar to Jesus' words: "Then shall the lame *man* leap as an hart, and the tongue of the dumb sing" [italics in KJV] (Isaiah 35:6). Isaiah's account of events at the time of the Messiah include, "to preach good tidings unto the meek" (Isaiah 61:1). John the Baptist would have understood that what he announced had arrived—Jesus was the promised Messiah and King of that kingdom. The "gospel," the "good news" (εὐαγγέλιον) was about the person and work of the Messiah who had come.

Jesus praised John the Baptist with whom proof of His identity was linked. Jesus quoted from Malachi 3:1; "For this is *he*, of whom it is written, Behold, I send my messenger before thy face, which shall prepare thy way before thee" [italics in KJV] (Matthew 11:10). The words in the Malachi quotation are followed by, "And the Lord, whom ye seek, shall suddenly come to his temple, even the messenger of the covenant, whom ye delight in" (Malachi 3:1), where the title "Lord" is a translation of "Adonay" (אֲדֹנָי). Although this part of the verse is not quoted by Jesus, it may well have been remembered by those hearing His words.

The judgment pronounced against Chorazin, Bethsaida, and Capernaum was the direct result of their rejection of Jesus' message of repentance in spite of the miracles performed. On that occasion Jesus expressed the exclusive relationship that exists between Himself and God the Father; "All things are delivered unto me of my Father: and no man knoweth the Son, but the Father; neither knoweth any man the Father, save the Son, and *he* to whomsoever the Son will reveal *him*" [italics in KJV] (Matthew 11:27). Jesus as the mediator between God and man is indicated by the use of the verb for "will" (βούλομαι) signifying "desire" or "intent" in the clause, "*he* to whomsoever the Son will reveal *him*" [italics in KJV] (Matthew 11:27). In the conclusion to this pericope Jesus said, "and ye shall find rest unto your souls" (Matthew 11:29). The "rest" (ἀνάπαυσιν) Jesus promised is predicated on their acceptance of His invitation to "Come unto me" (Matthew 11:28). Only the God/Man/Messiah could make such an offer.

Matthew Chapter 12

A conflict with the Pharisees in Matthew 12 started with the violation of the Sabbath: "At that time Jesus went on the sabbath day through the corn; and his disciples were an hungred, and began to pluck the ears of corn, and to eat" (Matthew 12:1). Jesus began His defense using David as an example of when the physical need for food trumped observance of the Law. "But he said unto them, Have ye not read what David did, when he was an hungred, and they that were with him; How he entered into the house of God, and did eat the shewbread, which was not lawful for him to eat, neither for them which were with him, but only for the priests?" (Matthew 12:3-4). The implication was that David's violation of the temple and its contents that were reserved for God was acceptable.

Jesus' second example was the priests who violated the Law by engaging in work on the Sabbath as they went about their temple duties: "Or have ye not read in the law, how that on the sabbath days the priests in the temple profane the sabbath, and are blameless?" (Matthew 12:5). Violation of the Law was written into the very fabric of the Law itself. Jesus then alluded to His own identity, saying, "But I say to you, that in this place is *one* greater than the temple" [italics in KJV] (Matthew 12:6). He then made it explicit, "For the Son of Man is Lord even of the Sabbath day" (Matthew 12:8). The only One with authority over the Sabbath was God Himself. The occasion had been the disciples' hunger that required immediate attention. Jesus reprimanded the mean-spirited attack of the Pharisees with a quotation of Hosea 6:6; "I will have mercy, and not sacrifice" (Matthew 12:7). Jesus reinforced His authority over the

Sabbath, and further illustrated that quote with a healing miracle, that same Sabbath day.

Jesus' went on to do more healing miracles on the Sabbath and warned those He healed not to broadcast what He had done for them. He "charged them that they should not make him known" (Matthew 12:16). The meaning of the Greek adjective translated "make. . .known" (φανερός), provided by the respected Greek lexicon of Bauer, Arndt, and Gingrich for this usage in Matthew 12:16 is to "reveal the identity of someone" (Walter Bauer, William F. Arndt, and Wilbur F. Gingrich, *A Greek-English Lexicon of the New Testament and Other Early Christian Literature* [Chicago: University of Chicago Press, 1957], 860). Matthew says this is a fulfillment of Isaiah 42:1-4:

> Behold my servant, whom I have chosen; my beloved, in whom my soul is well pleased: I will put my spirit upon him, and he shall shew judgment to the Gentiles. He shall not strive, nor cry; neither shall any man hear his voice in the streets. A bruised reed shall he not break, and smoking flax shall he not quench, till he send forth judgment unto victory. And in his name shall the Gentiles trust (Matthew 12:18-21).

This Old Testament passage is Isaiah's prophetic description of the messianic servant. Harris, Archer, and Waltke, under their entry for "servant" (עֶבֶד), write, "The most significant use of the term 'servant' is as a messianic designation, the most prominent personal, technical term to represent the OT teaching on the Messiah" (R. Laird Harris, Gleason L. Archer, Jr., Bruce K. Waltke, eds, *Theological Wordbook of the Old Testament* [Chicago: Moody, 1980], 2:639) (TWOT). While some may argue that the "servant" is national Israel, as TWOT also points out, the passage in question is one "in which the servant is differentiated from actual Israel and has a mission to Israel" (ibid., 2:640). The intent of Matthew's inclusion of the passage as being fulfilled by Jesus is to identify Him as the Messiah.

In the controversy over the exorcism and healing of the man who was blind and unable to speak in Matthew chapter 12, the subject of Jesus' identity is brought up by the multitude who asked the rhetorical question, "Is this not the son of David?" (Matthew 12:23). A. T. Robertson says, "The form of the question expects the answer 'no,' but they put it so because of the Pharisaic hostility towards Jesus" (*Word Pictures in the New Testament*, 1:95). The form of the question is the same as in the Gospel of John where the Samaritan woman at the well asked, "Is not this the Christ, is it?" (John 4:29). Louw and Nida's explanation of John's usage is applicable here as well:

> Some persons have argued that the occurrence of μήτι in Jn 4:29 is contradictory, since it would appear from the context that the individuals posing the question regarded Jesus as a possible Messiah. On the other hand, asking the question in this form would have certainly fit the circumstances in which there was strong opposition to anyone claiming that Jesus was the Messiah. This form of the question would have avoided an overt commitment, while at the same time indicating people's evident interest and concern (Johannes P. Louw and Eugene A. Nida, *Greek-English Lexicon of the New Testament Based on Semantic Domains*, 2nd ed. [New York: United Bible Societies, 2nd ed], 1989, 1:667).

The ever-present Pharisees heard the multitude and stepped in to refute the idea that Jesus could be the Son of David, the Messiah, and offered an alternative identity. They said, "This *fellow* doth not cast out devils, but by Beelzebub the prince of the devils" [italics in KJV] (Matthew 12:24). Jesus refuted their claim by showing the absurdity of it. The devil has a vested interest in maintaining not destroying his own minions. Jesus the Messiah was the dividing line between the divine and the demonic; "He that is not with me is against me; and he that gathereth not with me scattereth abroad" (Matthew 12:30). Anything and anyone associated with Jesus could not be associated with the devil.

In Matthew 12:46-50 there appears to be on the surface an insensitive response by Jesus when told that His family is waiting to talk with Him. He asks, "Who is my mother? And who are my brethren?" (Matthew 12:48). Family identity is part of who someone is and no less so in the first century, but Jesus brushed that aside "and he stretched forth his hand toward his disciples, and said, Behold my mother and my brethren!" (Matthew 12:49). Jesus indicated that His family extended beyond the disciples who were present; "For whosoever shall do the will of my Father which is in heaven, the same is my brother, and sister, and mother" (Matthew 12:50). The most significant part of Jesus' identity was spiritual and not physical.

Matthew Chapter 13

Parables provided proof that Jesus is the predicted Messiah. Jesus said that those who failed to understand His parables were foretold by the prophet Isaiah:

> By hearing ye shall hear, and shall not understand; and seeing ye shall see, and shall not perceive: For this people's heart is waxed gross, and *their* ears are dull of hearing, and their eyes they have closed; lest at any time they should see with *their* eyes, and hear with *their* ears, and should understand with *their* heart, and should be converted, and I should heal them [italics in KJV] (Matthew 13:14-15).

Isaiah's prophecy proved that denial did not disprove Jesus' claims but in fact proved them.

The question of Jesus' identity comes up again at the end of Matthew chapter 13 when He returned to His hometown of Nazareth. He had His roots there and people thought they knew Him but were beginning to wonder, "Whence hath this *man* this wisdom, and *these* mighty works?" [italics in KJV] (Matthew 13:54). The facts they knew did not account for what was happening, and so they asked, "Is not this the carpenter's son? Is not his mother called Mary and his brethren, James, and Joses, and Simon, and Judas? And his sisters, are they not all with us? Whence then hath this *man* all these things?" [italics in KJV] (Matthew 13:55-56). They could not reconcile who they thought He was with what they saw and heard and "they were offended in him" (Matthew 13:57) (ἐσκανδαλίζοντο ἐν αὐτῷ). What He claimed elevated Him to a status superior to their own. The chapter concludes with Matthew's explanation, "And he did not many mighty works there because of their unbelief" (Matthew 13:58). In the context the "unbelief" (ἀπιστίαν) was directly related to their refusal to accept Jesus' divine messianic identity.

Matthew Chapter 14

King Herod, plagued by a guilty conscience for his execution of John the Baptist, was also concerned about who Jesus is and he speculated, "And said unto his servants, This is John the Baptist; he is risen from the dead; and therefore mighty works do shew forth themselves in him" (Matthew 14:2). Matthew left no doubt about John the Baptist's death; "And his disciples came, and took up the body, and buried it" (Matthew 14:12). Herod attempted to reconcile what he knew about John the Baptist with Jesus' identity.

Jesus, upon hearing that His notoriety had reached Herod, took steps to lower His profile but couldn't get away from the multitude. "When Jesus heard *of it*, he departed thence by ship into a desert place apart: and when the people had heard *thereof*, they followed him on foot out of the cities" [italics in KJV] (Matthew 14:13). What followed was the miracle of the Feeding of the Five Thousand, an event that added to the evidence of Jesus' messianic identity.

Jesus and His disciples were finally able to get away from the multitude, first by having the disciples leave in a boat. After spending time in prayer alone, Jesus returned to the disciples who were in the midst of a frightening storm. Jesus did so by walking on the water, which in our day has become a metaphor for the supernatural. The subject of Jesus' identity came up as the disciples mistook Him for a ghost; "they were troubled, saying, It is a spirit; and they cried out for fear" (Matthew 14:26). Jesus responded by saying, "It is I" (Matthew 14:27) (ἐγώ εἰμι), or, "I am." While the disciples, in their frightened state no doubt did not fully apprehend the significance of those words, "I am" (ἐγώ εἰμι), as reminiscent of the God of the Old Testament who revealed Himself as "I am that I am" (אֶהְיֶה אֲשֶׁר אֶהְיֶה) to Moses (Exodus 3:14) at the burning bush, subsequent readers/listeners of Matthew's Gospel would have made the connection. Keil and Delitzsch write, "[God] designated Himself by this name as the absolute God of the fathers, acting with unfettered liberty and self-dependence" (C. F. Keil and F. Delitzsch, *Commentary on the Old Testament* [Grand Rapids: Eerdmans, 1981], 1:442).

Once the wind and the waves had subsided the disciples in the boat who had seen Jesus walk on the water responded. "Then they that were in the ship came and worshipped him, saying, Of a truth thou art the Son of God" (Matthew 14:33). They identified Him as God; otherwise their worship would have been blasphemy.

Matthew Chapter 15

The controversy with the Pharisees resumed in chapter 15 with the accusation that Jesus' disciples violated "the tradition of the elders" (Matthew 15:2) by failing to perform a washing ritual before meals. Jesus' response accused the Pharisees of elevating their traditions over God's commands. Jesus said, "Why do ye also transgress the commandment of God by your tradition?" (Matthew 15:3). Jesus gave an example of their failing to honor their parents by failing to provide for them by claiming to have set those resources aside for God. The disciples informed Jesus that this had "offended" (Matthew 15:12) (σκανδαλίζω) the Pharisees. Jesus reacted by condemning the Pharisees. He said, "Every plant, which my heavenly Father hath not planted, shall be rooted up. Let them alone: they be blind leaders of the blind. And if the blind lead the blind, both shall fall into the ditch" (Matthew 15:13-14). Jesus referred to God as "my heavenly Father" (Matthew 15:13) (ὁ πατήρ μου ὁ οὐράνιος), implying a highly personal association which would have offended His opponents and been regarded by them as blasphemous.

When Jesus healed a Canaanite woman (Matthew 15:22), a Gentile referred to Jesus as the "Son of David" (Matthew 15:22) (υἱὸς Δαυίδ). The designation by the woman, that identified Him specifically with Israel, preceded Jesus' words, "I am not sent but unto the lost sheep of the house of Israel" (Matthew 15:24). Jesus referred to the woman's response by saying, "great *is* thy faith" [italics in KJV] (Matthew 15:28). The "faith" (πίστις) of the woman was probably "trust in His person," although some might contend it was belief in the proposition that He could and would exorcize the demon from the woman's daughter. This incident foreshadowed that Jesus' ministry would have universal implications. But for the time being the primary emphasis would be on the Jews, as noted in Matthew's telling of the multitudes' response to His miraculous works, "and they glorified the God of Israel" (Matthew 15:31).

Matthew Chapter 16

The Pharisees and the Sadducees put Jesus to the "test" (πειράζω), asking Him for a "sign from heaven" (Matthew 16:1) (σημεῖον ἐκ τοῦ οὐρανοῦ). This sign may have been proof that He was from heaven and thus displayed His identity. Jesus' response included an element of His identity, the "sign of Jonah" (Matthew 16:4), that, as Matthew previously recorded (Matthew 12:40), referred to His coming death and resurrection. Jesus included the Pharisees and the Sadducees in His condemnation: "A wicked and adulterous generation seeketh after a sign; and there shall no sign be given unto it, but the sign of the prophet Jonas[h]" (Matthew 16:4). Jesus' death and resurrection would result in judgment because they rejected who He is.

Jesus initiated a discussion with His disciples about His identity by asking, "Whom do men say that I the Son of Man am?" (Matthew 16:13). The disciples told Jesus, "Some *say that thou art* John the Baptist: some, Elias; and others, Jeremias, or one of the prophets" [italics in KJV] (Matthew 16:14). Jesus was not engaging His disciples in a theoretical discussion when He asked them their opinions about the title "the Son of Man" (τὸν υἱὸν τοῦ ἀνθρώπου). He was asking them opinions about Himself. Additionally, Jesus was concerned not for the opinions of others, but for the conviction of His disciples. Jesus used the second person plural personal pronoun "you" (ὑμεῖς) in the emphatic initial position in His question, "But whom say ye that I am?" (Matthew 16:15) (ὑμεῖς δὲ τίνα με λέγετε εἶναι;). Peter, true to his outspoken character, answered,

"Thou art the Christ, the Son of the living God" (Matthew 16:16) (σὺ εἶ ὁ χριστὸς ὁ υἱὸς τοῦ θεοῦ τοῦ ζῶντος). Without divine revelation and illumination Peter would not have reached that conclusion. Jesus said, "flesh and blood hath not revealed *it* unto thee, but my Father which is in heaven" [italics in KJV] (Matthew 16:17).

Jesus warned His disciples not to publicize what they had just talked about. Matthew's indirect quotation of Jesus' words are a self-identification of Himself as the Messiah. "Then charged he his disciples that they should tell no man that he was Jesus the Christ" (Matthew 16:20). Jesus left no doubt about who He is. There can be no denying that Jesus explicitly stated that He is "the Christ" (ὁ χριστός), that is, the Messiah.

Peter's proclamation is a turning point in Matthew's Gospel which is seen in the transition statement that follows this passage. "From that time forth began Jesus to shew unto his disciples, how that he must go unto Jerusalem, and suffer many things of the elders and chief priests and scribes, and be killed, and be raised again the third day" (Matthew 16:21). Chapter 16 concludes with Jesus claiming for Himself the identity of "the Son of Man" (ὁ υἱὸς τοῦ ἀνθρώπου); and the One who will judge men: "For the Son of man shall come in the glory of his Father with his angels; and then he shall reward every man according to his works" (Matthew 16:27).

Matthew Chapter 17

The Transfiguration parallels Jesus' baptism as an event with a heavenly confirmation of His identity. Peter, James, and John are listed as contemporary witnesses, together with Moses and Elijah, two witnesses from the past whose testimony served to verify Jesus' claims. Additionally there were two supernatural phenomena; "a bright cloud overshadowed them: and behold a voice out of the cloud, which said, This is my beloved Son, in whom I am well pleased; hear ye him" (Matthew 17:5). What they witnessed: "And was transfigured before them: and his face did shine as the sun, and his raiment was white as the light" (Matthew 17:2). Peter, James, and John were told by Jesus not to relate what they had just witnessed; "Tell the vision to no man, until the Son of man be risen again from the dead" (Matthew 17:9). Later on they would testify to what they had seen and heard, Peter himself writing about it in his second epistle (2 Peter 1:17-18) and becoming part of the written record in the other two Synoptic Gospels (Mark 9:2-13; Luke 9:28-36).

 In the conversation following the Transfiguration (Matthew 17:10-13) the disciples asked about Elijah coming, "And his disciples asked him, saying, Why then say the scribes that Elias must first come?" (Matthew 17:10). Matthew identifies "Elijah" (Ἡλίας) in his editorial comment; "Then the disciples understood that he spake unto them of John the Baptist" (Matthew 17:13). Jesus said about him; "and they knew him not" (Matthew 17:12), speaking of their failure to identify John the Baptist for who he was. John the Baptist was not recognized as the herald of King Jesus. Jesus added, "Likewise shall also the Son of man suffer of them" (Matthew 17:12). Jesus would also fail to be identified by the religious leadership as who He is, and just as John the Baptist suffered martyrdom Jesus would be put to death.

In Matthew 17:14-21 Jesus uses the occasion of the disciples' failure to exorcize a demon to talk about faith. When Jesus said, "O faithless and perverse generation" (Matthew 17:17), with the adjective "faithless" or "unbelieving" (ἄπιστος) was He referring to the failure of the father wanting the demon driven out of his son and/or the disciples to believe a proposition such as, "Jesus is able to, and/or Jesus will deliver from this demon?" Or was it failure to put their trust in Him who would deliver? Or was it both? Perhaps in this instance it is better to understand the adjective "unbelieving" (ἄπιστος), together with the participle translated "perverted" (διεστραμμένη), as descriptive of the "generation" (γενεά), functioning as a negative counterpart to the participial use of "believer" (πιστευσάντων), which can function as a title meaning "a believer" or "a Christian." In the case of Matthew 17:17 it would be used as a title for "an unbeliever," or a "non-Christian." This would be a plenary or inclusive meaning incorporating both meanings, that of belief in a proposition and trust in a person, neither of which those referred to had done. In contrast to their failure Jesus spoke of "faith as a grain of mustard seed" (Matthew 17:20) with which those who exercise it "shall say unto this mountain, Remove hence to yonder place; and it shall remove; and nothing shall be impossible unto you" (Matthew 17:20). Semantically the noun "faith" (πίστις) could mean belief in a proposition related to the removal of the mountain or trust in Him who would accomplish it, or both.

The incident about paying the temple tax is used by Jesus to address the issue of His identity. In His illustration Jesus asked, "of whom do the kings of the earth take custom or tribute? of their own children, or of strangers?" (Matthew 17:25). The reasoning Jesus used is that for the Son of God to pay the temple tax would be the equivalent of a secular son paying tax to his father the king, a scenario which those who heard His illustration agreed did not happen. By going ahead and paying the tax Jesus was not denying who He is, "Notwithstanding, lest we offend them" (Matthew 17:27), because He was concerned with the level and timing of rising opposition.

Matthew Chapter 18

One of the most endearing pericopes in the entire Gospel of Matthew is Jesus' teaching about faith with a child as an example. He described securing entrance into the kingdom as "except ye be converted, and become as little children, ye shall not enter into the kingdom of heaven" (Matthew 18:3). There has been much debate over exactly what characteristic/s of the faith of "children" (τὰ παιδία) is/are to be taken from Jesus' visual object lesson, but what is certain are the words He used to describe them as "one of these little ones which believe in me" (Matthew 18:6). The Greek construction "believe in" (πιστεύω εἰς) is found only this one time in Matthew's Gospel, once in Mark (Mark 9:42), never in Luke, but 32 times in the Johannine Gospel, and several times elsewhere. The search goes on to find this exact construction in secular literature; however for now, it can be concluded that its usage is confined to the New Testament. More will be said later about its meaning, particularly in the Gospel of John, but here in Matthew the idea of "simple trust" in the person of Jesus is probable in the context of children, although belief in the truth of propositions about Him is also possible, and perhaps the two are not intended to be mutually exclusive.

Matthew chapter 18 concludes with Jesus teaching His disciples. In the instructions for dealing with a sinning brother the reason given for "take with thee one or two more" (Matthew 18:16), was what was established in the Old Testament "in the mouth of two or three witnesses every word may be established" (Matthew 18:16). The quotation is from Deuteronomy 19:15: "One witness shall not rise up against a man for any iniquity, or for any sin, in any sin that he sinneth: at the mouth of two witnesses, or at the mouth of three witnesses, shall the matter be established." Jesus and Matthew were aware of and followed the Old Testament principle and avoided solitary witnesses.

Matthew Chapter 19

In the account of what has become known as "the Rich Young Ruler" in Matthew 19:16-26 Jesus turned a request for instruction, "what good thing shall I do, that I may have eternal life?" (Matthew 19:16), into an inquiry into Jesus' identity: "Why callest thou me good? *There is* none good but one, *that is*, God" [italics in KJV] (Matthew 19:17). While Jesus was challenging him to acknowledge that He indeed was God, the rich young ruler did not take up His challenge.

Instead, when the question of keeping the commandments came up, "but if thou wilt enter into life, keep the commandments" (Matthew 19:17), the man claims perfection. The man said, "All these things have I kept from my youth up: what lack I yet?" (Matthew 19:20). The issue being discussed was the man's performance, not his willingness, desire, or commitment to do so. In fact the Greek word for "willing" (θέλω) is used in the immediate context, but not as a requirement for eternal life but the desire to do (actual performance) what it takes to obtain it. Jesus said, "but if thou wilt [θέλω = "wish" or "desire"] enter into life" (Matthew 19:17) he needed to do the following. Interestingly Jesus did not refute the man's claim of perfection although it was patently false.

The request Jesus made of the man was an additional requirement for perfection. The man said that he had kept the Law. The Gospel of Matthew demonstrates that perfection goes beyond legal requirements and includes mental aspects (lust, hate, etc.). Jesus dashed the man's hope of reaching heaven by his works. To water the requirement down to a wishing, willing, or committing to do but not actually doing, distorts the words of Jesus. Jesus said that what He was asking was impossible.

In the denouement of the pericope Jesus said, "Verily I say unto you, That a rich man shall hardly enter into the kingdom of heaven. And again I say unto you, It is easier for a camel to go through the eye of a needle, than for a rich man to enter into the kingdom of God" (Matthew 19:23-24). The ingenious interpretation of some Bible teachers notwithstanding, it was not a matter of unloading the camel to get him through a narrow opening. The context says nothing about the camel bearing a load although it is assumed by some that the riches of the man represent that load.

The astonishment of Jesus' disciples and His response to them proves that Jesus did not have that in mind. "When his disciples heard *it*, they were exceedingly amazed, saying,

Who then can be saved? But Jesus beheld *them*, and said unto them, With men this is impossible; but with God all things are possible" [italics in KJV] (Matthew 19:25-26). The disciples were amazed at what Jesus said and Jesus looked at them. Here was God standing before them saying that perfection was impossible unless you were God and Jesus was God. Jesus was not saying that God will remove man's materialism in order to be saved. Materialism is only the beginning. Perfection has so many facets that it is impossible for man. But God is perfect and provides forensic imputed perfection to men if they place their trust in Jesus. Only God is perfect, and Jesus is God. Unfortunately the man was seeking to earn his way to heaven, an utter impossibility.

The chapter ends with Peter asking Jesus what giving things up to follow Him would mean for himself and his fellow disciples; "Then answered Peter and said unto him, Behold, we have forsaken all, and followed thee; what shall we have therefore?" (Matthew 19:27). Jesus did not tell Peter, "Good job. You have thereby earned eternal life." Instead Jesus told Peter and His disciples what they could expect in the future; "And Jesus said unto them, Verily I say unto you, That ye which have followed me, in the regeneration when the Son of man shall sit in the throne of his glory, ye also shall sit upon twelve thrones, judging the twelve tribes of Israel" (Matthew 19:28).

Furthermore, Jesus said, "And every one that hath forsaken houses, or brethren, or sisters, or father, or mother, or wife, or children, or lands, for my name's sake, shall receive an hundredfold, and shall inherit everlasting life" (Matthew 19:29). The answer for Peter and anyone else who follows Jesus in a life of self-denial is that it will all be worthwhile. While doing the things that Jesus mentioned will result in receiving "many times as much" (Matthew 19:29 NASB) (ἑκατονταπλασίων), literally, one hundred times as much, eternal life cannot be earned by works, as explicitly taught elsewhere (Ephesians 2:8 etc.), and will be received by those who do not work for it but by those who believe in Him.

Jesus' followers could also anticipate a readjustment in the hereafter; "But many *that are* first shall be last; and the last *shall be* first" [italics in KJV] (Matthew 19:30). Not "all" but "many" (πολύς). Some who appear to have been faithful followers on earth, and even some who thought themselves to have been so, will find out in heaven that such was not the case. Who could authoritatively speak about such things? Only God Himself, and that is who Jesus is. Because of Jesus' divine identity His followers can rest assured that what He predicted will in fact take place, and they will receive what He promised.

Matthew Chapter 20

Matthew chapter 20 begins where Jesus left off in chapter 19. Jesus promised the disciples positions of power in the kingdom, but He also made the ominous pronouncement: "But many *that are* first shall be last; and the last *shall be* first" [italics in KJV] (Matthew 19:30). In chapter 20 that theme is continued in the Parable of the Laborers. Not all workers in God's harvest have equal opportunity or longevity.

Jesus warned about whining over wages and the ways of God. Since Jesus is God, He has the right to determine eternal remuneration.

Jesus is the King who will sit on His throne, but before that happened He would die. Those two concepts were difficult to reconcile. The mother of James and John, the sons of Zebedee, focused on the former and wanted to make sure her sons did not just reign with Jesus but had the most prominent positions; "Then came to him the mother of Zebedee's children with her sons, worshipping *him*, and desiring a certain thing of him. And he said unto her, What wilt thou? She saith unto him, Grant that these my two sons may sit, the one on thy right hand, and the other on the left, in thy kingdom" [italics in KJV] (Matthew 20:20-21). She failed to recognize that just as Jesus would die and reign, the disciples would suffer for Him and many would die for Him before reigning with Him. The invitation Jesus extended His disciples was to do both. Not that their death would save anyone, but they were called to follow Him, even to a martyr's death. As Jesus put it, "Even as the Son of man came not to be ministered unto, but to minister, and to give his life a ransom for many" (Matthew 20:28).

Two blind men would not be denied the opportunity to have Jesus heal them. Although they could not see Jesus, Matthew says, "And, behold, two blind men sitting by the way side, when they heard that Jesus passed by, cried out, saying, Have mercy on us, O Lord, *thou* Son of David" [italics in KJV] (Matthew 20:30). Even though they were told to keep silent, they persisted in calling on the One they identified as the Messiah. Jesus stopped and healed them. "So Jesus had compassion *on them*, and touched their eyes: and immediately their eyes received sight, and they followed him" [italics in KJV] (Matthew 20:34). They had witnessed firsthand Jesus' healing touch and followed Him, becoming eyewitnesses with their newly acquired sight.

Matthew Chapter 21

Twice in chapter 20 (verses 18 and 28) Jesus had referred to Himself as "The Son of Man" (ὁ υἱὸς τοῦ ἀνθρώπου) and two blind men (Matthew 20:30-31) had twice addressed Him as the "Son of David" (υἱὸς Δαυίδ), a title referring to His kingship. Those titles provided a fitting lead up to the Triumphal Entry, an event that is presented as significant evidence for Jesus' identity. Matthew used his familiar procedure of a description of an event followed by an Old Testament prophecy. The details of the preparations for the Passover made by the disciples are followed by the words, "All this was done, that it might be fulfilled which was spoken by the prophet" (Matthew 21:4). A quotation told what was being fulfilled; "Say to the daughter of Zion, behold your King is coming to you, gentle, and mounted on a donkey, even on a colt, the foal of a beast of burden" (Matthew 21:5 NASB). The quotation is of Zechariah 9:9: "Rejoice greatly, O daughter of Zion! Shout in triumph, O daughter of Jerusalem! Behold, your king is coming to you; He is just and endowed with salvation, humble, and mounted on a donkey, even on a colt, the foal of a donkey" (NASB). In this messianic passage the title of "king" (βασιλεύς) (מֶלֶךְ) is applied to Jesus.

Prophetic evidence of the identity of Jesus as the King/Messiah is followed by that of the assembled crowd, and another quotation. Matthew writes, "And the multitudes that went before, and that followed, cried, saying, Hosanna to the Son of David: blessed *is* he that cometh in the name of the Lord; hosanna in the highest" [italics in KJV] (Matthew 21:9). The issue was one of identity as seen in the question that was raised; "Who is this?" (Matthew 21:10). The multitudes focused on His place of origin for evidence of identity; "And the multitude said, This is Jesus the prophet of Nazareth of Galilee" (Matthew 21:11).

In the Cleansing of the Temple Jesus quoted what appears to be parts from two Old Testament passages. When He said, "It is written, My house shall be called the house of prayer; but ye have made it a den of thieves" (Matthew 21:13), the first part, "My house shall be called the house of prayer" comes from Isaiah 56:7: "For mine house shall be called an house of prayer for all people." The second part, "but ye have made it a den of thieves" is from Jeremiah 7:11: "Is this house, which is called by my name, become a den of robbers in your eyes?"

By boldly exercising the authority He did in clearing out the commercial interests from the temple and referring to it as "My house," Jesus' self-declared close association with God was not lost on the "chief priests and scribes" (Matthew 21:15). And while they feared the crowd, with its enthusiasm for Jesus and their messianic chant, they did not hesitate to confront Jesus about the title that children were giving to Him; "And when the chief priests and scribes saw the wonderful things that he did, and the children crying in the temple, and saying, Hosanna to the Son of David; they were sore displeased" (Matthew 21:15). If that wasn't enough to anger them, Jesus quoted Psalm 8, a messianic psalm (confirmed to be messianic in Hebrews 2:6-8) in His answer to them; "Out of the mouth of babes and sucklings thou hast perfected praise" (Matthew 21:16). Psalm 8:2 says: "Out of the mouth of babes and sucklings hast thou ordained strength." Jesus appropriated the messianic passage for Himself.

As the week prior to the crucifixion progressed so did the antagonism of the religious establishment, referred to as "the chief priests and elders of the people" (Matthew 21:23). They avoided speaking directly about His identity and instead asked where His authority came from and under whose auspices He acted: "By what authority doest thou these things? And who gave thee this authority?" (Matthew 21:23). Because they rejected that He possessed divine authority, they asked about delegated authority.

The appropriate time to answer that question had not arrived so Jesus stumped them with a question, "The baptism of John, whence was it? from heaven, or of men?" (Matthew 21:25), which they refused to answer: "And they answered Jesus, and said, We cannot tell" (Matthew 21:27). Jesus did likewise: "Neither tell I you by what authority I do these things" (Matthew 21:27).

Jesus told a parable about a landowner who planted a vineyard and rented it out to vine-growers who were to pay rent to the landowner. Instead of paying the rent to the landowner's slaves whom he had sent to collect it, they "took his servants, and beat one, and killed another, and stoned another" (Matthew 21:35). A second group of slaves was sent to collect the rent, and they met with the same fate. Hoping for a better outcome, the landowner "sent unto them his son, saying, They will reverence my son" (Matthew 21:37). However, the son fared no better than the slaves: "But when the husbandmen saw the son, they said among themselves, This is the heir; come, let us kill him, and let us seize on his inheritance. And they caught him, and cast *him* out of the vineyard, and slew *him*" [italics in KJV] (Matthew 21:38-39).

Jesus' opponents recognized who His parables were about. "And when the chief priests and Pharisees had heard his parables, they perceived that he spake of them" (Matthew 21:45). They were the evil vine-growers and Jesus was the landowner's son. They refused to agree who Jesus is. Their response was to attempt to do exactly what the vine-growers in the parable had done. "But when they sought to lay hands on him, they feared the multitude, because they took him for a prophet" (Matthew 21:46). The multitude was closer in their assessment of who Jesus is.

Matthew Chapter 22

At the end of chapter 21 the author tells his readers about the multitudes: "they took him for a prophet" (Matthew 21:46), and in the following chapter Jesus Himself moved the question of His identity a step further by asking the Pharisees, "What think ye of Christ? whose son is he? They say unto him, *The Son* of David" [italics in KJV] (Matthew 22:42). They responded, "*The Son* [contextually understood] of David." They equated "the Son of David" with "the Christ" (τοῦ χριστοῦ), that is, the Anointed One, the Messiah. If Jesus is "The Son of David," which the multitudes thought, and therefore is the Messiah, what else is true about Him?

Jesus gave evidence for the deity of that individual by citing a quotation from David himself: "The Lord said unto my Lord, Sit thou on my right hand, till I make thine enemies thy footstool" (Matthew 22:44). The quote is from Psalm 110:1 and forms the basis for the question Jesus then poses: "If David then call him Lord, how is he his son?" (Matthew 22:45). The Greek form is that of a first-class conditional sentence that assumes the truth of the protasis (the initial "if" part), for the purpose of argument, on the part of the speaker, in this case Jesus. The Pharisees agreed with Jesus that David called the Messiah "Lord" (κύριος). Jesus made sure they agreed to that premise by asking, "How then doth David in spirit call him Lord?" (Matthew 22:43) (κύριον). Jesus followed that up with the Psalm 110:1 quotation of David's Holy Spirit inspired words.

This was a package deal—The Messiah = The Son of David = Lord. With their theological interpretation the Pharisees had no way of reconciling the difficulties posed by their own Scripture, or more precisely, their interpretation of it. They either had to deny their interpretation or the Scripture itself, neither of which they would do. The equation, Son of David = Messiah = Jesus = Lord, would form the basis for the Christology of the New Testament church. The Pharisees were through talking: "And no man was able to answer him a word, neither durst any *man* from that day forth ask him any more *questions*" [italics in KJV] (Matthew 22:46). Instead they would concentrate on a plan to get rid of Jesus.

Matthew Chapter 23

Chapter 23 begins with Jesus warning the disciples about the Jewish religious leaders' pursuit of praise and desire to be in charge and to control others. He told the disciples they were to reject the religious leaders, not seek to be a replacement for them; "But be not ye called Rabbi: for one is your Master, *even* Christ; and all ye are brethren" [italics in KJV] (Matthew 23:8). Jesus was to be their one and only teacher.

They shared a brotherhood because they had a single heavenly father; "And call no *man* your father upon the earth: for one is your Father, which is in heaven" [italics in KJV] (Matthew 23:9). They were to be led by Jesus Himself. "Neither be ye called masters: for one is your Master, *even* Christ" [italics in KJV] (Matthew 23:10). Jesus identified Himself as "the teacher" (ὁ διδάσκαλος), "leader" (καθηγητὴς), and "the Christ" (ὁ Χριστός) the Messiah.

Matthew's methodology was to provide evidence and have his readers draw the inevitable conclusion about Jesus' identity, and that was Jesus' method as well. Jesus and Matthew "bear witness" which is frequently referred to with the Greek verb μαρτυρέω. This verb is usually used positively for evidence of Jesus' messianic identity but negatively by Him in His denunciation of the scribes and Pharisees: "Wherefore ye be witnesses unto yourselves, that ye are the children of them which killed the prophets" (Matthew 23:31).

The Pharisees attempted to associate themselves with the prophets rather than their executioners, but Jesus told them they were "children of them which killed the prophets" (Matthew 23:31). Their rejection of the evidence of Jesus' identity and their persecution of Him became evidence against them.

Chapter 23 concludes with Jesus placing Himself in an Old Testament messianic setting; "For I say unto you, Ye shall not see me henceforth, till ye shall say, Blessed *is* he that cometh in the name of the Lord" [italics in KJV] (Matthew 23:39). The quotation is of Psalm 118:26: "Blessed *be* he that cometh in the name of the Lord" [italics in KJV]. At the Messiah's Second Coming Jesus' countrymen will afford Him a far different reception than at His first coming. Instead of denial of the evidence there will be acceptance of His divine identity.

Matthew Chapter 24

The disciples understood the eschatological implications of Jesus' teaching and His place in those events and they asked, "Tell us, when shall these things be? and what *shall be* the sign of thy coming, and of the end of the world?" [italics in KJV] (Matthew 24:3). What follows is a remarkable self-identification of Jesus as the Messiah. Jesus' followers are not to be confused and misled by false Messiahs who will claim that they are He. "Take heed that no man deceive you. For many shall come in my name, saying, I am Christ; and shall deceive many" (Matthew 24:4-5). The identity of the imposters is to be rejected.

Jesus is identified as the key figure in the climax of history. Preceding His return, in addition to cataclysmic events, the end times will be characterized by worldwide dissemination of the gospel message. "And this gospel of the kingdom shall be preached in all the world for a witness unto all nations; and then shall the end come" (Matthew 24:14). The message is "good news" (τὸ εὐαγγέλιον) about "the kingdom" (τῆς βασιλείας), centered on its King who is about to return. The fundamental purpose of the kingdom/King message is to "provide testimony," a "witness" (εἰς μαρτύριον) that will lead men to put their trust in Him. According to John the Apostle, in his book of Revelation, during the Great Tribulation the principal presenters of that testimony will be two men; "And I will give *power* unto my two witnesses, and they shall prophesy a thousand two hundred *and* threescore days" [italics in KJV] (Revelation 11:3). Their primary distinguishing characteristic will be as "witnesses" (μάρτυς) who will provide evidence of the identity of Jesus as the King to "all nations." Jesus is the unique and universal Messiah.

Matthew Chapter 25

Throughout Matthew chapter 25 Jesus speaks of "the Son of Man" (ὁ υἱὸς τοῦ ἀνθρώπου). He is characterized as One with "glory" (δόξα), accompanied by "all the angels" (πάντες οἱ ἄγγελοι), who "will sit on His glorious throne" (καθίσει ἐπὶ θρόνου δόξης αὐτοῦ), and judge all men. "When the Son of man shall come in his glory, and all the holy angels with him, then shall he sit upon the throne of his glory" (Matthew 25:31). Using a word picture for judgment Jesus said, "And before him shall be gathered all nations: and he shall separate them one from another, as a shepherd divideth *his* sheep from the goats" [italics in KJV] (Matthew 25:32).

A negative judgment will be rendered against those who have rejected Him, and a reward awaits those who have received Him by faith: "Then shall the King say unto them on his right hand, Come, ye blessed of my Father, inherit the kingdom prepared for you from the foundation of the world" (Matthew 25:34). He is again referred to as the King: "And the King shall answer and say unto them, Verily I say unto you, inasmuch as ye have done *it* unto one of the least of these my brethren, ye have done *it* unto me" [italics in KJV] (Matthew 25:40). Jesus is of such importance that what is done to Him and His followers has eternal consequences. Whatever one's eschatological view on the place of this passage in the prophetic timetable, one thing is certain; the identity of Jesus as "the Son of Man" (ὁ υἱὸς τοῦ ἀνθρώπου).

Matthew Chapter 26

The anointing of Jesus' feet by Mary in Bethany is a case of special treatment for a unique individual. Matthew introduces the pericope with, "Now when Jesus was in Bethany, in the house of Simon the leper" (Matthew 26:6). Not only is Simon's name given but Matthew made sure that he would not be confused with another Simon, the disciple Simon Peter, so he added "the leper" (τοῦ λεπροῦ). When it came to identifying the woman, who was at least the second most important character in the story, Matthew introduces her simply as "a woman" (Matthew 26:7) (γυνὴ). Perhaps the author wanted to communicate that the gift and the One to whom it was given were more important than the giver.

After the anointing and the disciples' expression of indignation, Jesus asks, "Why trouble ye the woman?" (Matthew 26:10). Because of who Jesus is, the value of what she did took on an entirely unexpected significance. Jesus prophesied that what she did would receive notoriety. "Verily I say unto you, Wheresoever this gospel shall be preached in the whole world, *there* shall also this, that this woman hath done, be told for a memorial of her" [italics in KJV] (Matthew 26:13).

What gave significance to her action was the identity of the One for whom she did it. Jesus' repeated use of first person singular pronoun bears this out: "For she hath wrought a good work upon me" (Matthew 26:10); "but me ye have not always" (Matthew 26:11); "for in that she hath poured this ointment on my body" (Matthew 26:12); and "she did *it* for my burial" [italics in KJV] (Matthew 26:12). Just as this woman recognized who Jesus is and did something befitting that identity, the reader of Matthew's Gospel is implicitly invited to do likewise.

Before the crucifixion Jesus prepared the disciples by indicating Old Testament passages that His death would fulfill, so that even though they failed to understand their significance at the time, they would realize their importance and include them in their preaching in retrospect. Even their abandonment of Jesus just before His death would become supporting evidence of His messianic identity. Jesus quoted Zechariah 13:7: "I will smite the shepherd, and the sheep of the flock shall be scattered abroad" (Matthew 26:31). Zechariah 13:7 says, "Smite the shepherd, and the sheep shall be scattered." Jesus identified Himself as the Shepherd in that messianic prophecy.

The betrayal of Jesus by one of His twelve disciples included Judas identifying Him to His captors. "Whomsoever I shall kiss, that same is he: hold him fast" (Matthew 26:48). Matthew does not identify the disciple who cut off the ear of the high priest's slave and neither do the other two Synoptic Gospels, Mark and Luke, but John's Gospel says that it was Simon Peter (John 18:10-11). Jesus let Peter know that given His identity the circumstances of the arrest did not signify helplessness on His part. Far from it; "Thinkest thou that I cannot now pray to my Father, and he shall presently give me more than twelve legions of angels?" (Matthew 26:53). Jesus let Peter know that his precipitous act was an attempt, however futile, to jeopardize the divine plan. "But how then shall the scriptures be fulfilled, that thus it must be?" (Matthew 26:54). Jesus made a statement about what was happening to Him to those present; "But all this was done, that the scriptures of the prophets might be fulfilled" (Matthew 26:56).

In preparation for Jesus' trial it was natural that evidence in the form of testimony by witnesses would be sought. Matthew depicts the search with the words, "Now the chief priests, and elders, and all the council, sought false witness against Jesus, to put him to death" (Matthew 26:59). The search for witnesses is described as both a success and a failure at the same time: "But found none: yea, though many false witnesses came, *yet* found they none" [italics in KJV] (Matthew 26:60). Perhaps they were not convincing enough as liars. The religious establishment was not in the least deterred by the ninth Commandment, "Thou shalt not bear false witness against thy neighbour" (Exodus 20:16). In addition to offering "false testimony" (ψευδομαρτυρίαν) they were "testifying against" (καταμαρτυροῦσιν) (Matthew 26:62) Him. The mission to manufacture "false testimony" (ψευδομαρτυρίαν) is in contrast with Matthew's presentation of reliable "testimony" (μαρτύριον) to identify Jesus as the God/Man/Messiah.

The main issue the high priest had with Jesus at His trial was His identity. "And the high priest answered and said unto him, I adjure thee by the living God, that thou tell us whether thou be the Christ, the Son of God" (Matthew 26:63). Jesus responded in the affirmative. "Jesus saith unto him, Thou hast said" (Matthew 26:64), and went on to use Old Testament language relevant to the role and identification as the Messiah: "nevertheless I say unto you, Hereafter shall ye see the Son of man sitting on the right hand of power, and coming in the clouds of heaven" (Matthew 26:64). This was not a direct quotation but the high priest understood Jesus to be claiming divine prerogatives. The high priest reacted by tearing his robes as a sign of grief over what he considered to be blasphemy and said, "He hath spoken blasphemy; what further need have we of witnesses? behold, now ye have heard his blasphemy" (Matthew 26:65). They physically punished Him and said, "Prophesy unto us, thou Christ, Who is he that smote thee?" (Matthew 26:68). Even though they were doing so sarcastically, they were verbally affirming Jesus' messianic identity.

Matthew Chapter 27

The Jewish religious establishment reached a verdict, which Matthew communicated in writing about Judas, the disciple/betrayer: "Then Judas, which had betrayed him, when he saw that he was condemned" (Matthew 27:3). Too late Judas remorsefully acknowledged Jesus' innocence. Judas "repented himself, and brought again the thirty pieces of silver to the chief priests and elders, Saying, I have sinned in that I have betrayed the innocent blood" (Matthew 27:3-4). Even the chief priests and their co-conspirators inadvertently contributed evidence confirming Jesus' identity when it "was fulfilled that which was spoken by Jeremy the prophet, saying, And they took the thirty pieces of silver, the price of him that was valued, whom they of the children of Israel did value; and gave them for the potter's field, as the Lord appointed me" (Matthew 27:9-10). The quotation appears to be a paraphrase from Zechariah. Zechariah 11:12 says, "And I said unto them, If ye think good, give *me* my price; and if not, forbear. So they weighed for my price thirty *pieces* of silver" [italics in KJV]. Zechariah 11:13 reads, "And the Lord said unto me, Cast it unto the potter: a goodly price that I was prised at of them. And I took the thirty *pieces* of silver, and cast them to the potter in the house of the Lord" [italics in KJV].

When Jesus was examined by Pilate He was again asked who He is, "Art thou the King of the Jews? And Jesus said unto him, Thou sayest" (Matthew 27:11). The NASB says, "*It is as* you say" [italics in NASB]. In Pilate's response the issue of incriminating testimony is brought up: "Hearest thou not how many things they witness against thee?" (Matthew 27:13). As in Matthew 26:62, the Greek word for "to testify against" (καταμαρτυρέω) is used to refute Jesus' claim to messianic identity. In Pilate's review of the charges against Jesus, while considering his options for the decision he was about to make about the customary releasing of a condemned man at the time of the feast, he sarcastically referred to Jesus as "Jesus which is called Christ" (Matthew 27:17).

Pilate's wife, knowing of the decision her husband was about to make, made known her opinion that Jesus was innocent, saying, "Have thou nothing to do with that just man" (Matthew 27:19). Even Pilate's pagan wife had something to say about who Jesus is. Pilate enjoyed goading Jesus' Jewish adversaries and again referred to Jesus as "Jesus which is called Christ" (Matthew 27:22).

The soldiers into whose custody Jesus was placed, the Roman "cohort" (Matthew 27:27) (τὴν σπεῖραν), derisively addressed Him with "Hail, King of the Jews" (Matthew 27:29) (χαῖρε, βασιλεῦ τῶν Ἰουδαίων). Then at the crucifixion, the Roman authorities had a placard placed on His cross which read, "THIS IS JESUS THE KING OF THE JEWS" (Matthew 27:37) (οὗτός ἐστιν Ἰησοῦς ὁ βασιλεὺς τῶν Ἰουδαίων). Matthew also records the mocking by Jewish religious authorities present at the execution who referred to Him sarcastically with "He is the King of Israel" (Matthew 27:42) (βασιλεὺς Ἰσραήλ ἐστιν). They also derisively announced what it would take for them to believe in Him; "let him now come down from the cross, and we will believe him" (Matthew 27:42).

Playing to the crowd the religious leaders added an Old Testament quotation and the title He used of Himself; "He trusted in God; let him deliver him now, if he will have him: for he said, I am the Son of God" (Matthew 27:43). The part of Matthew 27:43 which they hurl at Jesus is an Old Testament quotation from the messianic Psalm 22: "He trusted on the Lord *that* he would deliver him: Let him deliver him, seeing he delighted in him" [italics in KJV] (Psalm 22:8).

The extraordinary events accompanying Jesus' death point to who He is. The curtain protecting the most holy of Jewish places was torn; there was an earthquake; rocks split open; and dead saved people came back to life; "and the graves were opened; and many bodies of the saints which slept arose" (Matthew 27:52). The events shook the Romans in charge of the execution and they concluded about His identity, "Truly this was the Son of God" (Matthew 27:54). The chief priests and the Pharisees held no such opinion. In their request to Pilate that he post guards to ensure that Jesus' disciples did not abscond with the body they did not refer to Him by name but called Him "that deceiver" (Matthew 27:63).

Matthew Chapter 28

The witnesses and testimony in the last chapter of Matthew attest to Jesus' resurrection. There "was a great earthquake" (Matthew 28:2) (σεισμὸς ἐγένετο μέγας). Perhaps what had precipitated the earthquake was "the angel of the Lord [who] descended from heaven, and came and rolled back the stone from the door, and sat upon it" (Matthew 28:2). The angel appeared. "His countenance was like lightning, and his raiment white as snow: and for fear of him the keepers did shake, and became as dead *men*" [italics in KJV] (Matthew 28:3-4).

Matthew highlights two women as witnesses; "Mary Magdalene and the other Mary" (Matthew 28:1) (Μαριὰμ ἡ Μαγδαληνὴ καὶ ἡ ἄλλη Μαρία) who were told by the angel to tell what they had seen and heard; "go quickly, and tell his disciples that he is risen from the dead" (Matthew 28:7). There was to be little delay between the time when they witnessed the resurrection and testified about it—no time to cloud or dim their memory. Of interest is the fact that there were two of them and not just one; sufficient for their report to qualify as credible evidence. That would not be all they witnessed. On their way to tell the disciples, Jesus Himself appeared to them with a message; "go tell my brethren that they go into Galilee, and there shall they see me" (Matthew 28:10). The disciples would also become witnesses.

While the women and Jesus' disciples would become true and faithful witnesses to what they had seen and heard, there would be those whose who would instead intentionally bear false witness. The chief priests and the elders conspired and paid off the guards at the tomb so that they would contradict the other eyewitness reports about what had happened. "Say ye, His disciples came by night, and stole him *away* while we slept" [italics in KJV] (Matthew 28:13). For the men to admit that they had been asleep at the time when the events to which they were testifying had occurred shows that their testimony is unreliable.

Jesus did appear to His eleven disciples—Matthew makes a point to write how many of them were there; "Then the eleven disciples went away into Galilee, into a mountain where Jesus had appointed them" (Matthew 28:16). Jesus appeared to them there; "and when they saw him, they worshiped him" (Matthew 28:17). The author points out that in spite of the evidence there were those who did not accept it: "but some doubted" (Matthew 28:17).

Matthew's Gospel concludes with the Great Commission. Those who signed on to the mission would recognize who Jesus is and believe it when He said, "all power is given unto me in heaven and in earth" (Matthew 28:18). Jesus' authority is absolute and those who participate in His program will enjoy the permanence of His presence; "and, lo, I am with you alway, *even* unto the end of the world" [italics in KJV] (Matthew 28:20). Having identified who Jesus is and put their trust in Him for eternal salvation, they were to seek others who would do likewise, visibly identifying with Him in baptism and becoming followers who learned from Him.

Chapter 5

Evidence for the Identity of Jesus in the Gospel of Mark

Man on a Mission

Mark, the author of this Gospel, was not one of Jesus' original twelve disciples. He may or may not have been an eyewitness to what he wrote. Traditionally it is held that Mark was in close contact with Jesus' disciple Simon Peter, writing down the recollections passed on to him by Peter. As will be shown, Mark's purpose and method was the same as that of his fellow Gospel writers, namely, to prove the identity of Jesus as the One in whom man must place his trust for eternal salvation.

Mark Chapter 1

Mark introduces his work with the words, "The beginning of the gospel of Jesus Christ, the Son of God" (Mark 1:1). The message of "the gospel" (τοῦ εὐαγγελίου) is "good news" about Jesus. Mark is the shortest of the four Gospels and leaves out material that the others include. For example, Mark does not have a genealogy, does not have a birth narrative, and he begins his account at the time of Jesus' baptism. As has been noted in Matthew's Gospel, the baptism of Jesus, together with the Transfiguration, was the supreme New Testament evidence of the identity of Jesus as the Messiah.

Mark, like Matthew, also identified Jesus as the Messiah with the use of the Old Testament. Early on, the church fathers noticed that although both Isaiah and Malachi appear to have been quoted in Mark 1:2-3, Mark mentions only Isaiah as the prophet who wrote what he quotes: "As it is written in Isaiah the prophet" (Mark 1:2 NASB). Variants in the manuscript evidence, which mention "prophets" in the plural, and may or may not include "Isaiah," may have been attempts to resolve this apparent difficulty.

The quotation here, from Malachi, is unique among the Gospel writers. However that question is resolved, the reason for Mark's use of Old Testament prophecy was to identify John the Baptist, who would, in turn, identify who Jesus is. The eccentricity of John the Baptist drew attention to his persona so that his message would be heard.

John the Baptist made sure there would be no confusion or misidentification of himself with the One whom he was introducing. The first characteristic that would distinguish John the Baptist from the One who would follow is stated in Mark 1:7: "There cometh one mightier than I after me, the latchet of whose shoes I am not worthy to stoop down and unloose." The distinction would be one of identity, not just ability.

A second comparison: "I indeed have baptized you with water: but he shall baptize you with the Holy Ghost" (Mark 1:8), indicates that the work of that One would be supernatural.

Mark's account of Jesus' baptism, just as in Matthew's Gospel, mentions two types of evidence, visual: "he saw the heavens opened, and the Spirit like a dove descending upon him" (Mark 1:10), and auditory: "there came a voice from heaven, *saying*, Thou art my beloved Son, in whom I am well pleased" [italics in KJV] (Mark 1:11). The words "Thou art" (Mark 1:11) are used for identity. There may be disagreement over whether anyone besides Jesus saw and heard what happened. The verb in verse 10 "he saw" (εἶδεν) is a third person singular and could refer to either Jesus or John the Baptist. Nevertheless, neither option takes away from the evidence the Gospel writer presents to prove who Jesus is.

In Mark 1:15 Jesus' message is described as "the gospel of God" (τὸ εὐαγγέλιον τοῦ θεοῦ), found in close proximity to "the gospel of Jesus Christ" (τοῦ εὐαγγελίου Ἰησοῦ Χριστοῦ) in the opening verse. The gospel, the "good news" from God the Father is about Jesus Christ, His Son. The response to the gospel Jesus asked for in His preaching was: "repent and believe in the gospel" (Mark 1:15).

The reader is referred to the first chapter of this book that discusses the Greek verb "repent" (μετανοέω) and the noun "repentance" (μετάνοια). The meaning here could very well be, "change your mind and believe the gospel."

The question arises whether "believe in the gospel" (πιστεύετε ἐν τῷ εὐαγγελίῳ), found here with the preposition "in" (ἐν), means "to believe something to be true" or "to put one's trust in something or someone." As discussed earlier, to assume that one of these possibilities does not exist, specifically trust in a person, or to subsume one meaning within the other, does not do justice to the semantic range of the verb "believe" (πιστεύω). However, while keeping that in mind, perhaps the attempt to pin down the present usage in question to one of these possible meanings is misguided, because when the term "the gospel" (τὸ εὐαγγέλιον) was used it was meant to convey both. It could have meant information received and believed to be true (Latin = *noticia* and *assensus*), and what was to be done with the accepted information, which was to put one's trust in the person identified by that data (Latin = *fiducia*). This could be what E. W. Bullinger refers to as "Synecdoche" or "Transfer," the specific type of which would be "Synecdoche of the Whole" and a subdivision under that where the whole idea is put for the parts integral to it (Ethelbert W. Bullinger, *Figures of Speech Used in the Bible Explained and Illustrated* [Grand Rapids: Baker, 1898], 635). "The gospel" (τὸ εὐαγγέλιον) would be the umbrella term encompassing the two salvifically significant meanings of the verb "believe" (πιστεύω).

In the call of the disciples to become part of Jesus' inner circle Mark uses the adverb "straightway" or "immediately (NASB)" (Mark 1:18 and 20) (εὐθύς) to demonstrate the authority He exuded and the magnetism with which they were drawn to Him. Mark makes a point to mention those who witnessed that sudden event: "and they left their father Zebedee in the ship with the hired servants, and went after him" (Mark 1:20). The uniqueness of Jesus is also seen in the reaction of those present in the Capernaum synagogue: "they were astonished at his doctrine: for he taught them as one that had authority, and not as the scribes" (Mark 1:22). The witnesses to these events were multiple, and their testimony uniform, except for that of the antagonistic religious establishment whose agenda prevented them from being unbiased observers.

While still in the synagogue a man with a demon called out to Jesus, saying, "what have we to do with thee, thou Jesus of Nazareth? art thou come to destroy us? I know thee who thou art, the Holy One of God" (Mark 1:24). Jesus responded to the demon's statement about His identity by telling him to "Be quiet" (Mark 1:25) (φιμώθητι), but the demon-possessed man's words had not been lost on those present, even though the time for His identity to be openly revealed had not yet come. To the testimony of the demon, who was a hostile witness, is added the miraculous evidence of the exorcism of the demon from the man.

Those present recognized something extraordinary had just occurred on a higher plane than their run-of-the mill religious experience. They asked, "What thing is this? what new doctrine *is* this? for with authority commandeth he even the unclean spirits, and they do obey him" [italics in KJV] (Mark 1:27). Their excitement revolved around Him: "And immediately his fame spread abroad throughout all the region round about Galilee" (Mark 1:28). Mark notes that the issue with demons was that they could identify Him and were not hesitant to do so. That did not stop Jesus from casting them out, but He "suffered not the devils to speak, because they knew him" (Mark 1:34). By means of His words and works Jesus was proving His identity, and would do so on His own terms and timing, not that of demons.

Describing Jesus' warning to a leper He healed not to broadcast what had happened to him, Mark used the strong words: "He straitly charged him" (Mark 1:43). The healed leper was, however, instructed to fulfill his duty to the law and present himself to the priest who would certify his cleansing, which would allow him to return to regular society. Interestingly, regarding the priests, Jesus told him this would be: "for a testimony unto them" (Mark 1:44). Perhaps this was just to let the priests know Jesus was concerned with fulfilling the law, although, considering Mark's concern for "testimony" (μαρτύριον) as proof of Jesus' identity, it may well have been to convey far more, namely that these antagonists were far from guiltless for their rejection of the testimony, which they personally had received.

Mark Chapter 2

In the incident of the paralytic who was let down through the ceiling, the occasion became more than one of Jesus' regular healings when He said to him, "thy sins be forgiven thee" (Mark 2:5). The identity question was brought up by the scribes who asked, "who can forgive sins but God only?" (Mark 2:7). Jesus answered their question with the declaration that "the Son of man hath power on earth to forgive sins" (Mark 2:10), and then proved He was the one having that power and identity by healing the paralytic. Mark made a point to mention the ever-present crowd who were multiple witnesses to this event, remarking that the healed man "went forth before them all" (Mark 2:12).

Following the paralytic's healing and forgiveness of his sins that demonstrated Jesus' divine prerogative, which included the spiritual as well as the physical realm, He told the disciples what His mission was. The occasion was dinner with a notorious sinner, Levi, also known as Matthew, a despised tax collector. When He was criticized for hob-knobbing with such a sinner, Jesus said, "I came not to call the righteous, but sinners to repentance" (Mark 2:17). His primary purpose was not physical healing but spiritual restoration, a mission only He could accomplish. He came "to call" (Mark 2:17) (καλέω) sinners to what? The previous context of the paralytic's forgiveness hints at it being an invitation to have sins forgiven.

The nature of testimony is that sometimes someone may see something or hear something, and not fully understand at the time what is seen or heard or what importance it might have. Later on, in light of subsequent events, those same things are looked back on and understood by the witnesses. Sometimes Jesus spoke in a veiled, or almost cryptic manner, such as with His use of parables. He spoke of "the bridegroom" (Mark 2:19) (ὁ νυμφίος), referring to Himself, which was or was not to a lesser or greater degree understood by His disciples. Later, after He was no longer physically present, with the benefit of hindsight, they and we, the intended audience, would have a deeper understanding.

Mark, as well as Matthew and Luke, records controversies about the Sabbath, which were often provoked by the actions of Jesus and His disciples. On one such occasion they were picking grain and eating it as they passed through a field and it happened to be on the Sabbath. Jesus countered the Pharisees' criticism by using David and his band of men as an example of someone having technically violated the Sabbath, in that case to satisfy their hunger. But Jesus went beyond the comparison with David and his men and the fact that "the sabbath was made for man, and not man for the sabbath" (Mark 2:27) to say that "the Son of man is Lord also of the sabbath" (Mark 2:28). No human being is above the law, and Jesus could not only interpret it, but He also claimed that He is the "master" or "Lord" (κύριός) (Mark 2:28) of it. Moses had received the law at Mount Sinai, but here was One who claimed to be greater than he, on a level with God Himself.

Mark Chapter 3

When the demon-possessed came in contact with Jesus, they consistently acknowledged who He is: "And unclean spirits, when they saw him, fell down before him, and cried, saying, Thou art the Son of God" (Mark 3:11). Mark vividly pictures it as an exhibition and expression of anguish as they: "would cry out" (Mark 3:11 NASB) (ἔκραζον). The author here uses the imperfect tense to capture the action. Daniel Wallace describes action depicted by the imperfect tense as "a *motion picture*, portraying the action as it unfolds" [italics in original] (*Greek Grammar beyond the Basics* [Grand Rapids: Zondervan 1996], 541). The imperfect is also used by Mark when he says the demon-possessed "fell down" (Mark 3:11) (προσέπιπτον). These were not assuming a posture of worship but of forced submission.

The demon's verbal identification of who Jesus is answered the question that Mark the author intended to ask and answer with his Gospel: "Thou art the Son of God" (Mark 3:11). Jesus did not deny the demon's declaration but "he straitly charged them that they should not make him known" (Mark 3:12). John Grassmick says, "In silencing their untimely cries Jesus reaffirmed His submission to God's plan for the *progressive* disclosure of His identity and mission" [italics in original] ("Mark," in *The Bible Knowledge Commentary, New Testament*, ed. John F. Walvoord, and Roy B. Zuck [Wheaton, IL: Victor, 1983; reprint, Colorado Springs: Cook, 1996], 116).

The subject of demon possession came up again when Jesus sent the Twelve out to preach. The disciples, no doubt, would encounter opposition just as He had, and although not explicitly stated in that manner, the demons would have been a likely adversary. Jesus' authority was such that He could delegate power over demons to the disciples to cast them out. They were given a message and the means to carry it out: "to have power to heal sicknesses, and to cast out devils" (Mark 3:15).

One might assume those who knew Jesus the best, "his friends" (Mark 3:21), would know who He is, but such was not the case. Rather than believe the message of His identity, backed up as it was by the miracles Jesus performed, instead the conclusion they reached was, "He is beside himself" (Mark 3:21). This was a misdiagnosis. On the other hand, they did have something right, Jesus is either who He said He is, or He had lost touch with reality. The conclusion they came to was cause for concern. What mischief or worse might someone with such delusions get into? Mark's description leads one to think they would have used force if necessary: "they went out to lay hold on him" (Mark 3:21). Perhaps well-intentioned, however misguided, at that point they were not ready to accept who He really is.

There were others who had less than kindhearted motives, to say the least, particularly those from the religious establishment. The scribes descended from Jerusalem offering another option for what was happening: "He hath Beelzebub" (Mark 3:22). And specifically: "by the prince of the devils casteth he out devils" (Mark 3:22). Their opinion: He was not insane, but He was in cahoots with the leader of those He cast out! Jesus' response was severe. He had little patience for their evil machinations because what He was doing was by the power of the Holy Spirit and not Satan. If His antagonists continued in willful denial of His true identity, and attribution of what the Holy Spirit was doing through Him, their condemnation was certain: "But he that shall blaspheme against the Holy Ghost hath never forgiveness, but is in danger of eternal damnation" (Mark 3:29).

The family, "his brethren and his mother" (Mark 3:31) arrived on the scene, no doubt with intervention on their minds. Today they may have wanted Him committed (to an institution). When Jesus was told of their arrival and that they had summoned Him, His answer appears, on the surface, to be rather abrupt and harsh: "Who is my mother, or my brethren?" (Mark 3:33). Jesus had more than His earthly identity in view when He responded with: "For whosoever shall do the will of God, the same is my brother, and my sister, and mother" (Mark 3:35). Included in "the will of God" would be the acceptance that Jesus was His divine Son.

Mark Chapter 4

In the Parable of the Soils that follows Jesus concludes with a quotation from the Old Testament before beginning His interpretation of it. It is prophetic messianic evidence of His parabolic pedagogic methodology, proving His identity: "That seeing they may see, and not perceive; and hearing they may hear, and not understand; lest at any time they should be converted, and *their* sins should be forgiven them" [italics in KJV] (Mark 4:12). It appears He was quoting Isaiah 6:9-10. Isaiah 6:9 says that although the message will be heard it will not be understood: "And he said, Go, and tell this people, Hear ye indeed, but understand not; and see ye indeed, but perceive not." Their ability to understand would be supernaturally impaired: "make their ears heavy, and shut their eyes; lest they see with their eyes, and hear with their ears, and understand with their heart, and convert, and be healed" (Isaiah 6:10).

Mark 4 concludes with Jesus calming the sea, after He had been asleep during a storm. The identity question it raised for the disciples: "What manner of man is this, that even the wind and the sea obey him?" (Mark 4:41). Only God, the One who had created the wind and the sea, by the word of His mouth, could command, and have them submit to His authority.

Mark Chapter 5

The demon-possessed man, living among the tombs, took the initiative and approached Jesus: "But when he saw Jesus afar off, he ran and worshipped him" (Mark 5:6). The verb translated "worshipped him" or "bowed down" (NASB) (προσεκύνησεν) is normally used for worship or to denote reverence, but here, more likely, it indicates fear. The man said, "What have I to do with thee, Jesus, *thou* Son of the most high God? I adjure thee by God, that thou torment me not" [italics in KJV] (Mark 5:7). The man's use of the superlative adjective "most high" (ὕψιστος), of God, which consequently elevated His Son Jesus to that level, revealed their superiority, that the demon was resisting: "For he said unto him, Come out of the man, *thou* unclean spirit" [italics in KJV] (Mark 5:8). Once again, a hostile witness, gave testimony to the divine identity of Jesus.

In raising the daughter of Jairus from death, Jesus gave the key to securing favor with God, in saying to her father, "only believe" (μόνον πίστευε) (Mark 5:36). The requirement for receiving temporal as well as eternal blessing is "believe" (πιστεύω). Did Jesus' use of the term here mean "to believe a proposition to be true," such as the statement, "Jesus is able to raise my daughter from death?" Or was he to "put his trust" in Jesus to raise her? Or perhaps, without an explicit referent, it is to be understood as both, with a combined, plenary meaning. Given the semantic possibilities of the verb "believe" (πιστεύω) perhaps the ambiguity was intentional.

One thing is apparent, Mark included detailed information about who witnessed this resurrection: "he taketh the father and the mother of the damsel, and them that were with him, and entereth in where the damsel was lying" (Mark 5:40). The witnesses included His disciples, who could have been accused of bias in favor of Jesus, as well as the girl's parents, who knew for certain that she had died. As evidence that she was now alive, Mark mentions the actions of the girl: "the damsel arose, and walked; for she was *of the age* of twelve years. And they were astonished with a great astonishment" [italics in KJV] (Mark 5:42).

And then Jesus elicited a second proof when He "commanded that something should be given her to eat" (Mark 5:43). This is reminiscent of the post-Resurrection appearance of Jesus where Luke, in his account, described the disciples: "But they were terrified and affrighted, and supposed that they had seen a spirit" (Luke 24:37). In that instance, as proof of the physical resurrection of His body, Jesus asked, "Have ye here any meat?" (Luke 24:41). And then Luke records, "And they gave him a piece of a broiled fish, and of an honeycomb. And he took *it*, and did eat before them" [italics in KJV] (Luke 24:42-43). Jesus was physically resurrected from the dead. The daughter of Jairus was physically brought back to life. The evidence did not lie.

Mark Chapter 6

Back in Jesus' hometown of Nazareth His opponents again had trouble reconciling who they thought He was with His words and works: "From whence hath this *man* these things? and what wisdom *is* this which is given unto him, that even such mighty works are wrought by his hands?" [italics in KJV] (Mark 6:2). Interestingly, His antagonists mention "His hands" (Mark 6:2). To them they were the hands of a carpenter, not a miracle worker. Certainly not the hands that would receive the nails of a cross as He died for the sins of man.

The identity question they asked was rhetorical, expecting an affirmative answer: "Is not this the carpenter, the son of Mary, the brother of James, and Joses, and of Juda, and Simon? and are not his sisters here with us?" (Mark 6:3). Jesus' self-identification, which conflicted with their assumption, displeased them: "And they were offended at him" (Mark 6:3).

Following Mark's remarks, of those in Nazareth, denying that Jesus had anything other than a colloquial origin and identity, there is a statement about His miracles, indicating that at least to some extent, they were contingent on people's faith. "And he could there do no mighty work, save that he laid his hands upon a few sick folk, and healed *them*" [italics in KJV] (Mark 6:5). While there is not a stated connection between the preceding context and this statement, it is sandwiched between the denial of His identity before it and the following words of Jesus: "And he marvelled because of their unbelief" (Mark 6:6). The "unbelief" (ἀπιστία) here could be either their not believing the proposition that Jesus could heal them, or the truths of the gospel of the kingdom, or not trusting in Him. Louw and Nida include the two possibilities, not believing in a proposition, or not trusting in a person, among other options, for the meaning of this noun "unbelief" (ἀπιστία). (Johannes P. Louw and Eugene A. Nida, *Greek-English Lexicon of the New Testament Based on Semantic Domains*, 2nd ed. [New York: United Bible Societies, 2nd ed], 1989, 1:378-79).

All three of the Synoptic Gospels tell of the confusion that existed between Jesus' identity with that of John the Baptist. Mark used the opportunity to explain the circumstances of John the Baptist's beheading. Herod, haunted by what he had done, feared that Jesus was a resurrected John the Baptist. Mark also mentions other possibilities that were entertained: "Others said, That it is Elias. And others said, That it is a prophet, or as one of the prophets" (Mark 6:15).

Mark's Gospel includes the miracle of Jesus walking on the water, which has become a universal reference for the supernatural. It is a great example of Jesus' work. Jesus identified Himself to the disciples with the words: "It is I" (Mark 6:50) (ἐγώ εἰμι). As mentioned in the comments on Matthew, in their frightened state of mind no doubt the disciples did not fully appreciate the significance of those words as reminiscent of how God revealed Himself to Moses at the burning bush (Exodus 3:14). While one may chalk it up to verbal coincidence, it is nonetheless striking. As Grassmick puts it, "The words **It is** (lit., 'I am,' ego eimi) may simply convey self-identification ('It is I, Jesus'), but they are probably intended here to echo the Old Testament formula of God's self-revelation: 'I am who I am' (cf. Exod. 3:14; Isa. 41:4; 43:10; 51:12; 52:6)" [bold and parentheses in original]. (John Grassmick , "Mark," in *The Bible Knowledge Commentary, New Testament*, ed. John F. Walvoord, and Roy B. Zuck [Wheaton, IL: Victor, 1983; reprint, Colorado Springs: Cook, 1996], 132).

Mark's intent, as well as it was presumably that of Jesus, was for the evidence of His identity to have a cumulative effect. Mark's account of the miracle of the multiplication of the loaves and fish, that preceded the incident of Jesus' walking on water, was intended to be interconnected in the author's purpose with what followed to prove Jesus' identity, and not simply a narrative of a subsequent event. Mark's editorial comment supports that conclusion. It would seem natural that the disciples, having seen Jesus walking on the water, and having witnessed that "the wind ceased" (Mark 6:51), would be "sore amazed" (Mark 6:51).

But Mark does not treat as natural or expected the disciples' reaction. Instead he puts it in a very negative light. Jesus' words and works had fallen on deaf ears and blind eyes: "For they considered not *the miracle* of the loaves: for their heart was hardened" [italics in KJV] (Mark 6:52). Today it could be described as "not connecting the dots." It had been intended to be a transferrable concept, one miraculous event after another, but astoundingly Mark described the disciples, who were eyewitnesses, as those whose "heart was hardened" (Mark 6:52).

This contrasts with Mark's comment about the reaction of the multitudes: "And when they [Jesus and His disciples] were come out of the ship, straightway they knew him" (Mark 6:54). And having identified who He was the people scurried about "and ran through that whole region round about, and began to carry about in beds those that were sick, where they heard he was" (Mark 6:55). Mark highlights the extent of their expectations when he says they "besought him that they might touch if it were but the border of his garment: and as many as touched him were made whole" (Mark 6:56). And they were not disappointed. Jesus had a 100 percent success rate: "and as many as touched him were made whole" (Mark 6:56). Their healing was evidence of who He is, and just as He had the power and they "were made whole" (ἐσῴζοντο from σῴζω "to rescue, save, or heal") of their physical ailments, because of who He is, He would be able "to save" (σῴζω) their eternal souls as well.

Mark Chapter 8

Mark, as do the other two Synoptic Gospels, Matthew (Matthew 16:13-23) and Luke (Luke 9:18-22), includes Peter's confession of Jesus as the Messiah. As they also do, Mark shows that Peter's declaration was elicited by Jesus' question about His identity, first the more general question, "Whom do men say that I am?" (Mark 8:27), followed by the more personal question put to His disciples, "But whom say ye that I am?" (Mark 8:29). Peter answered Jesus' question with: "Thou art the Christ" (Mark 8:29), that is, the Messiah. This confirmed His identity.

Mark Chapter 9

Mark, also with the other two Synoptic Gospels, records Jesus' Transfiguration. As stated previously when looking at Matthew's account (Matthew 17:1-13), the Transfiguration parallels Jesus' baptism as an event with heavenly confirmation of His identity. Again, as in Matthew, Mark mentions the three contemporary witnesses chosen by Jesus, namely, Peter, James, and John, whose eyewitness presence was in addition to the prophetic figures of Moses and Elijah. Mark adds to Matthew and Luke's description of Jesus' garments the fact that "his raiment became shining, exceeding white as snow; so as no fuller on earth can white them" (Mark 9:3). This account also refers to a supernatural cloud from which proceeded a voice stating who Jesus is: "This is My beloved Son: hear him" (Mark 9:7). Because of who Jesus is, it is imperative that people listen to what He has to say.

Returning from the Transfiguration, Jesus found the rest of the disciples discussing exorcism with a distraught father of a demon-possessed son. In that encounter the issue of the nature of faith came up with the much-discussed statement, "Lord, I believe; help thou mine unbelief" (Mark 9:24). Are there degrees of faith? Are there categories of faith that are deficient in some way, or is this an example of progression in faith? Since "believe" (πιστεύω), refers to "belief in a proposition" or "trust in a person," are both based on supporting evidence? Are progression and stages possible and usually the norm? As corroborating testimony is added, the stronger the case for Jesus' identity becomes and the greater the confidence of the believer becomes. Conversely, struggling while weighing the evidence is a common and expected occurrence. That is not to say that at some point a conclusion is not reached, which must happen before one can put his trust in Christ, but such is the reason for presenting the evidence.

Mark Chapter 10

All three of the Synoptic Gospels, Matthew, Mark, and Luke, include the account of Jesus receiving children, with the favorable comparison of their faith with the reception of the kingdom. Matthew's parallel passage makes it clear that reception involves belief by characterizing the children as: "one of these little ones which believe in me" (Matthew 18:6). Here in Mark, as stated about the Matthew passage, the idea of "simple trust," specifically in the person of Jesus in the context of children, is quite likely, although belief in the truth of propositions about Him is also possible, and must precede the former. With Jesus physically present, children could observe what He did, and hear what He said and what was said about Him, and come to an understanding and acceptance of His divine identity, and put their trust in Him.

Mark also follows the incident with children, with that of "the Rich Young Ruler" (Mark 10:17-22). As in Matthew's Gospel Jesus picks up on the man's reference to Him as "good" (Mark 10:18) (ἀγαθός), and He questions him, "Why callest thou me good? *there is* none good but one, *that is*, God" [italics in KJV] (Mark 10:18). Jesus does not press him on that issue of His identity but instead focuses on the man's performance. Jesus said, "One thing thou lackest: go thy way, sell whatsoever thou hast, and give to the poor, and thou shalt have treasure in heaven: and come, take up the cross, and follow me" (Mark 10:21). The next step in perfection would address the man's attachment to material possessions. The man's unwillingness to actually relinquish his riches demonstrated how far short of perfection he was. To inherit eternal life he would either have to attain perfection or accept the imputed righteousness of Christ by trusting in Him. Rather than acknowledge his own inability, the text says, "And he was sad at that saying, and went away grieved: for he had great possessions" (Mark 10:22). It was not his riches that kept him out of heaven but rather his inability to recognize his lack of righteousness.

Hearing Jesus' words, Peter spoke up and said, "we have left all, and have followed thee" (Mark 10:28). In Jesus' response to their sacrifice Jesus associated Himself with the gospel. What they have done has been "for My sake and for the gospel's sake" (Mark 10:29). Jesus could do that because "the gospel," "the good news" (τοῦ εὐαγγελίου) was all about Him, His arrival, and His agenda. The disciples would reap eternal rewards but not earn righteousness. Entrance into heaven is not the result of works or the willingness or commitment to do them.

Jockeying for positions in the coming kingdom was a recurring preoccupation with the disciples, particularly those within Jesus' inner circle of Peter, James, and John. They recognized that by virtue of who Jesus is, He has the power and authority to grant their request. James and John's request comes across as quite brazen: "Master, we would that thou shouldest do for us whatsoever we shall desire" (Mark 10:35). After rebuking them for a wrong attitude and approach to service, Jesus used Himself as an example: "For even the Son of man came not to be ministered unto, but to minister, and to give his life a ransom for many" (Mark 10:45). Because of who He is, His death could achieve what the death of no mere man could accomplish. The implication was, "If I, being who I am, serve others, what in the world are you thinking, seeking to aggrandize yourselves?"

Mark chapter 10 concludes with the restoration of sight to blind Bartimaeus, who, in spite of some people's attempts to silence him, kept on imploring, "Jesus, *thou* Son of David, have mercy on me" [italics in KJV] (Mark 10:47). Jesus asked blind Bartimaeus, "What wilt thou that I should do unto thee? The blind man said unto him, Lord, that I might receive my sight" (Mark 10:51). Jesus healed the man, commending his faith: "thy faith hath made thee whole" (Mark 10:52). The verb translated "made thee whole" is the same Greek word (σῴζω) sometimes rendered "to save" or "to deliver." In this context, no doubt, the meaning of the word is to deliver from physical blindness. However, the man's faith may very well have also brought him eternal salvation, which may be implied by Mark's words, "and immediately he received his sight, and followed Jesus in the way" (Mark 10:52). The addition of "in the way" (Mark 10:52) (ἐν τῇ ὁδῷ) may imply that his "following" (ἀκολουθέω) Jesus was not restricted to the physical realm.

Mark Chapter 11

The Gospel of Mark includes the Triumphal Entry, a signature event, for evidence of Jesus' identity. And, like Matthew, Mark uses Old Testament prophetic testimony for proof. Specifically, Mark's quotation, "Blessed *is* he that cometh in the name of the Lord" [italics in KJV] (Mark 11:9) is from Psalm 118:26: "Blessed *be* he that cometh in the name of the Lord" [italics in KJV]. In addition to quoting the Psalm, Mark records that the crowd was crying out, "Blessed *be* the kingdom of our father David" [italics in KJV] (Mark 11:10). The crowd recognized a connection between the arrival of the king and that of His kingdom.

All three of the Synoptic Gospels include Jesus' cleansing of the temple. Jesus took personal offense at its commercialization and desecration. He referred to it as "My house" (Mark 11:17), and He said, "Is it not written, My house shall be called of all nations the house of prayer? but ye have made it a den of thieves" (Mark 11:17). Indeed it had been written. And indeed they had made it a haven for highway robbers. Just as in Matthew's account, Jesus quotes what appears to be parts of two Old Testament passages, Isaiah 56:7 and Jeremiah 7:11.

Mark relates the hostile reaction of the priests and scribes to Jesus' direct reference to them and to the temple as "My house" (Mark 11:17). Mark comments, "And the scribes and chief priests heard *it*, and sought how they might destroy him" [italics in KJV] (Mark 11:18). By declaring ownership of the temple Jesus made a bold statement about His own identity.

The issue of Jesus' identity was sometimes couched in terms of His "authority" (ἐξουσία). The Jewish religious leadership asked Him, "By what authority doest thou these things? and who gave thee this authority to do these things?" (Mark 11:28). Jesus, in turn asked them, "The baptism of John, was *it* from heaven, or of men?

answer me" [italics in KJV] (Mark 11:30). This was not an attempt to evade the issue, but if they could not or would not answer a question about John the Baptist's baptism, they would have an even more difficult time answering the same question about Jesus. Furthermore, because the mission of John the Baptist was related to that of Jesus, the Messiah, to reject one was to reject the other.

Mark Chapter 12

Mark concludes his parable of the vineyard owner, and the treacherous dealing of the vine-growers with his heir, with an Old Testament quotation: "The stone which the builders rejected is become the head of the corner: This was the Lord's doing, and it is marvellous in our eyes?" (Mark 12:10-11). This is a quotation of Psalm 118:22-23. "The stone *which* the builders refused is become the head *stone* of the corner. This is the Lord's doing; it *is* marvellous in our eyes" [italics in KJV].

Although in the midst of a crowd, Jesus was interacting with "the chief priests, and the scribes, and the elders" (Mark 11:27), and they got the point He was making that He is "the head *stone* of the corner" [italics in KJV] (Mark 12:10). Mark has this summation of their reaction to the parable: "And they sought to lay hold on him, but feared the people: for they knew that he had spoken the parable against them" (Mark 12:12). They recognized themselves as the negative characters in the parable, and no doubt they also realized Jesus was equating Himself with the son and heir in the parable, which was God the Father and the messianic Son. What incited their ire was His indictment of them and His self-identification.

In the temple in Mark 12:35-37 Jesus brought up the issue of the identity of the Messiah in relation to David by asking, "How say the scribes that Christ is the Son of David?" (Mark 12:35). How could that idea, that the Messiah was David's son, which in Jewish thinking implied subordination of the son to the father, be reconciled with David's inspired words, "For David himself said by the Holy Ghost, The Lord said to my Lord, Sit thou on my right hand, till I make thine enemies thy footstool" (Mark 12:36). That was a quotation of Psalm 110:1: "The Lord said unto my Lord, Sit thou at my right hand, Until I make thine enemies thy footstool."

In that messianic passage David referred to the Messiah as his "Lord" (אָדוֹן). Jesus' question was, "How could David speak of his subordination to the Messiah and at the same time have the Messiah be his son, which would imply the opposite, that the Messiah was subordinate to him?" How is that inconsistency resolved? Jesus' asked, "whence is he *then* his son?" [italics in KJV] (Mark 12:37). The question is left tantalizingly unanswered. Grassmick writes, "Jesus' rhetorical question pointed His listeners to the only valid answer: the Messiah is David's Son *and* David's Lord at the same time. This strongly implies that the Messiah is both God (David's Lord) and man" [italics and parenthesis in original] (John Grassmick, "Mark," in *The Bible Knowledge Commentary, New Testament*, ed. John F. Walvoord, and Roy B. Zuck [Wheaton, IL: Victor, 1983; reprint, Colorado Springs: Cook, 1996], 165). The audience got the point that the Messiah is both David's son and Lord/God, whereas the religious hierarchy rejected the evidence for Jesus' dual identity.

Mark Chapter 13

In Mark's eschatological section Jesus emphasized His central role in future events. Jesus warned against those who would usurp His identity: "For many shall come in my name, saying, I am *Christ*; and shall deceive many" [italics in KJV] (Mark 13:6). It would not have been lost on the original audience that Jesus, in referring to Himself, used the words "I am" (Mark 13:6) (ἐγώ εἰμι). This expression coincides with Yahweh's self-designation in the Old Testament. Grassmick says, "This claim to deity is expressed in the formula of God's own self-revelation" (ibid., p. 168). At Jesus' first coming there was controversy over who He is. Likewise, leading up to the Second Coming the issue of His identity will arise again. The devil succeeds when he deceives people about who Jesus is. His end-time agenda will be to confuse people with a counterfeit Christ. Today cults may use biblical titles for deity, but those whom they so identify, are not Jesus, or God the Father, or the Holy Spirit of the Bible.

Christ's followers are to counter the false claims of imposters with evidence. Their persecution will be the result of their loyalty to Him: "for they shall deliver you up to councils; and in the synagogues ye shall be beaten: and ye shall be brought before rulers and kings for my sake, for a testimony against them" (Mark 13:9). And that very persecution, prophesied by Jesus, will constitute corroborating evidence of who He is: "for a testimony against them" (Mark 13:9). It is not surprising to find that Jesus' next words were, "And the gospel must first be published among all nations" (Mark 13:10). The mission is to proclaim a message, "the gospel," "the good news" (τὸ εὐαγγέλιον), which is evidence of Jesus and what should be done with that evidence. Jesus repeated what His followers would experience and why: "And ye shall be hated of all *men* for my name's sake" (Mark 13:13).

One's name is inextricably tied to one's identity and Jesus' name and identity is forever united with the name and title of "Christ," "Messiah" (Χριστός). In His description of the Great Tribulation, Jesus again warned His followers about mistaken identity: "And then if any man shall say to you, Lo, here *is* Christ; or, lo, *he is* there; believe *him* not" [italics in KJV] (Mark 13:21). Jesus used a compound word for the impersonators, which is translated, "false Christs" (Mark 13:22) (ψευδόχριστοι). They will be imposters, who by their very nature, attempt to deceive, by masking their true identity, to get people to believe they are someone they are not. However, at the end of the Great Tribulation, at Christ's Second Coming, there will be no mistaking who the Messiah is because "then shall they see the Son of man coming in the clouds with great power and glory" (Mark 13:26).

Mark Chapter 14

In Mark 14, when a woman anointed Jesus with perfume, He said something that would have been incredibly arrogant, had He not been who He is. He said to those who criticized her and said the perfume could instead have been sold and the proceeds given to the poor: "For ye have the poor with you always, and whensoever ye will ye may do them good: but me ye have not always" (Mark 14:7). Because of who Jesus is, His presence on earth had extraordinary significance. His identity was unlike that of any other individual, before or since.

As one would expect, at Jesus' trial before the Sanhedrin, there were witnesses providing testimony. Mark describes the futile effort to find testimony to secure conviction for a death penalty: "And the chief priests and all the council sought for witness against Jesus to put him to death; and found none" (Mark 14:55). There was no lack for witnesses, but their testimony was problematic: "For many bare false witness against him, but their witness agreed not together" (Mark 14:56). The abundance of witnesses, rather than promoting a guilty verdict which Jesus' antagonists sought, caused a problem, because their testimony was inconsistent. Later on, the consistent testimony of multiple witnesses to the truth of who Jesus is, as expressed in the written words of Scripture, would be astounding.

In his desperation the prosecuting high priest turned to Jesus to get Him to incriminate Himself: "Art thou the Christ, the Son of the Blessed?" (Mark 14:61). Jesus' response left no doubt whatsoever: "I am: and ye shall see the Son of man sitting on the right hand of power, and coming in the clouds of heaven" (Mark 14:62). Grassmick writes:

> This is the first time in Mark's Gospel that He openly declared He is the Messiah. . . .In proof of this—something the Jews expected the true Messiah to provide—Jesus made a startling prediction. Applying words from Psalm 110:1 and Daniel 7:13 to Himself, He stated, **And you** (His human judges) **will see the Son of Man...sitting at the right hand**, exalted to the place of highest honor and authority...[bold and parenthesis in original] (ibid., 183).

For the Sanhedrin this was proof enough. Jesus self-identification as the Messiah was not lost on them: "Then the high priest rent his clothes, and saith, What need we any further witnesses? Ye have heard the blasphemy: what think ye? And they all condemned him to be guilty of death" (Mark 14:63-64).

Mark Chapter 15

At Jesus' next trial the question of who He is also came up with Pilate asking, "Art thou the King of the Jews?" (Mark 15:2). The form of Jesus' admission was: "Thou sayest *it*" [italics in KJV] (Mark 15:2). This brief affirmation can be understood as Grassmick sees it: "It is best understood as a **yes** answer but with a qualification attached. As Messiah, Jesus is the King of the Jews but His concept of kingship differed from that implied in Pilate's question" [bold in original] (ibid, 185).

This same identification issue is taken up by the soldiers who taunted Jesus with the words: "Hail, King of the Jews!" (Mark 15:18). At the site of the crucifixion, the inscription on the placard on Jesus' cross read, "THE KING OF THE JEWS" (Mark

15:26). At the cross the chief priests and scribes, albeit in mocking, nevertheless identified Him correctly when they referred to Him as "Christ the King of Israel" (Mark 15:32). And then the centurion sincerely exclaimed, "Truly this man was the Son of God" (Mark 15:39). Indeed He was and continues to be.

Mark Chapter 16

In the final chapter of the Gospel of Mark, and the account of the Resurrection, the reliability of eyewitness testimony is a prominent theme. The angels at the tomb confirm the identity of the One the women seek: "Ye seek Jesus of Nazareth, which was crucified" (Mark 16:6). While there is some question as to the authenticity of Mark 16:9-20, and its presence or absence in the original autographs, that in no way takes away from the emphasis on the identity of Jesus that permeates Mark's Gospel until this point. If the longer ending of Mark is accepted as genuine, its contents reveal a continuation of the subject of identity and the question becomes, "Will the testimony be believed?"

The post-Resurrection appearances of Jesus begin with, "he appeared first to Mary Magdalene" (Mark 16:9). The response of the disciples to her testimony was immediate rejection: "And they, when they had heard that he was alive, and had been seen of her, believed not" (Mark 16:11). Two of the disciples had Jesus appear to them, and when they reported back what they had seen, their testimony was also rejected: "And they went and told *it* unto the residue: neither believed they them" [italics in KJV] (Mark 16:13).

When Jesus did appear to the eleven He scolded them for refusing to believe the eyewitness testimony about Him: "Afterward he appeared unto the eleven as they sat at meat, and upbraided them with their unbelief and hardness of heart, because they believed not them which had seen him after he was risen" (Mark 16:14). At the conclusion of this longer ending of Mark's Gospel we are given a reason for the miracles that accompanied the proclamation of the gospel. They were intended to serve as corroborating evidence "confirming the word" (Mark 16:20) (τὸν λόγον βεβαιοῦντος) about who Jesus is and what He had done.

Mark's Gospel is one more witness citing multiple instances that give evidence of the identity of Jesus. He is the One about whom Old Testament prophets spoke and wrote, whom heavenly witnesses proclaimed in person and in proclamation. It is all about Jesus, who identified Himself by means of supernatural works and sublime words. It is a record whose united testimony is ignored at one's eternal peril.

Chapter 6

Evidence for the Identity of Jesus in the Gospel of Luke

The Doctor's Diagnosis

*S*hortly after the Gospel of Luke was written, it was recognized that the subject matter it contained related to "the gospel," that is, "the good news" (τοῦ εὐαγγελίου) about Jesus Christ, and that it was penned by Luke, the physician and close associate of the Apostle Paul. Consequently, the title "according to Luke" (ΚΑΤΑ ΛΟΥΚΑΝ) was given to it, to designate it as Luke's record of what had occurred. Together with the Acts of the Apostles, considered to also have been written by Luke, it comprises a history of Jesus' life and ministry and the beginning of the New Testament church.

Luke Chapter 1

Luke's stated methodology was accuracy in recording testimony that could be relied on—his source would not be speculation. He was aware as well that he was not alone in this endeavor: "many have taken in hand to set forth in order a declaration of those things which are most surely believed among us" (Luke 1:1), but yet he saw a need to add his record to that of other written testimony.

Luke made a point to tell his readers that he was taking the testimony of "eyewitnesses" (Luke 1:2) (αὐτόπται), not hearsay, and that he had scrupulously checked them out: "having had perfect understanding of all things from the very first, to write unto thee in order" (Luke 1:3). Luke's stated purpose was for his material to be used for instructional purposes: "That thou mightest know the certainty of those things, wherein thou hast been instructed" (Luke 1:4). The verb translated "thou hast been instructed" (κατηχήθης) is the origin of the word "catechize" and "catechism." The meaning of the noun translated "the exact truth" (ἀσφάλεια), according to Louw and Nida's lexicon is "a state of certainty with regard to a belief—'certainty, being without doubt'" (Johannes P. Louw and Eugene A. Nida, *Greek-English Lexicon of the New Testament Based on Semantic Domains*, 2nd ed. [New York: United Bible Societies, 2nd ed], 1989, 1:371). Luke's purpose was to provide credible, admissible evidence on which belief could reliably rest.

The prediction of John the Baptist's birth was witnessed by Zacharias, who was given the twofold evidence of an appearance and an announcement by "an angel of the Lord" (Luke 1:11) (ἄγγελος κυρίου), as well as testimony from an Old Testament passage: "And he shall go before him in the spirit and power of Elias [Elijah]" (Luke 1:17). This appears to be a reference to Malachi 4:5-6. Malachi 4:5 speaks of Elijah's commissioning: "Behold, I will send you Elijah the prophet before the coming of the great and dreadful day of the Lord." Malachi 4:6 is about Elijah's mission: "And he shall turn the heart of the fathers to the children, and the heart of the children to their fathers, lest I come and smite the earth with a curse." John Martin says, "Jesus affirmed that John was the fulfillment of Malachi 3:1 (Matthew 11:10), and stated that John *would have* fulfilled Malachi 4:5-6 if the people had accepted his message" [italics in original] (Matthew 11:14). (John A. Martin, "Luke," in *The Bible Knowledge Commentary, New Testament*, ed. John F. Walvoord and Roy B. Zuck [Wheaton, IL: Victor, 1983; reprint, Colorado Springs: Cook, 1996], 204).

In spite of this evidence, Zacharias still had doubts about his wife and himself having a child at their advanced age and he asked, "Whereby shall I know this?" (Luke 1:18). In response the angel identified himself and gave his credentials: "I am Gabriel, that stand in the presence of God; and am sent to speak unto thee, and to shew thee these glad tidings" (Luke 1:19). While providing evidence for Zacharias, his inability to speak was also a fitting judgment for his failure to believe the words of the angel: "thou shalt be dumb, and not able to speak, until the day that these things shall be performed, because thou believest not my words" (Luke 1:20).

The angel Gabriel also had a message for Mary, most of which dealt with the identity of the child to whom she would give birth: "He shall be great, and shall be called the Son of the Highest: and the Lord God shall give unto him the throne of his father David: and he shall reign over the house of Jacob for ever; and of his kingdom there shall be no end" (Luke 1:32-33). This fivefold description would have been recognized by Mary as belonging to the Messiah as predicted in 2 Samuel 7, to David, through Nathan the prophet. As John Martin writes, "David stated that Yahweh had spoken of the distant future (2 Samuel 7:19). Mary would have understood that the angel was speaking to her of the Messiah who had been promised for so long" (ibid., 205). Luke identified Jesus as being a legitimate heir to the Davidic throne. Additionally, significant for the identification of her child, the angel told Mary, "that holy thing which shall be born of thee shall be called the Son of God" (Luke 1:35).

Elizabeth, and her yet unborn son John the Baptist, through the Holy Spirit, also testified to the identity of Jesus. When she was visited by Mary she experienced a Holy Spirit-induced "leaping" (σκιρτάω) (Luke 1:41) in her womb and called Mary "the mother of my Lord" (Luke 1:43), thereby identifying the One who would be born to her. When Elizabeth's husband Zacharias could finally speak, "filled with the Holy Ghost" (Luke 1:67), he identified whom his son would introduce: "For thou shalt go before the face of the Lord to prepare his ways" (Luke 1:76), equating the coming Messiah with Yahweh. He also speaks of Him as "the Sunrise from on high" (Luke 1:78 NASB), perhaps an allusion to Malachi 4:2 and a future day: "But for you who fear My name the sun of righteousness will rise with healing in its wings."

Luke Chapter 2

In the birth narrative Joseph is identified as being "of the house and lineage of David" (Luke 2:4), because legally, although not physically, the Messiah's lineage was traced through His earthly father. Again, an angel provides testimony as to the identity of the child born in Bethlehem: "For unto you is born this day in the city of David a Saviour, which is Christ the Lord" (Luke 2:11). Luke, the author of this Gospel, would also, in his Acts of the Apostles, in Peter's first sermon, record these two details of His identity: "that God hath made that same Jesus, whom ye have crucified, both Lord and Christ" (Acts 2:36).

The appearance of the angel with a message, in and of itself, was testimony to the extraordinariness of Jesus. Few births have been heralded in such a fashion. This is augmented by what the angel calls "a sign" (Luke 2:12) (σημεῖον). It will be seen, particularly in the Johannine Gospel, that signs are often used as evidence of Jesus' identity. The angel's identifying sign was for the shepherds: "And this *shall be* a sign unto you; ye shall find the babe wrapped in swaddling clothes, lying in a manger" [italics in KJV] (Luke 2:12). The shepherds then became plural witnesses to what they had observed: "And when they had seen *it*, they made known abroad the saying which was told them concerning this child" [italics in NASB] (Luke 2:17).

Jesus' circumcision was the next recorded event giving evidence of His identity. The aged priest Simeon was awaiting the arrival of "the consolation of Israel" (Luke 2:25) (παράκλησιν τοῦ Ἰσραήλ), understood as the Messiah, as explained by Luke in the promise "that he should not see death, before he had seen the Lord's Christ" (Luke 2:26). As he held the infant Jesus, Simeon's words identified Him as "thy salvation, which thou hast prepared before the face of all people; a light to lighten the Gentiles, and the glory of thy people Israel" (Luke 2:30-31). Simeon would soon die, but his words had been heard, and understood by His parents who "marvelled at those things which were spoken of him" (Luke 2:33).

Simeon also addressed Mary, saying, "Behold, this *child* is set for the fall and rising again of many in Israel; and for a sign which shall be spoken against; (Yea, a sword shall pierce through thy own soul also), that the thoughts of many hearts may be revealed" [parenthesis and italics in KJV] (Luke 2:34-35). Luke added to the priest's testimony that of the elderly widow Anna who "spake of him to all them that looked for redemption in Jerusalem" (Luke 2:38).

The only recorded event during Jesus' childhood occurred at the Passover in Jerusalem when He was twelve years old, when He confounded the Jewish theologians of His day. Luke describes the scene as Him "sitting in the midst of the doctors, both hearing them, and asking them questions. And all that heard him were astonished at his understanding and answers" (Luke 2:46-47). Jesus' response to His parents' expression of concern seems, on the surface at least, to be insensitive at best and almost disrespectful at worst: "How is it that ye sought me? wist ye not that I must be about my Father's business?" (Luke 2:49).

Luke tells his readers that Jesus' parents did not comprehend what He really meant: "And they understood not the saying which he spake unto them" (Luke 2:50). What they did not understand was that "My Father's *house*" [italics in NASB] (Luke 2:49), or his "business" (KJV) referred to His intimacy with God the Father, and how that superseded the relationship with His earthly parents. It was a piece to the puzzle of His identity that they would not put together until later.

Luke Chapter 3

Jesus' baptism by John the Baptist, as mentioned when looking at it in the other two Synoptic Gospels, Matthew and Mark, is one of two highly significant events with evidence of His identity, the other event being The Transfiguration. Luke brought up the question on the minds of many in that day, whether or not John the Baptist himself might be the Messiah: "And as the people were in expectation, and all men mused in their hearts of John, whether he were the Christ, or not" (Luke 3:15). Luke answered that question unequivocally by contrasting his ministry with that of the Messiah.

Of interest in Luke's Gospel is the inclusion of material about John the Baptist's ministry, not present in the other two Synoptic or Johannine Gospels. While Matthew (Matthew 3:2) and Mark (Mark 1:4) mention "repentance" (Matthew uses the verb "to repent," μετανοέω, and Mark uses the noun "repentance," μετάνοια), Luke elaborated with a list of examples of "fruits in keeping with repentance" (Luke 3:8) (καρποὺς ἀξίους τῆς μετανοίας). Any casual perusal of the items in this list leads to the conclusion that they are things to do, that is, they are works to be performed.

Because of the apparent conflict between works and Pauline statements that works are excluded from the soteriological equation, various possibilities have been entertained, as to their interpretation. Some interpreters relegate the Synoptic Gospels and these moral/ethical works to a "gospel of the kingdom" which do not apply to New Testament believers. Others say that works are required as postconversion proof of the reality of prior faith. Other interpretations have been proferred.

What we do find is John the Baptist contrasting his ministry, "I indeed baptize you with water" (Luke 3:16), with that of the coming Messiah: "He shall baptize you with the Holy Ghost and with fire" (Luke 3:16). "Baptism with the Holy Ghost [Spirit]" most likely refers to what happens at the time of New Testament conversion, and "fire" most naturally, means judgment, as it does in the following verse: "unquenchable fire" (Luke 3:17).

Any interpretation of John the Baptist's ethical appeal must take into consideration Luke's contrast that the conversion the coming Messiah will usher in is on a different and higher level than what he preached. In what ways that differed is the question that a correct interpretation of the Gospels must answer. This interpreter's view is that ethical standards in the Gospels usually have in view a post conversion scenario, which has been preceded by an acknowledgment of inability, and a subsequent placing of trust in the One who gives the power that enables performance. In some instances ethical standards should be understood in terms of perfection that must be attained for the acquisition of eternal life. The alternative to personal perfection is imputed righteousness granted on the basis of belief. The performance is real and must not be watered down; a wishing, or wanting, or willingness, or a promise to perform are not satisfactory substitutes.

Luke's summation of John the Baptist's ministry is of interest: "And many other things in his exhortation preached he unto the people." The NASB reads, "So with many other exhortations also he preached the gospel to the people" (Luke 3:18). What constituted the "good news" (εὐαγγέλιον) he preached was not only ethical demands in preparation for the Messiah, which honest self-assessment would result in the recognition of an utter insufficiency, but also news about His identity and imminent arrival as well. Luke indicated that in addition to Herod putting John the Baptist in prison because of the accusations he made against him, there was an additional motivation: "he added yet this above all" (Luke 3:20). What Herod added to his list of grievances was that John the Baptist was heralding the arrival of someone whom he recognized as a threat to his throne.

Luke, as the other Synoptic authors did, mentioned the two items of evidence present at Jesus' baptism that proved His identity. The first was the supernatural appearance of a dove as a symbol of the presence of the Holy Spirit: "and the Holy Ghost descended in a bodily shape like a dove upon him" (Luke 3:22), and the second, was an audible voice: "and a voice came from heaven, 'Thou art My beloved Son, in Thee I am well-pleased'" (Luke 3:22).

Right after the Holy Spirit and God the Father's affirmation of Jesus' identity as the Son, at His baptism, Luke traced the genealogy from His mother Mary, back through earthly ancestors, full circle, to God: "Which was *the son* of Enos, which was *the son* of Seth, which was *the son* of Adam, which was *the son* of God" [italics in KJV] (Luke 3:38). The result was that the evidence for the deity of Jesus was thereby reinforced.

Luke also took the opportunity, at the beginning of the genealogy, to affirm the virgin birth by saying: "being (as was supposed) the son of Joseph" [parenthesis in KJV] (Luke 3:23). The two Greek terms translated "being (as was supposed)" (ὡς ἐνομίζετο) literally mean "as" (ὡς) "was supposed, thought or believed" (ἐνομίζετο). According to Louw and Nida the verb "believe" or "thought" (νομίζω), used here, means "to regard something as presumably true, but without particular certainty—'to suppose, to presume, to assume, to imagine, to believe, to think'" (Johannes P. Louw and Eugene A. Nida, *Greek-English Lexicon of the New Testament Based on Semantic Domains*, 2nd ed. [New York: United Bible Societies, 2nd ed], 1989, 1:369). The imperfect tense, with a continuous nuance, communicates this was the people's general consensus, though it was erroneous.

Luke Chapter 4

As noted in the discussion of the temptation in Matthew's Gospel, in the first temptation the devil used a first-class conditional sentence that assumed Jesus' divine identity for the sake of argument: "If thou be the Son of God, command this stone that it be made bread" (Luke 4:3). Wallace, in his *Greek Grammar beyond the Basics*, uses this verse as an example of a first-class conditional sentence, and argues that it does not prove the devil believes the statement, that Jesus is God's Son. Wallace argues against noted grammarian A. T. Robertson: "for Robertson to argue that the devil used the first class condition in his temptation of Jesus (εἰ υἱὸς εἶ τοῦ θεοῦ in Luke 4:3) because 'the devil knew it to be true' is to make several faulty assumptions about the nature of language and its correspondence to reality" [parenthesis in original] (Daniel Wallace, *Greek Grammar beyond the Basics* [Grand Rapids: Zondervan 1996], 11). Wallace's comments are well taken. The most that can be said from the grammar is that the devil presented the temptation, with the *assumption* of Jesus' identity taken as a point of view for the sake of argument, not necessarily as a fact with which he (the devil) was in agreement.

Be that as it may, the issue of Jesus' identity is an important theme for the temptation of Christ. Matthew and Luke's Gospels reverse the order of the second and third temptation, but in both the devil repeats the use of the words "if thou be the Son of God," an assumption about Jesus' identity, as mentioned previously, for the sake of argument. Jesus concluded the confrontation by applying to Himself an Old Testament verse: "Thou shalt not tempt the Lord thy God" (Luke 4:12). The quotation comes from Deuteronomy 6:16. Whatever the devil believed, Jesus left no doubt as to His own identity—He was even the devil's Lord and God.

The objective identity of Jesus as "Lord" (κύριος) is often confused and conflated with subjective submission to Him as such. Jesus is, in reality, the devil's "Lord" (κύριος) objectively, whether he believes it or subjectively submits himself to Him or not. To hold that the subjective meaning is always in view is something to be proved, not automatically assumed.

In the famous passage of Jesus' Sabbath sermon at Nazareth's synagogue, where He abruptly stopped His reading of Isaiah, and pronounced the fulfillment of that prophecy, the emphasis is one of identity. Strikingly, the first-person singular personal pronoun "Me" is found three times: "The Spirit of the Lord *is* upon me, because he hath anointed me to preach the gospel to the poor; he hath sent me to heal the brokenhearted, to preach deliverance to the captives, and recovering of sight to the blind, to set at liberty them that are bruised" [italics in KJV] (Luke 4:18). This part of His quotation or paraphrase is from Isaiah 61:1: "The Spirit of the Lord God *is* upon me; because the Lord hath anointed me to preach good tidings unto the meek; he hath sent me to bind up the brokenhearted, to proclaim liberty to the captives, and the opening of the prison to *them that are* bound" [italics in KJV].

In Luke 4:22 the NASB has the words: "And all were speaking well of Him" which does not fully express how Luke describes it. The verb translated "were speaking well" is the Greek verb "to testify" (μαρτυρέω), although, to be fair to the NASB, they do insert "*testifying*" (italics in NASB) in the margin, as a possibility after the verse. Luke, by characterizing their words as "testimony" was emphasizing their qualification as eyewitnesses to what Jesus had just said. And although their testimony was reliable, those present did express confusion because the quotation/paraphrase was a messianic prophecy which did not seem to them to fit with what they knew of His humble origin, so they were asking, "Is not this Joseph's son?" (Luke 4:22). Their question expected an affirmative answer. But how could that identity be reconciled with Jesus being the fulfillment of a messianic prophecy?

Jesus responded knowing that what they really wanted was for Him to perform miracles, so He said, "Ye will surely say unto me this proverb, Physician, heal thyself: whatsoever we have heard done in Capernaum, do also here in thy country" (Luke 4:23). Jesus then responded to what He knew was going on in their hearts, giving two Old Testament examples of miracles that were experienced by individuals and not by the populace at large. Furthermore, Jesus chose examples; that of Elijah and the widow, and Elisha and Naaman, which involved non-Jews, appropriate to the idea of the absence of receptivity in one's hometown. It was too much for His fickle fellow Jews to handle, who answered with anger: "And all they in the synagogue, when they heard these things, were filled with wrath" (Luke 4:28). What followed was Jesus' escape from one of the closest encounters with execution He would experience before His crucifixion.

Jesus returned to the receptive city of Capernaum where again, the demon in a demon-possessed man, shouted out His identity. It happened on a Sabbath, in a synagogue, where one would expect spirituality, holiness, and purity, yet where Luke said there was "a spirit of an unclean devil" (Luke 4:33). The demon addressed Him with, "Jesus of Nazareth" (Luke 4:34), and also said, "I know thee who thou art; the Holy One of God" (Luke 4:33). The demon knew he was in the presence of more than a man.

What could not be separated was the man from His message, His identity from His instruction, His actions from His authority: "What a word *is* this! for with authority and power he commandeth the unclean spirits, and they come out" [italics in KJV] (Luke 4:36). He had "the message" or "the word" (ὁ λόγος) and the Apostle John, in his Gospel, would use that term "the word" (ὁ λόγος) as a title for Him who was the embodiment of the gospel message. Jesus exorcized the demon, a public action witnessed by many, and word spread through the Galilean grapevine: "And the fame of him went out into every place of the country round about" (Luke 4:37).

In the supernatural spiritual world His "authority" (Luke 4:36) (ἐξουσία) and "power" (δύναμις) were such that He could command a demon and it obeyed. Amazingly, in the healing of Peter's mother-in-law Luke puts it, He "rebuked the fever; and it left her" (Luke 4:39). Whether demon or disease, His word was their command. And His was not hit-and-miss healing—He had a one hundred percent healing success rate: "all they that had any sick with divers diseases brought them unto him; and he laid his hands on every one of them, and healed them" (Luke 4:40).

Luke repeated that demons would immediately recognize and shout out Jesus' identity, saying, "Thou art Christ the Son of God" (Luke 4:41). Luke also commented concerning Jesus' silencing of demons: "And he rebuking them, suffered *them* not to speak: for they knew that he was Christ" [italics in KJV] (Luke 4:41). With this editorial comment Luke, the author, affirms that what the demons were declaring about Jesus' identity was true, despite the source of the testimony being despicable.

Luke Chapter 5

In the account of the recruitment of Simon Peter to become one of the twelve disciples, Jesus' identity is highlighted. In Peter's response to the miracle catch of fish "he fell down at Jesus' knees, saying, Depart from me; for I am a sinful man, O Lord" (Luke 5:8). Luke gives the reason for Peter's action, which would have been considered blasphemy by his contemporaries: "For he was astonished, and all that were with him, at the draught of the fishes which they had taken" (Luke 5:9). Peter and his companions' conclusion as to Jesus' identity also explains their immediate acceptance of His invitation to follow Him: "And when they had brought their ships to land, they forsook all, and followed him" (Luke 5:11).

With the cleansing of the leper, as mentioned in comments about the incident in the other two Synoptic Gospels, Matthew and Mark, Jesus' ability to heal was assumed, contingent only on His willingness. Luke also included Jesus' prohibition to the cleansed leper not to spread word of the healing, but also that he was to present himself to the priest with the requisite offering for certification of cleansing. The reason given by Jesus was: "for a testimony unto them" (Luke 5:14). The nature of the "testimony" (μαρτύριον) could have been proof to the priest, and others who may have been present (αὐτοῖς is plural), of who Jesus is, because they would naturally have asked the leper how the cleansing had happened. It could have been proof that Jesus met all the Old Testament Law's requirements and encouraged others to do so as well. Or perhaps the testimony would serve as a witness or judgment against them, since they were being asked to render a verdict on the authenticity of Jesus' healing work, which would point to who Jesus is.

The interaction between Jesus and the scribes and Pharisees, over His forgiving the sins of the paralytic in Luke, is similar to that recorded by Mark in his Gospel. The question the scribes and Pharisees asked was: "Who is this which speaketh blasphemies? Who can forgive sins, but God alone?" (Luke 5:21). Again, as in the other Synoptic accounts, Jesus healed the man, which was proof of His identity, that qualified Him to forgive sins: "But that ye may know that the Son of man hath power upon earth to forgive sins, (he said unto the sick of the palsy), I say unto thee, Arise, and take up thy couch, and go into thine house" [parenthesis in KJV] (Luke 5:24). In his record of the emotional response of the witnesses to this event, Luke adds the detail that they "were filled with fear" (Luke 5:26).

Physical healing was one thing, it related to the here and now, but forgiveness of sins was quite another. It had ramifications for the life to come. It came as a surprise to them, as seen in their verbal response: "We have seen strange things today" (Luke 5:26) (εἴδομεν παράδοξα σήμερον). We get our English word "paradox" from that Greek adjective, παράδοξος ("strange"). Louw and Nida, in their lexicon, give two possible meanings: 1) "pertaining to being difficult to be believed;" and 2) "pertaining to that which is unusual in the sense of contrary to expectations—'unusual, remarkable'" (Johannes P. Louw and Eugene A. Nida, *Greek-English Lexicon of the New Testament Based on Semantic Domains*, 2nd ed. [New York: United Bible Societies, 2nd ed], 1989, 1:371 and 592). What they had witnessed could be explained in no other way than supernatural terms. Certainly Jesus' words gave them something to think about. They now had an additional characteristic to consider in coming to a conclusion about His identity. Not only was He a faith healer, He also claimed to be a forgiveness grantor.

Following Jesus' words about His ability to forgive sins, Luke told of the call of Matthew to discipleship, and the party he threw to celebrate his decision to follow Him. The scribes and Pharisees objected to Jesus' association with "publicans [tax-gatherers] and sinners" (Luke 5:30). Their supposed issue was contamination, whereas Jesus was concerned with conversion and compassion. These religious leaders had not learned from the paralytic experience before this occasion. To have one's sins forgiven one had to have sins to be forgiven of, or at the very least to recognize a personal need for forgiveness.

Without Jesus directly accusing them of sin, in a sort of tongue-in-cheek manner, He switched to a patient/physician analogy, which the author, Luke, a physician by vocation, would have appreciated: "They that are whole need not a physician; but they that are sick" (Luke 5:31). And then, switching back to His initial subject of sin, by way of application, Jesus related to them the nature of His mission: "I came not to call the righteous, but sinners to repentance" (Luke 5:32). The scribes and Pharisees needed to change their mind about their self-righteousness. To paraphrase, Jesus said in effect: "I have not come to call those who think, or say, or assume, that they are righteous to repentance," but He didn't have to—they, and we, get the point—the understood application is that the sinners were His fellow-diners, who made no pretention of being righteous, and the (so-called) righteous are the scribes and Pharisees who were anything but righteous.

At the beginning of Jesus' public ministry the disciples of John the Baptist had difficulty understanding how their mentor's teaching related to that of the newcomer, who seemed to be taking over. They did notice some similarities, between their master's teaching, with that of the Pharisees, that both differed from that of Jesus. Luke does not say who approached Jesus about this, whereas Matthew (Matthew 9:14) says they were disciples of John the Baptist and in Mark's account (Mark 2:21) they appear to be John's disciples, the Pharisees, or both. Whoever it was their question expressed a complaint: "Why do the disciples of John fast often, and make prayers, and likewise *the disciples* of the Pharisees; but thine eat and drink?" [italics in KJV] (Luke 5:33).

Jesus' response, using the figure of a bridegroom, which was a veiled reference to Himself, indicated His presence represented a different and superior order. His illustrations that follow, where a new cloth patch would tear an old garment, and old wineskins would burst if new wine were placed in them, are used by Jesus to show the incompatibility of the old order with the new. John the Baptist and the Pharisees represented the old, which required a renewal: "But new wine must be put into new bottles [or wineskins]" (Luke 5:38).

Continuing with the wine illustration, Jesus used it to show that acceptance of the new would naturally encounter reluctance and opposition: "No man also having drunk old *wine* straightway desireth new: for he saith, The old is better" (Luke 5:39). Just as Jesus previously stated that the recognition of need was a requirement for forgiveness of sins, those who would accept Jesus as the Messiah would have to recognize that the old order was superseded by the new.

Luke Chapter 6

In Luke 6 Jesus' disciples were accused of doing work on the Sabbath which was prohibited by the Mosaic Law. As they were going through a field they gathered grain and ate it. Jesus responded to the Pharisees by drawing a parallel between what His disciples had just done and what David's men did in I Samuel 21:6 when they ate sacred bread from the tabernacle. The exception to the Law was deemed acceptable because of physical necessity. On the other hand, Jesus claimed that the disciples had a right to violate the Law, and the reason He gave was that "the Son of man is Lord also of the sabbath" (Luke 6:5).

It should be noted that of the four meanings that Louw and Nida give in their Lexicon for this term "Lord" (κύριος) the usage here is most likely their second meaning which they indicate with the superscript "b," and is that of "one who owns and controls property, including especially servants and slaves, with important supplementary semantic components of high status and respect—'owner, master, lord'" (Johannes P. Louw and Eugene A. Nida, *Greek-English Lexicon of the New Testament Based on Semantic Domains*, 2nd ed. [New York: United Bible Societies, 2nd ed], 1989, 1:559). Since God created the Sabbath, for Jesus to claim ownership and thereby control of it, was equivalent to calling Himself God.

The identity of Jesus is implied in Luke 6:19: "And the whole multitude sought to touch him: for there went virtue out of him, and healed *them* all" [italics in KJV]. It was not just His actions, but His person that was considered to be extraordinary. They sensed that because of who Jesus is "virtue" or "power" (δύναμις) was emanating from Him. This may seem to border on the superstitious, and yet Luke states it without giving his readers/listeners any reason to question that it was so.

In Luke 6:46 Jesus brought up the term "Lord" (κύριος) and asked, "And why call ye me, Lord, Lord, and do not the things which I say?" In Matthew's Gospel (Matthew 7:21-23) there is a similar discussion in Jesus' Sermon on the Mount. Jesus was asking how they could legitimately address Him as their "Lord" (κύριος), or "master," which was a title that indicated ownership. Service and obedience are implicit rights of ownership. If they were not doing what He said, how could they lay claim to having Him as their owner; that they belonged to Him? Jesus' identity, who He is as "Lord" (κύριος), has consequences and ramifications for what He requires of men who have a relationship with Him.

Luke Chapter 7

The centurion, whose son Jesus healed, was an example of a Gentile who recognized something extraordinary about Jesus. Jesus' station in life was a humble one, and yet the centurion said to Him, "Lord, trouble not thyself: for I am not worthy that thou shouldest enter under my roof: wherefore neither thought I myself worthy to come unto thee" (Luke 7:6-7). The centurion, being a military man, was familiar with the chain of command, and he was careful not to come across as if he was commanding Jesus to do anything. The centurion drew a parallel between those he had at his disposal to command, and Jesus, who could also issue a command and have His bidding done: "Wherefore neither thought I myself worthy to come unto thee: but say in a word, and my servant shall be healed. For I also am a man set under authority, having under me soldiers, and I say unto one, Go, and he goeth; and to another, Come, and he cometh; and to my servant, Do this, and he doeth *it*" [italics in KJV] (Luke 7:7-8).

Normally others were the ones who were amazed at what Jesus did. On this occasion Luke records that "when Jesus heard these things, he marvelled at him, and turned him about, and said unto the people that followed him, I say unto you, I have not found so great faith, no, not in Israel" (Luke 7:9). The centurion had to believe something about who Jesus is, to think that He could speak and sickness would obey Him. The centurion's faith was all the greater because his sick son was not even present—this One could command and would be obeyed, even if what was commanded was beyond the range of his voice. No wonder Jesus "marvelled" (ἐθαύμασεν) at the man's faith.

The raising from the dead, of the widow of Nain's son, naturally brought up the issue of the identity of the One who could do such a thing. Luke emphasized the plurality of witnesses to this event. In Luke 7:11 he points out: "And it came to pass the day after, that he went into a city called Nain; and many of his disciples went with him, and much people." The following verse indicates that crowd was joined by those accompanying the grieving widow: "and much people of the city was [were] with her" (Luke 7:12). The raising from the dead itself was not done in private. Everyone in the funeral procession were present as witnesses: "And he came and touched the bier: and they that bare *him* stood still" [italics in KJV] (Luke 7:14).

Luke made the point that the son had really been dead by saying, "And he that was dead sat up, and began to speak" (Luke 7:15). Being a physician, Luke did not want to leave out that detail. The son was dead–really dead. The response of those who observed this raising from the dead was to exclaim that "a great prophet is risen up among us; and, that God hath visited his people" (Luke 7:16). They knew they were living in extraordinary days, similar to those of the prophets of old. Their exclamation, "God hath visited His people" (Luke 7:16) was more real than most of them probably realized. It was God Himself, in the person of Jesus.

Luke 7:17-23 is the parallel account to Matthew 11:2-6 of John the Baptist's inquiry from prison about the identity of Jesus. The question John the Baptist had two of his disciples ask was, "Art thou he that should come? or look we for another?" (Luke 7:19). This is identical to the question recorded in Matthew (Matthew 11:3). The answer Jesus gave John's disciples, to relay back to him, was identical in Luke and Matthew. John the Baptist, the wavering witness, was given Old Testament testimony as well as the evidence of on-going miracles, to strengthen his initial conviction that Jesus was the anticipated Messiah.

In closing his account of this incident Luke contrasted two responses to Jesus' words. On the one hand: "And all the people that heard *him*, and the publicans, justified God ["acknowledged God's justice" = NASB], being baptized with the baptism of John" [italics in KJV] (Luke 7:29). On the other hand: "But the Pharisees and lawyers rejected the counsel of God against themselves, being not baptized of him" (Luke 7:30). The latter observation indicates it is possible, in some manner, to reject "the counsel [purpose] of God" (τὴν βουλὴν τοῦ θεοῦ), while also recognizing Paul's assertion in the form of a question: "For who hath resisted His will?" (Romans 9:19) (τῷ γὰρ βουλήματι αὐτοῦ τίς ἀνθέστηκεν), which expects the answer, "No one." These two truths are probably best understood as referring to different nuances to God's purpose and will–one His permissive will, the other His decree.

Luke described the woman who anointed Jesus' feet with perfume as: "a woman in the city, which was a sinner" (Luke 7:37). The Pharisees used the incident as proof that Jesus could not be a prophet: "if he were a prophet, [he] would have known who and what manner of woman *this is* that toucheth him: for she is a sinner" [italics in KJV] (Luke 7:39). This is a second-class conditional sentence in Greek, in which the speaker assumes the first part, the protasis, the condition, not to be true–the Pharisees did not believe Jesus was a prophet. But their assumption was false and Jesus set about to prove it.

Contrary to the Pharisees' assumption that Jesus did not know the woman's notoriety as a sinner, the woman's identity as a sinner became an opportunity for Him to exercise His prerogative as the Savior and to implicitly give evidence of His own identity: "And he said unto her, Thy sins are forgiven" (Luke 7:48). The Pharisees had denied He was a prophet. Now they had to deal with His identity, not only as a prophet, but as One who forgave sins: "Who is this that forgiveth sins also?" (Luke 7:49).

The woman's sacrificial gift was not the cause of her forgiveness, but a sign of gratitude. Jesus had illustrated it in a parable about two debtors, one of whom had been forgiven ten times what the other had been forgiven. As He explained it, the greater gratitude was exhibited by this woman who had been forgiven "her sins, which are many" (Luke 7:47). Her gratitude was for forgiveness and as Jesus expressed it: "Your faith has saved you; go in peace" (Luke 7:50).

As Louw and Nida indicate in their lexicon, the verb "to save" (σῴζω), can mean: "to rescue; " "to save," and, "to heal." Here, in the context of forgiveness of sins, it fits with the first of these, "to save," which means, according to Louw and Nida: "to cause someone to experience divine salvation" (Johannes P. Louw and Eugene A. Nida, *Greek-English Lexicon of the New Testament Based on Semantic Domains*, 2nd ed. [New York: United Bible Societies, 2nd ed], 1989, 1:242). The question raised by the Pharisees was, "Who is this that forgiveth sins also?" (Luke 7:49). If it were true, and it was, that He had forgiven the woman's sins, it could only mean one thing–He was God.

Luke Chapter 8

As in the other two Synoptic Gospels, Matthew (Matthew 12:46-50), and Mark (Mark 3:31-35), Luke included the incident where Jesus downplayed the relationship with His earthly family compared to His heavenly identity. Jesus referred to the latter in Matthew 12:50: "For whosoever shall do the will of my Father which is in heaven, the same is my brother, and sister, and mother," and Mark 3:35: "For whosoever shall do the will of God, the same is my brother, and my sister, and mother." Luke has: "My mother and my brethren are these which hear the word of God, and do it" (Luke 8:21), which could refer to obeying Jesus' words because they are the word of God Himself. As in the other Synoptic Gospels Jesus asserted that spiritual identification with Him is superior to earthly familial relationships.

Jesus' calming of the storm also has parallels in the other two Synoptic Gospels. In the Matthew account the miracle elicits the disciples' question, "What manner of man is this, that even the winds and the sea obey him!" (Matthew 8:27), emphasizing the characteristics and identity of such an individual. Mark's account is similar. Luke likewise expressed the disciples' question with the words, "What manner of man is this! for he commandeth even the winds and water, and they obey him" (Luke 8:25). "The winds" (τοῖς ἀνέμοις) and "the water" (τῷ ὕδατι) are personified as they "obey Him" (ὑπακούουσιν αὐτῷ); the inanimate bowing to the will and word of their Creator. The miracle brought to light the identity of the person who had performed it.

Luke also mentioned the miraculous exorcism and casting of demons into swine. The demon-possessed man speaking through the demon immediately identified Jesus in Matthew as the "Son of God" (Matthew 8:29) (υἱὲ τοῦ θεοῦ), in Mark as "Son of the Most High God" (Mark 5:7) (υἱὲ τοῦ θεοῦ τοῦ ὑψίστου), and in Luke also "Son of the Most High God" (Luke 8:28) (υἱὲ τοῦ θεοῦ τοῦ ὑψίστου). Luke makes a point to mention that there were eyewitnesses to this event: "They also which saw *it* told them by what means he that was possessed of the devils was healed" [italics in KJV] (Luke 8:36). The verb translated "was healed" (ἐσώθη), is an aorist passive indicative form of the verb that can mean "to rescue," "to save," or "to heal" (σῴζω). Contextually, the best meaning here would be "to rescue" or "to deliver," as the man had been delivered from the demons and from the hermit's life among the tombs to which he had been relegated.

The raising of the daughter of Jairus from the dead included an interesting detail. Jesus' words to the distraught father were, "Fear not: believe only, and she shall be made whole" (Luke 8:50). The stated requirement for divine action, "believe only" (μόνον πίστευσον), is reminiscent of Luke's recorded response in his other book, The Acts of the Apostles, to the Philippian jailor's inquiry made to Paul and Silas. The jailor in Acts 16:30 asked: "Sirs, what must I do to be saved?" and the answer given by Paul and Silas was, "Believe on the Lord Jesus Christ, and thou shalt be saved, and thy house" (Acts 16:31).

In Luke's Gospel the desired divine action was a physical raising from the dead, in Luke's Acts of the Apostles it would be eternal deliverance from spiritual death. In both the same Greek verb "to rescue," "to save," or "to heal" (σῴζω) is used, in the former for deliverance from death, in the latter to secure a felicitous eternal destiny. In both of these instances, in the Gospel of Luke and the Acts of the Apostles, the verb "believe" (πιστεύω) is unaccompanied by any other action, physical or mental, in the former explicitly, with the addition of the adjective "only" (μόνος) used adverbially, and in the latter implicitly by the absence of added or qualifying caveats.

Luke Chapter 9

Luke Chapter 9 opens with Jesus equipping the Twelve: "Then he called his twelve disciples together, and gave them power and authority over all devils, and to cure diseases" (Luke 9:1). And having equipped them "And he sent them to preach the kingdom of God, and to heal the sick" (Luke 9:2). The ability to delegate presupposed that Jesus was One who had the authority to do so. Later on, having been eyewitnesses to the feeding of the five thousand, the Twelve, minus one, would be sent on a future Jewish/Gentile mission, to the whole world.

Herod the tetrarch was concerned who this man Jesus was, about whom he had heard so much. Herod had heard rumors, and entertained three possibilities: (1) "John [the Baptist] was risen from the dead" (Luke 9:7); (2) "Elias [Elijah] had appeared" (Luke 9:8); and (3) "one of the old prophets was risen again" (Luke 9:8). He had doubts about the first possibility, having personal knowledge of John the Baptist's execution, and he said so: "John have I beheaded: but who is this, of whom I hear such things?" (Luke 9:9). Perhaps, Herod thought, if he could just see Him, he could identify Him: "And he desired to see Him" (Luke 9:9).

The feeding of the five thousand provides proof of Jesus' identity by means of miracles. The first miracle was the multiplication of a meal. Luke notes that the twelve disciples came to Jesus telling Him of the need: "then came the twelve, and said unto him, Send the multitude away, that they may go into the towns and country round about, and lodge, and get victuals: for we are here in a desert place" (Luke 9:12). In spite of having only "the five loaves and the two fishes" (Luke 9:16), He "blessed them, and brake, and gave to the disciples to set before the multitude" (Luke 9:16). What was left over exceeded what was originally available: "and there was taken up of fragments that remained to them twelve baskets" (Luke 9:17). The Twelve had front-row seats, as it were, as witnesses to the miracle as they dispensed the food, and also as each took up one of the twelve baskets of leftovers.

Peter's confession of faith, expressed his conviction of who Jesus is. Jesus introduced the subject of His identity on that occasion by first asking the disciples, "Whom say the people that I am?" (Luke 9:18). The disciples' answer, recorded by Luke, is identical to the threefold speculation entertained by Herod in Luke 9:7-8: "They answering said, John the Baptist; but some *say*, Elias; and others *say*, that one of the old prophets is risen again" [italics in KJV] (Luke 9:19).

But more than a general response, what Jesus was after was the disciples' personal conviction: "But whom say ye that I am?" (Luke 9:20). Peter responded immediately, "The Christ of God" (Luke 9:20). Peter recognized Him as "the Messiah" (ὁ Χριστός) whom God had sent. Luke did not include the lengthier response of Peter's confessional affirmation found in Matthew's Gospel (Matthew 16:17-19) but did record Jesus' telling the disciples not to publicize His identity as the Messiah, which both of the other Synoptic Gospels also do (Matthew 16:20; Mark 8:30). Luke did place the prohibition in the context of upcoming events, "The Son of man must suffer many things, and be rejected of the elders and chief priests and scribes, and be slain, and be raised the third day" (Luke 9:22). The public identification of Jesus as the Messiah had to wait, adhering to the divine timeline.

In light of what Jesus would suffer, He gave the disciples the requirements for discipleship: "If any *man* will come after me, let him deny himself, and take up his cross daily, and follow me" [italics in KJV] (Luke 9:23). Jesus' requirement for someone to "come after Me" was, in Matthew's Gospel: "let him deny himself, and take up his cross, and follow Me" (Matthew 16:24); in Mark's Gospel, identical to what is found in Matthew: "let him deny himself, and take up his cross, and follow Me" (Mark 8:34).

This requirement for discipleship should not be equated or conflated with the requirement for eternal salvation from hell. There are several serious problems with doing so with this passage, but one is readily apparent. In all three of the Synoptic Gospels the reader/hearer who would embark on the discipleship journey is addressed with the words: "If anyone wishes" (Matthew 16:24) (εἴ τις θέλει); "If anyone wishes" (Mark 8:34) (εἴ τις θέλει); and "If any *man* will" [italics in KJV] (Luke 9:23) (εἴ τις θέλει). The word "wishes" is the Greek verb θέλω. The meaning in Louw and Nida's lexicon, which best fits this context, is: "to desire, to want, to wish" (Johannes P. Louw and Eugene A. Nida, *Greek-English Lexicon of the New Testament Based on Semantic Domains*, 2nd ed. [New York: United Bible Societies, 2nd ed], 1989, 1:289). It is used in contexts that have an object of the "desire," the "want," or the "wish."

In Matthew the object is to "come after Me" (Matthew 16:24), (ὀπίσω μου ἐλθεῖν–using the aorist active infinitive form of the verb "ἔρχομαι," translated "come" or "go"). In Mark the object is also translated to "come after me" (Mark 8:34) (ὀπίσω μου ἀκολουθεῖν–using a different verb–the present active infinitive form of the verb "ἀκολουθέω" regularly translated "to follow"). In Luke (Luke 9:23) the object of the "desire," "want," or "wish" is "to come after Me" (ὀπίσω μου ἔρχεσθαι–using the present middle or passive infinitive form of the verb "ἔρχομαι," usually translated "to come" or "to go"). In all three Synoptic Gospels the object of "willing" or "desiring" is discipleship.

It is erroneous to incorporate the meaning of the verb "to desire," "to want," or "to wish" (θέλω) into its object, that is, following Jesus. Jesus was addressing those with the desire to follow Him, and giving instructions for turning the desire into action. Desiring to follow cannot substitute for actual doing. The interpretational shift is subtle but significant. Jesus' requirement for following Him is not merely a "desire," a "want," or a "willingness," to take up one's cross, obey, sacrifice, etc. Significantly, in the immediate context of taking up one's cross, Jesus used the word "to desire" (θέλω), and could have used it to qualify the terms or requirements for discipleship, but He did not. Jesus' instructions for following Him must not be watered down–they require doing and not merely desiring to do so.

Ostensibly, this watering down of the requirement to an attitude instead of an action is done by some Bible teachers in order not to run afoul of the biblical doctrine of salvation apart from works. When confronted with the biblical distinction between actual work being required to be a disciple, and the fact that eternal salvation is secured by grace through faith alone, it is illegitimate to resort to a "willing to" or "commit to" position.

It is also illegitimate to resort to the expedient of declaring that God is the one who does the work, and that such work is thereby exempt from the clear biblical prohibition. As will be shown in the discussion of Ephesians 2:8, that loophole is untenable lexically, as well as logically. If Jesus had meant to say that it was good enough, as a requirement for "coming after" or "following Him" to be "willing" to deny oneself and take up one's cross, He would have said so. In fact, Jesus used the very word for being "willing" (θέλω) that a watering down position employs, but with the significant difference already discussed. Jesus' requirement for discipleship, contrary to such an interpretation of the text, was not to "desire" or be "willing" to deny oneself but rather to actually do it.

The Transfiguration, recorded by Luke (Luke 9:27-36), as it was also by the other two writers of the Synoptic Gospels, Matthew (Matthew 16:28-17:9) and Mark (Mark 9:1-9), is generally recognized as a significant event in Jesus' earthly life. It is important because of its contribution to the identity motif shared by authors of these Gospels. Luke, introduced his presentation of the Transfiguration with Jesus' words: "there be some standing here, which shall not taste of death, till they see the kingdom of God" (Luke 9:27).

Matthew's introduction to the same event is almost identical, with the exception that instead of ending with "the kingdom of God" (Luke 9:27) he has "the Son of Man coming in His kingdom" (Matthew 16:28). Mark ends it with: "till they have seen the kingdom of God come with power" (Mark 9:1). These variations, which can be attributed to being indirect rather than direct quotations, are probably referring to an event that will precede the death of some of the disciples, specifically, Peter, James, and John, whom Jesus would select to accompany Him and witness it.

These three disciples, likely a number not chosen arbitrarily, but conforming to the requisite number of required witnesses to confirm testimony, are described with the word for "seeing" (Luke 9:27) (ἴδωσιν–aorist, active, subjunctive, third person, plural form from "ὁράω" = "to see"). Luke lets the reader/listener know that despite their having just been awakened from sleep, the three were wide awake eyewitnesses of this event: "But Peter and they that were with him were heavy with sleep: and when they were awake, they saw his glory, and the two men that stood with him" (Luke 9:32). The mention of the "[fully] awake" (διαγρηγορήσαντες) condition of the witnesses adds to their credibility.

Luke referred to the three as "Peter and they that were with him" (Luke 9:32), perhaps reflecting that his (Luke's) information came by way of Peter. The latter in his second epistle was no doubt writing about this same event: "For we have not followed cunningly devised fables, when we made known unto you the power and coming of our Lord Jesus Christ, but were eyewitnesses of his majesty" (2 Peter 1:16). Peter, in his epistle, used the plural noun "eyewitnesses" (2 Peter 1:16) (ἐπόπται) to identify himself and his two fellow disciples, in relation to the events he was writing about.

Peter's written testimony about what he saw, in his second epistle, mirrors what Luke wrote in his Gospel. This is to be expected if Luke got his information from Peter. Peter wrote: "For he received from God the Father honour and glory, when there came such a voice to him from the excellent glory, This is my beloved Son, in whom I am well pleased" (2 Peter 1:17). Peter went on to verify the time and location where this happened: "And this voice which came from heaven we heard, when we were with him in the holy mount" (2 Peter 1:18). Peter wanted his readers/listeners to have no doubt about the reliability of his testimony. And Luke in his gospel was driven by the same motivation, to carefully produce a reliable record of an event that provided evidence of Jesus' identity.

When evidence is offered, often there is an attempt to verify it by means of corroborating testimony. When Luke was putting together what he would write, most of the other disciples, besides Peter, James, and John, were probably alive and available to be questioned about what happened on that day. Granted, the rest of the disciples were not there on the mountain, because they had been left behind. But surely with something so significant, they would have heard about it, if not from Jesus Himself, certainly from Peter, James, or John. And if they had not, would that not cast doubt on those three disciples' account of events that had happened earlier? How could they have kept that to themselves?

It appears Luke may have thought about that possibility, and checked it out. And so he wrote, "and they kept *it* close, and told no man in those days any of those things which they had seen" [italics in KJV] (Luke 9:36). Luke did not explain why they kept it secret, but Matthew did: "And as they came down from the mountain, Jesus charged them, saying, Tell the vision to no man, until the Son of man be risen again from the dead" (Matthew 17:9). Mark, in his gospel, also answers the question why the rest of the disciples did not know what had happened: "And as they came down from the mountain, he charged them that they should tell no man what things they had seen, till the Son of man were risen from the dead" (Mark 9:9). Unlike some whom Jesus healed and were told not to tell anyone, and yet did so anyway, to their credit, it appears that Peter, James, and John kept the secret until the time when Jesus had released them to tell it.

In our day many people are skeptical when they hear about exorcisms. And when charlatans are exposed it only serves to justify our skepticism. In Jesus' day demon possession was a recognized reality. One would expect that with the historical event of the Incarnation, the devil would redouble his efforts in that day and in that particular place, with spiritual warfare becoming all the more intense, relentless, and overt. Graphic demonstrations of demon possession and exorcisms were recognized and accepted as genuine. In Luke 9:37-42 a man in desperation asked Jesus to cast the demon out of his only son. Apparently the disciples had unsuccessfully attempted an exorcism, and the father now desperately looked to Jesus for help. On this occasion, unlike many others, the demon did not call out identifying who Jesus is. Luke succinctly reports that "Jesus rebuked the unclean spirit, and healed the child, and delivered him again to his father" (Luke 9:42).

Luke followed up the exorcism with these words: "And they were all amazed at the mighty power of God" (Luke 9:43). The crowd could have merely thought that this had been done by God's power, and that it had no ontological significance for Jesus' identity. It seems, however, that the crowd may have been about to crown Him king. Apparently the disciples had been caught up in all the excitement. Jesus sternly brought the disciples back down to earth: "But while they wondered every one at all things which Jesus did, he said unto his disciples, Let these sayings sink down into your ears: for the Son of man shall be delivered into the hands of men" (Luke 9:43-44). The identity of Jesus presented in the Gospels includes not only His deity and His humanity, but also the significant events that were a part of His mission; His death on a cross for the sins of mankind and His victorious resurrection from the dead.

Jesus' identity was intimately connected with His relationship with God the Father. To accept God the Father, as the religious leaders were claiming to do in His day, and at the same time reject Jesus, was not possible. To accept or reject One was to accept or reject the Other. Jesus put it this way: "whosoever shall receive me receiveth him that sent me" (Luke 9:48).

At the end of chapter 9 of Luke is another passage that some have misinterpreted to incorporate works as a requirement for eternal salvation. Jesus first addressed an individual who says, "Lord, I will follow thee whithersoever thou goest" (Luke 9:57). It is noteworthy that the person promised to do something specifically, physically, not figuratively, to "follow" (ἀκολουθέω). He no doubt had a desire to do so, but at that point in time it was just a verbal promise or expression of a desire. Jesus did not respond by saying something like, "I see your heart is right," or, "I accept your willingness; that's what I'm looking for." What Jesus did say was, "Foxes have holes, and birds of the air *have* nests; but the Son of man hath not where to lay *his* head" [italics in KJV] (Luke 9:58). In effect the person was told, "You do not know what you are in for."

There is nothing in the context that suggests that the requirements for "following" Jesus comprised an attitude instead of an action. We are not explicitly told what the individual's response was, although it may be presumed from Jesus' remark at the end of this chapter that the man failed to follow through, having been discouraged on learning what was involved. Jesus was not just looking for assent that was intellectually informed about the rigors endured by a first-century itinerant teacher; what He was asking for was immediate action.

In the next related incident Jesus was the initiator: "And he said unto another, Follow me" (Luke 9:59). This person did not outright refuse but asked for a "rain check": "But he said, Lord, suffer me first to go and bury my father" (Luke 9:59). Was it a matter of preparing him for burial? Was he on the brink of needing to be buried? Was he dead yet, or not quite? Whatever it was, it was not immediate obedience on the part of this person.

Again, with this individual the issue under consideration was an action, not an attitude. Jesus did not tell this person something like "I know you have personal responsibilities to attend to, and I know your heart. I'll give you a pass, go for it. Come back when you're ready." No, not exactly. Jesus' response was, "Let the dead bury their dead: but go thou and preach the kingdom of God" (Luke 9:60). Whatever Jesus was talking about, it required immediate action. Good intentions could not be substituted for genuine implementation.

Perhaps the disciples were wondering, as some today might suggest, that the delay or the leave of absence the person was asking for was too lengthy, if it was indeed true that the father was nowhere near dying. The next individual who was volunteered may have thought a shorter time period would pass muster: "And another also said, Lord, I will follow thee; but let me first go bid them farewell, which are at home at my house" (Luke 9:61). Jesus' response indicates that the length of time of the delay was not the problem with this potential follower: "And Jesus said unto him, No man, having put his hand to the plough, and looking back, is fit for the kingdom of God" (Luke 9:62).

The present writer spent his childhood in a third-world country with pre-mechanized agricultural technology, quite similar to that of the first century, where oxen and a primitive wooden plow were employed. Having had literal, first-hand experience "putting my hand to the plow," I can assure the reader that it requires one's full attention and energy. It is a strenuous three-dimensional physical task, in which one must keep both the oxen and the plow going in a straight line, not deviating to the left or the right, while using physical strength to lift or plunge the plow to make sure the plowing is neither too shallow nor too deep. It is impossible to "look back" and plow effectively. One must be fully and completely engaged in the activity of plowing. Jesus' illustration is of a first-century physical activity, and shows that singleness of purpose is required.

The more primitive the plow, the likelier it would have been for plows in Jesus' day to be of the one-handled type, unlike those of the popular TV show "Little House on the Prairie," which were of the high-tech two-handled variety. On that show even "Ma" could do the plowing if "Pa" were unexpectedly absent. There was no need to seek the help of the giant of a man, neighbor Jonathan Garvey, played by the late Merlin Olsen, of National Football League fame. The plow Jesus referred to required strength and stamina. Neither should the use of the singular "hand" (τὴν χεῖρα) in Luke 9:62 be seen as a reference to a tentative approach to the plowing task. Once plowing began, there was no turning back. While attitude would have been involved, what Jesus had in mind was action, not simply a willing attitude.

Matthew in his Gospel recorded this incident, whereas Mark did not. In Matthew's account only the first two individuals are mentioned with Jesus' response to the second proposal: "But Jesus said unto him, Follow me; and let the dead bury their dead" (Matthew 8:22). Perhaps Luke in his Gospel provides the key to a correct understanding of this incident. Jesus' response to the third person in this pericope, which appears to be addressed to all three individuals was this: "No man, having put his hand to the plough, and looking back, is fit for the kingdom of God" (Luke 9:62).

Jesus used a Greek adjective translated "fit" (εὔθετος), for which Louw and Nida in their lexicon provide the definitions "suitable" and "useful" as possible meanings (Johannes P. Louw and Eugene A. Nida, *Greek-English Lexicon of the New Testament Based on Semantic Domains*, 2nd ed. [New York: United Bible Societies, 2nd ed], 1989, 1:624 and 627). Anyone who has plowed, with a tractor or a plow, knows that in order to plow straight, you have to look ahead, not behind. Usefulness in the kingdom is negated or compromised by the act of "looking back" (βλέπων εἰς τὰ ὀπίσω), which in the context of the illustrations provided, are detours that prevent immediate action, but it also has a negative effect on effectiveness.

These detours are distractions that may come in a couple of forms. One is mental or attitudinal, to decline to enter into the contemplated journey, once its rigorous requirements are revealed. While this mental activity can be understood as a "willingness," or more precisely an "unwillingness" here, mere mental acquiescence will not meet the conditions to qualify as obedience to Jesus' command to "Follow me" (Luke 9:59) (ἀκολούθει μοι). The intended implication is that the excuses Jesus was discussing would be a hindrance to keep this individual from actually acting.

Whatever the obstacles might be, they preclude action. The implicit lesson is to immediately without hesitation "Follow me" (Luke 9:59) (ἀκολούθει μοι), which Jesus relates to "the kingdom of God" (Luke 9:62) (τῇ βασιλείᾳ τοῦ θεοῦ). Nothing in any of Luke's three illustrations warrants a watering down of the command "follow" to "be willing to follow." Any attempt to shore up a faulty perception of deficiency in the requirement for salvation, as found in the biblical gospel for the unsaved, unwittingly or purposefully, by gutting sanctification in the form of the discipleship of the saved, by reducing required action to an attitude, collapses salvation and sanctification. Such conflation breeds confusion.

Luke Chapter 10

In the mission to the seventy Jesus enigmatically alluded to His identity when He commissioned them. In light of the scarcity of reapers, "but the laborers *are* few" [italics in KJV] (Luke 10:2), He instructed them to "pray ye therefore the Lord of the harvest, that he would send forth laborers into his harvest" (Luke 10:2). One could assume that Jesus was referring to God the Father as "the Lord of the harvest" (τοῦ κυρίου τοῦ θερισμοῦ). However, immediately, Jesus says to them, "Go your ways; behold, I send you out as lambs in the midst of wolves" (Luke 10:3). It may be argued that different Greek verbs are translated "send" in verses 2 and 3. In Luke 10:2 in the phrase to "send forth labourers" (ἐργάτας ἐκβάλῃ) the Greek verb "to send out" is ἐκβάλλω, while in verse 3 the phrase "I send you forth" (ἀποστέλλω ὑμᾶς) the Greek verb ἀποστέλλω is used. Although these two Greek verbs are not synonymous, they do share the meaning "to send out" which is undoubtedly the meaning here. Both God the Father and Jesus, to whom the Father has given authority, participate in commissioning believers.

The close association Jesus claimed with God the Father is further seen in the summation of His commissioning of the seventy: "He that heareth you heareth me; and he that despiseth you despiseth me; and he that despiseth me despiseth him that sent me" (Luke 10:16). The same Greek verb used in verse 3 "to send out" (ἀποστέλλω) for the seventy, is used here in verse 16 of God the Father sending Jesus. Additionally when the seventy return, they tell Jesus about the exorcisms they had performed: "the devils are subject unto us through your name" (Luke 10:17). Bauer, Arndt, and Gingrich in their lexicon give the meaning "the demons are subject to us at the mention of your name" (Walter Bauer, William F. Arndt, and Wilbur F. Gingrich, *A Greek-English Lexicon of the New Testament and Other Early Christian Literature* [Chicago: University of Chicago Press, 1957], 576). That Jesus' personal presence was not required demonstrated the magnitude of even His delegated power. Jesus put his followers' exuberance over exorcism into perspective: "Notwithstanding in this rejoice not, that the spirits are subject unto you; but rather rejoice, because your names are written in heaven" (Luke 10:20).

Jesus made a comment that some might have considered egotistical or erroneous, if not outright blasphemous, concerning what His closest followers were witnessing: "And he turned him unto *his* disciples, and said privately, Blessed *are* the eyes which see the things that ye see: For I tell you, that many prophets and kings have desired to see those things which ye see, and have not seen *them*; and to hear those things which ye hear, and have not heard *them*" [italics in KJV] (Luke 10:23-24). The inclusion of these words of Jesus, specifically the mention of "the eyes" (οἱ ὀφθαλμοὶ), and that the disciples would "hear" (ἀκούω), serves Luke's purpose to support the authenticity of his record as based on the testimony of eyewitnesses. The nature of the testimony of the disciples, which some of them would record, would be both visual and auditory.

The introduction to the parable of the Good Samaritan is noticeably similar to that of the account of the Rich Young Ruler (Matthew 19:16-26; Mark 10:17-27; and Luke 18:18-27) with the inquiry: "what shall I do to inherit eternal life?" (Luke 10:25). Perhaps sensing this question from a "lawyer" (Luke 10:25) (νομικός) was rhetorical, Jesus asks him, "What is written in the law? how readest thou?" (Luke 10:26). Jesus affirmed the response to the summary of legal requirements by the lawyer: "Thou hast answered right: this do, and thou shalt live" (Luke 10:28). The word translated "right" is the Greek word ὀρθῶς from which we get the term "orthodox" or "orthodoxy." Orthodoxy, correct theology, was not the man's problem, it was obedience, as his follow-up question suggests: "But he, willing to justify himself, said unto Jesus, And who is my neighbour?" (Luke 10:29). The lawyer was attempting to sidetrack Jesus with a question about semantics.

Whatever Jesus was communicating, He was not saying that attitude could be substituted for action. The parable of the Good Samaritan that follows is bracketed by Jesus' use of the verb "to do" (ποιέω) in verse 28: "this do, and you will live," and verse 37: "Go, and do thou likewise." A subsidiary lesson from this parable is that one is to provide for the physical needs of anyone a person meets. The primary lesson is that perfect performance is a requirement for eternal life. As John Martin puts it: "The man's response should have been to ask, 'How can I do this? I am not able. I need help'" (John A. Martin, "Luke," in *The Bible Knowledge Commentary, New Testament*, ed. John F. Walvoord and Roy B. Zuck [Wheaton, IL: Victor, 1983; reprint, Colorado Springs: Cook, 1996], 234).

The parable of the Good Samaritan highlighted only one area of obedience. Jesus could have gone back to the first part of the lawyer's orthodox answer: "Thou shalt love the Lord thy God with all thy heart, and with all thy soul, and with all thy strength, and with all thy mind" (Luke 10:27). While parts of this requirement are mental, without a doubt, the inclusion of "with all thy strength" extends beyond the realm of attitude to that of action. It is impossible for man to meet the demands of sinless perfection. Deficiency in perfection is found in the particulars of performance.

Luke follows Jesus' words about "doing" in the parable of the Good Samaritan with an incident in which it appears that activity is disparaged. Jesus complimented Mary who "sat at Jesus' feet, and heard his word" (Luke 10:39), while He lovingly corrected Martha: "Martha, Martha, thou art careful and troubled about many things" (Luke 10:41). Jesus narrowed it down: "But one thing is needful" (Luke 10:42). Jesus said that what He said was the most important thing. Eternal life is found in the words of Jesus, not in any work that one may perform. Even work done on His behalf would not accomplish what belief in Him could do.

Luke Chapter 11

In Luke 11 Jesus cast out a demon that did not cry out His identity as on other occasions because "it was dumb" (Luke 11:14). The demon manifested itself in the man's being unable to speak: "And it came to pass, when the devil was gone out, the dumb spake" (Luke 11:14). While this demon itself does not offer evidence of Jesus' identity verbally, Luke mentions the presence of witnesses: "and the people wondered ["marveled" = NASB]" (Luke 11:14). Whether the demon identified Jesus or not the exorcism itself spoke volumes about who Jesus is.

Nobody who witnessed the exorcism denied that it happened, not even hostile witnesses who attributed the miracle to the devil: "But some of them said, He casteth out devils through Beelzebub the chief of the devils" (Luke 11:15). Jesus refuted them with logic. Why would the devil cast out those who were under his authority? Jesus' antagonists had colleagues who practiced exorcisms. Did His antagonists use the same logic with them? With a rhetorical conditional sentence Jesus said, "But if I with the finger of God cast out devils, no doubt the kingdom of God is come upon you" (Luke 11:20). If Jesus' exorcism was God's doing, then the kingdom of God was at hand and the presence of the king, in the person of Jesus Himself, could not be denied.

In worshiping God one is inclined to exalt what is connected to Him. With Jesus it can be a place, an object, or those who had an earthly relationship to Him. Mariolatry, the worship of Mary, Jesus' mother, which later became a major tenet of Roman Catholicism, was addressed and rejected by Him when it appeared in an incipient form, even during His earthly ministry: "one of the women in the crowd raised her voice, and said to Him, 'Blessed is the womb that bore You, and the breasts at which You nursed'" (Luke 11:27 NASB).

The woman's devotion was misdirected: "But he said, Yea rather, blessed *are* they that hear the word of God, and keep it" [italics in KJV] (Luke 11:28). Any earthly connection to Jesus, even that of His own mother, was superseded by a spiritual relationship with Him. Implicitly Jesus was identifying His own words with "the word of God" (τὸν λόγον τοῦ θεοῦ). To do what He said was equivalent to obeying God. Mary's position, while privileged, paled in comparison to that of Jesus, God's Son.

Jesus followed up the contrast between earthly and spiritual relationships with a contrast between acceptance and rejection of the kingdom and its King. Jesus introduced His comments, saying, "This is an evil generation: they seek a sign" (Luke 11:29). The "sign" (σημεῖον) sought was ostensibly for the purpose of rendering a verdict about who Jesus is, and what He was doing, in essence passing judgment on Him. Jesus turned the tables on them by saying that the only "sign" (σημεῖον) they would receive was one that would indict them at the judgment. Jonah's sudden appearance in a foreign land announced judgment against the inhabitants of the city of Nineveh. That type of sign, one of impending judgment, was what those who rejected Him had to look forward to: "For as Jonas was a sign unto the Ninevites, so shall also the Son of man be to this generation" (Luke 11:30).

Jesus thereby identified Himself as the One who would judge His antagonists. The kingdom, and Jesus Himself as its visible central figure, the King/Messiah, referred to with His self-identification as "the Son of Man" (Luke 11:30), would be the basis on which a verdict "at the judgment" (Luke 11:32) would be rendered. At that future tribunal those who rejected the kingdom and its King could expect to have testimony introduced from surprise witnesses. The unlikely and unexpected witnesses for the prosecution would be Gentiles, taken from two Old Testament settings.

The "queen of the south" (Luke 11:31) considered Solomon to be important enough for Gentile royalty to travel a great distance, "she came from the utmost parts of the earth to hear the wisdom of Solomon" (Luke 11:31) in person. Jonah's words of impending judgment were accepted by Gentile Ninevites as a message from God and "The men of Nineve[h] shall rise up in the judgment with this generation, and shall condemn it: for they repented at the preaching of Jonas[h]" (Luke 11:32). The testimony of the acceptance of Solomon and Jonah's words by Gentiles, made the rejection of the kingdom and Jesus by Jewish religious leaders all the more egregious.

Also their rejection would leave them without excuse because something more spectacular was going on in their day than in the days of Solomon and Jonah. Regarding Solomon, Jesus said, "a greater than Solomon *is* here" [italics in KJV] (Luke 11:31). Likewise for Jonah, "a greater than Jonas[h] *is* here" [italics in KJV] (Luke 11:32). It should be noted that Jesus regularly stated the acceptance/rejection option in terms of the kingdom, and not His person, although implicitly He was included. Even though it was articulated in terms of the kingdom, He was the primary sign of its arrival, and often a mention of the kingdom was not meant to exclude its King. As John Martin states, "That something was the kingdom of God, present in the person of Jesus" (John A. Martin, "Luke," in *The Bible Knowledge Commentary, New Testament*, ed. John F. Walvoord and Roy B. Zuck [Wheaton, IL: Victor, 1983; reprint, Colorado Springs: Cook, 1996], 236). Here in Luke 11:31 and 32 "a greater" is probably an inclusive reference to the kingdom as a program and a person, its King, as well.

Luke Chapter 12

Implicitly Jesus confirmed the significance of His identity when He asserted that the consequence for those confessing or denying Him on earth would be confession or denial, respectively, of them in heaven: "Whosoever shall confess me before men, him shall the Son of man also confess before the angels of God: but he that denieth me before men shall be denied before the angels of God" (Luke 12:8-9). The translation possibilities given by Louw and Nida in their lexicon for the verb "to confess" (ὁμολογέω) are "profess," "admit," and "declare" (Johannes P. Louw and Eugene A. Nida, *Greek-English Lexicon of the New Testament Based on Semantic Domains*, 2nd ed. [New York: United Bible Societies, 2nd ed], 1989, 1:413, 419, and 420). The One whom the confession, profession, admission, or declaration "before men" (Luke 12:8) was to be about was "me," a reference to Himself, that is, Jesus.

Bible students have debated whether this confession and denial is a requirement or a disqualifying factor, for eternal life or if it is related to the postconversion experience. Some see a parallel between this passage and Romans 10:9, "if thou shalt confess with thy mouth the Lord Jesus," as both presenting a requirement for eternal life. Romans 10:9 has been discussed in chapter 2, "Exegetical Eye-Openers," where it was shown to refer unambiguously to a postconversion experience. Perhaps with the reference to "the angels of God" (Luke 12:9), Jesus was referring to the future, throughout endless ages, when in heaven He would delight in telling the holy angels about the exploits of those who had placed their trust in Him. Perhaps Jesus was telling His audience, in effect, "You need to do what will give me something to talk about to God's angels in heaven."

In Luke 12, contextually, there is an emphasis on speech. Verse 10 has "whosoever shall speak a word against the Son of Man" and then "him that blasphemeth," which was done verbally. Verse 11 continues with "take ye no thought how or what thing ye shall answer, or what ye shall say," and verse 12 concludes with the words "for the Holy Ghost shall teach you in the same hour what ye ought to say." The Greek word translated "ye shall answer" (Luke 12:11) (ἀπολογήσησθε), in its immediate context, meant giving testimony in and to "the synagogues and *unto* magistrates, and powers" [italics in KJV] (Luke 12:11). Jesus addressed these words to the twelve disciples, who, with the exception of Judas Iscariot, would have experiences as described, giving testimony under duress as eyewitnesses of what and whom they had seen and heard.

In Luke 12:31 Jesus said, "But rather seek ye the kingdom of God; and all these things shall be added unto you." As in Matthew 6:33, believers are not to be frantically concerned about earthly material things but seek the advancement of God's kingdom. God promises to provide the necessities of life. Believers are not to live in dread but in dependence on God. Jesus says, "Fear not, little flock; for it is your Father's good pleasure to give you the kingdom" (Luke 12:32). Just as the Father gives to "the ravens" (Luke 12:24), that "neither sow nor reap," "the lilies" (Luke 12:27) that "neither toil or spin" (Luke 12:27), He will likewise do for them. Jesus said that "it is your Father's good pleasure to give you the kingdom" (Luke 12:32). Ultimately believers do not need to live in fear because their eternal salvation is indeed a free gift. "It is your Father's good pleasure to give you the kingdom" (Luke 12:32).

Louw and Nida define "good pleasure" (εὐδοκέω) "to be pleased with something or someone, with the implication of resulting pleasure" (Johannes P. Louw and Eugene A. Nida, *Greek-English Lexicon of the New Testament Based on Semantic Domains*, 2nd ed. [New York: United Bible Societies, 2nd ed], 1989, 1:299). It is the same Greek verb used in Matthew 3:17 for the voice of God the Father out of heaven which declared of Jesus, "This is My beloved Son, in whom I am well pleased." The same Greek verb is found in Mark 1:11 where the same incident, Jesus' baptism, is described. God derives pleasure from providing for His children who depend on Him and in granting salvation to those who believe in Him.

Believers can confidently obey Jesus' words, "Sell that ye have, and give alms" (Luke 12:33). Are possessions the price of paradise? Is heaven earned by hard work? Some would respond in the affirmative, or sort of. They think that, either the actions of verse 33 are required for eternal life, or, that selling your possessions and giving the proceeds to the poor is not really the price that has to be paid for heaven, but that the willingness to do so is what counts. But what did Jesus say? "Sell" and "give." He certainly meant more than just to "put it up for sale," or "put it on Craig's List." Both of the verbs "sell" (Πωλήσατε) and "give" (δότε) are imperatives–they are commands. Integrity demands that these imperatives not be watered down to fit a theology, or an agenda. The desire to do good is admirable, but is not an acceptable substitute for action. These are instructions for believers, not requirements for eternal life.

Jesus did have something to say in this context about desire, but it is the opposite of what some might propose. The right desire is not the requirement, but rather the result of doing what is required. Jesus said, "For where your treasure is, there will your heart be also" (Luke 12:34). He did not say, "where your heart is (where your "willingness" or your "desire" are) there will your treasure be also." Accumulating treasure in heaven requires action which will transform attitude, not the reverse.

Luke Chapter 13

In Luke 13:23 Jesus is asked a crucial question by an anonymous inquirer: "Lord, are there few that be saved?" Apparently Jesus' words about the kingdom had not given this individual much hope. On the one hand He had said, "it is your Father's good pleasure to give you the kingdom" (Luke 12:32). On the other hand, there were difficult things that God asked of an obedient believer. Jesus' response was less than encouraging: "Strive to enter in at the strait gate" (Luke 13:24).

Three things Jesus said stand out. The first is His use of the word "strive" (ἀγωνίζομαι). Louw and Nida give three possibilities for the meaning of this word, all of which are hard: (1) "to engage in intense struggle, involving physical or nonphysical force against strong opposition–'to struggle, to fight'"; (2) "to compete in an athletic contest, with emphasis on effort–'to compete, to struggle'" (3) "to strive to do something with great intensity and effort–'to make every effort to, to do everything possible to, to strain oneself to'" (Johannes P. Louw and Eugene A. Nida, Greek-English Lexicon of the New Testament Based on Semantic Domains, 2nd ed. [New York: United Bible Societies, 2nd ed], 1989, 1:496, 528, 663). Louw and Nida use Luke 13:24 as an example of the third usage. What Jesus commanded required "great intensity and effort." Jesus could not have stated it more strongly than He did.

The second word "narrow" (στενός) compounded the inquirer's discouragement, implying restricted access. The stern reason Jesus gave for striving and squeezing, as it were, through the narrow entrance, made it even worse: "for many, I say unto you, will seek to enter in, and shall not be able" (Luke 13:24). Obviously Jesus was speaking figuratively. Physical fitness is not a prerequisite for eternal life. Nor is physical exertion a requirement for the journey to heaven. Physical squeezing through a restricted opening is not how eternal salvation is accessed.

Mental gymnastics are required. Whatever is necessary must be done to work through the evidence for the identity of Jesus. Lingering doubts must be dealt with. Saints of the past have recounted the wrestling that has gone on in their minds, over the claims of Christ. The metaphorical passage is narrow because there is only one way and only one person in whom trust must be placed for eternal life. The inability of some was due to their rejection of the only way, and the only person who could grant them eternal salvation.

Jesus also had words that did not bode well for His audience. There was a "window of opportunity" they needed to take advantage of: "When once the master of the house is risen up, and hath shut to the door, and ye begin to stand without, and to knock at the door, saying, Lord, Lord, open unto us; and he shall answer and say unto you, I know you not whence ye are" (Luke 13:25). The statement, "I know not whence ye are" is repeated again in verse 27.

Jesus' audience, who took pride in their Jewish origin, would find that their ancestry would not grant them entrance into the kingdom. When He made reference to their origin a second time, Jesus added the words: "Depart from me, all *ye* workers of iniquity" [italics in KJV] (Luke 13:27). This was a quotation from Psalm 6:8: "Depart from me, all ye workers of iniquity; for the Lord hath heard the voice of my weeping." In Psalm 6 David was calling out to God about his enemies. For Jesus to imply that those in the audience being denied entrance to the kingdom could be referred to as God's enemies would have been difficult for them to accept.

When Jesus spoke positively of those granted entrance in the kingdom He did mention the Jewish patriarchs and prophets: "There shall be weeping and gnashing of teeth, when ye shall see Abraham, and Isaac, and Jacob, and all the prophets, in the kingdom of God, and you *yourselves* thrust out" [italics in KJV] (Luke 13:28). Jesus then unexpectedly included those who were not Jews as those who would enter: "And they shall come from the east, and *from* the west, and from the north, and *from* the south, and shall sit down in the kingdom of God" [italics in KJV] (Luke 13:29). That was not supposed to happen.

Another surprise would be in store for some: "And, behold, there are last which shall be first, and there are first which shall be last" (Luke 13:30). In the context of entrance/ denial of entrance, it is probably best to understand those who "are last who will be first" as those granted entrance, and those who "are first who will be last" as those refused entry into the kingdom. The "first" ($\pi\rho\tilde{\omega}\tau$οι) are those who think they are first in line and think of themselves as those who will make it in, and the "last" ($\check{\epsilon}\sigma\chi\alpha\tau$οι) are those thought of as least likely candidates for the kingdom, who will make it in. Taking the context into consideration this is preferable to taking the "first" ($\pi\rho\tilde{\omega}\tau$οι) and "last" ($\check{\epsilon}\sigma\chi\alpha\tau$οι) as both having entered the kingdom and their reversal as referring to a hierarchical readjustment taking place between them.

The question arises whether being denied kingdom entrance is on the basis of works because they are called "evildoers" (ἐργάται ἀδικίας). Some supporters would say that this is confirmation of "perseverance of the saints." In their view an "evildoer" is one whose life is characterized by sin, proved perhaps by a preponderance of the evidence. It might reasonably be asked what percentage of perfection must be attained to prevent being categorized an "evildoer" (ἐργάται ἀδικίας). Is there is a 99 percent plan, or would 51 percent suffice? The Bible does recognize relative perfection, as with the use of the Greek adjective τέλειος to describe maturity. Scripture never uses relative perfection in the context of the acquisition of eternal life, in fact, it expressly excludes it.

During His time on earth Jesus lived a life of sinless perfection, which qualified Him as the perfect substitute to die for the sins of men. He did not preach relative perfection as a path to entrance into the kingdom. The apostle Paul, referring to the Jews, which would include those present during the ministry of Jesus, described them with these words: "For they being ignorant of God's righteousness, and going about to establish their own righteousness, have not submitted themselves unto the righteousness of God" (Romans 10:3). In Luke 13 Jesus was addressing the issue of entrance or denial of entrance into the kingdom, and in that context denial of entrance is based on the words: "I know you not whence ye are; depart from me, all *ye* workers of iniquity" [italics in KJV] (Luke 13:27). Their credentials, who they were and what they had done, were unacceptable for kingdom access. Origin speaks of the issue of ownership and iniquity to their need of Christ as the perfect substitute, which those who were rejected, did not have.

Luke Chapter 14

Luke 14:25-35 is a passage with implications for sanctification and discipleship. The passage begins with the requirement "If any *man* come to me, and hate not his father, and mother, and wife, and children, and brethren, and sisters, yea, and his own life also, he cannot be my disciple" [italics in KJV] (Luke 14:26). This appears to contradict the second most important commandment to: "Thou shalt love thy neighbour as thyself" (Matthew 22:39), also found in Mark (Mark 12:31), unless it is argued that "neighbour" (πλησίον) excludes family members. Both record Jesus quoting Leviticus 19:18 "but thou shalt love thy neighbor as thyself." The contradiction with numerous passages such as Ephesians 5:25: "Husbands, love your wives," and I John 4:7: "Beloved, let us love one another," are problematic.

Of course, Jesus' requirement for being His disciple is regularly interpreted as E. W. Bullinger did, more than a century ago. Bullinger used the verse in question as an example where he labeled it as "Hyperbole; or, Exaggeration" (Bullinger, *Figures of Speech Used in the Bible: Explained and Illustrated*, 426). Bullinger wrote that Luke 14:26 means, "does not esteem them less than me. So the verb *to hate* is used" [italics in original] and saw two parallels. The first, Genesis 29:31, "the Lord saw that Leah *was* hated," [italics in KJV] where the Hebrew uses the verb "hate" (שָׂנֵא). The second parallel is Romans 9:13: "Jacob have I loved, but Esau have I hated," where Paul quotes Malachi 1:2-3. Malachi 1:2 ends with, "yet I loved Jacob," and Malachi 1:3 begins with, "and I hated Esau," again, the prophet using the Hebrew verb "hate" (שָׂנֵא).

It is virtually universally recognized that the requirement Jesus gave for discipleship in Luke 14:26 was hyperbole, a recognized figure of speech. The literal application, as Bullinger observes, is that one must esteem those closest to himself as less than Jesus in order to be His disciple. This requirement is not to be *willing* to esteem those closest to oneself as less than Jesus, but to actually do so. The requirement is for discipleship, that is, sanctification, not salvation.

Jesus continued with the requirements for being His disciple in Luke 14:27: "And whosoever doth not bear his cross, and come after me, cannot be my disciple." Whatever "bear his cross" means, it is not meant to be taken literally, but is a metaphor, that would certainly include what would be categorized as "works." It is not a "desire" or a "willingness" to do so, but rather to actually do whatever it entails. Jesus included no qualifier or caveat to justify replacing the requirement for discipleship from an activity to an attitude.

Jesus then talks about taking mental stock of the cost involved before beginning on the discipleship path. The first illustration He gives was that of construction: "For which of you, intending to build a tower, sitteth not down first, and counteth the cost, whether he have *sufficient* to finish *it*?" [italics in KJV] (Luke 14:28). To commence and not complete a project was to open oneself up to those who would "mock" (ἐμπαίζω) (Luke 14:29).

The second illustration was of warfare: "Or what king, going to make war against another king, sitteth not down first, and consulteth whether he be able with ten thousand to meet him that cometh against him with twenty thousand?" (Luke 14:31). Defeat, not merely derision, could be the result of a failure to count the cost. Recognizing the requirements beforehand was a prudent prerequisite before beginning to travel the road of discipleship. Jesus did not say that merely recognizing the requirements, or even being willing to fulfill the requirements, was an acceptable replacement for meeting those rigorous requirements. The wise thing to do is "look before you leap."

Jesus began His two-part conclusion/application by reiterating the requirement for being His disciple when He challenged the Rich Young Ruler with, "So likewise, whosoever he be of you that forsaketh not all that he hath, he cannot be my disciple" (Luke 14:33). Was this application to be taken literally or figuratively? Jesus' requirement for those who would follow Him physically, during His ministry, was no less than the abandonment of their material assets.

Jesus used figurative language to explain what He meant, but the application was to be understood and acted on literally. To take what Jesus required of them and to convert it into a watered-down solution, and mix it so that it is given soteriological significance, is to do violence to the text, make a travesty of the gospel, and produce a veritable theological witch's brew. The applicational question, contextualized for us today, one that is true to the text, is this: "What does Jesus ask of you, and of me, who are believers, to follow in obedience to Him?"

Luke Chapter 15

In chapter 15 of Luke are found the three parables of the Lost Sheep, the Lost Coin, and the Lost Son. J. Vernon McGee calls them "three pictures in a single frame" (*Thru the Bible with J. Vernon McGee* [Nashville: Thomas Nelson Publishers, 1983], 4:312). It appears that these three parables go together because they are all three about something lost. However, the consensus notwithstanding, these three parables are better taken as the first three members of a parable quartet. It begins in Luke 15:1 and ends with Luke 16:17. As will be shown, this helps in understanding the Parable of the Unjust Servant, the fourth member of the quartet, which is notoriously difficult to interpret because of Jesus' commendation of its undeniably dishonest main character. If the objection is raised that the Parable of the Unjust Servant or Unjust Steward is not to be included because it is preceded by the words, "and he said also unto his disciples" (Luke 16:1) in Luke 16:14 it says, "And the Pharisees also, who were covetous, heard all these things: and they derided him." They progressed from grumbling (Luke 15:2) to scoffing or sneering at Him (Luke 16:14).

Jesus' parables are introduced with the words, "Then drew near unto him all the publicans and sinners for to hear him" (Luke 15:1). The occasion was a meal, which prompted a reaction: "And the Pharisees and scribes murmured, saying, This man receiveth sinners, and eateth with them" (Luke 15:2). In the religious system of the Pharisees and the scribes, tax-gatherers and sinners were devalued and discarded, and Jesus' association with them, in the mind of the Jewish leaders, justified their rejection of Him.

Jesus dressed down "the Pharisees and the scribes" with four parables. In the first parable, that of the Lost Sheep, is a contrast between the grumbling of the religious leaders and the rejoicing of the shepherd with his friends and neighbors. The lost sheep that is found comprises merely one percent of the flock, yet Jesus' antagonists would have had to concede the value of even one percent to the shepherd.

The conclusion to the first parable is a not-so-veiled condemnation of the Pharisees and the scribes who represented "ninety and nine just persons, which need no repentance" (Luke 15:7). For the sake of argument Jesus went along with the assumption that they had no need to repent. Their erroneous assumption prevented them from the repentance they did indeed need. The greater joy experienced in heaven over the one compared with the ninety-nine was not to be taken as a measure of the relative value of a recent convert as opposed to those already saved, but was meant to elicit a reassessment by the Pharisees and scribes of their own eternal standing.

Many believe that in the Parable of the Lost Sheep the ninety-nine were already saved, but that was not the case. The ninety-nine only thought they were saved, and Jesus was comparing them to the antagonistic Pharisees and scribes. The lost sheep represented the tax-gatherers and sinners with whom Jesus was having a meal, so that He could rescue them from their sins and give them eternal salvation. With this parable Jesus was drawing his antagonists in. No one would begrudge the rescue of a single lost sheep, but they were grumbling about Jesus doing exactly that. This interpretation helps answer why it might seem inappropriate that there was no celebration over the ninety-nine.

In the second parable, that of the Lost Coin, ten percent, one of ten coins, has been lost. This time the subject is a search and subsequent find, which again elicits elation: "Rejoice with me; for I have found the piece which I had lost" (Luke 15:9). In the first two parables of this quartet no evidence supports the idea that either the lost sheep or the lost coin did anything that accounted for or facilitated their being found. Again, in keeping with the context, the nine coins correspond to the Pharisees and the scribes, whereas the one lost coin represented the low-life tax-gatherers and sinners.

The third parable, that of the Lost Son, or more familiarly known as the Parable of the Prodigal Son, also has something, this time someone, who was lost. The son who got to the point where he wished he could eat like a pig, represented the tax-gatherers and sinners, with whom Jesus was engaged in evangelism. The angry brother corresponded to the grumbling Pharisees and scribes, who were upset about how well those who they looked down on were being treated. The Pharisees and the Scribes thought that they were saved, but were in fact lost.

The justification that the elder son gave for his bad attitude was: "Lo, these many years do I serve thee, neither transgressed I at any time thy commandment" (Luke 15:29). The lost son figured that he would make the transition from the pigpen to the penthouse by working for his father: "make me as one of thy hired servants" (Luke 15:19). Those were the terms on which he figured he could return. But his father would have none of it. The father's mind was made up long before, not during, or after, they met. No terms of employment. No probation period. Not a peep about work, or what his son had been up to: "But the father said to his servants, Bring forth the best robe, and put *it* on him; and put a ring on his hand, and shoes on *his* feet" [italics in KJV] (Luke 15:22). A robe would mean that everyone would know he was the master's son, and a ring and sandals would mean he could follow everywhere his father went.

Luke Chapter 16

Then Jesus told a fourth parable. This one does not seem to fit the pattern of the previous three, but it is to be included with them. The lost son is described in the previous parable as having "wasted" (Luke 15:13) (διασκορπίζω) everything he had been given from his father's estate. Jesus used the same Greek verb "waste" or "squander" (διασκορπίζω), to describe what the unjust steward did in the fourth parable with what his master had entrusted to him: "There was a certain rich man, which had a steward; and the same was accused unto him that he had wasted his goods" (Luke 16:1).

The unjust steward was lost–no doubt about it. And he was shrewd. When he learned he was about to be fired, he made sure he got on the good side of his boss' debtors, by changing their debt totals, so that he would have somewhere to land, when the inevitable happened. Sure enough, he got fired. Amazingly, the boss said, in effect, "Good move": "And the lord commended the unjust steward, because he had done wisely: for the children of this world are in their generation wiser than the children of light" (Luke 16:8). Up until now, in these four parables, the word "righteous" or "unrighteous" had not been used. Now Jesus introduced the latter, and used it in His application of the parable: "And I say unto you, Make to yourselves friends of the mammon of unrighteousness; that, when ye fail, they may receive you into everlasting habitations" (Luke 16:9). Of course, it is not the intent of this parable to advise the unsaved to prepare their way for a future in hell.

In his wrap up with Pharisees who were mocking Jesus, He characterized them with these words: "Ye are they which justify yourselves [declare yourselves righteous] before men; but God knoweth your hearts: for that which is highly esteemed among men is abomination in the sight of God" (Luke 16:15). The verdict of their self-assessment, based on what people outwardly observed, was that they were innocent. The Pharisees' self-justification by works needed to be replaced by what only God could offer.

The Pharisees had developed a truncated version of God's requirements for entrance into His kingdom, and they wrongly assumed that because they had met them, they would be granted admittance. Jesus affirmed that the Law was still the standard, by first saying that: "The law and the prophets *were* until John" [italics in KJV] (Luke 16:16), and then after mentioning that: "since that time the kingdom of God is preached" (Luke 16:16). Jesus also said that "it is easier for heaven and earth to pass, than one tittle of the law to fail" (Luke 16:17). The Greek verb translated "fail" (from the aorist active infinitive of πίπτω = literally, "to fall") should be understood figuratively to mean either "to come to an end" or "to become inadequate" (Johannes P. Louw and Eugene A. Nida, *Greek-English Lexicon of the New Testament Based on Semantic Domains*, 2nd ed. [New York: United Bible Societies, 2nd ed], 1989, 1:160 and 680).

Interestingly, inserted between Jesus' statements about the Law, when He mentions that "the kingdom of God is preached" (Luke 16:16), He adds, "and every man presseth into it" (Luke 16:16). The Greek verb translated "presseth into" (from the third person, singular, present, middle or passive indicative of βιάζομαι) means "suffer violence" or "use violence." In this context Jesus may have been referring to trying to enter the kingdom by whatever means, such as the Pharisees' misguided attempts. The unjust servant is a parabolic example of one attempting, by whatever means he can, however unscrupulous, to secure his future.

This Greek verb is found only twice in the New Testament, here and in Matthew 11:12, and has been notoriously difficult to understand. However it is understood, it should not be taken to mean that work is a requirement for obtaining eternal salvation. That would be counter to the parables in the immediate context particularly that of the Lost Son, or Prodigal Son, whose offer to work was rejected by his father.

Jesus followed up His statement about the permanence of the Law, expanding the seventh commandment of the Decalogue, "Thou shalt not commit adultery" (Exodus 20:14), with the words, "Whosoever putteth away his wife, and marrieth another, committeth adultery: and whosoever marrieth her that is put away from *her* husband committeth adultery" [italics in KJV] (Luke 16:18). The Pharisees and the scribes (Luke 15:2), the tax-gatherers and sinners (Luke 15:1), as well as the disciples (Luke 16:1), who are mentioned as being present, would have all been astounded at these authoritative words, which spoke to the identity of this individual who could Himself expand the existing Law and not merely expound it.

Luke chapter 16 concludes with the Parable of the Rich Man and Lazarus that provides insight into the afterlife and human destiny. After death the no longer rich man, in his anguish, implores Abraham to send the previously poor man Lazarus to warn his five brothers, so that they will not meet with the same fate: "For I have five brethren; that he may testify unto them, lest they also come into this place of torment" (Luke 16:28). The verb translated "he may testify" (present, either middle or passive, subjunctive, third person, singular, from διαμαρτύρομαι = "testify," or "insist," or "warn") is a compound Greek verb with the prefixed preposition (δια) which serves to intensify the verb (μαρτυρέω) = "witness" or "speak well of." Only here in Luke 16:28 does Luke use this compound verb in his Gospel. However, he does use it nine times in the book of Acts (Acts 2:40; 8:25; 10:42; 18:5; 20:21, 23, 24; 23:11; and 28:23). The KJV consistently translates διαμαρτύρομαι in both Luke 16:28 and in Acts with "testify."

The rich man in the parable wanted Abraham to send Lazarus with a message, in essence "testify" to his living brothers, no doubt about the reality of the afterlife, and the agony that awaited them, if they were to continue on their present course as he had. The idea that a message to be believed is in view is supported by Abraham's reply: "They have Moses and the prophets; let them hear them" (Luke 16:29), which was written testimony, as well as his use of the verb "persuaded" (πεισθήσονται from πείθω = "to persuade") in Abraham's clinching remark, "neither will they be persuaded, though one rose from the dead" (Luke 16:31). Moses and the prophets all testified about who the one true God is, and that He required faith from man. Abraham's post-death pronouncement about unbelief, in spite of someone rising from the dead, foreshadowed the resurrection of Jesus which some people would likewise reject.

Luke Chapter 17

In Luke 17 there is an intriguing interchange between Jesus and His disciples. In response to Jesus' expansion of forgiveness: "And if he trespass against thee seven times in a day, and seven times in a day turn again to thee, saying, I repent; thou shalt forgive him" (Luke 17:4), the disciples appear to say in consternation: "Increase our faith" (Luke 17:5). Jesus' response to their request has been variously understood. John Martin says, "When the disciples asked Jesus for more **faith,** He answered that they needed not more faith but the right kind of faith. Even the smallest amount of faith (like **a mustard seed,** the smallest seed; cf. 13:19) could do amazingly miraculous things" [bold and parenthesis in original] (John A. Martin, "Luke," in *The Bible Knowledge Commentary, New Testament,* ed. John F. Walvoord and Roy B. Zuck [Wheaton, IL: Victor, 1983; reprint, Colorado Springs: Cook, 1996], 248). Martin's interpretive comment: "the right kind of faith" is unsupported by the text or context.

More likely Jesus was responding that the disciples did not need their faith augmented, but rather that they needed faith, period. They needed to trust God. They either trusted Him or they did not. This was not a matter of a type of trust, nor adding to what they already had, but rather simply relying on the One who could fulfill their request, to be able to forgive someone so extravagantly.

Without skipping a beat, in Luke's account, Jesus proceeds to discuss the relationship of a slave and his master. Perhaps Jesus was disabusing the disciples of the notion that faith could be used to grant whatever they desired. After all, He had said, "If ye had faith as a grain of mustard seed, ye might say unto this sycamine tree, Be thou plucked up by the root, and be thou planted in the sea; and it should obey you" (Luke 17:6). But that would reverse the relationship. They were to serve God, not vice versa, as Jesus' master/slave illustration demonstrated. Their attitude was to be: "We are unprofitable servants: we have done that which was our duty to do" (Luke 17:10).

In the account of the healing of the ten lepers there is an interesting use of the Greek word σῴζω, which can mean "to rescue," "to save," or "to heal." In His "goodbye" Jesus told the one cleansed leper who returned in gratitude: "Arise, go thy way: thy faith hath made thee whole" (Luke 17:19). The NASB translates σῴζω with "made...well," but does indicate in the margin the alternative "has saved you." One indication the latter may be the preferred translation is Luke's use of the word "cleansed" (ἐκαθαρίσθησαν aorist passive indicative from καθαρίζω = "to make clean") when he initially tells of the miracle: "And it came to pass, that, as they went, they were cleansed" (Luke 17:14). Even though the use of a different Greek verb σῴζω in verse 19 may be due to the nature of their ailment being emphasized in the prior verb, or that Jesus may have been employing stylistic variation, it appears something more was going on with the healed leper who returned.

Of significance is the contextual contrast between the nine who were healed and did not return, and the man who was also healed and did return to thank Jesus. Also what they experienced was not identical. When the one cleansed man who returned "with a loud voice glorifyied God" (Luke 17:15), but the nine did not: "There are not found that returned to give glory to God" (Luke 17:18). An additional distinction is made explicit by Luke in his editorial comment about the man who returned: "and he was a Samaritan" (Luke 17:16), as well as the fact that Jesus took note of that fact about the returnee, by adding, "save [except] this stranger" (Luke 17:18).

Furthermore the contrast between the nine and the one is accentuated by Jesus explicitly attributing faith to this latter individual at a point in time after the physical healing. If the grateful one had faith, and the neglectful nine did not, it is reasonable to understand that the "saving" the latter experienced, was eternal salvation, which was more than the physical healing they all received.

Also, if Jesus was understood by those who witnessed this event as pronouncing the eternal salvation of this leper, it would be in keeping with Luke's primary theme of presenting the identity of the Messiah. Who was this One, who could state that eternal salvation had been received? Even if it was not understood that way by those present at the time, Luke, and Jesus' intent, may well have been that those who read and heard this account later would "connect the dots," and recognize it as evidence that confirmed His messianic identity.

The subject of "the kingdom of God" (ἡ βασιλεία τοῦ θεοῦ) was in the minds of many, including the Pharisees who asked Jesus about its timing. Jesus' response was that its appearance would be sudden and subtle: "The kingdom of God cometh not with observation: Neither shall they say, Lo here! or, lo there! for, behold, the kingdom of God is within you" (Luke 17:20-21). The words translated "is within you" in the KJV are probably best understood as the NASB "is in your midst" (Luke 17:21). The latter translation seems likely because Jesus' answer is in reply to the Pharisees who were unsaved.

This is more likely an enigmatic reference to Jesus' presence as the primary representative of that kingdom. This interpretation is reinforced by the immediate inclusion of one of Jesus' favorite self-designations, "the Son of Man" (Luke 17:22) (τοῦ υἱοῦ τοῦ ἀνθρώπου). Those words are directed to the disciples who had the temporary privilege of His personal presence: "The days will come, when ye shall desire to see one of the days of the Son of man, and ye shall not see *it*" [italics in KJV] (Luke 17:22).

Luke Chapter 18

In the Parable of the Widow and the Judge (Luke 18:1-8) Jesus used a dissimilar comparison between God and the judge to encourage persistence in prayer. After making the comparison explicit, Jesus asked, "when the Son of man cometh, shall he find faith on the earth?" (Luke 18:8). While it may be that the question was rhetorical and remained unanswered purposely, the parable that follows in Luke, the Pharisee and the tax-gatherer, explains what that "faith" (τὴν πίστιν) looks like.

Luke alerted his readers/listeners that He was about to illustrate faith by describing Jesus' audience: "And he spake this parable unto certain which trusted in themselves that they were righteous, and despised others" (Luke 18:9). The issue having eternal consequences was what, or in whom, one placed his/her confidence and reliance. To express this Luke used the perfect form of the Greek verb πειθώ which can have the meaning "trust" that corresponds with the meaning of "trust" present in the semantic range of the noun "faith" (πίστις) used in the immediately preceding verse (Luke 18:8). The Greek verb πειθώ can also mean "obey," but not in the perfect tense, which is what

is used here, which means "trust." As Louw and Nida state, "πείθω (perf. stem only). .
.to believe in something or someone to the extent of placing reliance or trust in or on—
'to rely on, to trust in, to depend on, to have (complete) confidence in, confidence,
trust'" (Johannes P. Louw and Eugene A. Nida, *Greek-English Lexicon of the New
Testament Based on Semantic Domains*, 2nd ed. [New York: United Bible Societies,
2nd ed], 1989, 1:376).

This parable is bracketed with Luke's use of the adjective "righteous" (Luke 18:9)
(δίκαιος) in his introductory comment, and Jesus' conclusion that the tax-gatherer was
"justified" (δεδικαιωμένος perfect passive participle from δικαιόω = "to declare
righteous" or "to acquit") (Luke 18:14). The Pharisee, one of those who "trusted in
themselves that they were righteous" (Luke 18:9) had confidence in their self-
declaration of righteousness, rather than a declaration that was received from God on
the basis of trust in Him: "God, be merciful to me a sinner" (Luke 18:13). The tax-
gatherer put his trust in a merciful God to solve his sin problem, whereas the Pharisee
saw himself as the solution for his sin. The former's faith showed humility, the latter
exemplified pride. The tax-gatherer knew he as a sinner, and knew who the one and
only true God was, in whom he placed his trust. Jesus' authoritative declaration
pointed to His identity: "I tell you, this man went down to his house justified *rather
than the other*" [italics in KJV] (Luke 18:14). Who but God could know such a thing?

As in the other two Synoptic Gospels, Matthew (Matthew 19:13-15) and Mark (Mark
10:13-16), Luke includes an account of Jesus and some children (Luke 18:15-17). Luke
did not explicitly give a reason, what it was that the parents expected. He only says,
"And they brought unto him also infants, that he would touch them" (Luke 18:15). The
term translated by the NASB with "infants" (βρέφοις) denotes very young children.
When Jesus drew an application from His actions, He used the word normally
translated "child" (Luke 18:17) (παιδίον) which Louw and Nida understand as a child
"normally below the age of puberty" (Johannes P. Louw and Eugene A. Nida, Greek-
English Lexicon of the New Testament Based on Semantic Domains, 2nd ed. [New
York: United Bible Societies, 2nd ed], 1989, 1:110).

Jesus' said, "Verily I say unto you, Whosoever shall not receive the kingdom of God as
a little child shall in no wise enter therein" (Luke 18:17). Whatever Jesus was saying
appears to rule out complexity in the requirement for entrance into the kingdom of
God. Children are capable of exercising what the two ideas germane to eternal
salvation require, which are within the semantic range of "faith" (πίστις): "belief that
something is true" and "trust in a person or thing." On the word of Jesus Christ
Himself, not only are children capable of fulfilling the condition required for eternal
salvation, but everyone who enters must receive the kingdom of God "as a little child"
(Luke 18:17) (ὡς παιδίον), that is, in the same manner.

Luke's Gospel includes the account of the Rich Young Ruler (Luke 18:18-27) just as
Matthew (Matthew 19:16-26) and Mark (Mark 10:17-27) do. What was written when
commenting on Matthew and Mark apply here as well. In addition to the commentary
there, it was not mentioned there that in those two earlier Synoptic accounts (Matthew

19:25; Mark 10:26), and here in Luke as well, the audience hearing the parable asked Jesus, "Who then who can be saved?" (Luke 18:26). His response was, "The things which are impossible with men are possible with God" (Luke 18:27). The conclusion that must be drawn from this exchange is not that all the young man had to do was to "sell all that thou hast, and distribute unto the poor" (Luke 18:22). He could have done that. Nor does it mean as some would have it, that he should "be willing to sell...and willing to distribute." Instead the idea is that the requirement for eternal salvation required something above and beyond the rich young man's ability to perform.

In Luke 18:28-30 Peter reacted to Jesus' words following the encounter with the Rich Young Ruler, and His response to the disciples was that they would be rewarded for the sacrifices they made. Jesus' paraphrased Peter's reaction about the disciples' having "left all, and followed thee" (Luke 18:28) with: "left house, or parents, or brethren, or wife, or children" (Luke 18:29), and added the words, "for the kingdom of God's sake" (Luke 18:29). Louw and Nida give this Greek word translated "sake" (ἕνεκεν) the meaning, "a marker of cause or reason, often with the implication of purpose in the sense of 'for the sake of'—'on account of, because of'" (Johannes P. Louw and Eugene A. Nida, *Greek-English Lexicon of the New Testament Based on Semantic Domains*, 2nd ed. [New York: United Bible Societies, 2nd ed], 1989, 1:781).

Sacrificially following Jesus was doing something for God's kingdom and would be rewarded: "who shall not receive manifold more in this present time, and in the world to come life everlasting" (Luke 18:30). Eternal life would not be earned by doing those things, but would be the glorious destiny of those who had sacrificed so much in life. Delayed gratification would result in eternal glory. Jesus was not threatening them that if they did not sacrificially leave earthly relationships they would forfeit heaven, but rather that everything they were doing was worthwhile.

In all three Synoptic Gospels are found the prophetic words Jesus spoke about His own upcoming death and resurrection (Matthew 20:17-19; Mark 10:32-34; and Luke 18:31-34). "For he shall be delivered unto the Gentiles, and shall be mocked, and spitefully entreated, and spitted on: and they shall scourge *him*, and put him to death: and the third day he shall rise again" [italics in KJV] (Luke 18:32-33). These prophetic words of Jesus are about the fulfillment of a prophecy. At stake was not only the veracity of Old Testament prophecies about the death and resurrection of the Messiah, but also His own prophetic words that He would fulfill.

The identity of Jesus was once again brought to the reader/listener's attention with the healing of blind Bartemaeus. It began with the noise of a crowd approaching, which the blind man heard, and asked a passerby about: "And they told him, that Jesus of Nazareth passeth by" (Luke 18:37). Evidently the blind beggar had heard of "Jesus of Nazareth" (Ἰησοῦς ὁ Ναζωραῖος), and who He was, so when he called out to Him, not being able to see, addressed Him with, "Jesus, *thou* Son of David, have mercy on me" [italics in KJV] (Luke 18:38). The blind beggar, having been told Jesus' earthly identity by the crowd, addressed Him with the messianic designation as David's descendant.

As the man was shouting toward Jesus, people tried to get the blind man to be quiet. Matthew's Gospel says it was "the multitude" (Matthew 20:31) (ὁ ὄχλος), while Mark's Gospel refers to them as "many" (Mark 10:48) (πολλοὶ). Luke says they were "they which went before" (Luke 18:39) (οἱ προάγοντες). They may well have been some of the disciples, who were clearing the way for their Master, and in an act of misguided service, attempted to prevent the man whom they saw as a problem, from hindering their progress. We are not told whether Jesus could hear the man when he first called out. As the God-Man he could have chosen to hear him, even though the hubbub of the crowd may have drowned him out. Regardless, the effect of Jesus not responding to the blind beggar's initial call, with its messianic identification, resulted in his repeating it, this time more vociferously: "but he cried so much the more, *Thou* Son of David, have mercy on me" [italics in KJV] (Luke 18:39).

The iterative use of the imperfect tense, indicated by the NASB translation, "he kept crying out" (ἔκραζεν), indicates that the man was repeatedly crying out Jesus' messianic identity. While the repetition may or may not have been accompanied by an increase in volume, seen in the progression from "he cried" (Luke 18:38) (ἐβόησεν) to "he cried so much the more" (Luke 18:39) (ἔκραζεν), Louw and Nida say this about the latter use of "crying out" (κράζω): "to shout or cry out, with the possible implication of the unpleasant nature of the sound—'to shout, to scream'" (Johannes P. Louw and Eugene A. Nida, *Greek-English Lexicon of the New Testament Based on Semantic Domains*, 2nd ed. [New York: United Bible Societies, 2nd ed], 1989, 1:399). The context does include the possibility that he was irritating people.

After the blind beggar was healed, he became the pied piper of praise: "And immediately he received his sight, and followed him, glorifying God" (Luke 18:43). With that example, "and all the people, when they saw *it*, gave praise unto God" [italics in KJV] (Luke 18:43). While it may have been that those "glorifying God" (δοξάζων τὸν θεόν) and who "gave praise to God" (ἔδωκεν αἶνον τῷ θεῷ) were praising God for what He had done through Jesus, who in their mind was just a man, latter readers/listeners of these words would have understood that it was Jesus, identified by the blind beggar as the Messiah with the title "Son of David" (Luke 18:38 and 39) (υἱὲ Δαυίδ), who was Himself worthy of praise due only to God.

Luke Chapter 19

Luke's narration of Jesus' meeting with Zaccheus unambiguously refers to conversion with the noun "salvation" (Luke 19:9) (σωτηρία) and the verb "save" (Luke 19:10) (σῶσαι–aorist active infinitive of σῴζω). Jesus gave a reason for His declaration: "This day is salvation come to this house" (Luke 19:9) with the words, "forsomuch as [because] he also is a son of Abraham" (Luke 19:9). The reason why "salvation" (σωτηρία) had come to Zaccheus, and his entire family, was not because of their Jewish ancestry. Zaccheus' position as "a son of Abraham" (υἱὸς Ἀβραάμ), with soteriological implications, is what Paul explained in Romans 4:16: "to that also which is of the faith of Abraham; who is the father of us all."

Zaccheus had become a true spiritual son of Abraham by faith in Jesus. That was the reason he received eternal salvation. Just before Jesus' words affirming the source of his conversion, Zaccheus had said, "Behold, Lord, the half of my goods I give to the poor; and if I have taken any thing from any man by false accusation, I restore *him* fourfold" [italics in KJV] (Luke 19:8). Jesus did not say that Zaccheus' promise of restitution was the cause of his salvation. Instead He said that his salvation was the result of his being a son of Abraham, which he obtained by faith in Jesus. Jesus ignored entirely Zaccheus' words about restitution.

Luke did not give details of the exact chronology of events. If the promise of restitution came before the conversion, Jesus in fact ignored it, and rightfully so, or He would have had to explain to Zaccheus that he (Zaccheus) was barking up the wrong tree. For those who try to make restitution, or the willingness or a promise of such a condition for conversion, Jesus missed a golden opportunity to make that explicit. If Zaccheus' promise of restitution came after he put his trust in Jesus for salvation, restitution would be an effect, a result, not a cause; fruit, not the root, of his being born again.

Luke concluded his account of Zaccheus' conversion with Jesus' words, "For the Son of man is come to seek and to save that which was lost" (Luke 19:10). With his self-designation as "the Son of Man" (ὁ υἱὸς τοῦ ἀνθρώπου) Jesus was identifying Himself as One who could make the statement He did about Zaccheus' salvation. Jesus' mission was to find lost sinners and to provide the means by which they could be saved. No doubt Zaccheus would have been the last person to assert that his charitable giving or restitution, much less his promise to do so, could have contributed to his having been saved from his sins, or have added anything to his having put his trust in Jesus and Him alone for eternal salvation. He needed to, and did, according to Jesus (by his becoming a true son of Abraham), put his trust in the Him who alone was the solution to his sin problem.

In the Parable of the Ten Minas Jesus addressed the subject of the timing of the kingdom. As He was about to go up to Jerusalem, where the Triumphal Entry would take place, there was a sense of anticipation "because they thought that the kingdom of God should immediately appear" (Luke 19:11). The expectation was that Jesus would set up an earthly kingdom with Himself as its King. To disabuse people of that notion, Jesus told the Parable of the Ten Minas, which presented an impediment to the immediate establishment of that kingdom. The kingdom, whose king was represented by the nobleman in the parable, would have to wait while he "went into a far country to receive for himself a kingdom, and to return" (Luke 19:12).

The characters in the parable included protagonists and antagonists. The protagonists, in addition to the nobleman, are the two slaves who did not question the position or person of the "nobleman," but obeyed him by investing what had been entrusted to them and thereby increased their boss's net worth. There was a singular antagonist, the slave who was the eventual recipient of the nobleman's rebuke, as well as plural antagonists referred to as "his citizens" (Luke 19:14), introduced in a parenthesis at the beginning of the parable. Their opposition is described with the words, "But his citizens hated him, and sent a message after him, saying, We will not have this *man* to reign over us" [italics in KJV] (Luke 19:14). These words of the antagonists are the first part of an *inclusio* (bracketing) with the closure found in the concluding verse: "But those mine enemies, which would not that I should reign over them" (Luke 19:27).

Between the two bracketing statements a shift occurs, from the antagonists initially being presented as those who oppose the fictional nobleman in the parable, to their identification as Jesus' own enemies, whom He describes as "those enemies of mine" (Luke 19:27). These people are condemned at the denouement of the parable along with the slave who did not invest what had been given to him. The reason for their punishment, "slay *them* before me" [italics in KJV] (Luke 19:27), is their rejection of Jesus as their king. Their rejection was in spite of the evidence Luke has presented identifying Jesus as their messianic King. This was Jesus' reply to those who wanted to immediately make Him their king. They were enemies of His because they wanted Him to become their earthly king, not their savior. The earthly kingdom would come, and Jesus would reign, in the Millennium, but they would not dictate His timing, nor His terms.

The Triumphal Entry in Luke's Gospel (Luke 19:28-44) is essentially the same as that found in the other Synoptic Gospels (Matthew 21:1-9; Mark 11:1-10). Unique to Luke's Gospel is the Pharisees' reaction to the event and their request, or rather their demand: "Master, rebuke thy disciples" (Luke 19:39). The Pharisees viewed the multitude's unbridled, enthusiastic reception of Jesus' messiahship, as unwarranted and alarming. For the Pharisees, shutting up the multitude was the solution to their problem. But the expression of Jesus' identity could not be silenced so easily. Jesus told them, "I tell you that, if these should hold their peace, the stones would immediately cry out" (Luke 19:40).

Also unique to Luke's Gospel is the inclusion of Jesus' weeping over the city of Jerusalem. The Triumphal Entry was a pivotal turning point in time, as Jesus' words indicate: "If thou hadst known, even thou, at least in this thy day, the things *which belong* unto thy peace!" [italics in KJV] (Luke 19:42). The surface acceptance by the multitude would soon be replaced by rejection of the Messiah. The pivotal nature of these events is further amplified with Jesus' explanation of the reason for Jerusalem's destruction: "because thou knewest not the time of thy visitation" (Luke 19:44). They "knewest not the time" as one of singular importance, nor accepted the evidence for the Messiah's identity.

Luke Chapter 20

In what would be the last week, before Jesus' crucifixion, Luke said that "he taught the people in the temple, and preached the gospel" (Luke 20:1). Jesus preached the good news of the kingdom and the proof of its arrival, the presence of Himself as its King. Uncomfortable with that message, to say the least, "the chief priests and the scribes came upon *him* with the elders" [italics in KJV] (Luke 20:1) and questioned His legitimacy: "Tell us, by what authority doest thou these things? or who is he that gave thee this authority?" (Luke 20:2). The authenticity of the message, as well as the identity of the messenger hinged on its origin. If it was human it could be disregarded, or attacked as heretical blasphemy; if it was heavenly it had to be accepted.

 Rather than give a direct answer Jesus asked one of His famous, confounding questions: "The baptism of John, was it from heaven, or of men?" (Luke 20:4). Caught between the proverbial "rock and a hard place" the religious leaders punted: "And they answered, that they could not tell whence *it was*" [italics in KJV] (Luke 20:7). Instead of answering the religious leaders' initial question, which would have immediately escalated the conflict, Jesus said, "Neither tell I you by what authority I do these things" (Luke 20:8).

While Jesus did not answer them on that occasion, the question would not remain unanswered. The question of Jesus' identity would be answered by the disciples, when they testified as eyewitnesses to what they had seen and heard and experienced. Ultimately the answer to the question, about the human or heavenly origin of Jesus and His message, would determine whether one went to hell or to heaven. The gospel has the power to determine eternal destinies.

In Luke 20:39-44 the gospel writer included one of the most important passages dealing with the identity of Jesus as the Messiah. The other two Synoptic authors include it as well. It is proof of the Messiah's deity. The conclusive evidence Jesus used was from David's words in Psalm 110. The reader is referred to comments made earlier in this book on the parallel passages in Matthew 22:41-46 and Mark 12:35-37. The reader is also referred to comments on the parallel passages (Matthew 24:4-14, 23-26; Mark 13:5-6, 21-23) that refer to Jesus' second coming and false messiahs who will appear on the scene and claim, "I am" (Luke 21:8) (ἐγώ εἰμι). They all warn the reader/listener not to be fooled by future imposters who will assume a false identity. They would plot the ultimate identity theft, trying to take on the identity of the real Messiah.

Luke Chapter 21

In Jesus' prophetic words about the persecution His followers would experience on His account, and the opportunity it would afford, is found the biblical paradigm and the believer's role in the evangelistic endeavor. Jesus said about persecution: "And it shall turn to you for a testimony" (Luke 21:13). The NASB translates the same words "It will lead to an opportunity for your testimony." The word translated with the noun "testimony" (μαρτύριον) refers to the evidence of eyewitnesses whose firsthand knowledge of the events would be recorded in this and the other Gospels. The testimony of those witnesses will have a divine origin: "For I will give you a mouth and wisdom, which all your adversaries shall not be able to gainsay nor resist" (Luke 21:15).

In Matthew 5:18 Jesus said about the Law that, "Till heaven and earth pass, one jot or one tittle shall in no wise pass from the law, till all be fulfilled." In Luke 16:17, Luke also included Jesus words about the Law: "it is easier for heaven and earth to pass, than one tittle of the law to fail." Astounding His listeners, Jesus also said, about His own words, what He had said about the Law: "Heaven and earth shall pass away: but my words shall not pass away" (Luke 21:33). Who could say that? This was in the context of His explaining eschatological events. Jesus put His predictions about what would happen in the future right alongside those of Scripture. That would have been considered blasphemy. His words were the same as God's word!

Actually Jesus implied that His words were greater than the Law. In Matthew 5:18 with the use of the Greek word "till" or "until" (ἕως), when talking about the Law, Jesus spoke in relative terms—in relation to "heaven and earth" the Law would at least last "until" (ἕως) their destruction or "passing away" (παρέλθῃ aorist active subjunctive from παρέρχομαι "to cease to exist," "to pass away," or "to cease"). There would be a time when heaven and earth would pass away and the Law would last at least until then. But the Law would eventually come to an end.

On the other hand, Jesus' statement (Luke 21:33) about His own words was not relative, but absolute—even though "heaven and earth" would be destroyed or "will pass away" (παρελεύσονται future middle indicative from παρέρχομαι "to cease to exist," "to pass away," or "to cease"), His words would not meet the same fate. For someone to say that, in the presence of the Jewish religious hierarchy was beyond astounding. For those words to be true, the one making such a claim, that He was greater than the Law, would have to be none other than God Himself, the Law's creator.

Luke Chapter 22

In response to the disciples' debate over who among them was greatest Jesus made another of His amazing claims: "And I appoint unto you a kingdom, as my Father hath appointed unto me; That ye may eat and drink at my table in my kingdom, and sit on thrones judging the twelve tribes of Israel" (Luke 22:29-30). Only God could have such a position and wield such power. The disciples, at least to some degree at this point, recognized who He is, which explains why they seemed to be constantly elbowing one another to get what they thought He had to offer. Although they thought that the earthly kingdom would be set up soon, and they were mistaken about that, they were going to receive prominent positions in the future earthly kingdom. The disciples' selfish ambition was wrong, but they were not wrong about the identity of Jesus.

On the eve of His crucifixion Jesus identified Himself as one who would fulfill Old Testament messianic prophecy of that event by quoting: "And he was reckoned among the transgressors" (Luke 22:37). The citation is a part of Isaiah 53:12: "And he was numbered with the transgressors," located in perhaps the most undisputed messianic passage in the entire Old Testament. Jesus left no doubt that He Himself was the fulfillment of the prophecy by saying so before the citation: "For I say unto you, that this that is written must yet be accomplished in me" (Luke 22:37), and mentioning it again after it as well: "for the things concerning me have an end [or "fulfillment"]."

In Luke 22:48 in the garden of Gethsemane Judas betrayed Jesus with an identifying kiss. This was not the arrest of a common criminal. Jesus made sure Judas was aware of that with His rhetorical question, "Judas, betrayest thou the Son of man with a kiss?" (Luke 22:48). The person Judas was identifying was not a mere man but the Messiah. Everything surrounding the arrest, trial, execution, and resurrection of Jesus would point to who He is, His identity.

The only issue on the agenda in the trial of Jesus before the Sanhedrin mentioned by Luke is that of His identity. The accused could not refuse to appear as a witness and testify, so in the interrogation He was commanded, "If you are the Christ, tell us" (Luke 22:67 NASB). In the Greek this is a first-class conditional sentence. Daniel Wallace says that "The first class condition indicates *the assumption of the truth for the sake of argument*" (*Greek Grammar beyond the Basics*, 450, italics in original). Wallace's italics serve to emphasize that the speaker does not necessarily believe the protasis (the first, "if" part) to be true, although he is taking that position as a rhetorical strategy. Jesus, knowing those trying Him did not and would not accept His answer as the truth, responded, "If I tell you, ye will not believe" (Luke 22:67).

Then, in an oblique statement, alluding to an Old Testament passage, Jesus told them, "Hereafter shall the Son of man sit on the right hand of the power of God" (Luke 22:69). The implication that He was "the Son of Man" (ὁ υἱὸς τοῦ ἀνθρώπου), the same as "the Son of God" (ὁ υἱὸς τοῦ θεοῦ), was not lost on the Sanhedrin. Their response was to ask, "Art thou then the Son of God?" (Luke 22:70). Jesus' answer was affirmative. "Ye say that I am" (Luke 22:70). In English, Jesus' answer does not sound unambiguous. A. T. Robertson says this about Jesus' reply, and what it was that He was affirming:

> Note how these three epithets [Christ, Son of Man, and Son of God] are used as practical equivalents. They ask about "the Messiah." Jesus affirms that he is the Son of Man and will sit at the right hand of the power of God. They take this to be a claim to be the Son of God (both humanity and deity). Jesus accepts the challenge and admits that he claims to be all three (Messiah, the Son of man, the Son of God). Ye say (Humeis legete). Just a Greek idiom for "Yes" (compare "I am" in Mark 14:62 with "Thou has said" in Matt. 26:64) (*Word Pictures in the New Testament* [Nashville: Broadman, 1930], 2:277).

The context of Jesus' trial in Mark 14:62 and Matthew 26:64, as well as Luke 22:70, is that of His trial before the Sanhedrin. The verbal difference between Luke 22:70 "Ye say that I am" (λέγετε ὅτι ἐγώ εἰμι), Matthew 26:64 "Thou has said" (σὺ εἶπας), and Mark 14:62 which has "I am" (ἐγώ εἰμι), could be accounted for by being indirect quotations, recognizing that the Greek original did not use our present-day quotation mark punctuation. All three Synoptic Gospels are communicating that Jesus said He is the Son of God.

Luke's record, of the Sanhedrin's response to Jesus' affirmation, confirms that conclusion: "And they said, What need we any further witness? for we ourselves have heard of his own mouth" (Luke 22:71). Ironically, and unwittingly, the Jewish Sanhedrin became a hostile, corroborating witness to the "testimony" (μαρτυρία) of Jesus, the witness, and His claim of deity. And their rhetorical question, "What need we any further witness?" (Luke 22:71), whose expected answer was "none," speaks to the adequacy and sufficiency of the evidence to render that verdict.

Luke Chapter 23

Luke's account of the trial before Pilate raised the same identity question found in Matthew (Matthew 27:11) and Mark (Mark 15:2), which was, "Art thou the king of the Jews?" (Luke 23:3). Jesus' response, recorded by those three Gospels, was, "Thou sayest *it*" [italics in KJV] (σὺ λέγεις). The equivalent in our day would be: "You said it," as an affirmative response to a question that has been asked. Here again is Jesus Himself providing evidence, this time of His messianic kingship. All three of the Synoptic accounts of the trial before Pilate are brief, in contrast to the detail found in the Gospel of John, which will be discussed in our comments on that passage.

At the scene of the crucifixion, people mocking Jesus brought up the issue of His identity: "He saved others; let him save himself, if he be Christ, the chosen of God" (Luke 23:35). Grammatically the conditional part of the sentence is a first-class condition. Again, as Wallace says about a first-class condition: "The first class condition indicates *the assumption of the truth for the sake of argument*" (Daniel Wallace, *Greek Grammar beyond the Basics* [Grand Rapids: Zondervan 1996], 450, italics in original). Their words were sarcastic–they did not personally believe or identify Jesus as the "Christ, the chosen of God" (ὁ χριστὸς τοῦ θεοῦ ὁ ἐκλεκτός). The proof of Jesus' messiahship, the evidence tauntingly requested, would not come in the form they demanded, which was deliverance from the cross, but would be provided by His resurrection.

The Roman soldiers, no doubt recognizing that coming down from a cross, after having been crucified, was something they were there to prevent, got into the act as well. Their taunting was no less sarcastic than that of the other onlookers, and with their weapons menacingly at the ready, they said, "If thou be the king of the Jews, save thyself" (Luke 23:37). Perhaps they made reference to the placard on Jesus' cross, because, as Luke explains, "And a superscription also was written over him in letters of Greek, and Latin, and Hebrew, THIS IS THE KING OF THE JEWS" (Luke 23:38). For the soldiers, personally, the identity of the man they were executing was not what the sign said. Their allegiance was not to Him. He was not their king.

One of the criminals crucified with Jesus, who was interested if an escape plan was being contemplated, nevertheless, not to be left out, joined in mocking Him and said, "If thou be Christ, save thyself and us" (Luke 23:39). Because he did not believe that Jesus was who he had heard He said He was, he had no hope of His rescuing him from his predicament. Nor did he recognize that he had a far greater problem–that of his eternal destiny.

On the other hand, one of the other crucified criminals saw things differently. Even though it appeared that Jesus was one of them, suffering the consequences of crime, this criminal said to the other, "Dost not thou fear God, seeing thou art in the same condemnation? And we indeed justly; for we receive the due reward of our deeds: but this man hath done nothing amiss" (Luke 23:40-41). This criminal believed Jesus to be the very One who the naysayers were saying He was not.

Believing that to be true, that Jesus was the prophesied and promised Messiah, and recognizing his need, in light of what he was very soon to experience, he put his trust in the Messiah/Christ (ὁ χριστὸς), who was indeed the King (ὁ βασιλεὺς), as his only hope for heaven, and expressed it with the words: "Lord, remember me when thou comest into thy kingdom" (Luke 23:42). On the basis of his trust in Jesus, and that alone–no promises to perform, no wishing or willing or wanting to do anything–Jesus made His own solemn promise to him: "Verily I say unto thee, Today shalt thou be with me in paradise" (Luke 23:43).

If that criminal had somehow been pardoned in the nick of time, taken down from the cross, and lived another fifty years, nothing he committed to do, or could do, would have contributed to or altered his eternal destiny. As it turned out, what Jesus had promised, happened–he was with Him in paradise that very day.

Luke recounted that there was a three-hour period of darkness at the crucifixion: "And it was about the sixth hour, and there was a darkness over all the earth until the ninth hour. And the sun was darkened" (Luke 23:44-45). The Roman centurion, overseeing the execution, who was an eyewitness, reacted, but his response to the event was unexpected: "Now when the centurion saw what was done, he glorified God, saying, Certainly this was a righteous man" (Luke 23:47). The word translated "righteous" (δίκαιος) may indicate that the centurion not only thought Jesus was innocent of a crime worthy of crucifixion, but also thought of Him as "sinless." Furthermore, "he glorified God" (Luke 23:47) which may be evidence that he trusted in Jesus, thereby securing his eternal destiny. The reader/listener is not told, but the centurion may have overheard the conversation between Jesus and that criminal on the cross who was converted.

Luke, in keeping with his intention to present eyewitness testimony to the events about which he was writing, concluded his account of the crucifixion with a comment to that effect: "And all his acquaintance, and the women that followed him from Galilee, stood afar off, beholding these things" (Luke 23:49). The words translated "all his acquaintance[s]" show that the eyewitnesses were not just handpicked "true believers" who would be expected to testify as Luke wanted them to.

Jesus' resurrection proved beyond reasonable doubt and beyond that Jesus is who He said He is. Because of that, it was especially important for Luke to include multiple eyewitnesses to that critical event. First, to have a resurrection from the dead, there must be proof that the person has died. Luke's account does not include some of the details the other Gospels do, that prove Jesus died while on the cross. However, Luke does go into detail about His burial. Normally live people are not buried.

Luke's primary witness who could vouch for Jesus' death was Joseph of Arimathea, the man who buried Him. Luke went into more detail about who this man was than any of the other Gospel writers. And it is noteworthy that there were plural eyewitnesses who saw Joseph of Arimathea bury Jesus: "And the women also, which came with him from Galilee, followed after, and beheld the sepulchre, and how his body was laid" (Luke 23:55). Luke may have questioned the ladies to get their testimony.

Luke Chapter 24

These same women went to the tomb the next day and did not find Jesus' body, but instead encountered two angels who referred to Him as "the living" (Luke 24:5) (τὸν ζῶντα) and reminded them that He had referred to Himself as "the Son of man" (Luke 24:7) (τὸν υἱὸν τοῦ ἀνθρώπου). The women went back and told the disciples, and others, what they had seen and heard, but the mourners did not believe them: "And their words seemed to them as idle tales, and they believed them not" (Luke 24:11). They doubted that what the women were saying was true.

Some manuscripts containing Luke's account state that Peter went to the tomb to check things out for himself, while in other manuscripts that verse is missing. However, in the Gospel of John, in an undisputed passage (John 20:3-8), Peter and another unnamed disciple, presumably John, went to the tomb together. In that account, quite probably speaking from firsthand experience, it says, "Then went in also that other disciple, which came first to the sepulchre, and he saw, and believed" (John 20:8). If Peter was the one giving Luke material to write, he would have been an eyewitness to the empty tomb. Knowing Peter, he probably felt the slab to make sure he could trust what he saw. There was no body!

The agenda of all the Gospel writers was to provide evidence so that men might believe in Jesus for eternal life. And the process was beginning in which eyewitnesses would put things together—"connect the dots," as it were, to understand the significance of what they had seen and heard. Luke says this about the women at the tomb, their memory having been jogged by the angels: "And they remembered his words" (Luke 24:8). They remembered what Jesus had said.

Three of the women witnesses are mentioned by name: "It was Mary Magdalene, and Joanna, and Mary *the mother* of James" [italics in KJV] (Luke 24:10). There were other women with them who became witnesses as well: "and other *women that were* with them, which told these things unto the apostles" [italics in KJV] (Luke 24:10). These who had witnessed the missing body of Jesus, had heard the words, and had seen the angelic messengers, relayed their testimony to the disciples, which some of them, inspired by the Holy Spirit, would write down and become part of Scripture.

As two disciples, one named Cleopas (Luke 24:18), and the other unidentified, were walking from Jerusalem to Emmaus, they got into a conversation with a fellow-traveler whom they at first failed to recognize as Jesus Himself. The two disciples were astonished as they assumed, from a question Jesus asked that He did not know what had been going on. Jesus had asked, "And he said unto them, What manner of communications *are* these that ye have one to another, as ye walk, and are sad?" [italics in KJV] (Luke 24:17).

Their astonishment is reflected in Cleopas's words: "Art thou only a stranger in Jerusalem, and hast not known the things which are come to pass there in these days?" (Luke 24:18). All of it had occurred in public, not in secret, and was the frequent subject of conversation.

Not only was it common knowledge, but there had also been multiple witnesses to those events. In relating the recent events Cleopas and his fellow disciple identified Jesus as "Jesus of Nazareth, which was a prophet mighty in deed and word before God and all the people" (Luke 24:19). Again the public nature of Jesus' ministry is emphasized. It had all taken place "before God and all the people" (Luke 24:19). Not only were the occurrence of the events themselves proven by the presence of multiple witnesses, but the mention of God Himself as a witness, was not just a platitude; it was a significant statement.

The account of the two men on the road to Emmaus began with the identity of the stranger being hidden from them: "But their eyes were holden that they should not know him" (Luke 24:16). They were supernaturally prevented from recognizing Jesus. The account concludes with His identity being revealed: "And their eyes were opened, and they knew him" (Luke 24:31). Before the two disciples could react He disappeared: "and he vanished out of their sight" (Luke 24:31). The One whom they had not recognized had been revealed and the visible became invisible. Jesus had appeared to two men, not just to a lone individual. The evidence was credible because it was corroborated.

The next post-resurrection appearance by Jesus was to "the eleven gathered together, and them that were with them" (Luke 24:33). The two disciples who had been with Him on the road to Emmaus and began to share a meal with Him brought the message of their encounter. Interestingly, they began with, "The Lord is risen indeed, and hath appeared to Simon" (Luke 24:34). Simon may have been the unnamed disciple who was with Cleopas. If the report of this event is based on Peter's recollection, and he preferred an unassuming role, perhaps that explains why he was not mentioned initially. Considering Peter's stature as an apostle, Peter's testimony would have been important.

The purpose of this post-resurrection appearance was the identification of the risen Jesus with the pre-cross Jesus. Luke first mentions the mistaken identity in the minds of the witnesses who "supposed that they had seen a spirit" (Luke 24:37). Jesus proceeded to dispel that erroneous assumption. A spirit, or ghost, is not subject to the sense of touch, so He said, "handle me, and see; for a spirit hath not flesh and bones, as ye see me have" (Luke 24:39). Luke, the author of this Gospel, had an identity agenda. It coincided with Jesus' post-resurrection agenda–to prove that it was He. Jesus identified Himself: "it is I myself" (Luke 24:39) (ἐγώ εἰμι αὐτός).

Jesus' purpose was to dispel doubts about His identity: "Why are ye troubled? and why do thoughts arise in your hearts?" (Luke 24:38). And in spite of His words about the physical characteristics of His post-resurrection body, they still doubted: "And while they yet believed not for joy, and wondered" (Luke 24:41). They were having trouble recovering from the surprise of His appearance. Jesus had used the sense of touch to prove His identity, and then the sense of taste, and the fact that "a spirit" would not eat: "he said unto them, Have ye here any meat? and they gave him a piece of a broiled fish, and of an honeycomb. And he took *it*, and did eat before them" [italics in KJV] (Luke 24:41-43). With the words "before them" (Luke 24:43) (ἐνώπιον αὐτῶν), Luke lets the reader/listener know that those present witnessed Him eating, proving that it was indeed Jesus who had risen from the dead.

In what some consider to be Luke's "Great Commission" Jesus identified Himself as the Messiah who was prophesied in the entire Old Testament: "all things must be fulfilled, which were written in the law of Moses, and *in* the prophets, and *in* the psalms, concerning me" [italics in KJV] (Luke 24:44). The message was about Him, through whom was available "remission of sins" (Luke 24:47). Those present were to carry out the purpose "that repentance and remission of sins should be preached in his name among all nations, beginning at Jerusalem" (Luke 24:47).

Their qualification was that they had witnessed the works and words of Jesus: "ye are witnesses of these things" (Luke 24:48). They could testify to who Jesus is, and what He had done, so that many would believe their testimony and put their trust in Him and Him alone for the forgiveness of their sins, thereby ensuring that heaven would be their eternal destiny.

Chapter 7

Evidence for the Identity of Jesus in the Gospel of John

The Home Run Hitter

Like being fourth in the lineup in the game of baseball, the Apostle John batted "cleanup." With the bases loaded he was expected to hit a home run, driving all the base runners home. And he did not disappoint. This biblical book has been used more than any other, except perhaps Paul's epistle to the Romans, to present the gospel to the lost. Its importance for evangelism can hardly be overstated. It has long been in vogue, particularly in liberal scholarly circles, to postulate a theological purpose for this Gospel, at the expense of its historical value. Both are present and must be accounted for in a viable interpretation.

What has been presented previously in this study, specifically the theme of the identity of Jesus, as the primary theological thread that runs throughout the Synoptic Gospels, is intensified, and finds its culmination in the Gospel of John. It will be demonstrated how the fourth Gospel builds on the work of its canonical predecessors. Differences between this Gospel and the Synoptics, especially the inclusion of material absent from the latter, and present in the former, have been highlighted by many. The differences, however, are overshadowed by a unity of purpose, and a shared conceptual paradigm, common to the four Gospels. The unifying purpose and paradigm is to provide evidence proving that Jesus is the God/Man/Messiah, who provided the means by which those placing their trust in that divine/human Person secure eternal life.

John Chapter 1

John did not begin with Jesus' birth narrative, or genealogy. Instead the introduction includes theological statements affirming Jesus' deity, followed by those supporting His humanity. These statements of identification are foundational for understanding what the author unfolds in what follows. The rest of the fourth Gospel proves what the prologue asserts.

John refers to Jesus as "the Word" (John 1:1) (ὁ λόγος) in his opening statement, "In the beginning was the Word" (Ἐν ἀρχῇ ἦν ὁ λόγος). John uses the equative "to be" verb (from εἰμί) to identify Jesus as One who exists from all eternity. Daniel B. Wallace, in his grammar, uses John 1:1 as an example of the active voice with a "stative active" meaning where, "The subject exists in the state indicated by the verb" (*Greek Grammar beyond the Basics* [Grand Rapids: Zondervan, 1996], 412). The Greek imperfect tense of the verb translated "was" (ἦν the imperfect, active, indicative of εἰμί = "to be") additionally expresses that state as continuous. Louw and Nida's lexicon has the meaning for this use of the "to be" verb as "to exist, in an absolute sense–'to be, to exist'" (Johannes P. Louw and Eugene A. Nida, *Greek-English*

Lexicon of the New Testament Based on Semantic Domains, 2nd ed. [New York: United Bible Societies, 2nd ed], 1989, 1:157).

The Jehovah's Witnesses, in their theologically specialized New World Translation, have "a God," with the indefinite article, reflecting their Christological agenda, rather than the definite "God" found in the NASB and all other translations. As Wallace notes:

> It is interesting that the New World Translation [that of the Jehovah's Witnesses] renders θεὸς as "a god" on the simplistic grounds that it lacks the article. This is surely an insufficient basis. Following the "anarthrous" [no definite article] = "indefinite" principle would mean that ἀρχῇ should be "a beginning" (1:1,2), ζωὴ should be "a life" (1:4), παρὰ θεοῦ should be "from a god" (1:6), Ἰωάννης should be "a John" (1:6), Θεὸν should be "a god" (1:18), etc. Yet none of these other anarthrous nouns is rendered with an indefinite article. One can only suspect strong theological bias in such a translation (Daniel Wallace, *Greek Grammar beyond the Basics*, [Grand Rapids: Zondervan, 1996], 267).

By denying the uniqueness of Jesus, as the God/Man, Jehovah's Witnesses have undermined His identity, so that in their theology He is no longer the One revealed in Scripture. The Jehovah's Witnesses' faulty identity makes faith in Jesus impossible.

Jesus' identity is further revealed as He who was with God the Father, in His immediate presence: "and the Word was with God" (John 1:1). Edwin A. Blum comments that "the word 'with' translates the Greek *pros*, which here suggests 'in company with'" ("John," in *The Bible Knowledge Commentary, New Testament*, ed. John F. Walvoord and Roy B. Zuck [Wheaton, IL: Victor, 1983; reprint, Colorado Springs: Cook, 1996], 271, italics in original). Not only was Jesus in close association with God the Father, but He was in fact God: "and the Word was God" (John 1:1). Again we see the presence of the equative "to be" verb in the imperfect tense, which carries the sense of continuity. This identifies Jesus as equal to God the Father in His essence, and is implicit evidence of the Trinity as a biblical truth.

Wallace takes the position that here the lack of the article (anarthrous) with the predicate nominative "God" (θεὸς) is to be understood as qualitative. He says: "Such an option does not at all impugn the deity of Christ. Rather, it stresses that, although the person of Christ is not the person of the Father, their *essence* is identical" (Daniel Wallace, *Greek Grammar beyond The Basics*, [Grand Rapids: Zondervan, 1996], 269, italics in original). In that way, John the Apostle avoided confusion and conflation of the persons within the Godhead. In the following verse the eternal existence of Jesus, and His continuous communion with God the Father, is reiterated by John: "The same was in the beginning with God" (John 1:2). Jesus' eternal existence and experience were coterminous with that of God the Father.

Jesus was not only present at the time of the creation of the physical universe, He was also its creator: "All things were made by him; and without him was not any thing made that was made" (John 1:3). Wallace details how scripture attributes creation to God:

> The Logos is represented as the Creator in a "hands-on" sort of way, with the implication that God is the ultimate agent. This is the typical (though not exclusive) pattern seen in the NT: Ultimate agency is ascribed to God the Father (with ὑπό), intermediate agency is ascribed to Christ (with διά), and "impersonal" means is ascribed to the Holy Spirit (with ἐν or the simple dative) (ibid., 434).

Chief among what came into being by the creative agency of Jesus/the Word, was physical and spiritual life: "In him was life; and the life was the light of men" (John 1:4). He, the infinite, eternal possessor of life, could pass spiritual and physical life on to men.

Apart from divine initiative, people would be left without spiritual access to "the life" (ἡ ζωή) which required "the light" (τὸ φῶς) of supernatural communication and illumination. To begin to fill that void, a witness, John the Baptist, was divinely sent: "The same came for a witness, to bear witness of the Light, that all *men* through him might believe" [italics in KJV] (John 1:7). Jesus, having been referred to as "the Word" (ὁ λόγος), was now the personification of "the light" (τὸ φῶς), whom John the Baptist was about to introduce. The goal was that people "might believe" (πιστεύσωσιν aorist, active, subjunctive, from πιστεύω = "believe") in Jesus. For belief to occur, John the Baptist was an intermediate agent, expressed with the words "through him" (δι' αὐτοῦ). John, the Gospel writer, made sure the identity of John the Baptist would not be confused with that of Jesus: "He was not that Light, but *was sent* to bear witness of that Light" [italics in KJV] (John 1:8).

The identification of Jesus as the Creator, first stated in John 1:3, is repeated in verse 10: "and the world was made by Him." And although He had every right to be welcomed by those He had created, that was not what He experienced. John the Apostle, writing these words more than a half century after Jesus' time on earth, explained that, "He came unto his own, and his own received him not" (John 1:11). This rejection was spiritual and physical, individual and national.

In contrast to those who refused to welcome and accept Jesus for who He is, were those who received Him: "But as many as received him, to them gave he power to become the sons of God, *even* to them that believe on his name" [italics in KJV] (John 1:12). Those with spiritual reception are those that "believe in His name" (John 1:12 NASB). Louw and Nida understand "His name" (τὸ ὄνομα αὐτοῦ) as a figurative extension of a person's given name referring to his person, the referent here being Jesus Himself (Johannes P. Louw and Eugene A. Nida, *Greek-English Lexicon of the New Testament Based on Semantic Domains*, 2nd ed. [New York: United Bible Societies, 2nd ed], 1989, 1:106). The phrase "believe in His name" [NASB] (πιστεύω εἰς τὸ ὄνομα αὐτοῦ) has the same meaning as "believe in Him" (πιστεύω εἰς αὐτὸν), that is, to place one's trust in Jesus.

The expression "believe in" (πιστεύω εἰς), which appears to be unique to the New Testament, is the usual way in which John's Gospel refers to saving faith. The use of this phrase is best understood to refer to trust in a person as opposed to believing something to be true or that someone is telling the truth. In order to place trust in a person, one must believe that what he has said is true. Jesus spoke extensively about His own identity, words that must be believed as true, if saving faith/trust is to be placed in His person. What He did, dying for sins and rising from the dead, are part of what constitute His biblical identity. Every detail related to His identity need not be known and believed, but enough to insure that it is the Jesus who has been revealed in Scripture. If something revealed about Him is known to an individual but not believed, the identity of the One in whom trust is placed is thereby compromised and comes into question. Ultimately God is the One who decides if the One in whom trust has been placed is the One whom Scripture has revealed.

The identity of Jesus cannot be understood apart from the Incarnation, in which the eternal Word became a human being: "And the Word was made flesh, and dwelt among us" (John 1:14). John, the human author of this Gospel, counted himself among those who were eyewitnesses, and could testify to the truth of the Incarnation: "(and we beheld his glory, the glory as of the only begotten of the Father), full of grace and truth" [parenthesis in KJV] (John 1:14).

Although John did not include in his account the occasion when Jesus was "transfigured," as did the other Gospel writers (Matthew 17:1-13; Mark 9:2-13; Luke 9:28-36), he, along with Peter and James, witnessed that momentous event, and with John's mention of "glory" (δόξα), he may have been reminiscing about it. Certainly "glory" (δόξα), "grace" (χάρις), and "truth" (ἀλήθεια) characterized Jesus' works and words. Perhaps the Gospel writer, John the Apostle, did not include the Transfiguration because, having been one of three human witnesses to that event, he did not want to highlight himself. Not referring to himself by name seems to have been his preference. Instead he replaced it with "the disciple whom Jesus loved" (John 13:23; 19:26; 21:7 & 20).

Jesus, who is God Incarnate, is the One about whom John the Baptist bore witness: "John bare witness of Him" (John 1:15). The purpose of John the Baptist's testimony was that of identification: "This was he of whom I spake" (John 1:15). That included His position, as well as His pre-Incarnate existence: "He that cometh after me is preferred before me: for he was before me" (John 1:15). Only God could fulfill both the "after" (ὀπίσω) and the "before" (πρῶτός) criteria. This unique combination–of chronological precedence and subsequence–requires eternal existence.

The Gospel writer, John the Apostle, was not only an observer of what he wrote. He was also the object of divine favor: "And of his fulness have all we received, and grace for grace" (John 1:16). It must be emphasized that the objective value of the testimony of the witness, was not compromised by the subjectivity of his experience, but rather was enhanced by it. The author did recognize a difficulty that his prologue raised, "How could anyone be an eyewitness and experience the infinite God, One in whose presence no man could live?" (Exodus 33:20). The humanly inexplicable nature of the Incarnation is placed where it must rest, in the Person of Jesus Christ: "No man hath seen God at any time; the only begotten Son, which is in the bosom of the Father, he hath declared *him*" [italics in KJV] (John 1:18). The epistemological question, "How can God be known?" is answered in the person of Jesus. And the soteriological question, "How can man be saved eternally?" also finds its answer in that divine person.

John, the author of this Gospel, presents John the Baptist's confrontation with the priests and Levites in the witness/testimony form with the words, "And this is the record ["the witness" or "the testimony" = ἡ μαρτυρία] of John" (John 1:19). The issue of identity appears as they ask him, "Who art thou?" (John 1:19). Apparently they assumed John the Baptist claimed to be the Messiah. So he responded, "I am not the Christ" (John 1:20). After a verbal interaction about his personal identity, John the Baptist's self-identity is stated in terms of his relationship to the Messiah. As in all three of the Synoptic accounts (Matthew 3:3; Mark 1:3; Luke 3:4) John the Baptist quoted Isaiah 40:3, "I *am* the voice of one crying in the wilderness, Make straight the way of the Lord" [italics in KJV] (John 1:23).

When Jesus appeared on the scene, John the Baptist stepped up and identified Him with the words, "Behold the Lamb of God, which taketh away the sin of the world" (John 1:29). By identifying Jesus as "the Lamb of God" (ὁ ἀμνὸς τοῦ θεοῦ), he recognized Him as the ultimate sacrifice who would die for the sins of every man. In identifying Jesus, John the Baptist made a point to say twice that he did not recognize Him, "and I knew him not" (John 1:31, 33), perhaps indicating that his identification was not just a personal conclusion but had been divinely revealed.

Following his second declaration he gave the divine source of his identification: "but he that sent me to baptize with water, the same said unto me, Upon whom thou shalt see the Spirit descending, and remaining on him, the same is he which baptizeth with the Holy Ghost" (John 1:33). The Gospel of John does not say that this occurred at Jesus' baptism, but this affirmation of His identity no doubt took place during that event, as indicated by the Synoptic writers (Matthew 3:13-17; Mark 1:9-11; Luke 3:21, 22). John the Baptist's summary statement to the religious leaders told them and the readers/listeners of this Gospel his view of his personal role as an eyewitness giving testimony: "And I saw, and bare record that this is the Son of God" (John 1:34). The identifying designation, "the Son of God" (ὁ υἱὸς τοῦ θεοῦ), is a title of Davidic messianic kingship.

The next day John the Baptist pointed out Jesus to two of his followers, and identified Him again by alluding to His substitutionary mission: "Behold the Lamb of God!" (John 1:36). One of John's followers was Andrew, who told his brother Peter the identity of the teacher they were now following, "We have found the Messias[h]" (John 1:41). Luow and Nida define "Messiah" (Μεσσίας) as "literally 'one who has been anointed'" (Johannes P. Louw and Eugene A. Nida, *Greek-English Lexicon of the New Testament Based on Semantic Domains*, 2nd ed. [New York: United Bible

Societies, 2nd ed], 1989, 1:543). The words that follow in the text are probably those of John the writer of the Gospel of John who parenthetically adds, "which is, being interpreted, the Christ" (John 1:41).

As previously mentioned, the title "Christ" (Χριστός) identified Jesus as "the anointed One," that is, the Messiah. This parenthetical explanation reinforced the gospel writer's purpose to have the reader/listener know the identity of Jesus. That the words, "which is being interpreted [translated], the Christ," at the end of verse 41 are parenthetical, and not part of Andrew's words to Peter, is supported by John the author's obvious use of a parenthesis in the following verse, where Jesus referred to Peter as "Cephas" (Κηφᾶς), adding the parenthetical explanation, "(which is translated Peter)" [parenthesis in NASB] (John 1:42) (ὃ ἑρμηνεύεται Πέτρος).

When Jesus called Philip to follow Him, Philip in turn told Nathaniel details about His identity, "We have found him, of whom Moses in the law, and the prophets, did write, Jesus of Nazareth, the son of Joseph" (John 1:45). Hearing "Nazareth" mentioned, Nathaniel expressed disbelief, "Can there any good thing come out of Nazareth?" (John 1:46), to which Philip replied, "Come and see" (John 1:46). Philip encouraged Nathaniel to personally witness what he and other disciples had witnessed. Jesus immediately left no reason for doubting who He is, by first revealing His omniscient knowledge of Nathaniel's character: "Behold an Israelite indeed, in whom is no guile!" (John 1:47), and then showing the exercise of His omnipresence, when He said, "Before that Philip called thee, when thou wast under the fig tree, I saw thee" (John 1:48).

Having witnessed that supernatural demonstration, Nathaniel reacted by spontaneously exclaiming, "Rabbi, thou art the Son of God; thou art the King of Israel" (John 1:49), thereby identifying Him as the Messiah. Blum comments, "This does not mean that Nathaniel at this early date fully understood the Trinity or the Incarnation. Rather He understood Jesus to be the Son of God in the messianic sense (cf. Ps. 2:6-7). This future Davidic King would have God's Spirit on Him (Isa. 11:1-2) and thus would have supernatural knowledge" (Edwin A. Blum, "John," in *The Bible Knowledge Commentary, New Testament*, ed. John F. Walvoord and Roy B. Zuck [Wheaton, IL: Victor, 1983; reprint, Colorado Springs: Cook, 1996], 276). While Nathaniel probably did not realize the full implication of his words, those who would later read or listen to what he said, John the Apostle's intended audience, would grasp their significance.

The purpose for Jesus' supernatural activity was to elicit faith/trust in His person. His disciples would believe the truth about who He is, because they witnessed those events that proved His divine identity. Their faith would continue to grow as the amount of evidence increased. In effect Jesus is telling Nathaniel, "You have not seen anything yet!" with the words, "Because I said unto thee, I saw thee under the fig tree, believest thou? thou shalt see greater things than these" (John 1:50). Jesus also said to Nathaniel, "Verily, verily, I say unto you, Hereafter ye shall see heaven open, and the angels of God ascending and descending upon the Son of man" (John 1:51). In close textual proximity "the Son of God" (John 1:49) (ὁ υἱὸς τοῦ θεοῦ), and "the King of Israel"

(John 1:49) (ὁ βασιλεὺς τοῦ Ἰσραήλ), as well as "the Son of Man" (John 1:51) (τὸν υἱὸν τοῦ ἀνθρώπου) refer to the same divine person.

Twice Jesus told Nathaniel, "thou shalt see" (John 1:50) (ὄψῃ = singular), and then He said to the other disciples, "ye shall see" (John 1:51) (ὄψεσθε = plural), alluding to their future role as eyewitnesses. In verse 50 Jesus spoke to Nathaniel using the singular, "thou [Nathaniel, singular] shalt see greater things than these," then in verse 51 He used the plural, "Verily, verily, I say unto you [plural], Hereafter ye [plural] shall see heaven open." There would be multiple eyewitnesses, and their testimony would corroborate evidence proving the identity of Jesus as the Messiah/God, so that men might believe in Him.

John Chapter 2

In the account of Jesus turning water into wine, at the wedding in Cana of Galilee, is an oblique allusion to identity found in Jesus' response to His mother's words: "They have no wine" (John 2:3). Jesus responded with the enigmatic statement, "Woman, what have I to do with thee?" (John 2:4). A. T. Robertson refers to F. C. Burkitt's 1912 article, which interprets the words as, "What is it to us?" (*Word Pictures in the New Testament* [Nashville: Broadman, 1932], 5:34). Blum follows the NIV which translates the question as, "Why do you involve Me?" (Edwin A. Blum, "John," in *The Bible Knowledge Commentary, New Testament*, ed. John F. Walvoord and Roy B. Zuck [Wheaton, IL: Victor, 1983; reprint, Colorado Springs: Cook, 1996], 278), and he adds that this "was a common expression in Greek that referred to a difference in realms or relations" (ibid.). Blum continues, "Demons spoke these words when they were confronted by Christ ('What do You want with us?' [Mark 1:24]; 'What do You want with me?' [Mark 5:7])" (ibid., parenthesis and brackets in original).

If Blum's interpretation of "a difference in realms or relations" is correct, Jesus was alluding to His divine identity, as opposed to a human relationship with His mother. What is certain is that the disciples came away from this miracle with a knowledge of who He is, and more than that, as indicated by John, the author's, commentary, "This beginning of miracles did Jesus in Cana of Galilee, and manifested forth his glory; and his disciples believed on him" (John 2:11).

Many have commented on the correlation in John's Gospel between signs and belief. Here the writer specifically describes the "sign" (John 1:11) (σημεῖον) as something that "manifested forth his glory." "His glory" was evidence of who He is, and the evidence consisting of the first "sign" (σημεῖον), the miracle of turning water into wine, had as its purpose that the disciples would put their trust in Him, which the text indicates they did.

During Jesus' earthly ministry His disciples began making connections between what they were witnessing and what they knew from the Old Testament, and the author of this Gospel occasionally lets his readers/listeners in on what was going on in their minds. One such occasion was after Jesus cleansed the temple when "his disciples remembered that it was written, The zeal of thine house hath eaten me up" (John 2:17).

In contrast to the disciples who believed, "the Jews" (οἱ Ἰουδαῖοι), John's designation for the unbelieving and increasingly antagonistic Jewish religious hierarchy, disingenuously asked for more proof in the form of a miraculous sign: "Then answered the Jews and said unto him, What sign shewest thou unto us, seeing that thou doest these things?" (John 2:18). Rather than oblige them with a miracle, Jesus made a prediction about His coming death and resurrection, "Destroy this temple, and in three days I will raise it up" (John 2:19). Jesus' opponents immediately thought He was referring to the physical structure in which they were standing. But Jesus had Himself in mind, as John's editorial comment lets the reader/listener know: "But he spake of the temple of his body" (John 2:21).

The Gospel writer continued his editorial comment with the disciples' later understanding of what they had heard: "When therefore he was risen from the dead, his disciples remembered that he had said this unto them; and they believed the scripture, and the word which Jesus had said" (John 2:22). Here the verb "believe" (πιστεύω) has the meaning, "to think something to be true," which in the context is the words of Scripture.

The next verse has, "many believed in his name, when they saw the miracles which he did" (John 2:23). The purpose of "the signs" (τὰ σημεῖα) was to prove who He is, so that they "believed in His name" (ἐπίστευσαν εἰς τὸ ὄνομα αὐτοῦ), that is, placed their trust in Him. The meaning of this second use of "believe" (πιστεύω), found in the four verses (John 2:22-25), is to place "trust and reliance" in the person of Christ. The signs led to belief in propositions about His divine identity, which led to trust in the person of Jesus.

Having used those two meanings of the verb "believe" (πιστεύω), in the next verse the author employed a third meaning of that same verb, "But Jesus did not commit himself unto them" (John 2:24). Here the same Greek verb "believe" (πιστεύω) has the meaning "to entrust something to the care of someone." The trust that these individuals placed in Jesus was not reciprocated by Him. He knew He could not rely or count on them. He knew men generally, and these individuals in particular, "But Jesus did not commit himself ["not entrusting Himself" = NASB] unto them, because he knew all *men*, And needed not that any should testify of man: for he knew what was in man" [italics in KJV] (John 2:24-25).

The trusting relationship that Jesus did not enter into with the disciples is parallel to the opportunity for friendship which He offered them on another occasion when He said, "Ye are my friends, if ye do whatsoever I command you" (John 15:14). The contingency on which that relationship relies is obedience, "if ye do" (ἐὰν ποιῆτε); actual performance, not wishing, or wanting, or being willing, or committed to do, but actually obeying Christ's commands.

An observation to be drawn from John 2:23-25 is that eternal salvation, by means of faith in Jesus, is not a reciprocal transaction, and the term "exchange" is an improper word to use. One who has placed trust in Jesus is not left to wonder whether Jesus has placed trust in him to validate their conversion. The contrast in this passage, between the one believing and trusting, and the One in whom trust is placed, supports the opposite conclusion, which is that faith in Christ is not always matched by faithfulness on the part of the individual placing their faith in Him, a condition that He is omnisciently aware of. The faith of believers is in no way compromised or invalidated by the lack of confidence that Jesus might have in their deficient performance.

Another contrast in this passage is the means by which faith is exercised. People exercise faith based on evidence presented to them: "many believed in his name, when they saw the miracles which he did" (John 2:23). In contrast, because of Jesus' omniscience, He requires no testimony. "And needed not that any should testify of man: for he knew what was in man" (John 2:25). The author's mention of Jesus' omniscience is additional support for the view that the writer was concerned with what would contribute to his readers'/listeners' acceptance of Jesus' true identity.

Some interpreters would deny that those who "believed in His name" (ἐπίστευσαν εἰς τὸ ὄνομα αὐτοῦ) in John 2:23 were genuinely saved. They claim that this is an example of failed faith. At best that would be an implication drawn from the text and not an explicit statement. However, no qualifying adjectives or caveats are in the biblical text to question the quality of the trust that was placed in Jesus. Additionally, no one, to this writer's knowledge, takes the Greek verb "believe" (πιστεύω) to mean the same thing in both John 2:23 and 2:24. The presence of polysemy (a word having more than one meaning) is universally accepted. The verb "believe" (πιστεύω) in John 2:23 is taken to mean either "belief in a proposition" or "belief in a person," and in John 2:24, as "entrusting something to the care of someone," with the latter being translated by the NASB with "entrusting." Polysemy notwithstanding, to read failure into the meaning of the word "believe" (πιστεύω) in reference to those who believed in Jesus, and not to do so with "entrusting" (πιστεύω), which Jesus did not do, exposes an interpreter to the charge of theologically motivated special pleading.

John 1:12 uses the same words found in John 2:23 about belief "in His name" (εἰς τὸ ὄνομα αὐτοῦ). Those who believe in His name (1:12) are those to whom "He gave the right to become children of God." John 2:23 should not be understood differently because it uses the same terminology as in John 1:12, and the author mentions no difference in the meaning of the same two terms, nor does he modify the former with any qualifier or caveat. In both, belief in Jesus results in becoming a child of God.

John Chapter 3

In his meeting with Jesus, Nicodemus made a statement about His identity, "Rabbi, we know that thou art a teacher come from God: for no man can do these miracles that thou doest, except God be with him" (John 3:2). Nicodemus recognized that the origin and source of Jesus' power were keys to His identity. Jesus introduced what He would say about Himself with the axiom that testimony is based on firsthand knowledge: "We speak that we do know, and testify that we have seen" (John 3:11). Jesus said of Nicodemus and his contemporaries that in spite of the evidence available to them, "ye [plural] receive not our witness" (John 3:11). To "receive the witness" was to believe that the evidence was true, with the result that trust would be placed in the One whom the testimony was about.

The Old Testament example Jesus used, "as Moses lifted up the serpent in the wilderness" (John 3:14), pictured Jesus' death on the cross and what faith in Him would accomplish. Faith in the Old Testament type, the raised serpent that Jesus used to illustrate His point, resulted in restoration to health, and prevented physical death. Faith, in the New Testament, its antitype: "even so must the Son of man be lifted up" (John 3:14), was the antidote for spiritual death: "That whosoever believeth in him should not perish, but have eternal life" (John 3:15).

For John 3:16, and the surrounding context, the reader is referred back to chapter 2, "Exegetical Eye-Openers."

John 3:22-36 tells about a discussion that took place during the overlap of the ministries of Jesus and John the Baptist, with the latter's disciples having difficulty accepting the fact that their master's ministry was being eclipsed. As John's disciples discussed it with him, the central issue became the identity of Jesus. Without mentioning Jesus' name, John's disciples express their concern and consternation: "Rabbi, he that was with thee beyond Jordan, to whom thou barest witness, behold, the same baptizeth, and all *men* come to him" [italics in KJV] (John 3:26). John the Baptist's testimony about Jesus had been about His identity: "Behold the Lamb of God, which taketh away the sin of the world" (John 1:29). In John 3:26-36, the verb "witness" (μαρτυρέω) appears three times (vv. 26, 28, 32), and two times the noun "testimony" (μαρτυρία) is used (vv. 32-33). John the Baptist clarified who he was in contrast to who Jesus is: "I am not the Christ, but, I have been sent before Him" (John 3:28 NASB).

Using the illustration of a wedding John the Baptist identified Jesus as the "bridegroom" (John 3:29) (νυμφίος) and himself as the "friend of the bridegroom" (John 3:29) (φίλος τοῦ νυμφίου). Given that relationship, John's disciples were to understand that "He must increase, but I *must* decrease" [italics in KJV] (John 3:30). In downplaying who he was, compared to who Jesus is, John the Baptist said something about the relative weight that Jesus' testimony was to be given compared to his own. "He that cometh from above is above all: he that is of the earth is earthly, and speaketh of the earth: he that cometh from heaven is above all. And what he hath seen and heard, that he testifieth" (John 3:31-32).

If ever there was an expert witness Jesus was it. His credibility and veracity as a witness is equated with that of God Himself. "He that hath received his testimony hath set to his seal that God is true" (John 3:33). He, the God-Man, was giving testimony that was the very word of God, "For he whom God hath sent speaketh the words of

God" (John 3:34). Commenting on this verse, Blum says, "Thirty-nine times the Gospel of John refers to Jesus being sent from God. . . .This affirms Jesus' deity and heavenly origin, as well as God's sovereignty and love in initiating the Son's incarnation" (Edwin A. Blum, "John," in *The Bible Knowledge Commentary, New Testament*, ed. John F. Walvoord and Roy B. Zuck [Wheaton, IL: Victor, 1983; reprint, Colorado Springs: Cook, 1996], 283). The words that John the Baptist said next could only be true of God Himself, "for God giveth not the Spirit by measure *unto him*" [italics in KJV] (John 3:34). Men are capable of receiving only a portion of God's Spirit. Jesus, because He is part of the Trinity, has no such limitation.

The conclusion of John the Baptist's speech mirrors Jesus' words in John 3:16. Jesus said to Nicodemus that the result of belief in the "only begotten Son" (John 3:16) (τὸν υἱὸν τὸν μονογενῆ) would be, stated negatively, "should not perish" (μὴ ἀπόληται) and positively, "have eternal life" (ἔχῃ ζωὴν αἰώνιον). Similarly, John the Baptist said that the consequence for "He who believes in the Son" (John 3:36) (ὁ πιστεύων εἰς τὸν υἱὸν) would be that he, as stated positively, "has eternal life" (ἔχει ζωὴν αἰώνιον). Conversely John stated the cause negatively, "but he who does not obey the Son" (ὁ δὲ ἀπειθῶν τῷ υἱῷ), and the negative result, "shall not see life" (οὐκ ὄψεται ζωήν), and with the additional negative effect, "the wrath of God abides on him" (ἡ ὀργὴ τοῦ θεοῦ μένει ἐπ' αὐτόν).

The presence, in the text of John 3:36, of the words "but he who does not obey the Son" (ὁ δὲ ἀπειθῶν τῷ υἱῷ) has been used by some to insert obedience into belief. Not surprisingly, when that position is taken, obedience is watered down to a willingness or commitment to obey, because of the recognition that not doing so would violate passages that clearly exclude works from the salvation equation. The NASB version includes in its margin the word "believe" as an alternative. Louw and Nida indicate that this word can be translated as "unwillingness or refusal to comply with the demands of some authority—'to disobey, disobedience'" (Johannes P. Louw and Eugene A. Nida, *Greek-English Lexicon of the New Testament Based on Semantic Domains*, 2nd ed. [New York: United Bible Societies, 2nd ed], 1989, 1:468-69). But they note that it can also be translated, "to refuse to believe the Christian message—'to refuse to be a believer, to reject the Christian message, to refuse to believe'" (ibid., 1:379). Bauer, Arndt and Gingrich in their lexicon state:

> since, in the view of the early Christians, the supreme disobedience was a refusal to believe their gospel, [ἀπειθέω] may be restricted in some passages to the mng. disbelieve, be an unbeliever. This sense, though greatly disputed...seems most probable in J 3: 36; Ac 14: 12; 19: 9; Ro 15: 31, and only slightly less prob. In Ro 2:8; 1 Pt 2: 8; 3: 1, perh. also vs 20; 4: 17 ("ἀπειθέω" in Walter Bauer, William F. Arndt, and Wilbur F. Gingrich, *A Greek-English Lexicon of the New Testament and Other Early Christian Literature* [Chicago: University of Chicago Press, 1957], 82).

Having noted the parallels between Jesus' words in John 3:16 and what John the Baptist says in John 3:36, it would be highly unusual that the latter would introduce the notion of obedience (works), as an additional requirement for the reception of eternal life, whereas the former does not. The perceived need of those who do so, to waffle and water down the requirement for eternal life to a wanting, wishing, or willingness, or commitment to obey, rather than to actually obey, which their interpretation requires, exposes the untenable nature of this. The biblical text should be interpreted so that internal consistency is maintained, and attribute the use of the Greek verb "disbelieve" or "disobey" (ἀπειθέω) to stylistic variation rather than introduce an alien element into the context. The consistent theme of the Johannine Gospel is that the identity of Jesus is such that belief/trust, or conversely, disbelief/lack of trust in Him determines one's eternal destiny.

John Chapter 4

Jesus' conversation with a Samaritan woman at a well outside of Sychar centered on who He is. The woman immediately recognized Jesus as a Jew: "How is it that thou, being a Jew, askest drink of me, which am a woman of Samaria?" (John 4:9). In His answer Jesus advanced the issue of His identity a step further: "If thou knewest the gift of God, and who it is that saith to thee, Give me to drink; thou wouldest have asked of him, and he would have given thee living water" (John 4:10). The woman, no doubt did not understand completely Jesus' use of the term "water" in a spiritual sense, but she did refer to it as Jesus had, as "living water" (John 4:11).

Perhaps sarcastically, the woman said to Jesus, "Art thou greater than our father Jacob, which gave us the well, and drank thereof himself, and his children, and his cattle?" (John 4:12). She expected a negative reply, "No, I am not greater than Jacob." Instead of answering her question about His identity directly, Jesus addressed that by talking about the nature of the water He could supply. The water He offered would forever quench one's thirst and become a satisfying source of spiritual life, "But whosoever drinketh of the water that I shall give him shall never thirst; but the water that I shall give him shall be in him a well of water springing up into everlasting life" (John 4:14).

Who was the person who could give that kind of water? Jesus answered that question by telling her something about her past, something He could only have known supernaturally, "Thou hast well said, I have no husband: for thou hast had five husbands; and he whom thou now hast is not thy husband" (John 4:17-18). The woman's response was, "Sir, I perceive that thou art a prophet" (John 4:19). After initially assuming Jesus' inferiority to Jacob, she now elevated Him to equality with the patriarch.

The woman continued with what appears to be a change of subject, but may have been an attempt to salvage her Samaritan belief system, which she sensed was being undermined. She said, "Our fathers worshipped in this mountain; and ye say, that in Jerusalem is the place where men ought to worship" (John 4:20). Jesus' response to her was that a place of worship was not what was important. Most important is the God who is worshiped and the way in which He is worshiped. "God *is* a Spirit: and they that worship him must worship *him* in spirit and in truth" [italics in KJV] (John 4:24).

The construction in the Greek of the words "God is spirit" (John 4:24 NASB) (πνεῦμα ὁ θεός) does not have a verb but the "to be" verb is understood. Wallace demonstrates that the anarthrous (lacking the definite article) "spirit" (πνεῦμα ὁ θεός) is not to be understood as indefinite: "the KJV incorrectly renders this, 'God is *a* spirit'" (Daniel Wallace, *Greek Grammar beyond the Basics*, [Grand Rapids: Zondervan, 1996], 270, italics in original). The emphatic initial position of "spirit" (πνεῦμα) in the word order of the sentence militates against taking it as indefinite. Instead, as Wallace notes, "Here, πνεῦμα is qualitative–stressing the nature or essence of God" (ibid.). The Samaritan woman's argument about the physical location of worship recedes in light of the nature of the One who is worshiped. The manner of worship is dictated by the nature of God, and the channel of soteriological revelation that He has chosen is the Jewish people, "for salvation is of the Jews" (John 4:22). All arguments between Jew and Samaritan are settled by God's revelation culminating in the coming of the Messiah.

Not daring to venture whether Jesus was that One, the woman nevertheless brought up the subject, "I know that Messias[h] cometh, which is called Christ: when he is come, he will tell us all things" (John 4:25). Without equivocation, Jesus explicitly confirmed His identity to her. "I that speak unto thee am *he*" [italics in KJV] (John 4:26). She was a Samaritan, which may have been why He revealed His identity to her. Blum writes, "Normally in His ministry in Galilee and Judea (cf. 6:15) because of political implications, He veiled His office and used the title 'Son of Man.' But with this Samaritan the dangers of revolt by national zealots were not a problem" (Edwin A. Blum, "John," in *The Bible Knowledge Commentary, New Testament*, ed. John F. Walvoord and Roy B. Zuck [Wheaton, IL: Victor, 1983; reprint, Colorado Springs: Cook, 1996], 286).

When the woman, who was not a person of influence in that society, went and told her fellow townspeople whom she had met, she did not come right out and say He is the Messiah. Instead she gave them evidence of His supernatural revelation to her and invited them to come to their own conclusion. "Come, see a man, which told me all things that ever I did: is not this the Christ?" (John 4:29). She asked the question tentatively, in a form expecting a negative reply to pique their interest enough to make them want to check it out for themselves. Out of curiosity, they return with her to the well.

John, the author of the Gospel, in commenting on the response of the people of Sychar, depicts the woman as a witness, who testified about what she had seen. "And many of the Samaritans of that city believed on him for the saying of the woman, which testified, He told me all that ever I did" (John 4:39). For some of the townspeople, the woman's testimony alone was instrumental so that they "believed on Him" (ἐπίστευσαν εἰς αὐτὸν). For others, it was Jesus' words that brought about belief. "And many more believed because of his own word" (John 4:41). The Greek preposition translated "because of" (διὰ), is followed by the article and noun "the word" (τὸν λόγον) in the accusative case. As Wallace says, this is a basic use of this preposition with the accusative to indicate "Cause: *because of, on account of, for the sake of*" [italics in original] (Daniel Wallace, *Greek Grammar beyond the Basics*, [Grand Rapids: Zondervan, 1996], 368-69). It should be noted that the "belief" (ἐπίστευσαν aorist, active, indicative, from πιστεύω = "believe") was what resulted from "His word," the intermediate instrumental cause, resulting in trust in His divine person.

The pericope of the woman at the well ends with the words of Sychar's most recent converts to the woman who had introduced them to Jesus, "Now we believe, not because of thy saying: for we have heard *him* ourselves, and know that this is indeed the Christ, the Saviour of the world" [italics in KJV] (John 4:42). Again the preposition translated "because of" (διὰ) introduces the cause or reason for belief. First, hearsay evidence is mentioned. That reason or cause no longer applied, "thy saying" (John 4:42). Then the townspeople said that their conviction now rested on what they had personally witnessed, "for we have heard *him* ourselves" [italics in KJV]. The conclusion they had come to as eyewitnesses was, "[we] know that this is indeed the Christ, the Savior of the world" (John 4:42). They "believed in Him" (ἐπίστευσαν εἰς αὐτὸν), that is, they put their trust in Him, because they now knew His identity.

The reason Jesus told the woman about her previous and present relationships, was so that she would realize that He was more than a man. Jesus moved the conversation from her seeing Him as a prophet and her inquiry about His messianic identity, to His messianic self-identification. The pericope ends with the Samaritans' identifying exclamation, "this One is indeed the Christ, the Savior of the world" (John 4:42), which emphasizes the identity of the Savior. It should be noted that although some manuscripts do not include "the Christ," they still include the identifier, "the Savior of the world." The answer the Samaritan woman expected from her fellow Samaritans was not, "Yes, you are a sinner," or "Let us go see if He can tell us what sins we have committed," but rather, "Let us go see if he is the Christ or not." Jesus had exposed her iniquity in order to reveal His identity.

John Chapter 4 concludes with the healing of the nobleman's son. The author writes, "This *is* again the second miracle *that* Jesus did, when he was come out of Judaea into Galilee" [italics in KJV] (John 4:54). The first mention of a "sign" (σημεῖον) is in John 2:11, "This beginning of His signs Jesus did in Cana of Galilee," when He miraculously turned water into wine. John, the Gospel writer, says that that sign "manifested His glory" (John 2:11). It pointed to His identity, with the result that "His disciples believed in Him" (John 2:11). The "sign" in John Chapter 4 serves the same purpose.

The three times the verb "believe" (πιστεύω) is found in the present passage (John 4:46-54) are of interest. First, Jesus appears to rebuff "the royal official" (βασιλικὸς) who asked Him to heal His son, saying, "Except ye see signs and wonders, ye will not believe" (John 4:48). While the object of belief is not mentioned, it could mean to believe the proposition that Jesus could or would heal his son. However, Jesus may have been saying more than what the official would have understood at that moment, a reference to eternal salvation. While Jesus did not state the object of belief, it could mean that they would not believe the proposition "that Jesus is the Christ, the Son of

God" (John 20:31). However, Jesus could have been decrying the demand for miracles, not only for the purpose of believing a proposition to be true, but also to "believe in Him," that is, to put their trust in Him.

The meaning of the second use of the Greek verb "believe" (πιστεύω) in this passage is not ambiguous. After Jesus told the man: "Go thy way; thy son liveth" (John 4:50), it says, "The man believed the word that Jesus had spoken to him" (John 4:50). The object of the man's belief, "the word" (τῷ λόγῳ), was Jesus' words to him, "thy son liveth." The presence of the stated object of belief removes any ambiguity.

The object of the third use of "believe" (πιστεύω) in this passage is not explicitly stated. John 4:53 says, "So the father knew that *it was* at the same hour, in the which Jesus said unto him, Thy son liveth: and himself believed, and his whole house" [italics in KJV]. In the verse prior to this one, the father had asked his slaves exactly when the healing had happened. "Then inquired he of them the hour when he began to amend. And they said unto him, Yesterday at the seventh hour the fever left him" (John 4:52). The father was able to pinpoint the time of the healing and know that it coincided with the timing of Jesus' words to him. It could not have happened by chance or coincidence. Jesus had indeed healed his son.

Verse 53 could be a repetition of verse 50 where the royal official believed Jesus' word to be true. Or did he "believe" in another sense? It appears that the word "believe" (πιστεύω) in verse 53 conveys a meaning that is not limited to believing something Jesus said to be true, that his child would be healed. Did the man and his household believe that Jesus is who He said He is, because of what He had done, and had they put their trust in Him, the God-Man?

If this Gospel was written after the Acts of the Apostles, as is widely held, John the writer may have been aware of Luke's use of the term "household" (οἶκος) in relation to salvation. In Acts 11:14 when Peter recounted his Joppa experience he said, "Who shall tell thee words, whereby thou and all thy house shall be saved." The Philippian jailor in the familiar and often-quoted Acts 16:31 is told, "Believe on the Lord Jesus Christ, and thou shalt be saved, and thy house." Acts 18:8 says, "And Crispus, the chief ruler of the synagogue, believed on the Lord with all his house; and many of the Corinthians hearing believed, and were baptized."

In John 4:53 John the Apostle was likely indicating that the whole household of the royal official was converted. The healing miracle, validating Jesus' supernatural divine identity, led to the entire household trusting in Him for their eternal destiny.

John Chapter 5

In Jesus' healing of the paralytic on the Sabbath "the Jews" (οἱ Ἰουδαῖοι), a reference to the Jewish religious leadership who confronted the man, quizzed him on the identity of the One who had healed him. "What man is that which said unto thee, Take up thy bed, and walk?" (John 5:12). At that point the healed paralytic did not know the identity of the One who had healed him. Jesus sought him out and said to him, "Behold, thou art made whole: sin no more, lest a worse thing come unto thee" (John 5:14). Jesus must have told the man who He was because "The man departed, and told the Jews that it was Jesus, which had made him whole" (John 5:15). The reader/listener is told of an immediate result, "And therefore did the Jews persecute Jesus, and sought to slay him, because he had done these things on the sabbath day" (John 5:16). The use of the imperfect tense for the Greek word translated "was doing" (ἐποίει) could indicate that Jesus was making a habit of healing on the Sabbath.

If that was not enough to antagonize these people, what Jesus says to them next certainly did. Jesus says, "My Father worketh hitherto, and I work" (John 5:17). Jesus could have used inclusive language but He did not. As Blum notes, "Jesus did not say 'your Father' or even 'our father.' His opponents did not miss His claim to Deity" (Edwin A. Blum, "John," in *The Bible Knowledge Commentary, New Testament*, ed. John F. Walvoord and Roy B. Zuck [Wheaton, IL: Victor, 1983; reprint, Colorado Springs: Cook, 1996], 290). Jesus' relationship with God was not what theirs was. By not distinguishing His own work from that of God the Father, Jesus elevated Himself to the level of God. The brazenness of such a claim and its implications for Jesus' identity was not lost on "the Jews," the religious hierarchy.

The writer of the Gospel made this explicit with his editorial comment, "Therefore the Jews sought the more to kill him, because he not only had broken the sabbath, but said also that God was his Father, making himself equal with God" (John 5:18). Although present-day biblical scholars may argue over whether Jesus said He was God, His religious contemporaries concluded that He indeed made that claim.

Jesus' claim to deity continues in the verses that follow. Jesus claimed the actions of God to be the same as His own when He stated, "The Son can do nothing of himself, but what he seeth the Father do: for what things soever he doeth, these also doeth the Son likewise" (John 5:19). The greatest of miracles, the ability to raise someone from the dead, that only God could perform, was claimed by Jesus; "For as the Father raiseth up the dead, and quickeneth *them*; even so the Son quickeneth whom he will" [italics in KJV] (John 5:21).

The defining characteristic of deity is one's right to be worshiped. Jesus claimed that He is to be honored just as God the Father is honored "That all *men* should honour the Son, even as they honour the Father" [italics in KJV] (John 5:23). Jesus claimed that He is due the honor reserved for God alone. But also His intimate Trinitarian relationship with God the Father is such that it precluded an independent polytheistic identity. "He that honoureth not the Son honoureth not the Father which hath sent him" (John 5:23).

The Trinitarian relationship is one in which belief in the Father and the Son are inextricably intertwined. One cannot believe what one of them says is true and believe what the other says is false. One cannot put their trust in one, without thereby putting trust in the other. This was of such importance that Jesus prefaces His words with,

"Verily, verily, I say unto you. . . ." (John 5:24). Then Jesus said, ". . . . He that heareth my word, and believeth on him that sent me, hath everlasting life, and shall not come into condemnation; but is passed from death unto life" (John 5:24). The stated object of the present active participle with a definite article, translated as "he who hears" (ὁ ἀκούων), is "My word" (ὁ τὸν λόγον μου). Jesus' word is timeless, having universal application.

Jesus used a coordinating conjunction translated "and" (καὶ), followed by another present active participle translated "believes" (πιστεύων). While the coordinate Greek participles, "one who hears" (ἀκούων) and "believes" (πιστεύων), are parallel, the object of the former was what Jesus said, while the object of the latter is "him that sent me" (τῷ πέμψαντί με), that is, God the Father. While the NASB has the translation: "and believes Him who sent Me" (John 5:24), the KJV has, "and believeth on him that sent me," adding the preposition "on." The inclusion of the English preposition "on" in the KJV, and the lack thereof in the NASB, are both translating the dative case of the Greek article and participle, "the one who sent" (τῷ πέμψαντί). Writing about the use of the dative as a direct object with the verb "believe" (πιστεύω), Wallace says, "πιστεύω can be rendered 'I trust in'" (Daniel Wallace, *Greek Grammar beyond the Basics*, [Grand Rapids: Zondervan, 1996], 172). The KJV is not incorrect in its inclusion of the preposition "on," which could also have been "trust in," communicating an identical nuance, that of trust in a person.

In John 5:24 the question arises whether believing in God the Father is the same thing as believing the word of Jesus to be true and trusting in Him. Is it saying that, hearing that word and putting trust in the Father who sent Him, assures the acquisition of eternal life, "hath everlasting life" (John 5:24) (ἔχει ζωὴν αἰώνιον)? The result of doing that would be that judgment is averted, "and shall not come into condemnation" (καὶ εἰς κρίσιν οὐκ ἔρχεται), and passage from spiritual death to eternal life is secured, "but is passed from death unto life" (ἀλλὰ μεταβέβηκεν ἐκ τοῦ θανάτου εἰς τὴν ζωή).

John 5:24 brings up the relationship between trust in God the Father, and trust in Jesus. Given the truth of the Trinity, were both "trusts" functionally equivalent in that day, and are they now? Would trust in the God revealed in the Old Testament secure eternal salvation at the time of Jesus' earthly ministry? The answer to the latter is "yes," unless one had also received revelation of the identity of Jesus and had rejected it. Would trust in Jesus, during the time of His ministry, as He revealed Himself, be sufficient for eternal salvation? Yes. Today, trust in the Son whose identity is associated with the identity of the Father, is not independent of trust in the Father.

Tangentially relevant in John 5:24 is the issue of whether the present tense of the verb "believe" (πιστεύω) is to be given the meaning "keep on believing." As already mentioned, there are two Greek active, present tense participles in this verse, "one who hears" (ἀκούων), and "believes" (πιστεύων). Since they are parallel, they would be expected to carry the same nuance. One possibility would be that both of these terms have a continuous nuance, so that the meaning would be, "he who keeps on hearing My word, and keeps on believing Him who sent me." However, a better contextually consistent alternative is that both participles have a punctiliar meaning. For a discussion of the continuous versus punctiliar, or instantaneous rendering of the present tense, the reader is directed back to the remarks on John 3:16, in chapter 2, "Exegetical Eye-Openers."

Returning to the subject of resurrection that was raised in John 5:21, Jesus emphatically claims to be the agent of man's physical resurrection from the grave. Jesus says, "Verily, verily, I say unto you, The hour is coming, and now is, when the dead shall hear the voice of the Son of God: and they that hear shall live" (John 5:25). In case Jesus' audience did not think they heard what they thought they heard Him say, He repeated it; "Marvel not at this: for the hour is coming, in the which all that are in the graves shall hear his voice, and shall come forth" (John 5:28-29). In this discussion Jesus referred to Himself interchangeably as "the Son" (ὁ υἰὸς), "the Son of God" (τοῦ υἱοῦ τοῦ θεοῦ), and "the Son of Man" (υἰὸς ἀνθρώπου) who shares an intimate relationship with "the Father" (ὁ πατὴρ). The issue of identity is explicitly expressed by Jesus, when He provides legitimacy for the assertions He is making; "because he is the Son of Man" (John 5:27).

Astounding as the claims are, Jesus acknowledged the Jewish legal necessity for witnesses. "If I bear witness of myself, my witness is not true" (John 5:31). He then proceeded to provide two corroborating witnesses, the first of which was God the Father. "There is another that beareth witness of me; and I know that the witness which he witnesseth of me is true" (John 5:32). This was written testimony in the Old Testament where God identified who the Messiah would be. The second witness to Jesus' messianic identity is John the Baptist whom his listeners had heard. "Ye sent unto John, and he bare witness unto the truth" (John 5:33).

While men required the requisite number of credible witnesses to prove Jesus' identity claims, and He would comply with the law's requirement, He personally had no such need: "But I receive not testimony from man: but these things I say, that ye might be saved" (John 5:34). As God He is the only self-authenticating being. The provision of witnesses is an accommodation for man. Neither John the Baptist's testimony, nor Jesus' baptism by him, which identified Jesus to those who witnessed it, has any bearing on His ontological existence. The purpose of the Incarnation, and the evidence proving it, are for man's salvation; "but these things I say, that ye may be saved" (John 5:34).

Jesus realized that in the minds of many, words are cheap and people want physical evidence to back up oral testimony. Jesus' identity claims were corroborated by the physical evidence of the miracles He performed. "But I have greater witness than *that* of John: for the works which the Father hath given me to finish, the same works that I do, bear witness of me, that the Father hath sent me" [italics in KJV] (John 5:36). Unfortunately the words of God the Father, presented as evidence intended to bring those who heard them to faith, had not achieved their goal for those to whom Jesus addressed these words. "And the Father himself, which hath sent me, hath borne witness of me. Ye have neither heard his voice at any time, nor seen his shape. And ye have not his word abiding in you: for whom he hath sent, him ye believe not" (John 5:37-38). By not acknowledging the identity of Jesus as the Messiah, they had not observed "his shape" or "form," (εἶδος αὐτοῦ), the only manner in which God could be seen, by means of the Incarnation.

Their rejection of the testimony had a result: "And ye have not his word abiding in you" (John 5:38). The reason for the lack of God's word "abiding" (μένοντα), with its lexical nuance of "continuing," is introduced with the conjunction "for" (ὅτι), which here has a causal meaning "because." The abiding word was not being experienced "for [because] whom he hath sent, him ye believe not." Lack of trust in Jesus accounted for their lack of experiencing God's word.

In a court of law the prosecution and the defense attempt to present their respective evidence in terms that the jurors will understand, sometimes appealing to the values they hold. The audience to whom Jesus appealed shared a reverence for the Old Testament so He addressed them with, "Search the scriptures; for in them ye think ye have eternal life" (John 5:39). The Old Testament, which they treasured, was testimony that spoke of Jesus' identity as the Messiah; "and they are they which testify of me" (John 5:39). What they sought for, "eternal life" (ζωή αἰώνιος), could not be separated from Jesus, "And ye will not come to me, that ye might have life" (John 5:40).

During criminal and civil trials it is common to summon expert witnesses to give testimony relevant to the case being tried. Sometimes that is done in person, other times written testimony is introduced, and sometimes it is given in the form of sworn depositions. Jesus introduced the writings of Moses as evidence of who He is. Because Moses was dead and could not personally be summoned or subpoenaed, his writings were nevertheless introduced as evidence by Jesus, knowing that they would not be met with an objection.

In His closing argument Jesus said, "Do not think that I will accuse you to the Father: there is *one* that accuseth you, *even* Moses, in whom ye trust. For had ye believed Moses, ye would have believed me: for he wrote of me. But if ye believe not his writings, how shall ye believe my words?" (John 5:45-47). Jesus' opponents would not even accept Moses' testimony about His identity. If they rejected the testimony of one whom they professed to hold in high regard, there was no hope for them. There was no possible rebuttal to that argument. And with that, Jesus closed His case.

John Chapter 6

The Feeding of the Five Thousand, a miracle recorded in all four Gospels (Matthew 14:13-21; Mark 6:31-44; Luke 9:11-17; John 6:1-14), is called a "sign" (σημεῖον) by the author of the fourth Gospel, "Then those men, when they had seen the miracle ["sign" = σημεῖον] that Jesus did" (John 6:14). Louw and Nida say that a "sign" (σημεῖον) is a reference to "an event which is regarded as having some special meaning" (Johannes P. Louw and Eugene A. Nida, *Greek-English Lexicon of the New Testament Based on Semantic Domains*, 2nd ed. [New York: United Bible Societies,

2nd ed], 1989, 1:443). In the Gospel of John signs are used as evidence of Jesus' identity. That intended purpose was realized on this occasion and communicated by the author, "Then those men, when they had seen the miracle that Jesus did, said, This is of a truth that prophet that should come into the world" (John 6:14).

The people identified Jesus as the Messiah promised in the Old Testament and particularly zeroed in on His role as Davidic king. Their reaction and Jesus' response to their identification is included by the author; "When Jesus therefore perceived that they would come and take him by force, to make him a king, he departed again into a mountain himself alone" (John 6:15). Jesus intended that people come to the conclusion that He was the Messiah, but the timetable of the coming kingdom and that of events leading to the Crucifixion would be divinely and not humanly orchestrated.

The miracle of Jesus walking on water and the cluster of supernatural events accompanying it were also signs that proved His identity. The terror of the disciples was alleviated by Jesus identifying Himself to them, "But he saith unto them, It is I; be not afraid" (John 6:20). Their fear subsided as they recognized Jesus. "Then they willingly received him into the ship" (John 6:21). If Jesus' words "It is I" (ἐγώ εἰμι) did not immediately remind them of the Old Testament divine self-designation, "I am that I am" (Exodus 3:14; Isaiah 41:4), on later reflection it would.

In Jesus' day people were not that different from people today. People flock to ministries that emphasize their material needs and wants. In the first century, when Jesus fed people, they wanted to stick around for another free lunch. The author of the fourth Gospel spends several verses picturing the frantic search that took place when Jesus gave them the slip: "The day following, when the people which stood on the other side of the sea saw that there was none other boat there, save that one whereinto his disciples were entered, and that Jesus went not with his disciples into the boat, but *that* his disciples were gone away alone" [italics in KJV] (John 6:22). The author confirms that Jesus had not arrived there by boat. He had to have gotten there by some other means.

After the multitude took boats to where He was, they asked Him, "Rabbi, when camest thou hither?" (John 6:25). Jesus rebuked them for seeking physical rather than spiritual benefits. "Verily, verily, I say unto you, Ye seek me, not because ye saw the miracles, but because ye did eat of the loaves, and were filled. Labour not for the meat which perisheth, but for that meat which endureth unto everlasting life" (John 6:26-27). The source of eternal life was the Son of Man: "which the Son of Man shall give unto you" (John 6:27). Jesus was qualified to provide it because God the Father had set His imprimatur on Him; "for him hath God the Father sealed." The NASB reads, "for on Him the Father, *even* God, has set His seal" [italics in NASB] (John 6:27). In a context referring positively to "signs" (John 6:26) (σημεῖα), the verb translated "has set His seal" (John 6:27) (ἐσφράγισεν) is to be understood as God the Father's affirmation of Jesus' messianic identity and mission.

The multitude picked up on Jesus' reference to working, "Labour not" (John 6:27) (ἐργάζεσθε μὴ) and asked Him a question which may have been sarcastic, "What shall we do, that we might work the works of God?" (John 6:28). Their question was in line with the "works" mentality prevalent in that day. However, instead of giving them a "to do" list, Jesus deftly steered their mindset to a trust/rely requirement; "This is the work of God, that ye believe on him whom he hath sent" (John 6:29).

In His response Jesus changed the plural "the works of God" (τὰ ἔργα τοῦ θεοῦ) of the multitude's question, to a singular "the work of God" (τὸ ἔργον τοῦ θεοῦ). Ethelbert W. Bullinger uses this incident as an example of "Synœceiosis," which he defines as "The repetition of the same Word in the same Sentence with an Extended Meaning," and notes that "the word 'works' is used by the Jews in its proper acceptation: it is repeated by Christ in the same sense, but with another meaning altogether, as He goes on to explain" (*Figures of Speech used in the Bible* [Grand Rapids: Baker, 1898 reprint, 1968], 295). Jesus' explanation implied that "works" (ἔργα) were not to be done by man. Instead He stated that what was required was trust in Him, "that ye believe on Him [Jesus] whom he [God the Father] has sent" (John 6:29). If there is any "work" (ἔργον) to be done, it will be God's responsibility, whereas the requirement for man is to believe in Him. God would do what was needed on man's behalf. Jesus' substitutionary death on the cross for man's sin would be exactly that. All that man can do for eternal salvation is "trust" (πιστεύω) in Jesus.

The stubbornness of Jesus' audience is seen in their response. Although they mention belief, they insist on going back to the physical benefits that He could provide for them. In a crass attempt to manipulate Him to feed them again, they attempt to induce professional jealousy saying, "What sign shewest thou then, that we may see, and believe thee? what dost thou work? Our fathers did eat manna in the desert; as it is written, He gave them bread from heaven to eat" (John 6:30-31). Would Jesus equal or surpass what Moses had done for their ancestors?

Jesus turned the subject from the physical back to the spiritual; "Then Jesus said unto them, Verily, verily, I say unto you, Moses gave you not that bread from heaven; but my Father giveth you the true bread from heaven" (John 6:32). With those words Jesus implicitly placed Moses as subordinate to Himself and God the Father. The addition of the adjective "true" (ἀληθινός) turned the subject from the physical to the spiritual, but His listeners may have chosen to ignore the switch. Perhaps sarcastically they replied, "Lord, evermore give us this bread" (John 6:34). While they sought sustenance for physical life, His concern was for their spiritual well-being for which He was the source: "I am the bread of life: he that cometh to me shall never hunger; and he that believeth on me shall never thirst" (John 6:35).

Jesus' words elicited a negative response from some of them. "The Jews then murmured at him, because he said, I am the bread which came down from heaven" (John 6:41). The naysayers rejected His identity by arguing, "Is not this Jesus, the son of Joseph, whose father and mother we know? How is it then that he saith, I came down from heaven?" (John 6:42). Jesus' response excludes Himself from the realm of mankind. One of humanity's defining limitations, the inability to see God the Father (Exodus 33:20; John 1:18; 1 Timothy 6:16), does not apply to Jesus: "Not that any man hath seen the Father, save he which is of God, he hath seen the Father" (John 6:46). Jesus' opponents reject the identity that He invoked.

Continuing to use the metaphor of bread, Jesus makes a statement about His impending physical death, "the bread that I will give is my flesh, which I will give for the life of the world" (John 6:51). What people can receive from Jesus is eternally efficacious because He, the bread of life, would die on their behalf. Jesus is not looking for people to give, be willing to give, or to commit to give their lives sacrificially for Him, as part of what He requires in order for Him to give them eternal life. He gave His physical life, so that they might receive eternal, spiritual life. Jesus does not want people to give their lives in service to Him, in order to acquire eternal life, nor should that be watered down to their being willing to give their lives for Him as part of a saving transaction.

Some of Jesus' disciples were having a hard time getting their minds around His metaphorical language about eating His flesh; "Many therefore of his disciples, when they had heard *this*, said, This is an hard saying; who can hear it?" [italics in KJV] (John 6:60). This would have been a perfect opportunity for Jesus to expound on the adjective "hard" or "difficult" (σκληρός = "harsh" or "demanding") and say that the requirement for salvation is difficult in terms of works or a willingness or commitment to work. Instead, the gospel of Jesus, as spoken by Him, never wavers from the singular requirement; believe in Him.

How did Jesus explain the statement that the disciples found difficult, "Whoso eateth my flesh, and drinketh my blood, hath eternal life" (John 6:54)? Jesus asked, "Doth this offend you?" (John 6:61) (τοῦτο ὑμᾶς σκανδαλίζει;). According to Louw and Nida, the verb translated "offend" (or stumble) (σκανδαλίζω) has the meaning, "to cause someone to no longer believe–'to cause to give up believing, to make someone no longer believe.' τοῦτο ὑμᾶς σκανδαλίζει; 'does this cause you to no longer believe?' John 6:61" (Johannes P. Louw and Eugene A. Nida, *Greek-English Lexicon of the New Testament Based on Semantic Domains*, 2nd ed. [New York: United Bible Societies, 2nd ed], 1989, 1:376). Perhaps sensing a theological intrusion in that definition, which reads doctrine into their definition, and a violation of their stated lexical principle, Louw and Nida make reference to another possible meaning for the Greek verb σκανδαλίζω: "to cause someone to experience anger and/or shock because of what has been said or done–'to cause one to be offended, to offend'" (ibid, 1:308-9).

If the latter definition is accepted it could refer to the disciples' sensibilities, a revulsion to cannibalism, implied by the metaphor, "eateth my flesh" (John 6:53-57) (φάγητε τὴν σάρκα). If they had difficulty believing what Jesus said about eating His flesh, He reasoned with them, "*What* and if ye shall see the Son of man ascend up where he was before?" [italics in KJV] (John 6:62). The Ascension would be something even more unbelievable. The disciples' difficulty with what He said, stemmed from their literal interpretation, which Jesus corrected: "It is the spirit that quickeneth; the flesh profiteth nothing: the words that I speak unto you, *they* are spirit, and *they* are life" [italics in KJV] (John 6:63). The Holy Spirit is the One who gives eternal life in the spiritual realm and what Jesus spoke of has that as its result.

Unfortunately not everyone took advantage of what Jesus made available, "But there are some of you that believe not" (John 6:64). John, the author of the Gospel, lets the reader/listener know that what Jesus said was not speculation, a hunch, a possibility, or even a probability, but rather specific knowledge born of omniscience. "For Jesus knew from the beginning who they were that believed not, and who should betray him" (John 6:64). While there is a remote possibility that the words "who they were that believed not" (John 6:64) were not in the original manuscripts, there is no debate that Jesus, knowing who would betray Him, was in the original autograph. Jesus' knowledge of Judas' future betrayal is evidence of His omniscience and therefore His deity.

The following verse is probably one of the strongest verses in support of God the Father's activity in the salvation of men: "Therefore said I unto you, that no man can come unto me, except it were given unto him of my Father" (John 6:65). There was an immediate fallout to Jesus' words, "From that *time* many of his disciples went back, and walked no more with him" [italics in KJV] (John 6:66). Interestingly these who "went back" (ἀπῆλθον εἰς τὰ ὀπίσω), who made an exit, are referred to as "His disciples" (τῶν μαθητῶν αὐτοῦ). Some insist that there is no biblical distinction between being a disciple and being a believer, and that the terms always refer to saved individuals (except with the obvious exception of Judas Iscariot). In this context it is difficult to know for certain whether the departing disciples were saved but sanguine assertions that they had to be unsaved are based on theological rather than textual grounds.

In the same pericope, addressing His twelve disciples, perhaps as they were looking back at those disciples who had departed, Jesus asked, "Will ye also go away?" (John 6:67). Knowing what Jesus knew about Judas who would betray Him, one can almost feel a sense of sadness in His voice as He spoke those words. Simon Peter, perhaps feeling the emotion of the moment, quickly utters two of his most memorable sentences, a question followed by a response, "Lord, to whom shall we go? thou hast the words of eternal life" (John 6:68). Peter continued, with words that are just as momentous, "And we believe and are sure that thou art that Christ, the Son of the living God" (John 6:69).

Using the Greek perfect tense, in the active voice and indicative mood for both verbs, "we believe" or "we have believed" (John 6:69) (πεπιστεύκαμεν) and "are sure" or "we have come to know" (ἐγνώκαμεν), Peter indicates that they had known who Jesus is and believed, both events having been completed in the past but which now had ongoing results. Simon, as usual the spokesman for the group, got it right. His theology was impeccable, although his inclusive language was not quite on target. He probably got eleven out of twelve correct, or perhaps ten out of twelve, because doubting Thomas may not yet have been saved (John 20:26-29).

Jesus, aware of Judas Iscariot, did not stop to compliment Peter for his orthodox creedal confession but instead unleashed a rebuke, "Have not I chosen you twelve, and one of you is a devil?" (John 6:70). The adjective "devil" (διάβολος), used as a substantive (functioning as a noun), has the meaning of "slanderer." Failure to correctly identify Jesus is "slander." Those who refuse to believe in Jesus, have rejected His identity and replaced Him with something or someone other than "the Holy One of God" (John 6:69 NASB) (ὁ ἅγιος τοῦ θεοῦ), the title Peter used of Him.

John Chapter 7

Jesus got into a conversation with His blood brothers about going to Judea and making Himself known publicly in the center of Jewish religious power. Perhaps in the minds of His brothers He had become a source of embarrassment to them and they wanted Him out of there. It is difficult not to assign evil motives to them when they urged Jesus to go to Jerusalem where trouble awaited. John, the author, gives the reason why Jesus was in Galilee, "for he would not walk in Jewry [Judea], because the Jews sought to kill him" (John 7:1). His brothers subtly accused Him of being a "publicity hound" saying, "For *there is* no man *that* doeth any thing in secret, and he himself seeketh to be known openly" [italics in KJV] (John 7:4). Jesus' brothers rejected His messianic identity, proved by the miraculous signs he was performing, and mockingly said, "If thou do these things, shew thyself to the world" (John 7:4).

What were Jesus' brothers taunting Him to do? They wanted Him to reveal His identity, which they themselves rejected; "For neither did his brethren believe in him" (John 7:5). As seen in chapter 2, "Exegetical Eye-Openers," in the discussion of John 3:16 and the nature of saving faith, whether saving belief is punctiliar, taking place in a moment, or relatively short period of time, or continuous, the presence here of the imperfect tense in the indicative mood (ἐπίστευον) is not to be taken to mean that Jesus' brothers' saving belief, if it had occurred, would have been ongoing. The use of the iterative imperfect distributive, with the plural verb "believe" or "were believing" (ἐπίστευον) means that if Jesus' brothers had come to faith, each (distributive) would have come to faith at different times (iterative), prior in time (imperfect tense), to the writing of those words.

Jesus could not, and would not, comply with the urging of His brothers because to do so would have upset the divine timetable. The time for publicity had not yet come, but the opportunity for belief is always present. Jesus' future public identification did not keep him from offering a personal invitation: "My time is not yet come: but your time is alway ready" (John 7:6). Today the invitation is open, to examine the evidence for Jesus' identity and to conclude that He is who He claims to be, that He did what He claimed to do, dying for sins, and to place trust in Him for one's eternal destiny.

The issue of Jesus' identity inevitably became a topic of conversation when His name came up. In Jerusalem at the feast "there was much murmuring among the people concerning him: for some said, He is a good man: others said, Nay; but he deceiveth the people" (John 7:12). He was either a deceiver, or the Davidic messiah. The choice is clear. There are only two options; one either believes what Jesus says about Himself and places trust in Him, or does not believe who He is, and refuses to trust in Him.

When Jesus arrived in Jerusalem the buzz was all about who He is. The Gospel author mentions a question people were asking, "Do the rulers know indeed that this is the very Christ?" (John 7:26). The form of the question assumed a negative response that the rulers did not know who Jesus is. A. T. Robertson is undoubtedly correct in saying, "It was sarcasm about the leaders...there is ridicule of the rulers in the form of the question" (*Word Pictures in the New Testament*, 5:126). On His arrival, Jesus taught in the temple, where He said, "Ye both know me, and ye know whence I am" (John 7:28). The rulers' response was, "they sought to take him" (John 7:30), demonstrating their rejection and refusal to accept the truth of His identity.

In contrast to them, there were those who believed what Jesus said about Himself, and put their trust in Him. "And many of the people believed on him" (John 7:31). The multitude asked, "When Christ cometh, will he do more miracles than these which this *man* hath done?" [italics in KJV] (John 7:31). This is a rhetorical question because the text indicates that they had believed. The form in which the question was posed required a negative answer, "No, He would not perform more signs." Those who had believed used this rhetorical question as they debated those who rejected Jesus' claims.

One of the consequences of the failure to accept Jesus' claims about His identity was an inability to make sense of some of what He said. Jesus said: "Yet a little while am I with you, and *then* I go unto him that sent me. Ye shall seek me, and shall not find *me*: and where I am, *thither* ye cannot come" [italics in KJV] (John 7:33-34). Befuddlement resulted from a lack of belief, seen in those who rejected Jesus. "Then said the Jews among themselves, Whither will he go, that we shall not find him? will he go unto the dispersed among the Gentiles, and teach the Gentiles?" (John 7:35). The beginning of faith is knowing who Jesus is, without which nothing makes much sense.

Events were building during that week, and ended with Jesus saying, "If any man thirst, let him come unto me, and drink. He that believeth on me, as the scripture hath said, out of his belly shall flow rivers of living water" (John 7:37-38). The metaphor of drinking is explained as believing in Jesus. The source of the Old Testament quote may have been Isaiah 58:11, "And thou shalt be like a watered garden, and like a spring of water, whose waters fail not."

The editorial comment of the Gospel writer explains the enigmatically expressed result of drinking, "(But this spake he of the Spirit, which they that believe on him should receive: for the Holy Ghost was not yet *given*; because that Jesus was not yet glorified)" [parenthesis and italics in KJV] (John 7:39). Believers would experience the baptism by the Holy Spirit, but it would have been anachronistic to say during Jesus' ministry that those who believed in Him received the Holy Spirit in that way. The Gospel writer, who wrote this after believers had been baptized by the Holy Spirit was "connecting the dots" for his readers/listeners. Jesus' statement anticipated the day when that would happen.

Those who rejected Jesus' true identity were nevertheless awestruck by Him and still had to try to explain things some other way. Jesus' antagonists had been on a mission to apprehend Him, but their minions had come away empty-handed. When asked why they had not arrested Him, their answer was, "Never man spake like this man" (John 7:46). Such was the power of His words. One can sense the sneering of the Pharisees who responded to that reply with, "Are ye also deceived?" (John 7:47). The form of the question expects a negative reply but it appears from the context that the Pharisees thought that "the officers" (John 7:45) (οἱ ὑπηρέται) had indeed been taken in by Jesus. With withering words of condescension, the Pharisees pridefully boasted, "Have any of the rulers or of the Pharisees believed on him?" (John 7:48). The expected answer was something like, "Of course not."

Nicodemus was present and decided, however timidly, that it was time to speak up; "Nicodemus saith unto them, (he that came to Jesus by night, being one of them), Doth our law judge *any* man, before it hear him, and know what he doeth?" [parenthesis and italics in KJV] (John 7:50-51). The retort of the chief priests and Pharisees (τοὺς ἀρχιερεῖς καὶ Φαρισαίους) was sarcastic and swift, "Art thou also of Galilee? Search, and look: for out of Galilee ariseth no prophet" (John 7:52). Jesus did not fit their prophetic paradigm, and they thought that to identify with Him was beneath them. The reader/listener is not told for sure but it appears that Nicodemus says nothing in reply.

John Chapter 8

Jesus spoke of His identity with an "I am" statement, "I am the light of the world: he that followeth me shall not walk in darkness, but shall have the light of life" (John 8:12). Jesus saw Himself as the source of "the life" (τῆς ζωῆς). The Pharisees reject His claim, using as proof the lack of corroborating testimony, "The Pharisees therefore said unto him, Thou bearest record of thyself; thy record is not true" (John 8:13). They followed Old Testament protocol with its requirement of two or three witnesses (Deuteronomy 17:6; 19:15). To use a modern cliché, the Pharisees said, in effect, "You are just 'tooting your own horn.'" In that manner they justified their unbelief.

 The first point in Jesus' response to them relates to His identity. God is not bound by human standards for establishing truth. Jewish rules of evidence, required because of human fallibility, do not apply to God. What God says is true regardless of corroboration. By including Himself under the rules that apply to God alone, Jesus identified Himself as God. Jesus did that by saying, "Though I bear record of myself, *yet* my record is true: for I know whence I came, and whither I go; but ye cannot tell whence I come, and whither I go" [italics in KJV] (John 8:14).

The second part of Jesus' response was that even though what He said about His identity did not require corroboration, there are two witnesses. "It is also written in your law, that the testimony of two men is true. I am one that bear witness of myself, and the Father that sent me beareth witness of me" (John 8:17-18). Consequently, the Pharisees had no excuse for their unbelief. The evidence is sufficient.

Since He had appealed to the testimony of the Father, in order to try to have Him incriminate Himself they ask Him, "Where is thy Father?" (John 8:19). This question probably had a sarcastic implication with reference to Jesus' earthly father. That becomes explicit later in the chapter when they say, "We be not born of fornication" (John 8:41). Instead of answering their question Jesus addressed their unbelief. "Ye neither know me, nor my Father: if ye had known me, ye should have known my Father also" (John 8:19).

The meaning of the verb "know" (οἶδα) in this context goes beyond to "know about," "remember," or mere "acquaintance." Louw and Nida's following definition is applicable; "to acknowledge the high status of a person or event—'to honor, to show honor to, to respect'" (Johannes P. Louw and Eugene A. Nida, *Greek-English Lexicon of the New Testament Based on Semantic Domains*, 2nd ed. [New York: United Bible Societies, 2nd ed], 1989, 1:735). The Pharisees' failure to believe what Jesus said about His identity impugned the faith that they claim to have in God the Father. The God revealed by divine inspiration in the Old Testament could not be separated from His Incarnate Son who stood before them.

Because of the failure of the Jewish religious hierarchy to believe that Jesus is the Messiah they had to come up with an alternative explanation for what He said about Himself. Jesus told them, "I go my way, and ye shall seek me, and shall die in your sins: whither I go, ye cannot come" (John 8:21). Rather than accept that He was referring to a supernatural departure, they cynically insisted on taking what He said as suicidal, "Then said the Jews, Will he kill himself? because he saith, Whither I go, ye cannot come" (John 8:22). Jesus' response expressed the condemnation that they deserved, as well as its cause, "I said therefore unto you, that ye shall die in your sins: for if ye believe not that I am *he*, ye shall die in your sins" [italics in KJV] (John 8:24). In order for them to put their trust in the Messiah, they had to believe that He is the Messiah, as He claimed.

In the Jews' rejoinder they returned to the issue of Jesus' identity with the question, "Who art thou?" (John 8:25). The subject of Jesus' messianic identity was not new, but an integral part of His entire ministry. Jesus answers their question with one of His own, "What have I been saying to you *from* the beginning?" (John 8:25 NASB, italics in NASB), and added, among other things, "but He that sent me is true" (John 8:26). John, the author of this Gospel, picks up on Jesus' words, "He that sent me," and explains to the reader/listener that, "They understood not that he spake to them of the Father" (John 8:27). Their rejection blinded them to reality.

The realization of Jesus' identity would come with His crucifixion: "When ye have lifted up the Son of man, then shall ye know that I am *he*" [italics in KJV] (John 8:28). It was probably not lost on the original readers/listeners that Jesus used the words "I am" (ἐγώ εἰμι), which coincided with God the Father's Old Testament designation of Himself. For many in Jesus' audience, sufficient evidence of His identity is already in for them to draw a conclusion, and "As he spake these words, many believed on him" (John 8:30). They put their trust in Him.

Speaking to these individuals who were believers (those Jews which believed on him), Jesus uses the verb "abide" (μένω) in a conditional sentence, "If ye continue in my word, *then* are ye my disciples indeed" [italics in KJV] (John 8:31). He then added, "And ye shall know the truth, and the truth shall make you free" (John 8:32). Previously in this Gospel Jesus addressed His adversaries telling them, "And ye have not his word abiding in you" (John 5:38), a reference to the word of God the Father. The reason, Jesus said, was "for [because] whom he hath sent, him ye believe not" (John 5:38).

In John 8:31, Jesus was addressing individuals "who had believed Him" (τοὺς πεπιστευκότας αὐτῷ), they had been converted (πεπιστευκότας = perfect active participle from πιστεύω "believe"). As mentioned earlier, the pronoun "Him" (αὐτῷ) is in the dative case and can be translated "in Him." Jesus said to these believers, "If ye continue in my word," which was the contingent part of the conditional sentence, there would be three outcomes. The first would be "are ye my disciples indeed" (John 8:31), the second, "ye shall know the truth" (John 8:32), and the third, "the truth shall make you free" (John 8:32). The freedom experienced by the children of God, is made possible by becoming "disciples indeed," the key which is to know the truth of God's word.

Jesus' statement linking discipleship, truth, and freedom in John 8:31-32 is a parenthetical aside that Jesus addressed to those among the Jews who came to believe in Him. Before and after these verses Jesus engaged those who rejected Him and His message. In the preceding context Jesus describes their condition with, "Ye are from beneath" (John 8:23) and "ye are of this world" (John 8:23). Later Jesus told them, "Ye are of *your* father the devil" [italics in KJV] (John 8:44).

The response of unbelief was to reject Jesus' identity and accuse Him of the worst thing they could think of, "Say we not well that thou art a Samaritan" (John 8:48), and for good measure they added, "and hast a devil." After Jesus refuted their accusations, they came back with another assault on His identity and ask, "whom makest thou thyself?" (John 8:53). The NASB translates, "whom do you make Yourself out *to be?*" [italics in NASB]. Since "the Jews" (οἱ Ἰουδαῖοι), the Jewish religious leadership, were questioning His identity, Jesus made the astounding statement, "Your father Abraham rejoiced to see my day: and he saw *it*, and was glad" [italics in KJV] (John 8:56). Those who heard Jesus understood that He claimed an existence contemporaneous with that of Abraham, and they strenuously objected. "Thou art not yet fifty years old, and hast thou seen Abraham?" (John 8:57).

Their disbelief was met with an even more astounding claim, "Verily, verily, I say unto you, Before Abraham was, I am" (John 8:58). Not only did Jesus claim to be contemporaneous with Abraham, but He said that He preceded him chronologically as well. Again Jesus used the words "I am" (ἐγὼ εἰμί), reminiscent of the Old Testament divine name that God used of Himself. Jesus' self-proclaimed identity presented two options; either believe the claim or consider it blasphemy. His antagonists chose the latter option and reacted accordingly; "Then took they up stones to cast at him" (John 8:59).

John Chapter 9

Jesus made another of His enigmatic "I am" statements. "As long as I am in the world, I am the light of the world" (John 9:5). The author began his Gospel with "*That* was the true Light, which lighteth every man that cometh into the world" [italics in KJV] (John 1:9), and Jesus identified Himself as that One. In chapter 9 Jesus confirmed His words by giving sight to a man blind from birth. Asked by His disciples the reason for the man's blindness, which they assumed to have been caused by personal or parental sin, Jesus explained, "Neither hath this man sinned, nor his parents: but that the works of God should be made manifest in him" (John 9:3). Jesus essentially tells them that their assumption is a wrong application of reverse engineering. A result cannot necessarily be traced back mechanically to its cause. God's glory is the overarching agenda of the universe and He can righteously assign a lifelong affliction for His own divine purpose.

The now sighted man drew the attention of his neighbors who focused on the man's identity and asked, "Is not this he that sat and begged?" (John 9:8). The discussion went on, "Some said, This is he: others *said*, He is like him: *but* he said, I am *he*" [italics in KJV] (John 9:9). Because the man kept on insisting that he was indeed the same man, the neighbors turn to the subject of his sight and asked, "How were thine eyes opened?" (John 9:10). When the man attributes his healing to "a man that is called Jesus" (John 9:11), and said he did not know His whereabouts, they took him to the Pharisees. The healing had taken place on the Sabbath, so it triggered an investigation. Opinions quickly polarized over Jesus' identity. "Therefore said some of the Pharisees, This man is not of God, because he keepeth not the sabbath day. Others said, How can a man that is a sinner do such miracles?" (John 9:16).

Unable or unwilling to come to a resolution because of the conundrum it presented, they asked the former blind beggar who he thought Jesus is, "What sayest thou of him, that he hath opened thine eyes?" (John 9:17). The man probably thought, "Here I am among the religious leaders and they're asking me?" Nevertheless he ventured his opinion, "He is a prophet" (John 9:17), which was not what the Pharisees wanted to hear. The tactic they resorted to was, "If you cannot accept the result, deny the premise." They questioned whether the man had been born blind, "But the Jews did not believe concerning him, that he had been blind" (John 9:18).

When the man's parents were brought in for questioning they confirmed it was their son but they steered clear of saying who they thought Jesus is. They sensed a setup and fearing "the Jews" (οἱ Ἰουδαῖοι), the religious hierarchy, they in effect "threw their son under the bus." They said, "he is of age; ask him: he shall speak for himself" (John 9:21). Never mind that the man could not remember back to the time of his birth. John, the author, explains what was going on. "These *words* spake his parents, because they feared the Jews: for the Jews had agreed already, that if any man did confess that he was Christ, he should be put out of the synagogue" [italics in KJV] (John 9:22). Excommunication was the price to pay for believing Jesus' messianic identity.

The man who had been blind was brought in again. Because he was walking, talking evidence of who Jesus is, they attempted to intimidate him by bringing him down to headquarters and questioning him again; "Then again called they the man that was blind, and said unto him, Give God the praise: we know that this man is a sinner" (John 9:24). After continued harassment the man was losing his patience with his interrogators. With sarcasm "He answered them, I have told you already, and ye did not hear: wherefore would ye hear *it* again? will ye also be his disciples?" [italics in KJV] (John 9:27). Wrong answer.

Those questioning the man Jesus had healed said, "We know that God spake unto Moses: *as for* this *fellow*, we know not from whence he is" [italics in KJV] (John 9:29). One's origin is crucial to establishing identity. Repeatedly Jesus' heavenly origin was questioned. Amazingly the man who had been born blind showed greater spiritual insight than the religious leaders did. He said to them, "If this man were not of God, he could do nothing" (John 9:33). The interrogators had had enough of this smart aleck.

After the man was excommunicated Jesus approached him and asked, "Dost thou believe on the Son of God?" (John 9:35). In order for the man to put his trust in the Son of God he had to know who He is, so he asked, "Who is he, Lord, that I might believe on him?" (John 9:36). Jesus unequivocally identified Himself as the Son of God. "And Jesus said unto him, Thou hast both seen him, and it is he that talketh with thee" (John 9:37). The man's response was to put his trust in Jesus. He said, "Lord, I believe" (John 9:38).

The blindness of the beggar pictures the spiritual blindness of everyone and the restoration of his physical sight depicts the regeneration that is obtained by means of belief. The physical sight of those who refuse to believe belies a spiritual blindness of which they will not be healed because of their unbelief. Jesus expressed that paradox with the words, "For judgment I am come into this world, that they which see not might see; and that they which see might be made blind" (John 9:39). The Pharisees could not believe that what Jesus was saying applied to them, so Jesus stated it directly, "If ye were blind, ye should have no sin: but now ye say, We see; therefore your sin remaineth" (John 9:41). Believing requires the sinner to see himself or herself as a sinner and identify who the Savior is.

John Chapter 10

In John 10 Jesus used metaphors to identify who He is and to explain His role. His intent at that time and place was to veil the message. As the writer comments, "This parable spake Jesus unto them: but they understood not what things they were which he spake unto them" (John 10:6). Jesus established His legitimacy as a shepherd who had the right to enter the sheepfold. "But he that entereth in by the door is the shepherd of the sheep" (John 10:2). He also used the shepherd motif to explain His pastoral function, "I am the good shepherd: the good shepherd giveth his life for the sheep" (John 10:11).

Between those two statements Jesus shifted from the figure of a shepherd to that of a sheepfold door. "I am the door: by me if any man enter in, he shall be saved, and shall go in and out, and find pasture" (John 10:9). The means by which people are saved is His person, "by me" (δι' ἐμοῦ). The salvation experience and subsequent progressive sanctification are illustrated as someone who "enters" (εἰσέρχομαι) with a twofold result: (1) conversion, "he shall be saved;" and (2) the Christian walk, "and shall go in and out, and find pasture."

Jesus returned to the figure of Himself as a shepherd and foreshadowed His sacrifice for sin. "the good shepherd giveth his life for the sheep" (John 10:11). Twice more the sacrifice motif is brought up. Jesus said, "As the Father knoweth me, even so know I the Father: and I lay down my life for the sheep" (John 10:15), and "Therefore doth my Father love me, because I lay down my life, that I might take it again" (John 10:17). Those statements produced a sharp reaction. "There was a division therefore again among the Jews for these sayings" (John 10:19).

Again the issue of Jesus' identity arose, "And many of them said, He hath a devil, and is mad; why hear ye him? Others said, These are not the words of him that hath a devil. Can a devil open the eyes of the blind?" (John 10:20-21). The form of their question expected a negative reply, but where that led would have been unacceptable to them.

One can sense the exasperation of "the Jews" (οἱ Ἰουδαῖοι), Jesus' religious antagonists, in Jerusalem during the Feast of the Dedication when they approached Him saying, "How long dost thou make us to doubt? If thou be the Christ, tell us plainly" (John 10:24). In response Jesus said that He had already told them and pointed to the evidence of His identity. "I told you, and ye believed not: the works that I do in my Father's name, they bear witness of me" (John 10:25). The two items of evidence were Jesus' message, what He said (εἶπον), and His miracles, what He did (ἔργον), neither of which they were willing to accept. The requisite number of witnesses had been presented and their testimony summarily dismissed.

A crisis point was reached when Jesus unexpectedly said, "I and *my* Father are one" [italics in KJV] (John 10:30). Blum says:

> When Jesus said, I and the Father are One [bold in original], He was not affirming that He and the Father are the same Person. The Son and the Father are two Persons in the Trinity. This is confirmed here by the fact that the word 'One' is neuter. Instead, He was saying They have the closest possible unity of purpose. Jesus' will is identical to the Father's regarding the salvation of His sheep. And yet absolute identity of wills involves identity of nature. Jesus and the Father are One in will (and also in nature for both are God; cf. 20:28; Phil. 2:6; Col. 2:9) (Edwin A. Blum, "John," in *The Bible Knowledge Commentary, New Testament*, ed. John F. Walvoord and Roy B. Zuck [Wheaton, IL: Victor, 1983; reprint, Colorado Springs: Cook, 1996], 311-12).

The reaction of "the Jews" (οἱ Ἰουδαῖοι) was severe. They understood Him to be equating Himself to God ontologically, in His essence, which to them was blasphemy. When Jesus referred to the proof of His works which were those of God the Father, their response was; "For a good work we stone thee not; but for blasphemy; and because that thou, being a man, makest thyself God" (John 10:33).

Jesus' reasoning followed the form, "from the lesser to the greater," and He pointed out that His argument was based on the Old Testament, which is God's word which "cannot be broken" (John 10:35) (δύναται λυθῆναι). Jesus made the point that since the Old Testament appropriately uses the term "gods" of those who were only recipients of God's word, "unto whom the word of God came" (John 10:35), how much more fitting it is for Jesus to use the title "Son of God" (John 10:36) of Himself, "whom the Father hath sanctified, and sent into the world" (John 10:36). John's prologue had proclaimed that before them stood One who had been sent by God the Father Himself.

The intensity of the encounter at the Feast of the Dedication was such that Jesus sought refuge in a less populated region: "Therefore they sought again to take him: but he escaped out of their hand, and went away again beyond Jordan into the place where John at first baptized; and there he abode" (John 10:39-40). People in the area remembered John the Baptist's ministry and what he had said about Jesus. They connected his testimony and message with the One who was now in their midst: "And many resorted unto him, and said, John did no miracle: but all things that John spake of this man were true" (John 10:41). The author thereby tied the conversion of these people to the testimony of that prior witness. People who had heard John the Baptist's testimony and that of Jesus Himself made the correct doctrinal connection. And the intended purpose of the combined evidence was realized in these individuals. "And many believed on him there" (John 10:42). They put their trust in Jesus.

John Chapter 11

Lazarus of Bethany suffered from an unnamed sickness. And even though he would die from it, Jesus said, "This sickness is not unto death, but for the glory of God, that the Son of God might be glorified thereby" (John 11:4). For Lazarus, death would not be the final answer that day. Instead, death itself would serve the dual, divinely intertwined goal of bringing "glory" (δόξα) to Jesus and God the Father. What made that combined goal achievable is the deity shared by the Father and the Son. The resurrection of Lazarus would reveal Jesus' identity which would bring "glory" (δόξα) to God the Father and His Son.

Jesus deliberately delayed His journey to Bethany rather than depart immediately to attend to Lazarus. "When he had heard therefore that he was sick, he abode two days still in the same place where he was" (John 11:6). The delay was so that Lazarus would die; the greater the degree of difficulty the greater the glory. Humanly speaking, "Where there's life there's hope," but with Jesus there is always hope. Jesus pictured the life and death distinction as that between day and night, darkness and light: "Are there not twelve hours in the day? If any man walk in the day, he stumbleth not, because he seeth the light of this world. But if a man walk in the night, he stumbleth, because there is no light in him" (John 11:9-10). Jesus had told His disciples, "As long as I am in the world, I am the light of the world" (John 9:5). They were about to witness the power of His presence when faced with the darkness of death.

Martha, Lazarus' sister, appeared to be a "go-getter," more so than her sister Mary. "Then Martha, as soon as she heard that Jesus was coming, went and met him: but Mary sat *still* in the house" [italics in KJV] (John 11:20). Martha believed that Jesus could heal the sick, but it was too late for that. "Then said Martha unto Jesus, Lord, if thou hadst been here, my brother had not died" (John 11:21). She believed Jesus to be a healer, but He wanted her to believe that He is more than that. Martha believed that He is the conduit of divine blessing. "But I know, that even now, whatsoever thou wilt ask of God, God will give *it* thee" [italics in KJV] (John 11:22).

Jesus wanted her to know that He is the source of life, both spiritual and physical, and so He went from a discussion about physical healing to the subject of physical resurrection. "Jesus saith unto her, Thy brother shall rise again" (John 11:23). It was far from Martha's mind that the One talking to her could restore her brother to life. She believed in the theological truth of an eschatological future resurrection of the body, but not in the present possibility that Jesus could raise her brother from the dead. "Martha saith unto him, I know that he shall rise again in the resurrection at the last day" (John 11:24). She knew what would happen in the by-and-by, but not what Jesus could do in the present. We must not blame Martha. We who have put trust in Jesus for our eternal destiny many times have trouble depending on Him in our everyday trials, not to mention having faith that He will raise someone from the dead.

This was not the first time that Jesus came to Bethany. On previous occasions He had visited with Martha and her two siblings, Mary and Lazarus, and had stayed with them in their home. There is no reason to doubt that all three of them had put their trust in Jesus for their eternal destiny. Martha said as much about her deceased brother. She expressed confidence that her brother Lazarus would one day be included in the resurrection of dead believers (John 11:24). Martha's problem was not her eternal future, but her present feelings. She missed Lazarus and grieved because of his absence. Jesus is truly human and He also feels emotion. Exactly how He experiences grief is to some degree wrapped up in the mystery of the Incarnation. The inspired text does say that "Jesus wept" (John 11:35).

Martha needed additional insight into who it was who stood before her, and Jesus proceeded to tell her. "Jesus said unto her, 'I am the resurrection and the life'" (John 11:25). Not only is Jesus the source of life for physical bodies and spiritual souls, both here and now and for the hereafter, in His person He represents life. Jesus explained what He meant by that: "he that believeth in me, though he were dead, yet shall he live: and whosoever liveth and believeth in me shall never die" (John 11:25-26). Jesus' words were to be understood as follows: "he that believeth in me, though he were dead [spiritually], yet shall he live [spiritually]: and whosoever liveth [physically] and believeth in me shall never die [spiritually]" (John 11:25-26). The life that results from belief is spiritual life that physical death cannot defeat.

Belief resulting in spiritual life must take place during one's physical lifetime. The thread linking the two parts of the sentence is the person of Jesus. Trust in Jesus is the key to eternal salvation, and although we may fail to acknowledge it, Jesus is the sustainer of physical life as well. Jesus is the one who controls physical as well as spiritual life. Jesus asked Martha, "Believest thou this?" (John 11:26). Martha believed that Jesus is the source of spiritual life but she had difficulty facing the apparent finality of her brother being physically dead.

The pronouncement Jesus made was about His identity. Jesus' question to Martha was whether she believed Jesus is who He said He is. Did she believe that Jesus is the One on whom eternal and physical life depends? Did she believe that the One talking with her had those prerogatives and that power? Martha answered Jesus' question affirmatively and accordingly: "Yea, Lord: I believe that thou art the Christ, the Son of God, which should come into the world" (John 11:27). Martha believed that Jesus is the Messiah, but she was having difficulty believing that Jesus could physically raise her brother Lazarus from the dead. She knew that Jesus the Messiah was there and that was all that mattered.

If Jesus was able to accomplish the greater, bestow eternal life on one who believes in Him, which He could, those mourning Lazarus' death would soon see that He could do the lesser, restore physical life to a dead body. The raising of Lazarus from the dead would provide powerful evidence that Jesus is indeed God. In His prayer before He raised Lazarus Jesus referred to the benefit that those who witnessed this resurrection would receive, "Father, I thank thee that thou hast heard me. And I knew that thou hearest me always: but because of the people which stand by I said *it*, that they may believe that thou hast sent me" [italics in KJV] (John 11:41-42). Jesus' descent from the presence of God the Father identified Him as One with Him.

Jesus accomplished His mission. "Many of the Jews which came to Mary, and had seen the things which Jesus did, believed on him" (John 11:45). Jesus said, "if thou wouldest believe, thou shouldest see the glory of God" (John 11:40). For some, belief preceded Lazarus' being raised from the dead, for others it came as a result of the miracle: "Then many of the Jews which came to Mary, and had seen the things which Jesus did, believed on him" (John 11:45).

With the word translated "had seen" ("beheld" = NASB, θεασάμενοι aorist participle from θεάομαι) the reader/listener is reminded of the same Greek word for "beheld" (ἐθεασάμεθα aorist indicative, also from θεάομαι) that the Gospel writer used in his introduction, "and we beheld His glory" (John 1:14). These people exercised faith that was not just the belief in propositional truth about Jesus' divine identity, although they did do that. They put their trust in Jesus based on the evidence of the raising of Lazarus' from the dead.

The assertion has been made by some that Jesus' question to Martha, "Do you believe this?" (John 11:27) (πιστεύεις τοῦτο;) refers back to the propositional statement that Jesus made about Himself, and that belief in the truth of that statement is the requirement for obtaining eternal life. Jesus' words to Martha have been taken as a creedal mantra of sorts, representing the minimum "content" that must be believed to secure eternal life. Nothing is wrong with creeds or theological confessions. The question, however, is this: "Is the propositional truth they express about Jesus an end in itself, something to be believed to be true, or are they declarations identifying the One in whom trust is to be placed?"

The "content" driven "minimalist" approach (explained in chapter 1, "The Case for Minimum Content") seems to reduce to the following: I believe [the proposition to be true] that Jesus gives eternal life to those who believe [the proposition to be true] that He gives eternal life to those who believe [that proposition to be true]. The epistemological dog is chasing its proverbial tail. However, it seems doubtful that the New Testament writers had that in mind. That interpretation assumes a paradigmatic presuppositional conceptual construct of "content." True, content is critical. Without it no one would know who Jesus is. Is knowledge of His identity sufficient? No.

A valid interpretation must take into consideration the dual meaning of the verb "believe" (πιστεύω) that Jesus used three times in His words to Martha. The first two times it is used with a preposition and stated object, "believeth in Me" (John 11:25-26) (πιστεύων εἰς ἐμὲ). This construction conforms to the Johannine salvific formula for trust in the person of Jesus for eternal life. The third use of "believe" (πιστεύω) in these two verses (John 11:25-26) has the object as "this" (τοῦτο) in Jesus' question, "Do you believe this?" (John 11:26) (πιστεύεις τοῦτο;) and unambiguously refers to belief that a proposition is true. The proposition to be believed is that Jesus is who He says He is, One who because He is God can grant eternal life to those who put their trust in His person. An evidence/identity/trust paradigm, in contrast to a "content only" construct, does justice to the polysemantic (having more than one meaning) nature of the term "believe" (πιστεύω).

A religious council convened to determine what to do about the astounding miracle of Lazarus' resurrection. Caiaphas the high priest who would qualify as a hostile witness inadvertently testified to Jesus' identity. Caiaphas addressed the council saying, "Ye know nothing at all, nor consider that it is expedient for us, that one man should die for the people, and that the whole nation perish not" (John 11:49-50). His intent was to preclude Roman intervention, although religious self-interest cannot be excluded.

The Gospel writer reveals divine intervention acting behind the scenes, with Caiaphas unaware of the significance of his words. "And this spake he not of himself: but being high priest that year, he prophesied that Jesus should die for that nation; and not for that nation only, but that also he should gather together in one the children of God that were scattered abroad" (John 11:51-52). Caiphas's statement, motivated by expediency, by divine design became instead a statement about expiation. The Gospel writer thereby affirmed the truths of Jesus' substitutionary atonement and the universal character of the church. A man plotting the death of the Messiah was also prophesying in detail about His mission.

John Chapter 12

Lazarus achieved celebrity status. He was a living, walking, talking "Exhibit A"– evidence that proved Jesus' identity. Lazarus' testimony alarmed the chief priests. The solution they proposed was to get rid of the witness. They had already concluded that Jesus had to be put to death, and they added Lazarus to their hit list. "But the chief priests consulted that they might put Lazarus also to death" (John 12:10). The problem of the chief priests' was compounded. Not only were many convinced that Lazarus had been raised from the dead, but also they were putting their trust in Jesus who had performed his resurrection. "By reason of him many of the Jews went away, and believed on Jesus" (John 12:11). The NASB says that "on account of him [Lazarus] many of the Jews were going away, and were believing in Jesus."

The verb translated in the NASB "were believing" (ἐπίστευον) is a Greek imperfect active indicative. Normally the imperfect tense has the nuance of continuous past activity, however in the New Testament when it is found with a plural noun or pronoun, particularly with the verb "believe" (πιστεύω), the Greek imperfect has a distributive, iterative nuance. The text indicates that these Jews had each individually, at a time in the past, put their trust in Jesus. While these people could and probably did continue to believe in Jesus, the verb form does not necessarily make that assertion.

The reader is referred back to chapter 2 "Exegetical Eye-Openers" and the discussion of John 3:16 and the question of whether belief for eternal life is continuous.

The reaction of the crowd during Jesus' Triumphal Entry into Jerusalem was directly the result of the resurrection of Lazarus. The multitude was incited by the testimony of those who had witnessed that miracle. "The people therefore that was with him when he called Lazarus out of his grave, and raised him from the dead, bare record. For this cause the people also met him, for that they heard that he had done this miracle" (John 12:17-18). The NASB says, "And so the multitude who were with Him when He called Lazarus out of the tomb, and raised him from the dead, were bearing Him witness. For this cause also the multitude went and met Him, because they heard that He had performed this sign."

The multitude who were witnesses, and the multitude who heard the testimony of the witnesses, considered Jesus and not Lazarus to be the biggest celebrity. The Gospel writer points out the significance of Lazarus' resurrection as a "sign" (σημεῖον) (John 12:18), something that pointed to something and/or someone. Here the "something" was Jesus' identity and the "someone" was Jesus Himself. The cumulative significance of a multitude upon a multitude highlights the presence of a multiplicity of witnesses abundantly exceeding the minimal requirements for the credibility of evidence.

The appointed time for the crucifixion was near, and though from an earthly perspective the crucifixion would seem to be a tragic event, instead it became a moment of triumph. Jesus said, "The hour is come, that the Son of man should be glorified" (John 12:23). Jesus compared His upcoming death with what happens to grains of wheat, "Verily, verily, I say unto you, Except a corn of wheat fall into the ground and die, it abideth alone: but if it die, it bringeth forth much fruit" (John 12:24). Without the death of Christ there would be no salvation. If Jesus had held on to His physical life refusing to go to the cross, there would be no eternal life for mankind: "He that loveth his life shall lose it; and he that hateth his life in this world shall keep it unto life eternal" (John 12:25).

Not only was it true of Jesus Himself, that to "keep" (φυλάσσω, "guard" or "protect") His physical life would come at a price, there is also a sense in which anyone who clings to physical life "in this world" (ἐν τῷ κόσμῳ τούτῳ), ignoring the world to come, will find it costly. While the preservation of physical life by a human being, or giving it up in death, will not result in securing eternal salvation, there is an arena in which sacrifice is appropriate. The principle is this: "If any man serve me, let him follow me; and where I am, there shall also my servant be: if any man serve me, him will *my* Father honour" (John 12:26).

The recompense for "serving" (διακονέω) and "following" (ἀκολουθέω) Jesus is not eternal salvation but being "honored" (τιμάω) by God the Father. When Jesus said, "and where I am, there shall also my servant be" (John 12:26), which comes after the idea of "following" (ἀκολουθέω), perhaps he meant that following Him they would experience death (Edwin A. Blum, "John," in *The Bible Knowledge Commentary, New Testament*, ed. John F. Walvoord and Roy B. Zuck [Wheaton, IL: Victor, 1983; reprint, Colorado Springs: Cook, 1996], 317). Jesus died for the sins of man. Many of His disciples would die a martyr's death. The broadened application was parenthetical, and then Jesus returned to the main theme of His discourse. Jesus said, "Now is my soul troubled; and what shall I say? Father, save me from this hour: but for this cause came I unto this hour" (John 12:27).

Some have taken Jesus' words in this passage about dying vs guarding one's life as the presentation of a requirement for salvation. Any assertion that such is the case must take into consideration that the statement in verse 24 about a grain of wheat (σῖτος) might be associated with Jesus' words about His own glorification in verse 23 (δοξάζω). If that is correct, then the words, "keep it unto life eternal" (John 12:25), could apply to the eternal life that Jesus' death secured. Jesus was thinking about what He was about to do for people's salvation, certainly not what they would do to partially pay for it. The words "unto eternal life" (John 12:25) applied to man's endeavors could be a reference to that future time for which present efforts are being done, when toil on earth will translate into treasure in heaven.

The crucifixion weighed heavily on Jesus' mind and He returned to that subject: "Now is my soul troubled; and what shall I say? Father, save me from this hour: but for this cause came I unto this hour" (John 12:27). Jesus knew His crucifixion would exalt God the Father, and so He said, "Father, glorify thy name" (John 12:28) (πάτερ, δόξασόν σου τὸ ὄνομα). "The name" (τὸ ὄνομα) was a reference to His Person. God the Father's response was to speak audibly from heaven: "Then came there a voice from heaven, *saying*, I have both glorified *it*, and will glorify *it* again" [italics in KJV] (John 12:28).

In leading up to the raising of Lazarus from the dead Jesus had said, "Said I not unto thee, that, if thou wouldest believe, thou shouldest see the glory of God?" (John 11:40). God the Father may have been referring to that event when He spoke from heaven and said, "I have…glorified it" (John 12:28) (ἐδόξασα). The future "and will glorify *it* again" [italics in KJV] (John 12:28) (καὶ πάλιν δοξάσω), may refer to what Jesus spoke about in John 12:32: "And I, if I be lifted up from the earth, will draw all *men* unto me" [italics in KJV], which the Gospel writer explains with the words "This he said, signifying what death he should die" (John 12:33).

The Gospel writer leaves no doubt that the assembled crowd heard God's voice. "The people therefore, that stood by, and heard *it*" [italics in KJV] (John 12:29). The impact was such that some said "that it thundered" (John 12:29). Some had a different opinion: "others said an angel has spoken to Him" (John 12:29). As Jesus made clear, the testimony from heaven was for their benefit. Jesus said, "This voice came not because of me, but for your sakes" (John 12:30). Its purpose was to reveal the Father's approval of Jesus and His work, thereby signaling Him as the object of trust.

The multitude had trouble reconciling "the Son of Man" (τὸν υἱὸν τοῦ ἀνθρώπου), who they recognized as the Messiah (ὁ χριστὸς), with the idea of death or ascension. So they asked Jesus about that individual's identity: "We have heard out of the law that Christ abideth for ever: and how sayest thou, The Son of man must be lifted up? who is this Son of man?" (John 12:34). Alluding to His upcoming death and departure from earth Jesus said, "Yet a little while is the light with you. Walk while ye have the light, lest darkness come upon you: for he that walketh in darkness knoweth not whither he goeth" (John 12:35).

Jesus' physical presence illuminated the way to eternal life in a way they would not always have. Present rejection would make future belief more difficult. Alluding to Himself, Jesus invited them to respond: "While ye have light, believe in the light, that ye may be the children of light" (John 12:36). The response to Jesus' invitation was mixed. On the one hand, "But though he had done so many miracles before them, yet they believed not on him" (John 12:37). On the other hand there were "many" (πολλοὶ) unlikely converts: "Nevertheless among the chief rulers also many believed on him" (John 12:42). The NASB says, "Nevertheless many even of the rulers believed in Him," which better represents the Greek preposition "in" (εἰς), in the prepositional phrase, "in Him" (εἰς αὐτόν).

The Greek adverb (ὅμως) and the contrastive conjunction (μέντοι) together translated "nevertheless," convey the contrast between unbelievers (John 12:37) and believers (John 12:42). Some have argued that the latter were not genuinely saved because verse 42 then says of them: "but because of the Pharisees they did not confess *him*, lest they should be put out of the synagogue." In the Gospel of John the Greek verb translated "confess" (ὁμολογέω) occurs four times, twice in 1:20, and once each in 9:22 and 12:42. The fact that this verb is found so infrequently in the Gospel of John which was written for the express purpose that man might receive eternal life (John 20:31), should give pause to the interpreter who would include confession as a requirement for salvation.

The reader is referred to chapter 2 "Exegetical Eye-Openers" under Romans 10:9 and the use of the verb "confess" (ὁμολογέω).

The first two references to confess in John 1:20 are not soteriologically significant, referring to John the Baptist: "And he confessed, and denied not; but confessed, I am not the Christ." In John 9:22 the context is the healing of the blind man whose parents were brought in by the Jews and questioned. The Gospel writer comments, "for the Jews had agreed already, that if any man did confess that he was Christ, he should be put out of the synagogue." It was "the Jews" (οἱ Ἰουδαῖοι), Jesus' antagonists, who came up with confession as a criteria for expulsion from the synagogue.

The threat of excommunication is also present in the context in which "confess" (ὁμολογέω) occurs in John 12:42. The text does not say the threat of excommunication kept these people from believing; it says that they did believe, but that the threat of excommunication kept them from "confessing" (ὡμολόγουν imperfect, active, indicative from ὁμολογέω "confess"). Some say that the unconverted status of these individuals is proved by the additional words, "For they loved the praise of men more than the praise of God" (John 12:43). One could ask where else is loving "the praise of God" made a requirement for eternal salvation? The answer is, "Nowhere."

Jesus immediately said, "He that believeth on me, believeth not on me, but on him that sent me" (John 12:44). Jesus was equating trust in Him with trust in God the Father. If His audience did not realize He was equating Himself with God the Father, He added, "And he that seeth me seeth him that sent me" (John 12:45). Jesus could not have identified Himself as God any more clearly. And by linking "he that believeth on Me" (John 12:44) (ὁ πιστεύων εἰς ἐμὲ) with "he that seeth me" (John 12:45), He was emphasizing their role as eyewitnesses of what they had seen.

John Chapter 13

At the Last Supper Jesus indicated that all but one of His disciples were saved. He did that to counter Peter's request for a full bath rather than just having Jesus wash his feet. Jesus said, "He that is washed needeth not save to wash *his* feet, but is clean every whit: and ye are clean, but not all" [italics in KJV] (John 13:10). This shows that even Thomas, who would have doubts about the resurrection (John 20:26-29), was saved at the time of the Last Supper.

The notable exception of course was Judas Iscariot who would soon leave to carry out his betrayal. Before that event occurred, Jesus spoke of it as a fulfillment of Old

Testament prophecy. Even Judas's betrayal served the purpose of identifying who the Messiah is so "that the scripture may be fulfilled, He that eateth bread with me hath lifted up his heel against me. Now I tell you before it come, that, when it is come to pass, ye may believe that I am *he*" [italics in KJV] (John 13:18-19). The future belief Jesus was referring to would not involve the disciples' salvation because that had already happened (John 13:10). At this point in time, the progression of events and divine revelation did not yet include Jesus' crucifixion and resurrection, but that did not keep the eleven disciples from believing who He is and putting their trust in Him. From the later historical standpoint of the Gospel writer's readers/listeners, that revelation would be relevant to their understanding of Jesus' identity.

No doubt for Jesus' disciples His words, "that when it is come to pass, ye may believe that I am *he"* [italics in KJV] (John 13:19) would be a call to believe in His deity. Jesus associated His disciples and future converts with Himself and God the Father: "Verily, verily, I say unto you, He that receiveth whomsoever I send receiveth me; and he that receiveth me receiveth him that sent me" (John 13:20). The revelation of the Trinitarian composition of the Godhead would continue to proceed, reaching its apex in the prophecy of the coming of the Holy Spirit in John chapters 14 and 15. The veil of revelation related to the interconnection, interdependence, and yet independence within the Trinitarian unity is lifted to a finite degree in Jesus' description of His relationship with God the Father: "Now is the Son of man glorified, and God is glorified in him. If God be glorified in him, God shall also glorify him in himself, and shall straightway glorify him" (John 13:31-32).

Because Judas had made his exit (John 13:30) and those present were all believers, Jesus could speak intimately with them: "Little children, yet a little while I am with you. Ye shall seek me: and as I said unto the Jews, Whither I go, ye cannot come; so now I say to you" (John 13:33). Jesus' physical presence on earth would soon be a thing of the past but the disciples' spiritual connection with Him would continue and was to be demonstrated in their relationships with one another: "A new commandment I give unto you, that ye love one another; as I have loved you, that ye also love one another" (John 13:34). The physical absence of Jesus Incarnate was not to result in a loss of community or in the isolation of His disciples; instead they should become known for their care and concern for each other: "By this shall all *men* know that ye are my disciples, if ye have love one to another" [italics in KJV] (John 13:35). Observable love for each other was to be the outward sign of the invisible union they shared.

Simon Peter, who was quick to pick up on anything Jesus said, asked Him, "Lord, whither goest thou?" (John 13:36). When told by Jesus that he could not follow Him at that time, Peter responded with the words, "Lord, why cannot I follow thee now? I will lay down my life for thy sake" (John 13:37). At that point it would not be Peter who would lay down his life, but rather Jesus who would do so for him and the whole world. Even though Peter, as tradition has it, and Jesus predicted (Matthew 20:23), would follow and die for Jesus, in the short term he would choose denial over death: "Jesus answered him, Wilt thou lay down thy life for my sake? Verily, verily, I say unto thee, The cock shall not crow, till thou hast denied me thrice" (John 13:38). Peter's example sadly demonstrates that saved disciples are not immune to denial.

John Chapter 14

Jesus' identity as God is proved by the identical response that He and God the Father command. Jesus taught that trust in Him produced the same result as trust in God the Father: "Let not your heart be troubled: ye believe in God, believe also in me" (John 14:1). Furthermore God the Father lives in His heavenly home. "In my Father's house are many mansions" (John 14:2). And Jesus the Son lives there as well, and will also receive those who trust in Him to reside there: "I will come again, and receive you unto myself; that where I am, *there* ye may be also" [italics in KJV] (John 14:3).

Jesus taught the exclusive nature of the requirement for entrance into His eternal home. Reception into heaven, where God the Father dwells, is reserved for those who by faith receive Jesus as their Savior. Stated positively Jesus said, "I am the way, and the truth, and the life" (John 14:6). With the threefold use of the definite article "the" (ή) Jesus unambiguously expressed that He is the exclusive way, the embodiment of truth, and the only source of eternal life. Expressed negatively, to exclude the possibility of any other means of entrance into heaven and God the Father's home, Jesus said, "no man cometh unto the Father, but by me" (John 14:6).

In the Old Testament God the Father had been revealed and Jesus the divine Son had been implied but not completely identified. Through the Incarnation Jesus was officially introduced and identified. Because of the deity Jesus shares with God the Father, to know the former is to know the latter: "If ye had known me, ye should have known my Father also: and from henceforth ye know him, and have seen him" (John 14:7). Understandably this was difficult to comprehend. How could the invisible spirit God of the Old Testament be seen? If that were somehow possible, Jesus' disciples wanted in on it. Philip spoke up: "Lord, shew us the Father, and it sufficeth us" (John 14:8).

In His reply to Philip Jesus revealed His deity: "he that hath seen me hath seen the Father" (John 14:9). The evidence Jesus offered for the disciples to believe what He said was twofold: His words and His works. "Believe me that I *am* in the Father, and the Father in me: or else believe me for the very works' sake" [italics in KJV] (John 14:11). Jesus was inviting the disciples to choose the evidence for His identity that was most convincing to them: the statements or the signs; the words or the works; the message or the miracles.

In addition to what Jesus said about who He is and God the Father's corroborating testimony, the Holy Spirit would also become a witness to His identity, as well as the disciples' position in relation to Him: "At that day ye shall know that I *am* in my Father, and ye in me, and I in you" [italics in KJV] (John 14:20). That knowledge would result from the indwelling of the Holy Spirit: "*Even* the Spirit of truth; whom the world cannot receive, because it seeth him not, neither knoweth him: but ye know him; for he dwelleth with you, and shall be in you" [italics in KJV] (John 14:17). There would be continuity of the Spirit's presence, although at Pentecost a switch from empowerment to indwelling would take place. On that day the identity of Jesus would be confirmed supernaturally, and their faith in Him validated.

One of the disciples noticed that Jesus was not saying He would be revealed to them publicly: "Judas saith unto him, not Iscariot, Lord, how is it that thou wilt manifest thyself unto us, and not unto the world?" (John 14:22). In response Jesus drew a distinction between His teaching during His physical presence with them and the future ministry of the Holy Spirit: "These things have I spoken unto you, being *yet* present with you. But the Comforter, *which is* the Holy Ghost, whom the Father will send in my name, he shall teach you all things, and bring all things to your remembrance, whatsoever I have said unto you" [italics in KJV] (John 14:25-26). The Holy Spirit would affirm what Jesus had said to them; it would not be another message and they would not need to rely exclusively on their unaided memory. Particularly, as will be demonstrated, in the Acts of the Apostles the disciples would be indwelt and empowered to proclaim the identity of Jesus of Nazareth so that their hearers would place their faith in Him.

The fulfillment of Jesus' prediction of the changed role that the Holy Spirit would play in their lives and ministries, beginning at Pentecost, would itself be evidence confirming who He is and what He had taught them: "And now I have told you before it come to pass, that, when it is come to pass, ye might believe" (John 14:29). While each of the eleven disciples had already trusted in Jesus and were saved (John 13:10), when the prophecy of Pentecost was fulfilled they would believe that what He had said about it was true. Additionally the prediction of Pentecost would be incorporated into their message. Jesus pointed out that His purpose extended beyond the circle of the eleven who were present: "but that the world may know that I love the Father, and as the Father gave me commandment, even so I do" (John 14:31).

John Chapter 15

In another of Jesus' "I am" statements He again claimed exclusivity, "I am the true vine" (John 15:1), with the use of the definite article "the" (ἡ) and the adjective "true" (ἀληθινὴ). God the Father was identified in the extended metaphor as "the vinedresser" (ὁ γεωργός), or the farmer who tended the vineyard. Jesus further amplified the metaphor of "the vine" (ἡ ἄμπελος) by referring to a "branch" (κλῆμα) that was attached to it: "in me" (John 15:2) (ἐν ἐμοὶ).

In the metaphorical scenario Jesus described was the possibility of fruitlessness: "Every branch in me that beareth not fruit" (John 15:2). There is no reason to suppose that fruitlessness, "beareth not fruit," was a state that could not exist for one who was "in me" (ἐν ἐμοὶ), that is "in Jesus," but rather is explicitly contemplated by Him. The consequence for a fruitless branch was that the farmer would remove the branch: "he taketh away" (John 15:2) (αἴρει). Whatever one's opinion of branch removal, it is a consequence meted out to a saved individual.

Even fruitful branches are not spared the corrective cutting of the vinedresser. Jesus said this about a fruitful branch: "and every *branch* that beareth fruit, he purgeth it" [italics in KJV] (John 15:2), so that production would increase: "that it may bring forth more fruit" (John 15:2). It should not be ignored that contextually both the fruitless and the fruitful branches are "in me" (ἐν ἐμοί), that is, they are "in Jesus." With the fruitless the positional "in me" (ἐν ἐμοί) is explicitly stated, with the fruitful it is contextually implied. To hold that the former represent the unsaved and the latter the saved is to make a distinction not found in the text.

The Greek verb translated in the NASB as "prunes" (καθαίρει) is the present active indicative of the verb that can mean to "clean" or "prune" (καθαίρω) (John 15:2). The disciples, hearing about this cleansing activity performed by God the Father could have been confused. In John 13:10 Jesus, using the adjective "clean" or "pure" (καθαρός), had told them "and ye are clean, but not all" (the latter a reference to Judas Iscariot). How could it be that someone, who according to Jesus' own words, had just said was "in me" (ἐν ἐμοί), that is, in Jesus, need to be "cleaned" (καθαίρω)? Anticipating the possibility of confusion Jesus clarified what He meant by using a parenthesis.

Denying the presence of a parenthesis, the words which follow would be abrupt and Jesus' train of thought lacking in continuity. Jesus parenthetically said to His disciples, "ye are clean through the word which I have spoken unto you" (John 15:3). Conversion is not to be confused with divine correction. Louw and Nida see in John 15:2-3 a play on words:

> In John 15:2 the verb καθαίρω involves a play on two different meanings. The one meaning involves pruning of a plant, while the other meaning involves a cleansing process (79.49). This play on two meanings of καθαίρω serves to highlight the meanings of καθαρός as "clean" (79.48) or "pure" (53.29) in John 15:3 (Johannes P. Louw and Eugene A. Nida, *Greek-English Lexicon of the New Testament Based on Semantic Domains*, 2nd ed. [New York: United Bible Societies, 2nd ed], 1989, 1:517).

In John 15:2 the term translated "prunes" or "purgeth" (καθαίρω) is a verb and in verse 3 "clean" (καθαρός) is an adjective. In John 13:10 and 11 Jesus used the same adjective "clean" (καθαρός) to describe the eleven disciples who were saved: "and ye are clean" (John 13:10) and "but not all" (John 13:11).

In John 15:13 Jesus also uses the adjective "clean" (καθαρός) metaphorically to characterize the disciples as saved. Jesus was not telling the disciples that they were exempt from the application of the preceding verse because they were saved. Even saved fruitful disciples are subject to pruning. Jesus preempted a nonsalvation interpretation with His parenthesis.

Unfortunately some Bible teachers introduce confusion where Jesus communicated clearly. They have become fruit inspectors who have denied salvation to those who fail to meet their standards. Instead of the joy that Jesus intended for His disciples: "These things have I spoken unto you, that my joy might remain in you, and *that* your joy might be full" [italics in KJV] (John 15:11), the result has been to introduce a sense of spiritual angst, uneasiness and loss of assurance. Given the clarity of Jesus' communication the misinterpretation of this passage is inexcusable.

The message Jesus proclaimed was the means used in the disciples' salvation. They were saved "through the word which I have spoken to you" (John 15:3). Jesus said, "the word" (John 15:3) (ὁ λόγος), is the instrument used in salvation, and is also the means for sanctification, "If you abide in Me, and My words abide in you" (John 15:7).

The identification of the disciples with Jesus would invite persecution: "If they have persecuted me, they will also persecute you" (John 15:20). In turn their persecution would verify the connection Jesus claimed between Himself and God the Father: "But all these things will they do unto you for my name's sake, because they know not him that sent me" (John 15:21). To receive or reject Jesus was to do that to God the Father: "He that hateth me hateth my Father also" (John 15:23). Ironically, those who rejected Jesus, by their very rejection, became witnesses to Jesus' messianic identity which was prophesied in their own Scriptures: "But *this cometh to pass*, that the word might be fulfilled that is written in their law, They hated me without a cause" [italics in KJV] (John 15:25).

Proving Jesus' identity is a Trinitarian agenda of God the Father, the Son, and the Holy Spirit. Jesus attributed the evidence of miraculous works to Himself as well as God the Father: "If I had not done among them the works which none other man did, they had not had sin: but now have they both seen and hated both me and my Father" (John 15:24). Having "seen" (ἑωράκασιν perfect active indicative from ὁράω "see"), that is, having been eyewitnesses to Jesus' works and rejecting that evidence of Jesus' identity, was to sin against God the Father.

The Holy Spirit would become an additional witness to Jesus' identity: "But when the Comforter is come, whom I will send unto you from the Father, *even* the Spirit of truth, which proceedeth from the Father, he shall testify of me" [italics in KJV] (John 15:26). The curriculum the Holy Spirit would teach would be Christ. The instructional content would relate to Christ's identity, and the Holy Spirit would provide external (signs and wonders) and internal (writing of Scripture) evidence for the church which was about to be established.

Not only was it the mission of the Triune God to prove who the divine Son is, it would also become the responsibility of those who by virtue of their presence with Jesus to relate what they had observed: "And ye also shall bear witness, because ye have been with me from the beginning" (John 15:27). Perhaps the presence of the Greek present tense, translated as a future tense by the KJV with "shall bear witness" should not be translated as a future tense, to match the future tense of the previous verse, John 15:26 "shall testify" (μαρτυρήσει), where it refers to the ministry of the Holy Spirit. Instead the present tense indicates that the disciples' testimony was beginning even as Jesus spoke these words.

John Chapter 16

The threefold mission of the Holy Spirit is unified under the title of "conviction" (ἐλέγχω): "And when he is come, he will reprove the world" (John 16:8). The three areas of conviction will be "of sin, and of righteousness, and of judgment" (John 16:8). Because Jesus is the only solution for sin the Holy Spirit's conviction of sin will target those who refused to put their trust in Him, "Of sin, because they believe not on me" (John 16:9). The convicting activity includes their acknowledgement of sin, and the identity of the Savior. With the progress of revelation and redemptive history the Savior is identified by what He said about Himself and what He has done on behalf of man. The Holy Spirit will use Scripture, which He has inspired, to present evidence that individuals are to consider in deciding to trust in Christ. The convicting ministry of the Holy Spirit also relates to sin in the life of a believer.

The second sphere of the Holy Spirit's conviction will be "righteousness" (δικαιοσύνη). Jesus is the example and model of perfect righteousness. While on earth He confronted people about their lack of it and modeled what it is like. Once Jesus' physical presence was gone, the Holy Spirit took over that convicting role: "Of righteousness, because I go to my Father, and ye see me no more" (John 16:10). Because Jesus, the model of perfect righteousness, is no longer physically present on earth, the Holy Spirit convicts the unsaved about the need for Christ's imputed righteousness (although they probably do not understand it in those terms) and baptizes (1 Corinthians 12:13) and seals (2 Corinthians 1:22; Ephesians 1:13) them at conversion. The Holy Spirit's ministry would also convict believers concerning practical righteousness in their daily walk.

The third convicting ministry of the Holy Spirit predicted by Jesus would be: "judgment, because the prince of this world is judged" (John 16:11). This conviction of the Holy Spirit convinces people that God will judge sin. The certainty of divine judgment is based on the condemnation of Satan that has already taken place. The Holy Spirit's "conviction concerning judgment" (ἐλέγχω. . . περὶ. . . κρίσεως) consists of warning unbelievers that judgment awaits them as well if they ignore His prompting. Included under this ministry of the Spirit is His work in the conscience of believers, warning them of the earthly (temporal chastisement) and heavenly (loss of rewards) consequences of sin.

Jesus did not hesitate to put Himself on the same level as the Holy Spirit: "He shall glorify me: for he shall receive of mine, and shall shew *it* unto you" [italics in KJV] (John 16:14). And He completed the Trinitarian circle with the statement, "All things that the Father hath are mine: therefore said I, that he shall take of mine, and shall shew *it* unto you" [italics in KJV] (John 16:15). Claiming to possess everything that God the Father possesses is blasphemy unless it is true.

The disciples realized that Jesus meant exactly what He said about His origin and omniscience with its implications for His identity: "His disciples said unto him, Lo, now speakest thou plainly, and speakest no proverb. Now are we sure that thou knowest all things, and needest not that any man should ask thee: by this we believe that thou camest forth from God" (John 16:29-30). The disciples were referring to what they had just heard Jesus say, which they believed to be true.

John Chapter 17

In Jesus' high priestly prayer He spoke intimately with God the Father in a manner that revealed His divine identity: "Father, the hour is come; glorify thy Son, that thy Son also may glorify thee" (John 17:1). God the Father's glory is wrapped up in the glory of the Son, and the divine glory of God the Son is equal to that of God the Father: "And now, O Father, glorify thou me with thine own self with the glory which I had with thee before the world was" (John 17:5). Jesus claimed preexistence which only God can rightfully claim. The purpose of the Incarnation of the Son was to reveal God to man, and that mission has been accomplished: "Now they have known that all things whatsoever thou hast given me are of thee. For I have given unto them the words which thou gavest me; and they have received *them*, and have known surely that I came out from thee, and they have believed that thou didst send me" [italics in KJV] (John 17:7-8).

The pattern of "testimony delivered, testimony believed" was to be successively repeated down through generations of believers that would follow. Jesus prayed for His disciples and those who would continue the process: "Neither pray I for these alone, but for them also which shall believe on me through their word" (John 17:20). The chain of evidence was to continue unbroken. The gospel was to be carefully preserved and proclaimed. The evidence was to be believed in the united community and broadcast to the entire world: "I in them, and thou in me, that they may be made perfect in one; and that the world may know that thou hast sent me, and hast loved them, as thou hast loved me" (John 17:23).

John Chapter 18

The Gospel of John records that three times during Jesus' arrest He identified Himself with the words "I am" (ἐγώ εἰμι). The first instance came after Jesus asked those who had come looking for Him, "Whom seek ye?" (John 18:4) and they answered with, "Jesus of Nazareth" (John 18:5). Jesus responded by saying, "I am *he*" [italics in KJV] (John 18:5) (ἐγώ εἰμι). While this could have simply been Jesus identifying Himself to them, the Gospel writer makes a point to repeat the words "I am *he*" [italics in KJV] (John 18:6) (ἐγώ εἰμι) and adds the reaction that His words produced: "they went backward, and fell to the ground" (John 18:6). Their reaction supports the idea that although the meaning here of the words "I am *he*" [italics in KJV] (ἐγώ εἰμι) may be ambiguous, they may well have been interpreted as being a reference to His deity.

A second time Jesus asked those looking for Him whom they sought, and after they answered He replied, "I told you that I am *He*" [italics in KJV] (John 18:8) (εἶπον ὑμῖν ὅτι ἐγώ εἰμι). Jesus continued, "if therefore ye seek me, let these go their way" (John

18:8), referring to the disciples. Even in protecting them Jesus was fulfilling the will of God the Father (John 6:39), and His own words (John 17:12).

The requirement of plural witnesses to establish the validity of evidence was followed not only by the Gospel writers but also by Jesus Himself. In the trial before the high priest Annas Jesus made the point that everything He had done had been done publicly: "I spake openly to the world; I ever taught in the synagogue, and in the temple, whither the Jews always resort; and in secret have I said nothing" (John 18:20). Jesus was not guilty of having secretly conspired to subvert the Jewish religion or overthrow the Roman government. Jesus, who was both a witness and a defendant in His own case, told the court that they needed to look elsewhere for evidence of His guilt, and He questioned their judicial procedure: "Why askest thou me? ask them which heard me, what I have said unto them: behold, they know what I said" (John 18:21).

No doubt Jesus' implication was not lost on the court. Most if not all of the officials had heard what He had said on numerous occasions. Jesus was telling them to apply their own legal standard and seek corroboration of His testimony. For pointing that out He was accused of contempt of court and punishment came swiftly: "And when he had thus spoken, one of the officers which stood by struck Jesus with the palm of his hand, saying, Answerest thou the high priest so?" (John 18:22). In response Jesus asked the court to follow the Jewish judicial requirement for the acceptance of evidence, rather than accepting it without corroboration, and instead charge and punish Him for contempt. "Jesus answered him, If I have spoken evil, bear witness of the evil: but if well, why smitest thou me?" (John 18:23). Since they were the ones bringing the charges, they were required to produce evidence to prove their case.

In Jesus' next trial Pilate was curious about who Jesus is. Pilate had probably heard rumors about Jesus' claims, so he asked Him, "Art thou the King of the Jews?" (John 18:33). Jesus knew what prompted Pilate to ask his question, that he had been put up to it, so he asked Pilate, "Sayest thou this thing of thyself, or did others tell it thee of me?" (John 18:34). The NASB says, "Are you saying this on your own initiative?" Perhaps Jesus was probing Pilate for his personal opinion about Jesus' identity. For Pilate to answer that he had not been put up to it would be to admit that he personally wanted to know about Jesus. If he answered that he had been coached, Pilate would appear weak, and a pawn of the Jewish religious leadership. Pilate was not about to answer either question, so he evaded answering and said, "Am I a Jew?" (John 18:35). Because Jesus' questions had gotten too personal for Pilate he steered the conversation back to the subject of the charge against Jesus: "Thine own nation and the chief priests have delivered thee unto me: what hast thou done?" (John 18:35).

Jesus answered Pilate's question about His identity: "My kingdom is not of this world: if my kingdom were of this world, then would my servants fight, that I should not be delivered to the Jews: but now is my kingdom not from hence" (John 18:36). Jesus spoke of a kingdom that belongs to Him, the implication being that He indeed is a king. In response Pilate asked directly, "Art thou a king then?" (John 18:37), to which Jesus unambiguously answered affirmatively, "Thou sayest that I am a king" (John 18:37). The NASB says, "You say *correctly* that I am a king" [italics in NASB].

Jesus went on to state the purpose of His kingship: "To this end was I born, and for this cause came I into the world, that I should bear witness unto the truth" (John 18:37). The purpose of the Incarnation is to reveal God to man, and the testimony of Jesus' very person is that of His identity as the God-Man. Not everyone would accept it. Some would reject His claims. But others would believe that He is who He said He is, and they would learn from Him: "Every one that is of the truth heareth my voice" (John 18:37). That was the response of faith. It recognized the gravity of the matter; that truth could make the difference between heaven and hell, between glorification and condemnation, between eternal life and eternal loss.

Pilate's response revealed not the seriousness of faith but rather a flippancy of faithlessness when he asked, "What is truth?" (John 18:38). The most important question was not "What is truth?" Theoretical epistemology was not the crucial issue. The issue is, "Who is the way, the truth, and the life?" (John 14:6). "Who" asks a question of identity. Of course propositions are extremely important because they point to the identity of the divine person, but they were never intended to become a substitute for Him. Propositions have a place, but they were never meant to replace the person of Christ.

John Chapter 19

The issue of Jesus' identity continued to play center stage after His arrest. The Roman soldiers who were assigned to guard Jesus joined in with the mocking and said, "Hail, King of the Jews!" (John 19:3). When the enraged mob got no help in their pursuit of Jesus' execution, they told Pilate the real reason for their opposition to Him: "We have a law, and by our law he ought to die, because he made himself the Son of God" (John 19:7). Jesus' self-designation as "the Son of God" (ὁ υἱὸς τοῦ θεοῦ) was considered blasphemy because it was a claim to deity. The penalty for blasphemy laid out in the Old Testament was death: "And he that blasphemeth the name of the Lord, he shall surely be put to death, *and* all the congregation shall certainly stone him: as well the stranger, as he that is born in the land, when he blasphemeth the name *of the Lord*, shall be put to death" [italics in KJV] (Leviticus 24:16).

The accusation of blasphemy and the request for execution gave Pilate pause. He did not want to be accused of promoting blasphemy and thereby encouraging unrest among his subjects, since one of his duties was to promote peace among them. Because the imposition of the death penalty was reserved to him, Pilate reacted with fear. "When Pilate therefore heard that saying, he was the more afraid" (John 19:8).

Pilate once again asked Jesus about His identity, with a question about His origin, "Whence art thou?" (John 19:9). In spite of Jesus' refusal to answer him, Pilate was inclined to release Him. But bowing to the pressure of the crowd, he condemned Him to death. The inscription that Pilate ordered placed on Jesus' cross was a reference to the controversy over His identity: "JESUS OF NAZARETH THE KING OF THE JEWS" (John 19:19). Since this happened during the Passover and there was an international or intraempire presence in the city, it was also ordered that the placard be written in three languages; Hebrew, Latin, and Greek, thereby covering the religious, political, and cultural bases, respectively.

The description of the scene at the Crucifixion is punctuated by the fulfillment of Old Testament messianic prophecies. It begins with the soldiers' squabbling over Jesus' outer garment and their decision to cast lots for it. The Gospel writer points out that their action fulfilled Scripture: "that the scripture might be fulfilled, which saith, They parted my raiment among them, and for my vesture they did cast lots" (John 19:24). The Old Testament passage was Psalm 22:18, "They part my garments among them, and cast lots upon my vesture." John indicates the significance and purpose for what they did as fulfillment of the prophecy: "these things therefore the soldiers did" (John 19:24).

Another Old Testament fulfillment in John's crucifixion narrative is Jesus' statement consisting of one Greek word, "I thirst" (John 19:28) (διψῶ), which is introduced with, "that the Scripture might be fulfilled" (John 19:28). It appears Jesus was referring to the words of Psalm 22:15, "My strength is dried up like a potsherd; and my tongue cleaveth to my jaws." The Gospel writer mentions another fulfillment of an Old Testament prophecy: "Now there was set a vessel full of vinegar: and they filled a spunge with vinegar, and put *it* upon hyssop, and put *it* to his mouth" [italics in KJV] (John 19:29). This was a fulfillment of Psalm 69:21, "They gave me also gall for my meat; and in my thirst they gave me vinegar to drink." John, the Gospel writer again identified Jesus as the One who fulfilled Old Testament messianic prophecy. The account of the action of the Roman soldiers who did not break the bones in Jesus' legs but did spear Him in His side, are additional evidence of identity provided by prophetic fulfillment: "But when they came to Jesus, and saw that he was dead already, they brake not his legs: but one of the soldiers with a spear pierced his side, and forthwith came there out blood and water" (John 19:33-34).

The author John the Apostle tells why he is qualified to write and gives his reason for writing: "And he that saw *it* bare record, and his record is true: and he knoweth that he saith true, that ye might believe" [italics in KJV] (John 19:35). John gave reliable testimony that would result in his readers/listeners putting their trust in the One whom the testimony was about.

Two Old Testament prophecies are quoted. First, "For these things were done, that the scripture should be fulfilled, a bone of him shall not be broken" (John 19:36), which is a quotation from Psalm 34:20 "He keepeth all his bones: not one of them is broken." The second, "They shall look on Him whom they pierced'" (John 19:37). This is a quotation of Zechariah 12:10 which says, "And they shall look upon me whom they have pierced."

The burial of Jesus gives further evidence of His messianic identity. The two men, Joseph of Arimathea, who provided the place for His burial, and Nicodemus, who assisted him, were men of means. The Gospel writer implies that what Joseph of Arimathea gave for His burial was the best he had to offer, "a new sepulchre, wherein was never man yet laid" (John 19:41). How was it that Jesus who had nowhere to lay His head (Matthew 8:20; Luke 9:58) would be laid in a new tomb where a wealthy man would be buried? It was to further identify Him as the Davidic Messiah prophesied in the Old Testament. Isaiah had predicted: "And he made his grave with the wicked, and with the rich in his death" (Isaiah 53:9). The unexpected provided evidence that was undeniable.

John Chapter 20

Evidence of identity abounds in the account of Jesus' resurrection. The first witness was Mary Magdalene. "The first *day* of the week cometh Mary Magdalene early, when it was yet dark, unto the sepulchre, and seeth the stone taken away from the sepulchre" [italics in KJV] (John 20:1). Her observation was corroborated by the two disciples, Peter and "the other disciple, whom Jesus loved" (John 20:2), presumably John, to whom she had told what she had seen.

Verbs of visual perception are repeatedly used by the Gospel writer, as well as a description of where these two disciples were when they saw the empty tomb: "And he stooping down, *and looking in*, saw the linen clothes lying; yet went he not in. Then cometh Simon Peter following him, and went into the sepulchre, and seeth the linen clothes lie" [italics in KJV] (John 20:5-6). The Gospel writer, who was an eyewitness, then described the scene in great detail: "And the napkin, that was about his head, not lying with the linen clothes, but wrapped together in a place by itself" (John 20:7). Peter had been the first disciple to physically enter the tomb and was followed by John: "Then went in also that other disciple, which came first to the sepulchre, and he saw, and believed" (John 20:8).

John's description of his personal reaction to what He saw was that he "believed" (ἐπίστευσεν). His use of the verb "believe" (πιστεύω) probably means he believed that Jesus had risen from the dead as indicated from the following verse, "For as yet they knew not the scripture, that he must rise again from the dead" (John 20:9). Even though they had Old Testament prophecy that the Messiah would rise from the dead in Psalm 16:10, as well as Jesus' own predictions about His resurrection, it took this event for the fact of His resurrection to sink in.

The first person to see Jesus after he had risen from the dead was Mary Magdalene. The question of His identity surfaced as she failed to recognize Him. "And when she had thus said, she turned herself back, and saw Jesus standing, and knew not that it was Jesus" (John 20:14). In a moving dialogue between Jesus and the distraught Mary Magdalene, including the element of mistaken identity, she eventually recognized Him when He addressed her personally, "Jesus saith unto her, Mary. She turned herself, and saith unto him, Rabboni; which is to say, Master" (John 20:16).

The message Jesus wanted Mary Magdalene to convey to the disciples was, "I ascend unto my Father, and your Father; and *to* my God, and your God" [italics in KJV] (John 20:17). Mary Magdalene, as well as the disciples, would understand that Jesus' relationship with God the Father differed from theirs. The Gospel writer, as one of the disciples who recognized the uniqueness of Jesus, includes what Mary Magdalene said in addition to conveying His message. She said that, "she had seen the Lord" (John 20:18). She was a singular witness who would soon be joined by many eyewitnesses to the fact that Jesus had indeed risen from the dead.

The author's description of the reaction of the assembled disciples to Jesus' post-resurrection appearance to them mirrors Mary Magdalene's words. "Then were the disciples glad, when they saw the Lord" (John 20:20). In telling of the conversation with Thomas, who had been absent at that post-resurrection appearance, the Gospel writer includes the disciples' statement to Thomas, "We have seen the Lord" (John 20:25).

Thomas, the disciple famous for doubting, wanted to see and touch physical evidence for the resurrection before he would believe: "Except I shall see in his hands the print of the nails, and put my finger into the print of the nails, and thrust my hand into his side, I will not believe" (John 20:25). With the word "believe" (πιστεύω) Thomas conveyed that he wanted proof to "believe the proposition to be true" that Jesus had risen from the dead and that He was alive. As mentioned previously, Thomas had already put his trust in Jesus for eternal life (John 13:10; 15:3).

Jesus provided the proof Thomas wanted. While Jesus did commend those in the future who would believe without physical proof, one should not assume that belief on the basis of physical evidence is in some way deficient. In fact Jesus invited Thomas to both see and touch the physical evidence of His resurrection body: "Reach hither thy finger, and behold my hands; and reach hither thy hand, and thrust *it* into my side: and be not faithless, but believing" [italics in KJV] (John 20:27). In Jesus' invitation to Thomas, to transition from "not believing" (ἄπιστος) to "believing" (πιστός), the resultant belief was not expressed by Jesus using any qualifying modifier. The two adjectives, with the single equative "to be" verb (γίνου present middle of passive imperative from γίνομαι "be" or "become"), were used by Jesus to invite Thomas to move from a state of unbelief, or lack of faith, to a state of belief, or that of having faith. Jesus' appearances had the purpose of identifying Him as the very same person, before and after the resurrection.

We are not told whether Thomas actually physically touched Jesus' hands and side, but he concluded that Jesus had been resurrected and that the One who stood before him was He, and so he said, "My Lord and my God" (John 20:28). Jesus said that those who would believe the accounts of the eyewitnesses would be worthy of commendation because they had not personally been able to examine the evidence: "blessed *are* they that have not seen, and *yet* have believed" [italics in KJV] (John 20:29). Future generations of believers would not have firsthand access to the evidence.

The Gospel author acknowledged that his written record was not exhaustive. "Many other signs truly did Jesus in the presence of his disciples, which are not written in this book" (John 20:30). Some of the testimony had been recorded by the other Gospel writers. Also, there was probably more evidence than that, which was not recorded.

The point that John, the writer of this Gospel, made was that although his account is not exhaustive it is sufficient for his readers/listeners to come to a conclusion as to Jesus' identity and to put their trust in Him. As John put it, "but these are written, that ye might believe that Jesus is the Christ, the Son of God; and that believing ye might have life through his name" (John 20:31). This verse has been taken as a purpose statement for the entire Gospel of John, which it probably is. John is giving his readers/listeners the reason he included the contents he did.

The thesis of this present book is that the gospel has two parts reflected in the semantic range of the Greek verb "believe" (πιστεύω), which are: (1) belief in propositions to be true which prove the identity of Jesus; with the purpose of (2) trusting in that person for one's eternal destiny. In John 20:31 the clause, with the Greek conjunction translated with the first "that" (ἵνα), "that ye might believe" indicates purpose.

The second clause in this phrase has another Greek conjunction, also translated "that" (ὅτι), which introduces a propositional statement that is the content of that belief, namely, "that Jesus is the Christ, the Son of God" (ὅτι Ἰησοῦς ἐστιν ὁ χριστὸς ὁ υἱὸς τοῦ θεοῦ). This phrase, with its two clauses, refers to the identity of Jesus. The content of John's Gospel included Jesus' works and words that were intended to lead the reader/listener to the conclusion that Jesus is indeed "the Christ" (ὁ χριστὸς), that is the Messiah, who is "the Son of God" (ὁ υἱὸς τοῦ θεοῦ), that is God Himself in His essential nature.

The second part of the dual purpose of John's Gospel is expressed with the phrase, introduced again by the identical and coordinate conjunction translated "that" (ἵνα), indicating purpose: "and that believing ye might have life through His name" (John 20:31). With the prepositional phrase "through his name" (ἐν τῷ ὀνόματι αὐτοῦ), the author is saying the same thing as "in Him," or "in His person." The Gospel writer began in John 1:12 saying that the privilege of being included in God's family was for "as many as received Him" (ὅσοι . . . ἔλαβον αὐτόν). Here he says it is for "those who believe through His name" (τοῖς πιστεύουσιν εἰς τὸ ὄνομα αὐτοῦ).

Is the second part of this verse, "and that believing ye might have life through His name" (John 20:31) essentially a repetition of the first? Is the second use of "believe" (πιστεύω) a reference to the preceding "believe" (πιστεύω), with the same meaning? That is, is the second use of "believe" (πιστεύω) a repetition of the former? Is believing in a proposition the same thing as trusting in a person, or is the purpose of believing in the proposition ("that Jesus is the Christ, the Son of God"), a prerequisite for believing in Him as a person ("that by believing ye might have life through his name")?

This book contends that the latter better represents the biblical data. Would it be unusual for the two meanings of "believe" (πιστεύω), "to think that something is true," and "to put one's trust in something or someone," to be found in close proximity to each other? As demonstrated in the discussion of John 2:22-24, John, the author of this Gospel, placed that very same verb "believe" (πιστεύω), and three of its meanings: (1) to believe something to be true or someone to be telling the truth; (2) to place one's trust in a person or thing; and (3) to entrust something to one's care, in close proximity. In John 11:25-27, in His conversation with Martha, Jesus used the verb "believe" (πιστεύω) four times. In that passage two of the uses have the meaning "to place one's trust in a person or thing (John 11:25-26), and the other two convey "to believe something to be true or someone to be telling the truth (John 11:26-27).

In John 20:31 in its first appearance, "believe" (πιστεύω), in the clause "but these are written that ye might believe," has the meaning of concluding that what is said about Jesus, by the Gospel writer and by Jesus Himself is true, and that the evidence of the signs proves His identity as the divine Messiah. The meaning of the verb πιστεύω in the second use is built on that of the first in the clause "and that believing ye might have life through His name." Having accepted as true the proposition that Jesus is the Messiah and God, one is to put his trust in Him. The object of the latter is not the evidence but the person the evidence is about.

That is the gospel. The apostle Paul preached the very same gospel. He spoke of "our Saviour Jesus Christ, who hath abolished death, and hath brought life and immortality to light through the gospel" (2 Timothy 1:10). Concerning that One, identified as "Saviour" (σωτήρ) and "Christ" (Χριστός), that is the Messiah, Paul added, "for I know whom I have believed, and am persuaded that he is able to keep that which I have committed unto him against that day" (2 Timothy 1:12). Paul was sure of the identity of the One in whom he had placed his trust and confidence: "for I know whom I have believed" (2 Timothy 1:12). He was also sure of the supernatural ability of the One in whom that trust was placed: "and am persuaded that he is able to keep" (2 Timothy 1:12). In that divine person who has that supernatural ability, Paul had entrusted, "that which I have committed" ["entrusted" = NASB], his eternal destiny and lived in confident expectation "against that day." Paul described what all believers have experienced objectively and the subjective assurance he expressed can become a reality in the experience of every believer as well.

John Chapter 21

The post-resurrection appearances of Jesus are additional evidence of who He is. In the first verse of this chapter the Gospel writer introduces what he is about to write with the verb translated "shewed" ("manifested" = NASB) (ἐφανέρωσεν) to emphasize Jesus' physical presence. First, it tells who the witnesses were and where they were, "Jesus shewed himself again to the disciples at the sea of Tiberias" (John 21:1). The verb "shewed" or "manifest" (φανερόω) is repeated, "and on this wise shewed he *himself*" [italics in KJV] (John 21:1). Jesus made Himself visible to them, emphasizing that they were eyewitnesses and could testify to what they had seen.

In this appearance by Jesus after His resurrection there were seven witnesses, five of whom are mentioned by name, and the other two are referred to simply as disciples. "There were together Simon Peter, and Thomas called Didymus, and Nathanael of Cana in Galilee, and the *sons* of Zebedee, and two other of his disciples" [italics in KJV] (John 21:2). Identity is the first issue brought up by the Gospel writer, "But when the morning was now come, Jesus stood on the shore: but the disciples knew not that it was Jesus" (John 21:4). It was apparently the disciple John who finally realized who it was. "Therefore that disciple whom Jesus loved saith unto Peter, It is the Lord" (John 21:7). Jesus cooked fish and invited them to eat with him and again the Gospel writer brings up the subject of His identity. "And none of the disciples durst ask him, Who art thou? knowing that it was the Lord" (John 21:12). Their ambivalence can be attributed to their knowing that Jesus had died and now He was alive.

Not only were there more than the requisite two or three witnesses present to confirm Jesus' identity, but also John indicated it was not an isolated incident but that he had documented three such events: "This is now the third time that Jesus shewed himself to his disciples, after that he was risen from the dead" (John 21:14). One of the primary purposes for Jesus' post-resurrection appearances was to demonstrate that He was the same individual before and after that event. It was the Gospel writer's intent to show that the evidence for the resurrection of Jesus, the greatest of the signs confirming His identity as the divine Messiah, was incontrovertible.

John signed off with an affirmation of the veracity of his account based on his having been personally present when the events about which he had written took place. "This is the disciple which testifieth of these things, and wrote these things: and we know that his testimony is true" (John 21:24). When these words were written there were people alive who could vouch for him. Some of them had also been eyewitnesses who could testify to the identity of the One about whom John wrote. No doubt they could also testify to the fact that John did not have to scrounge around to come up with enough evidence to prove his point.

John, the Gospel writer, concludes by repeating what he had said in John 20:30 about his book not being an exhaustive account of the evidence. He implies that he has only scratched the surface. "And there are also many other things which Jesus did, the which, if they should be written every one, I suppose that even the world itself could not contain the books that should be written" (John 21:25). Those are the words of an eyewitness who was overwhelmed by the sheer volume of the evidence for the identity of Jesus as the Christ, the Son of God.

Chapter 8

Evidence for the Identity of Jesus in the Acts of the Apostles

Apostolic Application

A cts is important because it demonstrates how the early church put into practice what was introduced in the Gospel accounts. Particularly the content of the preaching described by Luke shows that the identity of Jesus, first and foremost, comprised its subject matter. The use of the verb "believe" (πιστεύω) coincides with that of the Gospel writers and the response that those who proclaimed the gospel expected was the same as what Jesus required. While revelation about Jesus, with the addition of information regarding His identity had increased, He remained the same individual, and trust in Him was the requirement for eternal salvation.

Acts Chapter 1

Luke begins with a reference to the Gospel that he had previously written. The content of that Gospel was about "all that Jesus began both to do and teach" (Acts 1:1). That information had been entrusted to individuals chosen by Jesus Himself: "unto the apostles whom He had chosen" (Acts 1:2); selected; and qualified as witnesses: "To whom also he shewed himself alive after his passion by many infallible proofs" (Acts 1:3). Jesus designated each of the disciples as a "witness" (μάρτυς) when He commissioned them: "and ye shall be witnesses unto me" (Acts 1:8). The witness/testimony motif used by all of the Gospel writers, one of whom was Luke, is applied by Jesus to His followers in the Acts of the Apostles.

In Luke's account in this book the emphasis on the disciples as eyewitnesses is seen on the occasion of Jesus' ascension to heaven. Acts 1:9 describes the disciples' actions during that event with the words, "while they were looking on" (βλεπόντων αὐτῶν) and Jesus' disappearance with, "a cloud received him out of their sight." The stage set for the appearance of the angels is that of the disciples' continuing to stare heavenward: "And while they looked stedfastly toward heaven as he went up" (Acts 1:10). The angels referred to what the disciples had just witnessed with their question, "why stand ye gazing up into heaven?" (Acts 1:11), and again the emphasis on sight is found in saying that Jesus' return would happen in the same manner. "This same Jesus, which is taken up from you into heaven, shall so come in like manner as ye have seen him go into heaven" (Acts 1:11).

In seeking a replacement for Judas Iscariot, the betrayer, to become an apostle, Peter recognized that the primary qualification was that he be an eyewitness of the words and works of Jesus. "Wherefore of these men which have companied with us all the time that the Lord Jesus went in and out among us, beginning from the baptism of John, unto that same day that he was taken up from us, must one be ordained to be a witness with us of his resurrection" (Acts 1:21-22). A witness had to have witnessed what he was to testify about, and Matthias fit the bill and was chosen.

Acts Chapter 2

This chapter tells of the beginning of the church. Jesus was no longer with them, so His followers felt a sense of sadness. They were gathered together expectantly waiting for what would happen next. In Jesus' parting words He had said, "but ye shall receive power, after that the Holy Ghost is come upon you" (Acts 1:8). They had never experienced that and with Jesus gone they felt powerless. They took care of corporate housekeeping details; they chose Matthias as a replacement for Judas Iscariot who had betrayed their beloved Jesus. They knew that in the future they would be "witnesses" (μάρτυς) because Jesus had told them so. Just before He was taken up into heaven He had told the disciples, "and ye shall be witnesses unto me" (Acts 1:8). The criteria they used as they chose Judas's replacement was that he qualified to be a "witness" (μάρτυς).

And they waited. Suddenly it happened. It started with physical phenomena. "And suddenly there came a sound from heaven as of a rushing mighty wind, and it filled all the house where they were sitting" (Acts 2:2). As they looked around they saw something on each other; "And there appeared unto them cloven tongues like as of fire, and it sat upon each of them" (Acts 2:3). Perhaps it reminded them of Moses who saw a burning bush that did not burn up. For Moses it was related to God's presence. Now they were experiencing something similar. What happened next was supernatural. "And they were all filled with the Holy Ghost, and began to speak with other tongues, as the Spirit gave them utterance" (Acts 2:4). The church age had been inaugurated with visible and audible expressions of the presence of the Holy Spirit. Similar phenomena would be experienced to validate the presence of the Holy Spirit in those who were included in the infant church.

Peter took the opportunity to preach the first sermon with Jesus as its subject. Peter began with, "Ye men of Israel, hear these words; Jesus of Nazareth" (Acts 2:22). Peter proceeded to point out that what he was about to say concerning Jesus was backed up by evidence that was irrefutable; "a man approved of God among you by miracles and wonders and signs, which God did by him in the midst of you, as ye yourselves also know" (Acts 2:22). The greatest witness was God the Father Himself and Peter's audience, who had heard and observed what Jesus had done by God's power, were corroborating witnesses.

Peter's appeal in this sermon included those who had been hostile witnesses and complicit in the death of Jesus. "Him, being delivered by the determinate counsel and foreknowledge of God, ye have taken, and by wicked hands have crucified and slain" (Acts 2:23). God's determinative involvement notwithstanding, they had been the human actors in the divine drama. Jesus, whom these hostile witnesses were determined to identify as a mere man, was shown by God to have been much more by means of the Resurrection: "Whom God hath raised up, having loosed the pains of death: because it was not possible that he should be holden of it" (Acts 2:24).

It was impossible for death to have the last word because of the identity of the One whom they had put to death. In support of his assertion Peter used the Old Testament and specifically the beloved psalmist David who carried weight with his Jewish audience. David had spoken of resurrection in Psalm 16, a messianic psalm. In his quotation Peter picked out parts of that psalm that dealt with the identity of the One of whom David had written. The first indicator of identity is found in Psalm 16:8, "I have set the Lord always before me: because *he is* at my right hand, I shall not be moved" [italics in KJV]. Acts 2:25 says, "I foresaw the Lord always before my face, for he is on my right hand, that I should not be moved." The second Old Testament quotation is Psalm 16:10, "Neither wilt thou suffer thine Holy One to see corruption." In the KJV Acts 2:27 is identical to Psalm 16:10.

Peter went on to explain that the psalm could not refer to David himself since he had not been raised from the dead; "Men *and* brethren, let me freely speak unto you of the patriarch David, that he is both dead and buried, and his sepulchre is with us unto this day" [italics in KJV] (Acts 2:29). What David had in mind was the fulfillment of the Davidic covenant which promised him an heir to the throne. "Therefore being a prophet, and knowing that God had sworn with an oath to him, that of the fruit of his loins, according to the flesh, he would raise up Christ to sit on his throne" (Acts 2:30). Some manuscripts do not include "Christ." The NASB omits "Christ" and translates: "And so, because he was a prophet, and knew that God had sworn to him with an oath to seat *one* of his descendants upon his throne" [italics in NASB] (Acts 2:30). In both the KJV and the NASB the one Peter is referring to is Jesus.

David identified his future dynastic heir as "the Christ" (ὁ Χριστός), that is the Messiah whose resurrection would fulfill the prediction made in Psalm 16. "He seeing this before spake of the resurrection of Christ, that his soul was not left in hell, neither his flesh did see corruption" (Acts 2:31). Peter identified that individual of whom David spoke as Jesus: "This Jesus hath God raised up, whereof we all are witnesses" (Acts 2:32). Because his audience had been eyewitnesses to Jesus' death and resurrection that identified Him as the Messiah, Peter appealed to them to make the connection.

The Pentecost event had implications for the identity of Jesus. Peter had quoted the prophet Joel (Acts 2:16-21) and his prediction as having been partially fulfilled with the phenomena occurring just before this sermon and now linked it to a person, Jesus. "Therefore being by the right hand of God exalted, and having received of the Father the promise of the Holy Ghost, he hath shed forth this, which ye now see and hear" (Acts 2:33). The prediction was about a person who was not to be identified as David but Jesus his successor. "For David is not ascended into the heavens: but he saith himself, The Lord said unto my Lord, Sit thou on my right hand, until I make thy foes thy footstool" (Acts 2:34-35). Jesus' ascension to heaven and predicted present position proved that He is more than a man, which was all that David could claim for himself. In fact, David had distanced himself from who Jesus is by calling Him "My Lord" and put Him on a par with God the Father by picturing them in intimate conversation.

Peter bracketed what he said; he began by addressing the audience as "men of Judaea, and all *ye* that dwell at Jerusalem" [italics in KJV] (Acts 2:14), and closed with an exhortation to "all the house of Israel" (Acts 2:36). In his summation to them Peter emphasized the sufficiency of the evidence he had presented for Jesus' identity. "Therefore let all the house of Israel know assuredly" (Acts 2:36); and explicitly expressed who Jesus is: "that God hath made that same Jesus, whom ye have crucified, both Lord and Christ" (Acts 2:36). Jesus was nothing less than "Lord" (κύριος) that is, God and the long-awaited Davidic divine Messiah "Christ" (Χριστός). The audience's response to the information about Jesus' identity was appropriate. "Now when they heard *this*, they were pricked in their heart, and said unto Peter and to the rest of the apostles, Men *and* brethren, what shall we do?" [italics in KJV] (Acts 2:37).

The answer Peter gave was, "Repent, and be baptized every one of you in the name of Jesus Christ for the remission of sins, and ye shall receive the gift of the Holy Ghost" (Acts 2:38). Historically this response was used by the Campbellites beginning in the mid-nineteenth century as the main support for their belief that water baptism, in addition to belief, is a requirement for eternal salvation. Their ecclesiastical and doctrinal descendants are present today. Since they rely primarily on this text as their *crux interpretum* (Latin for the central point of an argument) it is important to understand what Peter said.

The reader is referred to the discussion of this verse in chapter 2, "Exegetical Eye-Openers."

The author of Acts describes Peter's ministry as providing evidence and exhortation; "And with many other words did he testify and exhort, saying, Save yourselves from this untoward generation" (Acts 2:40). What set apart those in the church was that they had believed in the One about whom Peter preached. They are described by the author with the words, "And all that believed were together" (Acts 2:44).

Acts Chapter 3

The healing of the lame man at the temple gate set the stage for Peter's second sermon. People had regularly seen the man begging at the temple and knew who he was. After he had been healed when they saw him "walking and leaping" (Acts 3:8) (περιπατῶν καὶ ἁλλόμενος), they knew something miraculous had happened. Luke's description of the reaction to the healing was "And they knew that it was he which sat for alms at the Beautiful gate of the temple: and they were filled with wonder and amazement at that which had happened unto him" (Acts 3:10). In his second sermon Peter followed the same pattern he used in his first sermon. He began by identifying who Jesus is. God Himself has exalted Jesus: "The God of Abraham, and of Isaac, and of Jacob, the God of our fathers, hath glorified his Son Jesus" (Acts 3:13). Many in Peter's audience had willingly become accomplices and hostile witnesses against Jesus: "whom ye delivered up, and denied him in the presence of Pilate, when he was determined to let *him* go" [italics in KJV] (Acts 3:13). Peter revealed the One whose identity and claim to be the Messiah had been "denied" (ἠρνήσασθε) by them. Peter identified Him as "the Holy One and the Just" (Acts 3:14).

The juxtaposition of death and life was stark. They had "killed the Prince of life" (Acts 3:15) (τὸν δὲ ἀρχηγὸν τῆς ζωῆς ἀπεκτείνατε). They had initiated the death of the "initiator" (ἀρχηγός) of life. Peter also identified Jesus as having been resurrected: "whom God hath raised from the dead" (Acts 3:15). Peter was qualified to speak, and could do so confidently because he and his fellow apostles had seen the risen Christ, "whereof we are witnesses" (Acts 3:15).

The lame man had been healed because of his faith in that person whom Peter had identified: "And his name through faith in his name hath made this man strong, whom ye see and know: yea, the faith which is by him hath given him this perfect soundness in the presence of you all" (Acts 3:16). "Faith in His name" (τῇ πίστει τοῦ ὀνόματος αὐτοῦ) is belief or trust in His person. Salvation and healing both require trust in Jesus.

What the lame man had experienced could happen to Peter's audience as well. The healing of his lame body and the rescue of his lost soul came by faith in Jesus alone. Peter knew that the words about his audience's complicity in Jesus' death had been harsh, so he began his invitation by telling them he recognized they had not acted with full knowledge of what they had done. "And now, brethren, I wot [know] that through ignorance ye did *it*, as *did* also your rulers" [italics in KJV] (Acts 3:17). They were not thereby absolved of their responsibility for His death, but there was a way back.

The solution was that they "Repent ye therefore, and be converted [return]" (Acts 3:19) (μετανοήσατε οὖν καὶ ἐπιστρέψατε). Interestingly in this invitation Peter did not include baptism as he had in the first sermon in Acts 2:38. That parenthetical aside was not indispensable to the gospel that Peter and the rest of the apostles preached. Peter's audience could be saved without water baptism but they could not be saved without a change of mind (repent) about who the One was whom they had put to death, and recognize who He really was. Those who needed a solution to their sin problem had to revisit the conclusion they had come to regarding Jesus' identity and to put their trust in Him. They could experience what Jesus had come to earth for: "that your sins may be blotted out, when the times of refreshing shall come from the presence of the Lord; and he shall send Jesus Christ, which before was preached unto you" (Acts 3:19-20). Because they had rejected Jesus when He was on earth, their subsequent reception of Him could be pictured as a "revisitation" specifically for them. Present reception could remedy their past rejection.

Jesus was the "Christ" (Χριστός), the "Messiah," whose arrival ushered in an age anticipated by the prophets: "the times of restitution of all things, which God hath spoken by the mouth of all his holy prophets since the world began" (Acts 3:21). Moses had called the central prophetic figure a "prophet" (προφήτης), and their reception/rejection of Him would determine their eternal destiny. "For Moses truly said unto the fathers, A prophet shall the Lord your God raise up unto you of your brethren, like unto me; him shall ye hear in all things whatsoever he shall say unto you. And it shall come to pass, *that* every soul, which will not hear that prophet, shall be destroyed from among the people" [italics in KJV] (Acts 3:22-23). Moses had recorded in Deuteronomy 18:15-19 what God told him about the future prophet and his was not a lone prophetic voice. The messianic age had been the subject of every Old Testament prophet. "Yea, and all the prophets from Samuel and those that follow after, as many as have spoken, have likewise foretold of these days" (Acts 3:24).

The people in Peter's Jewish audience were to be the recipients of the blessings of salvation. "Ye are the children of the prophets, and of the covenant which God made with our fathers, saying unto Abraham, And in thy seed shall all the kindreds of the earth be blessed" (Acts 3:25). Salvation was initially offered to them. "Unto you first God, having raised up his Son Jesus, sent him to bless you, in turning away every one of you from his iniquities" (Acts 3:26). Salvation centered on Jesus.

Acts Chapter 4

The Jewish religious leadership got upset with the apostles because Jesus was the subject of their preaching, and particularly the Sadducees took offense to the message of the resurrection. "And as they spake unto the people, the priests, and the captain of the temple, and the Sadducees, came upon them, being grieved that they taught the people, and preached through Jesus the resurrection from the dead" (Acts 4:1-2). In spite of opposition many believed what the Apostles said and put their trust in Jesus. "Howbeit many of them which heard the word believed; and the number of the men was about five thousand" (Acts 4:4).

Jesus had proved who He was by performing miracles and now the apostles were doing the very same thing and they understood that what they were doing was a continuation of His ministry. In their defense before those who had arrested them, Peter said, "be it known unto you all, and to all the people of Israel, that by the name of Jesus Christ of Nazareth, whom ye crucified, whom God raised from the dead, *even* by him doth this man stand here before you whole" [italics in KJV] (Acts 4:10).

Peter emphasized Jesus' identity and continued, "This is the stone which was set at nought of you builders, which is become the head of the corner" (Acts 4:11). Stanley Toussaint notes the difficulties associated with the use of Psalm 118:22, where Peter identifies Jesus:

> The background of this verse is disputed. The rejected stone, (Ps. 118) may be (a) an actual building stone, (b) the nation of Israel, or (c) David. Or it may also be a proverb with no specific application. Most probably, to David the rejected stone in Psalm 118:22 meant Israel, a nation spurned by other nations. At any rate, the verse finds its ultimate fulfillment in Christ Jesus who is the "ideal" Israel ("Acts," in *The Bible*

Knowledge Commentary, New Testament, ed. John F. Walvoord and Roy B. Zuck [Wheaton, IL: Victor, 1983; reprint, Colorado Springs: Cook, 1996], 363).

Peter's purpose was to identify Jesus as indispensable to man's salvation. "Neither is there salvation in any other: for there is none other name under heaven given among men, whereby we must be saved" (Acts 4:12).

Peter and John were bold, confident, and articulate in the delivery of their message that did not go unnoticed by the religious establishment. "Now when they saw the boldness of Peter and John, and perceived that they were unlearned and ignorant men, they marvelled; and they took knowledge of them, that they had been with Jesus" (Acts 4:13). Their testimony had no other explanation than that they had spent time in the presence of the One of whom they spoke. In their response and refusal to stop speaking about Jesus, Peter and John mentioned that theirs was the testimony of eyewitnesses. "For we cannot but speak the things which we have seen and heard" (Acts 4:20).

Peter and John understood that the threats they received and the injunction not to speak about Jesus were an extension of the opposition that the Messiah Himself had experienced and connected it with David's words. "The kings of the earth stood up, and the rulers were gathered together against the Lord, and against his Christ" (Acts 4:26). Psalm 2:2 says, "The kings of the earth set themselves, and the rulers take counsel together, Against the Lord, and against his anointed [or "Messiah"]." The association and application that Peter and John saw between these words of Psalm 2:2 about the Messiah and what had been done to Jesus, is explicitly stated. "For of a truth against thy holy child Jesus, whom thou hast anointed, both Herod, and Pontius Pilate, with the Gentiles, and the people of Israel, were gathered together" (Acts 4:27).

Luke, the author of the book of Acts, saw the mission of the apostles as giving testimony to what they had witnessed. Sometimes the writer used the resurrection, the greatest sign and proof of who Jesus is, as shorthand to express all that had gone on. "And with great power gave the apostles witness of the resurrection of the Lord Jesus" (Acts 4:33).

Acts Chapter 5

The judgment of instant death experienced by Ananias and Sapphira struck fear in the hearts of everyone who heard about it. "And great fear came upon all the church, and upon as many as heard these things" (Acts 5:11). Nothing in the text casts doubt on the salvation of Ananias and Sapphira. They are placed by the author among those described in Acts 4:32 with, "And the multitude of them that believed were of one heart and of one soul: neither said any *of them* that ought of the things which he possessed was his own; but they had all things common" [italics in KJV].

Additionally, when Sapphira was rebuked by Peter, he asked her, "How is it that ye have agreed together to tempt the Spirit of the Lord?" (Acts 5:9). The question was appropriate to ask of one indwelt by the Holy Spirit and militates against the position that they were unbelievers. If they were indeed believers does not their experience put in jeopardy the perseverance of these two saints? Perhaps if theological reverse engineering or regression analysis were employed, it would be discovered that these two were never saved in the first place. But we digress.

Juxtaposed with this sobering example of deathly supernatural judgment is that of the apostles who continued their miracle ministry. "And by the hands of the apostles were many signs and wonders wrought among the people" (Acts 5:12). The net result was that in spite of the scary seriousness of God's dealing with the sin of Ananias and Sapphira, many still put their trust in Christ for salvation. "And believers were the more added to the Lord, multitudes both of men and women" (Acts 5:14). The object of faith, the One in whom their trust was placed, was "the Lord" (ὁ κύριος), identified in the apostles' preaching as Jesus, who is the Messiah.

The high priest, who led the opposition to the apostles and had them put in prison, was associated with the party of the Sadducees who denied the resurrection. "Then the high priest rose up, and all they that were with him, (which is the sect of the Sadducees), and were filled with indignation, and laid their hands on the apostles, and put them in the common prison" [parenthesis in KJV] (Acts 5:17-18). When an angel delivered them from the prison, his instruction to the apostles specifically mentioned "life" (ζωή). In Acts 5:20 the angel commanded them, "Go, stand and speak in the temple to the people all the words of this life."

Stanley Toussaint writes that the angel's command to continue preaching "**the full message of this new life** (lit., "all the words of this life," [was] an unusual way to refer to the gospel)" [bold and parenthesis in original] ("Acts," in *The Bible Knowledge Commentary, New Testament*, ed. John F. Walvoord and Roy B. Zuck [Wheaton, IL: Victor, 1983; reprint, Colorado Springs: Cook, 1996], 366). The angel's use of the term "life" (ζωή) was similar to the shorthand for the gospel message that Luke, the author of this book, used in Acts 4:33 where he says that "with great power gave the apostles witness of the resurrection of the Lord Jesus." Luke's parenthetical mention of the Sadducees, who were well known for their denial of the resurrection, fits well with the interpretation that "life" (ζωή) is to be understood as a reference to the gospel message's emphasis on Jesus' resurrection and the eternal life that believers receive by trusting in Him; it probably does not refer to the Christian way of life.

The gospel message preached by the apostles revolved around Jesus' identity, and their antagonists were concerned with what they were saying about who Jesus is. In the follow-up to their injunction not to talk about Jesus they said, "Did not we straitly command you that ye should not teach in this name? And, behold, ye have filled Jerusalem with your doctrine, and intend to bring this man's blood upon us" (Acts 5:28).

Instead of being apologetic Peter and the rest of the apostles responded with their famous statement, "We ought to obey God rather than men" (Acts 5:29). The reader is not told by Luke how this was done, whether in unison or if they took turns, or if Peter was their spokesman since he is singled out. What they did do was reiterate who Jesus is: "The God of our fathers raised up Jesus, whom ye slew and hanged on a tree. Him hath God exalted with his right hand *to be* a Prince and a Saviour, for to give repentance to Israel, and forgiveness of sins" [italics in KJV] (Acts 5:30-31). The identity of Jesus is grounded in historical events and the apostles viewed themselves as witnesses to those events: "And we are his witnesses of these things" (Acts 5:32).

The apostles and the assembled crowd, as well as the Jewish religious leaders, had witnessed the phenomenon of Pentecost. In addition to all of those witnesses the apostles added the Holy Spirit as a witness; "And we are his witnesses of these things; and *so is* also the Holy Ghost, whom God hath given to them that obey him" [italics in KJV] (Acts 5:32). Concerning the disciples and the Holy Spirit Jesus had said, "But when the Comforter is come, whom I will send unto you from the Father, *even* the Spirit of truth, which proceedeth from the Father, he shall testify of me: and ye also shall bear witness, because ye have been with me from the beginning" [italics in KJV] (John 15:26-27).

One of the primary ministries of the Holy Spirit is that of conviction; "And when he is come, he will reprove [convict] the world" (John 16:8). One of the things unbelievers will be convicted about is their sin and their need for Jesus as its solution. Jesus said this about the convicting work of the Holy Spirit in relation to sin: "of sin, because they believe not on me" (John 16:9). Peter told unbelievers to "repent" (Acts 2:38) (μετανοήσατε) and those who did so are described as those who (Acts 2:44) "believed" (οἱ πιστεύοντες). At the end of Acts 5:32 it says, "the Holy Ghost, whom God hath given to them that obey him." Given the Holy Spirit's convicting ministry in unbelievers because of their sin, means that for them to obey the Holy Spirit was to believe in Jesus, thereby dealing with their sin problem.

The apostles were told again "that they should not speak in the name of Jesus" (Acts 5:40). Instead of using persecution as an excuse to keep silent about Jesus, they saw it as an incentive to continue doing so. "And they departed from the presence of the council, rejoicing that they were counted worthy to suffer shame for his name" (Acts 5:41). Luke made sure his readers knew that the issue of contention was the message of Jesus' identity. "They ceased not to teach and preach Jesus Christ." The NASB says that, "they kept right on teaching and preaching Jesus *as* the Christ" [italics in NASB] (Acts 5:42), that is that He is the Messiah.

Acts Chapter 6

Deacons were selected by the church congregation in Jerusalem so that the apostles could attend to their primary responsibilities. "But we will give ourselves continually to prayer, and to the ministry of the word" (Acts 6:4). The church continued to grow as a result. "And the word of God increased; and the number of the disciples multiplied in Jerusalem greatly; and a great company of the priests were obedient to the faith" (Acts 6:7).

Some Bible teachers say that being "obedient to the faith" (ὑπήκουον τῇ πίστει) means that obedience and faith were synonymous in the minds of New Testament believers. Sometimes the help of Rudolph Bultmann is enlisted because he wrote, "'to believe' is 'to obey'" (*Theological Dictionary of the New Testament* [Grand Rapids: Eerdmans, 1968], 6:205). Without going into James Barr's criticisms of the linguistic methodology of that theological dictionary, the context of Bultmann's words quoted above should not be ignored. Bultmann wrote: "The fact that 'to believe' is 'to obey,' as in the OT (—> 199, 19ff.), is particularly emphasized in Hb. 11. Here πιστεύειν ["to believe"] of OT characters has in some instances the more or less explicit sense of obedience" (ibid.).

Bultmann apparently recognized how tenuous his assertion was, necessitating the "more or less" qualifier. He did add,

> How naturally πιστεύειν ["to believe"] includes obeying may be seen from the use of πείθεσθαι ["to obey"] rather than πιστεύειν ["to believe"] for receiving the Christian message, —> 4, 18 ff. Unbelief can be denoted not merely by ἀπιστεῖν ["to disbelieve"] but also by ἀπειθεῖν, ["to disobey"] —> 11. 16 ff. Paul in particular stresses the element of obedience in faith. For him πίστις [faith] is indeed ὑπακοή, [obedience]. . . Faith is for Paul ὑπακούειν τῷ εὐαγγελίῳ, ["to obey the gospel"] R. 10:16. To refuse to believe is not to obey the righteousness which the Gospel offers for faith, R. 10:3 (ibid., 205-6).

Regarding Bultmann's last biblical reference, Romans 10:3, Paul's discussion in Romans 10 explicitly excludes effort expended to keep the Law (works) in favor of faith alone. Bultmann's lexicography and his followers notwithstanding, neither the New Testament apostles nor their converts considered the terms "obedience" and "faith" to be synonymous and consequently they did not conflate faith and works. As the rest of the book of Acts demonstrates, Luke observed the biblical distinction between faith and works. The famous Jerusalem Council of Acts 15 and the apostle Paul's ministry as described by Luke are testimony to the importance of that foundation for accurate biblical interpretation.

When deacon Stephen was brought before the Council, the accusation centered on what he was saying about Jesus. And the character of Stephen's accusers is brought up by Luke. "And [they] set up false witnesses, which said, This man ceaseth not to speak blasphemous words against this holy place, and the law: for we have heard him say, that this Jesus of Nazareth shall destroy this place, and shall change the customs which Moses delivered us" (Acts 6:13-14). They recognized Stephen was claiming that the One of whom he spoke was superior to Moses whom they revered.

Acts Chapter 7

Stephen's defense began with an extensive rehearsal of Israel's redemptive history. He included the words of Moses whom he had been accused of dishonoring. "This is that Moses, which said unto the children of Israel, A prophet shall the Lord your God raise up unto you of your brethren, like unto me; him shall ye hear" (Acts 7:37). This proved that Moses believed the prophet whose coming he predicted was at least on a par with him. And the rejection to which Moses was subjected would picture what the coming One would endure. "To whom our fathers would not obey, but thrust *him* from them, and in their hearts turned back again into Egypt" [italics in KJV] (Acts 7:39). The ancestors of Stephen's accusers had not treated Moses in a manner commensurate with who he was and Jesus would receive even worse treatment.

Stephen completed his annotated history lesson and made the application to his accusers. "Ye stiffnecked and uncircumcised in heart and ears, ye do always resist the Holy Ghost: as your fathers *did*, so *do* ye" [italics in KJV] (Acts 7:51). Stephen accused the ancestors of his persecutors of having murdered the Old Testament prophets who prophesied about Jesus' coming. "Which of the prophets have not your fathers persecuted? And they have slain them which shewed before of the coming of the Just One [or "Righteous One"]" (Acts 7:52).

With the mention of "the Just One" or "the Righteous One" Stephen had arrived at the climax of his defense. Stephen was identifying "the Just One" or "the Righteous One" as Jesus and his accusers as His murderers: "whose betrayers and murderers you have now become" (Acts 7:52). The implication of Stephen's words and the identification he made were understood and the reaction was immediate. "When they heard these things, they were cut to the heart, and they gnashed on him with *their* teeth" [italics in KJV] (Acts 7:54).

The courtroom scene erupted out of control and Stephen was supernaturally shown the One of whom he spoke. Luke described what Stephen experienced. "But he, being full of the Holy Ghost, looked up stedfastly into heaven, and saw the glory of God, and Jesus standing on the right hand of God" (Acts 7:55). Stephen identified the One he saw as the Son of Man, "Behold, I see the heavens opened, and the Son of man standing on the right hand of God" (Acts 7:56). Stephen's testimony of whom he saw is contrasted with the witnesses who stoned him: "and the witnesses laid down their clothes at a young man's feet, whose name was Saul. And they stoned Stephen" (Acts 7:58-59). The law was scrupulously followed with plural witnesses providing testimony to produce a verdict authorizing Stephen's murder. But the scene resembled a lynching more than an orderly court proceeding.

The dying words of Stephen recorded by Luke are a prayer of forgiveness addressed to Jesus whom he had just seen at the right hand of God the Father and whom he identifies as "Lord" (κύριος). Stephen prayed, "Lord Jesus, receive my spirit. And he kneeled down, and cried with a loud voice, Lord, lay not this sin to their charge. And when he had said this, he fell asleep" (Acts 7:59-60). The prayer of forgiveness was not unlike that of Stephen's Savior Jesus as He died to secure Stephen's eternal salvation.

Acts Chapter 8

Persecution caused believers to scatter from Jerusalem. At the forefront of the persecution rampage was Saul. "As for Saul, he made havock of the church, entering into every house, and haling men and women committed *them* to prison" [italics in KJV] (Acts 8:3). The unintended result was, "Therefore they that were scattered abroad went every where preaching the word" (Acts 8:4). "The word" (ὁ λόγος) that was preached is explained by the author in his description of the activities of Philip, one of those driven from Jerusalem who escaped to Samaria. "Then Philip went down to the city of Samaria, and preached Christ unto them" (Acts 8:5). "The word" (ὁ λόγος) he preached was about Jesus Christ.

The message about the Messiah (ὁ Χριστός) was further explained as "preaching the good news about the kingdom of God and the name of Jesus Christ" (Acts 8:12). The person of "Jesus" (Ἰησοῦς), "the Messiah" (ὁ Χριστός), was integral to the new order, "the kingdom of God" (ἡ βασιλεία τοῦ θεοῦ); without the messianic King there would be no messianic kingdom. What Philip preached was also referred to as God's word: "Now when the apostles which were at Jerusalem heard that Samaria had received the word of God" (Acts 8:14).

Peter and John were dispatched from Jerusalem to confirm what had happened in Samaria and to express their unity with the new group of believers. The selection of Peter and John was important because they were recognized as witnesses who could confirm the truth of the message about Jesus. Luke, the author of Acts, made a point to describe their ministry in that way. "And they, when they had testified and preached the word of the Lord, returned to Jerusalem, and preached the gospel in many villages of the Samaritans" (Acts 8:25).

Philip's conversation with the Ethiopian eunuch emphasized the identity of Jesus. The Old Testament passage the eunuch was reading was the messianic prophecy of Isaiah 53:7-8. Luke quoted it from the Greek translation, the Septuagint (LXX): "He was led as a sheep to the slaughter; and like a lamb dumb before his shearer, so opened he not his mouth: in his humiliation his judgment was taken away: and who shall declare his generation? for his life is taken from the earth" (Acts 8:32-33). The eunuch's question was about the identity of the person in the passage. He asked Philip, "I pray thee, of whom speaketh the prophet this? of himself, or of some other man?" (Acts 8:34).

Philip's answer is found in the author's retelling of the conversation that follows. "Then Philip opened his mouth, and began at the same scripture, and preached unto him Jesus" (Acts 8:35). Luke does not specifically state what Philip said. Acts 8:37 does provide a clue to the content, if one accepts that verse as being in the original. The verse in question, Acts 8:37 says, "And Philip said, If thou believest with all thine heart, thou mayest. And he answered and said, I believe that Jesus Christ is the Son of God." Bruce Metzger in his textual commentary says this about Acts 8:37:

There is no reason why scribes should have omitted the material, if it had originally stood in the text. It should be noted too that τὸν Ἰησοῦν Χριστόν is not a Lukan expression. The formula πιστεύω ... Χριστόν was doubtless used by the early church in baptismal ceremonies, and may have been written in the margin of a copy of Acts. Its insertion into the text seems to have been due to the feeling that Philip would not have baptized the Ethiopian without securing a confession of faith, which needed to be expressed in the narrative. Although the earliest known New Testament manuscript that contains the words dates from the sixth century (ms. E), the tradition of the Ethiopian's confession of faith in Christ was current as early as the latter part of the second century, for Irenaeus quotes part of it (Against Heresies, III.xii.8).

Although the passage does not appear in the late medieval manuscript on which Erasmus chiefly depended for his edition (ms. 2), it stands in the margin of another (ms. 4), from which he inserted it into his text because he "judged that it had been omitted by the carelessness of scribes (arbitror omissum librariorum incuria)" (*A Textual Commentary on the Greek New Testament*, 359-60).

Whether Acts 8:37 was a part of the original Greek text, its appearance in the latter part of the second century is an indication that the early church saw the identity of Jesus as integral to the gospel message.

The question the eunuch had was about the identity of the One about whom the prophet Isaiah wrote. Philip showed the eunuch what the rest of Old Testament Scripture said about Jesus. Luke called this "preaching the gospel" (εὐηγγελίζετο), telling the "good news" as seen in his summary statement, "But Philip was found at Azotus: and passing through he preached in all the cities, till he came to Caesarea" (Acts 8:40). The NASB translates, "But Philip found himself at Azotus; and as he passed through he kept preaching the gospel to all the cities, until he came to Caesarea." The Greek uses the term "preached the good news" (εὐηγγελίζετο). The ministry of Philip was an extension of the mission of the Jerusalem church and his message was the same as that of Peter and the rest of the apostles.

Acts Chapter 9

The conversion of Saul on the road to Damascus lays a foundation for most of the remainder of the book of Acts as well as much of the rest of the New Testament. It explains how a persecutor of Christians became a preacher of what those whom he persecuted believed. It began with a dazzling appearance by Jesus: "and suddenly there shined round about him a light from heaven" (Acts 9:3). Jesus identified Himself as the person whom Saul was in the process of persecuting, saying, "Saul, Saul, why persecutest thou me?" (Acts 9:4). Saul needed further identification so he asked Jesus who He is: "Who art thou, Lord?" (Acts 9:5). Jesus identified Himself to Saul: "I am Jesus whom thou persecutest" (Acts 9:5).

The term "believe" (πιστεύω) is not used in Luke's conversion account but Saul knew who the One was in whom he would believe. Paul, whose name would be changed from Saul, would write to Timothy about it: "for I know whom I have believed, and am persuaded that he is able to keep that which I have committed unto him against that day" (2 Timothy 1:12). There Paul used the Greek perfect tense "I have believed" (πεπίστευκα) to describe his conversion as having taken place at a time in the past, and having ongoing results.

Confirmation in Acts of Saul/Paul having been converted prior to his meeting with Ananias in Damascus (not the Ananias from Jerusalem who had been slain by the Holy Spirit in Acts chapter 5) is found in Jesus' words to Ananias where Ananias is told, "inquire in the house of Judas for *one* called Saul, of Tarsus: for, behold, he prayeth" [italics in KJV] (Acts 9:11). Also when Ananias greeted Saul he addressed him as "Brother Saul" (Acts 9:17) (Σαοὺλ ἀδελφέ).

Having seen Jesus, knowing who He is, and having put his trust in Him for his eternal destiny, Saul lost no time in introducing Jesus as the Son of God to others: "and straightway he preached Christ in the synagogues, that he is the Son of God" (Acts 9:20). Jesus' identity became the focal point of the gospel that Paul preached. He proclaimed that Jesus is God, and the promised Messiah. "But Saul increased the more in strength, and confounded the Jews which dwelt at Damascus, proving that this is very Christ" (Acts 9:22).

Barnabas defended Saul to those who feared him in the Jerusalem church and told them that Saul had personally seen Jesus, spoken with Him, and fearlessly testified about Him to the people of Damascus. "But Barnabas took him, and brought *him* to the apostles, and declared unto them how he had seen the Lord in the way, and that he had spoken to him, and how he had preached boldly at Damascus in the name of Jesus" [italics in KJV] (Acts 9:27). The authenticity of Saul's ministry was based on his having met Jesus personally, which established his qualification as an eyewitness.

In describing the healing ministry of Peter the author of Acts showed that the early church identified Jesus as "Christ" (Χριστός), the Messiah, and as "Lord" (κύριος), that is, God Himself. Peter told a paralyzed man, "Aeneas, Jesus Christ maketh thee whole: arise, and make thy bed" (Acts 9:34). Luke summarized what resulted from the healing. "And all that dwelt at Lydda and Saron saw him, and turned to the Lord" (Acts 9:35). To "turn" (ἐπιστρέφω) to "the Lord" (ὁ κύριος) referred to their switching from something and someone else to "Jesus Christ" (Ἰησοῦς Χριστός) by whose power Peter had healed the paralyzed man. Those who had observed the healing were convinced about Jesus' identity in whom they then placed their trust.

In Joppa Peter prayed over the dead body of a woman believer. She is described with the words, "there was at Joppa a certain disciple named Tabitha, which by interpretation is called Dorcas: this woman was full of good works and almsdeeds which she did" (Acts 9:36). Luke gives details surrounding her death to leave no doubt that she had indeed died. "And it came to pass in those days, that she was sick, and died: whom when they had washed, they laid *her* in an upper chamber" [italics in KJV] (Acts 9:37).

A miracle of such magnitude would undergo intense scrutiny. Accordingly, Luke carefully included in his account those who could corroborate what had happened. Peter was summoned from Lydda to Joppa by two men who told him of Tabitha's death. "And forasmuch as Lydda was nigh to Joppa, and the disciples had heard that Peter was there, they sent unto him two men, desiring *him* that he would not delay to come to them" [italics in KJV] (Acts 9:38). Grieving "widows" (χῆραι) are mentioned as being present in the room with Tabitha's body. "And all the widows stood by him weeping, and shewing the coats and garments which Dorcas made, while she was with them" (Acts 9:39). They were witnesses to her sacrificial life, death, and her coming back to life.

Acts 9:40-41 says, "But Peter put them all forth, and kneeled down, and prayed; and turning *him* to the body said, Tabitha, arise. And she opened her eyes: and when she saw Peter, she sat up. And he gave her *his* hand, and lifted her up, and when he had called the saints and widows, presented her alive" [italics in KJV]. Although only Peter was present for the actual miracle, many became witnesses to her resurrection because they knew she had died and was then alive. The miracle resulted in many conversions. "And it was known throughout all Joppa; and many believed in the Lord" (Acts 9:42). Many Joppites came to place their trust in the One who had raised Dorcas from the dead. That One was "the Lord" (ὁ κύριος), understood to be Jesus the God/Man/Messiah in whose name miracles were performed and in whose name, or divine person, people put their trust.

Acts Chapter 10

Cornelius, the Roman centurion, knew about God the Father and revered Him. Luke says that he was a "devout *man*, and one that feared God with all his house, which gave much alms to the people, and prayed to God alway" [italics in KJV] (Acts 10:2). Peter was sent by God to tell him who Jesus is and what God requires.

Cornelius was pious but he had much to learn, as His actions when Peter arrived demonstrate. "And as Peter was coming in, Cornelius met him, and fell down at his feet, and worshipped *him*" [italics in KJV] (Acts 10:25). The situation required immediate corrective action on Peter's part. "But Peter took him up, saying, Stand up; I myself also am a man" (Acts 10:26). The presence in the Greek of the personal pronoun "myself" (αὐτὸς) shows that Peter was emphatic.

Peter helped Cornelius understand the relationship between the God of the Old Testament and Jesus. The identity of Jesus had been revealed in the Old Testament. "The word which *God* sent unto the children of Israel, preaching peace by Jesus Christ: (he is Lord of all)" [italics and parenthesis in KJV] (Acts 10:36). Jesus had been identified as God, the Master in control of everyone and everything.

The centurion was not unaware of Jesus; what He had done was not done in secret. "Ye know, [that] which was published throughout all Judaea, and began from Galilee, after the baptism which John preached" (Acts 10:37). It was common knowledge that what

Jesus did was supernaturally empowered. "How God anointed Jesus of Nazareth with the Holy Ghost and with power: who went about doing good, and healing all that were oppressed of the devil; for God was with him" (Acts 10:38).

Peter presented his own credentials to the centurion, affirming why Peter was qualified to make assertions about Jesus' identity. Peter used the plural when talking about himself. He was not a solitary witness but part of a select chosen group. "And we are witnesses of all things which he did both in the land of the Jews, and in Jerusalem" (Acts 10:39). The events of Jesus' life centered in the country of God's chosen people and at the epicenter of the worship of God. Three important particulars Peter mentioned about Jesus to identify Him were His death, resurrection, and postresurrection appearances: "whom they slew and hanged on a tree: Him God raised up the third day, and shewed him openly" (Acts 10:39-40).

In contrast to Jesus' public ministry His postresurrection appearances were targeted to certain individuals and groups. Although there were others outside the circle of the disciples who saw Him, God determined that they would be the official eyewitnesses of those events. Peter spoke of the uniqueness of the postresurrection apostolic witness: "Not to all the people, but unto witnesses chosen before of God, *even* to us, who did eat and drink with him after he rose from the dead" [italics in KJV] (Acts 10:41). The singular event of the Resurrection required officially designated witnesses whose testimony was incontrovertible.

Not only were the disciples specially qualified official witnesses; also to them was given the mission to proclaim what they had seen and heard: "And he commanded us to preach unto the people, and to testify that it is he which was ordained of God *to be* the Judge of quick and dead" [italics in KJV] (Acts 10:42). The Greek verb translated "solemnly to testify" (διαμαρτύρασθαι aorist, middle, infinitive from διαμαρτύρομαι = "testify," "insist," or "warn"), can include the idea of giving a warning. Since Jesus is "ordained by God to be the Judge of quick [living] and dead" (Acts 10:42), the disciples' gospel message had a sense of urgency about it. The Old Testament prophets concurred that Jesus was the only One who could deal with the problem of sin: "To him give all the prophets witness, that through his name whosoever believeth in him shall receive remission of sins" (Acts 10:43). Sin's solution is found in putting one's trust in the one and only Savior, Jesus.

The whole Cornelius episode was extraordinary. Cornelius was a Gentile and so were many of those in his household and those he had gathered to hear Peter. The church had been inaugurated in Jerusalem among Jews and accompanied by supernatural phenomena showing that the Holy Spirit was a vital part of that new entity. What happened next indicated that Gentiles were also included in the church with all its rights and privileges: "While Peter was still speaking these words, the Holy Spirit fell upon all those who were listening to the message" (Acts 10:44) (Ἔτι λαλοῦντος τοῦ Πέτρου τὰ ῥήματα ταῦτα ἐπέπεσεν τὸ πνεῦμα τὸ ἅγιον ἐπὶ πάντας τοὺς ἀκούοντας τὸν λόγον).

Luke expresses the surprise of the Jews from Jerusalem who had come along with Peter: "And they of the circumcision which believed were astonished, as many as came with Peter, because that on the Gentiles also was poured out the gift of the Holy Ghost" (Acts 10:45). Luke explains how they knew that the Holy Spirit had been experienced by these Gentiles: "For they heard them speak with tongues, and magnify God" (Acts 10:46). The church did indeed include Gentiles. Peter would have some explaining to do when he returned to Jerusalem. The opportunity to do so presented itself as soon as he got back.

Acts Chapter 11

Luke records that no sooner had Peter returned to Jerusalem when he was challenged about what he had just done. Word had spread quickly. "And the apostles and brethren that were in Judaea heard that the Gentiles had also received the word of God" (Acts 11:1). It should have been good news but there were those who did not take it as such. "And when Peter was come up to Jerusalem, they that were of the circumcision contended with him, saying, Thou wentest in to men uncircumcised, and didst eat with them" (Acts 11:2-3). They were not merely upset about the eating; they were just getting started. Peter probably took a deep breath as he began his defense: "But Peter rehearsed *the matter* from the beginning, and expounded *it* by order unto them" [italics in KJV] (Acts 11:4).

When Peter recalled the events that took place in Caesarea, he reported that the centurion repeated to him what an angel had said, "Send men to Joppa, and call for Simon, whose surname is Peter; who shall tell thee words, whereby thou and all thy house shall be saved" (Acts 11:13-14). In the NASB translation, Peter's report of belief and the gift of the Holy Spirit make the timing of the latter sound subsequent to the former, "If God therefore gave to them the same gift as He gave to us also after believing in the Lord Jesus Christ" (Acts 11:17). That chronology is not required by the grammar. It is more likely an example of the aorist participle "after believing" (πιστεύσασιν) having instead a coincident or contemporaneous meaning. That is, believing in Jesus and the giving of the Holy Spirit were most likely simultaneous events.

A. T. Robertson writes, "Acts, however, is particularly rich in examples of the coincident aorist participle which follows the verb. . . .It is in point of fact a characteristic of Luke's style to use frequently the coincident participle (both aorist and present) placed after the principal verb" (*A Grammar of the Greek New Testament in Light of Historical Research*, 1113). Wallace similarly notes, "The *aorist* participle, for example, usually denotes *antecedent* time to that of the controlling verb. But if the main verb is also aorist [which is the case in Acts 11:17], this participle *may* indicate contemporaneous time" [italics in original] (Daniel B. Wallace, *Greek Grammar beyond the Basics*, [Grand Rapids: Zondervan, 1996], 614). At the time they became believers they received the Holy Spirit that was accompanied by supernatural phenomena, indicating that they were included in the New Testament church.

After Peter's report about the events in Caesarea in the home of Cornelius his audience in Jerusalem said, "Then hath God also to the Gentiles granted repentance unto life" (Acts 11:18). As elsewhere in the book of Acts, to "believe" (πιστεύω) is referred to alternatively as "repentance" (μετάνοια). The change of mind on the part of Cornelius may have been the transition from thinking he could earn salvation by works, being a "devout *man*, and one that feared God with all his house, which gave much alms to the people, and prayed to God alway" [italics in KJV] (Acts 10:2), to one who knew who "the Lord Jesus Christ" (ὁ κύριος Ἰησοῦς Χριστός) is and had put his trust in Him.

The scattering that resulted from Stephen's martyrdom saw the gospel work its way to Antioch. Some of those displaced believers focused their attention on the Jews of Antioch, "preaching the word to none but unto the Jews only" (Acts 11:19). Others evangelized Grecians. The author writes about "men of Cyprus and Cyrene, which, when they were come to Antioch, spake unto the Grecians, preaching the Lord Jesus" (Acts 11:20). Louw and Nida see this as a description of "a Greek-speaking Jew in contrast to one speaking a Semitic language–'Greek-speaking Jew.'…basically Jewish in culture and religion, but they had adopted certain customs typical of the larger Greco-Roman world in which many of them lived. This inevitably resulted in certain suspicions and misunderstandings" (Johannes P. Louw and Eugene A. Nida, *Greek-English Lexicon of the New Testament Based on Semantic Domains*, 2nd ed. [New York: United Bible Societies, 2nd ed], 1989, 1:135-36).

Luke refers to those who were receptive to the gospel with the words, "and a great number believed, and turned unto the Lord" (Acts 11:21). The orientation of the mind had to be "turned" (ἐπέστρεψεν aorist, active, indicative from ἐπιστρέφω "turn," "return," "change one's beliefs," or "change one's ways" Johannes P. Louw and Eugene A. Nida, *Greek-English Lexicon of the New Testament Based on Semantic Domains*, 2nd ed. [New York: United Bible Societies, 2nd ed], 1989, 1:194, 373-4, 510) from whatever it had been focused on as an object of its trust to "the Lord" (ὁ κύριος) in whom they "believed" (πιστεύσας aorist active participle from πιστεύω "believe"). The meaning of "change one's ways" is ruled out because of the association of "turn" with "believe."

Luke records that Barnabas went to Antioch to see what was happening there: "Who, when he [Barnabas] came, and had seen the grace of God, was glad, and exhorted them all, that with purpose of heart they would cleave unto the Lord" (Acts 11:23). Having found out that they were indeed believers, he encouraged them to "cleave unto the Lord." Their "cleaving" was a condition that Barnabas knew was not assured nor was it automatic. For it to be a reality, Barnabas enlisted Saul's help discipling the new believers and Luke indicates that "the disciples were called Christians first in Antioch" (Acts 11:26). Their association with Jesus, and belief in Him whom they recognized as the "Messiah" (ὁ Χριστός) was the reason they were known by that name.

Acts Chapter 12

Herod imprisoned Peter and probably intended to execute him as he had James, the brother of John (Acts 12:2). Instead an "angel of the Lord" (ἄγγελος κυρίου) delivered Peter from prison. Luke gives details of Peter's release. First came the shackles, "And his chains fell off from *his* hands" [italics in KJV] (Acts 12:7). Then Peter followed the angel out of prison as the gates opened before them. "And he went out, and followed him. . . .When they were past the first and the second ward, they came unto the iron gate that leadeth unto the city; which opened to them of his own accord: and they went out, and passed on through one street" (Acts 12:9-10).

Understandably Peter was in a daze; he thought he was dreaming. On further contemplation the truth of what had just happened sunk in. "And when Peter was come to himself, he said, Now I know of a surety, that the Lord hath sent his angel, and hath delivered me out of the hand of Herod, and *from* all the expectation of the people of the Jews" [italics in KJV] (Acts 12:11). In the Old Testament the angel of the Lord is considered by some to have been appearances of the preincarnate Christ. Perhaps here Peter witnessed a postresurrection appearance of Christ. Peter was finally let inside the home of those praying for his deliverance who were having trouble believing that it had actually happened. Peter "declared unto them how the Lord had brought him out of the prison" (Acts 12:17). Perhaps it was Luke's way of indicating the Lord was the One who had orchestrated Peter's deliverance, or Peter could have understood that it was actually Jesus who led him out of prison.

At the end of the chapter "an angel of the Lord" (ἄγγελος κυρίου) makes another appearance, this time in judgment, when Herod blasphemed by allowing his subjects to worship him. "And immediately the angel of the Lord smote him, because he gave not God the glory: and he was eaten of worms, and gave up the ghost" (Acts 12:23). As in the case of Ananias and Sapphira divine judgment resulted in the expansion of the church. "But the word of God grew and multiplied" (Acts 12:24). Luke used a figure of speech called "metonymy" or "change of noun" described by Bullinger under "Metonymy of the Cause" (Ethelbert W. Bullinger, *Figures of Speech Used in the Bible*, 538). "Metonymy of the *Cause* is when the cause is put for the effect: *i.e.*, when the doer is put for the thing done; or, the instrument for that which is effected; or, where the action is put for the effect produced by the action" [italics in original] (ibid.). In Acts 12:24 cause is put for effect; the cause being the word of God, the effect being conversions.

Acts Chapter 13

In this chapter Luke begins to refer to Saul as Paul. The first instance is Acts 13:9. "Then Saul, (who also *is called* Paul)" [italics and parenthesis in KJV]. A result of the preaching of Paul and the blinding of Elymas, the magician and false prophet, was the conversion of Sergius Paulus, the proconsul. "Then the deputy, when he saw what was done, believed, being astonished at the doctrine [teaching] of the Lord" (Acts 13:12). In the phrase "the teaching of the Lord" (τῇ διδαχῇ τοῦ κυρίου), "the Lord" (τοῦ κυρίου = genitive, singular), should be taken as an objective genitive; the teaching was about the Lord, that is, Jesus. Information about Jesus' identity was communicated by Paul so that the proconsul could put his trust in Him.

Paul was invited to say some words in the synagogue in Psidian Antioch on the Sabbath. He began by rehearsing Israel's history from the time in Egypt to the time of David and introduced Jesus as David's promised son. "Of this man's seed hath God according to *his* promise raised unto Israel a Saviour, Jesus" [italics in KJV] (Acts 13:23). Paul proceeded to identify who Jesus is beginning with the one who introduced Him, John the Baptist, who made sure that he was not confused with Jesus. John the Baptist said, "Whom think ye that I am? I am not *he*. But, behold, there cometh one after me, whose shoes of *his* feet I am not worthy to loose" [italics in KJV] (Acts 13:25).

Paul identified the One who had been prophesied in the Old Testament and the Jewish nation's religious leaders and those who followed them had not recognized but rather had rejected: "For they that dwell at Jerusalem, and their rulers, because they knew him not, nor yet the voices of the prophets which are read every sabbath day" (Acts 13:27). Jesus was further identified as the One whose execution they had orchestrated, "And though they found no cause of death *in him*, yet desired they Pilate that he should be slain" [italics in KJV] (Acts 13:28). His identification was also proven by His burial and resurrection. "They took *him* down from the tree, and laid *him* in a sepulchre. But God raised him from the dead" [italics in KJV] (Acts 13:29-30).

Paul appealed to his audience in the synagogue of Psidian Antioch to accept the testimony of Jesus' disciples who had witnessed the resurrection and His entire ministry, and who could vouch for who He is. "And he was seen many days of them which came up with him from Galilee to Jerusalem, who are his witnesses unto the people" (Acts 13:31). The disciples considered themselves official witnesses and Paul considered them as such as well. For Paul the key identifying event was Jesus' resurrection and he used three quotations to prove it.

First Paul said, "And we declare unto you glad tidings, how that the promise which was made unto the fathers, God hath fulfilled the same unto us their children, in that he hath raised up Jesus again; as it is also written in the second psalm, Thou art my Son, this day have I begotten thee" (Acts 13:32-33). Second, Paul quoted Isaiah 55:3: "And as concerning that he raised him up from the dead, *now* no more to return to corruption, he said on this wise, I will give you the sure mercies of David" [italics in KJV] (Acts 13:34). Third, from Psalm 16, "Wherefore he saith also in another *psalm*, Thou shalt not suffer thine Holy One to see corruption" [italics in KJV] (Acts 13:35).

The resurrection uniquely identified Jesus. As Peter had done in his sermon Paul made sure it was understood that David's words were not about himself but about someone else. "For David, after he had served his own generation by the will of God, fell on sleep, and was laid unto his fathers, and saw corruption: but he, whom God raised again, saw no corruption" (Acts 13:36-37).

Jesus, the one identified by Paul, was the instrument God used to bring salvation to men. "Be it known unto you therefore, men *and* brethren, that through this man is preached unto you the forgiveness of sins" [italics in KJV] (Acts 13:38). Through Jesus what the Law could not accomplish was provided: "And by him all that believe are justified from all things, from which ye could not be justified by the law of Moses" (Acts 13:39). The word translated "justified" (δικαιόω), is used twice in this verse (δικαιωθῆναι aorist passive infinitive, and δικαιοῦται present passive indicative, both from δικαιόω = "justify" or "declare righteous"). Trust in Jesus results in justification. "And by him all that believe are justified" (Acts 13:39), and there is no one who has trusted in Him and not been justified.

Paul and Barnabas's ministry to the Jews in the synagogue was rejected resulting in their focusing instead on Gentiles. The Gentile response was, "they were glad, and glorified the word of the Lord" (Acts 13:48). "The word of the Lord" (ὁ λόγος τοῦ κυρίου) was the message about Jesus. Jesus was both its source and its subject. It told them who Jesus was so that they could put their trust in Him for their eternal destiny. And that is what they did: "and as many as were ordained to eternal life believed" (Acts 13:48). Interpreters may not agree on what is meant by God having "ordained" or "appointed" (τεταγμένοι perfect passive participle from τάσσω "appoint" or "designate") them, but belief or trust is what they did and consequently were saved.

Acts Chapter 14

The narration of Paul and Barnabas's ministry in the Iconium synagogue states that "a great multitude both of the Jews and also of the Greeks believed" (Acts 14:1) (πιστεῦσαι Ἰουδαίων τε καὶ Ἑλλήνων πολὺ πλῆθος). Others rejected the message: "But the unbelieving Jews" (Acts 14:2) (οἱ δὲ ἀπειθήσαντες Ἰουδαῖοι). For the converts the Greek verb for "believe" is πιστεύω and for the unsaved the verb translated by "disbelieved" is ἀπειθέω. The close contextual proximity of these two verbs is reminiscent of John the Baptist's words, where the same verbal parallel is used in John 3:36. "He that believeth [πιστεύω] on the Son hath everlasting life: and he that believeth not [ἀπειθέω] [NASB = "does not obey"] the Son shall not see life."

In Acts 14:1-2 the same two Greek verbs are used and the NASB and the KJV both translate the terms πιστεύω and ἀπειθέω with "believe" and "disbelieve," respectively. The consistency reflects the overlap of semantic range of the two Greek words. There is no need to introduce the idea of "disobey" with its connotation of "works" into either Acts 14:1-2 or John 3:36. Furthermore if the nuance of works is introduced, employing the term "disobey" or "believe not" (ἀπειθέω) to mean a lack of willingness or commitment to "obey" is unwarranted. The presumed presence of either a works or willingness or commitment to work in the term "disbelieve" or "disobey" (ἀπειθέω) creates a lexical distinction between it and the term "believe" (πιστεύω) that is both lexically unnecessary and theologically untenable. The lexical change in this context is a stylistic choice by the author with the meaning of the two verbs being functionally synonymous. In both John 3:36 and Acts 14:1-2 the issue is trust in Jesus and not obedience to ethical requirements or the intention to do so.

In Acts 14 Paul was a witness, along with Barnabas, as they preached the gospel. Luke indicates that the Lord Himself corroborated their testimony. "Long time therefore abode they speaking boldly in the Lord, which gave testimony unto the word of his grace, and granted signs and wonders to be done by their hands" (Acts 14:3). The NASB says, "Therefore they spent a long time *there* speaking boldly *with reliance* upon the Lord, who was bearing witness to the word of His grace, granting that signs and wonders be done by their hands" [italics in NASB]. The missionary team was run off by a conspiracy between the Jews and the Gentiles of Iconium from continuing their ministry there, "And when there was an assault made both of the Gentiles, and also of the Jews with their rulers, to use *them* despitefully, and to stone them, they were ware of *it*, and fled unto Lystra and Derbe, cities of Lycaonia, and unto the region that lieth round about" [italics in KJV] (Acts 14:5-6). Persecution did not prevent them from continuing to evangelize the adjacent areas, "and there they preached the gospel" (Acts 14:7).

Paul's proclamation of the gospel continued to be miraculously corroborated. A lame man was healed, and Luke made sure that his readers/listeners would be convinced of the authenticity of the miracle by giving details of the man's prior condition. "And there sat a certain man at Lystra, impotent in his feet, being a cripple from his mother's womb, who never had walked" (Acts 14:8). The genuineness of the miracle is further substantiated by the response of those who witnessed it. The pagan audience exclaimed, "The gods are come down to us in the likeness of men" (Acts 14:11).

This erroneous identification was corrected by Barnabas and Paul who preached a gospel that identified a person far superior to any human being and pagan idols. The preaching began with who God is: "We also are men of like passions with you, and preach unto you that ye should turn from these vanities unto the living God, which made heaven, and earth, and the sea, and all things that are therein" (Acts 14:15). Testimony to the identity of God is found in His providential provision: "Nevertheless he left not himself without witness, in that he did good, and gave us rain from heaven, and fruitful seasons, filling our hearts with food and gladness" (Acts 14:17). Barnabas and Paul had difficulty turning the people's attempted object of worship away from themselves and onto God. "And with these sayings scarce restrained they the people, that they had not done sacrifice unto them" (Acts 14:18). The crowds focused on the messengers rather than the message they preached.

The treatment Paul received in Lystra went from worship to attempted execution, from deification to a literal near-death experience. "And there came thither *certain* Jews from Antioch and Iconium, who persuaded the people, and, having stoned Paul, drew *him* out of the city, supposing he had been dead" [italics in KJV] (Acts 14:19). Barnabas and Paul went on to the city of Derbe where they "preached the gospel to that city" (Acts 14:21). Their ministry is also described as one in which they "taught many" (Acts 14:21). Having accepted the gospel these new believers were now on the path of discipleship.

Although Paul had experienced a brush with death in Lystra, on the return trip they passed through there again. Luke describes their ministry as "Confirming the souls of the disciples, *and* exhorting them to continue in the faith" [italics in KJV] (Acts 14:22). Barnabas and Paul recognized that they shared with these disciples the certain prospect of persecution: "we must through much tribulation enter into the kingdom of God" (Acts 14:22). "Tribulation" (θλῖψις) was not a requirement for entrance into the kingdom but a consequence of their identification with Jesus. As Barnabas and Paul left these converts, "they commended them to the Lord, on whom they believed" (Acts 14:23). With the use of the Greek pluperfect tense translated as "they had believed" (πεπιστεύκεισαν) Luke indicates they had done something (believed) that was completed in the past and had ongoing results.

Acts Chapter 15

At the famous Jerusalem Council those who ended up on the losing side of the debate are nevertheless depicted as being saved. From their description the reader understands that they had to have gotten it right when they got saved but then they went awry. Luke wrote, "But there rose up certain of the sect of the Pharisees which believed" (Acts 15:5). The NASB says, "But certain ones of the sect of the Pharisees who had believed." Luke used the Greek perfect tense of the participle translated "who had believed" (πεπιστευκότες), meaning that they had believed in the past, a completed event that had an ongoing effect even as they were promoting their heresy. Perhaps because of their Pharisaic past they wandered from the way in which they had personally been saved. There is no reason to doubt their sincerity, but their theology was suspect.

The text does not state that there was anything wrong with their conversion, but they had now come up with what they thought was a better theology than what had originally resulted in their salvation. They stood and addressed those assembled, among them the apostles and elders, who were going to make a decision. Their contention was, "that it was needful to circumcise them, and to command *them* [Gentiles] to keep the law of Moses" [italics in KJV] (Acts 15:5). The following context shows that although their proposal recorded by Luke does not explicitly say that it was a requirement for salvation that they were insisting on, such was indeed the case.

Peter had been the first of the apostles to publicly preach the gospel, having done so at Pentecost. And having dealt with the issue of Gentiles being saved with the centurion coming to Christ it was natural that he would be the first one to speak, not that he would need a lot of prodding. Peter recounted his relevant prior experience with Gentile conversion: "Men *and* brethren, ye know how that a good while ago God made choice among us, that the Gentiles by my mouth should hear the word of the gospel, and believe" [italics in KJV] (Acts 15:7). Believing had been sufficient for the Gentiles to be saved as proven by Cornelius and his household.

Peter also recounted God's seal of approval that validated that those Gentiles had been saved: "And God, which knoweth the hearts, bare them witness, giving them the Holy Ghost, even as *he did* unto us" [italics in KJV] (Acts 15:8). God had shown Peter that there was not one way of salvation for Jews and another for Gentiles: "And put no difference between us and them, purifying their hearts by faith" (Acts 15:9). It was not faith alone for Jews, or the apostles and an "inner circle," and faith plus circumcision or the Law for Gentiles; salvation for all was by faith alone. Peter made the biblical position clear: "But we believe that through the grace of the Lord Jesus Christ we shall be saved, even as they" (Acts 15:11). Additional evidence for salvation by faith alone, without circumcision or observance of the Law, was introduced by Barnabas and Paul who testified about the miracles that authenticated Gentile conversion. "Then all the multitude kept silence, and gave audience to Barnabas and Paul, declaring what miracles and wonders God had wrought among the Gentiles by them" (Acts 15:12).

With that the case presented before the council for salvation without works rested and James gave a closing argument. First, he argued for the legitimacy of Gentile conversion by linking Peter's testimony with the Old Testament. "Simeon hath declared how God at the first did visit the Gentiles, to take out of them a people for his name. And to this agree the words of the prophets" (Acts 15:14-15). For evidence James quoted from Amos 9:11-12, "After this I will return, and will build again the tabernacle of David, which is fallen down; and I will build again the ruins thereof, and I will set it up: that the residue of men might seek after the Lord, and all the Gentiles, upon whom my name is called, saith the Lord, who doeth all these things" (Acts 15:16-17).

In his summation James proposed a verdict. "Wherefore my sentence ["judgment" = κρίνω] is, that we trouble not them, which from among the Gentiles are turned to God: but that we write unto them, that they abstain from pollutions of idols, and *from* fornication, and *from* things strangled, and *from* blood" [italics in KJV] (Acts 15:19-20). Salvation on the basis of faith alone in Christ should not be compromised. Those who were turning from trusting in pagan idols to trusting in Christ need not undergo circumcision, nor were they required to obey the Law in order to be saved.

James recognized the cultural environment of the cities in which Gentile ministry was taking place. He made his recommendation with an explanation, "For Moses of old time hath in every city them that preach him, being read in the synagogues every sabbath day" (Acts 15:21). Jewish sensibilities should not be unnecessarily offended. After all, the Gentile mission would not be conducted to the exclusion of Jewish evangelism. In that spirit what would be considered most egregious to the Jewish populace would be avoided.

James's recommendation was accepted by the Jerusalem Council and the church at large. Luke described the decision to send a letter to the churches that spelled out their findings. "Then pleased it the apostles and elders, with the whole church, to send chosen men of their own company to Antioch with Paul and Barnabas; *namely*, Judas surnamed Barsabas [Barnabas], and Silas, chief men among the brethren" [italics in

KJV] (Acts 15:22). The letter made clear that those members from the Jerusalem church who had come with a message that added to the gospel had not done so with the leaders' approval. "Forasmuch as we have heard, that certain which went out from us have troubled you with words, subverting your souls, saying, *Ye must* be circumcised, and keep the law: to whom we gave no *such* commandment" [italics in KJV] (Acts 15:24). What could be more "subverting" ("unsettle" = NASB) (ἀνασκευάζω = "cause distress") spiritually to one's very soul than to shake the biblical foundation for the assurance of salvation?

Having settled the issue of the requirement for salvation, the church in Antioch could get on with the task of evangelism and discipleship. "Paul also and Barnabas continued in Antioch, teaching and preaching the word of the Lord, with many others also" (Acts 15:35). The One about whom they taught and preached was "the Lord" (ὁ κύριος), that is Jesus. "The word of the Lord" (ὁ λόγος τοῦ κυρίου) was the message that had Jesus as its subject. It was about Him in whom trust needed to be placed for eternal salvation.

When Paul suggested that he and Barnabas go on a second missionary journey, he described their first trip as one in which they had preached that message. "Paul said unto Barnabas, Let us go again and visit our brethren in every city where we have preached the word of the Lord, *and see* how they do" [italics in KJV] (Acts 15:36). Jesus was the One on whom the message centered, and it was also He, Jesus, and the Holy Spirit who would empower the evangelistic endeavor. The sendoff of Paul and his new partner Silas after the split with Barnabas is described by Luke as their "being recommended by the brethren unto the grace of God" (Acts 15:40).

Acts Chapter 16

Luke brings up the issue of Timothy's circumcision or rather the lack thereof before Paul's arrival. The rationale given for Timothy's being circumcised at this point was "because of the Jews which were in those quarters: for they knew all that his father was a Greek" (Acts 16:3). This might seem to contradict what the Jerusalem council had decided. Their decision spelled out in the encyclical letter had purposefully not mentioned circumcision as something that was to be done to accommodate Jewish sensibilities.

Luke was aware of the possibility that his readers could misunderstand Timothy's circumcision as being contrary to the Jerusalem council's decision so he specifically mentioned the letter and that Paul and Silas were delivering it to the churches they visited. "And as they went through the cities, they delivered them the decrees for to keep, that were ordained of the apostles and elders which were at Jerusalem" (Acts 16:4). What Paul had done in regard to Timothy was consistent with the decision of the council. Circumcision was not to be added to belief as a requirement for salvation but Timothy's salvation was not in question. Timothy is called a "disciple" (Acts 16:1) (μαθητής) but if he had not been circumcised it could have kept him from entering Jewish synagogues as he accompanied Paul and Silas.

On the second missionary journey the steps of the first journey were partially retraced and had as one of its goals the edification of existing believers. "And so were the churches established in the faith" (Acts 16:5). The evangelistic imperative also continued. In addition to discipleship Luke says the churches were being "established in the faith, and increased in number daily" (Acts 16:5). The mission to Macedonia is depicted as an outreach to the unsaved. The text says about Paul the leader of the expedition, "And after he had seen the vision, immediately we endeavoured to go into Macedonia, assuredly gathering that the Lord had called us for to preach the gospel unto them" (Acts 16:10). This is the first of the "we" sections (Acts 16:10-17), the others being Acts 20:5-21:18 and Acts 27:1-28:16, that include Luke the book's author as an eyewitness of what he reports.

Just as demons identified Jesus as the Davidic Messiah, Paul and his companions had a slave-girl with "a spirit of divination" (Acts 16:16) (πνεῦμα πύθωνα) identify them and their mission. "These men are the servants of the most high God, which shew unto us the way of salvation" (Acts 16:17). Just as Jesus had exorcised the demons identifying Him, by Jesus' power Paul exorcised the spirit following them around, "And this did she many days. But Paul, being grieved, turned and said to the spirit, I command thee in the name of Jesus Christ to come out of her. And he came out the same hour" (Acts 16:18).

The conflict created by the exorcism set the stage for Paul and Silas to be thrown into prison in Philippi and the scene of one of the most memorable question/answer sequences in all of Scripture. The distraught Philippian jailor asked, "Sirs, what must I do to be saved?" (Acts 16:30). The soteriologically significant answer is, "Believe on the Lord Jesus Christ, and thou shalt be saved, and thy house" (Acts 16:31). The Majority Text includes "Christ" (Χριστός) in the title of Paul and Silas's identification of the One in whom the jailer was to place his trust, while the critical text does not. Whether "Christ" (Χριστός) was in the original autograph or not, there is no question that Jesus is the object of trust. To be saved eternally one must "believe in Him": nothing more, nothing less, no One else.

No doubt Paul and Silas went on and elaborated, giving their listeners abundant evidence to prove who Jesus is. Luke says, "And they spake unto him the word of the Lord, and to all that were in his house" (Acts 16:32). At some point during the ensuing conversation the jailer and those in his home each put their trust in Jesus to save them.

Luke tells how the jailer wanted to make things right by Paul and Silas. "And he took them the same hour of the night, and washed *their* stripes" [italics in KJV] (Acts 16:33). Then the whole household did what Jesus had commanded that new converts should do: "and was baptized, he and all his, straightway" (Acts 16:33). The jailer offered hospitality. "And when he had brought them into his house, he set meat before them" (Acts 16:34). It was a joyous occasion in which they "rejoiced greatly" (Acts 16:34) (ἠγαλλιάσατο).

Luke summarized what had happened and why. It was because the jailer and his household had put their trust in the One who was and is none other than God Himself. Luke stated that unequivocally: "believing in God with all his house" (Acts 16:34) (πανοικεὶ πεπιστευκὼς τῷ θεῷ). To believe in Jesus is to believe in God. They "had believed" (πεπιστευκὼς). Luke used the perfect tense so as to leave no doubt that they had put their trust in Jesus, an event that was completed in the past and had ongoing results. Such is the nature of saving faith.

Acts Chapter 17

In every city Paul went he made a practice of speaking first in the local synagogue. In Thessalonica the author says that "they came to Thessalonica, where was a synagogue of the Jews: and Paul, as his manner was, went in unto them, and three sabbath days reasoned with them out of the scriptures" (Acts 17:1-2). The strategy was to present evidence of Jesus' identity as the Messiah, "opening and alleging, that Christ must needs have suffered, and risen again from the dead; and that this Jesus, whom I preach unto you, is Christ" (Acts 17:3). The NASB says, "explaining and giving evidence that the Christ had to suffer and rise again from the dead, and *saying*, 'This Jesus whom I am proclaiming to you is the Christ'" [italics in NASB]. The death and resurrection of Jesus were integral to His identity. In order to put their trust in the Messiah they had to be convinced about who He is. Among those who were persuaded by Paul, the Greek-speaking Jews were particularly receptive. "And some of them believed, and consorted with Paul and Silas; and of the devout Greeks a great multitude, and of the chief women not a few" (Acts 17:4).

Inevitably the hostility of the religious leaders was aroused and they attempted to engage the civil authorities against Paul and his entourage. The strategy of their accusation was a misrepresentation of Paul's message about Jesus' identity. The indictment was, "these that have turned the world upside down are come hither also; whom Jason hath received: and these all do contrary to the decrees of Caesar, saying that there is another king, *one* Jesus" [italics in KJV] (Acts 17:6-7). Those who rejected the message and those who accepted it were both right; the issue was the identity of Jesus and what they would do about Him. Would they put their trust in Him or not?

Those who rejected Paul's preaching in Thessalonica are contrasted with those who diligently examined the Scriptures in Berea. "These were more noble than those in Thessalonica, in that they received the word with all readiness of mind, and searched the scriptures daily, whether those things were so" (Acts 17:11). Many today use the Bereans as examples for Bible study by believers. There are innumerable churches, Sunday School classes, groups, etc., who call themselves Bereans. Contextually these were Jewish unbelievers consulting their Old Testament to see "whether those things were so" (Acts 17:11). That they were Jewish unbelievers is confirmed by the sentence before the description of "more noble" which says, "And the brethren immediately sent away Paul and Silas by night unto Berea: who coming *thither* went into the synagogue of the Jews" [italics in KJV] (Acts 17:10). In the synagogue they were unbelieving

Jews. The subject matter of their inquiry was the identity of Jesus whom Paul was teaching.

Having investigated the issue to their satisfaction, many were convinced and "Therefore many of them believed; also of honourable women which were Greeks, and of men, not a few" (Acts 17:12). The latter two of the three groups mentioned, the "honourable women" who were "Greeks" and "men" may have been converted as a result of the witness of the first group mentioned, Jewish Bereans from the synagogue. Confirmation that the same message was preached by Paul in both Thessalonica and Berea is found in Luke's depiction of the opposition encountered. "But when the Jews of Thessalonica had knowledge that the word of God was preached of Paul at Berea, they came thither also, and stirred up the people" (Acts 17:13).

In Athens Paul encountered pagan philosophers involved in idol worship. They heard what Paul said and some of them concluded that "he seemeth to be a setter forth of strange gods" (Acts 17:18). Luke explained that they thought that "because he preached unto them Jesus, and the resurrection" (Acts 17:18). Paul was proclaiming who Jesus is and his listeners knew that he was ascribing deity to Him.

In contrast to the Jewish audience in the Berean synagogue, who did not need to be convinced of the existence of the true God, the Athenians held no such presupposition. With them Paul began with "Theology 101." It was theology proper, the existence of God. Paul introduced his subject by contrasting what he was about to present with idols: "*Ye* men of Athens, I perceive that in all things ye are too superstitious. For as I passed by, and beheld your devotions, I found an altar with this inscription, TO THE UNKNOWN GOD" [italics in KJV] (Acts 17:22-23).

Paul's subject was that of identity: "Whom therefore ye ignorantly worship, him declare I unto you" (Acts 17:23). Specifically Paul would speak of the identity of the One true God: "God that made the world and all things therein, seeing that he is Lord of heaven and earth, dwelleth not in temples made with hands; neither is worshipped with men's hands, as though he needed any thing, seeing he giveth to all life, and breath, and all things" (Acts 17:24-25). The animate and inanimate world are God's creation, and humanity, corporately and individually, is subject to Him: "And hath made of one blood all nations of men for to dwell on all the face of the earth, and hath determined the times before appointed, and the bounds of their habitation" (Acts 17:26).

While people as God's creatures are separate from their divine Creator, they are dependent on Him for their very existence and are responsible to Him alone. Every human being was created so "that they should seek the Lord, if haply they might feel after him, and find him, though he be not far from every one of us: for in him we live, and move, and have our being" (Acts 17:27-28). Human beings are responsible for their response to general revelation. The existence of God is not shrouded in obscurity.

Furthermore man's relationship to God is personal, not impersonal: "as certain also of your own poets have said, For we are also his offspring. Forasmuch then as we are the offspring of God, we ought not to think that the Godhead is like unto gold, or silver, or stone, graven by art and man's device" (Acts 17:28-29). If men have life, how can their god (an idol) not have life? Paul's reasoning was, "How can the animate be related to the inanimate?" Offspring must share in the nature of the one whose offspring they are. The nature of the one must correspond to the nature of the other.

For Paul's audience the time for ignorance about the identity of God and what He required of them was over. "And the times of this ignorance God winked at; but now commandeth all men every where to repent" (Acts 17:30). The reason why it behooves human beings for their eternal well-being to do what God commands is "because he hath appointed a day, in the which he will judge the world in righteousness by *that* man whom he hath ordained; *whereof* he hath given assurance unto all *men*, in that he hath raised him from the dead" [italics in KJV] (Acts 17:31). Jesus' resurrection proved His identity, and people are to trust in Him for their eternal destiny. As Paul put it, "all everywhere should repent" (Acts 17:30) (τοῖς ἀνθρώποις πάντας πανταχοῦ μετανοεῖν). Whatever man-made notions they had about God, Jesus, and eternal salvation required a radical revelationally driven reorientation.

The resurrection of Jesus was a stumbling block to some; "And when they heard of the resurrection of the dead, some mocked" (Acts 17:32). Others were not yet ready or perhaps were veiling their rejection with politeness: "and others said, We will hear thee again of this *matter*" [italics in KJV] (Acts 17:32). Some were receptive to Paul's message. "Howbeit certain men clave unto him, and believed: among the which *was* Dionysius the Areopagite, and a woman named Damaris, and others with them" [italics in KJV] (Acts 17:34). Luke's naming specific names is like his saying, "You do not believe me? Ask these people." Those who believed the witnesses in turn became witnesses themselves. And on and on, as it was meant to be.

Acts Chapter 18

In Corinth Paul followed his pattern of speaking first in the synagogue. His message in Corinth was the same as elsewhere; the identity of Jesus. Paul "testified to the Jews *that* Jesus *was* Christ" [italics in KJV] (Acts 18:5). Jesus' identity as "the Christ" (ὁ Χριστός), that is, the Messiah, means that He is God, and Paul's teaching was understood that way by the Jews. Because of that Luke characterized the Jewish rejection with the words, "And when they opposed themselves, and blasphemed" (Acts 18:6). The charge of blasphemy expressed by Luke was an opinion shared by Paul. From the Jewish point of view Paul was a blasphemer for asserting that Jesus is divine. However, the ones who were blaspheming were the Jews who refused to accept Jesus' identity. In spite of Jewish opposition the head of the synagogue came to faith in Jesus. "And Crispus, the chief ruler of the synagogue, believed on the Lord with all his house" (Acts 18:8).

Paul's preaching is described with the words, he "testifyied to the Jews *that* Jesus *was* the Christ" [italics in KJV] (Acts 18:5), and the result was that people "believed on the Lord" (Acts 18:8). Perhaps referring to Gentile converts or as a summary Luke says, "and many of the Corinthians hearing believed, and were baptized" (Acts 18:8). The verbs are translated in the NASB, "were believing" (ἐπίστευον) and "being baptized" (ἐβαπτίζοντο). The KJV has, "and many of the Corinthians hearing believed, and were baptized." Both verbs are in the Greek imperfect tense and as previously discussed (chapter 2, "Exegetical Eye-Openers"), although the regular aspectual nuance of that tense denotes continuous action, it can carry the connotation of iterative action by different individuals (distributive) in the past, which in fact it does here. The text is not saying that each of these individuals was continuing to believe in the past and that each one was continuing to be baptized. Each one, individually, had put his trust in Jesus in the past. Likewise each one who believed was baptized once, identifying himself with Christ and the Christian community. That does not mean that these people stopped believing; the grammar does not indicate that, but it complements Scripture that depicts saving faith in Jesus as an event at a specific time.

The Jews who opposed Paul and brought him before Gallio accused Paul, saying, "This *fellow* persuadeth men to worship God contrary to the law" [italics in KJV] (Acts 18:13). Gallio characterized the Jews' charges as "a question of words and names, and *of* your law" [italics in KJV] (Acts 18:15). The "names" referred to Paul having identified Jesus as "Christ" (or "the Messiah") (Acts 18:5) (ὁ Χριστός). This was a supposed violation of religious law, not civil law, and Gallio refused to get involved. "And Gallio cared for none of those things" (Acts 18:17).

Apollos was a preacher whose knowledge about Jesus was incomplete. "This man was instructed in the way of the Lord; and being fervent in the spirit, he spake and taught diligently the things of the Lord, knowing only the baptism of John" (Acts 18:25). John the Baptist had done his job well. He had told people about the Messiah who was to come, and Apollos was a good disciple of John's and got the message right. And what Apollos taught others was exactly what John the Baptist had taught him.

However, Apollos was like a person who had been transported into a later time by a time machine. He was in a time warp. He did not know that the Messiah had come and gone. Priscilla and Aquila brought him up to speed. "They took him unto *them*, and expounded unto him the way of God more perfectly" [italics in KJV] (Acts 18:26). Having been better informed Apollos continued his ministry. Luke described those whom Apollos encountered next as believers. They were people who "had believed through grace" (Acts 18:27). Luke uses the perfect active participle of "believe" (πιστεύω), for those who had believed in the past with ongoing results. What Apollos learned from Priscilla and Aquila was who Jesus is. Apollos's subsequent ministry is described by Luke: "For he mightily convinced the Jews, *and that* publickly, shewing by the scriptures that Jesus was Christ" (Acts 18:28). The NASB says, "for he powerfully refuted the Jews in public, demonstrating by the Scriptures that Jesus was the Christ."

A question that arises is this, "When was Apollos saved?" He was already saved when Priscilla and Aquila talked with him. Luke says that the couple "expounded unto him the way of God more perfectly" (Acts 18:26). Apollos had "the way" (ὁ ὁδός) to God which was trust in Him, but he needed to add to it information about the person and work of Jesus the Messiah. Apollos had John the Baptist's message about the coming One, and now with Priscilla and Aquila's instruction he was able to identify Jesus as that One.

Old Testament believers and those who received additional information by way of John the Baptist shared a similar knowledge base but neither group had information that told them that Jesus, the figure of history, was the Messiah. For the former group such a physical identification was historically and chronologically impossible and the latter experienced something of a time warp caused by their ignorance. In neither case were individuals in a state of limbo. They could be saved by trusting in God. What people knew varied and included more or less information about Jesus Christ, the second person of the Trinity.

Acts Chapter 19

In Ephesus Paul followed where Apollos had ministered before Apollos had received the knowledge of the gospel. Perhaps Paul had heard that Apollos had been there and when Paul met some of Apollos's "disciples" (Acts 19:1) (μαθητής), he got a sense that something was missing. Paul asked them a question that began with the effect and worked back to the cause: "Have ye received the Holy Ghost since ye believed?" The NASB "Did you receive the Holy Spirit when you believed?" (Acts 19:2) better reflects the Greek contemporaneous aorist participle (εἰ πνεῦμα ἅγιον ἐλάβετε πιστεύσαντες). If they had not heard about the Holy Spirit, they would not have heard about Jesus. As Paul expected, they answered, "We have not so much as heard whether there be any Holy Ghost" (Acts 19:2).

If they had not heard of the Holy Spirit's existence, Paul reasoned, how had their water baptism been conducted? Jesus, in His instructions for water baptism had said, "baptizing them in the name of the Father, and of the Son, and of the Holy Ghost" (Matthew 28:19). So Paul asked them, "Unto what then were ye baptized?" (Acts 19:3). Apollos's disciples answered, "Unto John's baptism" (Acts 19:3). Their answer explained it all. Their teacher Apollos knew of only John the Baptist's baptism (Acts 18:25).

Paul needed to explain things to Apollos's followers just as Priscilla and Aquila did to Apollos. Paul reminded them that "John verily baptized with the baptism of repentance, saying unto the people, that they should believe on him which should come after him, that is, on Christ Jesus" (Acts 19:4). John the Baptist had taught that they were to put their trust in the One who would come after him, and when Jesus came on the scene, John the Baptist had identified Him as the One.

Apparently Apollos had not known that Jesus had come and so neither had Apollos's disciples. They were like Old Testament believers who knew about the coming One, but not specifically who He is. With their updated understanding they knew that the baptism of John they had received from Apollos was not the same as baptism in the New Testament church. They had been saved and now wanted to be baptized. "When they heard *this*, they were baptized in the name of the Lord Jesus" [italics in KJV] (Acts 19:5).

These disciples of Apollos, who had been disciples of John the Baptist, are significant because they represent the last of the Old Testament saints. The time of partial knowledge of Jesus the Messiah was now over. No longer could one trust in a Messiah who was to come because He had already come. Jewish people cannot say that they believe in a messiah to come and ignore Jesus the Messiah who came to earth and died for sins and was resurrected.

The Old Testament era was officially over, and Paul, led by the Holy Spirit, officiated over its conclusion. "And when Paul had laid *his* hands upon them, the Holy Ghost came on them; and they spake with tongues, and prophesied" [italics in KJV] (Acts 19:6). The supernatural phenomena that took place were what those at Pentecost (Acts 2:3-4) had experienced that signaled the inauguration of the church. The same phenomena were symbolic of God's imprimatur on the inclusion of Gentiles in the church at the home of Cornelius (Acts 10:44-46). Old Testament believers were now officially incorporated into the New Testament church as well.

Luke makes the comment, "And all the men were about twelve" (Acts 19:7). The symbolism as a reference to the nation of Israel would not have been lost on Luke's readers. God's redemptive plan had now shifted from a national emphasis to the church. Not that the physical children of Abraham would be forgotten, but for now the focus would move away from them. To be saved one now had to place his trust in Jesus and Him alone for eternal salvation.

After straightening out the doctrine and filling in the gaps of Apollos's students, Paul began teaching in the local synagogue in Ephesus. His three-month ministry there is described by Luke as "disputing and persuading the things concerning the kingdom of God" (Acts 19:8). Jesus the Messiah would become the ruler of a future worldwide kingdom, and in the meantime people could align themselves with its king by putting their trust in Him for their eternal destiny. Paul's method was "disputing [or "reasoning"] and persuading" (διαλεγόμενος καὶ πείθων). The "persuading" (πείθων) was helping them to identify Jesus as the messianic Davidic king.

But some refused to do so: "divers were hardened, and believed not, but spake evil of that way" (Acts 19:9). The NASB says, "But some were becoming hardened and disobedient, speaking evil of the Way." The Greek verb translated "disobedient" (ἠπείθουν) by the NASB is rendered "believed not" in the KJV. The Greek participle in the previous verse (Acts 19:8) translated "persuading" (πείθων) is from the verb πειθώ. The verb in verse 9 translated by the NASB "disobedient" (ἠπείθουν) is the verb ἀπειθέω which has an "alpha privative," a prefix that serves to negate or indicate the lack of something, which in the context is a lack of being persuaded.

The presence of the verb translated "disobedient" (ἠπείθουν) is not introducing to the salvation equation works, the willingness to obey, or a commitment to obey. Louw and Nida in their lexicon define ἀπειθέω: "to refuse to believe the Christian message–'to refuse to be a believer, to reject the Christian message, to refuse to believe'" (Johannes P. Louw and Eugene A. Nida, *Greek-English Lexicon of the New Testament Based on Semantic Domains*, 2nd ed. [New York: United Bible Societies, 2nd ed], 1989, 1:379).

Paul spent the next two years teaching in the school of Tyrannus. His students came from all over Asia Minor (it is generally understood that "Asia" refers to Asia Minor), or they later went and evangelized there because Luke mentions that the result of Paul's teaching was, "all they which dwelt in Asia heard the word of the Lord Jesus, both Jews and Greeks" (Acts 19:10).

The name of Jesus is prominent in the account of the seven sons of Sceva and their attempt at exorcism. The prospective exorcists employed what they thought was a sure-fire way to get results, pronouncing, "We adjure you by Jesus whom Paul preacheth" (Acts 19:13). They wanted to make sure they had the right person. The demon told them that it knew the identity of Jesus and Paul (apparently they were familiar antagonists of the demonic world) but did not know who they (the seven sons of Sceva) were: "Jesus I know, and Paul I know; but who are ye?" (Acts 19:15).

Without giving the men a chance to say, "We're the seven sons of Sceva," the demon caused the man it possessed to brutally attack them. Ironically the misuse of Jesus' name resulted in His name being exalted. "And this was known to all the Jews and Greeks also dwelling at Ephesus; and fear fell on them all, and the name of the Lord Jesus was magnified" (Acts 19:17). The incident had a sobering effect on believers: "And many that believed came, and confessed, and shewed their deeds" (Acts 19:18). These were believers who were still practicing magic. They were those "that believed" (τῶν πεπιστευκότων), a perfect active participle, which indicates that they had put their trust in Jesus at a time in the past and it had ongoing results. One of the results, as is demonstrated here, was the conviction and confession of sin.

Acts Chapter 20

In his address to the elders of Ephesus Paul said that his message consisted of "testifying both to the Jews, and also to the Greeks, repentance toward God, and faith toward our Lord Jesus Christ" (Acts 20:21). "Repentance toward God" (τὴν εἰς θεὸν μετάνοιαν) was a reordering of one's mind in some way. What exactly that consisted of is not stated but a recognition of one's sinful condition could be a part of that. Jesus Himself said that those who are not sick do not need a physician (Matthew 9:12 and Mark 2:17), an allusion to the acknowledgment of sin and need of a Savior.

What it cannot consist of is a promise to do something about it. For Jews, whom Paul had just mentioned, it would be a reorientation of their understanding of the one true God as existing in a Trinity, consisting of God the Father, Jesus, and the Holy Spirit. For a Jew, that would not be easy. It would require a review of the Old Testament and recognition of the identity of Jesus as the promised Messiah. "Faith toward our Lord Jesus Christ" (πίστιν εἰς τὸν κύριον ἡμῶν Ἰησοῦν) would require believing the evidence that proved the identity of Jesus and putting trust in Him for eternal salvation.

Paul characterized his ministry as having been given to him by Jesus Himself: "the ministry, which I have received of the Lord Jesus" (Acts 20:24), and his marching orders were "to testify the gospel of the grace of God" (Acts 20:24). To proclaim "the gospel" (τὸ εὐαγγέλιον), the good news, consisted of preaching about Jesus' identity and inviting people to trust in Him. Jesus' crucifixion as the God/Man/Messiah identified Him as the Savior. Paul included that concept when he exhorted the Ephesian elders "to feed the church of God, which he hath purchased with his own blood" (Acts 20:28).

Salvation is by the grace of God: "the gospel of the grace of God" (Acts 20:24) (τὸ εὐαγγέλιον τῆς χάριτος τοῦ θεοῦ) and by grace God and His word empower sanctification: "And now, brethren, I commend you to God, and to the word of his grace, which is able to build you up, and to give you an inheritance among all them which are sanctified" (Acts 20:32).

Acts Chapter 21

Back in Jerusalem Paul told James and the elders of the church about his ministry to the Gentiles. The reaction Paul's report received was positive: "And when they heard *it*, they glorified the Lord" [italics in KJV] (Acts 21:20). The leaders of the church in Jerusalem were also eager to share about their ministry to Jews in Jerusalem and they told Paul, "thou seest, brother, how many thousands of Jews there are which believe" (Acts 21:20). The NASB says, "You see, brother, how many thousands there are among the Jews of those who have believed." It should be noted that the Greek articular participle translated "those who have believed" (τῶν πεπιστευκότων) is in the perfect tense, signifying that these individuals had put their trust in Jesus in the past and it had ongoing results at the time when James and the Jerusalem elders were speaking.

They told Paul and his entourage about the Jewish converts: "and they are all zealous of the Law" (Acts 21:20). Those who had believed and thereby received salvation were Law-keepers and James and the Jerusalem elders had no problem with that because they were not keeping the Law in order to be saved or in addition to belief to be saved. Those believers, and James and the Jerusalem elders, were able to keep salvation and sanctification separate.

The Jerusalem Jews had more than a passing interest in what they had heard about how Paul dealt with Jewish sanctification in the environment of the predominately Gentile mission. The Jerusalem church leadership told Paul that "they are informed of thee, that thou teachest all the Jews which are among the Gentiles to forsake Moses, saying that they ought not to circumcise *their* children, neither to walk after the customs" [italics in KJV] (Acts 21:21). The Greek verb at the beginning of the verse translated "are informed" (κατηχήθησαν aorist passive indicative from κατηχέω "teach," "inform in a relatively detailed manner" Johannes P. Louw and Eugene A. Nida, *Greek-English Lexicon of the New Testament Based on Semantic Domains*, 2nd ed. [New York: United Bible Societies, 2nd ed], 1989, 1:410) indicates that they had detailed knowledge about it.

Paul, about whom they had heard from a distance, was now at their doorstep, and the leaders of the church in Jerusalem expressed their concern. "What is it therefore? the multitude must needs come together: for they will hear that thou art come" (Acts 21:22). They would not be able to keep his presence quiet for long. There was a difference between the sanctification practiced by Jewish converts in Jerusalem and Jewish converts among communities of Gentiles.

Salvation was uniform, but sanctification was not. There would always be the danger of legalism where one group of believers thought that the Christian life should be lived one way and others another, who would attempt to impose their preference on others. Sometimes opinions would be so tightly held that for the purpose of peace it would be better to accede to the preferences of other believers.

That was the proposal James and the Jerusalem elders made to Paul. "Do therefore this that we say to thee: we have four men which have a vow on them; them take, and purify thyself with them, and be at charges with them, that they may shave *their* heads: and all may know that those things, whereof they were informed concerning thee, are nothing; but *that* thou thyself also walkest orderly, and keepest the law" [italics in KJV] (Acts 21:23-24). Jewish converts had gotten the mistaken notion that Paul had prohibited Jewish converts in predominately Gentile congregations from doing such things. Paul had no opinion either way, as long as they did not take them to be requirements for eternal salvation. Paul demonstrated that by going along with the Jerusalem church leadership's recommendation.

Those who wanted Paul to do this recognized that Gentile converts, even in a predominately Gentile environment, should not run roughshod over Jewish sensibilities, and so they added, "As touching the Gentiles which believe, we have written *and* concluded that they observe no such thing, save only that they keep themselves from *things* offered to idols, and from blood, and from strangled, and from fornication" [italics in KJV] (Acts 21:25). This was a reiteration of the decision of the Jerusalem Council, to which Paul had been a party. Paul took their advice and did what was proposed. Salvation was in no way compromised but a signal was sent that sanctification was not to be guided by rigid inflexible rules.

Jumping to conclusions often gives birth to conflict. Paul had not even completed quelling potential dissension with Jewish converts when he was falsely accused by

Jews from Asia Minor of promoting violation of the Law who assumed he had violated the temple by taking Gentiles into it. They went public with their accusations. They were "crying out, Men of Israel, help: This is the man, that teacheth all *men* every where against the people, and the law, and this place: and further brought Greeks also into the temple, and hath polluted this holy place" [italics in KJV] (Acts 21:28).

Paul was accused of being "against. . .the law" (κατὰ. . .τοῦ νόμου). Paul, as many down through the ages who would follow in his footsteps preaching the gospel of the grace of God, was accused of antinomianism. "Anti," of course, is a prefix meaning "against," "nomos" refers to "law," originating from the Greek νόμος, and "ism," a distinctive doctrine, theory, system, or practice. Those who preach the biblical gospel of God's grace, and are pejoratively accused of "antinomianism," are in good company, that of the apostle Paul.

Acts Chapter 22

When Paul defended himself before the crowd in Jerusalem he recounted his origin and history of persecuting believers before he became one himself. As proof he said, "And I persecuted this way unto the death, binding and delivering into prisons both men and women, as also the high priest doth bear me witness, and all the estate of the elders: from whom also I received leters unto the brethren, and went to Damascus, to bring them which were there bound unto Jerusalem, for to be punished" (Acts 22:4-5). In telling about his Damascus road experience Paul recounted that he had asked the identity of the One who was speaking to him and was told, "I am Jesus of Nazareth, whom thou persecutest" (Acts 22:8). Paul understood that Jesus was God and addressed Him and referred to Him as "Lord" (κύριος), that is, God. "And I said, What shall I do, Lord? And the Lord said unto me, Arise, and go into Damascus" (Acts 22:10).

Ananias in Damascus identified the One who had appeared to Paul on the road as "that Just One" or "the Righteous One" (Acts 22:14) (ὁ δίκαιος). It was the same title Stephen had given to Jesus in Acts 7:52 where he said, "and they have slain them which shewed before of the coming of the Just One; of whom ye have been now the betrayers and murderers." In Acts 22:14 Ananias told Paul, "The God of our fathers hath chosen thee, that thou shouldest know his will, and see that Just One, and shouldest hear the voice of his mouth." Paul's role, having personally seen Jesus, was to testify: "For thou shalt be his witness unto all men of what thou hast seen and heard" (Acts 22:15).

A second time Jesus appeared to Paul, this time in Jerusalem; "And it came to pass, that, when I was come again to Jerusalem, even while I prayed in the temple, I was in a trance; and saw him saying unto me, Make haste, and get thee quickly out of Jerusalem: for they will not receive thy testimony concerning me" (Acts 22:17-18). Paul knew that those he persecuted had put their trust in Jesus and said, "I imprisoned and beat in every synagogue them that believed on thee" (Acts 22:19).

Paul now gave testimony about Jesus and recognized that Stephen, whose martyrdom Paul had witnessed and facilitated, had also been a witness. "And when the blood of thy martyr Stephen was shed, I also was standing by, and consenting unto his death, and kept the raiment of them that slew him" (Acts 22:20). And it had come full circle. The cloak watcher now watched as men cast aside their cloaks preparing to stone him: "they cried out, and cast off *their* clothes, and threw dust into the air" [italics in KJV] (Acts 22:23). A Roman commander had Paul rescued from that attempted execution: "The chief captain commanded him to be brought into the castle, and bade that he should be examined by scourging; that he might know wherefore they cried so against him" (Acts 22:24). Paul avoided the enhanced interrogation by asserting his Roman citizenship.

Acts Chapter 23

For Paul Jerusalem was a stepping stone that would propel him to the heart of the Roman Empire, Rome itself. Persecution in Jerusalem would serve God's purpose in the spread of the gospel. When the Jewish council brought him in for questioning Paul succeeded in pitting one part of the council against the other. "But when Paul perceived that the one part were Sadducees, and the other Pharisees, he cried out in the council, Men *and* brethren, I am a Pharisee, the son of a Pharisee: of the hope and resurrection of the dead I am called in question" [italics in KJV] (Acts 23:6). Everyone wanted a piece of Paul and the commander was alarmed that "Paul should have been pulled in pieces of them" (Acts 23:10).

In custody, Paul experienced another appearance by Jesus, confirming his mission and the part he was to play in it. The motif of testimony/witness is emphasized once again, this time by Jesus Himself: "And the night following the Lord stood by him, and said, Be of good cheer, Paul: for as thou hast testified of me in Jerusalem, so must thou bear witness also at Rome" (Acts 23:11). The subject matter of the testimony is translated in the NASB with "witnessed to My cause" (τὰ περὶ ἐμοῦ). The KJV has "testified of me." The Greek preposition περὶ here means "about" or "concerning." The phrase is literally "the things about, or concerning Me." The subject matter of the testimony was Christ. The argument between the Pharisees and the Sadducees was over the resurrection, and there was no doubt about Paul's preaching that Jesus had risen from the dead, which was central to the Christian message. "Of the hope and resurrection of the dead I am called in question" (Acts 23:6).

Acts Chapter 24

Ananias, the high priest, and the Jewish elders appeared before Felix, the Roman procurator or governor in Caesarea, and charged Paul with agitation and promotion of a divisive cult that followed Jesus. "For we have found this man *a* pestilent *fellow*, and a mover of sedition among all the Jews throughout the world, and a ringleader of the sect of the Nazarenes" [italics in KJV] (Acts 24:5). The identity of Jesus as a "Nazarene" (Ναζωραῖος) followed Him even after His ascension.

Paul admitted to having promoted "the way" (ἡ ὁδός), a reference to those who followed Jesus. "But this I confess unto thee, that after the way which they call heresy, so worship I the God of my fathers, believing all things which are written in the law and in the prophets" (Acts 24:14). Christianity does not contradict the Old Testament but is a continuation of what it communicates. By serving Jesus, the Son, Paul was serving God the Father. When Paul got an opportunity later on to speak to Felix and his wife Drusilla, Luke tells the reader that they "heard him concerning the faith in Christ" (Acts 24:24). Other related subjects that came up were "righteousness, temperance [or "self-control"], and judgment to come" (Acts 24:25).

Acts Chapter 25

Festus, the Roman procurator, talked to the visiting King Agrippa about unfinished business Festus had inherited from Felix. It concerned Paul, the prisoner who had been accused by Jewish religious leaders in Jerusalem. Festus was of the opinion that it was not a legitimate legal issue but a religious squabble: "but [they] had certain questions against him of their own superstition, and of one Jesus, which was dead, whom Paul affirmed to be alive" (Acts 25:19). The resurrection of Jesus was central to the gospel message that Paul preached. Jesus and his identity was at the center of the controversy. Agrippa agreed to hold a hearing to help Festus come up with an indictment to send along with Paul to Rome, where Paul insisted on going.

Acts Chapter 26

At the hearing King Agrippa let Paul make a statement in his own defense. Asking for the king's indulgence Paul told of his relationship with his accusers and that they shared a common religious heritage and hope. "And now I stand and am judged for the hope of the promise made of God unto our fathers" (Acts 26:6). In recounting his having jailed believers, Paul said he was trying to get them to "blaspheme" (Acts 26:11) (βλασφημέω). Just as Jesus' antagonists had tried to get him to identify Himself as God, and thereby in their mind to blaspheme, Paul, as an unbeliever, attempted to get Jesus' followers to do the same thing; identify Jesus as God. "And I punished them oft in every synagogue, and compelled *them* to blaspheme; and being exceedingly mad against them, I persecuted *them* even unto strange cities" [italics in KJV] (Acts 26:11).

Paul explained to King Agrippa how he had done an "about-face," from persecuting Jesus' followers to promoting Him. Paul mentioned that Jesus had identified Himself to him; "and he said, I am Jesus whom thou persecutest" (Acts 26:15). Paul was told by Jesus that his role was to be "a minister and a witness both of these things which thou hast seen, and of those things in the which I will appear unto thee" (Acts 26:16). Jesus promised future appearances to Paul who was to view himself as a "minister" (ὑπηρέτης), that is, a servant, and a "witness" (μάρτυς), one who gives testimony. Jesus told Paul his primary target would be Gentiles and the goal was "To open their eyes, *and* to turn *them* from darkness to light, and *from* the power of Satan unto God, that they may receive forgiveness of sins, and inheritance among them which are sanctified by faith that is in me" [italics in KJV] (Acts 26:18). Paul's agenda was to inform people so that their eyes would be open to the truth of Jesus' identity and so they would put their trust in Him.

Paul viewed his ministry holistically. Just as the "Great Commission" (Matthew 28:19-20) commanded seeking converts and instructing them to follow Jesus' commands, Paul was driven to evangelize so that people might believe in Jesus and to educate them which would result in a change of behavior. Paul expressed his goal to Agrippa in this way: "that they should repent and turn to God, and do works meet for repentance" (Acts 26:20). The decision to put one's trust in Jesus was to be followed by deeds consistent with it. The deeds were to be "meet for" or "appropriate" (ἄξιος = "worthy," "proper," or "fitting"), not because converts had previously promised to do them, or previously been willing to do them, but because it was fitting that the life of one who had put his trust in Jesus would be lived in the manner in which He lived.

Paul rightly understood biblical revelation of Jesus' identity in the Old and New Testaments as a continuum rather than a contrast. Paul said, "I continue unto this day, witnessing both to small and great, saying none other things than those which the prophets and Moses did say should come: that Christ should suffer, *and* that he should be the first that should rise from the dead, and should shew light unto the people, and to the Gentiles" [italics in KJV] (Acts 26:22-23). The identity of Jesus includes the fact that One who was once dead is now alive. To Festus it did not make sense, and he told Paul as much; "Paul, thou art beside thyself; much learning doth make thee mad" (Acts 26:24). Paul respectfully disagreed. "But he said, I am not mad, most noble Festus; but speak forth the words of truth and soberness" (Acts 26:25). The living Christ is a reality.

Paul asserted that his testimony about Jesus concerned things that had taken place in public not in private; "For the king knoweth of these things, before whom also I speak freely: for I am persuaded that none of these things are hidden from him; for this thing was not done in a corner" (Acts 26:26). King Agrippa acknowledged Paul's persuasiveness. He said, "Almost thou persuadest me to be a Christian" (Acts 26:28). The biblical author does not say what King Agrippa did, but King Agrippa, his wife Bernice, Festus, and the reader are not left in doubt about what it takes "to be [or rather, "become"] a Christian." It requires identifying Jesus as the One whom He and Paul said He is and putting one's trust in Him for eternal salvation.

Acts Chapter 27

This chapter tells of part of Paul's journey to Rome by ship. In verse 20 is an example of the secular use of the Greek verb "save" (σῴζω). It is the same verb used in the Philippian jailor's famous question, "Sirs, what must I do to be saved?" (Acts 16:30). In Acts 27:20 it is used to refer to being kept from shipwreck or drowning. Luke says, "all hope that we should be saved was then taken away." The same verb is used by Paul: "Except these abide in the ship, ye cannot be saved" (Acts 27:31).

The Greek noun (σωτηρία) related to this verb can mean "salvation," "deliverance," or "preservation." It can refer either to eternal salvation or temporal deliverance of some kind. Paul exhorted his shipmates, "wherefore I pray you to take *some* meat: for this is for your health ["salvation" or "preservation" (NASB) = σωτηρία]" [italics in KJV] (Acts 27:34). Needless to say, contextual considerations determine the meaning of the verb "save" (σῴζω) and the noun "preservation" or "salvation" (σωτηρία).

The compound verb related to this verb, διασῴζω, is found eight times in the New Testament (Matthew 14:36; Luke 7:3; Acts 23:24; 27:43, 44; 28:1, 4; 1 Peter 3:20), and while it can be synonymous with σῴζω, the New Testament writers never use it for eternal salvation. It is used exclusively for physical healing or safety. Luke, the author of Acts, uses it in Acts 27:43, 44 and 28:1, 4, for physical safety from drowning, perhaps for stylistic variation.

Acts Chapter 28

In Rome, Paul immediately contacted the leaders of the Jews living there. He let them know that he was not a prisoner because he was a criminal but because of what he had said about Jesus, "that for the hope of Israel I am bound with this chain" (Acts 28:20). Although they had not received word from Jerusalem about Paul they had heard about the movement he was involved with. They said, "We neither received letters out of Judaea concerning thee, neither any of the brethren that came shewed or spake any harm of thee. But we desire to hear of thee what thou thinkest: for as concerning this sect, we know that every where it is spoken against" (Acts 28:21-22). A time was set up when they could get more people together and hear what Paul had to say in more detail.

What Paul said to them at that meeting is described by Luke: "he expounded and testified the kingdom of God, persuading them concerning Jesus, both out of the law of Moses, and *out of* the prophets" [italics in KJV] (Acts 28:23). The subject was the identity of Jesus and the evidence was the Jews' own Old Testament. The results and reaction to Paul's presentation were mixed; "some believed the things which were spoken, and some believed not" (Acts 28:24). Paul told them that even their rejection had been anticipated and predicted by the prophet Isaiah. Paul said, "Well spake the Holy Ghost by Esaias [Isaiah] the prophet unto our fathers" (Acts 28:25). Paul applied Isaiah's prophecy to those who disagreed with him over what he said about who Jesus is. The prophecy Paul quoted is Isaiah 6:9-10:

> Go to this people and say, you will keep on hearing, but will not understand; and you will keep on seeing, but will not perceive; for the heart of this people has become dull, and with their ears they scarcely hear, and they have closed their eyes; lest they should see with their eyes, and hear with their ears, and understand with their heart and return, and I should heal them (Acts 28:26-27).

Rejection of God in the Old Testament would be followed prophetically by rejection of Jesus in the time of the New Testament. For Paul, Jewish rejection vindicated Old

Testament prophecy and validated Gentile evangelism. "Be it known therefore unto you, that the salvation of God is sent unto the Gentiles, and *that* they will hear it" [italics in KJV] (Acts 28:28).

The book of Acts concludes with Paul preaching and teaching, fulfilling the purpose for which he had gone to Rome. His message remained unchanged. It was about the new community God was building, founded on the foundation of the identity of His Son and those who put their trust in Him. Paul was "preaching the kingdom of God, and teaching those things which concern the Lord Jesus Christ, with all confidence, no man forbidding him" (Acts 28:31). The One whom Paul preached is "Lord" (κύριος) who has given the requirement for eternal salvation. Salvation comes when one puts his trust in Him, the God/Man/Messiah who walked this earth, died, rose again, and has ascended into heaven.

Chapter 9

Evidence for the Identity of Jesus in the Epistles:
Part 1 – Romans through 1 Timothy

Instructions in Identity

Evidence for Jesus' identity is primarily contained in the Gospels. Luke's history, the Acts of the Apostles, tells what the original church leaders did to introduce that information in evangelism and edification. The New Testament from the Epistles to the book of Revelation provide the interpretation and application of His identity in the doctrine and life of the Christian community.

Evidence for the Identity of Jesus in the Epistle of Romans

Paul's letter to believers in Rome explains and applies the doctrine of justification by faith, understood negatively in its exclusion of works and positively as putting one's trust in Jesus and Him alone for eternal salvation. As seen in Luke's description of Paul's ministry in the book of Acts the identity of Jesus was the foundation and focus of the gospel. For Paul the gospel and the person of Jesus were nearly synonymous.

Paul understood his life's mission to be the dissemination of the gospel. He had been "separated unto the gospel of God" (Romans 1:1) (ἀφωρισμένος εἰς εὐαγγέλιον θεοῦ). After saying the gospel was predicted in the Old Testament, "(Which he had promised afore by his prophets in the holy scriptures)" [parenthesis in KJV] (Romans 1:2), Paul states that it (the gospel) was about the One whose identity was ultimately proven by the resurrection: "Concerning his Son Jesus Christ our Lord, which was made of the seed of David according to the flesh; and declared *to be* the Son of God with power, according to the spirit of holiness, by the resurrection from the dead" [italics in KJV] (Romans 1:3-4).

It was this person who had enabled and enlisted Paul and his fellow apostles: "By whom we have received grace and apostleship" (Romans 1:5) for the purpose of bringing Gentiles to faith in Jesus: "for obedience to the faith among all nations, for his name" (Romans 1:5). Whatever Paul meant by his words "obedience to the faith" (ὑπακοὴν πίστεως) he did not mean that "faith" (πίστις) equals or is synonymous with "work" (ἔργον). He also did not mean that "faith" (πίστις) is the same as a willingness to work or a commitment to do works. Paul was clear about that in many of his other epistles but particularly in Romans. In Romans 4:4-5 he says, "Now to him that worketh is the reward not reckoned of grace, but of debt. But to him that worketh not, but believeth on him that justifieth the ungodly, his faith is counted for righteousness."

Paul's reasoning is based on work generally, of any kind, not on a particular species or type of work. He did not qualify the works as "works of the Law" nor as a prohibition against "meritorious works." Instead it is a categorical statement. Any attempt to blend the biblical distinction between the two is disingenuous at best and doctrinally deceitful at worst. Paul states it another way in Romans 11:6: "And if by grace, then *is it* no more of works: otherwise grace is no more grace" [italics in KJV]. The fundamental character of faith is altered by incorporating works into the requirement for eternal salvation.

In Romans 16:26 the same Greek phrase "obedience of faith" (ὑπακοὴν πίστεως) is used as in Romans 1:5. In neither instance is Paul introducing works as a requirement for eternal life with his use of the term "obedience" (ὑπακοή). Some writers state that in these verses Paul "equates" obedience with faith. But the use of the word "equates" as a reference to linguistic synonymy is problematic. The word "equates" belongs to the jargon of mathematics. Equations in mathematics are axiomatically reciprocal or bi-directional: $A + B = C$ and $C = A + B$. In language the meaning when equative verbs are employed is often uni-directional and not bi-directional: "All horses are animals" does not mean that "All animals are horses." In biology the terms "genus" and "species" are used in which the latter is a subset of the former. Both a horse and a rabbit may be animals but that does not mean that a horse is a rabbit. Neither mathematics nor biology should provide the methodology for biblical exegesis.

Who would propose that "obedience always means faith" and "faith always means obedience?" Sometimes the proposition is softened to say, "faith often means obedience." The question then arises whether "often" is occurring in a specific instance, as in Romans 1:5 and 16:26. For two terms to be even remotely synonymous (and no two terms are completely synonymous), they must share a measure of their semantic range and function. Although their meanings can overlap, a general term and a specific term cannot be synonymous. On one level, in the theological realm, such is the case with "obedience" (ὑπακοή) and "faith" (πίστις). "Believe" is one form that "obedience" can take, but not all exhortations to "believe" are commands to "obey." "Work" is "work," and "faith" is "faith." Where semantic conflation resides, serious confusion reigns.

News of the conversion of those in Rome was widespread, a fact that Paul described with the word "faith" (πίστις). Paul told his readers that he was grateful to God for them: "First, I thank my God through Jesus Christ for you all, that your faith is spoken of throughout the whole world" (Romans 1:8). Faith in Jesus is the initial act of obedience commanded of unbelievers. Paul expressed his gratitude to God, not for their "obedience" (ὑπακοή) in the form of works but for the "faith" (πίστις) the Romans had in Jesus. This was not Paul using stylistic variation; it reflected a basic biblical doctrine. Paul's message is referred to by him as "the gospel of his Son" (Romans 1:9). The gospel is about who Jesus is and putting one's trust in Him.

Paul majored in evangelism and made no excuse for that emphasis. His boldness is apparent in Romans 1:16; "For I am not ashamed of the gospel of Christ: for it is the power of God unto salvation to every one that believeth; to the Jew first, and also to the Greek." In the following verse Paul explains why he could speak boldly without shame. "For therein is the righteousness of God revealed from faith to faith" (Romans

1:17). The Greek pronoun translated "therein" or "it" (αὐτῷ) is neuter in gender, and the only neuter antecedent article and noun to which it can refer back to is "the gospel" (τὸ εὐαγγέλιον) in verse 16. The gospel reveals God's righteousness. For Paul the gospel revealed how God's righteousness can be credited (imputed) to man, described by the theological term "justification."

Many interpretations have been proposed for the phrase, "from faith to faith" (Romans 1:17) (ἐκ πίστεως εἰς πίστιν). Interpretations range from the growth of pre-conversion faith, to conversion faith, to faith exercised in sanctification, and many possibilities in between. Perhaps what Paul had in mind in the first instance "from faith" (ἐκ πίστεως) was faith involved in believing the propositions related to the identity of Jesus to be true; and the second, "to faith" (εἰς πίστιν), faith that consisted of putting one's trust in Him. The former would coincide with what the Reformers referred to with the Latin word "assensus," agreeing to the truth of propositions about Jesus, and the latter to "fiducia," placing trust and confidence in that person for one's eternal destiny.

In contrast to the felicitous eternal destiny that will be enjoyed by those who exercise faith in Jesus are the consequences for those who refuse to believe: "For the wrath of God is revealed from heaven against all ungodliness and unrighteousness of men, who hold the truth in unrighteousness" (Romans 1:18). The NASB describes them as those "who suppress the truth in unrighteousness." The truth that is suppressed is His identity: "Because that which may be known of God is manifest in them; for God hath shewed *it* unto them. For the invisible things of him from the creation of the world are clearly seen, being understood by the things that are made, *even* his eternal power and Godhead; so that they are without excuse" [italics in KJV] (Romans 1:19-20). No one can ever say that he does not know who the One is in whom he is supposed to put his trust.

Their just condemnation is confirmed by their substitution of the One identified by means of His creation. Paul explained what man does: "And changed the glory of the uncorruptible God into an image made like to corruptible man, and to birds, and fourfooted beasts, and creeping things" (Romans 1:23). Man even stoops to replacing the God of universal general revelation with unclean reptiles. Idolatrous substitution inevitably leads to sinful activities. Paul summed up what takes place: "Who changed the truth of God into a lie, and worshipped and served the creature more than the Creator, who is blessed for ever. Amen" (Romans 1:25).

The downward spiral of sin is universal; it infects Jew and Gentile, pagan and pious: "For all have sinned, and come short of the glory of God" (Romans 3:23). This verse is sandwiched between statements about the solution for sin. In the prior two verses Paul says, "But now the righteousness of God without the law is manifested, being witnessed by the law and the prophets; even the righteousness of God *which is* by faith of Jesus Christ unto all and upon all them that believe: for there is no difference" [italics in KJV] (Romans 3:21-22). The Old Testament served as a "witness" (μαρτυρέω) to the "righteousness of God" (δικαιοσύνη θεοῦ) that would be credited (imputed) only to those who put their trust in Jesus "through faith in Jesus Christ for all those who believe" (διὰ πίστεως Ἰησοῦ Χριστοῦ εἰς πάντας τοὺς πιστεύοντας).

Those who hold to "the new perspective on Paul" and "covenantal nomism" take the Greek genitive case form of "Jesus Christ" (Ἰησοῦ Χριστοῦ) in Romans 3:22 as a subjective genitive to mean "the faithfulness of Jesus Christ" rather than as an objective genitive, "faith in Jesus Christ." Making Jesus the actor in relation to faith in this context introduces an unusual and unexpected element into the text. As López says, "This new perspective on Paul. . .subverts and contradicts everything Paul says in Romans 3-5 and 9:30-33" (René López, *Romans Unlocked: Power to Deliver* [Springfield, MO: 21st Century Press, 2005], 74). Of course, Jesus Christ is faithful, but the replacement of His faithfulness in passages relating to trust that is to be placed in Jesus, introduces ideas that were not even contemplated by Paul.

The solution for sin is picked up again in verse 24: "Being justified freely by his grace through the redemption that is in Christ Jesus" (Romans 3:24). The NASB translates Romans 3:25 with, "whom God displayed publicly as a propitiation in His blood through faith." The Greek confirms López's conclusion that it is better to take "in His blood" (ἐν τῷ αὐτοῦ αἵματι) as modifying "faith" (πίστεως), as the KJV and the NIV do ("faith in His blood"), rather than "propitiation" (ἱλαστήριον) as the NASB does with "propitiation in His blood" (ibid., 79). Propitiation takes place when faith is placed in Jesus whose substitutionary death provided redemption.

God cannot be charged with injustice for declaring people righteous on the basis of faith alone. God's infinite righteousness remains intact. In fact justification, declaring people righteous on the sole condition of faith, is done for the purpose of showing that God is righteous: "To declare, *I say*, at this time his righteousness: that he might be just, and the justifier of him which believeth in Jesus" [italics in KJV] (Romans 3:26). Because righteousness is declared on the basis of faith in Jesus and excludes works, no one can take credit for it. Paul makes that point by posing a question, "Where *is* boasting then?" [italics in KJV] (Romans 3:27). He answers his own question immediately, "It is excluded" (Romans 3:27). The exclusion of any type of works excludes any and all boasting.

Paul expected to be challenged, so he brought up a possible objection, "By what law?" (Romans 3:27). What right did Paul have to exclude works? What rule or principle gave him the authority to exclude works? It seemed obvious, but Paul's exclusion of works could not be based on a principle that included works, could it? Paul put the question in the mouth of a potential objector, "of works?" (Romans 3:27). Paul's answer, "Nay: but by the law of faith" (Romans 3:27). "Faith" has its own set of rules that are not to be run roughshod over. The principle of faith itself has the right to require faith to the exclusion of works. With a play on two semantic meanings of "law" (νόμος), that of a rule or principle and its established technical reference to the Law of Moses, Paul switches from the former meaning to the latter and draws the conclusion, "For we maintain that a man is justified by faith apart from the works of the Law" (Romans 3:28). So that there would be no misunderstanding about the exclusion of works as a requirement for justification Paul was explicit; the Mosaic Law itself was excluded as a means to obtain justification.

How could that be? Paul followed up his astounding conclusion with another question: "*Is he* the God of the Jews only?" [italics in KJV] (Romans 3:29). Before answering, Paul asked, "*is he* not also of the Gentiles?" [italics in KJV] (Romans 3:29). Again, Paul answered his own question, "Yes, of the Gentiles also: seeing *it is* one God, which shall justify the circumcision by faith, and uncircumcision through faith" [italics in KJV] (Romans 3:29-30). There is one true God, one faith, and one means of justification that excludes work of any kind.

What about the Law of Moses? God gave it to Moses; so is it to be summarily tossed out? Paul asked, "Do we then make void the law through faith?" (Romans 3:31). Is the Mosaic Law to be treated as if it never existed, or as if it is no longer useful? Paul's answer, "God forbid" (Romans 3:31) (μὴ γένοιτο). The denial uses the optative form of the "to be" verb γίνομαι. The English "Perish the thought!" approximates what Paul thought of the Law's nullification.

Positively, Paul said, "yea, we establish the law" (Romans 3:31). Among the meanings that Louw and Nida include for the verb translated "establish" (ἵστημι) are "to acknowledge the validity of something–'to uphold, to maintain, to accept the validity of'" (Johannes P. Louw and Eugene A. Nida, *Greek-English Lexicon of the New Testament Based on Semantic Domains*, 2nd ed. [New York: United Bible Societies, 2nd ed], 1989, 1:682). The Law is to be retained as long as its original purpose is maintained. It is useful in pre-evangelism as a standard from which man falls short, and a guide to God's holiness in sanctification, but not as a means of salvation.

With the Old Testament example of Abraham Paul proves that faith is the universal and sole requirement for justification. Paul chose Abraham as an example for a reason. Abraham was universally respected, but more importantly he preceded the Mosaic Law. Whatever Paul says about the exclusion of works in relation to Abraham, cannot be taken to mean "works of the Law" because the Law had not yet been given. The first line of evidence Paul used was to demonstrate by means of Abraham's example what faith is not.

Paul did not have a statement by Abraham himself to quote directly but he did have Moses' pronouncement about Abraham in Genesis 15:6, "For what saith the scripture? Abraham believed God, and it was counted unto him for righteousness" (Romans 4:3). Paul's point is that because works are not mentioned in Scripture they played no role in the reckoning. Paul explains why work is excluded. The reason is that there is a difference between wages paid for work done and a declaration of righteousness granted on the basis of belief.

The first part of his argument, "Now to him that worketh is the reward not reckoned of grace, but of debt" (Romans 4:4). It would be an insult for a worker to be told by his employer that the wages he is receiving are a favor or a gift. As Jesus said, "for the worker is worthy of his support" (Matthew 10:10 NASB). And Luke wrote, "for the laborer is worthy of his wages" (Luke 10:7 NASB). Paul was probably quoting Jesus when he told Timothy, "The laborer is worthy of his wages" (1 Timothy 5:18). The payment of wages for work done is a matter of justice and God is not unjust. The first part of Paul's argument that excludes work as a requirement for righteousness relates to the nature of employment.

The second part of Paul's reasoning is rooted in the nature of God's declaration of righteousness. In contrast to a work/wages arrangement salvation is a grace/gift: "But to him that worketh not, but believeth on him that justifieth the ungodly, his faith is counted for righteousness" (Romans 4:5). In the work/wages setup where Paul said it was not a "favor," he used the Greek word for a "gift" (χάρις). God's declaration of righteousness on the basis of belief is a "gift" (χάρις) precisely because it is not given for work done.

Paul provides additional evidence for the principle that righteousness is reckoned without works. The principle of pure faith is corroborated by David, "Blessed *are* they whose iniquities are forgiven, and whose sins are covered. Blessed *is* the man to whom the Lord will not impute sin" [italics in KJV] (Romans 4:7-8). Paul could use the Davidic quote as proof for his premise because man inevitably does sinful works, and those would have to be factored in if works were the basis for righteousness.

The experience of Abraham provides more evidence. Paul's argument is that Abraham's faith preceded his work of circumcision. Paul uses circumcision as an example of a work that can be extended to represent all works. The reason he takes the example of that specific work is because of the chronological sequence of events on which he will base his argument. Furthermore circumcision was a matter of Jewish pride that needed to be explicitly excluded from the requirement for God's imputed righteousness. The account of Abraham's faith is located in Genesis 15, while his circumcision is in chapter 17.

The fact that Paul considered circumcision, the physical identifying mark of the covenant, to be a work, should give serious pause to those who think that water baptism, the act of identification of the New Testament believer, is required for salvation in addition to faith. (The reader is referred to the discussion of Acts 2:38 in chapter 2, "Exegetical Eye-Openers").

Circumcision and its later codification in the Mosaic Law, both of which were chronologically subsequent to Abraham's faith, are not to be added to the requirement for eternal salvation. Paul gives this reason: "For the promise, that he should be the heir of the world, *was* not to Abraham, or to his seed, through the law, but through the righteousness of faith" [italics in KJV] (Romans 4:13). God made sure that the Mosaic Law would not be the vehicle of imputed righteousness. The Law could not be that vehicle because, as Paul writes, Abraham received justification long before Moses' time. An interesting implication is that those who lived before Abraham, from the dawn of creation, were also saved by faith in God and not by works.

Paul continued with an illustration of how faith without works operated in the giving of the promise of a seed to Abraham. This thread is interwoven with the theme of the identity of the God who made the promise and would fulfill it, and was therefore the One in whom Abraham could confidently place his trust. The primary identifying characteristic of God in whom Abraham trusted was that of Creator and giver of life: "God, who quickeneth the dead, and calleth those things which be not as though they were" (Romans 4:17). The NASB says, "God, who gives life to the dead and calls into being that which does not exist." Abraham had to believe that God was who He claimed to be in order for him to place his trust in Him.

Abraham's faith was not nullified by his thinking that he could contribute to the production of an heir. Neither did he have any illusions about his wife. If they were to produce an heir, it would have to be God's doing: "And being not weak in faith, he considered not his own body now dead, when he was about an hundred years old, neither yet the deadness of Sara's womb" (Romans 4:19).

For the God who had revealed Himself to Abraham age was not an issue when it came to procreation. By believing the promises that God made, in the form of propositions, to be accepted as true, Abraham was able to trust in the one true God. This accounts for the progressive idea found in Romans 4:20. "He staggered not at the promise of God through unbelief; but was strong in faith, giving glory to God." The NASB says that "with respect to the promise of God, he did not waver in unbelief, but grew strong in faith, giving glory to God." Incrementally Abraham came to that conclusion that he could trust in God. Paul explains how Abraham's faith culminated: "And being fully persuaded that, what he had promised, he was able also to perform" (Romans 4:21).

It was not that Abraham believed a specific proposition, although he did do that and more, but having believed propositions that identified God to him, he put his trust in that Person. Years later Abraham's descendants would refer to the One in whom they trusted as the God of Abraham, Isaac, and Jacob. In Galatians Paul also quotes Genesis 15:6 and draws the conclusion, "Know ye therefore that they which are of faith, the same are the children of Abraham" (Galatians 3:7). Paul then explains that Abraham had the gospel preached to him in advance. "And the scripture, foreseeing that God would justify the heathen through faith, preached before the gospel unto Abraham, *saying*, In thee shall all nations be blessed" [italics in KJV] (Galatians 3:8). The quotation is from Genesis 12:3, "and in thee shall all families of the earth be blessed." Abraham knew that it would take his progeny to fulfill that promise and that was out of the realm of natural possibility. Abraham trusted in the God who would bring that about.

As discussed in commenting on Genesis 15:6, that verse is grammatically independent of its immediate surrounding context. It is difficult to tie the statement to a specific proposition to be believed as being true, and even if it could be done the content of that proposition would not have been applicable to those who lived before Abraham and those who were saved subsequently. René López interprets it as belief in a proposition. He writes, "Obviously, **He** (God) is powerful enough to **perform** the incredible promise of providing a Savior from Sarah's dead womb and Abraham's dead body. This is exactly what Abraham became convinced/believed" (*Romans Unlocked: Power to Deliver*, 98, emphasis and parenthesis in original). López adds, "The object and basis of Abraham's faith in Genesis 15:6 are in God's power to produce the promised Seed from Abraham's dead body. . . .Now Paul reveals this same object and basis of the believer's faith as **Jesus our Lord** *resurrected* **from the dead**" (ibid., 99, emphasis and italics in original). However, in applying the illustration of Abraham, Paul does not say that the object of faith is Jesus, but rather God the Father who raised Jesus from the dead: "But for us also, to whom it shall be imputed, if we believe on him that raised up Jesus our Lord from the dead" (Romans 4:24).

Because of Paul's Christology and Trinitarian understanding of God the Father and Jesus, he viewed the object of faith for Abraham and Paul as one and the same. Godet in his commentary refers to the object of faith and asks, "But what in our position now will be the object of faith?" (Frederic Louis Godet, *Commentary on Romans* [1883; reprint, Grand Rapids: Zondervan, 1956; reprint, Grand Rapids: Kregel, 1977], 183). To which he answers, "Faith in the biblical sense can only have one object. Whether Abraham or we be the parties in question, this object, always the same, is God and His manifestation" (ibid.). The one object of faith is best understood as the triune God revealed as God the Father in the Old Testament with the progressive revelation of the Son and the Holy Spirit completed in the New Testament. Godet admits as much. "But it must not be imagined that, because it falls to us to believe in an accomplished fact, faith is now nothing more than historical credence given to this fact [Jesus' resurrection]. The apostle at once sets aside this thought when he says, not: 'when we believe in the resurrection of Jesus,' but: 'when we believe in *God who raised Jesus*'" (ibid., 183-84, emphasis in original).

Similarly Murray writes, "Abraham's faith was focused upon God in his character as omnipotent, an omnipotence exemplified in his making alive the dead. Our faith likewise is focused upon God in the character that is exemplified by the miracle of the resurrection of Jesus from the dead" (John Murray, *The Epistle to the Romans*, The New International Commentary on the New Testament [Grand Rapids: Eerdmans, 1979], 153). Murray correctly observes that "Our faith in God as the one who raised Jesus from the dead is, for this reason, Christologically conditioned" (ibid.). Murray does hold to a "content" construct although that may have been tempered by his understanding of the object of faith. He says, "that our faith has different content and different objects" (ibid.). The present writer holds that the historical fact of the resurrection of Jesus is content or information that comprises evidence to correctly identify the One in whom trust is to be placed for eternal salvation.

In Romans chapter 5 Paul contrasts the believer's past condition and prior conversion with his/her present privileges and practice. It is instructive to observe the Greek tenses Paul uses which keep them distinct. He first mentions conversion, "Therefore being justified by faith" (Romans 5:1) (Δικαιωθέντες οὖν ἐκ πίστεως). "Being justified by faith" (Δικαιωθέντες) is an aorist passive participle that refers to an event completed in the past in relation to the time when Paul was writing. The KJV translates the aorist participle with "being justified," which could mistakenly be taken as an ongoing process. Justification was not an ongoing process that was not yet completed, but a past event. Even though Paul did not use the perfect tense in that verse (Romans 5:1), in the following verse (Romans 5:2) where he mentions conversion again, he uses the perfect tense in the indicative mood which speaks of a past completed event with ongoing results.

Before that Paul describes a believer's present condition, "we have peace with God through our Lord Jesus Christ" (Romans 5:1). "We have" (ἔχομεν) is a Greek present active indicative, that refers to something ongoing at the time Paul was writing. Since Koine Greek does not have a separate form for a single event and an ongoing event or condition in the present, and the present tense must serve both functions, the choice must be based on contextual and lexical considerations. Here the contrast is between a completed past event (conversion) with a present progressive condition (peace with God). In this passage Paul goes back and forth between the two.

In verse 2 Paul goes back to the past, "By whom also we have access by faith into this grace wherein we stand" (Romans 5:2), to explain how the present state of affairs came about. The NASB "we have obtained our introduction," and the KJV words "we have" translate the perfect active indicative ἐσχήκαμεν, which refers to something that happened in the past and had results that continued into the time in which the writing took place. Justification in the past resulted in present access to God's grace: "access by faith into this grace wherein we stand" (Romans 5:2). The verb translated "we stand" (ἑστήκαμεν) is a perfect active indicative.

The translation of the perfect tense as a present tense is what Wallace describes as an "Intensive Perfect" or a "Resultative Perfect." As Wallace explains, "The perfect may be used to *emphasize* the results or present state produced by a past action" (*Greek Grammar beyond the Basics*, 574, emphasis in original). Wallace notes that "This use of the perfect does not exclude the notion of a completed act; rather, it *focuses* on the resultant state" (ibid., 575, emphasis in original). The specificity of the indicative perfect tense in Romans 5:2 governs the general summary expressed by the aorist participle in Romans 5:1. It is understood that a believer's present standing is the result of prior justification.

Paul mentions additional results of justification: "and rejoice in hope of the glory of God" (Romans 5:2), and "we glory in tribulations also" (Romans 5:3). The latter, "tribulation" (θλῖψις), can produce the results of "patience" (ὑπομονὴ), "experience" (δοκιμὴ), and "hope" (ἐλπὶς) (Romans 5:4). And "hope" (ἐλπίς), "does not disappoint" (Romans 5:5) (οὐ καταισχύνει). All of these things are present or possible for a believer. At least one item on the list, "experience" (δοκιμὴ) suggests an accomplishment that is not guaranteed to every believer.

The last item listed, "hope" (ἐλπίς), "maketh not ashamed" (οὐ καταισχύνει) "because the love of God is shed abroad in our hearts by the Holy Ghost which is given unto us." Not expressing this love could be caused by a believer "quenching" (1 Thessalonians

5:19) (σβέννυμι) the Spirit. Paul then switches back to the event of conversion that makes the present possible. He continues to speak of the past and elaborates on love as God's motivation for the salvation of man: "But God commendeth his love toward us, in that, while we were yet sinners, Christ died for us" (Romans 5:8).

In Romans 5:9-10 Paul switches back and forth between the past and the future: "Much more then, being now justified [δικαιωθέντες = aorist participle] by his blood, we shall be saved [σωθησόμεθα = future indicative] from wrath through him. For if, when we were enemies, we were reconciled [κατηλλάγημεν = aorist indicative] to God by the death of his Son, much more, being reconciled [καταλλαγέντες = aorist participle], we shall be saved [σωθησόμεθα = future indicative] by his life." What was now in the past from the point of view of Paul's readers had consequences for the future. Future glorification is in store for those who have experienced justification in the past.

Justification is complete in relation to sin: "But where sin abounded, grace did much more abound: that as sin hath reigned unto death, even so might grace reign through righteousness unto eternal life by Jesus Christ our Lord" (Romans 5:20-21). Grace is sufficient for all sin. If it was sufficient for all sin committed before justification and thereafter, the question arises, "Shall we continue in sin, that grace may abound?" (Romans 6:1). Paul rejects that response to what God has done, "God forbid" (μὴ γένοιτο). That is an inappropriate response because of their new relationship.

Paul then counters a libertarian interpretation with a godly alternative in Romans 6:11-13:

> Likewise reckon ye also yourselves to be dead indeed unto sin, but alive unto God through Jesus Christ our Lord. Let not sin therefore reign in your mortal body, that ye should obey it in the lusts thereof. Neither yield ye your members *as* instruments of unrighteousness unto sin: but yield yourselves unto God, as those that are alive from the dead, and your members *as* instruments of righteousness unto God [italics in KJV].

Paul uses the Greek imperative mood for these commands. It is important to keep in mind what Wallace says about the imperative mood:

> The imperative mood is the mood of intention. It is the mood furthest removed from certainty. (Those who have strong-willed children understand this!) Ontologically, as one of the potential or oblique moods, the imperative moves in the realm of volition (involving the imposition of one's will upon another) and possibility [emphasis and parenthesis in original] (Daniel Wallace, *Greek Grammar beyond the Basics*, 485).

It was not Paul's intention to communicate that all believers would obey the commands he mentioned. To hold that all "true" believers will do so is to introduce an element not present in the text.

After a discussion of the benefits of holy living in contrast to the bondage of sin, Paul makes a summary statement. "But now being made free from sin, and become servants to God, ye have your fruit unto holiness, and the end everlasting life" (Romans 6:22).

The noun translated "holiness" (ἁγιασμόν), is probably best understood as referring to their present progressive walk rather than their positional identity. The question arises whether the words, "and the end everlasting life" (Romans 6:22) refers to eternal life being earned by the avoidance of sin in sanctification. Paul's argument earlier in the chapter is that based on what has happened to the believer in the past and what will happen in the future the believer is to live in the present in light of those truths. One case in point is Romans 6:5, "For if we have been planted together in the likeness of his death, we shall be also *in the likeness* of *his* resurrection" [italics in KJV]. Another example is Romans 6:8, "Now if we be dead with Christ, we believe that we shall also live with him."

In the immediate context of Romans 6:22, lest Paul's readers mistakenly assume that eternal life is earned by their effort he adds by way of explanation, "For the wages of sin *is* death; but the gift of God *is* eternal life through Jesus Christ our Lord" [italics in KJV] (Romans 6:23). Paul saw a difference between a "wage" (ὀψώνιον) and a "gift" (χάρισμα); the former is worked for, the latter is freely given. Paul reminds his readers that death never pays a living wage either before conversion or after but rather a dying one. Just as Adam and Eve received death, as an immediate spiritual recompense as well as their future physical demise as a result of their sin, their descendants would experience nothing other than sin's deadly consequences as well. All believers who read and hear Paul's words need to take heed and act accordingly.

In chapter 9 after Paul relates to his readers the blessings that God's people, the Jews, possessed collectively, he made a distinction between those who were more than physical descendants of Abraham but were also children of God: "They which are the children of the flesh, these *are* not the children of God: but the children of the promise are counted for the seed" [italics in KJV] (Romans 9:8). They were "the children of the promise" because they fulfilled the promise made to Abraham, recorded in Genesis 12:3, "and in thee shall all families of the earth be blessed." What made the difference was faith, something available to Gentiles as well as Jews. What they acquired by that means Paul called "righteousness which is of faith" (Romans 9:30).

For many Jews instead of faith becoming a stepping stone to salvation it became a stumbling block. They balked at the notion of placing their trust in the Messiah whom their own Old Testament had identified. Paul saw Christ in Isaiah 28:16: "As it is written, Behold, I lay in Sion a stumblingstone and rock of offence: and whosoever believeth on him shall not be ashamed" (Romans 9:33). Paul's quotation in Romans 9:33 is from the Septuagint (LXX), the Greek translation of the Old Testament, that has "he who believes" (ὁ πιστεύων), which translates the Hebrew Hiphil form of אָמַן "believe" or "trust." This means either to believe that something is true or someone is telling the truth, or it means to place trust in a person or thing. Since there is a stated object, the pronoun "him" (αὐτῷ), in this quotation, the latter is most likely the meaning here. The one who trusts in the Messiah will not find that their trust has been misplaced. Unfortunately the Jews refused to put their trust in Jesus, their Messiah.

There has been considerable debate and controversy regarding Romans 10:9 and the verses that follow. It is ironic that in a context where Paul expresses the principle and the certainty of clear communication from God there would be such confusion. For a discussion of Romans chapter 10 the reader is referred back to chapter 2, "Exegetical Eye-Openers."

Paul was a living example of the fact that the rejection of the gospel by the Jewish people did not mean God had rejected the nation in its entirety: "I say then, Hath God cast away his people? God forbid. For I also am an Israelite, of the seed of Abraham, *of the tribe of Benjamin*" [italics in KJV] (Romans 11:1). Widespread rejection was never proof of universal unbelief. As evidence Paul gave the Old Testament prophet Elijah as an example of God's ongoing redemptive program. Elijah complained to God that he was the last living believer. Paul asks, "But what saith the answer of God unto him?" (Romans 11:4). God's response was, "I have reserved to myself seven thousand men, who have not bowed the knee to *the image of* Baal" [italics in KJV] (Romans 11:4).

By extension, the existence of such a multitude at the time of Elijah bode well for their presence in Paul's day. "Even so then at this present time also there is a remnant according to the election of grace" (Romans 11:5). Paul inserts a comment about a general principle that he considered paramount in the gracious work of God on man's behalf: "And if by grace, then *is it* no more of works: otherwise grace is no more grace" [italics in KJV] (Romans 11:6). Paul's parenthetical comment is a categorical denial of works.

Exceptions are not carved out for "nonmeritorious works," or "works prepared beforehand," or "works performed by God through man," nor is there a caveat that Paul was only talking about "works of the Law." By definition, any amount of any kind of work done by man erases grace. To use an example in mathematics, if any of the factors in multiplication is a zero, it does not matter what any of the other factors are. The product is still zero. In reality, the addition of works does not doom grace; it never was grace to begin with.

Paul concludes the predominately doctrinal section of Romans at the end of chapter 11 with a doxology. He exclaims, "O the depth of the riches both of the wisdom and knowledge of God! how unsearchable *are* his judgments, and his ways past finding out!" [italics in KJV] (Romans 11:33). Man cannot completely know God or understand what He does, although he can know Him to the extent that He is revealed in Scripture. Man's knowledge is finite, given human limitations. In verse 34 Paul quotes from the book of Isaiah in the Septuagint (LXX), the Greek translation of the Old Testament, with the rhetorical question, "For who hath known the mind of the Lord? or who hath been his counseller?" (Romans 11:34, from LXX, Isaiah 40:13). The expected answer is, "No one." God does not seek man's advice.

And who better than Job could ask the question he does in Job 41:11, which Paul quotes, "Or who hath first given to him, and it shall be recompensed unto him again?" (Romans 11:35). Again, the expected answer is, "No one." The questions themselves border on the absurd. The latter question lays to rest any notion of conversion as an "exchange." Paul concludes with the reason why those two questions are to be categorically and emphatically answered in the negative, "For of him, and through him, and to him, *are* all things: to whom *be* glory for ever. Amen" [italics in KJV] (Romans 11:36). In bestowing eternal salvation to man God does not share His glory with him.

In Romans 14:9 Paul says, "For to this end Christ both died, and rose, and revived, that he might be Lord both of the dead and living." The context of this verse is an admonition not to judge the actions of a fellow believer who "regardeth the day" (Romans 14:6), or "he that eateth" (Romans 14:6), or "he eateth not" (Romans 14:6). Instead one should leave the judging to God. The One to whom believers are accountable is God and not fellow believers. Judgment is to be left where it belongs, with God who is the believer's "Lord" (κύριος), that is, his or her "Master."

Sometimes this passage (Romans 14:1-12) and its use of "Lord," (κύριος) has been taken to imply that the gospel includes submission to God, a willingness or commitment to obey, if not outright works in the gospel message. A theology that must find its support by violating contextual considerations and/or must rely on contrived implications is suspect at best and heretical at worst. Paul's point is that God has the sovereign right to dictate to His own children who are accountable to Him alone.

In the context of exhorting believers Paul appears to combine two passages, quoting the LXX (Greek translation of the Old Testament) from Isaiah, Isaiah 49:18 and Isaiah 45:23; "*As* I live, saith the Lord, every knee shall bow to me, and every tongue shall confess to God" [italics in KJV] (Romans 14:11). The Greek verb translated "shall confess" (ἐξομολογήσεται, future middle indicative of ἐξομολογέω, "agree," "confess," "admit"), is a verb that can mean "agree with" or "admit." While believers may have differing convictions, all will one day agree with God's assessment of their lives and activities. That Paul's application is meant for believers is confirmed by the statement that comes before it that he is explaining: "for we shall all stand before the judgment seat of Christ" (Romans 14:10). This is the "Bema" (βῆμα) judgment where the works of believers will be assessed.

In Romans 15:18 Paul wrote about the results he hoped to accomplish in his mission to Gentiles: "For I will not dare to speak of any of those things which Christ hath not wrought by me, to make the Gentiles obedient, by word and deed." The phrase translated "by word and deed" (λόγῳ καὶ ἔργῳ) can be taken as descriptive of Paul's ministry, characterized by the words he preached and works he performed (The NIV has "by what I have said and done"). Unbelievers would be obedient when they put their trust in Jesus for their eternal destiny.

Pauline oratory was supernaturally authenticated. The next verse completes the Greek sentence by expanding on the subject of Paul's ministry that was "through mighty signs and wonders, by the power of the Spirit of God; so that from Jerusalem, and round about unto Illyricum, I have fully preached the gospel of Christ" (Romans 15:19). While some may be called to consolidate the evangelistic efforts of others by discipling believers and strengthening churches, what drove Paul was to reach the unevangelized: "Yea, so have I strived to preach the gospel, not where Christ was named, lest I should build upon another man's foundation" (Romans 15:20). Paul viewed his ministry as an example and fulfillment of what Isaiah said in Isaiah 52:15, "But as it is written, To whom he was not spoken of, they shall see: and they that have not heard shall understand" (Romans 15:21).

While the words in Romans 15:18 translated "by word and deed" (λόγῳ καὶ ἔργῳ), could be taken to refer to the result and effect of the Gentile mission, rather than Paul's evangelistic method, he does not thereby infuse works into the gospel paradigm. He could be saying that the obedience of the Gentiles was demonstrated by their speech and actions, but these effects or the willingness or commitment to do them cannot legitimately be turned back chronologically and incorporated into the cause of their conversion, or as a requirement for it. To do so reveals more about the theological agenda of the interpreter than the meaning of the inspired text. To speak of them as the result is biblically permissible, but to take the result and incorporate it into the cause is not only scripturally unacceptable and logically questionable, but is many times a thinly disguised proverbial camel's nose trying to find its way into the evangelistic theological tent.

Christ is the bedrock of believers, and membership in the New Testament church rests on the foundation of the gospel. The church is comprised of individuals who know the identity of the Messiah and have put their trust in Him for their eternal salvation. If the last two verses of Romans was a part of the original autograph, (and some have questioned whether it was), Paul concluded the book of Romans, his theological *tour de force*, entrusting his readers to God; "Now to him that is of power to stablish you according to my gospel, and the preaching of Jesus Christ, according to the revelation of the mystery, which was kept secret since the world began" (Romans 16:25).

That was not to say that the Old Testament had not mentioned Him. Jesus would not be fully revealed until He came: "But now is made manifest, and by the scriptures of the prophets, according to the commandment of the everlasting God, made known to all nations for the obedience of faith" (Romans 16:26). At the time Paul wrote, Christ had come and the mission of the church was to make Him "known" (γνωρίζω) so that all peoples could exercise "faith" (πίστις) in Him for their eternal destiny, the initial act of "obedience" (ὑπακοή) that Jesus the "Lord" (κύριος) had commanded of unbelievers.

Evidence for the Identity of Jesus in the Epistle of 1 Corinthians

Paul addressed those who comprised the church at Corinth with the words, "to them that are sanctified in Christ Jesus" (1 Corinthians 1:2) (ἡγιασμένοις ἐν Χριστῷ Ἰησοῦ). The Greek perfect passive participle translated substantively (functioning as a noun) as "them that are sanctified" (ἡγιασμένοις) retains the aspect of a past completed action followed by results that continued to the time when Paul was writing. This is a reference to positional sanctification which coincided with the past justification of his audience.

The present status of these saved individuals was further described as "saints by calling" (1 Corinthians 1:2) (κλητοῖς ἁγίοις). They had been invited, "called" (κλητός), set apart for a life of holiness, and were part of a host of fellow believers "with all that in every place call upon the name of Jesus Christ our Lord, both theirs and ours" (1 Corinthians 1:2). The articular participle translated with "that. . .call upon" (τοῖς ἐπικαλουμένοις) is from the same verb "call" or "invite" (ἐπικαλέω), that Paul used in Romans 10:13: "whosoever shall call upon the name of the Lord shall be saved." The Corinthian Christians, as well as believers from all over, were calling on the One in whom they had previously placed their trust.

Paul concurred with Peter (Acts 2:38–see chapter 2 "Exegetical Eye-Openers") that water baptism was not a requirement for the reception of eternal life. Paul distinguished between water baptism and belief, and in 1 Corinthians 1:17 he says, "for Christ sent me not to baptize, but to preach the gospel." If the gospel had included baptism, Paul would have been an eager participant and it would have been included in his gospel message, which it was not. Paul contrasted water baptism with the simplicity of the gospel he preached: "not with wisdom of words, lest the cross of Christ should be made of none effect" (1 Corinthians 1:17). No baptismal supplement, nor any amount of eloquence, could substitute for faith in the crucified Christ.

Christ's crucifixion, central to the gospel message, was meaningless to the unsaved, "for the preaching of the cross is to them that perish foolishness" (1 Corinthians 1:18), but it has meaning for believers: "but unto us which are saved it is the power of God" (1 Corinthians 1:18). Paul continued with the words, "For it is written, I will destroy the wisdom of the wise, and will bring to nothing the understanding of the prudent" (1 Corinthians 1:19). Paul's readers were evidence of what the gospel could accomplish. God's way appeared strange to the world, but "it pleased God by the foolishness of preaching to save them that believe" (1 Corinthians 1:21). The preaching of the gospel gave the way of eternal salvation. The gospel identified Jesus as the One who had been crucified: "But we preach Christ crucified" (1 Corinthians 1:23).

In reminiscing about the early days of his ministry among the Corinthian believers Paul emphasized the centrality of Jesus' crucifixion. He was "declaring unto you the testimony of God" (1 Corinthians 2:1). This is explained with the words, "for I determined not to know any thing among you, save Jesus Christ, and him crucified" (1 Corinthians 2:2). Supporting evidence for the message of Jesus' identity and crucifixion was corroborated by supernatural phenomena: "And my speech and my preaching *was* not with enticing words of man's wisdom, but in demonstration of the Spirit and of power" [italics in KJV] (1 Corinthians 2:4). Moving oratory was not Paul's method. His goal was the establishment of a firm foundation for faith: "That your faith should not stand in the wisdom of men, but in the power of God" (1 Corinthians 2:5). God used ignorance and unbelief to accomplish His purpose: "But we speak the wisdom of God in a mystery, *even* the hidden *wisdom*, which God ordained before the world unto our glory: Which none of the princes of this world knew: for had they known *it*, they would not have crucified the Lord of glory" [italics in KJV] (1 Corinthians 2:7-8).

The present condition of the Corinthian Christians was not commendable, and Paul addressed this problem. "And I, brethren, could not speak unto you as unto spiritual, but as unto carnal, *even* as unto babes in Christ" [italics in KJV] (1 Corinthians 3:1). In spite of their carnality, "for ye are yet carnal: for whereas *there is* among you envying, and strife, and divisions" [italics in KJV] (1 Corinthians 3:3), Paul had no doubt about their position. He could call them "brethren" (1 Corinthians 3:1) (ἀδελφοί) and refer to their past conversion by saying "ye believed" (1 Corinthians 3:5) (ἐπιστεύσατε, aorist active indicative from πιστεύω, "believe" or "trust").

Paul used an agricultural metaphor for his ministry and that of his fellow worker Apollos. "I have planted, Apollos watered; but God gave the increase" (1 Corinthians 3:6). Evangelism of the unsaved and the discipleship of believers were recognized by Paul as distinct ministries. Paul was careful not to blur the two. The next metaphor used is of a building and the distinction between evangelism and discipleship is maintained: "According to the grace of God which is given unto me, as a wise masterbuilder, I have laid the foundation, and another buildeth thereon" (1 Corinthians 3:10). The foundation corresponds to evangelism with the hallmark, "For other foundation can no man lay than that is laid, which is Jesus Christ" (1 Corinthians 3:11). The gospel imperative is to make clear the identification of Jesus Christ so that the unsaved can put their trust in Him.

Without the foundation of faith future construction is futile. Once the right foundation has been built, only then can the next phase of construction begin. Ministries today that emphasize following Jesus without a firm biblical foundation of faith in Jesus alone, are not building His church, either individually or corporately. Contextually Paul's words applied to himself and his fellow laborers. Those, such as Apollos, who engaged in a ministry of discipleship, building on the foundation of evangelism, were to be careful in their construction as well. Their future reward would depend on it. In the eschatological future there will be an evaluation in which "the fire shall try every man's work of what sort it is" (1 Corinthians 3:13). A life spent building a structure that will go up in smoke is a possibility. "If any man's work shall be burned, he shall suffer loss" (1 Corinthians 3:15). Leading others astray will have consequences.

As tragic as that outcome will be, Paul makes the point that such a fellow worker will not be in danger of losing his eternal salvation; "but he himself shall be saved; yet so as by fire" (1 Corinthians 3:15). Nothing can or will undo what occurs when trust is placed in Jesus Christ for eternal life. Nevertheless the consequences are still chilling. "If any man defile the temple of God, him shall God destroy; for the temple of God is holy, which *temple* ye are" [italics in KJV] (1 Corinthians 3:17). Leading God's people astray is a serious matter. The positional sanctification of God's people is not to be polluted with heretical teaching related to the believer's practice. Anything short of eternal damnation can be the consequence for one who does so. Being called home to heaven is one possibility.

In 1 Corinthians 4:6 Paul exhorts his readers with the following: "And these things, brethren, I have in a figure transferred to myself and *to* Apollos for your sakes; that ye might learn in us not to think *of men* above that which is written, that no one of you be puffed up for one against another" [italics in KJV]. The readers were trying to outdo each other, claiming "bragging rights" on the basis of who their spiritual mentor was. However, they needed to realize that the supremacy of God and Christ far supersede any advantage they claim by human association. To elevate something or someone "above" (ὑπέρ) the written text puts the interpreter over the text rather than in submission to it, and ventures into unbiblical territory. Some who teach "above [or "beyond"] that which is written" may insert a theological view that is not in the text, or may introduce a meaning beyond a term's semantic range. Sound interpretation is possible only within the limits of the text.

Paul pictured his relationship to the Corinthian believers as that of a father to his children. "I write not these things to shame you, but as my beloved sons I warn *you*" [italics in KJV] (1 Corinthians 4:14). This was a unique relationship: "For though ye have ten thousand instructors in Christ, yet *have ye* not many fathers: for in Christ Jesus I have begotten you through the gospel" [italics in KJV] (1 Corinthians 4:15). What brought Paul and the Corinthians together was Christ Jesus, the subject of the gospel.

In addition to schismatic issues in the Corinthian church there was also a problem with immorality. "It is reported commonly *that there is* fornication among you, and such fornication as is not so much as named among the Gentiles, that one should have his father's wife" [italics in KJV] (1 Corinthians 5:1). What was anathema among Gentiles was being arrogantly accepted by the Corinthians. One can sense the embarrassment the apostle felt because the Corinthian believers felt no shame over it. Addressing the church Paul referred to that individual as one who was "among you" (ἐν ὑμῖν). The natural assumption is that this man was a believer. Confirmation that he was a believer is found in the absence of explicit evidence to the contrary. While it might be suggested that this is an argument from silence, it is an absence in the presence of overwhelming contrary evidence. Paul's approach to the matter was that of a father grieving over the sin of his son.

Paul's decision "to deliver such an one unto Satan for the destruction of the flesh, that the spirit may be saved in the day of the Lord Jesus" (1 Corinthians 5:5) and his rationale, "know ye not that a little leaven leaveneth the whole lump?" (1 Corinthians 5:6) includes the sinning individual as part of the whole, the whole being the church. It was incongruous for such a man to remain undisciplined.

Paul tells them to deal with the issue of sin so that their practical situation will match their saved condition, "Purge out therefore the old leaven, that ye may be a new lump, as ye are unleavened" (1 Corinthians 5:7). The thought of being "unleavened" (ἄζυμος) brought to the reader's mind the Passover in which unleavened bread was served, which depicted the sinlessness of the coming sacrifice for their sins. The sinlessness of that sacrifice, Jesus, is referred to by Paul as an additional reason for dealing with sin in the church. "For even Christ our passover is sacrificed for us" (1 Corinthians 5:7). Just as Jesus' death dealt with sin, the church needed to deal with sin appropriately.

The mention of the "Passover" (πάσχα) led Paul to comment on the Lord's Supper. Paul points out the disparity between the church celebrating Communion, in which the death of Christ the sinless sacrifice is remembered, while at the same time condoning serious sin: "Therefore let us keep the feast, not with old leaven, neither with the leaven of malice and wickedness; but with the unleavened *bread* of sincerity and truth" [italics in KJV] (1 Corinthians 5:8).

Such a powerful indictment of sin would naturally lead believers to distance themselves as far away from it as possible. The readers may have remembered what Paul wrote them in a previous letter, so he brought it up, "I wrote unto you in an epistle not to company with fornicators" (1 Corinthians 5:9). Paul wanted to clarify that what he had just said about contamination did not apply to association with unbelievers: "Yet not altogether with the fornicators of this world, or with the covetous, or extortioners, or with idolaters; for then must ye needs go out of the world" (1 Corinthians 5:10). What he wrote was not an exhortation to exit the world. Short of death, rubbing shoulders with unbelievers was unavoidable.

However, when it came to fellow believers, that was a different matter. "But now I have written unto you not to keep company, if any man that is called a brother be a fornicator, or covetous, or an idolater, or a railer, or a drunkard, or an extortioner; with such an one no not to eat" (1 Corinthians 5:11). The theologically loaded translation in the NASB "so-called brother" is a possibility but must be proven and not just assumed. The contrast in the context is between those inside and those outside the church; those saved and those unsaved. The one about to undergo discipline was saved.

Paul previously pointed out the incongruity of believers engaging in activity that should have been characteristic only of unbelievers and yet was being practiced by a believer. The presumptive presence of a third group–not "called" (saved), not "uncalled" (unsaved), but "so-called" (unsaved but pretending to be saved)–upsets the clear contrast set up by Paul. The consternation Paul expressed at the beginning of the chapter over egregious immorality does not seem appropriate if the individual was not even a believer. The NKJV translation is "anyone named a brother" (ἀδελφὸς ὀνομαζόμενος). Considering the seriousness with which identity was associated with a "name" (ὄνομα), it is better to take the person being contemplated to be a believer.

It would be strange for God to have a hands-off approach and delegate the judgment of unbelievers within the church to those who were not that person's fellow believers. Paul says, "But them that are without God judgeth. Therefore put away from among yourselves that wicked person" (1 Corinthians 5:13). Paul considered this an internal disciplinary matter. He was not questioning the man's identity as a believer, but rather assumed it, no doubt from evidence that he considered satisfactory. If the man had been an unbeliever what was missing was conversion, not correction.

In Paul's denunciation of internecine litigation in the church his reasoning is that the godly and ungodly realms represent irreconcilable differences. By their very nature those who constitute the church possess a greater competence than the world when it comes to dealing with disputes. Unbelievers are referred to as "unrighteous" (1 Corinthians 6:9) (ἄδικοι). Paul's use of the adjective substantively (functioning as a noun), and anarthrously (without the definite article in the Greek), emphasized the character rather than the identity of unbelievers. The qualification of an unbeliever to judge a believer is being questioned: "Know ye not that the unrighteous shall not inherit the kingdom of God?" (1 Corinthians 6:9). It does not make any sense to have someone not destined for God's kingdom adjudicating matters among those who are so destined. Did Paul's readers not realize the significance of their differences? The rhetorical question expects an affirmative reply. Yes, unbelievers have a different eternal destination than believers. It makes no sense to have unbelievers judge believers.

The real problem was that lawsuits even existed among believers in the first place. "Now therefore there is utterly a fault among you, because ye go to law one with another. Why do ye not rather take wrong? why do ye not rather *suffer yourselves to* be defrauded?" [italics in KJV] (1 Corinthians 6:7). The defeat or "fault" (ἥττημα) was the loss of reputation of Christ and His church. Worse yet was that not only were believers the defendants in lawsuits from fellow believers, but they were also the plaintiffs, the initiators of the lawsuits. "Nay, ye do wrong, and defraud, and that *your* brethren" [italics in KJV] (1 Corinthians 6:8).

Unbelievers are disqualified as arbiters because of what characterizes them, "Be not deceived: neither fornicators, nor idolaters, nor adulterers, nor effeminate, nor abusers of themselves with mankind, nor thieves, nor covetous, nor drunkards, nor revilers, nor extortioners, shall inherit the kingdom of God" (1 Corinthians 6:9-10). These are the people believers were asking to referee their disputes. A court comprised of criminals does not make sense. Similarly it is not rational for believers to submit their complaints to the jurisdiction of the unsaved.

Lest his readers become smug, Paul reminded them that they were once unsaved. "And such were some of you: but ye are washed, but ye are sanctified, but ye are justified in the name of the Lord Jesus, and by the Spirit of our God" (1 Corinthians 6:11). "And such were some of you." Not all of them had committed all the sins, crimes, and misdemeanors on the list, but they had all been in the same unbelieving boat. The difference between the Corinthian believers and their unbelieving counterparts is introduced with the contrastive conjunction "but" (ἀλλά). With three terms Paul explained what set them apart.

The Corinthian believers "are washed" (ἀπελούσασθε), "are sanctified" (ἡγιάσθητε), and "are justified" (ἐδικαιώθητε). All three verbs are in the Greek aorist indicative tense, indicating that what they referred to had already happened to these addressees. Each of these verbs, "wash" (ἀπολούω), "sanctify" (ἁγιάζω), and "justify" (δικαιόω), had occurred simultaneously, at the time of and because they had placed their trust "in the name" (1 Corinthians 6:11) (ἐν τῷ ὀνόματι) of the One identified as "the Lord Jesus Christ" (τοῦ κυρίου Ἰησοῦ Χριστοῦ), and by the power of or in the sphere of "the Spirit of our God" (ἐν τῷ πνεύματι τοῦ θεοῦ ἡμῶν). In their previous unregenerate state the Corinthians had the negatives in I Corinthians 6:9-10 minus the positives in verse 11 that were true of the saved. Because the Corinthian converts possessed the latter, they were qualified to judge their own.

The question arises whether the statement of the Corinthians' past condition, "and such were some of you" (1 Corinthians 6:11) (καὶ ταῦτά τινες ἦτε), can be applied to the present life of a believer, to prove that he or she can no longer do or be known for those things. To take this passage as support for such a proposition is probably going too far, because this is not stated explicitly in the text. To draw such a significant theological conclusion from a possible, but not necessary, implication is a dubious endeavor.

In 1 Corinthians chapter 10 Paul warns his Christian readers about disobedience, using the Old Testament example of the children of Israel in the wilderness. The experience of the Israelites is emphasized in a verbal staccato reaching a crescendo: "all our fathers were under the cloud, and all passed through the sea; and were all baptized unto Moses in the cloud and in the sea; and did all eat the same spiritual meat; and did all drink the same spiritual drink: for they drank of that spiritual Rock that followed them: and that Rock was Christ" (1 Corinthians 10:1-4). The same metaphor of drinking is used by Paul to refer to himself and fellow believers in 1 Corinthians 12:13, "For by one Spirit are we all baptized into one body, whether *we be* Jews or Gentiles, whether *we be* bond or free; and have been all made to drink into one Spirit" [italics in KJV].

In spite of physical and spiritual blessings many of the Israelites in the wilderness displeased God and bore the consequences: "But with many of them God was not well pleased: for they were overthrown in the wilderness" (1 Corinthians 10:5). Paul's Jewish readers would have noted that even Moses, who had just been mentioned, suffered the same fate. Only two Israelites, Caleb and Joshua, advanced beyond the wilderness. The lesson to be learned from their tragic experience was not intended to be lost on Paul and the Corinthian believers: "Now these things were our examples, to the intent we should not lust after evil things, as they also lusted" (1 Corinthians 10:6). Just as Moses was included with the Israelites, Paul included himself with his readers by using the first person plural pronoun translated "our" (ἡμῶν).

In 1 Corinthians 10:6-10 Paul mentions five specifics from the negative example of the Israelites that he and the Corinthian believers were to avoid: (1) "we should not lust after evil things"; (2) "neither be ye idolaters"; (3) "neither let us commit fornication"; (4) "neither let us tempt Christ"; (5) "neither murmur." Paul introduces the list of prohibitions with a statement that the Old Testament experience was an example for them (1 Corinthians 10:6), and he ends it on a similar note: "Now all these things happened unto them for ensamples: and they are written for our admonition, upon whom the ends of the world are come" (1 Corinthians 10:11). Far from being hypothetical situations that were impossible for Paul and his Corinthian believing readers to commit, Paul considered it imminently possible. "Wherefore let him that thinketh he standeth take heed lest he fall" (1 Corinthians 10:12). Standing is no guarantee against stumbling and falling.

Fortunately the believer is not left to his or her own devices. Temptation is subject to divine limits, and divine leading is available. "There hath no temptation taken you but such as is common to man: but God *is* faithful, who will not suffer you to be tempted above that ye are able; but will with the temptation also make a way to escape, that ye may be able to bear *it*" [italics in KJV] (1 Corinthians 10:13). Those identified with Moses experienced divine judgment along with him. Paul desired that he and those he mentored would avoid a similar fate.

Divine discipline experienced by God's children is not to be confused with the condemnation that will be experienced by those who have not believed in Jesus. Paul made that distinction clear in his discussion of the Lord's Supper. Those who partake in an unworthy manner are subject to discipline. Paul gives the alternatives: "For if we would judge ourselves, we should not be judged. But when we are judged, we are chastened of the Lord, that we should not be condemned with the world" (1 Corinthians 11:31-32). What the believer experiences for the purpose of correction signifies something different than the condemnation of unbelievers. The former confirms a saved status because God does not discipline those who are not His children; the latter foreshadows future judgment for the unsaved.

Paul's introduction to spiritual gifts in 1 Corinthians 12:1-3 begins with the statement, "Now concerning spiritual *gifts*, brethren, I would not have you ignorant" [italics in KJV] (1 Corinthians 12:1). He contrasts their past with their present. Their pagan past was characterized by idolatrous demonic domination: "Ye know that ye were Gentiles, carried away unto these dumb idols, even as ye were led" (1 Corinthians 12:2). First, they had been "carried away," "led astray" or "mislead" (ἀπάγω), and then they were "led" (ἄγω). First they were deceived and then they were directed. While the physical idol was "dumb" or "mute" (ἄφωνος), the demons behind them were anything but silent and induced pagan worshipers to be engaged in ecstatic utterances.

Conversely, Paul wrote about speech controlled by the Holy Spirit. Whatever superficial similarities might exist between the ecstatic speech of pagans and a believer's speaking, they were polar opposites because of the source of control. The source of the former was Satan, while that of the latter was the Holy Spirit. In contrast to the blasphemous pronouncements of demons, a believer was one who identified Jesus as the God-Man, and would never agree to or articulate what a demon would. "Wherefore I give you to understand, that no man speaking by the Spirit of God calleth Jesus accursed: and *that* no man can say that Jesus is the Lord, but by the Holy Ghost" [italics in KJV] (1 Corinthians 12:3). A believer could say the words, "Jesus is accursed," but never when under the control of the Holy Spirit.

Correct identification of Jesus is key to the gospel message and a salvific response to it. A believer is someone who has come to the opposite conclusion that an unbeliever has come to concerning who Jesus is. In Paul's day pagans had been deceived and then directed by demons. A believer was one who, based on the evidence, had correctly identified who Jesus was, put his or her trust in Him, and now received instruction from Him. Control by and direction of the Holy Spirit was a benefit bestowed only on believers: "no man can say that Jesus is the Lord, but by the Holy Ghost" (1 Corinthians 12:3). Although the unsaved can articulate the words, "Jesus is the Lord," just as the demons declared Jesus' identity when He was on earth, the true meaning of those words belongs to believers. Believers are those who can say "Jesus is the Lord" and He can be so for them because they do so "by the Holy Spirit" (1 Corinthians 12:3).

The Holy Spirit is in complete control of dispensing spiritual gifts and directing their exercise. According to Paul a purpose for the gift of tongues was evangelistic: "Wherefore tongues are for a sign, not to them that believe, but to them that believe not" (1 Corinthians 14:22). On the other hand, prophecy did not have evangelism as its primary purpose: "but prophesying *serveth* not for them that believe not, but for them which believe" [italics in KJV] (1 Corinthians 14:22). For Paul, the evidential value of speaking in tongues was primarily significant for evangelism. The supernatural ability to speak in an unknown language would serve to confirm the gospel message of Jesus' identity to unbelievers.

While the sign of tongues provided corroborating evidence for Jesus' identity, prophecy on the other hand focused on the spiritual edification of believers. However, prophecy could also have an evangelistic effect on an unbeliever: "But if all prophesy, and there come in one that believeth not, or *one* unlearned, he is convinced of all, he is judged of all: and thus are the secrets of his heart made manifest" [italics in KJV] (1 Corinthians 14:24-25). Prophecy could reveal something personal about an unbeliever who was present which would lead to his salvation: "and so falling down on *his* face he will worship God, and report that God is in you of a truth" [italics in KJV] (1 Corinthians 14:25). The authenticity of New Testament worship was apparent because God's presence could be sensed. An unbeliever could conclude that Jesus is God and put his or her trust in Him for eternal life.

In 1 Corinthians chapter 15 is Paul's famous passage on the gospel. Insight into Paul's thinking is found in his introduction and conclusion to this section, which come before going into detail about Jesus' resurrection. The bottom line for the gospel is "believe" (πιστεύω). Paul brackets his discussion of the gospel with it. The beginning of the *inclusio* (bracketing) is in the first Greek sentence, where at the end of 1 Corinthians 15:2 Paul writes, "unless ye have believed in vain." The bracket is closed in 1 Corinthians 15:11, "therefore whether *it were* I or they, so we preach, and so ye believed" [italics in KJV]. The saving response to the gospel is to believe to be true the evidence for the identity of Jesus which it contains and then placing trust in Him for one's eternal destiny.

Paul saw the gospel as something his readers had responded to in the past and which had present results. After stating what his subject is, "the gospel which I preached unto you" (1 Corinthians 15:1), he goes into their past and present response. In the past they had "received" (παρελάβετε) the gospel. Paul's use of "receive" (παραλαμβάνω) would be similar to what the apostle John would later write in the Gospel of John (John 1:12) where "receive" (λαμβάνω) is defined as "believe in His name" (πιστεύω εἰς τὸ ὄνομα αὐτοῦ), that is, put one's trust in Jesus. As indicated by the indicative aorist tense "received" (παρελάβετε) in 1 Corinthians 15:1, that event had occurred in the readers' past.

What had happened in their past had a present result: "wherein ye stand" (1 Corinthians 15:1) (ἐν ᾧ καὶ ἑστήκατε). The words "you stand" are in the indicative perfect tense (ἑστήκατε) which refers to a past event with results extending into the present. Paul's emphasis seems to be on the present result of to "stand." The Greek verb "stand" (ἵστημι) could refer either to their unchanging position or to a changeable contingent condition. The latter could well be Paul's meaning, which would coincide with his use of the same Greek verb "stand" (ἵστημι) in 1 Corinthians 10:12: "Wherefore let him that thinketh he standeth take heed lest he fall." Both the Corinthians' present position and saved condition were made possible by their past reception of the gospel.

What Paul says about the Corinthian believers in 15:2 refers to a present contingent condition: "by which also ye are saved" (δι᾽ οὗ καὶ σῴζεσθε). This condition had the same source as the previously mentioned position, "by which also" (δι᾽ οὗ καὶ), but unlike having been saved by receiving the gospel, this one has a proviso added to it, "if ye keep in memory what I preached unto you" (1 Corinthians 15:2). The NASB says, "if you hold fast the word which I preached to you."

The Greek form is a first class condition which assumes the truth or existence of the condition for the sake of argument. While contingent, Paul was assuming the best of his audience. The use of the verb "saved" (σῴζω), is not a reference to their eternal salvation, but is the more common use, that of deliverance. The benefits of having been converted, were being experienced by the Corinthians in their Christian walk because they were meeting the contingency, "keep in memory" or "hold fast" (κατέχω).

In addition to that proviso another conditional element is introduced: "unless ye have believed in vain" (1 Corinthians 15:2). The Greek form here is also a first class condition, which assumes for the sake of argument that Paul's audience had indeed not "believed in vain." This conditional element adds another contingency to one that precedes it, to "keep in memory" or "hold fast" (κατέχω). If the Corinthians had "believed in vain," both their salvation and sanctification would be undermined. This prepares the reader for a discussion about the resurrection where Paul will argue, "and if Christ be not raised, your faith *is* vain; ye are yet in your sins" [italics in KJV] (1 Corinthians 15:17).

That alternative, a contrary to fact scenario (that Jesus did not rise from the dead), coincides with "believed in vain" (1 Corinthians 15:2). Without the resurrection, Jesus would not be the One revealed in Scripture, and trust in Him would accomplish nothing. On the other hand, the reality of the resurrection shows that faith is not futile. The ramifications of the resurrection are enormous, as Paul goes on to point out. When he wrote, "your faith is worthless" (1 Corinthians 15:17), he did not mean the believer's faith was deficient. He meant that a Savior who was not risen was a faulty foundation of one's faith.

Paul gives the details of the gospel: Jesus' identity revealed in His substitutionary sacrifice, resurrection, and evidence for it. Paul's purpose, as well as that of the rest of the New Testament writers, was to provide relevant, compelling evidence that was variegated and verifiable. Many have mistakenly taken this passage and come up with a certain number of items, as a sort of checklist of what is to be believed for eternal salvation. The result has been endless arguments. As stated in the introductory chapter of this work, to use the construct of "content" to ascertain exactly what proposition/s is/are to be believed to be true to obtain eternal salvation, does not do justice to the authors' intent or method. In the witness or testimony matrix of Scripture, the more evidence the better. Certain evidence will convince some individuals more than others. The goal in presenting the gospel is to communicate who the Jesus revealed in Scripture is, so that trust in Him for eternal life can occur.

The Jesus of the New Testament is the same individual who was identified prophetically in the Old Testament. Twice in this passage Paul emphasizes the connection: (1) "that Christ died for our sins according to the scriptures" (1 Corinthians 15:3); (2) "and that He was buried, and that he rose again the third day according to the scriptures" (1 Corinthians 15:4). In addition to the written testimony of the Old Testament there was credible eyewitness testimony that backed up the prophecies about Jesus.

In listing the witnesses Paul repeatedly uses the Greek verb translated "was seen" (ὁράω): "and that he was seen of Cephas, then of the twelve" (1 Corinthians 15:5); "After that, he was seen of above five hundred brethren at once, of whom the greater part remain unto this present, but some are fallen asleep" (1 Corinthians 15:6); "After that, he was seen of James; then of all the apostles" (1 Corinthians 15:7); "And last of all he was seen of me also, as of one born out of due time" (1 Corinthians 15:8). The emphasis on the appearance of Jesus to eyewitnesses is difficult to ignore. This is as if Paul was inviting skeptics to do their own investigation. The information was not hidden. With the scattering of believers from Jerusalem, the Corinthian believers may have been acquainted with someone who had been there when those things took place.

Paul himself was exhibit "A" of what the gospel could do. He who had been a prime persecutor of believers was now a preacher of the gospel, which identified the One whom he had previously reviled. The evidence was overwhelming. The witnesses were numerous and Paul was not in competition with any of them. For Paul the bottom line was belief; "Therefore whether *it were* I or they, so we preach, and so ye believed" [italics in KJV] (1 Corinthians 15:11). The means and the messenger could vary but what was communicated remained constant, namely, the identity of the One in whom trust is to be placed.

Paul was aware of the witness/testimony mindset and took seriously his own responsibility as an eyewitness. He wrote in 1 Corinthians 15:15, "Yea, and we are found false witnesses of God; because we have testified of God that he raised up Christ: whom he raised not up, if so be that the dead rise not." For Paul, to be a "false witness" (ψευδόμαρτυς) would be a violation of his own missional self-identity.

Paul's Christology was not limited to what Jesus had done in the past and what His power was accomplishing in the present: it will culminate in His central eschatological role: "Then *cometh* the end, when he shall have delivered up the kingdom to God, even the Father; when he shall have put down all rule and all authority and power" [italics in KJV] (1 Corinthians 15:24). In the divine plan Jesus vanquishes every one of God's enemies: "For he must reign, till he hath put all enemies under his feet. The last enemy *that* shall be destroyed *is* death" [italics in KJV] (1 Corinthians 15:25-26).

Woven throughout this passage is an interesting discussion with inter/intra-Trinitarian implications. First Corinthians 15:24, "Then *cometh* the end, when he shall have delivered up the kingdom to God, even the Father; when he shall have put down all rule and all authority and power" [italics in KJV]. Because of the inclusive nature of "all" (πᾶσαν) being under Christ's rule Paul made sure that God the Father was not included as being subject to the Son. In a doxological detour Paul quoted from Psalm 8:6, "For He hath put all things under His feet" (1 Corinthians 15:27). Then he included the caveat, "For he hath put all things under his feet. But when he saith, all things are put under *him, it is* manifest that he is excepted, which did put all things under him" [italics in KJV] (1 Corinthians 15:27). The rule of God the Son would not extend to God the Father.

Trinitarian distinctions and prerogatives will continue throughout eternity: "And when all things shall be subdued unto him, then shall the Son also himself be subject unto him that put all things under him, that God may be all in all" (1 Corinthians 15:28). Although Paul stated this clearly, even he did not understand it completely. We are to believe what is revealed while the full extent of the intricacies of the Trinity will forever be bound in infinite mystery.

Evidence for the Identity of Jesus in the Epistle of 2 Corinthians

The recipients of the epistle of 2 Corinthians were believers, both local and regional, "unto the church of God which is at Corinth, with all the saints which are in all Achaia" (2 Corinthians 1:1). Because believers are addressed, perhaps it is best to understand Paul's use of the term "salvation" (σωτηρία) in 2 Corinthians 1:6 as a reference to his readers' deliverance when he says, "And whether we be afflicted, *it is* for your consolation and salvation, which is effectual in the enduring of the same sufferings which we also suffer: or whether we be comforted, *it is* for your consolation and salvation" [italics in KJV]. The possibility exists that Paul had in mind evangelism that was taking place in the Corinthian church but the coordinate word "comfort" (παράκλησις) or "encouragement" lends support for "salvation" (σωτηρία) to be taken as a reference to Paul's efforts on behalf of believers.

The gospel Paul preached revealed the identity of Jesus and those who refused to accept the message: "But if our gospel be hid, it is hid to them that are lost" (2 Corinthians 4:3). This "hiding" or "veiling" was because of a satanically induced inability, "in whom the god of this world hath blinded the minds of them which believe not" (2 Corinthians 4:4). What they were kept from accepting was who Jesus is: "lest the light of the glorious gospel of Christ, who is the image of God, should shine unto them" (2 Corinthians 4:4). Paul and his fellow missionaries were not to be the focus of attention, but Jesus whom the gospel was about: "For we preach not ourselves, but Christ Jesus the Lord" (2 Corinthians 4:5). The NASB has "Christ Jesus as Lord" (Ἰησοῦν Χριστὸν κύριον), whereas the KJV renders it "the Lord Jesus Christ." The Greek could be translated "Jesus Christ the Lord."

The NASB translation has been taken by some to support their inclusion of being willing, wanting, wishing, or committing to do works, if not outright works, as a requirement for acquiring eternal life. Such an interpretation is grammatically unnecessary and unbiblical. The focus of Paul's evangelistic preaching was on the person of Christ as identified by His title. One part of the title ("Lord") should not be infused with a nuance that shifts the focus from the identity of the One in whom trust is to be placed to that of a prospective believer and additional requirements for his or her eternal salvation.

Paul's primary concern was to preach the gospel, which he did in the face of persecution and other perils: "*We are* troubled on every side, yet not distressed; *we are* perplexed, but not in despair; persecuted, but not forsaken; cast down, but not destroyed" [italics in KJV] (2 Corinthians 4:8-9). He viewed what was detrimental to him and his fellow workers as beneficial for those to whom he ministered: "So then death worketh in us, but life in you" (2 Corinthians 4:12). Paul persevered in preaching the gospel as he remembered his own conversion: "We having the same spirit of faith, according as it is written, I believed, and therefore have I spoken; we also believe, and therefore speak" (2 Corinthians 4:13).

The quotation from Psalm 116:10 used the Hebrew verb אָמַן in the Hiphil form, which can mean either "believe" (something or someone to be telling the truth) or "trust" (in something or someone). Paul trusted in God to sustain him through persecution and peril. The psalmist expressed in Psalm 116:10: "I believed when I said, 'I am greatly afflicted.'" The psalmist's words are preceded by this statement: "I shall walk before the Lord in the land of the living" (Psalm 116:9). The psalmist could say that because he had experienced God's deliverance: "For Thou hast rescued my soul from death, my eyes from tears, my feet from stumbling" (Psalm 116:8). The psalmist trusted in the Lord.

The One who made an eternal difference for Paul and his audience is the same God the psalmist trusted: "Knowing that he which raised up the Lord Jesus shall raise up us also by Jesus, and shall present *us* with you" [italics in KJV] (2 Corinthians 4:14). The bottom line for Paul was that in collaboration with Corinthian believers there would be more and more who would believe in Jesus: "For all things *are* for your sakes, that the abundant grace might through the thanksgiving of many redound to the glory of God" [italics in KJV] (2 Corinthians 4:15). The purpose of every endeavor was God's glory.

No one will be exempt from answering to God for what he or she has done in their lifetime. That future appearance is obligatory, not optional. Every theological system that is biblical must address eschatological reality and include the saved as well as the unsaved. Believers will be held accountable at the judgment seat of Christ and unbelievers at the great white throne judgment. Paul stated what awaited him and fellow believers: "For we must all appear before the judgment seat of Christ; that every one may receive the things *done* in *his* body, according to that he hath done, whether *it be* good or bad" [italics in KJV] (2 Corinthians 5:10).

The knowledge of coming judgment motivated Paul in his ministry of evangelism to the unsaved as well as the edification of believers, both of which involved persuasion: "Knowing therefore the terror of the Lord, we persuade men" (2 Corinthians 5:11). Paul's method with the unsaved was to provide evidence of Jesus' identity to convince them of who He is so that they could put their trust in Him. He persuaded the saved that it is eternally worthwhile to lead lives of obedience by the power of and for the glory of God.

Jesus was the lens through which Paul viewed believers: "Wherefore henceforth know we no man after the flesh: yea, though we have known Christ after the flesh, yet now henceforth know we *him* no more" [italics in KJV] (2 Corinthians 5:16). Because of their position in Christ Paul's optimism for believers was unbounded: "Therefore if any man *be* in Christ, *he is* a new creature: old things are passed away; behold, all things are become new" [italics in KJV] (2 Corinthians 5:17). A whole new vista of possibilities awaited those who had put their trust in Jesus. This had come about not because of something that they had done, promised to do, or been willing to do, but by the work of God alone: "And all things *are* of God" [italics in KJV] (2 Corinthians 5:18). These were the effects, the results, not to be confused with the cause.

The evangelistic mandate is to tell people about Christ. Paul referred to it as "the ministry of reconciliation" (2 Corinthians 5:18). Paul said "that God was in Christ, reconciling the world unto himself, not imputing their trespasses unto them; and hath committed unto us the word of reconciliation" (2 Corinthians 5:19). Jesus' substitutionary atonement is integral to His identity, which Paul summarizes in these words: "For he hath made him *to be* sin for us, who knew no sin; that we might be made the righteousness of God in him" [italics in KJV] (2 Corinthians 5:21).

Paul's example of dealing with persecution enhanced the preaching of the gospel message, and he exhorted his Corinthian colleagues to do the same in response to their circumstances: "We then, *as* workers together *with him*, beseech *you* also that ye receive not the grace of God in vain" [italics in KJV] (2 Corinthians 6:1). The support Paul mustered was from Isaiah 49:8: "(For he saith, I have heard thee in a time accepted, and in the day of salvation have I succoured thee: behold, now *is* the accepted time; behold, now *is* the day of salvation)" [parenthesis and italics in KJV] (2

Corinthians 6:2). Paul's readers could count on God to deliver them in their time of suffering. A Godly response to persecution would keep the gospel from being viewed in a less than favorable light: "Giving no offence in any thing, that the ministry be not blamed" (2 Corinthians 6:3). The NASB says, "giving no cause for offense in anything, in order that the ministry be not discredited." The way they handled persecution could either help or hinder the proclamation of the gospel.

Those who have put their trust in Jesus for eternal salvation and proclaim what they have done are exhorted to back up their words with works. Paul's appeal was that the transformation resulting from conversion become apparent in a Christian's walk. That was Paul's reasoning when asking the Corinthian church to take up a collection for needy believers in Jerusalem. Their giving would supply a need and would cause the recipients to praise God:

> For the administration of this service not only supplieth the want of the saints, but is abundant also by many thanksgivings unto God; whiles by the experiment of this ministration they glorify God for your professed subjection unto the gospel of Christ, and for *your* liberal distribution unto them, and unto all *men* [italics in KJV] (2 Corinthians 9:12-13).

Their "professed subjection unto the gospel of Christ," which the NASB translates as their "obedience to your confession of the gospel of Christ" was to be a result of their conversion and was not a part of it. Generosity is not to be added to the gospel as a requirement for eternal salvation.

Paul's use of the term "gospel" (εὐαγγελίῳ), "good news," was reserved for what we would call "evangelism." Paul supported his apostolic authority and paternal spiritual concern for the Corinthian believers, saying, "for we were the first to come even as far as you in the gospel of Christ" (2 Corinthians 10:14 NASB). Paul referred to how his evangelistic outreach had come to include them. Paul used the same expression to communicate his evangelistic urgency and goal: "To preach the gospel in the *regions* beyond you, *and* not to boast in another man's line of things made ready to our hand" [italics in KJV] (2 Corinthians 10:16). He sought to share the gospel with those who had yet to hear about Jesus and what He had done to secure their eternal salvation.

Paul was concerned about those who might follow up his converts and subvert the gospel he had originally preached to them. He used the metaphor of matchmaking and marriage: "For I am jealous over you with godly jealousy: for I have espoused you to one husband, that I may present *you as* a chaste virgin to Christ" [italics in KJV] (2 Corinthians 11:2). Paul, who had introduced them to the groom (Christ), expressed alarm over what was going on with a comparison to Eve and the Fall: "But I fear, lest by any means, as the serpent beguiled Eve through his subtlety, so your minds should be corrupted from the simplicity that is in Christ" (2 Corinthians 11:3). According to Louw and Nida the Greek noun the NASB renders "simplicity" (ἁπλότητος), expresses "the quality of sincerity as an expression of singleness of purpose or motivation" (Johannes P. Louw and Eugene A. Nida, *Greek-English Lexicon of the New Testament*

Based on Semantic Domains, 2nd ed. [New York: United Bible Societies, 2nd ed], 1989, 747). The gospel Paul preached is uncomplicated. The gospel is about who Christ is and putting trust in Him for eternal salvation.

Paul commended the Corinthians for their recognition and rejection of a perverted gospel: "For if he that cometh preacheth another Jesus, whom we have not preached, or *if* ye receive another spirit, which ye have not received, or another gospel, which ye have not accepted, ye might well bear with *him*" [italics in KJV] (2 Corinthians 11:4). The NASB says, "For if one comes and preaches another Jesus whom we have not preached, or you receive a different spirit which you have not received, or a different gospel which you have not accepted, you bear *this* beautifully" [italics in NASB]. By the words, "you bear this beautifully" (καλῶς ἀνέχεσθε), Paul did not mean that they tolerated heresy. While they rightfully rejected it, the verb "bear" (ἀνέχομαι) has the idea of patient endurance.

Paul may have been empathizing with what they had been subjected to and was complimenting them for their appropriate response. However, the verb "bear" (ἀνέχομαι) can have a negative connotation. If that is the case Paul may have been speaking sarcastically, making fun of their acceptance of what they should have rejected. Paul uses the term sarcastically when he uses this same verb twice later on: "For ye suffer fools gladly, seeing ye *yourselves* are wise. For ye suffer, if a man bring you into bondage, if a man devour *you*, if a man take *of you*, if a man exalt himself, if a man smite you on the face" [italics in KJV] (2 Corinthians 11:19-20). The NASB says, "For you, being *so* wise, bear with [ἀνέχεσθε] the foolish gladly. For you bear with [ἀνέχεσθε] anyone if he enslaves you, if he devours you, if he takes advantage of you, if he exalts himself, if he hits you in the face" [italics in NASB].

Paul may have intended sarcasm in 2 Corinthians 11:4, but there is no doubt about his genuine concern for his readers. Paul reluctantly defended his selfless ministry that was not motivated by personal gain. He stated his intention to continue ministering in that manner even though it might be called "boasting" (καύχησις). He wrote, "As the truth of Christ is in me, no man shall stop me of this boasting in the regions of Achaia" (2 Corinthians 11:10). Paul asked rhetorically, "Wherefore? because I love you not? God knoweth" (2 Corinthians 11:11).

The "gospel" Paul was warning about was probably a heretical hybrid. He did not mince words in describing the purveyors of such heresy: "For such *are* false apostles, deceitful workers, transforming themselves into the apostles of Christ" [italics in KJV] (2 Corinthians 11:13). They were imitators of the devil, the one who inspired them: "And no marvel; for Satan himself is transformed into an angel of light. Therefore *it is* no great thing if his ministers also be transformed as the ministers of righteousness; whose end shall be according to their works" [italics in KJV] (2 Corinthians 11:14-15). Those who imitated the method and manner of Satan would attempt to make themselves indistinguishable from genuine preachers of the gospel. The attractive appearance of their ministries notwithstanding, the heretical nature of their gospel would be revealed.

At the end of Paul's second epistle to Corinthian believers is a verse that has been used by some as a test for the genuineness and assurance of salvation. Second Corinthians 13:5 states, "Examine yourselves, whether ye be in the faith; prove your own selves. Know ye not your own selves, how that Jesus Christ is in you, except ye be reprobates?" The NASB says, "Test yourselves *to see* if you are in the faith; examine yourselves! Or do you not recognize this about yourselves, that Jesus Christ is in you– unless you fail the test?" [italics in NASB]. Some bible teachers take this to refer to examining one's works to ascertain if one is saved. The reader is referred to chapter 2 "Exegetical Eye-Openers" for a discussion of this passage.

The desire of Paul and his colleagues was not to make themselves look good but that the readers would live godly lives. As Paul put it, "Now I pray to God that ye do no evil; not that we should appear approved, but that ye should do that which is honest, though we be as reprobates" (2 Corinthians 13:7). Paul was willing to have his own reputation destroyed, knowing that he was doing what was best for the Corinthian believers, and that God would see through appearances. Sin in the life of a believer was serious. It did damage to the church's reputation, but ultimately it met with God's disapproval not Paul's. The maturity of the Corinthian believers was Paul's goal: "For we are glad, when we are weak, and ye are strong: and this also we wish, *even* your perfection" [italics in KJV] (2 Corinthians 13:9). The NASB says, "this we also pray for, that you be made complete." Whatever admonishment he administered was "to edification, and not to destruction" (2 Corinthians 13:10). The NASB says, "for building up and not for tearing down." Such was Paul's desire.

Evidence for the Identity of Jesus in the Epistle of Galatians

The emphasis Paul placed on the gospel is found in the beginning of this epistle. He mentions Jesus and God the Father as the source of his apostleship. God the Father is referred to as the One, "who raised him [Jesus] from the dead" (Galatians 1:1). In the salutation Jesus is called the "Lord Jesus Christ" (Galatians 1:3) (κυρίου Ἰησοῦ Χριστοῦ) and is identified as the One "who gave himself for our sins, that he might deliver us from this present evil world" (Galatians 1:4). The importance of the gospel is emphasized by Paul's use of strong language in its defense. The gospel had a fixed quality; it was not to be reinvented. Paul expressed shock and dismay that the Galatian believers even considered altering and abandoning it: "I marvel that ye are so soon removed from him that called you into the grace of Christ unto another gospel" (Galatians 1:6).

Replacing the gospel with an alternative is the equivalent of leaving Jesus whom the gospel is about and abandoning grace. Paul refused to dignify the gospel replacement by even calling it "another" (ἄλλος) gospel: "Which is not another" (Galatians 1:7). The distortion of the gospel disquiets believers: "but there be some that trouble you, and would pervert the gospel of Christ" (Galatians 1:7). The peaceful settled dependence on God enjoyed by believers in the churches in the region of Galatia was being destroyed by those who distorted the gospel.

The readers of the epistle could rest assured that neither Paul himself, nor even additional revelation, could change the gospel: "But though we, or an angel from heaven, preach any other gospel unto you than that which we have preached unto you, let him be accursed" (Galatians 1:8). In case the reader wondered if they read him correctly Paul repeated himself: "As we said before, so say I now again, If any *man* preach any other gospel unto you than that ye have received, let him be accursed" [italics in KJV] (Galatians 1:9). The Greek "to be" (εἰμί) verb rendered by the NASB with "let him be" (ἔστω) is a third person imperative which is not present in the English language. The KJV and NASB translations do not do justice to the command nuance present in the Greek. Paul says, "I command him to be accursed." Whether the curse was Paul's own or if he was calling down a curse from God might be debated; but in either case the intensity of the imprecation is difficult to exaggerate. Changing the gospel affects everyone; the saved and the unsaved.

Paul was confident that what he preached was the genuine gospel because Jesus had personally identified Himself to him. "But I certify you, brethren, that the gospel which was preached of me is not after man. For I neither received it of man, neither was I taught *it*, but by the revelation of Jesus Christ" [italics in KJV] (Galatians 1:11-12). Paul's reception of the gospel had not just been information about Jesus; he had seen the personal presence of Jesus. He did not have to rely on others; he himself was an eyewitness to Jesus' identity.

Paul had asked on the Damascus road, "Who art Thou, Lord" (Acts 9:5), and Jesus had identified himself: "And the Lord said, I am Jesus whom thou persecutest" (Acts 9:5). As additional evidence that the gospel Paul preached was genuine Paul noted that he had not consulted with the leadership of the church in Jerusalem: "Neither went I up to Jerusalem to them which were apostles before me; but I went into Arabia, and returned again unto Damascus. Then after three years I went up to Jerusalem to see Peter, and abode with him fifteen days" (Galatians 1:17-18).

Paul knew he was not alone in having received the gospel. When he went to Jerusalem, he saw that his gospel and what had been given to the other apostles coincided. For the unity of the church it appears that Paul was told by God to make contact with Jerusalem leadership: "And I went up by revelation, and communicated unto them that gospel which I preach among the Gentiles, but privately to them which were of reputation, lest by any means I should run, or had run, in vain" (Galatians 2:2). Understandably Paul was worried that because his evangelistic ministry was to the Gentiles and the Jerusalem church reached out to Jews, there might be some difference in the gospel that was preached. He was relieved to find out they all preached the same gospel. Paul's gospel did not need tweaking: "they who seemed *to be somewhat* in conference added nothing to me" [italics in KJV] (Galatians 2:6). The NASB says, "those who were of reputation contributed nothing to me."

Paul did get into a confrontation with Peter later on because he (Peter) was succumbing to the pressure of Jewish legalists who tried to impose Jewish customs on Gentiles as a requirement for salvation. Paul used that opportunity with Peter, and in writing to the

Galatian churches, to clearly state the gospel: "Knowing that a man is not justified by the works of the law, but by the faith of Jesus Christ, even we have believed in Jesus Christ, that we might be justified by the faith of Christ, and not by the works of the law: for by the works of the law shall no flesh be justified" (Galatians 2:16). Three times in that one verse Paul mentions faith in Christ.

Because Paul was dealing with the gospel in relation to Jews, he contrasts "faith" (πίστις) with "works of the Law." This does not give license to those who say that other kinds of works, that are not "works of the Law" (ἔργων νόμου), such as "non-meritorious works" or "God-wrought works" can legitimately be added to "faith" (πίστις) as a requirement for eternal salvation. As has been demonstrated from Romans chapters 3 and 4 and will be shown in Ephesians 2:8-9, Paul made no such distinction. Works are not a requirement for eternal salvation. Trust in Jesus is the singular requirement for salvation to the exclusion of every species of works.

Paul's summary argument for faith uses the example of a human covenant and the fact that once a deal is made the matter is settled and is not subject to subsequent deletions or additions: "Brethren, I speak after the manner of men; though *it be* but a man's covenant, yet *if it be* confirmed, no man disannulleth, or addeth thereto" [italics in KJV] (Galatians 3:15). In human contracts dates are important. The chronology of the promise to Abraham and the introduction of the Law is critical; it establishes the priority of the promise: "And this I say, *that* the covenant, that was confirmed before of God in Christ, the law, which was four hundred and thirty years after, cannot disannul, that it should make the promise of none effect" [italics in KJV] (Galatians 3:17).

The principle of faith that precedes the Law includes Christ in whom trust is placed. Paul argues that the singular "seed" (σπέρματι), in the Abrahamic Covenant, as opposed to the plural "seeds" (σπέρμασιν), is significant because it identifies Him: "Now to Abraham and his seed were the promises made. He saith not, And to seeds, as of many; but as of one, And to thy seed, which is Christ" (Galatians 3:16). In a preliminary summation of the subject Paul emphasizes Jesus as the object of faith: "But the scripture hath concluded all under sin, that the promise by faith of Jesus Christ might be given to them that believe" (Galatians 3:22). The NASB says, "faith in Jesus Christ," that takes the Greek genitive as an objective genitive and not a subjective genitive as the KJV has, "faith of Jesus Christ." If the KJV translation is taken as being in agreement with the "new perspective on Paul" interpretation, it is to be rejected.

The purpose of the Law was not to provide a way to eternal life but to point to a Person who would. With the Incarnation the object of faith, who had been implicit in the Old Testament, became explicit: "But before faith came, we were kept under the law, shut up unto the faith which should afterwards be revealed. Wherefore the law was our schoolmaster *to bring us* unto Christ, that we might be justified by faith" [italics in KJV] (Galatians 3:23-24). That is not to say that faith was not the requirement for salvation before Jesus came. In the Old Testament it was trust in God. People knew God the Father who had revealed Himself and they had some information about His Son, the Messiah, who would come.

Abraham's paternal legacy was complicated. Not only was he the father of the Jewish people but as God promised in Genesis 17:4, "thou shalt be a father of many nations." God additionally promised Abraham, "And I will make thee exceeding fruitful, and I will make nations of thee, and kings shall come out of thee" (Genesis 17:6). The Jews considered themselves as the pinnacle in a hierarchy of Abrahamic progeny. But that paradigm would not apply to Abraham's spiritual descendants. Among the "sons of God" (υἱοὶ θεοῦ) there would be no spiritual hierarchy, "For ye are all the children of God by faith in Christ Jesus" (Galatians 3:26). Only Abraham's spiritual descendants–believers–are sons of God. Christ is the common denominator that overrides distinctions: "For as many of you as have been baptized into Christ have put on Christ" (Galatians 3:27). That included all believers. More important than individual diversity is communal identity: "There is neither Jew nor Greek, there is neither bond nor free, there is neither male nor female: for ye are all one in Christ Jesus" (Galatians 3:28).

The requirement for membership in the Christian community with its position and privileges is faith in Christ: "And if ye *be* Christ's, then are ye Abraham's seed, and heirs according to the promise" [italics in KJV] (Galatians 3:29). The church is to be a caring community that operates much like a loving home, being a blessing to each other and those around them: "As we have therefore opportunity, let us do good unto all *men*, especially unto them who are of the household of faith" [italics in KJV] (Galatians 6:10). The church is to care for unbelievers and nurture the special bond that exists between believers.

Evidence for the Identity of Jesus in the Epistle of Ephesians

The introduction that lists the believer's blessings is a lengthy Greek sentence that ends with a statement about the goal of God's work in salvation: "That we should be to the praise of his glory, who first trusted in Christ" (Ephesians 1:12). The NASB says, "to the end that we who were the first to hope in Christ should be to the praise of His glory." Paul used the Greek perfect participle translated "who were the first to hope" (προηλπικότας) from the compound verb (προελπίζω) that combines what came "before" (προ) and "hope" (ἐλπίδος). At conversion Paul and his readers as well as his companions experienced that when they put their trust in Christ.

Paul elaborates on what they had done that resulted in the Holy Spirit securing their position in Christ: "In whom ye also *trusted*, after that ye heard the word of truth, the gospel of your salvation: in whom also after that ye believed, ye were sealed with that holy Spirit of promise" [italics in KJV] (Ephesians 1:13). The NASB says, "In Him, you also, after listening to the message of truth, the gospel of your salvation–having also believed, you were sealed in Him with the Holy Spirit of promise." Paul's readers had believed the message of who Jesus is and what He has done and placed their trust in Him for eternal salvation.

Paul was thankful for what had happened and what was going on in the lives of the Ephesian believers and desired that they experience all that was now available to them. Ephesians 1:15 says, "Wherefore I also, after I heard of your faith in the Lord Jesus, and love unto all the saints." Although the Ephesian believers continued trusting in the Lord it would be too much to dogmatically derive that from the grammar of this verse. Interpreting it as saving faith, a prior event, is more likely, and relates it to the preceding context.

The famous passage, Ephesians 2:8-9, is preceded by a discussion of the pre-salvation condition of believers which begins in Ephesians 2:1: "And you *hath he quickened*, who were dead in trespasses and sins" [italics in KJV]. The description is figurative; the reference to death is spiritual and not physical. The passage continues, saying, "Wherein in time past ye walked" (Ephesians 2:2). They were "dead men walking." Some writers affirm that because the unsaved are spiritually dead, they have no ability to respond to the gospel. Therefore God regenerates (gives life to) the unbeliever, and then he exercises faith. However, this erroneously makes a person saved (regenerated) *before* he places his faith in Christ. A better view is to see the words "dead in trespasses and sins" (νεκροὺς τοῖς παραπτώμασιν καὶ ταῖς ἁμαρτίαις) as a figure of speech, which shows that because an unsaved person is dead, he cannot save himself.

The contrast is between the subjects who participate in salvation. The preconversion condition has "you" (Ephesians 2:1) (ὑμᾶς), "we" (Ephesians 2:3) (ἡμεῖς), and "the rest" (Ephesians 2:3) (οἱ λοιποί) as the subjects for the verbs. Beginning in Ephesians 2:4 the primary subject is God: "But God, who is rich in mercy" (ὁ δὲ θεὸς πλούσιος ὢν ἐν ἐλέει). God the Father, who took the divine initiative in man's salvation, did so by the instrumentality of Jesus, the Son. God the Father "hath quickened us together with Christ" (Ephesians 2:5). Louw and Nida recognize that theological difficulties could arise from an interpretation of the verb "made us alive together with" (συζωοποιέω). They write,

> There are serious semantic difficulties involved in a literal translation of συνεγείρω or συζωοποιέω, for a literal rendering could either be interpreted as 'to be raised to life at the same time with' or 'to be raised to life in the same way as,' but the reference in Col 3.1 and Eph 2.5 is to a spiritual existence more than to a literal resurrection of the body. This means that both συνεγείρω and συζωοποιέω must be understood as highly figurative (Johannes P. Louw and Eugene A. Nida, *Greek-English Lexicon of the New Testament Based on Semantic Domains*, 2nd ed. [New York: United Bible Societies, 2nd ed], 1989, 1:263).

Paul lets the reader know that he is referring to man's spiritual resurrection with a parenthesis, "(by grace ye are saved)" [parenthesis in KJV] (Ephesians 2:5). Man's spiritual resurrection (salvation) is not to be equated with Jesus' physical resurrection in which God the Father culminated the divine work on His behalf.

With the use of a Greek periphrastic perfect passive participle and finite verb, "ye are saved" ("you have been saved" = NASB) ἐστε σεσῳσμένοι, the past event of salvation with ongoing results is communicated. Wallace shows that the periphrastic construction consisting of a present tense finite "to be" (εἰμί) verb plus the perfect participle is the equivalent of the finite (indicative) perfect tense in meaning (Daniel Wallace, *Greek Grammar beyond the Basics*, [Grand Rapids: Zondervan, 1996], 648-

49). Wallace does entertain the possibility that the meaning is that of the present tense, "you are saved."

Although Wallace does not discuss this verse specifically he refers the reader to his discussion of the perfect tense where he states that because of lexical intrusion, "They are resultative perfects to the point that the act itself has virtually died; the results have become the act" (ibid., 579-80). If such a conclusion is reached, it should be noted that Wallace qualifies his statement with the term "virtually." The completed past event or act has not entirely disappeared. If a present meaning is accepted, it is an emphasis with the causal event still having existed in the past.

Wallace says that the present sense or meaning "of the perfect is always *lexically influenced* (i.e., it occurs only with certain verbs)" [italics and parenthesis in original] (ibid., 580). Wallace mentions several Greek verbs that are stative and used in this way; the verb "save" (σῴζω) is not among them, nor is the verb "believe" (πιστεύω) (ibid.). It could be argued that the verb "believe" (πιστεύω) is functionally a stative verb when used in salvation contexts and that when it is in the perfect tense it is virtually understood to have the meaning of a present tense. For more on that issue the reader is referred back to chapter 2, "Exegetical Eye-Openers," and the discussion of John 3:16.

Returning to the question of spiritual versus physical resurrection in Ephesians 2:5, in addition to Paul's parenthesis the rest of his sentence shows that he was referring to the spiritual resurrection of man. He finishes the sentence with, "And hath raised *us* up together, and made *us* sit together in heavenly *places* in Christ Jesus: that in the ages to come he might shew the exceeding riches of his grace in *his* kindness toward us through Christ Jesus" [italics in KJV] (Ephesians 2:6-7). The resurrection of believers Paul refers to is spiritual while that of Jesus was physical. Man needs both physical and spiritual resurrection. Jesus has no need of spiritual resurrection, but He required physical resurrection because He died for the sins of men.

In Ephesians 2:8-9 the identical phrase of the parenthesis at the end of verse 5 is repeated, "by grace are ye saved" (Ephesians 2:8), with additional explanatory information: "For by grace are ye saved through faith; and that not of yourselves: *it is* the gift of God: not of works, lest any man should boast" [italics in KJV] (Ephesians 2:8-9). In the phrase "and that not of yourselves" (Ephesians 2:8), the Greek demonstrative pronoun translated "that" (τοῦτο), which is neuter in gender, most likely refers to what precedes. Because "that" (τοῦτο) is neuter it does not, however, refer specifically to "faith" (πίστις), which is feminine in gender, but rather to the entire preceding concept of salvation by grace.

However, Sam Storms, writing about the antecedent of "that" (τοῦτο), takes a different view. He says "that" refers to "faith."

> Clearly the "gift" of God is salvation in its totality, a salvation that flows out of God's grace and becomes ours through faith. From beginning to end, from its inception to its

> consummation, salvation is a gift of God to his elect. Consequently, that faith by which we come into experiential possession of what God in grace has provided is as much a gift as any and every other aspect of salvation. One can no more deny that faith is wrapped up in God's gift to us than he can deny it of God's grace. *All is of God!* Salvation is of the Lord! [italics in original] (*Chosen for Life: The Case for Divine Election* [Wheaton, IL: Crossway, 2007], 71).

Storms is unconvincing in his conclusion that the reference to the gift of salvation as a whole must include the particulars in the way his Reformed theology requires.

Storms marshals support for his interpretation from 2 Peter 1:1 that says, "Simon Peter, a servant and an apostle of Jesus Christ, to them that have obtained like precious faith with us through the righteousness of God and our Saviour Jesus Christ." Storms writes,

> What is of paramount importance here is the word translated "have obtained" or "have received." It is related to a verb that means "to obtain by lot" (see Luke 1:9; John 19:24; Acts 1:17). Thus, faith is removed from the realm of human free will and placed in its proper perspective as having originated in the sovereign and altogether gracious will of God (ibid., 72).

In the KJV the words "them that have obtained" (τοῖς. . . λαχοῦσιν) translate an articular (with an article) substantival (functioning as a noun) participle. The meaning "to obtain by lot" that Storms relies on more likely is associated with the person chosen by lot and not to the "faith" (πίστις) that supposedly is thereby "removed from the realm of human free will" (ibid.). The "faith" (πίστις) Peter's readers had, was theirs because they had been chosen by God. Therefore, 2 Peter 1:1 does not necessarily support the position that faith itself is a gift of God and that man's will is not involved.

Ephesians 2:8 says that the cause of salvation is God and not man: "not of yourselves," and his faith is "not of works" (Ephesians 2:9). Everyone without exception is unable to secure his or her own eternal salvation. Paul's statement is universally applicable. No one person, past, present, or future, is the source of or contributor to his or her salvation. Paul categorically denies works as a requirement for obtaining eternal salvation. There is a conspicuous absence of any qualifier/s for either man or his works. All works of man–prior works, present works, and subsequent works–are excluded, as are promises to work, or works willing to be done, or commitments willing to be made.

Also, to say that God's works are allowed is to evade the clear meaning of the text. God's work in securing eternal salvation is not to be mixed with man's attempts to help God out. This would seem obvious because even the idea that "nonmeritorious works" are not prohibited, does not deny that man is involved in some way. Because man and/or his works as the agent and/or instrumental cause, cannot contribute to salvation, man has no basis for pride in securing salvation: "lest any man should boast" (Ephesians 2:9). If an exception is allowed for either man and/or his works, an exception for boasting must also be conceded. The text provides for neither.

With the explanatory causal conjunction "for" (γάρ) Paul introduces a statement that places work in its proper context: "For we are his workmanship" (Ephesians 2:10). Rather than salvation being the result of man's work, those who are saved constitute the product of divine "workmanship" (ποίημα). Whatever work it took, God and God alone did it. God was the cause with the effect being salvation. God's work in securing man's salvation, the divine cause, was to ultimately affect man's performance: "created in Christ Jesus unto good works, which God hath before ordained that we should walk in them" (Ephesians 2:10). God planned salvation from eternity past as well as the work that could be performed by those whom He would save.

Jesus was central to the formation of the church and the inclusion of Gentiles in it: "That the Gentiles should be fellowheirs, and of the same body, and partakers of his promise in Christ by the gospel" (Ephesians 3:6). The gospel is about Jesus; who He is and what is promised to those who put their trust in Him. In addition to eternal life, equal access to God the Father is granted to believers: "According to the eternal purpose which he purposed in Christ Jesus our Lord: in whom we have boldness and access with confidence by the faith of him ["faith in Him" = NASB]" (Ephesians 3:11-12). Paul's desire, "that he would grant you" (Ephesians 3:16), for believers is that what begins for them by God's grace through dependence on His Son Jesus for eternal life, will continue in their walk: "That Christ may dwell in your hearts by faith" (Ephesians 3:17). Eternal salvation is promised to those who put their trust in Jesus, and everyday progressive sanctification is experienced by those who depend on Him for it.

The second half of the Ephesians epistle is primarily devoted to the subject of the believer's sanctification. With the Greek imperative, prohibitions and commands are frequently found in this section. One of the reasons Paul gives for obedience has become the subject of controversy: "For this ye know, that no whoremonger, nor unclean person, nor covetous man, who is an idolater, hath any inheritance in the kingdom of Christ and of God. Let no man deceive you with vain words: for because of these things cometh the wrath of God upon the children of disobedience" (Ephesians 5:5-6).

Whether believers can or cannot commit these sins has been the subject of controversy. One proposed solution has been to say that these can be occasional or habitual sins and that true believers cannot commit the latter. But that interpretation conflicts with the near context in which three of the items on the list are specifically mentioned. Ephesians 5:3 says: "But fornication, and all uncleanness, or covetousness, let it not be once named among you, as becometh saints." Paul does not say that occasional lapses are acceptable and that making a habit of committing them is not.

It should be noted that in Ephesians 5:5, Paul identifies the individual who commits these sins as someone "who is an idolater" (ὅ ἐστιν εἰδωλολάτρης), probably identifying the individual as a pagan. No pagan "hath any inheritance in the kingdom of Christ and of God;" he or she will be excluded from the kingdom and presence of God. Pagans will be excluded from anything having to do with the kingdom, ruling or otherwise, and from God's presence. Ephesians 5:6 makes their unsaved status clear: "Let no man deceive you with vain words: for because of these things cometh the wrath of God upon the children of disobedience."

Of significance is the fact that Paul distinguishes his readers from them: "Be not ye therefore partakers with them" (Ephesians 5:7). The partaking or sharing (συμμέτοχος) that Paul is exhorting believers to avoid is not the eternal destiny of unbelievers but their sinful behavior, as seen in the remainder of the sentence: "For ye were sometimes ["formerly" = NASB] darkness, but now *are ye* light in the Lord: walk as children of light: (For the fruit of the Spirit *is* in all goodness and righteousness and truth); proving what is acceptable unto the Lord" [parenthesis and italics in KJV] (Ephesians 5:8-10).

Believers are those who are "in the Lord" (Ephesians 5:8) (ἐν κυρίῳ). To say that those who commit the sins mentioned, either occasionally or habitually, are not saved is to go beyond what the text is saying. What the text does say is that there are those who commit such sins and are destined for eternal separation from God and will experience His wrath, and it exhorts believers not to do the very same things that hell-bound sinners do. Such activity is inappropriate, unfitting, and unbecoming to believers. To say that the believers who do such things prove that they were not saved to begin with is to say more than the text says. To hang a consequential theological conclusion on a nonverbal implication rather than an explicit statement is doctrinally dangerous. Theological "reverse engineering" or regression analysis employs a dubious hermeneutic.

The danger Paul warned his readers about was real and not merely theoretical or hypothetical. This is seen in the contrast set up between a prohibition and a positive command in Ephesians 5:11, both of which are to be obeyed and neither of which is impossible for a believer: "And have no fellowship ["do not participate" = NASB] with the unfruitful works of darkness, but rather reprove *them*" [italics in KJV]. They were not to join their club but call them out. The prohibition is as capable of being obeyed or disobeyed as is the positive command. To single out the former as theoretical and impossible for a believer and not do so with the latter is to beg the question, and employ interpretational inconsistency.

The context of this passage is one of imitation. Ephesians 4:32 enjoins loving behavior toward fellow believers by following God's example: "And be ye kind one to another, tenderhearted, forgiving one another, even as God for Christ's sake hath forgiven you." The divine pattern is to be emulated. Paul says, "Be ye therefore followers of God, as dear children; and walk in love, as Christ also hath loved us, and hath given himself for us an offering and a sacrifice to God for a sweetsmelling savour" (Ephesians 5:1-2). The sweet smell of obedience is then contrasted with the scent of sin.

Believers were faced with a choice: either imitate the Son of God or the sons of disobedience. In Paul's communication of the contrast he did not use the language of possibility/impossibility, but rather that of consistency/inconsistency, congruence and incongruence. The prohibitions were couched in terms of what was "proper" (πρέπει), consistent with the positional identity of a believer, rather than that of a pagan: "as is proper among saints" (Ephesians 5:3) (καθὼς πρέπει ἁγίοις). The prohibition was they are not to engage in behavior contrary to their permanent saved position as believers. Their practice is to be consistent with their position.

It is to be "believer appropriate" rather than inappropriate behavior: "which are not convenient" ("which are not fitting" = NASB, ἀνήκω = "fitting" or "proper") (Ephesians 5:4) (ἃ οὐκ ἀνῆκεν). Believers are wise to obey the command to imitate Christ: "See then that ye walk circumspectly, not as fools, but as wise" (Ephesians 5:15). And it is foolish to fail to do so: "Wherefore be ye not unwise, but understanding what the will of the Lord *is*" [italics in KJV] (Ephesians 5:17). For a believer, failure to do God's will is always in the realm of possibility but is never the prudent thing to do.

Evidence for the Identity of Jesus in the Epistle of Philippians

The introduction includes Paul and Timothy as those who greet the Philippian believers: "Paul and Timotheus, the servants of Jesus Christ, to all the saints in Christ Jesus which are at Philippi" (Philippians 1:1). After the inclusion of Timothy, Paul, presumably the writer of the epistle, uses the first person singular with the verb "I thank" (Philippians 1:3) (Εὐχαριστῶ) to express gratitude to God for his readers: "I thank my God upon every remembrance of you." He was thankful "For your fellowship in the gospel from the first day until now" (Philippians 1:5). This could include their initial positive reception of the gospel at the time of their conversion together with their partnership by way of monetary contributions to Paul's evangelistic endeavors. The impression is that of a warm personal bond between Paul and these believers.

On the basis of Paul's personal knowledge of and relationship with his readers he boldly asserts about them: "Being confident of this very thing, that he which hath begun a good work in you will perform *it* until the day of Jesus Christ" [italics in KJV] (Philippians 1:6). The question arises whether this statement, directed to a specific group of believers, can be universally applied to all believers. Is it legitimate to use this as a proof text for the Reformed doctrine of "perseverance of the saints?" Paul did not expect his expression of desire for and confidence in the Philippian believers to be elevated to the level of universal applicability.

It could be argued that if the universal character of this text is denied, because it is talking to and about a specific group of individuals in the first century, very few passages would survive the criteria for present-day application. The danger inherent in the employment of that hermeneutic is readily acknowledged. However, this verse under discussion (Philippians 1:6) has contextual considerations that must be taken into account. Paul defends the assertion he makes about these believers: "Even as it is meet for me to think this of you all, because I have you in my heart; inasmuch as both in my bonds, and in the defence and confirmation of the gospel, ye all are partakers of my grace" (Philippians 1:7). The NASB says, "For it is only right for me to feel this way about you all, because I have you in my heart, since both in my imprisonment and in the defense and confirmation of the gospel you all are partakers of grace with me." The word translated by the NASB with "feel" (φρονέω) could just as well be translated "think," as the KJV renders it. In effect, Paul acknowledges that he is biased in his optimistic opinion about them because they had been his co-laborers.

Paul further explains the assertion he makes about them: "For God is my record, how greatly I long after you all in the bowels of Jesus Christ" (Philippians 1:8). The NASB translates the verse, "for God is my witness, how I long for you all with the affection of Christ Jesus." His motivation was Christlike compassion. Paul reasoned that their past practice was a good predictor of future performance and prayed that it might be so: "And this I pray, that your love may abound yet more and more in knowledge and *in* all judgment; that ye may approve things that are excellent" [italics in KJV] (Philippians 1:9-10). God's positive assessment would take into account what they had done in the past, and would also be contingent on what they would continue to do: "that ye may be sincere and without offence till the day of Christ; being filled with the fruits of righteousness, which are by Jesus Christ, unto the glory and praise of God" (Philippians 1:10-11). Did Paul say that what he was confident would take place in the lives of his readers would be the experience of every believer in every age who would read his words? That would put more weight on Paul's words than he intended.

Right after Paul painted this rosy picture of the Philippian believers, he told them about believers in Rome where he was being held prisoner and what he had to say about some of them was less than complimentary. A positive outcome of his incarceration was an increase in evangelism by believers: "And many of the brethren in the Lord, waxing confident by my bonds, are much more bold to speak the word without fear" (Philippians 1:14). Still writing about believers, Paul says, "Some indeed preach Christ even of envy and strife; and some also of good will" (Philippians 1:15).

For some of them, Paul's words were complimentary. They proclaimed the gospel out "of love, knowing that I am set for the defence of the gospel" (Philippians 1:17). They knew that Paul had a heart for evangelism and knowing that because of his imprisonment Paul was unable to continue his mission they "stepped up to the plate" out of love for him. They sounded like the Philippian believers for whom Paul had just prayed, "that your love may abound yet more and more" (Philippians 1:9).

In contrast there were the other believers of whom Paul says, "The one preach Christ of contention, not sincerely, supposing to add affliction to my bonds" (Philippians 1:16). In Philippians 1:10 Paul prays that his readers who are believers will one day be commended by God for having motives that are "sincere" (εἰλικρινής), and in Philippians 1:17 he accuses believers of evangelizing with less than pure motives. To preach the gospel is to proclaim who Christ is in order that the unsaved might put their trust in Him, and Paul was thrilled if believers were doing that regardless of their less than laudable motives. Paul said, "What then? notwithstanding, every way, whether in pretence, or in truth, Christ is preached; and I therein do rejoice, yea, and will rejoice" (Philippians 1:18). For Paul a clear message trumped a corrupt motivation. Were these Romans who were evangelizing "even of envy and strife" (Philippians 1:15) and out "of contention, not sincerely" (Philippians 1:16) believers? Yes. Would Paul have made a glowing prediction about their personal spiritual prospects? He did not and probably would not have.

Just as he did in his epistle to the Ephesians Paul in Philippians urges believers to behave in a manner consistent with their identity as believers. Having put their trust in Christ, Christlike conduct would reflect well on the gospel which had Him as its subject: "Only let your conversation be as it becometh the gospel of Christ" (Philippians 1:27). The NASB says, "Only conduct yourselves in a manner worthy of the gospel of Christ." The way in which they were to do that was to "stand" (στήκω) and "strive" (συναθλέω).

They could stand because they were believers and they were to strive for the same gospel by which they had been saved so that others would come to put their trust in Jesus: "that ye stand fast in one spirit, with one mind striving together for the faith of the gospel" (Philippians 1:27). Paul knew it would not be easy and that they would face opposition. He told them to be, "in nothing terrified by your adversaries" (Philippians 1:28). Antagonism was to be expected and would be evidence or proof of the destiny that awaited those who opposed them: "which is to them an evident token of perdition" (Philippians 1:28).

Conversely antagonism would prove to believers that they were on the right track: "but to you of salvation, and that of God" (Philippians 1:28). "Salvation" (σωτηρία) probably refers here to deliverance from the persecution they would encounter. As Paul explained, "For unto you it is given in the behalf of Christ, not only to believe on him, but also to suffer for his sake; having the same conflict which ye saw in me, and now hear *to be* in me" [italics in KJV] (Philippians 1:29-30). For Paul, suffering because of his identification with Christ was a special privilege that would be shared by his readers. This is indicated by the word translated "it is given" (ἐχαρίσθη). The Greek verb means to "give generously" (χαρίζομαι). Louw and Nida say that χαρίζομαι means, "to give or grant graciously and generously, with the implication of good will on the part of the giver" (Johannes P. Louw and Eugene A. Nida, *Greek-English Lexicon of the New Testament Based on Semantic Domains*, 2nd ed. [New York: United Bible Societies, 2nd ed], 1989, 1:569). These words set the stage for the famous "kenosis" passage in Philippians chapter 2 with its exhortation to humility.

Without getting into specific interpretations of the nature of the Incarnation in Philippians 2:6-11, the passage includes subject matter about Jesus' identity. Jesus is identified from His preincarnate existence to the eternal state. Eventually everyone will completely submit to Him: "That at the name of Jesus every knee should bow, of *things* in heaven, and *things* in earth, and *things* under the earth; and *that* every tongue should confess that Jesus Christ *is* Lord, to the glory of God the Father" [italics in KJV] (Philippians 2:10-11). Everyone, human, angelic, or demonic, will submit to the One to whom God the Father has delegated universal authority.

Paul urges his readers to obey and imitate Christ because of who He is. They had begun to do so by obeying the command to put their trust in Jesus for their eternal destiny. Now Paul lovingly encourages them to continue the Christian walk they had begun: "Wherefore, my beloved, as ye have always obeyed, not as in my presence only, but now much more in my absence, work out your own salvation with fear and trembling" (Philippians 2:12). This "salvation" (σωτηρία), or "deliverance," was an ongoing exercise they were to be engaged in, made possible by divine energizing and enabling: "For it is God which worketh in you both to will and to do of *his* good pleasure" [italics in KJV] (Philippians 2:13).

Paul expresses the twofold motivation for his instructions. First, "that ye may be blameless and harmless, the sons of God, without rebuke, in the midst of a crooked and perverse nation, among whom ye shine as lights in the world" (Philippians 2:15). They were already children of God; now they needed to demonstrate themselves "to be blameless and harmless," as well as "above reproach." The way to do that is by "holding forth [or "holding fast" = NASB] the word of life" (Philippians 2:16). Scripture was to be their instruction manual for living life.

The second motivation Paul had for their living godly lives was for himself: "that I may rejoice in the day of Christ, that I have not run in vain, neither laboured in vain" (Philippians 2:16). Paul's future reward was contingent on his readers' present performance. This was not an idle threat or manipulation on Paul's part, nor was he pessimistic that they would not follow through. He fully expected Timothy's report about them to be positive: "But I trust in the Lord Jesus to send Timotheus shortly unto you, that I also may be of good comfort, when I know your state" (Philippians 2:19). As an anxious spiritual parent Paul awaited a good report.

Paul contrasted false teachers whom he described as "the false circumcision" (Philippians 3:2 NASB) (τὴν κατατομήν), literally "the mutilation," in contrast to, "the *true* circumcision" (Philippians 3:3 NASB, italics in NASB) (ἡ περιτομή). Paul said, "For we are the circumcision, which worship God in the spirit, and rejoice in Christ Jesus, and have no confidence in the flesh" (Philippians 3:3). For Paul the crucial difference between the two was in what or in whom trust or "confidence" (πεποιθότες perfect active participle from πείθω = "trust") was placed.

As Louw and Nida state, this means "believe in something or someone to the extent of placing reliance or trust in or on–'to rely on, to trust in, to depend on, to have (complete) confidence in, confidence, trust'" (Johannes P. Louw and Eugene A. Nida, *Greek-English Lexicon of the New Testament Based on Semantic Domains*, 2nd ed. [New York: United Bible Societies, 2nd ed], 1989, 1:376). Paul and his co-workers were among those "which worship God in the spirit, and rejoice in Christ Jesus, and have no confidence in the flesh" (Philippians 3:3). The "flesh" (σάρξ), literally a physical act in which false teachers taught that confidence was to be placed in order to be saved, was circumcision.

Paul went into detail about his having physically undergone circumcision and met many other requirements in the Law and even battled those who disagreed. And yet he wrote, "But what things were gain to me, those I counted loss for Christ" (Philippians 3:7). Paul's Jewish privileges, his piety, prior performance, and persecution of believers amounted to nothing. By putting his trust in Christ and Him alone for his eternal salvation, Paul lost everything he had trusted in and spent his life building: "Yea doubtless, and I count all things *but* loss for the excellency of the knowledge of Christ Jesus my Lord: for whom I have suffered the loss of all things, and do count them *but* dung, that I may win Christ" [italics in KJV] (Philippians 3:8). Jesus could not be an add-on to his accomplishments. He had to let go of them in order to achieve righteousness by faith: "And be found in him, not having mine own righteousness, which is of the law, but that which is through the faith of Christ, the righteousness which is of God by faith" (Philippians 3:9).

What did Paul mean in Philippians 3:11: "If by any means I might attain unto the resurrection of the dead?" Does it mean Paul included works to earn eternal life or be resurrected? No. Paul's desire as a believer was to identify in any way possible with his Savior. In life or in death he wanted to partake of "the fellowship of his sufferings, being made conformable unto his death" (Philippians 3:10). If it were possible Paul even wanted to imitate Christ's resurrection. Because that was not possible in the same way that Christ was resurrected, Paul qualified his statement with "if somehow" (εἴ πως) or "in some way."

Some have taken the Greek compound term translated "resurrection" (ἐξανάστασιν) as a reference to the rapture, an "out resurrection" from among the dead. In the context it could be contrasting the rapture with Christ's resurrection in verse 10 that uses the uncompounded term ἀνάστασις. Perhaps this was the meaning Paul intended in 1 Corinthians 6:14 where he first uses the common verb "raise" (ἐγείρω) and then its compound form "raise" (ἐξεγείρω): "And God hath both raised up the Lord, and will also raise up us by his own power." However, the variation in the same verse could be attributed to stylistic variation rather than refer to the "rapture."

Paul's conversion had resulted in union with Christ, by having placed his trust in Him who had died and been resurrected. Paul wanted to be like Christ in every way possible, and the question was whether he had accomplished that desire. For anyone assuming that he had, Paul writes, "Not as though I had already attained, either were already perfect: but I follow after, if that I may apprehend that for which also I am apprehended of Christ Jesus" (Philippians 3:12). Beyond Paul's conversion, Jesus had a mission for him that was still in progress.

The Greek verb rendered in the NASB with "perfect" (τελειόω) has a broad range of meaning which accounts for its use in Philippians 3:15 where the English translation sounds contradictory. In Philippians 3:12 Paul denied that he was "already perfect" (ἤδη τετελείωμαι) with the words, "Not as though I had already attained, either were already perfect" and in Philippians 3:15 he writes, "Let us therefore, as many as be perfect" (Ὅσοι οὖν τέλειοι, τοῦτο φρονῶμεν). The verb "perfect" (τελειόω) can refer to absolute moral perfection, maturity, or attaining a goal or purpose.

Not until death would Paul do all that Jesus wanted him to do, but he (Paul) could refer to himself and some of his readers as mature believers. He exhorted his readers and applied his instruction to himself as well: "Nevertheless, whereto we have already attained, let us walk by the same rule, let us mind the same thing" (Philippians 3:16). Reaching a plateau in the Christian life should not be a time for rest but for renewed advance.

Evidence for the Identity of Jesus in the Epistle of Colossians

Paul received a report about the church he had planted in Colossae and expressed his gratitude to God for them and interceded in prayer on their behalf: "We give thanks to God and the Father of our Lord Jesus Christ, praying always for you, since we heard of your faith in Christ Jesus, and of the love *which ye have* to all the saints" [italics in KJV] (Colossians 1:3-4). Paul's readers were believers to whom the gospel message had been preached: "For the hope which is laid up for you in heaven, whereof ye heard before in the word of the truth of the gospel" (Colossians 1:5). The gospel had been heard and understood: "Which is come unto you, as *it is* in all the world; and bringeth forth fruit, as *it doth* also in you, since the day ye heard *of it*, and knew the grace of God in truth" [italics in KJV] (Colossians 1:6). They had heard the evidence of Jesus' identity, and believing it to be true they understood their need to trust in Him and Him alone for eternal salvation, which they had done.

News of their conversion drove Paul to prayer on their behalf: "For this cause we also, since the day we heard *it*, do not cease to pray for you" [italics in KJV] (Colossians 1:9). Paul did not take their spiritual progress for granted. He was driven by a godly realism to pray for them, knowing that spiritual growth was not guaranteed. His prayer was, "that ye might be filled with the knowledge of his will in all wisdom and spiritual understanding" (Colossians 1:9). By knowing what to do they would in fact be able to do it: "That ye might walk worthy of the Lord unto all pleasing, being fruitful in every good work, and increasing in the knowledge of God" (Colossians 1:10). Paul's prayer was that the Colossian believers would follow through and live lives of obedience to God. Paul was under no delusion that their perseverance was automatic. In 1 Corinthians, in the context of the Lord's Supper, Paul expresses his understanding that a believer is capable of behaving and participating in that meal in a less than worthy manner. Paul wrote, "Therefore whoever eats the bread or drinks the cup of the Lord in an unworthy manner" (1 Corinthians 11:27). Paul harbored no illusion of believer invulnerability.

Paul interceded on behalf of the believers in Colossae for the power of God to enable and empower them; "strengthened with all might, according to his glorious power, unto all patience and longsuffering with joyfulness" (Colossians 1:11). Joy in the midst of suffering required divine strength. In spite of difficult circumstances Paul was grateful for his own eternal salvation and that of his readers: "Giving thanks unto the Father, which hath made us meet to be partakers of the inheritance of the saints in light" (Colossians 1:12). Specifically what had taken place: "Who hath delivered us from the power of darkness, and hath translated *us* into the kingdom of his dear Son: in whom we have redemption through his blood, *even* the forgiveness of sins" [italics in KJV] (Colossians 1:13-14).

Whether eternal salvation or daily sanctification is in view, the identity of Jesus is the foundation. The One in whom trust is placed to secure one's eternal destiny is the same One who enables the believer's everyday walk. Paul's passage on the identity of Christ is a hinge that ties together his readers' shared history of salvation and his instructions to them as believers. Jesus is God and the Incarnation is the instrument whereby God who could not be seen physically became visible to man: "Who is the image of the invisible God, the firstborn of every creature" (Colossians 1:15).

Using what may have been an early hymn sung by believers, Jesus' identity as the Creator is affirmed. The term "firstborn" (πρωτότοκος) should be understood as a description of Jesus' preeminence and divine superiority and not taken to mean that He had a beginning and that He Himself had been created. "For by him were all things created, that are in heaven, and that are in earth, visible and invisible, whether *they be* thrones, or dominions, or principalities, or powers: all things were created by him, and for him" [italics in KJV] (Colossians 1:16). Jesus has existed from all eternity and all that He created continues to exist because of Him: "And he is before all things, and by him all things consist" (Colossians 1:17). Jesus is the originator of the church, and believers have an obligation to obey Him: "And he is the head of the body, the church: who is the beginning, the firstborn from the dead; that in all *things* he might have the preeminence" [italics in KJV] (Colossians 1:18).

The divine nature is not deficient in Jesus in any way. He is no less God than God the Father is God: "For it pleased *the Father* that in him should all fulness dwell" [italics in KJV] (Colossians 1:19). By means of Jesus' death He provided a bridge between sinful man and a holy God: "And, having made peace through the blood of his cross, by him to reconcile all things unto himself; by him, *I say*, whether *they be* things in earth, or things in heaven" [italics in KJV] (Colossians 1:20).

To his believing audience Paul could confidently say, "and you, that were sometime alienated and enemies in *your* mind by wicked works, yet now hath he reconciled in the body of his flesh through death" [italics in KJV] (Colossians 1:21-22). The Colossian believers already possessed that reconciliation and eternal salvation because they had put their trust in Jesus. Yet this was intended to have a future outcome: "to present you holy and unblameable and unreproveable in his sight" (Colossians 1:22). While the requirement for reconciliation is a one-time trust in Jesus, for Him to stand with them in the presence of God the Father with a favorable report as "holy and unblameable and unreproveable in his sight" (Colossians 1:22), had as its prerequisite, "If ye continue in the faith grounded and settled, and *be* not moved away from the hope of the gospel, which ye have heard, *and* which was preached to every creature which is under heaven; whereof I Paul am made a minister" [italics in KJV] (Colossians 1:23).

For their sanctification the Colossian believers were to continue to hold firm to the gospel Paul had preached to them. Without that they would experience all sorts of problems. Among them would be a loss of the assurance of salvation and ineffectiveness in evangelism, both of which would have far-reaching effects on other areas of their sanctification. Paul's desire was that those who had begun by believing in Jesus would continue on and that Paul and his fellow workers would be able to stand with Jesus before God the Father with believers having followed through on their initial faith: "Whom we preach, warning every man, and teaching every man in all wisdom; that we may present every man perfect in Christ Jesus" (Colossians 1:28). The initial message was the identity of Jesus and the need to put their trust in Him for eternal salvation, and the mission was not completed until those who had accepted the message had continued on to maturity.

Just as the gospel message is about Christ and putting one's trust in Him, the path to Christian maturity continues with the conviction of who Christ is and depending on Him. Paul was concerned for the Colossian believers as well as those in Laodicea and elsewhere: "For I would that ye knew what great conflict I have for you, and *for* them at Laodicea, and *for* as many as have not seen my face in the flesh" [italics in KJV] (Colossians 2:1). Paul's concern for them was, "that their hearts might be comforted, being knit together in love, and unto all riches of the full assurance of understanding, to the acknowledgement of the mystery of God, and of the Father, and of Christ" (Colossians 2:2). Christ could supply every spiritual need they might have: "In whom are hid all the treasures of wisdom and knowledge" (Colossians 2:3). Christ alone was enough, and Paul was concerned that there were those who were attempting to convince the believers in Colossae otherwise: "And this I say, lest any man should beguile you with enticing words" (Colossians 2:4).

From what Paul heard, his readers had not succumbed to those who were attempting to subvert them: "For though I be absent in the flesh, yet am I with you in the spirit, joying and beholding your order, and the stedfastness of your faith in Christ" (Colossians 2:5). Trusting in Christ, which had happened at the time of their conversion, was key to their present progressive sanctification as well. "As ye have therefore received Christ Jesus the Lord, *so* walk ye in him" [italics in KJV] (Colossians 2:6). The NIV renders it, "just as you received Christ Jesus as Lord, continue to live in Him."

The Greek adverbial comparative conjunction "as" (ὡς) is used once in the verse at the beginning of the sentence and not in the place or manner that the NIV translates it. The NIV wording "Christ Jesus *as* Lord" is an unnecessary and unwarranted interpretive nuance. The NASB says, "as you therefore have received Christ Jesus the Lord, *so* walk in Him" [italics in NASB]. The term "as" should not be used to import a wanting, a willingness or a commitment to do works. The title "Christ Jesus the Lord" identifies the One who was received through faith (Ephesians 2:8-9). Because they had the foundation of saving faith, they could build their lives in dependence on Christ: "Rooted and built up in him, and stablished in the faith, as ye have been taught" (Colossians 2:7).

The importance Paul placed on his readers staying with what they had originally been taught is seen in the repetition of his warning not to depart from it: "Beware lest any man spoil you through philosophy and vain deceit, after the tradition of men, after the rudiments of the world, and not after Christ" (Colossians 2:8). Whatever ideas men had to offer could add nothing to what they had been offered in Christ and what they had received when they put their trust in Him alone for eternal salvation. Jesus' identity as God is affirmed: "For in him dwelleth all the fulness of the Godhead bodily. And ye are complete in him, which is the head of all principality and power" (Colossians 2:9-10). Christ is to have the final word.

Rituals are not a requirement for salvation and there is no reason for them to become the means of sanctification: "Let no man therefore judge you in meat, or in drink, or in respect of an holyday, or of the new moon, or of the sabbath *days*: which are a shadow of things to come; but the body *is* of Christ" [italics in KJV] (Colossians 2:16-17). The NASB says, "but the substance belongs to Christ." Why seek the shadow if you have the Savior? Why pursue ritual when you have reality? The tone of concern in Paul's exhortation conveys that he thought they could indeed succumb to what he warned against or that they had already done so: "Wherefore if ye be dead with Christ from the rudiments of the world, why, as though living in the world, are ye subject to ordinances, Touch not; taste not; handle not" (Colossians 2:20-21).

Believers who are obedient can anticipate that they will be rewarded in the life to come. Paul addressed slaves who probably had few incentives to work hard because they were not being paid by their masters. Paul encouraged them to recognize who their real master is and to act accordingly: "And whatsoever ye do, do *it* heartily, as to the Lord, and not unto men; knowing that of the Lord ye shall receive the reward of the inheritance: for ye serve the Lord Christ" [italics in KJV] (Colossians 3:23-24). The believing slave's incentive was not only positive but also negative: "But he that doeth wrong shall receive for the wrong which he hath done: and there is no respect of persons" (Colossians 3:25). Disobedience by Christian slaves would have negative consequences in the life to come. If Christ is the one whom slaves served, it is no less true that all believers are accountable to Him.

Evangelism was always on Paul's agenda. When he asked believers at Colossae to pray for him and his associates, it was that they would be effective evangelists: "Withal praying also for us, that God would open unto us a door of utterance, to speak the mystery of Christ, for which I am also in bonds" (Colossians 4:3). Paul was eager to communicate the gospel and was concerned about the way in which he did so. We should do likewise.

Evidence for the Identity of Jesus in 1 Thessalonians

The gospel message originally received by the Thessalonians came with several types of evidence. First was the gospel message itself which had proof of Jesus' identity: "For our gospel came not unto you in word only" (1 Thessalonians 1:5). Corroborating evidence came by means of the supernatural activity of the Holy Spirit: "but also in power, and in the Holy Ghost" (1 Thessalonians 1:5). Additional evidence was provided by the confident testimony of Paul and his co-workers: "and in much assurance" (1 Thessalonians 1:5). The message was not delivered timidly or tentatively but authoritatively. Paul's personal testimony was compelling, having seen Jesus' on the road to Damascus. The evidence of transformed lives corroborated the truth of the gospel: "as ye know what manner of men we were among you for your sake" (1 Thessalonians 1:5). Personal testimony has a legitimate place in evangelism.

The message, the messengers, and their method had all contributed to the conversion of the believers in Thessalonica. The gospel message that brought salvation also resulted in life transformation: "And ye became followers of us, and of the Lord, having received the word in much affliction, with joy of the Holy Ghost: so that ye were ensamples to all that believe in Macedonia and Achaia" (1Thessalonians 1:6-7). The changed lives of the Thessalonians added to the evidence for the validity and effectiveness of the gospel: "For from you sounded out the word of the Lord not only in Macedonia and Achaia, but also in every place your faith to God-ward is spread abroad" (1 Thessalonians 1:8).

In his missionary travels Paul encountered those who had heard of the believers in Thessalonica: "so that we need not to speak any thing. For they themselves shew of us what manner of entering in we had unto you, and how ye turned to God from idols to serve the living and true God" (1 Thessalonians 1:8-9). Those who had served idols now served God. It happened because they had put their trust in the "living and true God," that is, in Jesus Christ. Not only did they have the opportunity to serve God in the present, they now had hope for the future: "And to wait for his Son from heaven, whom he raised from the dead, *even* Jesus, which delivered us from the wrath to come" [italics in KJV] (1 Thessalonians 1:10). Past trust led to present transformation and the certain hope of a future translation to heaven. The resurrection of Jesus proved that they would not experience punishment but the eternal life that they had been promised.

Those to whom Paul addressed this epistle were believers. Not only did he say so in his introduction but also when he wrote of his desire to visit them. Paul asked them twice rhetorically, "For what *is* our hope, or joy, or crown of rejoicing? *Are* not even ye in the presence of our Lord Jesus Christ at his coming?" [italics in KJV] (1 Thessalonians 2:19). The response, "For ye are our glory and joy" (1 Thessalonians 2:20). Concerning these saved individuals Paul communicated his apprehension: "For this cause, when I could no longer forbear, I sent to know your faith, lest by some means the tempter have tempted you, and our labour be in vain" (1 Thessalonians 3:5). What Paul felt was not over a theoretical impossibility nor was it hyperbolic exaggeration on his part, but the danger he agonized over was all too real.

What a sense of relief Paul must have felt when he was told about them. Paul writes, "But now when Timotheus came from you unto us, and brought us good tidings of your faith and charity" (1 Thessalonians 3:6). Paul also says, "we were comforted over you in all our affliction and distress by your faith" (1 Thessalonians 3:7). That the

Thessalonian believers would faithfully continue what had begun at conversion was not a foregone conclusion.

This is proven to be the case by Paul's inclusion of a conditional element: "For now we live, if ye stand fast in the Lord" (1 Thessalonians 3:8). Paul spoke for himself and his fellow-workers when he asked, "For what thanks can we render to God again for you, for all the joy wherewith we joy for your sakes before our God; night and day praying exceedingly that we might see your face, and might perfect that which is lacking in your faith?" (1 Thessalonians 3:9-10). Paul commended these believers into God's hands: "And the Lord make you to increase and abound in love one toward another, and toward all *men*, even as we *do* toward you" [italics in KJV] (1 Thessalonians 3:12). If Paul's desire was granted, the result at Christ's return would be positive: "To the end he may stablish your hearts unblameable in holiness before God, even our Father, at the coming of our Lord Jesus Christ with all his saints" (1 Thessalonians 3:13).

The first epistle to the Thessalonians ends with commands to be obeyed in light of Christ's return. There are about twenty of them depending on how they are counted, and whether some of them are combined. The commands are both positive and negative. The list is not exhaustive but it is extensive. Obviously it would not be overstating the case to say that no believer always obeys all of them. For instance, what believer would lay claim to having obeyed the commands to: "Rejoice evermore" (1 Thessalonians 5:16); "pray without ceasing" (1 Thessalonians 5:17); "in every thing give thanks" (1 Thessalonians 5:18); and "abstain from all appearance of evil" (1 Thessalonians 5:22)? Does interpreting these to mean, "Do not make a habit of doing/not doing them," or "Do not be characterized as doing/not doing them," do justice to the text? To ask such questions is to answer them. Of course not.

In his conclusion to 1 Thessalonians Paul says, "And the very God of peace sanctify you wholly; and *I pray God* your whole spirit and soul and body be preserved blameless unto the coming of our Lord Jesus Christ" [italics in KJV] (1 Thessalonians 5:23). Paul employs the Greek optative mood for the two verbs in the sentence translated, "may. . .sanctify" (ἁγιάσαι), and "be preserved" (ἁγιάσαι). Wallace notes that New Testament writers use the optative sparingly: "There are less than 70 optatives in the entire NT" (Daniel Wallace, *Greek Grammar beyond the Basics*, [Grand Rapids: Zondervan, 1996], 480). Wallace describes the optative mood: "the optative mood is the mood used when a speaker wishes to portray an action as *possible*. . .It. . .may be used to appeal to the volition. . .the optative is one of the potential or oblique moods" (ibid., italics in original). Wallace uses this verse as an example of a "voluntative optative" in which "There is every likelihood that the author expected such blessings for his audience" (ibid., 483). This verse does not support the position of the inevitability of continual improvement in progressive sanctification (sanctification that takes place in the life of the believer after his conversion).

Wallace observes that the use of the optative mood by Hellenistic writers (of which the New Testament writers are included) is significant because that mood was being absorbed into the subjunctive mood as the Greek language was shifting away from the classical Attic Greek. Wallace emphasizes the significance of his observation with his use of italics and bold print, *"When one morpho-syntactic feature is becoming absorbed by another in Hellenistic Greek and when a Hellenistic author uses the **rarer** form, he normally does so consciously and with understanding"* (ibid., 480). Paul's use of the oblique optative mood to indicate potentiality and not certainty must be taken seriously. Paul desired that his readers' sanctification would progress satisfactorily but was not making a dogmatic statement about its inevitability.

As Wallace states about the use of the voluntative optative in the language of prayer:

> The prayers offered to him [God] depend on his sovereignty and goodness. Thus, although the *form* of much prayer language in the NT has the tinge of remote possibility, when it is offered to God. . .its *meaning* often moves in the realm of expectation. If uncertainty is part of the package, it is not due to questions of God's ability, but simply to the petitioner's humility before the transcendent one (italics in original) (ibid., 481).

Paul's words in 1 Thessalonians 5:23 are in the form of a prayer. It is presumptive for any believer, even the apostle who wrote these words, to pray and expect or demand that God act. Paul's use of the optative mood is indicative that his words are not to be interpreted in such a fashion. A biblical understanding of God's sovereignty does not dictate that it must always be exercised in a deterministic fashion to avoid doing violence to His sovereignty. In fact to do so is to circumscribe His sovereignty.

Evidence for the Identity of Jesus in 2 Thessalonians

Trust in Jesus at the point in time when conversion occurs is an "all or nothing" occurrence, you either do or you do not trust in Jesus and Him alone for your eternal destiny. Dependence on Jesus subsequent to that in the process of progressive sanctification can and should increase. New situations and circumstances continue to arise in which trust in Jesus can be exercised. Paul included that idea in his expression of gratitude to God for the progress that the Thessalonian believers were making: "We are bound to thank God always for you, brethren, as it is meet, because that your faith groweth exceedingly, and the charity of every one of you all toward each other aboundeth" (2 Thessalonians 1:3). The growth of their faith was taking place while they were experiencing tremendous hardship: "So that we ourselves glory in you in the churches of God for your patience and faith in all your persecutions and tribulations that ye endure" (2 Thessalonians 1:4).

While the faithful perseverance of the Thessalonian believers did not contribute in any way to their eternal salvation, it would count for something in the kingdom of God which was to come: *"Which is* a manifest token of the righteous judgment of God, that ye may be counted worthy of the kingdom of God, for which ye also suffer" [italics in KJV] (2 Thessalonians 1:5). The difficulties they were experiencing were proof of the legitimacy of God's future action when He would "turn the tables" and their afflicters would be on the receiving end of divine judgment: "Seeing *it is* a righteous thing with

God to recompense tribulation to them that trouble you; and to you who are troubled rest with us, when the Lord Jesus shall be revealed from heaven with his mighty angels" [italics in KJV] (2 Thessalonians 1:6-7).

Paul identifies those who will be subject to that judgment: "taking vengeance on them that know not God, and that obey not the gospel of our Lord Jesus Christ" (2 Thessalonians 1:8). Leaving no doubt that these individuals are unsaved Paul adds, "who shall be punished with everlasting destruction from the presence of the Lord, and from the glory of his power" (2 Thessalonians 1:9). The timing of the defeat of the unsaved will coincide with the deliverance of the saved: "When he shall come to be glorified in his saints, and to be admired in all them that believe (because our testimony among you was believed) in that day" [parenthesis in KJV] (2 Thessalonians 1:10).

Paul includes what is required for one to be counted among those who will not face judgment. Paul's readers were included "in all them that believe (because our testimony among you was believed)" [parenthesis in KJV]. (2 Thessalonians 1:10). The testimony of Paul and his co-workers he refers to was the gospel. It was testimony about who Jesus is so that trust could be placed in Him and Him alone for their eternal destiny. Paul's words about "believe" (πιστεύω), the sole requirement for eternal salvation, are contextually juxtaposed with what the unsaved had failed to do: "on them that know not God, and that obey not the gospel of our Lord Jesus Christ" (2 Thessalonians 1:8). For Paul, to "obey the gospel" (ὑπακούουσιν τῷ εὐαγγελίῳ) meant to do what the gospel message proclaimed was necessary to do to receive eternal salvation, which was to believe who Jesus is identified to be and place one's trust in Him (cf. Rom. 1:5). Paul's use of the verb "obey" (ὑπακούω) should not be used as an interpretive wedge with which to introduce works or a willingness or commitment to do them as a requirement for salvation.

The biblical relationship of faith and works and the exclusion of the latter in the acquisition of eternal salvation is made clear by Paul. He is also clear about the inclusion of both faith and works in progressive sanctification. After stating and repeating that their past believing (πιστεύω = both aorist tenses) was the only requirement for his readers' participation in a glorious future (2 Thessalonians 1:10), Paul's prayer on their behalf for the present was, "that our God would count you worthy of *this* calling, and fulfil all the good pleasure of *his* goodness, and the work of faith with power" [italics in KJV] (2 Thessalonians 1:11). Paul did not conflate or confuse work and faith when it came to conversion but he did combine them in his instructions for Christian living. Believers could engage in "the work of faith with power" (2 Thessalonians 1:11), activity enabled by dependence on God.

Faith plus work in salvation fails to bring glory to God, and in fact does the opposite because it is a denial of the biblical gospel. On the other hand faith plus works in sanctification glorifies God. Paul prayed to that end, "that the name of our Lord Jesus Christ may be glorified in you, and ye in him, according to the grace of our God and the Lord Jesus Christ" (2 Thessalonians 1:12).

Paul described the coming of "that Wicked" ("that lawless one" = NASB) (2 Thessalonians 2:8) (ὁ ἄνομος), a reference to the Antichrist: "And then shall that Wicked be revealed, whom the Lord shall consume with the spirit of his mouth, and shall destroy with the brightness of his coming" (2 Thessalonians 2:8). The Antichrist will try to duplicate the miraculous signs that proved Jesus' identity in order to deceive people into thinking he is the Messiah: "And with all deceivableness of unrighteousness in them that perish; because they received not the love of the truth, that they might be saved" (2 Thessalonians 2:10). The truth that the Antichrist and his followers will hate instead of love is that of the identity of Jesus. Paul clearly states what they lacked. Rejection replaced reception of the truth. If they accept the truth about who Jesus is and put their trust in Him, they will be saved but they will not. Instead they will accept a counterfeit Christ, the Antichrist, and believe in him.

Because of their rejection of Jesus: "And for this cause God shall send them strong delusion, that they should believe a lie" (2 Thessalonians 2:11). "The lie" (τῷ ψεύδει), translated in the NASB with "what is false," is that the Antichrist is the messiah, rather than the true Messiah being Jesus. The divinely ordained consequence of that will be: "That they all might be damned who believed not the truth, but had pleasure in unrighteousness" (2 Thessalonians 2:12).

In contrast to the deserved destruction that awaits the future Antichrist and his followers Thessalonian believers could expect deliverance (σωτηρία). Paul's context was again that of gratitude to God for them: "But we are bound to give thanks alway to God for you, brethren beloved of the Lord, because God hath from the beginning chosen you to salvation through sanctification of the Spirit and belief of the truth" (2 Thessalonians 2:13). The "salvation" (σωτηρία) could be a reference either to conversion or subsequent physical and/or spiritual deliverance. The noun translated "sanctification" (ἁγιασμός) that means "setting apart," "consecration," or "dedication," could refer to either their saved position or their practical sanctification. What it does not mean is that eternal salvation is acquired by means of progressive sanctification.

Paul was encouraging his readers to continue in their present progressive sanctification, made possible by their past conversion. The latter Paul was certain about, and regarding the former he had confidence that they would continue: "And we have confidence in the Lord touching you, that ye both do and will do the things which we command you" (2 Thessalonians 3:4). The NASB says, "And we have confidence in the Lord concerning you, that you are doing and will *continue to* do what we command" [italics in NASB]. Their past performance gave Paul every reason to think that they would follow through in the future. Paul was not speaking prophetically that the believers in Thessalonica would definitely persevere. And he was not making an ironclad, universally applicable statement on perseverance.

In the form of a prayer Paul is expressing his expectation that God will guide them: "And the Lord direct your hearts into the love of God, and into the patient waiting for Christ" (2 Thessalonians 3:5). The NASB says, "And may the Lord direct your hearts into the love of God and into the steadfastness of Christ." With the Greek optative mood translated "may. . .direct" (κατευθύναι) Paul indicates that there is a volitional element involved. Believers have a choice whether they will follow divine guidance or reject it. God would not force his will on the Thessalonian believers nor was Paul promising them "patient waiting" or "steadfastness" (ὑπομονή).

Proof that all believers would not take what Paul commanded to heart, and that such was not just a theoretical but an actual possibility, is found in the immediate context. In stern words of warning Paul writes, "Now we command you, brethren, in the name of our Lord Jesus Christ, that ye withdraw yourselves from every brother that walketh disorderly, and not after the tradition which he received of us" (2 Thessalonians 3:6). Perhaps referring to the same individuals Paul added, "For we hear that there are some which walk among you disorderly, working not at all, but are busybodies" (2 Thessalonians 3:11).

Instead of following their negative example believers were exhorted, "but ye, brethren, be not weary in well doing" (2 Thessalonians 3:13). These words cannot be taken to mean that no one who is a believer can ever do such a thing because Paul adds, "and if any man obey not our word by this epistle, note that man, and have no company with him, that he may be ashamed" (2 Thessalonians 3:14). The saved can experience shame and being excluded by other believers can help produce that shame. Paul's final words on the subject should clinch the conclusion that a believer is in view: "Yet count *him* not as an enemy, but admonish *him* as a brother" [italics in KJV] (2 Thessalonians 3:15). Wayward Christians are to be dealt with in a Christlike way.

Evidence for the Identity of Jesus in 1 Timothy

Paul's introduction tells Timothy his purpose for having him stay on at Ephesus: "As I besought thee to abide still at Ephesus, when I went into Macedonia, that thou mightest charge some that they teach no other doctrine, neither give heed to fables and endless genealogies, which minister questions, rather than godly edifying which is in faith: *so do*" [italics in KJV] (1 Timothy 1:3-4). The NASB translates 1 Timothy 1:4, "nor pay attention to myths and endless genealogies, which give rise to mere speculation rather than *furthering* the administration of God which is by faith" [italics in NASB]. At the beginning of the church, "faith," its central tenet, was being undermined. "Faith" is the key to eternal salvation and progressive sanctification.

Paul pejoratively referred to the heretical activity with the terms, "to teach other doctrines" (ἑτεροδιδασκαλεῖν), "fables" (μύθοις), and "endless genealogies" (γενεαλογίαις ἀπεράντοις). For some these had become the building blocks for theological fantasy: "which give rise to mere speculation" (1 Timothy 1:4 NASB). On the other hand, faith is the foundation and guiding principle of biblical orthodoxy. Paul summed up the Christian message, mission, and method as "the administration of God which is by faith" (1 Timothy 1:4 NASB) (ἡ οἰκονομίαν θεοῦ τὴν ἐν πίστει).

In the first century a relentless assault began against faith and faith alone as the sole requirement for eternal salvation that continues to this day. Down through history human effort has been packaged and repackaged, qualified and modified, but the end result has been the same as it was in Paul's day when the Law was used to insert works as a requirement for eternal life. Paul describes the heretical activity going on in his day: "From which some having swerved have turned aside unto vain jangling; desiring to be teachers of the law; understanding neither what they say, nor whereof they affirm" (1 Timothy 1:6-7). The NASB says, "For some men, straying from these things, have turned aside to fruitless discussion, wanting to be teachers of the Law, even though they do not understand either what they are saying or the matters about which they make confident assertions." Dogmatism did not then and will not now ultimately succeed in displacing biblical doctrine. Sanguine assertions do not guarantee scriptural authenticity.

The Law, in and of itself, is not bad but the misuse of it is. Paul says, "But we know that the law *is* good, if a man use it lawfully" [italics in KJV] (1 Timothy 1:8). What is good and true can be used improperly. That is what makes it so insidious. The most dangerous heresies use biblical ingredients. The Law has a proper place in the preaching of the gospel.

Paul explains the Law's proper role. The Law serves no purpose for perfect people: "Knowing this, that the law is not made for a righteous man" (1 Timothy 1:9). Jesus said something slightly different with a similar intent, "They that be whole need not a physician, but they that are sick" (Matthew 9:12 cf. Mark 2:17; Luke 5:31). The Law is not needed for perfect people who already meet its demands. It applies to the imperfect, which is everyone. Paul goes through a litany of the worst offenders, to show the Law's intended use. Those to whom the Law applies are: "the lawless and disobedient, for the ungodly and for sinners, for unholy and profane, for murderers of fathers and murderers of mothers, for manslayers, for whoremongers, for them that defile themselves with mankind, for menstealers, for liars, for perjured persons, and if there be any other thing that is contrary to sound doctrine" (1 Timothy 1:9-10). From the worst sinners to the least the Law is intended to indict everyone.

Everyone needs to come to terms with their failure to meet the righteous demands of a holy God. The Jewish people had those demands spelled out for them in the Law. An acknowledgement of one's sinfulness and inability to do anything about sin to earn entrance into heaven is a prerequisite to putting faith in Jesus. Those who are self-righteous do not need (or do not think they need) a Savior from sin, but they do. That is why Paul ends his long sentence with the words, "according to the glorious gospel of the blessed God, which was committed to my trust" (1 Timothy 1:11) (κατὰ τὸ εὐαγγέλιον τῆς δόξης τοῦ μακαρίου θεοῦ, ὃ ἐπιστεύθην ἐγώ). The gospel is the good news that covers the bad news. If you do not believe the bad news about sin, you will not believe the good news about the One who died to solve the sin problem.

Paul offers himself as an example. He thanks Jesus that in spite of his past, Jesus has given him his present ministry: "I thank Christ Jesus our Lord, who hath enabled me, for that he counted me faithful, putting me into the ministry; who was before a blasphemer, and a persecutor, and injurious" (1 Timothy 1:12-13). Paul considered his own unsaved behavior egregious. However, sinful behavior is to be expected of unbelievers: "but I obtained mercy, because I did *it* ignorantly in unbelief" [italics in KJV] (1 Timothy 1:13). Before coming to a knowledge and acceptance of the truth of the gospel unbelievers can be characterized as "ignorant" (ἀγνοῶν). Salvation removes the blinders of spiritual ignorance.

The One without whom eternal salvation would be impossible is Jesus: "This *is* a faithful saying, and worthy of all acceptation, that Christ Jesus came into the world to save sinners" [italics in KJV] (1 Timothy 1:15). Jesus' identity, informed by the Incarnation, His sacrificial death for sinners, and His resurrection all constitute "faithful" or "trustworthy" (πιστός) information. The gospel that tells who Jesus is and that sinners, no matter how bad they are, can place their trust in Him for eternal life, can be relied on. Paul viewed himself as "Exhibit A," proof of the truthfulness of the evidence: "Howbeit for this cause I obtained mercy, that in me first Jesus Christ might shew forth all longsuffering, for a pattern to them which should hereafter believe on him to life everlasting" (1 Timothy 1:16). What was true for Paul is true of all sinners. Those who place their trust in Jesus, "believe on Him" (πιστεύειν ἐπ' αὐτῷ) "to life everlasting" (εἰς ζωὴν αἰώνιον), will have eternal life freely given to them.

Paul's personal words to Timothy at the beginning of this epistle end with a command and a warning. The command is placed in the context of prior prophecies concerning Timothy, of which we have no additional information: "This charge I commit unto thee, son Timothy, according to the prophecies which went before on thee, that thou by them mightest war a good warfare" (1 Timothy 1:18). Paul gives Timothy examples of those who have failed as a warning: "Holding faith, and a good conscience; which some having put away concerning faith have made shipwreck: of whom is Hymenaeus and Alexander" (1 Timothy 1:19-20). Perhaps applying apostolic authority Paul said about them, "whom I have delivered unto Satan" (1 Timothy 1:20). The stated purpose for that severe consequence was "that they may learn not to blaspheme" (1 Timothy 1:20).

Although the language resembles that of restoring a believer by discipline, these two individuals may not have been saved. Many Bible teachers have strong opinions whether they were or were not saved. Perhaps in Paul's day there was also debate about their spiritual status, a controversy that the author did not intend to incite nor a question that he answered. Paul mentions Hymenaeus again in his second letter to Timothy. Perhaps because debate over Hymanaeus's saved status had erupted, Paul in 2 Timothy 2:19 wrote the words, "Nevertheless the foundation of God standeth sure, having this seal, The Lord knoweth them that are his. And, Let every one that nameth the name of Christ depart from iniquity." Paul's intent was not to draw theological battle lines but to inspire holy living.

For those who suppose that Hymenaeus and Alexander could not have been "delivered unto Satan" (1 Timothy 1:20) if they had been believers, one need only look at the example of Job in the Old Testament. God told Satan concerning Job, "Behold, all that he hath *is* in thy power; only upon himself put not forth thine hand" [italics in KJV]

(Job 1:12). A second time God basically delivered Job to Satan: "And the Lord said unto Satan, Behold, he *is* in thine hand; but save his life" [italics in KJV] (Job 2:6). If Job who "was perfect and upright, and one that feared God, and eschewed evil" (Job 1:1) could have this happen to him, how can it be held that it could never happen to a believer? To teach that the saved cannot be disciplined by being "delivered unto Satan" (1 Timothy 1:20) is to offer an unbiblical assurance.

The apostle Paul's evangelistic mindset is apparent in his words about prayer. He urged prayer on behalf of everyone and particularly those in leadership positions: "I exhort therefore, that, first of all, supplications, prayers, intercessions, *and* giving of thanks, be made for all men; For kings, and *for* all that are in authority" [italics in KJV] (1 Timothy 2:1-2). Specifically the purpose of prayer for them was "that we may lead a quiet and peaceable life in all godliness and honesty" (1 Timothy 2:2). Contextually the request is for favorable actions and edicts from rulers, not so that believers could lead comfortable and contented lives, but that there would be a climate conducive to evangelism: "For this *is* good and acceptable in the sight of God our Saviour; who will have all men to be saved, and to come unto the knowledge of the truth" [italics in KJV] (1 Timothy 2:3-4).

The specific truth that Paul was concerned about communicating was the gospel; the identity of Jesus, who was the One in whom trust was to be placed: "For *there is* one God, and one mediator between God and men, the man Christ Jesus; who gave himself a ransom for all, to be testified in due time" [italics in KJV] (1 Timothy 2:5-6). The NASB translation indicates that Jesus Himself is "the testimony *borne* at the proper time" [italics in NASB] (1 Timothy 2:6). Jesus Himself is the evidence, or "testimony" (μαρτύριον), who by word and deed proved who He is. Paul, in turn, having been an eyewitness to what he had seen and heard concerning who Jesus is, corroborated that evidence and was commissioned to communicate it: "Whereunto I am ordained a preacher, and an apostle, (I speak the truth in Christ, *and* lie not;) a teacher of the Gentiles in faith and verity" [parenthesis and italics in KJV] (1 Timothy 2:7). Paul was a living example and evidence of the evangelistic message he proclaimed.

Instructions about the conduct of believers are placed in the context of the identity of Jesus. Paul stated his purpose for writing Timothy in these words: "that thou mayest know how thou oughtest to behave thyself in the house of God, which is the church of the living God, the pillar and ground of the truth" (1 Timothy 3:15). The church was to be the repository of the truth, to guard and conserve it without corruption. Truth consisted primarily of information about the identity of Jesus who was the foundation of the New Testament church. Paul mentions what may well be an early creed recited corporately by the church. He introduces it with the words, "And without controversy great is the mystery of godliness" (1 Timothy 3:16). The NASB says, "And by common confession great is the mystery of godliness."

The confession or creed is about Christ: "God was manifest in the flesh, justified in the Spirit, seen of angels, preached unto the Gentiles, believed on in the world, received up into glory" (1 Timothy 3:16). The creed brings together the identity of Jesus as the

Person whom heaven and earth acknowledges, the subject and object of the gospel message preached, and the One in whom trust is to be placed for eternal life.

As discussed earlier, the Greek verb "save" (σῴζω) many times means to "deliver" from physical peril, death, or present circumstances. Similarly the same is true for the noun translated "Savior" (σωτήρ), which does not always have the specialized meaning of the One who delivers from eternal condemnation, but can generically refer to one who rescues. Such is the case in 1 Timothy 4:10: "we trust in the living God, who is the Saviour of all men, specially of those that believe." What one is delivered from must be determined contextually. Here Paul uses the term "savior" or "rescuer" in the sense of general providence experienced by the unsaved as well as the saved, with the addition of what is extended exclusively to the latter.

The substantival participle of the verb "believe" or "trust" (πιστεύω) is frequently used in the New Testament as a title for Christians. Here the substantival use of the verb's derivative adjective "believer" (πιστός) is used as a title to refer to Christian converts. The adjective is used by Paul in the same way in 1 Timothy 4:12. The NASB says: "Let no one look down on your youthfulness, but *rather* in speech, conduct, love, faith *and* purity, show yourself an example of those who believe" [italics in NASB]. The KJV explicitly translates the words "of those who believe" (τῶν πιστῶν) as a title with "of the believers."

The generic, rather than the specialized, meaning of eternal salvation, for the Greek verb to "save" or "rescue" (σῴζω) is found in Paul's instruction in 1 Timothy 4:16: "Take heed unto thyself, and unto the doctrine; continue in them: for in doing this thou shalt both save thyself, and them that hear thee." Although Paul uses the verb, the NASB version makes it appear to be a noun, "you will insure salvation." The KJV represents the Greek verb and reflexive pronoun of the original with "save thyself" (σεαυτὸν σώσεις). This verse does not teach that perseverance is a prerequisite for eternal salvation, but rather that continuing in what Paul taught would result in a present deliverance, both physical and/or spiritual.

The church at Ephesus may have had an unusually large contingent of widows. Paul gave specific instructions to Timothy regarding their conduct and care. Contextually it is evident that the widows were believers. Paul described godly widows in these words: "Now she that is a widow indeed, and desolate, trusteth in God, and continueth in supplications and prayers night and day" (1 Timothy 5:5). Conversely Paul indicates the possibility of the existence of widows who led less than godly lives: "But she that liveth in pleasure is dead while she liveth" (1 Timothy 5:6). These latter widows, described as "the living dead," although eternally saved, were a poor example and testimony of what a believer was to be. So Paul saw the need to give further instructions: "And these things give in charge, that they may be blameless" (1 Timothy 5:7). A good reputation was something to be cultivated and not taken for granted.

The desperate and destitute condition of many widows in the first century was all too common, and it was a disgrace if believers did not do something to relieve their situation, especially if they were living in a believer's home: "But if any provide not for his own, and specially for those of his own house, he hath denied the faith, and is worse than an infidel" (1 Timothy 5:8). Regrettably a believer can act or fail to act in such a manner that he can be characterized by the words, "he hath denied the faith" (1 Timothy 5:8), and "is worse than an infidel [or "unbeliever" = NASB]" (1 Timothy 5:8). The text does not say, "appears to be worse" or "is almost worse" but "worse." One can sense that Paul was incensed that such a situation would even exist, but he did not deny the possibility. Regarding practical sanctification this is an expression of Pauline realism.

If a widow had no household member to provide for her, or her believing household played the part of an unbeliever, the church was to step in and help her: "Let not a widow be taken into the number under threescore years old, having been the wife of one man" (1 Timothy 5:9). Paul was concerned that the church's program for the assistance of widows be administered properly. He was concerned that a program with good intentions could be used by the devil for his own nefarious purposes: "give none occasion to the adversary to speak reproachfully. For some are already turned aside after Satan" (1 Timothy 5:14-15). There is no textual or contextual indication that these individuals who "turned aside after Satan" (ἐξετράπησαν ὀπίσω τοῦ σατανᾶ) were anything other than believers. Such was the sad albeit regrettable realistic possibility.

Near the end of Paul's first epistle to Timothy is a warning about money. Contentment is the cure for coveting: "And having food and raiment let us be therewith content" (1 Timothy 6:8). The alternative to contentment can have dire consequences: "But they that will be rich fall into temptation and a snare, and *into* many foolish and hurtful lusts, which drown men in destruction and perdition" [italics in KJV] (1 Timothy 6:9). The reason why this is so is that "the love of money is the root of all evil" (1 Timothy 6:10). The results may not be confined to physical consequences but can include spiritual ones as well: "which while some coveted after, they have erred from the faith, and pierced themselves through with many sorrows" (1 Timothy 6:10). The thought of the emotional pain of being pierced with spiritual pangs is heartrending. Paul specifically addressed this warning to Timothy, "But thou, O man of God, flee these things" (1 Timothy 6:11). Paul did not want Timothy to be among those believers who "have erred from the faith" (1 Timothy 6:10). The denials by some present-day Bible teachers notwithstanding, the apostle Paul considered such a possibility a reality.

Paul mentions positive things for Timothy to pursue: "follow after righteousness, godliness, faith, love, patience, meekness" (1 Timothy 6:11). In the context of sanctification "faith" (πίστις) is something to "pursue" (διώκω) and can be "erred from" ("wandered away from" = NASB) (ἀποπλανάω) or one can be "lead astray" from. "Patience" or ("perseverance" = NASB) (ὑπομονή) also needs to be pursued and is not automatic; it is not inevitable. "Faith" (πίστις) was not only something Timothy was to "follow after" or ("pursue" = NASB) (διώκω), it was also worth fighting for and was to be contended for: "Fight the good fight of faith, lay hold on eternal life, whereunto thou art also called, and hast professed a good profession before many witnesses" (1 Timothy 6:12). Timothy's contending for "the faith" (τῆς πίστεως) would require work, the exertion of effort. His initial exercise of saving faith excluded work as a requirement or it would not have resulted in eternal salvation. As a believer Timothy could appropriate those things that had eternal significance. In that way he would "lay hold on eternal life" (1 Timothy 6:12).

Paul was serious about Timothy obeying his instructions: "I give thee charge in the sight of God, who quickeneth all things, and *before* Christ Jesus, who before Pontius Pilate witnessed a good confession; that thou keep *this* commandment without spot, unrebukeable" [italics in KJV] (1 Timothy 6:13-14). The serious nature of the matter is conveyed by mentioning that it is commanded in the sight of the creator God and that of His Son Jesus who led an exemplary life, whom Pilate exonerated while allowing Him to be executed. Timothy's obedience to the commands was to continue "until the appearing of our Lord Jesus Christ" (1 Timothy 6:14). If Timothy failed to persevere, he would not be "without spot, unrebukeable" (1 Timothy 6:14).

While Paul probably had confidence in Timothy that he would persevere, or he would not have placed him in the position of responsibility that he had, he was not guaranteeing Timothy's spiritual success. It was a relative confidence. Paul did express his absolute confidence in Jesus' return: "the appearing of our Lord Jesus Christ: which in his times he shall shew, *who is* the blessed and only Potentate, the King of kings, and Lord of lords" [italics in KJV] (1 Timothy 6:14-15).

For Timothy, as is true for every believer in Jesus, His glorious return will be a time for either regret or reward. Paul's expectation that Timothy's perseverance would continue until Jesus' return is evidence that Paul believed in his Savior's imminent return. Believers are promised rewards for faithful service but are not each given the promise that they will in fact persevere. The guarantee of reward for steadfastness and faithful service for those who meet the criteria is ironclad because of who God is: "the blessed and only Potentate, the King of kings, and Lord of lords; who only hath immortality, dwelling in the light which no man can approach unto" (1 Timothy 6:15-16). The Person of the Godhead referred to here is probably God the Father, rather than Jesus the Son. Syntactically and grammatically either is possible. However, the statement, "whom no man hath seen, nor can see" (1 Timothy 6:16) is difficult, if not impossible, to reconcile with Jesus' Incarnation.

The epistle of 1 Timothy ends with a final word of warning, "O Timothy, keep that which is committed to thy trust, avoiding profane *and* vain babblings, and oppositions of science falsely so called" [italics in KJV] (1 Timothy 6:20). Again, the seriousness of the warning is conveyed by the mention of those who had failed: "Which some professing have erred concerning the faith" (1 Timothy 6:21). Paul and Christ were to be imitated. Those who were not to be imitated were real individuals. Paul did not add, "By the way, Timothy, you could never do that." To have done so, even implicitly would have emasculated the exhortation. Negative examples are normally presented to prevent them from being followed. To hold that there is an inherent impossibility in the imitation of a negative example reduces a warning to an inanity.

Chapter 10

Evidence for the Identity of Jesus in the Epistles:
Part 2 – 2 Timothy through Jude

Instructions in Identity

Paul's epistles continue and are followed by those of other authors. Paul and his fellow epistle writers' experience is brought to bear on subjects of significance for the nascent New Testament church. Many of the issues are in response to problems or circumstances that have come to the authors' attention. The New Testament church in many ways did not differ much from present-day congregations. The inspired instructions and doctrinal information given by the authors can be applied to Christian communities in the twenty-first century.

Evidence for the Identity of Jesus in 2 Timothy

This epistle is so similar to 1 Timothy that even those who question Pauline authorship view them as having the same author. The personal relationship that Paul had with Timothy is evident throughout. Second Timothy takes on special significance since it may well be the last epistle Paul wrote. Paul hoped that Timothy would be able to visit him so that he could see him one last time (2 Timothy 4:9). Realizing that his life was drawing to a close Paul writes as a man who is "tying up loose ends." In spite of the sense of melancholy that a farewell communication evokes, a sweetly mellow spiritual maturity pervades the epistle.

In 2 Timothy 1:9 Paul uses the verb "save" (σῴζω) to refer to a believer's eternal salvation that was planned and designed by God in eternity past: "Who hath saved us, and called *us* with an holy calling, not according to our works, but according to his own purpose and grace, which was given us in Christ Jesus before the world began" [italics in KJV]. The manner "according to" (κατὰ) or "in accordance with" whereby salvation was not to be accomplished was human "works" (ἔργα). That is contrasted with the manner in which salvation is accomplished, namely, God's "purpose and grace" (πρόθεσιν καὶ χάριν). The exclusion of "works" (ἔργα) from salvation's requirement was not a Pauline invention but God's intention. Implementation was by "grace" (χάρις) that left no room for "works" (ἔργα).

The One through whom salvation would be accomplished is Jesus. And the gospel is the vehicle used by God to inform people about Him and the necessity of trusting in Him: "But is now made manifest by the appearing of our Saviour Jesus Christ, who hath abolished death, and hath brought life and immortality to light through the gospel" (2 Timothy 1:10). "The gospel" (τοῦ εὐαγγελίου) provided the core curriculum and preaching of Paul. It was the mandate of his mission: "Whereunto I am appointed a preacher, and an apostle, and a teacher of the Gentiles" (2 Timothy 1:11).

Paul personally experienced and endured the persecution and humiliation of which he spoke: "For the which cause I also suffer these things: nevertheless I am not ashamed: for I know whom I have believed, and am persuaded that he is able to keep that which I have committed unto him against that day" (2 Timothy 1:12). Paul was "persuaded" or "convinced" (πέπεισμαι perfect passive indicative of πείθω = "convinced," "persuaded," or "assured") of the identity of the One in whom he had placed his trust "for I know whom I have believed" (οἶδα γὰρ ᾧ πεπίστευκα), the One whom he was relying on for his eternal salvation.

Paul's confidence in the security of his eternal destiny rested on his conviction of the reliability of Jesus: "he is able to keep" (δυνατός ἐστιν. . .φυλάξαι). What Paul had entrusted Jesus to guard was his eternal destiny. On "that day" (ἐκείνην τὴν ἡμέραν) what Paul preached would be vindicated; it was all worthwhile. He would enter into a new phase of eternal life because he had placed his trust in Jesus, and in Him alone for his eternal salvation. All who heard the gospel Paul preached would experience the same thing if they put their trust in Jesus as well.

Paul had entrusted his eternal destiny to Jesus, the One whom the gospel identified. Paul and his co-workers were in turn entrusted with that gospel that spoke of Him. Paul instructed Timothy to maintain the integrity of the gospel: "That good thing which was committed unto thee keep by the Holy Ghost which dwelleth in us" (2 Timothy 1:14). If the gospel was compromised, it would not lead to conversion.

Every generation is entrusted with the "treasure," literally "the good deposit" (τὴν καλὴν παραθήκην) of the gospel. Paul passed it on to Timothy, who was personally responsible for it: "Thou therefore, my son, be strong in the grace that is in Christ Jesus" (2 Timothy 2:1). The chain of custody was to remain unbroken as Timothy passed the gospel on to the next generation of believers: "And the things that thou hast heard of me among many witnesses, the same commit thou to faithful men, who shall be able to teach others also" (2 Timothy 2:2). As in a relay race, a proper passing of the baton of the gospel was crucial.

Some might argue that Paul was including here much more than the gospel. That may very well be true. Paul preached and taught "all the counsel of God" (Acts 20:27) (πᾶσαν τὴν βουλὴν τοῦ θεοῦ) that included truth related to progressive sanctification as well as eternal salvation. Teaching both, without confusing or conflating them, is the task of the Christian community. Paul uses three illustrations, that of the soldier, athlete, and farmer to get his point across. He says this about the athlete: "And if a man also strive for masteries, *yet* is he not crowned, except he strive lawfully" [italics in KJV] (2 Timothy 2:5). The NASB says, "And also if anyone competes as an athlete, he does not win the prize unless he competes according to the rules."

In American football, touchdowns are not scored by athletes who run with or catch the ball out of bounds. Violation of a rule results in a penalty, not validation, by means of yards or points. In communicating the gospel linguistic norms are not to be ignored. The task of biblical interpretation may not be easy but help is available: "Consider what I say; and the Lord give thee understanding in all things" (2 Timothy 2:7). The place to start is with the basics, the identity of Jesus found in the gospel message: "Remember that Jesus Christ of the seed of David was raised from the dead according to my gospel" (2 Timothy 2:8). Jesus, and preaching the gospel that was about Him, was what kept Paul going: "Therefore I endure all things for the elect's sakes, that they may also obtain the salvation which is in Christ Jesus with eternal glory" (2 Timothy 2:10).

Paul's entire message could be summarized in what was possibly a creed or hymn familiar to the readers of the epistle. Paul gave it his personal imprimatur, saying, "*It is a faithful saying*" [italics in KJV] (2 Timothy 2:11) (πιστὸς ὁ λόγος). There are four conditional sentences in 2 Timothy 2:11-13 that are all first-class conditional sentences in Greek. For the sake of argument Paul assumes to be true the first part of each sentence (the protasis). The first sentence is the only one of the four that refers to something that had taken place in the past, as indicated with the use of the aorist tense, "we be dead" ("we died with" = NASB) (συναπεθάνομεν). Paul included himself and Timothy, and his Christian readers: "For if we died with Him" (2 Timothy 2:11).

This is figurative language. In Colossians 2:20 is a similar use of the aorist tense, "If ye be dead with Christ" (Εἰ ἀπεθάνετε σὺν Χριστῷ) that refers to the readers' past conversion. The believer did not literally physically die when Jesus did at the time of the crucifixion, but rather it is a figurative reference to conversion. Paul's choice of the figure of death with Jesus for conversion was obviously not random, but central to the gospel, an event that secured man's eternal salvation and identified Jesus. This is a shorthand figurative reference for what believers had done; they had put their trust in the One who had died in their place. If that condition was met, and Paul assumed for the sake of argument that it had, then the result would be that in the future, as indicated with the future tense, "we shall also live with *him*" [italics in KJV] (2 Timothy 2:11). Eternal life with Jesus is assured for those who have put their trust in Him.

The second conditional sentence begins the conditional element (protasis) with the Greek present tense "if we suffer" ("if we endure" = NASB) (2 Timothy 2:12) (εἰ ὑπομένομεν). Paul, Timothy, and the readers could "endure" (ὑπομένω) in the present, and if they did they could be assured that in the future "we shall also reign with *him*" [italics in KJV] (2 Timothy 2:12). To "reign with" (συμβασιλεύω) Jesus required that one "remain," or "endure" (ὑπομένω) in the present walk. Nothing in the context indicates that if enduring happens in the present it will inevitably continue. In fact the stern warning that follows leaves open the possibility that it could fail to occur and thereby result in forfeiture of the privilege of being part of the administration in the future kingdom.

There is a chronological progression in this creed or hymn: from past (tense) salvation, to present (tense) patient endurance, followed by the future (tense) in the Greek "if we deny him" [italics in KJV] (2 Timothy 2:12) (εἰ ἀρνησόμεθα). Paul, Timothy, and his readers, while not presently denying Jesus, could in light of persecution do so in the future. The apostle Peter is a prime example of a believer who denied Jesus not once but three times at the time of Jesus' arrest. Past conversion and present obedience is not a guarantee of future performance.

What is meant by the consequences of denial, "he also will deny us" (2 Timothy 2:12) (κἀκεῖνος ἀρνήσεται ἡμᾶς), has been a point of controversy. Some interpreters tie this passage with Jesus' words in Matthew 10:33: "But whosoever shall deny me before men, him will I also deny before my Father which is in heaven." Those words were addressed to the twelve disciples in the context of instruction about persecution that they would face. Jesus did not say that denial was impossible for them but spoke negatively about not being "worthy" (Matthew 10:37, 38) (ἄξιος) of Him and positively of receiving a "reward" (Matthew 10:41-42) (μισθός).

Interpreting these as the possibility of loss of salvation would contradict other biblical passages. To use reverse theological engineering or regression analysis to say that anyone who denies Jesus never was saved to begin with introduces a guaranteed perseverance in the face of persecution not found in Scripture. That interpretation subjects persecuted believers to an unbiblical threat. Perhaps from the comfort of early twenty-first century American evangelicalism such a position is easy to maintain. Contemporary Christians in other parts of the world and in the second half of the first century and beyond enjoy and enjoyed, respectively, no such hermeneutical luxury.

The creed or hymn concludes with the conditional sentence, "If we believe not [or "are faithless" = NASB, ἀπιστέω], *yet* he abideth faithful: he cannot deny himself" [italics in KJV] (2 Timothy 2:13). Some question whether the verb translated "we believe not" or "we are faithless" (2 Timothy 2:13) (ἀπιστοῦμεν = present active indicative of ἀπιστέω = "not think true," "not believe," or "not trust") is a reference to a believer's lack of faithfulness or a loss of faith. Whatever it means, with the conditional sentence it is presented as a possibility, and in fact is contrasted with an inability or impossibility on the part of Jesus: "he abideth faithful" (2 Timothy 2:13).

In Scripture the faithfulness of God is always positive and a source of comfort for believers. Faithfulness is considered one of His attributes. Paul seems to be alluding to faithfulness as a divine attribute when he writes, "he cannot deny himself" (2 Timothy 2:13). While the use of the first person plural "we" in the beginning of the conditional sentence, "if we believe not" or "if we are faithless" (2 Timothy 2:13) (εἰ ἀπιστοῦμεν) may be explained as an editorial or rhetorical use where Paul did not intend to include himself, Timothy or other believers as being capable of denial or unfaithfulness, it would be strange if a hymn of the New Testament church would be about something that did not apply to believers. If it was an early creed, were they affirming what did not apply to them? An author's use of the editorial "we" always includes himself, while politely, albeit rhetorically including others, and never excludes himself while including others. Paul did not exclude himself from the possibility of failure entertained in this creed.

Paul expected Timothy to communicate what he had written to the church: "Of these things put *them* in remembrance, charging *them* before the Lord that they strive not about words to no profit, *but* to the subverting of the hearers" [italics in KJV] (2 Timothy 2:14). New Testament teaching is clear. Understanding it does not require special knowledge of allegorical meanings or secret terminology. Paul wanted endless disputes about the meaning of commonly used words to end. Instead of debating those who were being argumentative over the meaning of words Timothy was to communicate accurately: "Study to shew thyself approved unto God, a workman that needeth not to be ashamed, rightly dividing the word of truth" (2 Timothy 2:15). May we who follow in the footsteps of Paul and Timothy do likewise.

Confusion was the result of constant wrangling. A result Paul mentions "Who concerning the truth have erred, saying that the resurrection is past already; and overthrow the faith of some" (2 Timothy 2:18). The NASB says, "and thus they upset the faith of some." Some Bible teachers have sanguinely asserted that these people who had their faith shaken were not believers. Amid such chaos it would have been difficult to determine who was saved and who was not. It would be better to leave matters where Paul left them: "Nevertheless the foundation of God standeth sure, having this seal, The Lord knoweth them that are his" (2 Timothy 2:19). As Paul did, we should leave matters in God's hands and teach and preach what he did: "Let every one that nameth the name of Christ depart from iniquity" (2 Timothy 2:19). Believers are to be exhorted to live righteously. To "depart from iniquity" (ἀποστήτω ἀπὸ ἀδικίας), is literally to "keep away from unrighteousness." It was a command – and not a promise that they would indeed do so.

Paul used the metaphor of containers found in a home to illustrate holy and unholy living by believers. The former were made of the precious metals gold and silver, while the latter were of wood and clay: "But in a great house there are not only vessels of gold and of silver, but also of wood and of earth" (2 Timothy 2:20). The use to which they were put related to their value: "and some to honour, and some to dishonour" (2 Timothy 2:20). The metaphor breaks from reality at this point because the containers Paul pictured could choose which of those they wanted to be. What made a difference was whether a vessel was "purged" ("cleansed" = NASB, ἐκκαθαίρω), and hence was more valuable and the greater the use to which the master (God) could put it: "If a man therefore purge himself from these, he shall be a vessel unto honour, sanctified, and meet for the master's use, *and* prepared unto every good work" [italics in KJV] (2 Timothy 2:21).

The "these" (τούτων) from which someone aspiring to be "useful" (εὔχρηστος) to God needed to be "cleansed" (ἐκκαθαίρω) refer to the need to avoid doing certain things and do others: "Flee also youthful lusts: but follow righteousness, faith, charity, peace, with them that call on the Lord out of a pure heart" (2 Timothy 2:22). The use of the Greek singular imperative "flee" (φεῦγε) indicates that Timothy was being addressed. He could choose to flee or not.

Because Timothy was a pastor, of special importance for him was what Paul said next. "But foolish and unlearned questions avoid, knowing that they do gender strifes" (2 Timothy 2:23). The NASB says, "But refuse foolish and ignorant speculations, knowing that they produce quarrels." Timothy was to watch the way in which he "avoided" or "refused" (παραιτέομαι) to engage: "And the servant of the Lord must not strive; but be gentle unto all *men*, apt to teach, patient, in meekness instructing those that oppose themselves" [italics in KJV] (2 Timothy 2:24-25). A pastor's purpose in confronting error is to be corrective and not punitive: "if God peradventure will give them repentance to the acknowledging of the truth; and *that* they may recover themselves out of the snare of the devil, who are taken captive by him at his will" [italics in KJV] (2 Timothy 2:25-26). This "repentance" (μετάνοια) is a change of mind from error "to the acknowledging of the truth" (εἰς ἐπίγνωσιν ἀληθείας).

Some biblical interpreters have taken these individuals to be saved while others hold that they are unsaved. The command to correct error is to be obeyed whether the salvation of the offender can be determined or not. That does not relieve a pastor of the responsibility to be concerned about the souls of the unsaved. Certainly if unsaved individuals are teaching heresy conversion is in order. However, to assume that false teachers are never saved flies in the face of ecclesiastical biblical reality. Attempting to figure out someone's spiritual status can prove futile. As Paul put it, "the Lord knoweth them that are his'" (2 Timothy 2:19). God also knows those who are not His.

One of the individuals singled out by Paul in 2 Timothy 2:17 is Hymenaeus, who is also mentioned in 1 Timothy 1:20. In 1 Timothy he is described as being among those who "concerning faith have made shipwreck" ("suffered shipwreck in regard to their faith" = NASB) (1 Timothy 1:19). Consequently Paul included Hymenaeus among those "whom I have delivered unto Satan, that they may learn not to blaspheme" (1 Timothy 1:20). As mentioned in the discussion of 1 Timothy 1:19-20 Paul's intention was not to stir up theological controversy over the saved or lost status of individuals but rather to inspire holiness.

The same can be said about the spiritual condition of the contemporaries of Moses, Jannes, and Jambres (2 Timothy 3:8) in the passage in 2 Timothy that follows, and their comparison to false teachers in Paul's day. The details given about these individuals weigh the debate toward a conclusion that they were not saved. However, Paul's point was not to take their spiritual temperature but to get Timothy not to follow their teaching. In contrast to following false teachers Paul tells Timothy, "But continue thou in the things which thou hast learned and hast been assured of, knowing of whom thou hast learned *them*" [italics in KJV] (2 Timothy 3:14).

While the truth had come to Timothy by means of human messengers Scripture was the primary source: "from a child thou hast known the holy scriptures, which are able to make thee wise unto salvation through faith which is in Christ Jesus" (2 Timothy 3:15). Only Scripture can "make thee wise" (σοφίζω), identifying Jesus as the God/Man /Messiah, the only way of "salvation" (σωτηρία) that is available to those who put their trust in Him: "through faith which is in Christ Jesus." Timothy had believed what Scripture said and had initially placed his faith in Jesus; that had secured his eternal destiny and now that same Scripture was sufficient for his own spiritual life, growth, and ministry: "All scripture *is* given by inspiration of God, and *is* profitable for doctrine, for reproof, for correction, for instruction in righteousness: that the man of God may be perfect, throughly furnished unto all good works" [italics in KJV] (2 Timothy 3:16-17). Paul used the term "Scripture" (γραφὴ) to refer to the Old Testament writings and not to what he and the other apostles were in the process of writing. However, Paul considered his own teaching to have come from God and was therefore authoritative.

Paul may have been concerned that the threat of persecution was causing Timothy to think that it would be a good time to back off. Paul's instruction was to forge ahead: "I charge *thee* therefore before God, and the Lord Jesus Christ, who shall judge the quick and the dead at his appearing and his kingdom; Preach the word; be instant in season, out of season; reprove, rebuke, exhort with all longsuffering and doctrine" [italics in KJV] (2 Timothy 4:1-2). Paul himself knew that he did not have long to live and was giving it all he had. Being in prison Paul's ministry was curtailed but it continued and his epistles have accomplished far more than his physical presence ever could have.

Timothy could look at Paul's example. Paul told Timothy, "For I am now ready to be offered, and the time of my departure is at hand. I have fought a good fight, I have finished *my* course, I have kept the faith" [italics in KJV] (2 Timothy 4:6-7). It had not been easy, nor had it been guaranteed to him, but with God's enabling power, and Paul's submission to the work of the Holy Spirit in him, Paul had achieved what he had. Paul's words were those of a man whose obedience had not wavered although it could have. Consequently he could say of himself that "henceforth there is laid up for me a crown of righteousness, which the Lord, the righteous judge, shall give me at that day: and not to me only, but unto all them also that love his appearing" (2 Timothy 4:8). Christ's return can be looked forward to by believers who live lives of obedience. Paul invited Timothy to follow the same path.

While Paul believed in the possibility of divine deliverance he did not believe he would be spared persecution or difficulties. He wrote that "the Lord stood with me, and strengthened me; that by me the preaching might be fully known, and *that* all the Gentiles might hear: and I was delivered out of the mouth of the lion" [italics in KJV] (2 Timothy 4:17). Details of "Paul in the lion's den" await all those who will join Paul for eternity. Paul viewed his imprisonment as deliverance and also his imminent martyrdom: "And the Lord shall deliver me from every evil work, and will preserve *me* unto his heavenly kingdom: to whom *be* glory for ever and ever" [italics in KJV] (2 Timothy 4:18). This was not a theological statement of the inevitability of perseverance but an expression of his trust in God whom he knew to be trustworthy.

Evidence for the Identity of Jesus in the Epistle of Titus

Paul identified himself in terms of his relationship to God the Father and Jesus the Messiah and his evangelistic mission: "Paul, a servant of God, and an apostle of Jesus Christ, according to the faith of God's elect, and the acknowledging of the truth which is after godliness" (Titus 1:1). The gospel message was consistent with the holy character of God and its reliability was based on a divine attribute: "in hope of eternal life, which God, that cannot lie, promised before the world began" (Titus 1:2). Paul preached the gospel that comes from God in whom there is no deceit and that came to Paul directly from God: "but hath in due times manifested his word through preaching, which is committed unto me according to the commandment of God our Saviour" (Titus 1:3). The message was of divine origin and so was its dissemination by His chosen messenger. That Paul had "committed" to him ("entrusted" = NASB = ἐπιστεύθην, aorist passive indicative of πιστεύω = "believe," "trust," or "entrust") the message he was to communicate meant that he was not free to change its content. The message was not peculiar to Paul, but was shared by the entire Christian community that included Titus: "To Titus, *mine* own son after the common faith" [italics in KJV] (Titus 1:4).

Paul instructed Titus to appoint elders qualified to teach: "Holding fast the faithful word as he hath been taught, that he may be able by sound doctrine both to exhort and to convince the gainsayers" (Titus 1:9). Of particular concern was those who were attempting to insert circumcision as an additional requirement in the gospel as well as for godly living: "For there are many unruly and vain talkers and deceivers, specially they of the circumcision: whose mouths must be stopped, who subvert whole houses, teaching things which they ought not" (Titus 1:10-11). They had the wrong message and a wrong motivation: "for filthy lucre's sake" (Titus 1:11). They were motivated by money.

The less than altruistic motivation of these men is revealed in the way they talked behind the back of the people of Crete whom Titus was trying to reach. Paul gave an example of what was going on: "One of themselves, *even* a prophet of their own, said, The Cretians *are* alway liars, evil beasts, slow bellies ["lazy gluttons" = NASB]" [italics in KJV] (Titus 1:12). Paul then wrote, "This witness is true" (Titus 1:13) (ἡ μαρτυρία αὕτη ἐστὶν ἀληθής). Paul was not saying it was true that those of Crete were liars, evil beasts, and slow bellies or lazy gluttons, but it was true that that was what was being said behind the backs of the believers in the church in Crete. It made no sense to follow the teachings and ways of false teachers who were bad-mouthing them behind their backs. Paul instructed Titus, "Wherefore rebuke them sharply, that they may be sound in the faith; not giving heed to Jewish fables, and commandments of men, that turn from the truth" (Titus 1:13-14).

Those promoting circumcision were to be seriously reprimanded. Their error was compounded because it was not just that they held personal heretical beliefs, they were proselytizing among believers. Believers were to steer clear of these individuals because their behavior was in sharp contrast to godly expectations: "Unto the pure all things *are* pure: but unto them that are defiled and unbelieving *is* nothing pure; but even their mind and conscience is defiled. They profess that they know God; but in works they deny *him*, being abominable, and disobedient, and unto every good work reprobate" [italics in KJV] (Titus 1:15-16).

The question arises, what exactly was the danger that Paul was warning about? Was it that the believers in Crete would succumb to heretical beliefs, adding circumcision as a requirement for eternal life, and/or as a matter of Christian obedience in sanctification? Was it that they could be influenced to commit some of the same sins that the false teachers were guilty of? If a believer could do neither, what was the point of the warning? The text should be taken at face value and seen as a warning that Titus should be on guard for either or both eventualities. An interpretation employing reverse engineering or regression analysis (they were never saved to begin with if they commit any of these sins or fall for any of these beliefs) is alien to the author's intent.

Paul was concerned that behavior would match belief and that actions be appropriate: "But as for you, speak the things which are fitting for sound doctrine" (Titus 2:1). Titus was to model the message: "In all things shewing thyself a pattern of good works: in doctrine *shewing* uncorruptness, gravity, sincerity, sound speech, that cannot be condemned; that he that is of the contrary part may be ashamed, having no evil thing to say of you" [italics in KJV] (Titus 2:7-8). Satan and those who supported him were the ones who should be ashamed of themselves rather than having believers feel shame. There was to be no divide between deeds and doctrine.

Without the slightest hint that believing slaves were incapable of failing to obey Paul told Titus to, "*Exhort* servants to be obedient unto their own masters, *and* to please *them* well in all *things*; not answering again; not purloining, but shewing all good fidelity; that they may adorn the doctrine of God our Saviour in all things" [italics in KJV] (Titus 2:9-10). Slaves could either decorate the doctrine that they believed or detract from it. To hold that they could not do the latter makes a mockery of the Pauline warning.

The rationale Paul gives for righteous living is rooted in God's gracious purpose for believers: "For the grace of God that bringeth salvation hath appeared to all men, teaching us that, denying ungodliness and worldly lusts, we should live soberly, righteously, and godly, in this present world" (Titus 2:11-12). Paul believed in the universal availability of salvation. God's saving grace is directed to "all men" (Titus 2:11) (πᾶσιν ἀνθρώποις).

Paul employs a panoramic view of the believer's life that commences in salvation, continues in a life of sanctification, and culminates in the coming of the Savior. God's grace extended in salvation is present in sanctification where it is "teaching us that, denying ungodliness and worldly lusts, we should live soberly, righteously, and godly, in this present world" (Titus 2:12). The final phase will be the eagerly anticipated return of Jesus: "Looking for that blessed hope, and the glorious appearing of the great God and our Saviour Jesus Christ" (Titus 2:13).

Paul affirms Jesus' deity in Titus 2:13, referring to Him as "the great God and our Saviour Jesus Christ." Grammarians have debated whether this Greek construction refers to one individual, Christ Jesus, or if it also includes another Person, God the Father. The Granville Sharp Rule in Greek grammar applies here. It proves that Paul was referring to one Person, Jesus, who is God. Sharp discovered that "when the construction article-substantive-καὶ-substantive (TSKS) involved personal nouns which were singular and not proper names, they always referred to the same person" (Daniel Wallace, *Greek Grammar beyond the Basics*, [Grand Rapids: Zondervan, 1996], 270-71). Wallace writes about the Granville Sharp Rule and uses Titus 2:13 as an example:

> It [the Granville Sharp Rule] has been applied only with great hesitation to Titus 2:13 and 2 Pet 1:1 by Trinitarians in the past two centuries. However, a proper understanding of the rule shows it to have the highest degree of validity within the NT. Consequently, these two passages are as secure as any in the canon when it comes to identifying Christ as θεός [God]. (ibid., 290).

Jesus is both God (θεός) and the Messiah (Χριστός). For an individual to be saved he/she must believe that Jesus is God, placing trust in the Person whom Scripture has revealed.

The purpose of Jesus' provision of salvation is so that believers will live lives of obedience: "Who gave himself for us, that he might redeem us from all iniquity, and purify unto himself a peculiar people, zealous of good works" (Titus 2:14). The objective was obedience and Paul probably realistically anticipated that Titus would run into objections: "These things speak, and exhort, and rebuke with all authority. Let no man despise thee" (Titus 2:15). The inclusion of the verb "rebuke" (ἐλέγχω) implies that some would in fact fail to obey and would be in need of correction.

Paul then gave more instructions to believers: "Put them in mind to be subject to principalities and powers, to obey magistrates, to be ready to every good work, to speak evil of no man, to be no brawlers, *but* gentle, shewing all meekness unto all men" [italics in KJV] (Titus 3:1-2). The reason Titus should do this is stated in verse 3: "For we ourselves also were sometimes foolish, disobedient, deceived, serving divers lusts and pleasures, living in malice and envy, hateful, *and* hating one another" [italics in KJV] (Titus 3:3). The actions, attitudes, and emotions are true of Paul and Titus and anyone else in an unregenerate state.

If one holds that they could not apply to a believer in any manner that would be an implication not found explicitly in the text. In fact, the warning is for believers not to engage in the behavior of their unregenerate past. Items in one list are juxtaposed with their opposite in the other list. Titus 3:1 instructs believers "to obey" (πειθαρχεῖν) and in Titus 3:3 unbelievers are "disobedient" (ἀπειθεῖς). Titus 3:2 says, "to speak evil of no man, to be no brawlers, *but* gentle, shewing all meekness unto all men" and Titus 3:3 says "living in malice and envy, hateful, *and* hating one another." The parallels are apparent. There is no textual indicator to differentiate the positive commands from the negative prohibitions qualitatively or quantitatively. Believers failing to obey the positively stated commands would be committing their negative counterpart that was characteristic of unbelievers.

While believers are "to be ready to every good work" (Titus 3:1), Paul is quick to distance those actions from the acquisition of eternal salvation: "Not by works of righteousness which we have done, but according to his mercy he saved us, by the washing of regeneration, and renewing of the Holy Ghost" (Titus 3:5). Regeneration by the Holy Spirit was made possible by Jesus in whom trust had been placed: "Which he shed on us abundantly through Jesus Christ our Saviour; that being justified by his grace, we should be made heirs according to the hope of eternal life" (Titus 3:6-7). Paul, Titus, and the believers in Crete presently had hope for their eternal future because they had placed their trust in Jesus in the past, at which time they had been "justified" (δικαιόω).

Paul put what had happened to them in the past in proper perspective with what they were being exhorted to do in the present in his emphatic statement, *"This is* a faithful saying, and these things I will that thou affirm constantly, that they which have believed in God might be careful to maintain good works. These things are good and profitable unto men" [italics in KJV] (Titus 3:8). Paul separated salvation from progressive sanctification. The former had taken place in the past to "they which have believed in God," while the latter "good works" (καλῶν ἔργων) could be engaged in only because the former had taken place. The KJV legitimately translates the dative "God" (θεῷ) with "in God." Titus was to exhort "they which have believed in God" (Titus 3:8). (οἱ πεπιστευκότες θεῷ). Because of Paul's Trinitarianism, for him Jesus and God could be interchanged.

While it was possible for a believer to be engaged in them certain behaviors were to be avoided: "But avoid foolish questions, and genealogies, and contentions, and strivings about the law; for they are unprofitable and vain" (Titus 3:9). Paul was no doubt aware of Jesus' words about forgiving, "until seventy times seven" times (Matthew 18:22), yet Paul showed little tolerance for divisiveness: "A man that is an heretick ["a factious man" = NASB] after the first and second admonition reject; knowing that he that is such is subverted, and sinneth, being condemned of himself" (Titus 3:10-11). Paul held to a "three strikes and you're out" rule. Church unity was to be maintained by removing the unrepentant source of the problem.

Good works were always in order. Fruitfulness in the form of "good works" (καλόν ἔργον) was to be learned. "And let ours also learn to maintain good works for necessary uses, that they be not unfruitful" (Titus 3:14). Paul concludes with a farewell that indicates what united him with fellow believers: "Greet them that love us in the faith" (Titus 3:15). Their common trust in Jesus is what bound them together.

Evidence for the Identity of Jesus in the Epistle of Philemon

Paul's appeal to Philemon to consider freeing his slave Onesimus was based on Philemon's relationship to Paul, and the fact that Philemon was a believer. To review Philemon's relationship to Paul the apostle used the words "fellowlabourer" (Philemon 1) (συνεργός) and "partner" (Philemon 17) (κοινωνός), and the words, "thou owest unto me even thine own self besides." Paul wrote that he thanked God "hearing of thy love and faith, which thou hast toward the Lord Jesus, and toward all saints" (Philemon 5). There is a question whether "love" (ἀγάπη) and "faith" (πίστις) are both to be associated with "the Lord Jesus" (τὸν κύριον Ἰησοῦν) and with "the saints" (τοὺς ἁγίους). Robertson suggests the possibility of a chiasm where love is for the saints and faith is in Jesus (A. T. Robertson, *Word Pictures in the New Testament*, 4:465). Paul thanked God for Philemon's relationship with Jesus that was based on his having placed his trust in Him. Paul had also heard of the love that Philemon had for fellow believers. These were two things that Paul and Philemon had in common and would become the basis of Paul's appeal to Philemon.

Paul referred to "the communication of thy faith" ["the fellowship of your faith" = NASB] (Philemon 6) (ἡ κοινωνία τῆς πίστεώς σου). Paul prayed that "fellowship" or "partnership" (κοινωνία) within the community of believers would result in Philemon's spiritual growth: "and I pray that the fellowship of your faith may become effective through the knowledge of every good thing which is in you for Christ's sake" (Philemon 6 NASB). In this epistle Paul's gracious appeal to Philemon, as his spiritual father, neither deterministic nor threatening, mirrored God's appeal for the obedience of his spiritual children. Paul's exhortations were backed up by the consistency of his own gracious example so that he could seamlessly conclude with the words, "The grace of our Lord Jesus Christ *be* with your spirit" [italics in KJV] (Philemon 25).

Evidence for the Identity of Jesus in the Epistle of Hebrews

This epistle is famous for its extended passages on the identity of Jesus and begins by saying that God has communicated through Jesus who "hath in these last days spoken unto us by *his* Son, whom he hath appointed heir of all things, by whom also he made the worlds" [italics in KJV] (Hebrews 1:2). Jesus is to be listened to because of His exalted position, "whom he hath appointed heir of all things" (Hebrews 1:2), and power: "by whom also he made the worlds" (Hebrews 1:2). God could delegate these to Jesus because of who Jesus is: "Who being the brightness of *his* glory, and the express image of his person" [italics in KJV] (Hebrews 1:3). Jesus' essential nature is equal to that of God the Father. The universe continues to exist as it does because of Jesus: "upholding all things by the word of his power" (Hebrews 1:3).

The Incarnation was not an interruption in Jesus' divine identity; it was integral to it: "When he had by himself purged our sins, sat down on the right hand of the Majesty on high" (Hebrews 1:3). In heaven Jesus is now in the presence of the holy angels, but His position is far superior to theirs, "Being made so much better than the angels, as he hath by inheritance obtained a more excellent name than they" (Hebrews 1:4). The "name" (ὄνομα) of Jesus, His very identity, is infinitely superior to angels because of His eternal existence. Because angels were nonexistent they could not have been a party to inter-Trinitarian relationships: "For unto which of the angels said he at any time, Thou art my Son, this day have I begotten thee? And again, I will be to him a Father, and he shall be to me a Son?" (Hebrews 1:5). The answer to the rhetorical question is: "To none of them." Angels were not even present.

Jesus' identity as One worthy of praise further proves that angels are inferior to Him: "And again, when he bringeth in the firstbegotten into the world, he saith, And let all the angels of God worship him" (Hebrews 1:6). The Greek word translated "world" (οἰκουμένη) includes the idea of the inhabited world which God administers. The verb rendered "let. . .worship" (προσκυνησάτωσαν) is an aorist active imperative, third person imperative. There is no third person imperative in the English language but there is one in Greek. The meaning in the Greek is that of a command, not the implied concession inherent in the English translation "let." God the Father and Jesus, who are included in the Trinitarian Godhead, demand and command worship from the entire creation and that includes angelic beings.

Not only is angelic inferiority to Jesus proved by His divine identity and the fact that they worship Him; also angels serve Him: "And of the angels he saith, Who maketh his angels spirits, and his ministers a flame of fire" (Hebrews 1:7). Angelic inferiority to Jesus is proved by their subservience to Him. In contrast, Jesus' superiority is proved by His prerogative of eternal divine authority: "But unto the Son *he saith*, Thy throne, O God, *is* for ever and ever: a sceptre of righteousness *is* the sceptre of thy kingdom" [italics in KJV] (Hebrews 1:8). Jesus' rule is characterized by righteousness on which its legitimacy rests.

Some of the angels sinned and lost the privilege of spending eternity in God's presence, and will receive eternal punishment. Jesus' divine superiority prevents Him from ever sinning or suffering a similar fate: "Thou hast loved righteousness, and hated iniquity; therefore God, *even* thy God, hath anointed thee with the oil of gladness above thy fellows" [italics in KJV] (Hebrews 1:9). The Greek preposition translated "above" (παρά), could be rendered "instead of" or "rather than," which would highlight the contrast between Jesus' eternal righteousness and that of angels.

Additional testimony proving the superiority of Jesus is provided by creation:

> And, Thou, Lord, in the beginning hast laid the foundation of the earth; and the heavens are the works of thine hands: they shall perish; but thou remainest; and they all shall wax old as doth a garment; and as a vesture shalt thou fold them up, and they shall be changed: but thou art the same, and thy years shall not fail (Hebrews 1:10-12).

Jesus is in charge of and will outlast what He created. To emphasize the contrast between Jesus and angels, the writer of the Epistle asks a rhetorical question, "But to which of the angels said he at any time, Sit on my right hand, until I make thine enemies thy footstool?" (Hebrews 1:13). The expected answer is "None." No angel has ever had or been given such a position. In fact besides angels serving Jesus, they have been sent to serve the saved: "Are they not all ministering spirits, sent forth to minister for them who shall be heirs of salvation?" (Hebrews 1:14). The expected answer is "Yes, they are." The inferior status of angels is thereby further substantiated.

The writer of Hebrews discusses the superiority of Jesus over angels for the purpose of having the saving message about Him accepted. In the Old Testament angels communicated messages from God, but even more important words had recently been delivered: "Therefore we ought to give the more earnest heed to the things which we have heard, lest at any time we should let *them* slip. For if the word spoken by angels was stedfast, and every transgression and disobedience received a just recompence of reward; how shall we escape, if we neglect so great salvation; which at the first began to be spoken by the Lord, and was confirmed unto us by them that heard *him*?" [italics in KJV] (Hebrews 2:1-3). The consequences for rejecting communication through angels were serious and certain. The negative consequences that result from ignoring the message of salvation are just as certain and far more serious.

Accountability cannot be avoided because the message of salvation is supported by overwhelming evidence: "God also bearing *them* witness, both with signs and wonders, and with divers miracles, and gifts of the Holy Ghost, according to his own will" [italics in KJV] (Hebrews 2:3-4). The gospel involved the entire Trinity. There was not a "gospel according to God the Father," or a "gospel according to Jesus," that differed from a "gospel according to the apostles." It was one gospel that the Trinity, Paul, and the rest of the apostles preached. It had been accurately and divinely communicated, apostolically corroborated, and confirmed by the Holy Spirit.

Further proof of Jesus' superiority over angels is the fact that the latter were not given authority as Jesus was: "For unto the angels hath he not put in subjection the world to come, whereof we speak" (Hebrews 2:5). The author provides evidence from the Old Testament without specifically mentioning David, the psalmist to whom Psalm 8, a messianic psalm, is attributed:

> But one in a certain place testified, saying, What is man, that thou art mindful of him? or the son of man, that thou visitest him? Thou madest him a little lower than the angels; thou crownedst him with glory and honour, and didst set him over the works of thy hands: Thou hast put all things in subjection under his feet (Hebrews 2:6-8).

There is some question whether David was talking about man in general and man's having been given dominion over creation. However, the writer of Hebrews applies it to Jesus.

Jesus' position while He walked this earth was in some ways inferior to that of angels. Nevertheless it was temporary and His true identity was veiled and infinitely contrasts with that of angels over whom He has authority: "For in that he put all in subjection under him, he left nothing *that is* not put under him" [italics in KJV] (Hebrews 2:8). Angels are included under the category of "all [things]" (τὰ πάντα). Jesus' exalted position is not negated by the apparent present state of affairs: "But now we see not yet all things put under him" (Hebrews 2:8). The apparent present lack of subjection of all things to Jesus does not diminish His actual "glory and honor" (δόξα καὶ τιμή). Present inactivity does not translate into inability.

The paradox is that apparent defeat by death on the cross was Jesus' crowning achievement; the procurement of eternal salvation by Him who is explicitly mentioned as the One about whom the author of Hebrews is speaking: "But we see Jesus, who was made a little lower than the angels for the suffering of death, crowned with glory and honour; that he by the grace of God should taste death for every man" (Hebrews 2:9). The NASB says, "But we do see Him who has been made for a little while lower than the angels, *namely*, Jesus, because of the suffering of death crowned with glory and honor, that by the grace of God He might taste death for everyone" [italics in NASB]. What appeared to be defeat was instead His greatest deed and something God the Father had qualified Jesus to do: "For it became him, for whom *are* all things, and by whom *are* all things, in bringing many sons unto glory, to make the captain of their salvation perfect through sufferings" [italics in KJV] (Hebrews 2:10).

Jesus' Incarnation brought deity and humanity together and made possible His sacrifice for sin. Being one of them Jesus could die for them. God the Father unites Jesus with those for whom He died. "For both he that sanctifieth and they who are sanctified *are* all of one" [italics in KJV] (Hebrews 2:11). Jesus' identification with humanity does not compromise His holiness: "for which cause he is not ashamed to call them brethren" (Hebrews 2:11). The writer of Hebrews uses Psalm 22, an instance of prophetic typology, to prove that Jesus considers believers to be His brothers: "Saying, I will declare thy name unto my brethren, in the midst of the church will I sing praise unto thee" (Hebrews 2:12). The quotation is from Psalm 21:23 in the Greek translation of the Old Testament, the Septuagint (LXX) (διηγήσομαι τὸ ὄνομά σου τοῖς ἀδελφοῖς μου, ἐν μέσῳ ἐκκλησίας ὑμνήσω σε).

Additional proof of the bond between Jesus and believers is a shared trust in God the Father: "And again, I will put my trust in him" (Hebrews 2:13). The quotation is from Isaiah 8:17 in the Greek translation, the Septuagint (LXX) (πεποιθὼς ἔσομαι ἐπ' αὐτῷ). The writer of Hebrews emphasizes that he is referring to Jesus and believers: "And again, Behold I and the children which God hath given me" (Hebrews 2:13). This is from Isaiah 8:18, again from the LXX (ἰδοὺ ἐγὼ καὶ τὰ παιδία, ἅ μοι ἔδωκεν ὁ θεός). The Incarnation that has been alluded to is now made explicit: "Forasmuch then as the children are partakers of flesh and blood, he also himself likewise took part of the same; that through death he might destroy him that had the power of death, that is, the devil; and deliver them who through fear of death were all their lifetime subject to bondage" (Hebrews 2:14-15). Deliverance from the devil, a fallen angel, requires a greater power than that possessed by any of the angels and the only One who qualifies is Jesus because He is God.

Jesus shares a brotherhood with believers for whom He provides salvation. The opportunity is not offered to angels: "For assuredly He does not give help to angels, but He gives help to the descendant of Abraham" (Hebrews 2:16 NASB). The help Jesus provides for man's redemption required the Incarnation: "Wherefore in all things it behoved him to be made like unto *his* brethren, that he might be a merciful and faithful high priest in things *pertaining* to God, to make reconciliation for the sins of the people" [italics in KJV] (Hebrews 2:17). To die on man's behalf Jesus had to become one of them. What Jesus experienced uniquely qualifies Him to give compassionate assistance: "For in that he himself hath suffered being tempted, he is able to succour them that are tempted" (Hebrews 2:18).

Even in salvation man is not asked to do something Jesus did not do. When a person makes the decision to trust in Jesus for eternal life, he has the example and empathy of One who placed His trust in God the Father at the most critical moment of His time on earth. People are invited to put their trust in Christ, the One who entrusted His Spirit to God the Father at the Crucifixion. Jesus' last words on the cross were spoken so that all would hear: "And when Jesus had cried with a loud voice, he said, Father, into thy hands I commend my spirit" (Luke 23:46).

Not only is Jesus superior to angels; He is also superior to Moses, the one from whom the Mosaic Law and system derived its name. Faithfulness characterized both Jesus and Moses: "Wherefore, holy brethren, partakers of the heavenly calling, consider the Apostle and High Priest of our profession, Christ Jesus; who was faithful to him that appointed him, as also Moses *was faithful* in all his house" [italics in KJV] (Hebrews 3:1-2). Of course there is a distinct difference between Jesus and Moses. Jesus is the Creator and not a part of His creation: "For this *man* was counted worthy of more glory than Moses, inasmuch as he who hath builded the house hath more honour than the house. For every house is builded by some *man*; but he that built all things *is* God" [italics in KJV] (Hebrews 3:3-4). Here the author of Hebrews clearly identifies Jesus as God, "he that built all things" (Hebrews 3:4).

The author shifts the house metaphor slightly to compare its occupants, with Moses relegated to the role of a household servant: "And Moses verily *was* faithful in all his house, as a servant, for a testimony of those things which were to be spoken after" [italics in KJV] (Hebrews 3:5). Moses' faithfulness is not questioned, but his was a subordinate position in a supporting role. His faithful testimony would serve to corroborate the identity of Jesus his superior. Continuing the metaphor of the household's occupants, Jesus' position is made clear: "But Christ as a son over his own house; whose house are we, if we hold fast the confidence and the rejoicing of the hope firm unto the end" (Hebrews 3:6).

The contingent part of the sentence, "if we hold fast the confidence and the rejoicing of the hope firm unto the end" (Hebrews 3:6), has caused some controversy, consternation, and confusion. Does this clause say that those who fail to "hold fast" (κατέχω) will lose their eternal salvation or never had it to begin with? The key to the author's intent is found in his use of the adjective "faithful" (πιστός), in the immediate context, Hebrews 3:2 and 5. Jesus was "faithful" (Hebrews 3:2) (πιστός), Moses was "faithful" (Hebrews 3:5) (πιστός), and the writer of Hebrews and his readers would be faithful as well (Hebrews 3:6) if they held on to what they had originally been taught. This was an invitation to become members of a faithful household.

Jesus was completely faithful in everything He did. Although Moses failed to the extent that he was denied entry into the Promised Land that is not the focus of the household metaphor. Instead his faithfulness is highlighted by the author. Likewise the prospect that the author holds forth for himself and his readers is positive. To extrapolate significant theological implications as to a believer's eternal security or lack thereof, or to employ "reverse engineering" in denying salvation to unfaithful believers is to run far afield from the intent of the author and his use of the metaphor. The author's intent is to exhort himself and his believing readers to follow Jesus' and Moses' examples of faithfulness. One who fails to do so cannot claim identification with their example of faithfulness.

Jesus is referred to by the author as the "great high priest" (Hebrews 4:14) (ἀρχιερεύς μέγας) of believers. The high priest and the tabernacle/temple that they served were the pivotal points of connection between a believer and his or her worship of God. Jesus is superior to all high priests because whereas the Old Testament high priest was confined to earth, Jesus has direct access to God's presence in heaven. He is "a great high priest, that is passed into the heavens, Jesus the Son of God" (Hebrews 4:14). Jesus' transcendence does not mean He is unable to relate to man's humanity: "For we have not an high priest which cannot be touched with the feeling of our infirmities; but was in all points tempted like as *we are*" [italics in KJV] (Hebrews 4:15). The crucial caveat is that Jesus is sinless. Jesus is "without sin" (Hebrews 4:15) (χωρὶς ἁμαρτίας).

The superiority of Jesus' as a high priest is illustrated by Melchizedek. Evidence for Jesus' superiority is found in Psalm 110:4: "Thou *art* a priest for ever after the order of Melchisedec" [italics in KJV] (Hebrews 5:6). The description of Jesus' sacrifice is intriguing. "Who in the days of his flesh, when he had offered up prayers and supplications with strong crying and tears unto him that was able to save him from death, and was heard in that he feared" (Hebrews 5:7). The NASB says, "In the days of His flesh, He offered up both prayers and supplications with loud crying and tears to the One able to save Him from death, and He was heard because of His piety." God the Father could have saved Jesus from death, but Jesus desired the Father's will. Jesus was heard by God the Father whose will it was to accept His Son's death as a payment for sin.

The hallmark of Jesus' sacrifice was obedience: "Though he were a Son, yet learned he obedience by the things which he suffered" (Hebrews 5:8). This was a result of Jesus' sacrifice: "And being made perfect, he became the author of eternal salvation unto all them that obey him" (Hebrews 5:9). Some Bible teachers have taken this to mean that the obedience of works is required for eternal life; or the wanting, the willingness, or the commitment to do them. The latter seems to be a desperate theological expedient. Others hold that "eternal salvation" (σωτηρίας αἰωνίου) refers to eschatological rewards that believers can earn.

A better view is to see the statement in light of the context in which the disobedience of Israel is followed by the example of the obedience of Jesus. Just as Jesus was obedient to the will of God the Father, believers are to obey Jesus. Jesus said that people must believe in Him to obtain eternal life: "that whosoever believeth in him should not perish, but have everlasting life" (John 3:16). To add anything to "believe" (πιστεύω) is to fail to obey Jesus. Jesus' words about the way to heaven cannot be ignored. Jesus is "the way" (John 14:6) (ἡ ὁδὸς) and His way is the only way. Only by trusting in Jesus does He become "the author [or "source" NASB] of eternal salvation" (Hebrews 5:9) (αἴτιος σωτηρίας αἰωνίου) for lost sinners.

The doctrine that believers know at conversion is referred to in Hebrews 6:1 as "the principles of the doctrine of Christ." The NASB says, "the elementary teaching about the Christ" (τὸν τῆς ἀρχῆς τοῦ Χριστοῦ λόγον). This is the gospel which has information about Jesus' identity. Knowing who Jesus is must be followed by placing one's trust in Him and Him alone. Trusting in one's works is excluded. The writer of Hebrews refers to that with the words, "not laying again the foundation of repentance from dead works, and of faith toward God" (Hebrews 6:1). "Repentance" (μετάνοια) here is a change of mind about the efficacy of "works." "Works" are referred to as "dead" (νεκρός) because they do not play a role in receiving eternal life. They are useless for the purpose of obtaining eternal salvation. "Faith toward God" (Hebrews 6:1) (πίστεως ἐπὶ θεόν), namely, trust in Jesus, is the only requirement for eternal life.

The individuals the author is referring to in Hebrews 6:1-8 are saved. This is evident from the author's remarks about them. He describes them with the words, "those who were once enlightened, and have tasted of the heavenly gift, and were made partakers of the Holy Ghost, and have tasted the good word of God, and the powers of the world to come" (Hebrews 6:4-5). If this description appeared in any other context than that of a controversial passage, they would be understood to be referring to believers.

The author sees no need for "laying again the foundation" (Hebrews 6:1). The foundation of salvation was already in place. The solution for those who "fall away" (Hebrews 6:6) (παραπεσόντας) was not that these individuals be converted. In fact, the author states the obvious fact that it is "impossible" (Hebrews 6:6) (ἀδύνατος) for saved people to do so. The adjective "impossible" (ἀδύνατος) is in the emphatic initial position in verse 4 in the Greek, as the KJV has it. The NASB places it later on in the sentence in verse 6.

Contextually "repentance" (μετάνοια), used in verse 1 and verse 6, both refer to the change of mind that occurs at the time of salvation. The only other time the author of Hebrews uses the term "repentance" (μετάνοια) is in Hebrews 12:17 where Esau attempted to get his father Isaac to change his mind about giving him the birthright. The writer says, "For ye know how that afterward, when he would have inherited the blessing, he was rejected: for he found no place of repentance, though he sought it carefully with tears." The "change of mind" that Esau sought was from his father. It had nothing to do with sin on the part of Isaac his father.

In Hebrews 6:6 "renew them again unto repentance" is semantically equivalent to "repentance from dead works" in verse 1. They both refer to the change of mind that happens at conversion. Not even God Himself can "re-save" someone who is already saved. In fact, if that were possible, it would be tantamount to "re-crucifying" (Hebrews 6:6) (ἀνασταυρόω) Christ. The author states that hypothetical consequence with the words, "seeing they crucify to themselves the Son of God afresh" (Hebrews 6:6). An added result would be that they "put *him* to an open shame" [italics in KJV] (Hebrews 6:6). To do so would be saying that accepting Jesus' payment for their sins once was not enough. Being saved once was not sufficient. Shame would replace the glory of Jesus' once-for-all sacrifice for sin because it would subject Jesus to ridicule.

The crucifixion, and its efficacy applied to an individual, are both events never to be repeated. Believers who "fall away" (Hebrews 6:6) (παραπίπτω) cannot be "re-saved." It is impossible.

Using an agricultural metaphor the author contrasts believers who "fall away" (παραπίπτω) with those who have not. The latter are described with the words, "For the earth which drinketh in the rain that cometh oft upon it, and bringeth forth herbs meet for them by whom it is dressed, receiveth blessing from God" (Hebrews 6:7). In the metaphor these believers are the "earth" (γῆ). They are characterized by usefulness. They are pictured "drinking" (πίνω), perhaps a reference to receiving and applying divine instruction. Moving outside the metaphor, the author, then makes application to this believer who "receiveth blessing from God," perhaps a reference to God's approval and/or rewards.

Resuming the agricultural metaphor, the author associates another type of "earth" (γῆ) with believers who "fall away" (παραπεσόντας): "But that which beareth thorns and briers *is* rejected, and *is* nigh unto cursing; whose end *is* to be burned" [italics in KJV] (Hebrews 6:8). Such a believer is subject to the refining fire that will take place at the judgment seat of Christ. What has been produced will go up in smoke (1 Corinthians 3:12-15). The "earth" (γῆ) remains, but what is "rejected" (Hebrews 6:8) ("worthless" = NASB, ἀδόκιμος), that is, not worthy of approval, will be removed. Salvation is not lost but God's approval and/or rewards will be absent.

In contrast to the one who "receiveth blessing from God" (Hebrews 6:7), the author adds to his description of the opposite situation with the words, "nigh unto cursing" (Hebrews 6:8) ("close to being cursed" = NASB, καὶ κατάρας ἐγγύς). The author's inclusion of the qualifier "close" (ἐγγύς), is a tacit recognition of the sad situation in which such a believer has placed himself or herself. Believers who "fall away" (παραπίπτω) are not subject to the condemnation of a "curse" (κατάρα), but will experience a loss of divine commendation and reward.

The warning is to be taken seriously. However, the author and his colleagues were convinced his readers/listeners would take heed and not take that route: "But, beloved, we are persuaded better things of you, and things that accompany salvation, though we thus speak" (Hebrews 6:9). The severity of the warning is tempered by pastoral encouragement. This expectation was a desire and not a foregone conclusion. The author expressed as much: "And we desire that every one of you do shew the same diligence to the full assurance of hope unto the end" (Hebrews 6:11).

The author's desire should not be taken as a promise that his readers will persevere. The author adds, "be not slothful, but followers of them who through faith and patience inherit the promises" (Hebrews 6:12). Believers can be "slothful" (νωθρός), ("sluggish" = NASB) or "lazy." Instead they are to follow examples of "faith" (πίστις) and "patience" (μακροθυμία). "Faith" (πίστις) is exercised at conversion and throughout the life of a believer. Louw and Nida define the term translated "patience" (μακροθυμία) as "a state of emotional calm in the face of provocation or misfortune and without complaint or irritation–'patience'" (Johannes P. Louw and Eugene A. Nida, *Greek-English Lexicon of the New Testament Based on Semantic Domains*, 2nd ed. [New York: United Bible Societies, 2nd ed], 1989, 1:307). The relevance of this exhortation should be recognized in light of the persecution experienced by first-century believers.

The author uses Abraham, a man whose faith in God was exemplary. Abraham's interaction with Melchizedek is an opportunity for the author to give identifying characteristics that Melchizedek shares with Jesus. Melchizedek was "King of righteousness, and after that also King of Salem, which is, King of peace; without father, without mother, without descent, having neither beginning of days, nor end of life; but made like unto the Son of God; abideth a priest continually" (Hebrews 7:2-3). Melchizedek's lack of recorded ancestry mirrors Jesus' being a priest who, according to the Law, came from the wrong tribe. Jesus was from the tribe of Judah rather than the priestly tribe of Levi. The author of Hebrews describes Jesus as a priest "who is made, not after the law of a carnal commandment, but after the power of an endless life" (Hebrews 7:16). The NASB says, "who has become *such* not on the basis of a law of physical requirement, but according to the power of an indestructible life" [italics in NASB]. Jesus' qualifications to be a high priest far supersede that of any earthly high priest.

Jesus as a high priest is identified with the new covenant in contrast to the old covenant: "By so much was Jesus made a surety of a better testament" (Hebrews 7:22). Because of who Jesus is, the differences between Him as a high priest and those of high priests under the old covenant quickly become apparent: "And they truly were many priests, because they were not suffered to continue by reason of death: but this *man*, because he continueth ever, hath an unchangeable priesthood" [italics in KJV] (Hebrews 7:23-24). Because of their mortality old-covenant high priests, while serving one at a time, had to do so consecutively. Jesus is immortal and eternal and can permanently preside over the new covenant.

Jesus' permanence equips Him to offer salvation that is eternal: "Wherefore he is able also to save them to the uttermost that come unto God by him, seeing he ever liveth to make intercession for them" (Hebrews 7:25). Jesus' identity qualifies Him to do so: "For such an high priest became us, *who is* holy, harmless, undefiled, separate from sinners, and made higher than the heavens" [italics in KJV] (Hebrews 7:26). The NASB says, "For it is fitting that we should have such a high priest, holy, innocent, undefiled, separated from sinners and exalted above the heavens."

Jesus' identity affects the efficacy of His sacrifice. His perfection results in the permanence of His sacrifice: "who needeth not daily, as those high priests, to offer up sacrifice, first for his own sins, and then for the people's: for this he did once, when he offered up himself" (Hebrews 7:27). A multiple of fallible old-covenant high priests made an even greater number of sacrifices necessary. But the sinless sacrifice of Jesus was singular. The high priests of the old-covenant and Jesus in the new covenant, had contrasting ministries: "for the law maketh men high priests which have infirmity; but the word of the oath, which was since the law, *maketh* the Son, who is consecrated for evermore" [italics in KJV] (Hebrews 7:28). The NASB says, "for the Law appoints men as high priests who are weak, but the word of the oath, which came after the Law, *appoints* a Son, made perfect forever" [italics in NASB]. A perfect sacrifice need not be repeated.

The place where Jesus performs His priestly duties identifies Him as superior to all human high priests. "Now of the things which we have spoken *this is* the sum: We have such an high priest, who is set on the right hand of the throne of the Majesty in the heavens; a minister of the sanctuary, and of the true tabernacle, which the Lord pitched, and not man" [italics in KJV] (Hebrews 8:1-2). Not only "was Jesus made a surety of a better testament" (Hebrews 7:22), "He is also the mediator of a better covenant, which has been enacted on better promises" (Hebrews 8:6 NASB). The superiority of the new covenant is based on Jesus' sacrifice.

The uniqueness of Jesus' sacrifice made it like no other: "Neither by the blood of goats and calves, but by his own blood he entered in once into the holy place, having obtained eternal redemption *for us*" [italics in KJV] (Hebrews 9:12). Jesus' uniqueness and distinction from earthly priests is seen in the way He functions in contrast to them: "And every priest standeth daily ministering and offering oftentimes the same sacrifices, which can never take away sins: but this man, after he had offered one sacrifice for sins for ever, sat down on the right hand of God" (Hebrews 10:11-12). The high priests' sacrifices were repeated but Jesus' sacrifice was not. Why? Because of the nature of Jesus' sacrifice: "For by one offering he hath perfected for ever them that are sanctified" (Hebrews 10:14). "Those who are sanctified" (τοὺς ἁγιαζομένους) are those who put their trust in Jesus for their eternal destiny.

Because of who Jesus is and the fact that we have access to Him, believers are exhorted to do several things. Three commands are in the Greek subjunctive mood: (1) "Let us draw near with a true heart in full assurance of faith, having our hearts sprinkled from an evil conscience, and our bodies washed with pure water" (Hebrews 10:22); (2) "Let us hold fast the profession of *our* faith without wavering; (for he *is* faithful that promised)" [parenthesis and italics in KJV] (Hebrews 10:23); and (3) "And let us consider one another to provoke unto love and to good works" (Hebrews 10:24). The subjunctive mood in these instances are "hortatory" or "volitive." They express appeals to the will, exhortations or commands that may or may not be followed. The probability that what they exhort or command will be obeyed does not negate the fact that there always exists some degree of uncertainty. While it may seem obvious, for instance, when the author of Hebrews urges himself, his associates, and his addressees, with the words, "Let us hold fast the profession of *our* faith without wavering; (for he *is* faithful that promised)" [parenthesis and italics in KJV] (Hebrews 10:23), he is not promising that all believers will do that.

Hebrews 10:25 has often been used to tell believers to be regular in their church attendance. It says, "not forsaking the assembling of ourselves together, as the manner of some *is*; but exhorting *one another*" [italics in KJV]. In the context something more serious than sporadic church attendance is being addressed. And furthermore, instead of being a warning not to hold private worship in the woods, the command is addressing the problem of people "forsaking" (ἐγκαταλείπω) or "abandoning" the Christian community altogether. This is an example of one who fails to "hold fast the confession of *our* faith [or "hope"]" [italics in KJV] (Hebrews 10:23) (κατέχωμεν τὴν ὁμολογίαν τῆς ἐλπίδος). The command is given in light of Jesus' imminent return: "and so much the more, as ye see the day approaching" (Hebrews 10:25).

The author states the serious consequences for anyone contemplating abandoning the Christian community: "for if we sin wilfully after that we have received the knowledge of the truth, there remaineth no more sacrifice for sins" (Hebrews 10:26). The reader/listener is brought up short by the placement of the adverb "wilfully" (ἑκουσίως) in the initial emphatic position in the sentence. The subject under consideration is intentional abandonment. The situation is serious because for one who abandons the Christian community "there remaineth no more sacrifice for sins" (Hebrews 10:26).

First John 1:9 tells believers that "If we confess our sins, he is faithful and just to forgive us *our* sins, and to cleanse us from all unrighteousness" [italics in KJV]. That is the means by which believers find forgiveness. The author of Hebrews is contemplating a situation in which a believer no longer avails himself or herself of that provision. What is left for that believer: "but a certain fearful looking for of judgment and fiery indignation, which shall devour the adversaries" (Hebrews 10:27). Opposing God is serious business. Why would anyone purposefully subject himself or herself to the judgment of God?

The reader/listener is invited to consider the example of Old Testament believers: "He that despised Moses' law died without mercy under two or three witnesses" (Hebrews 10:28). After due process the loss of physical life was the prospect faced by Old Testament believers who committed certain sins. Reasoning from the lesser to the greater, the former referring to how matters were handled under the old covenant and the latter to the privileged position of believers under the new covenant, the rhetorical question is asked, "Of how much sorer punishment, suppose ye, shall he be thought worthy, who hath trodden under foot the Son of God, and hath counted the blood of the covenant, wherewith he was sanctified, an unholy thing, and hath done despite unto the Spirit of grace?" (Hebrews 10:29). Louw and Nida say that the verb translated "trodden under foot" (καταπατέω) is "(a figurative extension of [the] meaning of καταπατέω 'to trample on,') to thoroughly despise someone or something–'to despise, to treat with complete disdain'" (Johannes P. Louw and Eugene A. Nida, *Greek-English Lexicon of the New Testament Based on Semantic Domains*, 2nd ed. [New York: United Bible Societies, 2nd ed], 1989, 1:763, parentheses in original).

The adjective "unholy" ("unclean" = NASB) (κοινός) describes something that in the Old Testament was to be avoided in order not to be contaminated by it. That was what someone abandoning their Christian walk would be doing. Not only would Jesus be treated shabbily by a believer abandoning the faith; but also the Holy Spirit who indwelt him or her would be "done despite" ("insulted" = NASB) (ἐνυβρίζω): "and hath done despite unto the Spirit of grace" (καὶ τὸ πνεῦμα τῆς χάριτος ἐνυβρίσας). The very One who could help would thereby be rejected.

The writer leaves no doubt that he is referring to a believer by saying, "the blood of the covenant wherewith he was sanctified" (Hebrews 10:29). Additional confirmation that believers are in view are seen in the words, "The Lord will judge his people" (Hebrews 10:30). The quotation is from Psalm 135:14 that says, "For the Lord will judge his people, and he will repent himself concerning his servants." The divine judgment of a believer is summed up with the words, "*It is* a fearful thing to fall into the hands of the living God" [italics in KJV] (Hebrews 10:31). The NASB says that, "It is a terrifying thing to fall into the hands of the living God."

The inspired writer wished that fate on no one, so he implored his readers/listeners, "But call to remembrance the former days, in which, after ye were illuminated, ye endured a great fight of afflictions" (Hebrews 10:32). They were to remember the "good old days" of their Christian walk and "cast not away" ("throw away" = NASB) (ἀποβάλλω) what they had worked so diligently for: "Cast not away therefore your confidence, which hath great recompence of reward" (Hebrews 10:35). They could not lose their salvation but the same could not be said about their "reward" (μισθαποδοσία). They needed "endurance" (ὑπομονή) to finish the course of the Christian life that they had begun so well: "For ye have need of patience, that, after ye have done the will of God, ye might receive the promise" (Hebrews 10:36). "The promise" is a reference to reward.

If some were contemplating abandoning the faith, the writer expresses his resolve and that of those close to him to persevere. He says, "But we are not of them who draw back unto perdition; but of them that believe to the saving of the soul" Hebrews 10:39). The NASB says, "But we are not of those who shrink back to destruction, but of those who have faith to the preserving of the soul." The "preserving of the soul" (περιποίησιν ψυχῆς) should be taken as the preservation of their physical lives. The term translated "soul" (ψυχή) can mean "physical life," and that is what is in view.

In the context the example of the Israelites under the Law is that of physical death as a consequence for those who "despised Moses' Law" ("set aside the Law of Moses" = NASB ἀθετήσας. . .νόμον Μωϋσέως). "He that despised Moses' law died without mercy under two or three witnesses" (Hebrews 10:28). The consequence of God prematurely taking His child home as a form of chastisement can be averted. The author's words about his personal resolve were not intended to be taken as a promise to all believers that they will in fact endure to the end of life. His warning to the contrary is proof of that. Joshua expressed the same sentiment with the words, "but as for me and my house, we will serve the Lord" (Joshua 24:15). Similar to the words of the writer of Hebrews this was an expression of intention, not inevitability.

Hebrews chapter 11 is an extended discussion of faith. Many have taken it, and particularly the opening verse, as a definition of faith: "Now faith is the substance of things hoped for, the evidence of things not seen" (Hebrews 11:1). The NASB says, "Now faith is the assurance of *things* hoped for, the conviction of things not seen" [italics in NASB]. Machen writes the following about this verse: "These words are not a definition or a complete account of faith: they tell what faith is, but they do not tell all that it is, and they do not separate it from all that it is not" (J. Gresham Machen, *What is Faith?* [Grand Rapids: Eerdmans, 1925], 229). The support Machen gives for his statement bears repeating:

> There are other utterances also in the New Testament, which are sometimes treated as definitions and yet are not definitions at all. Thus when James says that "pure religion and undefiled before God and the Father is this, To visit the fatherless and widows in their affliction, and to keep himself unspotted from the world [James 1:27]," he is not giving a definition or a complete description of religion; he is telling what religion is, but he is not telling all that it is: pure religion is to keep himself unspotted from the world, but it is far more than that (ibid., 229-30).

The way to determine if something is a definition is to view it as an equation. As with an equation a definition should be reversible: if A = B, it is also true that B = A. Machen's discussion that follows the quotation above is a prime example:

> Or when it is said that "God is love" [1 John 4:8], that does not mean at all that God is only love. It is a very great logical error to single out such an affirmation and treat it as though it were a definition; many such affirmations would be necessary in order to obtain anything like a complete account of God; God is love, but He is many other things as well (ibid., 230).

Machen holds the following view concerning "faith" (πίστις) in Hebrews 11:1 "The aspect of faith which is here placed in the foreground is one special part of the intellectual aspect of it" (ibid.). Machen sees in Hebrews 11:1 a partial definition of faith.

The author of Hebrews does not intend to give a definition of "faith" (πίστις) in Hebrews 11:1. "Faith" (πίστις) is a mental activity that includes philosophical/ epistemological and psychological elements.

The former involves believing something to be true or someone to be speaking the truth and the later a state of mind described as relying or depending on something or someone. Both are included in the author's discussion that begins in Hebrews chapter 11 and continues into chapter 12. Both aspects are not always emphasized in each usage but the author's intent lies elsewhere.

Two Greek nouns in Hebrews 11:1 have proved challenging to English translators. The first (ὑπόστασις) is translated "assurance" in the NASB, "Now faith is the assurance of *things* [italics in NASB] hoped for" (Ἔστιν δὲ πίστις ἐλπιζομένων ὑπόστασις) and "substance" in the KJV. Louw and Nida have two possible definitions for this noun ὑπόστασις: (1) "the essential or basic nature of an entity—'substance, nature, essence, real being'" (Johannes P. Louw and Eugene A. Nida, *Greek-English Lexicon of the*

New Testament Based on Semantic Domains, 2nd ed. [New York: United Bible Societies, 2nd ed], 1989, 1:586) and; (2) "that which provides the basis for trust and reliance–'trust, confidence, assurance'" (ibid., 1:376).

If the second definition is accepted, then "faith" (πίστις) is being equated with the "evidence" (ὑπόστασις) that provides the basis for "*things* [italics in NASB] hoped for" (ἐλπιζομένων)–the ellipsis is required because the noun ὑπόστασις is singular and feminine while the participle ἐλπιζομένων is plural and neuter or masculine. In essence the instrumental cause, "faith" (πίστις), would be equated with its antecedent cause, the "evidence" (ὑπόστασις) on which it is based. However, if the first definition for ὑπόστασις is the author's intended meaning, then he is equating "faith" (πίστις) with the "reality" (ὑπόστασις) of the expectation, "*things* hoped for" [italics in NASB] (ἐλπιζομένων). That is what the author is conveying. The fulfillment of what faith is exercised for is so certain that it is to be equated with the reality of what it will obtain, even though the fulfillment is not present when faith is exercised but is future to it. The phrase that follows builds on that thought.

In the phrase "the conviction of things not seen" (NASB) (πραγμάτων ἔλεγχος οὐ βλεπομένων) the noun, ἔλεγχος, has proven difficult to translate and is rendered "conviction" in the NASB and "evidence" by the KJV. Louw and Nida define ἔλεγχος as "the evidence, normally based on argument or discussion, as to the truth or reality of something—'proof, verification, evidence for'" (ibid., 1:673). The author views "faith" (πίστις) as "proof," "verification" or "evidence" (ἔλεγχος) for what will be fulfilled, "of things not seen" (πραγμάτων. . .οὐ βλεπομένων). Faith itself is viewed as providing certainty. The writer's Old Testament examples that follow show that the invisible and yet-to-be-experienced fulfillments are certain because of the One whose words and in whose person confidence is placed.

The value of faith in God that the writer of Hebrews is applauding and exhorting his readers to emulate is based on the trustworthiness of the One who has promised and will perform. Faith is foundational, both for acquiring eternal salvation and living a life pleasing to God. "But without faith *it is* impossible to please *him*" [italics in KJV] (Hebrews 11:6). Faith begins with an understanding of who God is and believing the revelation about Him to be true. One must accept as true His personal, eternal existence: "for he that cometh to God must believe that he is" (Hebrews 11:6). Faith in God, the object of it, is directed toward a desired outcome. The one exercising faith believes that God will act on his or her behalf: "*that* he is a rewarder of them that diligently seek him" [italics in KJV] (Hebrews 11:6). Those who put their trust in God initially will find that He is ready to accept them into His family and then will fulfill what He has promised and grant their petitions according to His sovereign will.

The account of Noah in Hebrews 11 describes his temporal and eternal salvation that resulted from faith: "By faith Noah, being warned of God of things not seen as yet, moved with fear, prepared an ark to the saving of his house; by the which he condemned the world, and became heir of the righteousness which is by faith" (Hebrews 11:7). Because of Noah's "faith" (πίστις) he and his family experienced "salvation" (σωτηρία), a reference to physical deliverance from the fatal worldwide flood. Noah was also eternally saved by faith. "By faith Noah. . .became heir of the righteousness which is by faith" (Hebrews 11:7).

The "righteousness" Noah received was imputed righteousness and was not a reward for or the result of building the ark. The two results of building the ark by faith were: (1) "to the saving of his house" (from physical death by drowning) (Hebrews 11:7) (εἰς σωτηρίαν τοῦ οἴκου αὐτοῦ); and (2) "by which he condemned the world" (Hebrews 11:7) (δι' ἧς κατέκρινεν τὸν κόσμον). With the latter, the relative pronoun translated "which" (ἧς) is feminine and can refer back to either "faith" (πίστις) or the "ark" (κιβωτός) both of which are feminine. Both Noah's faith and the ark were testimony against those who rejected God and the message of coming judgment by means of a worldwide flood and served to condemn them.

Noah's eternal salvation, the divine imputation of righteousness to him, is not to be taken as a reward earned for obedience. Noah's "righteousness" (δικαιοσύνη) was explicitly and exclusively "righteousness which is by faith" (Hebrews 11:7) ("according to faith" = NASB) (κατὰ πίστιν). With that having been made clear in the text, Abraham's example that follows is not to be construed as introducing obedience (works) as a requirement for eternal salvation when it says, "By faith Abraham, when he was called to go out into a place which he should after receive for an inheritance, obeyed" (Hebrews 11:8). The "inheritance" (κληρονομία) was not heaven or eternal life but land. A possible indication of that are the words, "and he went out, not knowing whither he went" (Hebrews 11:8). God had not given Abraham a GPS coordinate, or its historical equivalent.

Additional confirmation that actions are not a requirement for the acquisition of eternal life is the Genesis account of Abraham and the quotations of it by Paul in Romans and Galatians where works are excluded. Abraham's descendants would receive the geographical land, but in the meantime he, his children and grandchildren would wander about without settling down: "By faith he sojourned in the land of promise, as *in* a strange country, dwelling in tabernacles with Isaac and Jacob, the heirs with him of the same promise" [italics in KJV] (Hebrews 11:9).

In addition to the promise of land Abraham looked forward to something far more valuable and permanent than an earthly location. The author refers to it as a "city" (πόλις) designed and built by God: "For he looked for a city which hath foundations, whose builder and maker *is* God" [italics in KJV] (Hebrews 11:10). If God's purpose had been for Abraham to find an earthly city, he came from one in Ur of the Chaldees and could have returned: "And truly, if they had been mindful of that *country* from whence they came out, they might have had opportunity to have returned" [italics in KJV] (Hebrews 11:15). There were cities back in Mesopotamia. But by faith Abraham and his descendants knew that what they were looking forward to would not be found on earth: "But now they desire a better *country*, that is, an heavenly" [italics in KJV] (Hebrews 11:16).

In Hebrews 11:6 the author writes about "faith" as the requirement for one who desires to "please" God: "But without faith *it is* impossible to please *him*" [italics in KJV]. In Hebrews 11:16 the author emphasizes that God was pleased with the "faith" (πίστις) of Abraham and his descendants, and he does so by negating an opposite: "wherefore God is not ashamed to be called their God." God looks favorably on human "faith" (πίστις) because He has made heavenly preparations for those who put their faith in Him: "for he hath prepared for them a city" (Hebrews 11:16).

After writing in detail about the faith of many Old Testament individuals, the author names six others and mentions the prophets. Concerning them he says, "Who through faith subdued kingdoms, wrought righteousness, obtained promises, stopped the mouths of lions, quenched the violence of fire, escaped the edge of the sword, out of weakness were made strong, waxed valiant in fight, turned to flight the armies of the aliens" (Hebrews 11:33-34). The result of women's faith is also mentioned, "Women received their dead raised to life again" (Hebrews 11:35). With that the author has come to the temporal culmination of what can be obtained by faith. From an earthly point of view what follows is a descent from lofty heights of accomplishment but it actually soars even higher. Faith does not always result in visible triumphs or successes.

From physical resurrection the writer of Hebrews ascends to the thought of spiritual life: "and others were tortured, not accepting deliverance; that they might obtain a better resurrection" (Hebrews 11:35). The author continues with a litany of additional affliction and suffering endured by saints who exercised faith in the past, "and others had trial of *cruel* mockings and scourgings, yea, moreover of bonds and imprisonment: they were stoned, they were sawn asunder, were tempted, were slain with the sword: they wandered about in sheepskins and goatskins; being destitute, afflicted, tormented" [italics in KJV] (Hebrews 11:36-37). With the insertion of a parenthetical comment the author interrupts his enumeration of persecution and gives his opinion of those who experienced such mistreatment: "(Of whom the world was not worthy)" [parenthesis in KJV] (Hebrews 11:38). The author's list ends with his referring to those who "wandered in deserts, and *in* mountains, and *in* dens and caves of the earth" [italics in KJV] (Hebrews 11:38).

Even those who from an earthly point of view met with success did not obtain the heavenly prize during their lifetime: "And these all, having obtained a good report through faith, received not the promise" (Hebrews 11:39). In a surprising twist the author departs from the expected explanation that what was promised was heaven and detours to what saints of the past accomplish in believers in the present: "God having provided some better thing for us, that they without us should not be made perfect" (Hebrews 11:40). Their physical lives came to an end but their examples live on. The story of their lives would be incomplete without including the effect that God intended their faith to have.

The example of the faith of people in the past is applied to the present: "Wherefore seeing we also are compassed about with so great a cloud of witnesses, let us lay aside every weight, and the sin which doth so easily beset *us*, and let us run with patience the race that is set before us" [italics in KJV] (Hebrews 12:1). The picture of a "cloud of witnesses" (νέφος μαρτύρων) is not a group of spectators in a stadium watching believers "run" (τρέχω). The testimony of the "witnesses" is the account of their lives of faith that tell later believers that a life of faith is well worth living. Old Testament believers put their trust in God and New Testament believers are exhorted to follow their example by trusting in Jesus: "Looking unto Jesus the author and finisher of *our* faith" [italics in KJV] (Hebrews 12:2). Jesus is the One in whom trust is placed initially at the time of conversion and He will bring the believer's faith to perfection. The present position of Jesus in the place of power and authority at God's right hand is proof that Jesus can complete the sanctification that follows a believer's salvation: "and is set down at the right hand of the throne of God" (Hebrews 12:2).

Apparently the writer of Hebrews did not have a high regard for his reader's spiritual progress. Knowing that difficult times were ahead for them, he advised, "For consider him that endured such contradiction of sinners against himself, lest ye be wearied and faint in your minds" (Hebrews 12:3). Persecution would test the readers' faith in the future or they were already undergoing it and were failing: "Ye have not yet resisted unto blood, striving against sin" (Hebrews 12:4). The readers are warned about God's chastisement either because they had forgotten or perhaps it was the writer's way of saying that in essence they may as well have forgotten because they were ignoring the consequences of sin in a believer's life: "And ye have forgotten the exhortation which speaketh unto you as unto children, My son, despise not thou the chastening of the Lord, nor faint when thou art rebuked of him" (Hebrews 12:5).

The readers are reminded that the purpose of God's discipline is "that *we* might be partakers of his holiness" [italics in KJV] (Hebrews 12:10). Those who respond appropriately to divine discipline experience a positive outcome: "nevertheless afterward it yieldeth the peaceable fruit of righteousness unto them which are exercised thereby" (Hebrews 12:11). What the readers needed was spiritual strength and enablement: "Wherefore lift up the hands which hang down, and the feeble knees; and make straight paths for your feet, lest that which is lame be turned out of the way; but let it rather be healed" (Hebrews 12:12-13). If something was not done, matters would get worse.

In the midst of exhortations and warnings the author includes a verse that unfortunately has caused controversy. Hebrews 12:14 says, "Follow peace with all *men*, and holiness [τὸν ἁγιασμόν], without which no man shall see the Lord" [italics in KJV. The NASB says, "Pursue peace with all men, and the sanctification without which no one will see the Lord." The last clause of the verse is the part in question: "and holiness, without which no man shall see the Lord" or "and the sanctification without which no one will see the Lord."

There are two types of biblical "holinesses" or "sanctifications" that believers experience; one is positional, the other progressive. Positional sanctification is absolute holiness that is the possession of every believer which he receives the moment he places his faith in Jesus because of His imputed righteousness. On the other hand, progressive sanctification is not absolute holiness but is relative to the progress a believer is making in his or her Christian walk. Progressive sanctification is in view in Hebrews 12:14 because positional sanctification that believers already have is not to be "pursued" (διώκω) by them; it is already their possession.

The verb translated "will see" (ὄψεται–future, middle, indicative from ὁράω = "see") may have a figurative sense. Louw and Nida include that as a possibility for this term: "to experience an event or state, normally in negative expressions indicating what one will not experience–'to experience, to undergo'" (Johannes P. Louw and Eugene A. Nida, *Greek-English Lexicon of the New Testament Based on Semantic Domains*, 2nd ed. [New York: United Bible Societies, 2nd ed], 1989, 1:809). Louw and Nida give examples of the negative use. In Hebrews 12:14 the figurative meaning of "to experience an event" is used positively; believers will experience Jesus' presence at His return. However, it may have a literal meaning and be a reference to the visual experience of seeing Jesus. Whatever choice is made, it is a reference to a future experience anticipated by all believers.

But how is progressive sanctification to be understood as a requirement for "seeing" (ὁράω) Jesus in the future? The degree to which progressive sanctification is pursued and achieved by a believer varies. But on that future day when believers see Jesus there will be a convergence of positional and progressive sanctification. Whatever is lacking in a believer's progressive sanctification will be completed. There will no longer be a dissonance between position and practice, and the deficiencies of human experience will be filled in by the sufficiency of the Savior. Every believer will be one hundred percent sanctified both positionally and practically.

Paul anticipated that future day: "For now we see through a glass, darkly; but then face to face: now I know in part; but then shall I know even as also I am known" (1 Corinthians 13:12). The apostle John likewise foresaw that time: "Beloved, now are we the sons of God, and it doth not yet appear what we shall be: but we know that, when he shall appear, we shall be like him; for we shall see him as he is" (1 John 3:2). John uses the same verb "see" (ὁράω) as is used in Hebrews 12:14 to refer to the same event.

John uses the anticipation of that future event to exhort believers to lead holy lives: "And every man that hath this hope in him purifieth himself, even as he is pure" (1 John 3:3). The writer of Hebrews in Hebrews 12:14 also ties the present pursuit of progressive sanctification with that future event. He says, "Follow peace with all *men*" [italics in KJV] and follows it with, "looking diligently lest any man fail of the grace of God" (Hebrews 12:15). In light of the future when salvation and sanctification, the positional and progressive aspects of the believer's identity, will converge, he or she is exhorted to keep progressing in godliness. The same thought is present when believers are encouraged to pursue "Christlikeness," even though no one will fully achieve it during his lifetime. A believer does so, knowing that in the future all deficiencies will be made up and one day "Christlikeness" will be an actuality.

Consider the following alternative to the correct biblical interpretation. Someone may say, "You as a believer are exhorted to pursue a plan of sanctification that is less than one hundred percent; perhaps seventy, eighty, or even ninety-nine percent that is your personal requirement for seeing Jesus. If you are not on one of these plans, you will not see Jesus because you are not saved." In such a scenario a leader can tell his followers that their own personal ninety-five or ninety-nine percent plan will get them an audience with Jesus but they are not sure of the prospects of anyone else whose plan is less than theirs or who have achieved less than they have. This unbiblical scheme promotes pride and minimizes sin.

"The sanctification without which no one will see the Lord" (Hebrews 12:14 NASB) is absolute and complete holiness. Anything short of that fails to meet the perfect requirements. The author of Hebrews describes the heavenly scene with these words, "But ye are come unto mount Sion, and unto the city of the living God, the heavenly Jerusalem, and to an innumerable company of angels, to the general assembly and church of the firstborn, which are written in heaven, and to God the Judge of all, and to the spirits of just men made perfect" (Hebrews 12:22-23). On that future day believers will stand in heaven and see Jesus, having been made perfect positionally and practically.

And in heaven believers will be with, "Jesus the mediator of the new covenant, and to the blood of sprinkling, that speaketh better things than *that of* Abel" [italics in KJV] (Hebrews 12:24). The new covenant is entered into by putting trust in Jesus, the all-sufficient sacrifice for sin. The reason trust can reliably be placed in Him is because "Jesus Christ [is] the same yesterday, and to day, and for ever" (Hebrews 13:8).

Evidence for the Identity of Jesus in the Epistle of James

Perhaps as no other epistle James has been employed in support of diametrically opposed doctrinal positions. Without repeating the arguments of many who have wrestled with its contents, a few comments pertinent to the subject at hand will be offered. Any valid interpretation, particularly of the controversial passage, James 2:14-26, revolves around two points. The first of them is the issue of the addressees of the epistle. Was James writing to saved or unsaved individuals or a mixture of the two? Some Bible teachers hold that the epistle was addressed to both believers and professing believers, the latter being unsaved individuals in the church. Those teachers see a mixed audience in many New Testament passages. The present writer is reminded of the verbal bromide that when the only tool in your toolbox is a hammer everything appears to be a nail. Obviously one would be ill-advised to employ the use of a hammer if the fastener presenting itself is a screw. Before automatically assuming a mixed audience as recipients of this epistle the interpreter should assess the data.

In this epistle James repeatedly emphasizes that his readers are indeed saved and he does so in a personal way. Specifically, leading up to the controversial passage in chapter 2 the author refers to them as "my brethren" (James 1:2) (ἀδελφοί μου), and in the admonition about prejudice in James 2:1 he does so as well. The specific reference to a saved readership is also used in advising believers, "the brother" (James 1:9) (ὁ ἀδελφὸς), who is poor is to "boast" (Καυχάσθω present, either middle or passive, imperative third person singular of καυχάομαι = "boast") in his destitution. In 1:16, 19, and 2:5 James addresses his readers as "my beloved brethren" (ἀδελφοί μου ἀγαπητοί).

In addition to these six times that the author refers to his audience as fellow believers with the term "brother" (ἀδελφός), that term is used in the controversial passage as well, particularly in its introduction: "What *doth it* profit, my brethren, though a man say he hath faith, and have not works?" [italics in KJV] (James 2:14). The example the author offers continues to restrict the addressees as fellow believers: "If a brother or sister be naked, and destitute of daily food, and one of you say unto them, Depart in peace, be *ye* warmed and filled; notwithstanding ye give them not those things which are needful to the body; what *doth it* profit?" [italics in KJV] (James 2:15-16).

In the passage immediately preceding the controversial passage on faith the author makes it doubly clear that he is addressing Christians, not only addressing them as such but also embedding it in his exhortation: "My brethren, have not the faith of our Lord Jesus Christ, *the Lord* of glory, with respect of persons" [italics in KJV] (James 2:1). The readers had "faith" (πίστις) in Jesus and are being exhorted or admonished about how they "hold" (ἔχω), that is, how they exhibit or exercise that faith in their Christian life. The implication is that they could indeed do so negatively and the illustration that follows makes the negative possibility explicit: "For if there come unto your assembly a man with a gold ring, in goodly apparel, and there come in also a poor man in vile raiment; and ye have respect to him that weareth the gay clothing, and say unto him, Sit thou here in a good place; and say to the poor, Stand thou there, or sit here under my footstool" (James 2:2-3). Considering that the subject continues to be faith as it relates to a believer, it would seem strange in the extreme that the intended audience would be switched in James 2:14-26 without the slightest textual indication that the author is doing so.

The controversial passage on faith begins with the question, "What *doth it* profit, my brethren, though a man say he hath faith, and have not works?" [italics in KJV] (James 2:14). The articular noun translated "profit" (τὸ ὄφελος), is used only three times in the Greek New Testament. It is present in this verse and in verse 16, as well as 1 Corinthians 15:32, where Paul applies it to himself: "If after the manner of men I have fought with beasts at Ephesus, what advantageth it me." The NASB says, "If from human motives I fought with wild beasts at Ephesus, what does it profit me?" Here in James the word "profit" (ὄφελος) refers to a benefit or advantage.

In James 2:15-16 the noun is used to indicate that ignoring someone's need does not benefit them: "If a brother or sister be naked, and destitute of daily food, and one of you say unto them, Depart in peace, be *ye* warmed and filled; notwithstanding ye give them not those things which are needful to the body; what *doth it* profit?" [italics in KJV]. The answer expected is that it is of no use. In this instance words without actions are worthless.

In James 2:14 the question, which James answers, is that faith with no works is of no benefit. Before answering that, a follow-up question is asked, "Can faith save him?" (James 2:14). Earlier in James the verb "save" (σῴζω) is used in a sanctification context where "deliver" or "rescue" is the appropriate meaning: "Wherefore lay apart all filthiness and superfluity of naughtiness, and receive with meekness the engrafted word, which is able to save your souls. But be ye doers of the word, and not hearers only, deceiving your own selves" (James 1:21-22). The Greek word translated "soul" (ψυχή) can refer either to the spiritual immaterial part of man or to his physical life. Since the readers are explicitly included in the circle of the saved and their spiritual eternal destiny is already secure, the reference is to their physical life.

One of the beneficial consequences of living in obedience to God's Word is the preservation of physical life. One would expect that the author would employ the same meaning in James 2:14 unless he provided a reason not to do so. The anticipated answer to the second question in James 2:14 is "No, it cannot save him," that is, it cannot "deliver" or "rescue" him. What the reader cannot be delivered from if he has faith but does not have works is found in the following context. The illustration that follows pertains not to eternal condemnation but the temporal consequences of inaction.

It should be noted that in the margin the NASB translation has the alternative for the English word "that" (James 2:14): "Can that faith save him?" (μὴ δύναται ἡ πίστις σῶσαι αὐτόν), which is the word "the," as in "the faith." While "Can the faith save him?" sounds awkward in English, it can be translated without the word "the," "Can faith save him?" This is because Greek often uses the definite article with an abstract noun such as "faith," whereas English does not. The question can be translated as the KJV has it: "Can faith save him?" The "that" included in the NASB has been taken pejoratively by some to mean "that kind of faith" with the interpretation that the "kind" of faith intended by James was a false, nonsaving, professing, but not possessing species of faith.

In that view the Greek definite article "the" (ἡ) is taken as an anaphoric use, that of previous reference. Wallace uses James 2:14 as an example of an anaphoric use of the article and writes: "The use of the article both points back to a certain kind of faith as defined by the author and is used to particularize an abstract noun" (Daniel Wallace, *Greek Grammar beyond the Basics*, [Grand Rapids: Zondervan, 1996], 219). Wallace also writes, "In particular, the author examines two kinds of faith in 2:14-26, defining a non-working faith as a non-saving faith and a productive faith as one that saves" (ibid.). Wallace assumes that the verb "save" (σῴζω) refers to eternal salvation and not temporal deliverance, a contextually suspect conclusion. He also assumes that a "non-working," "non-saving" faith is what the anaphoric article is referring back to. In a certain sense it may, but not in the way Wallace proposes.

As Wallace himself observes in his discussion: "the antecedent needs to be examined in its own immediate context" (ibid.). The immediate context does not require Wallace's interpretation. Wallace assumes that the author had in mind "two kinds of faith" (ibid.). There are not "two kinds of faith," if by that one means a negative and a positive Greek semantic range of the word "faith" (πίστις). No Greek lexicon has a nonsalvific type of "faith" (πίστις) as one of the possible meanings. The possible presence of a negative "faith" (πίστις) would have to be established contextually and not semantically. James is not coining a new meaning for "faith" (πίστις), one that has a negative connotation. Biblical faith is exercised in at least two arenas: in the realm of salvation, and in sanctification. Because James is addressing fellow believers, one would expect that what he applies to them would be about their sanctification.

In James 2:14 the article is most likely used anaphorically, but what it refers back to must be examined. Wallace assumes that the meaning of the term "faith" (πίστις), must be fundamentally salvifically deficient in some way. However, the word "faith" (πίστις) does not require or need to acquire the negative nuance Wallace gives it. The faith James refers to is "faith" (πίστις) that is not accompanied by "works" (ἔργα). The absence of "works" (ἔργα) in association with "faith" (πίστις) does not mean that the term "faith" (πίστις) be something or mean something different from what it normally is and means. Its usefulness has been compromised by the lack of the presence of something else (works) but its fundamental character is not necessarily altered. "Faith" (πίστις), dependence on God, independent of action empowered by the Holy Spirit, has no practical benefit.

For James and the rest of the Bible, "faith" (πίστις) and "works" (ἔργα) in the Christian life are parallel. They are not two parts necessary for obtaining eternal salvation. James's careful explanation and choice of Old Testament examples that illustrate the point he is making show that such a heretical conclusion is not to be reached.

When faith and works are both present in the life of a believer, there are beneficial results for him or her and for fellow believers. James's real-life illustration is that of someone just telling a fellow believer to have his physical needs met but not actually doing something about it (James 2:15-16). His point is that there is no benefit of doing one without also doing the other. James applies the illustration and explicitly states the need for both: "Even so faith, if it hath not works, is dead, being alone" (James 2:17). The issue may be raised that applying the adjective "dead" (νεκρός), as a predicate to "faith" (πίστις), says something intrinsically about the nature of "faith" (πίστις) that is being referred to.

Part of the confusion stems from the idea that the author is referring to a single "faith/works" event in which "works," or the lack thereof, are somehow linguistically integrated into the semantic range of "faith." However, "works" can be contextually included or excluded as results of "faith," or as a simultaneous event, but they each remain separate linguistic entities. Attempts to define "faith" (πίστις) on the basis of a subsequent (result) or simultaneous occurrence, that is separate from it, employ linguistically and rationally flawed methodology. The semantic ranges of the terms "faith" (πίστις) and "work" (ἔργον) do not overlap. The words themselves cannot be forced to share common meaning.

In James 2:17 the term "dead" (νεκρός) has been understood in various ways. Some say it refers to a faith that is nonredemptive in the context of eternal salvation. Others hold that it is faith that was once alive and is now dead. Others hold that it never existed in the first place. James's use of the adjective "dead" (νεκρός) is figurative rather than literal because it modifies an abstract noun, that is, "faith" (πίστις). Of the New Testament figurative uses of the adjective "dead" (νεκρός), one that deserves attention is in the book of Hebrews where it modifies the noun "work" (ἔργον). Hebrews 6:1 speaks of "not laying again the foundation of repentance from dead works, and of faith toward God." The adjective "dead" (νεκρῶν) modifies the noun "works" (ἔργα), a vivid figurative description of their failure and uselessness in acquiring salvation which faith alone can achieve.

Hebrews 9:14 has a similar meaning: "How much more shall the blood of Christ, who through the eternal Spirit offered himself without spot to God, purge your conscience from dead works to serve the living God?" The works were not dead because they were the wrong kind of works. To say that they are dead does not mean that they did not exist. They existed but did not serve the purpose that those who did them thought they would achieve. James has the same thought when he refers to faith as being dead. It was not that faith did not exist. It did exist but it did not accomplish anything because it was unaccompanied by works in the context of their sanctification. The writer exhorts his Christian readers away from reliance on useless faith.

James has the thought of "usefulness" or the lack thereof in his use of the adjective "dead" (νεκρός). Three times James says that "faith" (πίστις), when it is unaccompanied by "works" (ἔργα), fails the "usefulness" test: (1) "What *doth it* profit?" [italics in KJV] (James 2:14) (Τί τὸ ὄφελος); (2) "what *doth it* profit?" [italics in KJV] (James 2:16) (τί τὸ ὄφελος;); and (3) "faith without works is dead?" (James 2:20) ("that faith without works is useless?" = NASB) (ὅτι ἡ πίστις χωρὶς τῶν ἔργων ἀργή ἐστιν;). The Greek adjective translated by the KJV as "dead" (ἀργή) and the NASB by "useless" is not "dead" but "useless" or "accomplishes nothing."

A relevant question is, "Useful in what way, and for what?" James gives a fourfold answer to that question in which he steers clear of the issue of heaven and hell, never compromising the requirement of faith alone for eternal salvation, because that is not his subject. James supports the assertion that faith plus no works is useless with four proofs, two that are negative and two that are positive.

James first uses an imaginary objector who supports his proposition about faith without works: "Yea, a man may say, Thou hast faith, and I have works: shew me thy faith without thy works, and I will shew thee my faith by my works" (James 2:18). The point is that faith is invisible while works are demonstrable. Someone with faith but no works has no way to "show" (δείκνυμι) that he has faith, whereas someone with both faith and works can "show" (δείκνυμι) that he does indeed have faith that goes with his works.

To that drawback of faith without simultaneous works is added another. Not only is faith without accompanying works invisible; it also imitates the faith of demons: "Thou believest that there is one God; thou doest well: the devils also believe, and tremble" (James 2:19). There is a textual question whether the original Greek had "God is one" (εἷς ἐστιν ὁ θεός), or "There is one God" (εἷς ἐστιν θεός), with the presence or absence of the article, respectively. Both textual variants refer to belief in a theological proposition related to the existence of God. To believe but fail to act is to do what demons do; they know that God exists and only exhibit fear as they "tremble" ("shudder" = NASB) (φρίσσω).

Attempts to analyze the salvific or nonsalvific faith of demons go beyond the author's intent. The parallel James draws is confined to the negative comparison of faith without accompanying activity to that of demons. The shock felt by modern readers of being compared to demons was shared by the original audience and is the effect that the author intends. These two reasons for avoiding having faith without works are summarized in these words: "But wilt thou know, O vain man, that faith without works is dead?" (James 2:20). The better translation is that of the NASB: "But are you willing to recognize, you foolish fellow, that faith without works is useless?" The question expects agreement: "Yes, faith without accompanying works is useless."

In contrast to the two negative reasons James gives why his readers are not to fail to have both faith and works, he gives the example of two Old Testament individuals in whose lives both faith and works were present. In contrast to demons whose example is not to be followed, the faith and works of these two are to be imitated. The first positive example is that of Abraham: "Was not Abraham our father justified by works, when he had offered Isaac his son upon the altar?" (James 2:21).

The answer James expected was, "Yes, Abraham was justified by works when he did that work." This question would have gotten the immediate attention of James's readers. Theological red flags went up with them even as it does with believers today. They knew about justification by faith alone in Christ alone, but being "justified" (δικαιόω) by works?

Chronology is the key to a correct understanding of James's words. From the earliest days of the New Testament church, believers were taught that Abraham had been saved by faith without works. Abraham was saved before the account of it was recorded in Genesis 15 and he was circumcised after that in Genesis 17. This fact is proof that works are not a requirement for eternal salvation.

The justification James is talking about fit in after both of those events described in Genesis 15 and 17. James gave an example of Abraham's works, recorded in Genesis 22. James says, "when he had offered Isaac his son upon the altar" (James 2:21). James follows up his question with the statement, "Seest thou how faith wrought with his works, and by works was faith made perfect" (James 2:22). The NASB says, "You see that faith was working with his works, and as a result of works, faith was perfected."

Some Bible teachers try to make "works" (ἔργα) the result, demonstration, or proof of "faith" (πίστις), something that comes after faith. But James does not write about works as a result. In his example from the life of Abraham, James chose the verb translated "wrought with" ("working with" = NASB) (συνεργέω), from which our English word "synergy" comes; a combined action or functioning. The "works" (ἔργα) James was talking about were not something that happened subsequent to "faith" (πίστις); they took place at the very same time. By definition results come after their cause and not at the same time.

What did James mean when he said that Abraham was "justified" (δικαιόω) at this juncture, long after he originally had "righteousness" (δικαιοσύνη) imputed to him? James uses the term "perfected" or "completed" (James 2:22) (ἐτελειώθη) to indicate what happened. God's purpose does not end with justification by faith alone without works but intends that it be followed by a life of faith plus works. Abraham's initial faith subsequently matured when it was combined with works. James also describes it as faith that was "fulfilled" (James 2:23) (ἐπληρώθη).

God's initial verdict was based on Abraham's faith alone and imparted imputed righteousness to him. The faith and works that followed resulted in another verdict based on that obedient faith. On the basis of the latter practical righteousness that included both faith and works Abraham achieved intimacy with God: "and he was called the Friend of God" (James 2:23). Jesus similarly told His disciples that they could have intimacy with Him by means of obedience: "Ye are my friends, if ye do whatsoever I command you" (John 15:14).

Because James's readers had been taught about justification by faith alone, they were probably shocked by the use of justification terminology in combination with works even as believers are today. That was James's way of getting their attention and he repeated that thought when he summed up his illustration from the life of Abraham: "Ye see then how that by works a man is justified, and not by faith only" (James 2:24). Hodges has noted that because the Greek word translated "alone" (μόνον) is an adverb and not an adjective it modifies the implied verb "justified" (δικαιοῦται) in the final clause in the sentence and not the noun "faith" (πίστεως) ("Hebrews" Zane Hodges, *Grace New Testament Commentary*, Robert N. Wilkin, ed. [Denton, TX: Grace Evangelical Society, 2010], 2:1122). A clearer translation for James 2:24 would be, "You see that a man is justified by works, and not only justified by faith."

Hodges holds that justification by faith is "before God" and justification by works is "before men" (ibid.). Because justification by faith alone that results in eternal salvation is a verdict rendered by God, it would be better to see them both as declarations by God with justification by faith plus works related to sanctification. There is a justification or divine declaration that excludes works and one that includes works. The justification that excludes works imparts imputed righteousness. The one that includes works is equivalent to what the master told two of his servants in the parable of the talents, "Well done, *thou* good and faithful servant" [italics in KJV]

(Matthew 25:21 and 23). James is expressing God's declared evaluation of the actions or lack thereof of believers.

The unlikely example of Rahab is mentioned by James: "Likewise also was not Rahab the harlot justified by works, when she had received the messengers, and had sent *them* out another way?" [italics in KJV] (James 2:25). James expects his question to be answered affirmatively: "Yes, Rahab was justified by works." Two of Rahab's actions are mentioned: (1) "when she had received the messengers" (James 2:25); and (2) "had sent *them* out another way" [italics in KJV] (James 2:25). She had faith as she did those things that were preceded by having placed her trust in the God of the Israelites.

We are not told about that initial prior exercise of faith alone, but what James is not saying is that her initial faith that resulted in the imputation of righteousness to her was on the basis of works or faith plus works. The fact that the two separate actions that are mentioned probably took place at least a day apart militates against faith for eternal salvation being referred to because they would not fit the instantaneous nature of saving faith. The justification by works that James envisions does not conflict with Paul's justification by faith alone because James's justification occurs after that of Paul's in the life of a believer.

James concludes his discussion with a summary statement: "For as the body without the spirit is dead, so faith without works is dead also" (James 2:26). The picture of a lifeless body vividly portrays a believer who is inactive. Nowhere in the entire discussion does James question the presence of faith, in fact he asserts that it is present. What he does explicitly state is the presence of one, "faith" (πίστις) with the absence of the other, "works" (ἔργα). To assume that James was questioning the existence of the believers' faith introduces unnatural elements in the passage.

James had some serious words to believers about the use of their tongues when it came to teaching fellow believers: "My brethren, be not many masters, knowing that we shall receive the greater condemnation" (James 3:1). The NASB translation better reflects the presence of the noun "teachers" (διδάσκαλοι): "Let not many *of you* become teachers, my brethren, knowing that as such we shall incur a stricter judgment" [italics in NASB]. James is addressing believers and including himself in their number. The seriousness of out-of-control speech (out of the Holy Spirit's control) is scathingly described in its comparison to an out-of-control raging inferno: "And the tongue *is* a fire, a world of iniquity: so is the tongue among our members, that it defileth the whole body, and setteth on fire the course of nature; and it is set on fire of hell" [italics in KJV].

If there is any question in the reader's mind about whom James is talking about, he writes, "Therewith bless we God, even the Father; and therewith curse we men, which are made after the similitude of God. Out of the same mouth proceedeth blessing and cursing" (James 3:9-10). One can almost sense James's exasperation with some of his readers who were probably guilty of that against which he was railing: "My brethren, these things ought not so to be" (James 3:10). To presume that believers could not do what James was explicitly warning them about is to make a mockery of the text and disagree with the inspired author.

The fire metaphor is followed by that of a fountain and a fig tree: "Doth a fountain send forth at the same place sweet *water* and bitter? Can the fig tree, my brethren, bear olive berries? either a vine, figs? so *can* no fountain both yield salt water and fresh" [italics in KJV] (James 3:11-12). One can almost sense the author's consternation. The equivalent of what was impossible in nature had been accomplished by believers whose speech failed to match their spiritual nature. Believers were being oblivious to what was obvious.

James continues his barrage against sin in the lives of believers: "Who *is* a wise man and endued with knowledge among you? Let him shew out of a good conversation his works with meekness of wisdom. But if ye have bitter envying and strife in your hearts, glory not, and lie not against the truth" [italics in KJV] (James 3:13-14). Reminiscent of James's comparing worthless, workless faith with the faith of demons (James 2:19), sin in the life of a believer ultimately has a demonic source: "This wisdom descendeth not from above, but *is* earthly, sensual, devilish ["demonic" = NASB]" [italics in KJV] (James 3:15).

Addressing believers James has some serious words in James 4:7-10:

> Submit yourselves therefore to God. Resist the devil, and he will flee from you. Draw nigh to God, and he will draw nigh to you. Cleanse *your* hands, *ye* sinners; and purify *your* hearts, *ye* double minded. Be afflicted, and mourn, and weep: let your laughter be turned to mourning, and *your* joy to heaviness. Humble yourselves in the sight of the Lord, and he shall lift you up [italics in KJV].

Calling believers "sinners" (James 4:8) (ἁμαρτωλός) is a serious matter, but James does so. To deny that they are believers is to fly in the face of the biblical facts. To say that these words are addressed to unbelievers telling them what they need to do to be saved is preposterous.

James viewed sins of "omission" just as seriously as those of "commission": "Therefore to him that knoweth to do good, and doeth *it* not, to him it is sin" [italics in KJV] (James 4:17). James held that believers would not be condemned eternally for their sins, but he did hold to the possibility of a judgment of some sort, perhaps confined to the temporal: "Grudge not one against another, brethren, lest ye be condemned: behold, the judge standeth before the door" (James 5:9). James considered swearing by believers to be a very serious issue: "But above all things, my brethren, swear not, neither by heaven, neither by the earth, neither by any other oath: but let your yea be yea; and *your* nay, nay; lest ye fall into condemnation" [italics in KJV] (James 5:12). The NASB says, "so that you may not fall under judgment."

James also recognized the susceptibility of the saved to be swayed from what they believed, and he concludes his epistle with these words: (James 5:12) "Brethren, if any of you do err from the truth, and one convert him; let him know, that he which converteth the sinner from the error of his way shall save a soul from death, and shall hide a multitude of sins" (James 5:19-20). The NASB says, "My brethren, if any among you strays from the truth, and one turns him back, let him know that he who turns a sinner from the error of his way will save his soul from death, and will cover a multitude of sins." In the context, the NASB translation "turn" is a better rendition of the verb ἐπιστρέφω that the KJV translates "convert." The context is that of correction rather than conversion.

In spite of James saying that his words are to "my brethren" (Ἀδελφοί μου) some Bible teachers think that this is not addressed to believers. But this is an inaccurate assumption. The word translated "soul" (ψυχή) is just as easily rendered "life," and "death" (θάνατος) can be physical death and need not be a reference to eternal death. James explicitly states that the one "erring," "straying" or "being led astray" (James 5:19) (πλανάω) and the one causing him or her to "turn back" (ἐπιστρέφω) are believers. Sin among believers is serious business.

Evidence for the Identity of Jesus in the Epistle of 1 Peter

Peter understood that faith in Jesus alone is the requirement for eternal salvation. His saved readers could be confident about their eternal destiny because they were among those "who are kept by the power of God through faith unto salvation ready to be revealed in the last time" (1 Peter 1:5). Their confident assurance was based on their trust in Jesus whom they loved and was the source of great joy: "Whom having not seen, ye love; in whom, though now ye see *him* not, yet believing, ye rejoice with joy unspeakable and full of glory" [italics in KJV] (1 Peter 1:8). Peter singled out their "faith" (πίστις) which would bring about their eternal salvation: "Receiving the end of your faith, *even* the salvation of *your* souls" [italics in KJV] (1 Peter 1:9).

A person was central to the eternal salvation of the people of God that was predicted from the beginning of the Old Testament: "Of which salvation the prophets have inquired and searched diligently, who prophesied of the grace *that should come* unto you: searching what, or what manner of time the Spirit of Christ which was in them did signify, when it testified beforehand the sufferings of Christ, and the glory that should follow" [italics in KJV] (1 Peter 1:10-11). The circumstances of the timing of His coming would identify His person, and Peter confirmed that his audience was indeed living in that day: "unto whom it was revealed, that not unto themselves, but unto us they did minister the things, which are now reported unto you by them that have preached the gospel unto you with the Holy Ghost sent down from heaven; which things the angels desire to look into" (1 Peter 1:12).

Peter's exhortations about Christian living made sense because of the One in whom they had placed their trust in for their eternal destiny: "Wherefore gird up the loins of your mind, be sober, and hope to the end for the grace that is to be brought unto you at the revelation of Jesus Christ" (1 Peter 1:13). Now that they were God's children, just as earthly children were expected to obey their parents, they were to obey God: "As obedient children, not fashioning yourselves according to the former lusts in your ignorance" (1 Peter 1:14). Obedience was not to prove that they were God's children, nor would disobedience disprove their identity.

They were to imitate the character of their heavenly Father: "But as he which hath called you is holy, so be ye holy in all manner of conversation; because it is written, Be ye holy; for I am holy" (1 Peter 1:15-16). Their heavenly Father was the One to whom they were ultimately accountable: "And if ye call on the Father, who without respect of persons judgeth according to every man's work, pass the time of your sojourning *here* in fear" [italics in KJV] (1 Peter 1:17). They were not to "fear" that they were not God's children but live in reverent obedience to Him.

Peter reiterated that his readers' relationship with God was not in doubt: "Forasmuch as ye know that ye were not redeemed with corruptible things, *as* silver and gold, from your vain conversation *received* by tradition from your fathers" [italics in KJV] (1 Peter 1:18). Their position as children of their heavenly Father contrasted with that of their earthly fathers. All they could hope to inherit from human ancestors were "silver" (ἀργύριον) and "gold" (χρυσίον). In contrast their spiritual inheritance was purchased with something far superior to what earthly fathers could pass on to them: "But with the precious blood of Christ, as of a lamb without blemish and without spot" (1 Peter 1:19).

The price paid for man's sin by Jesus' death is put to the account of those who put their faith in Him: "Who verily was foreordained before the foundation of the world, but was manifest in these last times for you, who by him do believe in God, that raised him up from the dead, and gave him glory; that your faith and hope might be in God" (1 Peter 1:20-21). The unity of the Trinity is such that placing one's trust in Jesus is inseparable from faith in God the Father. As Peter put it, believers are those "who by him [Jesus] do believe in God" (1 Peter 1:21). There is no biblical "Jesus only" salvation that excludes God the Father. And there is no biblical "Jehovah only" salvation that denies Jesus. The identity of Jesus cannot be understood without that of God the Father. Placing trust in Jesus cannot occur without accepting the truth of His deity.

The foundation of faith in God for eternal salvation and for following in obedience is found in God's Word. The reliability of Scripture is the basis for initial belief and subsequent behavior: "Seeing ye have purified your souls in obeying the truth through the Spirit unto unfeigned love of the brethren, *see that ye* love one another with a pure heart fervently" [italics in KJV] (1 Peter 1:22). Because of the unity of Scripture it is applicable and trustworthy: "Being born again, not of corruptible seed, but of incorruptible, by the word of God, which liveth and abideth for ever" (1 Peter 1:23).

Peter provides evidence that his words about the Word of God are corroborated in the Old Testament: "For all flesh *is* as grass, and all the glory of man as the flower of grass. The grass withereth, and the flower thereof falleth away: but the word of the Lord endureth for ever" [italics in KJV] (1 Peter 1:24-25). Peter's quotation includes parts of Isaiah 40:6-8 from the Septuagint (LXX) the Greek translation of the Hebrew Old Testament (Πᾶσα σὰρξ χόρτος, καὶ πᾶσα δόξα ἀνθρώπου ὡς ἄνθος χόρτου, ἐξηράνθη ὁ χόρτος, καὶ τὸ ἄνθος ἐξέπεσεν, τὸ δὲ ῥῆμα τοῦ θεοῦ ἡμῶν μένει εἰς τὸν αἰῶνα). The gospel that had been preached to Peter's readers was God's Word: "And this is the word which by the gospel was preached to you" (1 Peter 1:25) (τοῦτο δέ ἐστιν τὸ ῥῆμα τὸ εὐαγγελισθὲν εἰς ὑμᾶς).

The difference between the saved and the unsaved, those bound for heaven and those for hell, was an important distinction for Peter and should be for the church today. Addressing believers, Peter writes, "To whom coming, *as unto* a living stone, disallowed indeed of men, but chosen of God, *and* precious, ye also, as lively ["living" = NASB] stones, are built up a spiritual house, an holy priesthood, to offer up spiritual sacrifices, acceptable to God by Jesus Christ" [italics in KJV] (1 Peter 2:4-5).

In the Old Testament Isaiah confirmed that the way to benefit from what Jesus offers is by believing: "Wherefore also it is contained in the scripture, Behold, I lay in Sion a chief corner stone, elect, precious: and he that believeth on him shall not be confounded ["disappointed" = NASB]" (1 Peter 2:6). Peter's quotation is from Isaiah 28:16 in the Septuagint (LXX), the Greek translation of the Hebrew Old Testament (Ἰδοὺ ἐγὼ ἐμβαλῶ εἰς τὰ θεμέλια Σιων λίθον πολυτελῆ ἐκλεκτὸν ἀκρογωνιαῖον ἔντιμον εἰς τὰ θεμέλια αὐτῆς, καὶ ὁ πιστεύων ἐπ᾽ αὐτῷ οὐ μὴ καταισχυνθῇ).

Peter states what differentiates the saved from the unsaved: "Unto you therefore which believe *he is* precious: but unto them which be disobedient, the stone which the builders disallowed, the same is made the head of the corner, and a stone of stumbling, and a rock of offence" [italics in KJV] (1 Peter 2:7-8). The explanation given for the fate of the unsaved is twofold: (1) they failed to believe "being disobedient" [by not believing] (1 Peter 2:7); and (2), "they were appointed" (1 Peter 2:8). The NASB says, "to this *doom* they were also appointed" [italics in NASB] (1 Peter 2:8) (εἰς ὃ καὶ ἐτέθησαν).

Whatever one's view of "appointed" (τίθημι), believers were direct participants only in the requirement to "believe" (πιστεύω). It should also be noted that the meaning of the clause translated "because they are disobedient to the word" (τῷ λόγῳ ἀπειθοῦντες) is informed contextually by the preceding phrase "for those who disbelieve" (ἀπιστοῦσιν). To disobey the word and to disbelieve are equivalent. The verb "disobey" (ἀπιστέω) cannot take on a life of its own and introduce works, or the promise of future works, or a desire or disposition toward works as an additional requirement for acquiring eternal salvation.

Peter's ethical exhortations for Christian living find their example in Jesus' perfect life and are applied directly to the environment of persecution his readers were presently experiencing: "For even hereunto were ye called: because Christ also suffered for us, leaving us an example, that ye should follow his steps" (1 Peter 2:21). Some have recently attempted to prove the inevitability and certainty of a believer's behavior by holding that Jesus' perfect life, which they refer to as His "active obedience," is a righteousness of actions imputed to believers and is differentiated from His "passive obedience," His sacrifice on the cross. Peter had no illusions about the frailty of believers and exhorted and implored them to follow Jesus' example.

The solution Peter presents to believers for living holy lives and enduring persecution is to "sanctify the Lord God in your hearts" (1 Peter 3:15). Those who set themselves apart (ἁγιάζω) for their Master's service mentally will be prepared to bear verbal witness for Him: "and *be* ready always to *give* an answer to every man that asketh you a reason of the hope that is in you with meekness and fear" [italics in KJV] (1 Peter 3:15).

The manner in which witnessing is to be done is "with meekness and fear" (μετὰ πραΰτητος καὶ φόβου) accompanied by holy behavior to back it up: "Having a good conscience; that, whereas they speak evil of you, as of evildoers, they may be ashamed that falsely accuse your good conversation in Christ" (1 Peter 3:16). The NASB says, "and keep a good conscience so that in the thing in which you are slandered, those who revile your good behavior in Christ may be put to shame." It should not go unnoticed that in 1 Peter 3:15 the Greek imperative "sanctify" (ἁγιάσατε) is addressed to believers. It would be highly inappropriate to ask unbelievers to do that ("sanctify Christ as Lord in your hearts" NASB) as a condition for receiving eternal salvation.

The apostle Peter was consistent in his insistence that water baptism was not a requirement for salvation. In Peter's sermon recorded by Luke in the second chapter of Acts Peter made clear that baptism is not a requirement for the forgiveness of sins in addition to repentance (see chapter 2, "Exegetical Eye-Openers" on Acts 2:38). In Peter's first epistle he again uses a parenthetical aside to exclude water baptism from the salvific formula. He uses the Old Testament example of Noah and his family's physical deliverance from drowning to illustrate the salvation of believers.

In doing so Peter recognizes that the presence of water in the case of Noah could be taken to imply that water also prefigures salvation. Peter is careful to say, "The like figure whereunto *even* baptism doth also now save us (not the putting away of the filth of the flesh, but the answer of a good conscience toward God), by the resurrection of Jesus Christ" [parenthesis and italics in KJV] (1 Peter 3:21). Rather than water baptism being a requirement for salvation, God uses the instrument of "the answer of a good conscience toward God." In his sermon in Acts 2 Peter spoke in terms of "the forgiveness of sins" (Acts 2:38) (ἄφεσιν τῶν ἁμαρτιῶν). In this epistle he phrases it: "an appeal to God for a good conscience" (1 Peter 3:21). "A good conscience" is the result of having sins forgiven through faith placed in Jesus. Peter said this comes about "through the resurrection of Jesus Christ" (1 Peter 3:21).

First Peter 4:6 is an enigmatic statement that has caused confusion for some: "For this cause was the gospel preached also to them that are dead, that they might be judged according to men in the flesh, but live according to God in the spirit." Because the conjunction translated at the beginning of the verse by the word "for" (γὰρ) connects it to what precedes it, verse 6 cannot be interpreted correctly without understanding the preceding context. Peter was discussing the sins of the unsaved that his readers had committed while being unsaved and the inability of the unsaved to understand why believers were no longer participating with them in their sinful behavior: "Wherein they think it strange that ye run not with *them* to the same excess of riot, speaking evil of *you*" [italics in KJV] (1 Peter 4:4). The astonishment and antagonism of the unsaved does not negate the reality of divine judgment: "Who shall give account to him that is ready to judge the quick [living] and the dead" (1 Peter 4:5). The apparent absence of immediate divine judgment of the unsaved in the present does not mean that they are not subject to God's judgment both in this life and the next.

Accountability cannot be avoided, but even for the unsaved (which as Peter has previously stated was a position previously shared by his audience) there is an escape available. And it cuts both ways. It is an escape if one accepts it, and it renders one without excuse if it is rejected: "For this cause was the gospel preached also to them that are dead" (1 Peter 4:6). The previous verse speaks of the accountability of the physically alive and the physically dead.

Verse 6 refers to the physically dead having had the gospel preached to them. The Greek indicative, aorist tense of the verb, rendered by the NASB with "has. . .been preached" (εὐηγγελίσθη), indicates that the preaching occurred sometime in the past. The past can be understood that it happened during their lifetime, not after their death. Peter can simply mean that during their life they had heard the gospel. Just because they are dead does not mean that they have escaped divine judgment. Peter is directly addressing a specific audience and he may well have had in mind local unsaved individuals who had died and now faced judgment.

Both the KJV and NASB translations split the verb from its helping verb. The NASB makes it look more like a perfect tense than simple past tense: "For the gospel has for this purpose been preached even to those who are dead" (1 Peter 4:6). The KJV better conveys the original: "For this cause was the gospel preached also to them that are dead." Both of these renderings may wrongly suggest that the gospel was preached to people after they were dead. They were dead at the time when Peter wrote, but they were not dead at the time they heard the gospel. The proverbial pirate cliché says, "Dead men tell no tales." They also are not around to hear the gospel or anything else. Peter was not introducing an otherwise biblically unheard of postmortem salvation opportunity.

The reason the unsaved were evangelized while they were alive is introduced by Peter with the Greek conjunction translated "that" (ἵνα), understood as "in order that" conveying purpose or result. The twofold reason is expressed in Greek with the coordinating, correlative (paired) conjunctions (μὲν. . . δὲ), a construction that conveys a parallel and is understood in English as "on the one hand. . .on the other hand" (Daniel Wallace, *Greek Grammar beyond the Basics*, [Grand Rapids: Zondervan, 1996], 672). The NASB concessive nuance, "though they are judged in the flesh as men" (1 Peter 4:6) (κριθῶσι. . . κατὰ ἀνθρώπους σαρκὶ) is an interpretive decision not required by the original. That interpretation makes the clause subordinate to the following clause rather than parallel with it.

It is better to render the two coordinate clauses as two alternative outcomes of the preaching of the gospel that precedes them. "On the one hand" if they rejected the gospel, they would be "judged according to men in the flesh" (1 Peter 4:6). "On the other hand" if they accepted the gospel, "but live according to God in the spirit" (1 Peter 4:6). The preaching of the gospel brings men to a point of decision. Only two alternatives are possible, acceptance or rejection. In Greek the two parallel options that follow the "on the one hand" and "on the other hand" (μὲν. . . δὲ) format are expressed with an identical grammatical construction, the former "according to men in the flesh" (κατὰ ἀνθρώπους σαρκὶ) and the latter with "according to God in the spirit" (κατὰ θεὸν πνεύματι). People are accountable to God for what they do with the gospel that they hear while they are alive, a decision with serious implications for their eternal destiny. Some will remain in the realm of the flesh. Others will be regenerated by the Holy Spirit.

In contrast to believers who believe the gospel, Peter refers to unbelievers as those who fail to obey the gospel: "them that obey not the gospel of God" (1 Peter 4:17). What the gospel demands is not work/s, the promise to do work/s, or the desire to do work/s, but rather having rejected work/s in any form to believe that Jesus did all that was required as both necessary and sufficient for eternal life, and believing that to be true, putting one's trust in Him to bring it about. Peter's readers who had entrusted their eternal souls to Jesus' safekeeping and were now going through persecution because of Him are exhorted to entrust their physical lives to Him: "Wherefore let them that suffer according to the will of God commit the keeping of their souls [lives] *to him* in well doing, as unto a faithful Creator" [italics in KJV] (1 Peter 4:19).

Peter was qualified to speak about Jesus' suffering as well as His sacrifice because he had been an eyewitness to those events: "The elders which are among you I exhort, who am also an elder, and a witness of the sufferings of Christ, and also a partaker of the glory that shall be revealed" (1 Peter 5:1). As an eyewitness Peter could speak with the utmost confidence, "exhorting, and testifying that this is the true grace of God wherein ye stand" (1 Peter 5:12). The NASB says, "Stand firm in it!" Peter knew what he was talking about because he had spent time in both Jesus' physical and spiritual presence.

Evidence for the Identity of Jesus in the Epistle of 2 Peter

This epistle begins with a declaration that the faith of the readers is the same as that of the writer, the apostle Peter, and that of his associates: "Simon Peter, a servant and an apostle of Jesus Christ, to them that have obtained like precious faith with us" (2 Peter 1:1). Louw and Nida indicate that the Greek adjective translated "like precious" (ἰσότιμος) has the meaning, "pertaining to that which is of equal significance or value" (Johannes P. Louw and Eugene A. Nida, *Greek-English Lexicon of the New Testament Based on Semantic Domains*, 2nd ed. [New York: United Bible Societies, 2nd ed],

1989, 1:589). Peter did not doubt the genuineness or authenticity of his faith or that of his audience. Peter did not imply that there was another species of spurious faith that differed from his own. The addressees shared genuine faith with the apostle and his associates.

Peter's introduction reflects his view of Jesus' identity. The faith in Jesus that he and his associates shared with his addressees was nothing short of faith in God: "through the righteousness of God and our Saviour Jesus Christ" (2 Peter 1:1). (The reader is referred to the discussion of Titus 2:13 and the Granville Sharp Rule that applies here). One person of the Trinity is in view. "Jesus Christ" (Ἰησοῦς Χριστός) is both "God" (θεός) and "Savior" (σωτήρ).While sharing the divine nature with God the Father, Jesus is separate from God the Father as the immediate context reveals: "Grace and peace be multiplied unto you through the knowledge of God, and of Jesus our Lord" (2 Peter 1:2). God progressively revealed Himself, first as God the Father and then as the Son, and Peter desired that his readers grow in their knowledge of Him.

The results of conversion are supernaturally empowered: "According as his divine power hath given unto us all things that *pertain* unto life and godliness, through the knowledge of him that hath called us to glory and virtue" [italics in KJV] (2 Peter 1:3). The new birth has completely equipped the believer. It is astounding what it includes: "Whereby are given unto us exceeding great and precious promises: that by these ye might be partakers of the divine nature, having escaped the corruption that is in the world through lust" (2 Peter 1:4).

Everything that believers share with God when they become "partakers of the divine nature" (2 Peter 1:4) may not be understood, but by virtue of the new birth they have a capacity for and experience a degree of holiness. Peter refers to it as "having escaped the corruption that is in the world through lust" (2 Peter 1:4). Peter exhorts his readers to add to their initial faith the following attributes and actions: "And beside this, giving all diligence, add to your faith virtue; and to virtue knowledge; and to knowledge temperance; and to temperance patience; and to patience godliness; and to godliness brotherly kindness; and to brotherly kindness charity" (2 Peter 1:5-7). Then Peter mentioned what can stem from these attributes. "For if these things be in you, and abound, they make *you that ye shall* neither *be* barren nor unfruitful in the knowledge of our Lord Jesus Christ" [italics in KJV] (2 Peter 1:8). Stated positively, usefulness and fruitfulness will result if these are added to initial faith and combined with ongoing faith.

Peter then describes believers who fail to have these attributes. "But he that lacketh these things is blind, and cannot see afar off, and hath forgotten that he was purged from his old sins" (2 Peter 1:9). Peter does not say that the lack of these qualities proves that one was not saved in the first place. Instead he says the opposite. He describes a believer with an absence of these in his life as having "forgotten that he was purged from his old sins" (2 Peter 1:9). The author is not using "forgetfulness" (λήθη) as a euphemism for a lack of a person's having been forgiven. He used the word charitably as a motive for them to remedy their failure. Peter leaves no doubt about the spiritual condition of his audience when he addresses them as "brethren" (2 Peter 1:10) (ἀδελφοί).

The exhortation in 2 Peter 1:10 has been the source of some debate: "Wherefore the rather, brethren, give diligence to make your calling and election sure: for if ye do these things, ye shall never fall." Does the text imply that a failure to "give diligence to make your calling and election sure" prove that one was not saved in the first place? Posing the question positively, does the text imply that all believers will "give diligence to make your calling and election sure?" Peter's answer to both questions is "No." Peter follows up the imperative with a reason why his readers are to do as he says, and it does not include their doubting the reality of their conversion. With the causal use of the conjunction "for" (γὰρ) Peter gave two reasons: (1) "for if ye do these things, ye shall never fall" (2 Peter 1:10); and (2) "for so an entrance shall be ministered unto you abundantly into the everlasting kingdom of our Lord and Saviour Jesus Christ" (2 Peter 1:11).

Regarding Peter's first reason for doing what he exhorts, "Can believers 'fall' ["stumble" = NASB] (2 Peter 1:10) (πταίω)?" Yes. Louw and Nida note that the New Testament never uses this verb literally but only figuratively: "(a figurative extension of meaning of πταίω 'to stumble,' not occurring in the NT) [the literal meaning is absent in the NT] to fail to keep the law (of God)–'to stumble, to err, to sin'" (Johannes P. Louw and Eugene A. Nida, *Greek-English Lexicon of the New Testament Based on Semantic Domains*, 2nd ed. [New York: United Bible Societies, 2nd ed], 1989, 1:774). Practicing what Peter exhorts will keep one from sin. To deny that believers sin is self-deception (1 John 1:8).

The second reason given by Peter mentions "[entrance] into the everlasting kingdom" (2 Peter 1:11) (εἴσοδος εἰς τὴν αἰώνιον βασιλείαν). Peter does not say or imply that failure will result in a denial of entry but rather that it "shall be ministered unto you abundantly" (πλουσίως ἐπιχορηγηθήσεται). A legitimate implication is the possibility that entrance into the eternal kingdom can be supplied less than abundantly but still be entrance. The introduction of a negative implication into an understanding of the text such as denial of entry adds an element unintended by the author. Care must be taken with possible negative implications of positive statements and caution exercised in supporting doctrine with implications that are possible but neither probable nor biblical.

Another reason for not taking 2 Peter 1:10 as a "proof of salvation" text is the author's use of the adjective translated in the NASB as "certain" (βέβαιος) in the clause, "to make certain about His calling and choosing of you" [NASB] (βεβαίαν ὑμῶν τὴν κλῆσιν καὶ ἐκλογὴν ποιεῖσθαι). In 2 Peter 1:19 the comparative form of this same adjective is used in the context of prophecy: "We have also a more sure word of prophecy." The NASB says, "And *so* we have the prophetic word *made* more sure" [italics in NASB]. What made the prophetic word "*more* sure" [italics in NASB] (βεβαιότερον) was Peter's eyewitness confirmation that he had just mentioned, "For we have not followed cunningly devised fables, when we made known unto you the power and coming of our Lord Jesus Christ, but were eyewitnesses of his majesty" (2 Peter 1:16).

The occasion Peter refers to is Jesus' Transfiguration which Peter, James, and John had witnessed: "For he received from God the Father honour and glory, when there came such a voice to him from the excellent glory, This is my beloved Son, in whom I am well pleased. And this voice which came from heaven we heard, when we were with him in the holy mount" (2 Peter 1:17-18). Confirmation by means of additional evidence did not add to prophetic truth or the identity of Jesus. If Peter, James, and John had not been present to see the Transfiguration or if the event had never happened, that would not have been proof that Jesus was not God's beloved Son.

The absence of particular evidence may not be proof that something is not so. Proof confirms what is already true. Proof does not affect the existence of the reality that it corroborates. Because of cumulative evidence of Jesus' identity Peter could say, "And *so* we have the prophetic word *made* more sure" [italics in NASB] (2 Peter 1:19) (καὶ ἔχομεν βεβαιότερον τὸν προφητικὸν λόγον). Similarly Peter's readers would have their "calling and election" (2 Peter 1:10) (τὴν κλῆσιν καὶ ἐκλογὴν) cumulatively confirmed if they followed what Peter told them to do. If they failed to do so, they would be missing corroborating evidence of the eternal salvation that they possessed but it would not prove that they had never believed in Jesus for their eternal destiny.

Old Testament prophecy in which "holy men of God spake *as they were* moved by the Holy Ghost" [italics in KJV] (2 Peter 1:21) was attacked by "false prophets" (2 Peter 2:1) (ψευδοπροφῆται). Similarly, "false teachers" (2 Peter 2:1) (ψευδοδιδάσκαλοι) would be a problem New Testament believers would face: "But there were false prophets also among the people, even as there shall be false teachers among you" (2 Peter 2:1). Peter describes the agenda of "false teachers" (ψευδοδιδάσκαλοι): "who privily shall bring in damnable heresies, even denying the Lord that bought them" (2 Peter 2:1). Jesus had paid the price that was sufficient for the sins of all men but the false teachers rather than put their trust in Him for their salvation would deny who He is. By doing so they would "bring upon themselves swift destruction" (2 Peter 2:1).

Peter warned that unsaved "false teachers" (ψευδοδιδάσκαλοι) would have a following: "And many shall follow their pernicious ways; by reason of whom the way of truth shall be evil spoken of" (2 Peter 2:2). The readers of Peter's epistle would not be exempt from their enticements: "and through covetousness shall they with feigned words make merchandise of you" (2 Peter 2:3). Peter then warns that the activity of these individuals will not be ignored by God: "whose judgment now of a long time lingereth not, and their damnation slumbereth not" (2 Peter 2:3). The individuals experiencing this are not those being enticed but those doing the enticing.

Peter's proof is threefold: (1) the judgment of sinning angels, perhaps an allusion to angels in Genesis 6:1-4, "For if God spared not the angels that sinned, but cast *them* down to hell, and delivered *them* into chains of darkness, to be reserved unto judgment" [italics in KJV] (2 Peter 2:4); (2) the judgment of the world's inhabitants, with the exception of Noah and his family, in the worldwide flood, "and spared not the old world, but saved Noah the eighth *person*, a preacher of righteousness, bringing in the flood upon the world of the ungodly" [italics in KJV] (2 Peter 2:5); and (3) the judgment of the inhabitants of Sodom and Gomorrah, "and turning the cities of Sodom and Gomorrha into ashes condemned *them* with an overthrow, making *them* an ensample unto those that after should live ungodly" [italics in KJV] (2 Peter 2:6).

God's judgment is not indiscriminate. He is able to rescue the godly from among the ungodly: "And delivered just Lot, vexed with the filthy conversation of the wicked. . . the Lord knoweth how to deliver the godly out of temptations, and to reserve the unjust unto the day of judgment to be punished" (2 Peter 2:7 & 9). The NASB says, "And *if* He rescued righteous Lot, oppressed by the sensual conduct of unprincipled men" [italics in NASB] (2 Peter 2:7). The Greek noun in 2 Peter 2:7 translated "sensual" (ἀσέλγεια) in the NASB is the same noun rendered by "pernicious" in the KJV and "sensuality" in the NASB in verse 2. The author is comparing what his readers will encounter with what Lot faced.

Just as there was a way out for Lot, there was a way of escape for them. Later in Peter's discussion of the activity and character of "false teachers" (ψευδοδιδάσκαλοι) he uses the Greek noun translated "sensuality" (NASB) (ἀσέλγεια) to describe their allure: "For when they speak great swelling *words* of vanity, they allure through the lusts of the flesh, *through much* wantonness, those that were clean escaped from them who live in error" [italics in KJV]. The NASB says, "For speaking out arrogant *words* of vanity they entice by fleshly desires, by sensuality, those who barely escape from ones who live in error" [italics in NASB] (2 Peter 2:18).

The Greek adverb and participle translated "those that clean escaped" ("those who barely escape" = NASB) (2 Peter 2:18) does not unambiguously describe the spiritual condition of these whom the false teachers will attempt to ensnare. However, using the same verb "escape" (ἀποφεύγω), (in verse 18 as a present participle and in verse 20 an aorist participle) the author does make it clear that they were saved. Verse 20 says, "For if after they have escaped the pollutions of the world through the knowledge of the Lord and Saviour Jesus Christ." They were saved and yet Peter says that "they are again entangled therein, and overcome, the latter end is worse with them than the beginning" (2 Peter 2:20).

Shockingly Peter seems to characterize a believer who succumbs to error as being worse off than an unbeliever. For a believer who should know better and has the power and potential to think and live differently it is indeed worse that he or she should be caught up in sinful thoughts and actions. Peter tops it off with the statement, "For it had been better for them not to have known the way of righteousness, than, after they have known *it*, to turn from the holy commandment delivered unto them" [italics in KJV] (2 Peter 2:21). The question arises whether Peter is saying that it is better that such a person had not been saved in the first place, rather than having been saved and then fallen for false teaching.

The key to understanding what Peter says is how he says it. He uses the imperfect tense of the "to be" verb (εἰμί), translated "would be" in the NASB and "had been" in the KJV, both translations giving the nuance of potentiality. This is probably a conative use of the imperfect, either voluntative/tendential in which the impersonal subject of the "to be" verb εἰμί is understood rather than stated, and the predicate nominative, the adjective "better" (κρεῖττον) is an unrealized state of being (Daniel Wallace, *Greek Grammar beyond the Basics*, [Grand Rapids: Zondervan, 1996], 550-52) The imperfect is used for a vivid portrayal of a contemplated state that is in fact not possible. While coming just short of saying it is better to be unsaved than saved, Peter does not deny that believers could behave or think in that way. He views such a possibility as disgusting–not a proverb one would want to emulate: "But it is happened unto them according to the true proverb, The dog *is* turned to his own vomit again; and the sow that was washed to her wallowing in the mire" [italics in KJV] (2 Peter 2:22). Following after false teaching is repulsive but not impossible.

While being unsaved is never better than being saved because of the judgment that the former will incur, Peter is nevertheless warning believers against following the instruction of false teachers. The warning was real and not just hypothetical: "Ye therefore, beloved, seeing ye know *these things* before, beware lest ye also, being led away with the error of the wicked, fall from your own stedfastness" [italics in KJV] (2 Peter 3:17). Those are among Peter's closing words. He ends the epistle as be began it by again mentioning the word "grace" (χάρις) (2 Peter 1:2): "But grow in grace, and *in* the knowledge of our Lord and Saviour Jesus Christ" [italics in KJV] (2 Peter 3:18). Peter identifies Jesus as "Lord and Saviour Jesus Christ" (τοῦ κυρίου. . . καὶ σωτῆρος Ἰησοῦ Χριστοῦ). Because of who Jesus is Peter can say: "To him *be* glory both now and for ever. Amen" [italics in KJV] (2 Peter 3:18).

Evidence for the Identity of Jesus in the Epistle of 1 John

John's Gospel account introduced Jesus' identity and his first epistle begins with the gospel that is about Him and results in eternal life. Jesus' identity reaches back to eternity past and the gospel message begins with information about the Incarnation: "That which was from the beginning, which we have heard, which we have seen with our eyes, which we have looked upon, and our hands have handled, of the Word of life" (1 John 1:1). The gospel message that produces eternal life is about a person whose life and ministry John and his fellow disciples had witnessed and could therefore communicate to others: "(For the life was manifested, and we have seen *it*, and bear witness, and shew unto you that eternal life, which was with the Father, and was manifested unto us)" [parenthesis and italics in KJV] (1 John 1:2). Because the gospel message is about Jesus, who is the source of eternal life, John blends the person with the proclamation when he writes, "which was with the Father" (1 John 1:2), a clause reminiscent of John 1:1, "and the Word was with God." The relative pronoun rendered "which" (ἥτις) is feminine in gender referring back to "the eternal life" (τὴν ζωὴν τὴν αἰώνιον).

The ultimate purpose of the gospel goes beyond the reception of eternal life to the experience of a relationship of fellowship and communion with fellow believers and with the Godhead itself: "That which we have seen and heard declare we unto you, that ye also may have fellowship with us: and truly our fellowship *is* with the Father, and with his Son Jesus Christ" [italics in KJV] (1 John 1:3). John's motivation for writing is the joy that is experienced when fellowship flourishes: "And these things write we unto you, that your joy may be full" (1 John 1:4).

Concerning God's attribute of holiness, John writes the words: "This then is the message which we have heard of him, and declare unto you, that God is light, and in him is no darkness at all" (1 John 1:5). Recognition of the author's use of absolutist language is key to understanding his letter. God is characterized not by relative holiness but by absolute holiness.

John uses the metaphor of "darkness" (σκότος) for sin and says that its presence precludes fellowship with God: "If we say that we have fellowship with him, and walk in darkness, we lie, and do not the truth" (1 John 1:6). Some have taken the words, "walk in the darkness" (ἐν τῷ σκότει περιπατῶμεν) as a relative term that means "making a habit of it" or "doing so as a way of life." That interpretation does not square with the absolute nature of the statement: "God is light, and in him is no darkness at all" (1 John 1:5) that precedes these words and what John says next, "but if we walk in the light, as he is in the light" (1 John 1:7). The adverbial comparative "as" (ὡς) and the emphatic pronoun "Himself" (αὐτός) militate against a relative meaning.

Having a relativistic view of "light" (φῶς) and "darkness" (σκότος) may seem justified because the following verse, 1 John 1:8, says, "If we say that we have no sin, we deceive ourselves, and the truth is not in us." John has not thereby diminished God's holiness but has juxtaposed Him and sinful man between whom there can be no fellowship. God's holiness will not allow Him to lower His absolute standard.

Fortunately for the saved God has provided a solution so that they can have fellowship with Him: "If we confess our sins, he is faithful and just to forgive us *our* sins, and to cleanse us from all unrighteousness" [italics in KJV] (1 John 1:9). Confession is the requirement for communion with God. Specific sins and sins generally are to be confessed "to cleanse us from all unrighteousness." John reiterates the need for confession with the inclusion of past sin: "If we say that we have not sinned, we make him a liar, and his word is not in us" (1 John 1:10). The denial of sin questions the veracity of God.

The reason the author gives for writing in 1 John 1:4 is, "that your joy may be full." In 1 John 2:1 an ancillary reason for writing is stated, "My little children, these things write I unto you, that ye sin not." Sin produces sorrow rather than joy. Being a biblical realist the author names the One who is the solution for a believer's sin: "And if any man sin, we have an advocate with the Father, Jesus Christ the righteous" (1 John 2:1). The advocacy of Jesus is on behalf of believers whose saved status they owe to Him:

"And he is the propitiation for our sins: and not for ours only, but also for *the sins of the whole world*" [italics in KJV] (1 John 2:2). Salvation is available to everyone.

The two purpose statements in 1 John 1:4 and 1 John 2:1 indicate that what John writes is for believers. The contents that follow the first purpose statement and continue to the second statement are unequivocally directed to those who are saved. There is no doubt that the words that follow the second purpose statement also address believers. Some Bible teachers hold that John's intention was to have believers examine the genuineness of their salvation and/or to expose the unsaved status of unbelievers. That interpretation, however, conflicts with the apostle's stated purpose, "My little children, these things write I unto you, that ye sin not" (1 John 2:1). The tender tone conveyed by John in this address is incompatible with an abrupt questioning of whether the readers are God's children or not.

The relationship between "knowing" (1 John 2:3, 4) (γινώσκω) and "keeping" (1 John 2:3, 4, 5) (τηρέω) or obeying God's commands, the "perfecting" (1 John 2:5) (τελειόω) of His "love" (1 John 2:5) (ἀγάπη) in them, "abiding" (1 John 2:6) (μένω) and "walking" (1 John 2:6) (περιπατέω) are all issues that affect the avoidance of sin in the life of a believer. To take them all as measures of the authenticity of saving faith places a burden on the believer that any reasonable assurance of salvation is unable to bear.

The words, "hereby know we that we are in him" (1 John 2:5) should be interpreted the same as John 15:1-11. In both the 1 John 2 and John 15 passages the word "abide" (μένω) is used. Also the words in the purpose statement of 1 John, "And these things write we unto you, that your joy may be full" (1 John 1:4) reflect Jesus' words about abiding in Him: "These things have I spoken unto you, that my joy might remain in you, and *that* your joy might be full" [italics in KJV] (John 15:11). The reader is referred to the discussion of John 15 on the application of that passage to believers.

Fellowship requires a knowledge of God that the author associates with obedience: "And hereby we do know that we know him, if we keep his commandments" (1 John 2:3). Knowledge without obedience does not result in fellowship with God. In salvation, "love" (ἀγάπη) is what God has for the unsaved world (John 3:16), and love is what a believer is to cultivate toward God and others: "but whoso keepeth his word, in him verily is the love of God perfected" (1 John 2:5). The divine example is to be emulated, not in order to earn eternal life or be entitled to it or to prove that one has received it but because imitating Jesus is incumbent on one who claims to be abiding in Him: "He that saith he abideth in him ought himself also so to walk, even as he walked" (1 John 2:6). Obedience is the proof of abiding, not proof of the possession of eternal salvation.

The author's words "I write no new commandment unto you" (1 John 2:7) and "I am writing a new commandment to you" (1 John 2:8) (ἐντολὴν καινὴν γράφω ὑμῖν) seem to be contradictory. But in the first instance John is telling his readers they have already heard about loving fellow believers. The instruction is not new, "but an old commandment which you have had from the beginning; the old commandment is the word which you have heard" (1 John 2:7) (ἀλλ᾽ ἐντολὴν παλαιὰν ἣν εἴχετε ἀπ᾽ ἀρχῆς· ἡ ἐντολὴ ἡ παλαιά ἐστιν ὁ λόγος ὃν ἠκούσατε). John himself recorded in his Gospel the words that Jesus spoke to His disciples at the Last Supper: "A new commandment I give to you, that you love one another, even as I have loved you, that you also love one another. By this all men will know that you are My disciples, if you have love for one another" (John 13:34-35) (Ἐντολὴν καινὴν δίδωμι ὑμῖν, ἵνα ἀγαπᾶτε ἀλλήλους, καθὼς ἠγάπησα ὑμᾶς ἵνα καὶ ὑμεῖς ἀγαπᾶτε ἀλλήλους. ἐν τούτῳ γνώσονται πάντες ὅτι ἐμοὶ μαθηταί ἐστε, ἐὰν ἀγάπην ἔχητε ἐν ἀλλήλοις).

Yet Jesus' command was not new in the sense that the disciples had never before been commanded to love. The Old Testament had commanded, "but you shall love your neighbor as yourself" (Leviticus 19:18). What was new was that they were to do so in light of the manner in which Jesus loved them, "as I have loved you" (John 13:34). This would communicate that they were His followers, "By this shall all *men* know that ye are my disciples, if ye have love one to another" [italics in KJV] (John 13:35). Jesus' presence signaled a new understanding of the Old Testament commandment that He modeled.

In 1 John 2:8 the author introduces a new understanding of the same commandment: "Again, a new commandment I write unto you, which thing is true in him and in you: because the darkness is past, and the true light now shineth." In addition to the presence and love of Jesus that is to inform a believer's obedience, another element is added. The author did not include eschatological themes in his Gospel, as the Synoptic writers had done, but now he does. The Synoptic writers' "already, not yet," "unrealized eschatology" viewpoint is shared by John. Jesus is present but not yet in the sense that He will be in the future. In the present "the darkness is passing away" (1 John 2:8 NASB) (ἡ σκοτία παράγεται) but "darkness" (σκοτία), that is, sin, is still very much present.

In the "already, not yet" present there are two realms or spheres in which believers can operate; John describes one with the word "light" (φῶς) and the other with the word "darkness" (σκοτία). In the eschatological future the "light" (φῶς) will take over, and "darkness" (σκοτία) will disappear. At that time believers will each personally experience the disappearance of sin when there is a convergence of their positional and practical sanctification. Until then a believer is capable of stepping into either the dark sphere of sin or the bright sunshine of God's divine Son.

John describes a situation in which the path of sin is selected by a believer: "He that saith he is in the light, and hateth his brother, is in darkness even until now" (1 John 2:9). While it might be argued that the word "brother" refers to a physical sibling the use of the word in the rest of the epistle militates against that interpretation. By contrast, "He that loveth his brother abideth in the light, and there is none occasion of stumbling in him" (1 John 2:10). In such a state he or she will not experience a "stumbling" (σκάνδαλον) and will not cause others to fall either.

The writer of the epistle does not propose the alternative of a shadowland in which obedience and disobedience, "light" (φῶς) and "darkness" (σκοτία) peacefully coexist. The choice believers are faced with consists of two stark alternatives, and there is something fundamentally wrong with a believer who makes the wrong decision. He or she is not thinking straight: "But he that hateth his brother is in darkness, and walketh in darkness, and knoweth not whither he goeth, because that darkness hath blinded his eyes" (1 John 2:11). Spiritually he is stumbling around in the darkness of sin. A believer's sinful decisions cause directionless living.

The writer's compassionate pastoral concern for his readers is evident in the way he addresses them. Some of them have not known Christ very long, and he says to them, "I write unto you, little children, because your sins are forgiven you for his name's sake" (1 John 2:12). Because they have put their trust in Jesus they have had their sins forgiven. For them to make the wrong choice would be to return to that from which they had recently been rescued. Others would read the epistle who had been believers for quite a while and the author addresses them as he would a "father" (πατήρ). John reminds them about the one whom they have come to know: "I write unto you, fathers, because ye have known him *that is* from the beginning" [italics in KJV] (1 John 2:13). Putting this together with what the apostle wrote earlier in this letter (1 John 2:3), the readers would understand that obedience is included in the author's understanding of knowledge. John also addresses those who are neither novices nor veterans in the faith: "I write unto you, young men, because ye have overcome the wicked one" (1 John 2:13). They have been the direct targets of the devil and are commended for the victories they have won.

The author goes through the three groups again to encourage and commend them. New believers, having recently become a part of God's family are commended for their knowledge of God their heavenly Father: "I write unto you, little children, because ye have known the Father" (1 John 2:13). A spiritual "father" (πατήρ) is told the exact same thing as earlier, "I have written unto you, fathers, because ye have known him *that is* from the beginning" [italics in KJV] (1 John 2:14). The repetition is not intended to encourage them to "rest on their laurels" but to keep on doing what they have been doing, that is, living obedient lives of knowing and doing. A "young man" (νεανίσκος) in the faith is encouraged by singling out his qualities of spiritual strength and knowledge and obedience to the Scriptures that have been his weapons in the spiritual battle: "I have written unto you, young men, because ye are strong, and the word of God abideth in you, and ye have overcome the wicked one" (1 John 2:14).

The transient nature of sin and the sinful world system are reason for avoiding them both. Not only is "darkness" (σκοτία), a metaphor for sin, "passing away" (1 John 2:8 NASB) (παράγω), but the "world" (1 John 2:17) (κόσμος), the sinful system organized by Satan, is also on its way out. It too "passeth away" (παράγω): "And the world passeth away, and the lust thereof" (1 John 2:17). Everything associated with sin will one day disappear. The process is underway. In contrast to choosing what is transient, the reader is exhorted to be one of those who is living in light of what is permanent: "but he that doeth the will of God abideth for ever" (1 John 2:17).

John views the eschatological future as imminent and that lends urgency to his exhortations: "it is the last time: and as ye have heard that antichrist shall come, even now are there many antichrists; whereby we know that it is the last time" (1 John 2:18). The NASB says, "it is the last hour; and just as you heard that antichrist is coming even now many antichrists have arisen; from this you know that it is the last hour." The church age, John writes, would be characterized by attacks on the identity of Jesus. They would attack His person and attempt to usurp His rightful place in the church and the world.

The fundamental truth of Christianity is the identity of Christ, and opposition to Christianity focuses on a doctrinal and practical denial of truths related to it: "Who is a liar but he that denieth that Jesus is the Christ? He is antichrist, that denieth the Father and the Son. Whosoever denieth the Son, the same hath not the Father" (1 John 2:22-23). The Trinity and the identity of Jesus as a member of it cannot be separated. God is a unity in a Trinity, and although the divine persons within it can be understood separately no one Person in the Trinity can be denied as a part of it. Biblical theism is Trinitarianism.

The author's pastoral concern is that believers lead obedient lives in light of the return of Jesus: "And now, little children, abide in him; that, when he shall appear, we may have confidence, and not be ashamed before him at his coming" (1 John 2:28). The return of Jesus, the perfect Son of God whose children believers are, is to inform and inspire every aspect of their lives: "If ye know that he is righteous, ye know that every one that doeth righteousness is born of him" (1 John 2:29). "Righteousness" (δικαιοσύνη) is the product of the relationship believers have with Jesus.

They have been "born of Him" (1 John 2:29) (ἐξ αὐτοῦ γεγέννηται), that is, they originate from Him. "Righteousness" (δικαιοσύνη) is a quality shared by the Savior and the saved. It is not one-hundred percent righteousness on the part of the Savior and fifty percent or even ninety-nine percent on the part of the believer. Jesus is the source of perfect "righteousness" (δικαιοσύνη), not degrees or percentages of it. If believers sin, and the author says that they do in fact sin (1 John 1:10), that sin cannot be traced back to the Savior.

There is a fundamental incompatibility between the saved and the unsaved. The unsaved find the intimacy of the relationship between God and believers incomprehensible: "Behold, what manner of love the Father hath bestowed upon us, that we should be called the sons of God: therefore the world knoweth us not, because it knew him not" (1 John 3:1). The relationship enjoyed by God's children is in an "already, not yet" phase, an "unrealized eschatology." In the future believers will realize fully their relationship with God: "Beloved, now are we the sons of God, and it doth not yet appear what we shall be: but we know that, when he shall appear, we shall be like him; for we shall see him as he is" (1 John 3:2).

The appearance of the Savior will result in the believer's transformation, whose primary characteristic will be holiness: "And every man that hath this hope in him purifieth himself, even as he is pure" (1 John 3:3). A Christological perspective will produce purity. The expectation and promise of future transformation should lead to present purification. Participation in sin is the opposite of purification from sin, which in essence is lawlessness: "Whosoever committeth sin transgresseth also the law: for sin is the transgression of the law" (1 John 3:4).

Jesus' second coming will have an effect on sin just as His first coming did: "And ye know that he was manifested to take away our sins; and in him is no sin" (1 John 3:5). Jesus led a life of perfect holiness and came to remove sin. Maintaining a relationship of fellowship with Him requires that sin be dealt with. When believers see Jesus at His second coming, sin will vanish from their practice and if they want to see Him and know Him in the present they need to deal with sin: "Whosoever abideth in him sinneth not: whosoever sinneth hath not seen him, neither known him" (1 John 3:6).

Nurturing sin and maintaining fellowship with Jesus at the same time is impossible. When believers recognize that their sins are forgiven and they practice righteous conduct, they are identifying with their Savior: "Little children, let no man deceive you: he that doeth righteousness is righteous, even as he is righteous" (1 John 3:7). Believers can experience in the present what will continuously be true in the eschatological future. Just as a child who has sinned then asks for forgiveness from his parent, a believer who seeks God's forgiveness can experience the joy of restored fellowship with God.

The ability to practice "righteousness" (δικαιοσύνη) has been bestowed on believers. The inability to do so is a characteristic of unbelievers. All that an unbeliever is capable of doing is sinning: "He that committeth sin is of the devil; for the devil sinneth from the beginning" (1 John 3:8). Believers have the God-given ability to imitate their Savior and heavenly Father, whereas unbelievers can follow only the devil. Jesus came to do away with the deeds of the devil: "For this purpose the Son of God was manifested, that he might destroy the works of the devil" (1 John 3:8). The devil himself and all that he has accomplished will be abolished. In light of that future believers are invited to join Jesus' mission by avoiding sin.

The absolute language of 1 John 3:9 appears to refer to a believer not sinning: "Whosoever is born of God doth not commit sin; for his seed remaineth in him: and he cannot sin, because he is born of God." However, at the beginning of the epistle John wrote that believers do in fact sin (1 John 1:8, 10). Various attempts have been made to resolve this apparent contradiction. One view takes the present tenses to mean habitual rather than occasional sin. Wallace describes that solution in reference to the four present tenses in 1 John 3:6, 9:

> Many older commentaries have taken the. . .presents. . .as customary (a view popularized by British scholars, principally Westcott): *does* not *continually sin. . .does not continually sin. . .does* not *practice* sin. . .*is* not *able to habitually sin*. Taking the presents this way seems to harmonize well with 1:8-10, for to deny one's sin is to

disagree with God's assessment (Daniel Wallace, *Greek Grammar beyond the Basics*, [Grand Rapids: Zondervan, 1996], 524-25, italics in original).

Wallace rejects this "tense solution." One reason he gives for rejecting this view is that "the very subtlety of this approach is against it" (ibid., 525). Another reason Wallace gives for rejecting the "tense solution" is that

> It seems to contradict 5:16 (ἐάν τις ἴδη τὸν ἀδελφὸν αὐτοῦ ἁμαρτάνοντα ἁμαρτίαν μὴ πρὸς θάνατον [if anyone sees his brother sinning a sin not unto death]). The author juxtaposes "brother" with the present tense of ἁμαρτάνω with the proclamation that such might not lead to death. On the customary present view, the author should not be able to make this statement (ibid.).

The inability Wallace refers to is that with the "tense solution" view a Christian brother would not be able to continuously (present tense) commit the less than "unpardonable sin" that does not lead to death, and yet the text contemplates that exact scenario. Wallace then discusses a third problem with this view.

> Gnomic presents most frequently occur with generic subjects (or objects). Further, "the sense of a generic utterance is usually an absolute statement of what each one does once, and not a statement of the individual's customary or habitual activity" (quotation from Buist M. Fanning, *Verbal Aspect in New Testament Greek*, [Oxford: Clarendon, 1990], 217). This certainly fits the pattern (Daniel Wallace, *Greek Grammar beyond the Basics*, [Grand Rapids: Zondervan, 1996], 525).

Thus the "tense solution" is untenable and creates as many problems as it solves.

The evident eschatological context that has been discussed earlier perhaps provides the best solution to understanding the enigmatic statements the author makes and is the lens through which the author intended for his words to be understood. The "not yet" part of the "already, not yet" paradigm is emphasized in those statements that appear to promote perfectionism. Wallace articulates that possibility:

> The immediate context seems to be speaking in terms of a projected eschatological reality. The larger section of this letter addresses the bright side of the eschaton: Since Christians are in the last days, their hope of Christ's imminent return should produce godly living (2:28-3:10). The author first articulates how such an eschatological hope should produce holiness (2:28-3:3). Then, without marking that his discussion is still in the same vein, he gives a proleptic ["an anachronistic representation of something as existing before its proper or historical time"–www.freedictionary.com] view of sanctification (3:4-10)–that is, he gives a hyperbolic picture of believers vs. unbelievers, implying that even though believers are not yet perfect, they are moving in that direction (3:6, 9 need to be interpreted proleptically), while unbelievers are moving away from truth (3:10; cf. 2:19). Thus, the author states in an absolute manner truths that are not yet true, because he is speaking within the context of eschatological hope (2:28-3:3) and eschatological judgment (2:18-19) (ibid.).

Wallace's words are well taken, with the exception that his comment that believers are "moving in that direction" (ibid.) might be interpreted by some as a guarantee that no detours into "darkness" (σκότος) are a possibility, something that the text warns believers not to do. The proposed view accounts for the absolutist language that will be reality only in the eschatological future.

Holy lives are a visible expression of the believer's inner reality: "In this the children of God are manifest, and the children of the devil: whosoever doeth not righteousness is not of God, neither he that loveth not his brother" (1 John 3:10). The natural reaction of the unsaved toward the saved is hatred: "Marvel not, my brethren, if the world hate you" (1 John 3:13). In this life a believer is capable of stepping into the sphere of life or into the realm of death: "We know that we have passed from death unto life, because we love the brethren. He that loveth not *his* brother abideth in death" [italics in KJV] (1 John 3:14). Believers are being told that they should love other believers and not be like those who abide "in death."

The author explains salvation and sanctification: "And this is his commandment, That we should believe on the name of his Son Jesus Christ, and love one another, as he gave us commandment" (1 John 3:23). Faith in Jesus alone is the requirement for salvation and it comes first, followed by a life of obedience that includes loving fellow believers. The two are sequential and not simultaneous. An individual who obeys Jesus is described as mutually "abiding" (μένω) in Him: "And he that keepeth his commandments dwelleth in him, and he in him" (1 John 3:24).

The existence of the mutually "abiding" (μένω) state is confirmed by the Holy Spirit: "And hereby we know that he abideth in us, by the Spirit which he hath given us" (1 John 3:24). The reader is not told in what way the Holy Spirit confirms that a believer is "abiding" (μένω), but the following context discusses the Holy Spirit's involvement in a verbal expression of the identity of Jesus: "Hereby know ye the Spirit of God: Every spirit that confesseth that Jesus Christ is come in the flesh is of God" (1 John 4:2). In some way the Holy Spirit confirms that the sanctification process is in progress.

Some Bible teachers hold that the purpose of the entire epistle of 1 John is to provide proofs of salvation. However, this verse alone (1 John 4:2) gave first-century believers sufficient proof that they had been saved. The view that assurance of salvation is an involved procedure that includes meeting multiple requirements seems unlikely. This is because believers could know that they were saved by the Holy Spirit's inspired words and works that were performed through them. Without a clear indication of intention by the author of a "proof of salvation" purpose, an audience hearing the text read to them would be hard pressed to remember each requirement and come to a conclusion at the end whether they were saved or not.

The author's description of a believers' capacity and ability to be either in or out of fellowship with Jesus and fellow believers militates against that major section of the epistle (1 John 1:5-5:5), being taken as a litmus test for salvation. The twofold possibility presented there is expressed with the conditional construction, "If we say that we have fellowship with him, and walk in darkness, we lie, and do not the truth: but if we walk in the light, as he is in the light, we have fellowship one with another, and the blood of Jesus Christ his Son cleanseth us from all sin" (1 John 1:6-7).

The identity of Jesus is integral to faith in Him and one of Satan's strategies is to promote confusion on that very issue. John warns his readers, "Beloved, believe not every spirit, but try the spirits whether they are of God: because many false prophets are gone out into the world" (1 John 4:1). Doctrinal deception is part of the demonic agenda, but God has provided a test for legitimacy: "Hereby know ye the Spirit of God: Every spirit that confesseth that Jesus Christ is come in the flesh is of God: and every spirit that confesseth not that Jesus Christ is come in the flesh is not of God: and this is that *spirit* of antichrist, whereof ye have heard that it should come; and even now already is it in the world" [italics in KJV] (1 John 4:2-3). The identity of Jesus as the God-Man is the focus of the devil's attack. If people are in error about Jesus' identity, they will be unable to put their trust in Him for eternal salvation.

The identity of Jesus consists not only of His humanity but also His deity. John and his fellow apostles were commissioned to communicate that message: "And we have seen and do testify that the Father sent the Son *to be* the Saviour of the world" [italics in KJV] (1 John 4:14). The writer then repeats the message of the identity of Jesus: "Whosoever shall confess that Jesus is the Son of God, God dwelleth in him, and he in God" (1 John 4:15). There is no salvific belief without the right object of belief. There is no new birth without belief in the Messiah: "Whosoever believeth that Jesus is the Christ is born of God" (1 John 5:1).

The new birth provides what makes victorious Christian living possible. The author uses the inclusive neuter adjective "whatever" (πᾶν) to indicate that what God provides conquers everything related with evil: "For whatsoever is born of God overcometh the world" (1 John 5:4). Victory is attributed to the new birth that is accessed by "faith" (πίστις): "and this is the victory that overcometh the world, *even* our faith" [italics in KJV] (1 John 5:4). Because of their "faith" (πίστις) believers presently possess eternal life; this is victory for Jesus and defeat for the devil.

Assurance of salvation is present in 1 John 5:6-13. The author's purpose statement includes "believe" (πιστεύω) as the requirement for salvation on which assurance rests: "These things have I written unto you that believe on the name of the Son of God; that ye may know that ye have eternal life" (1 John 5:13). Only those who "believe" (πιστεύω) can have assurance of salvation.

The section on assurance of salvation hinges on the requirement to "believe" (πιστεύω) and begins with acknowledging the identity of Jesus. The personal object of salvific faith must be the Jesus of biblical revelation as manifested in the Incarnation. With a rhetorical question John transitions from the thought of "the one who overcomes" (1 John 5:4) (ὁ νικῶν) to salvation which makes victory possible: "Who is he that overcometh the world, but he that believeth that Jesus is the Son of God" (1 John 5:5).

Jesus is identified in a twofold manner: "This is he that came by water and blood, *even* Jesus Christ; not by water only, but by water and blood" [italics in KJV] (1 John 5:6) Scholars debate the meaning of "by water" (δι' ὕδατος). Some see it as a reference to Jesus' baptism, and others say it refers to His birth. "Blood" (αἷμα) is usually taken to refer to Jesus' death. To these two are added the Holy Spirit as a third witness to Jesus' identity. "And it is the Spirit that beareth witness, because the Spirit is truth" (1 John 5:6).

Perhaps because of pre-Gnostic attacks on Jesus' humanity the epistle of 1 John is introduced with proofs of Jesus' physical nature: "which we have heard, which we have seen with our eyes, which we have looked upon, and our hands have handled, of the Word of life" (1 John 1:1). Additional evidence of Jesus' humanity is seen in 1 John 4:2, "Jesus Christ is come in the flesh." Because of the emphasis on that aspect of Jesus' identity the term "water" (ὕδωρ) in chapter 5 should probably be taken as a reference to His birth. Additional support is that the third witness is the Holy Spirit: "And there are three that bear witness in earth, the spirit, and the water, and the blood: and these three agree in one" (1 John 5:8). The Holy's Spirit's corroboration could be His identification of Jesus at His baptism. If "water" (ὕδωρ) in 1 John 5:7-8 refers to Jesus' baptism, two of the witnesses would be corroborating the same event.

God the Father is an additional witness that Jesus is His divine Son: "for this is the witness of God which he hath testified of his Son" (1 John 5:9). Believers themselves are also witnesses to Jesus' identity by virtue of the eternal life they have received: "He that believeth on the Son of God hath the witness in himself" (1 John 5:10). Unbelievers who deny Jesus' identity in essence place their credibility above that of God Himself: "he that believeth not God hath made him a liar; because he believeth not the record that God gave of his Son" (1 John 5:10).

God the Father has provided evidence of the identity of Jesus and evidence of the requirement of trust in His Son Jesus for eternal life: "And this is the record, that God hath given to us eternal life, and this life is in his Son" (1 John 5:11). The NASB says, "And the witness is this, that God has given us eternal life, and this life is in His Son." John then comments on the exclusivity of Jesus as the source of eternal life: "He that hath the Son hath life; *and* he that hath not the Son of God hath not life" [italics in KJV] (1 John 5:12).

The author returns to the relationship that believers who are in fellowship with God experience, and he mentions specifically their access to God in prayer: "And this is the confidence that we have in him, that, if we ask any thing according to his will, he heareth us: and if we know that he hear us, whatsoever we ask, we know that we have the petitions that we desired of him" (1 John 5:14-15). The "blank check" of prayer is qualified by the words "according to His will" (κατὰ τὸ θέλημα αὐτοῦ). A believer should not want to have what is not God's desire or a part of His divine plan.

Sometimes a believer's sin may be so serious that although he possesses eternal life that can never be lost, he may be subject to a premature physical death as a consequence of sin. Forgiveness is available (1 John 1:9) and the author does not want to dampen the believer's confidence in prayer, but sometimes a deadly consequence has been divinely determined. The author indicates that the sinning individual being contemplated is a fellow believer; he uses the term "brother" (ἀδελφός) to refer to him or her: "If any man see his brother sin a sin *which is* not unto death, he shall ask, and he shall give him life for them that sin not unto death. There is a sin unto death: I do not say that he shall pray for it" [italics in KJV] (1 John 5:16). The author notes that not all sin bears such consequences, although all sin is to be taken seriously because it is "unrighteousness" (ἀδικία): "All unrighteousness is sin: and there is a sin not unto death" (1 John 5:17). Not all sins lead to immediate or premature physical death.

In his conclusion the apostle returns to the duality of the believer's earthly experience: "We know that whosoever is born of God sinneth not; but he that is begotten of God keepeth himself, and that wicked one toucheth him not. *And* we know that we are of God, and the whole world lieth in wickedness" [italics in KJV] (1 John 5:18-19). Believers are surrounded by evil, yet in them resides one who, although He cannot be visibly seen, is nonetheless present: "And we know that the Son of God is come, and hath given us an understanding, that we may know him that is true, and we are in him that is true, *even* in his Son Jesus Christ" [italics in KJV] (1 John 5:20).

The author identifies who Jesus Christ is: "This is the true God and eternal life" (1 John 5:20). The demonstrative pronoun translated "this" (οὗτός) refers back to "Jesus Christ" (Ἰησοῦ Χριστῷ) who is "the true God" (ὁ ἀληθινὸς θεὸς). Believers need to keep their Christology correct; Jesus is God. They are not to idolatrously replace the Jesus of revelation either in their doctrine or in their deeds with anyone or anything other than Him: "Little children, keep yourselves from idols" (1 John 5:21).

Evidence for the Identity of Jesus in the Epistle of 2 John

In the introduction the apostle John identifies Jesus with the title "Jesus Christ" (2 John 3) (Ἰησοῦς Χριστός) and as "the Son of the Father" (2 John 3) (τοῦ υἱοῦ τοῦ πατρὸς). The author's concern with "truth" (ἀλήθεια) is evident in his use of the term five times in the letter's thirteen verses. Four of those instances are clear references to theological truth. The possible exception is the writer's description of his relationship to his addressees, "unto the elect lady and her children, whom I love in the truth" (2 John 1), although it may also express a common spiritual bond based on doctrine. Shared beliefs are probably in view because John adds, "and not I only , but also all they that have known the truth" (2 John 1). The author's concern is for the "truth" (ἀλήθεια) that he and his readers share: "for the truth's sake, which dwelleth in us, and shall be with us for ever" (2 John 2). The Apostle's position on eternal security is evident from his words, "and will be with us forever" (2 John 2). Eternal security is possible because the faith which secures it is based on truth that has a timeless quality.

For John "truth" (ἀλήθεια) can be "known" (2 John 1) (γινώσκω), "abided in" (2 John 2) (μένω ἐν), be "with" (2 John 2) (μετά), and "walked in" (2 John 4) (περιπατέω ἐν). The latter unequivocally refers to sanctification that includes behavior and beliefs. In 2

John 4 the author may be conveying that "walking in truth" is not true of all believers when he says, "I rejoiced greatly that I found of thy children walking in truth" (2 John 4). The NASB says, "I was very glad to find *some* of your children walking in truth" [italics in NASB] (Ἐχάρην λίαν ὅτι εὕρηκα ἐκ τῶν τέκνων σου περιπατοῦντας ἐν ἀληθείᾳ). It might be argued that the term "children" (2 John 1, 4) (τέκνον) is simply a reference to physical progeny and does not denote their spiritual condition. Or, it could convey both, that they are in her family and are saved. Their relationship to "truth" (ἀλήθεια) in verse 1 seems to indicate that they are saved.

The NASB adds "*some*" in italics in verse 4 to show that it is understood but not explicitly present in Greek. The KJV seems to avoid a commitment to the partitive (the selection of a part or quantity out of a group) interpretation by rendering the clause, "I rejoiced greatly that I found of thy children walking in truth." The NASB and the KJV are dealing with the presence of the preposition "from" or "out of" (ἐκ) and the unexpected absence of the indefinite pronoun "some" (τινὰς). A. T. Robertson points out that in John 16:17 the same author (John) leaves "some" (τινὰς) out and uses the preposition ἐκ to mean "some of" or "some from among" (*Word Pictures in the New Testament*, 6:251). John 16:17 says, "Then said *some* of his disciples among themselves" [italics in KJV]. The NASB says, "*Some* of His disciples therefore said to one another" [italics in NASB].

Other instances in which John the author uses the identical construction to refer to some within a group are: John 3:25; 6:39; 9:40; 18:17, 25; and Revelation 2:10. Wallace discusses the rarity of the genitive of separation and states that "In Koine Greek, however, the idea of separation was increasingly made more explicit by the presence of the preposition ἀπὸ or sometimes ἐκ" (Daniel Wallace, *Greek Grammar beyond the Basics*, [Grand Rapids: Zondervan, 1996], 108). In 2 John 4 the author expresses joy that "some" of the children of the "elect lady" (2 John 1) are "walking in truth" (2 John 4). The implication is that not all of them were "walking in truth."

The author was concerned that his readers would be subverted by heretical teaching related to Jesus' identity: "For many deceivers are entered into the world, who confess not that Jesus Christ is come in the flesh. This is a deceiver and an antichrist" (2 John 7). John was concerned that his readers would be taken in by the false teachers who were denying the cardinal truth of Jesus' humanity. John says, "Look to yourselves, that we lose not *those things* which we have wrought" [italics in KJV] (2 John 8). The contemplated possibility was very serious, as indicated by the author's use of the word translated "lose" (ἀπόλλυμι). False doctrine could destroy the work that the apostle John had "wrought" ("accomplished" = NASB ἐργάζομαι). He was concerned about a future consequence for his readers: "but *that* we receive a full reward" [italics in KJV] (2 John 8). The heresy did not put heaven in jeopardy. Their reward, not their redemption, was at stake. The author's desire was that his readers receive a "full reward" (μισθὸν πλήρη). Wrong thinking would result in a reduction of reward.

Tampering with the theological truths of Jesus' identity can involve adding to what Scripture has revealed and is to be rejected: "Whosoever transgresseth, and abideth not in the doctrine of Christ, hath not God. He that abideth in the doctrine of Christ, he hath both the Father and the Son" (2 John 9). The NASB says, "Anyone who goes too far and does not abide in the teaching of Christ, does not have God (Πᾶς ὁ προάγων καὶ μὴ μένων ἐν τῇ διδαχῇ τοῦ Χριστοῦ θεὸν οὐκ ἔχει). The verb translated "goes too far" (προάγω) can mean "to go beyond established bounds of teaching or instruction, with the implication of failure to obey properly–'to go beyond bounds, to fail to obey'" (Johannes P. Louw and Eugene A. Nida, *Greek-English Lexicon of the New Testament Based on Semantic Domains*, 2nd ed. [New York: United Bible Societies, 2nd ed], 1989, 1:468). New York: United Bible Societies.

Christological addition results in soteriological subtraction. To alter the biblical identification of either the Father or the Son means that eternal life is denied to the unsaved because it fundamentally changes the gospel. Also it means that believers forfeit future heavenly rewards. The truth of the Trinity and specifically the identity of Jesus is not only theologically significant; it also has applicational implications: "Whosoever transgresseth, and abideth not in the doctrine of Christ, hath not God" (2 John 9).

The author exhorts his readers that Christological correctness is to be maintained: "If there come any unto you, and bring not this doctrine, receive him not into *your* house, neither bid him God speed: for he that biddeth him God speed is partaker of his evil deeds" [italics in KJV] (2 John 10-11). Welcoming heretics into one's home, or even greeting them, adds to their credibility and can unwittingly promote their agenda. In Romans 12:13 Paul says believers are to be "given to hospitality" (τὴν φιλοξενίαν διώκοντες). Louw and Nida define the noun translated "hospitality" (φιλοξενία) in this way: "to receive and show hospitality to a stranger, that is, someone who is not regarded as a member of the extended family or a close friend–'to show hospitality, to receive a stranger as a guest, hospitality'" (ibid., 1:454-55).

"Hospitality" (φιλοξενία) made possible the survival of believers who were fleeing persecution but it was not to be extended to those who held heretical views on the identity of Jesus. Louw and Nida give the following definition for the verb translated "give. . .a greeting" (χαίρω): "to employ a formalized expression of greeting, implying a wish for happiness on the part of the person greeted–'hail, greetings'" (ibid., 1:392). The social correctness of extending a common courtesy of inviting someone into one's home or even greeting him was not to be extended to those who denied Jesus' identity.

Evidence for the Identity of Jesus in the Epistle of 3 John

In this epistle John is also concerned with "truth" (ἀλήθεια). He used the term six times in fourteen verses. "Truth" (ἀλήθεια) is to be practiced and not just known. The letter is addressed to one person, Gaius, who is commended because "of the truth *that is* in thee, even as thou walkest in the truth" [italics in KJV] (3 John 3). The author's desire was that everyone he ministered to would do likewise. He writes, "I have no greater joy than to hear that my children walk in truth" (3 John 4). For believers "walking in the truth" (ἐν τῇ ἀληθείᾳ περιπατοῦντα) is not automatic or an inevitable result of salvation. As with every worthwhile endeavor in the Christian life, its accomplishment is the result of diligent effort. Encouraging him to help fellow workers, John tells Gaius, "Beloved, thou doest faithfully whatsoever thou doest to the brethren, and to strangers" (3 John 5).

A believer's behavior is to reflect his or her relationship with God. God is the standard by which actions are to be measured: "and you will do well to send them on their way in a manner worthy of God" (3 John 6 NASB) (οὓς καλῶς ποιήσεις προπέμψας ἀξίως τοῦ θεοῦ). The author had no problem shifting between mentioning "the Name" (ὁ ὄνομα), a reference to Jesus, and God the Father. The way Jesus is treated reflects on the way God is treated because Jesus is God. The primary "truth" (ἀλήθεια) that fellow workers were promoting was related to Jesus, who He is and what He has done: "because that for his name's sake they went forth" (3 John 7). The NASB says, "for they went out for the sake of the Name." Supporting the messengers of God supported the message about His divine Son: (3 John 7) "Therefore we ought to support such men, that we may be fellow workers with the truth" (3 John 8).

Diotrephes was a church leader who attacked the message of the apostle John and his fellow workers and exercised tyrannical control over church members. The author does not say whether Diotrophes was saved, although the assumption seems to be that he was. Diotrophes's problem is that of egomaniacal aggrandizement: "who loveth to have the preeminence among them" (3 John 9). John's instruction to Gaius was, "Beloved, follow not *that which is* evil, but *that which is* good" [italics in KJV] (3 John 11). A believer who does "good" (ἀγαθοποιέω) imitates the one who is completely "good" (ἀγαθός): "He that doeth good is of God" (3 John 11). The one who does the opposite is blind to who God is: "but he that doeth evil hath not seen God" (3 John 11). This recalls the author's words in 1 John 3:6: "whosoever sinneth hath not seen him." The author is emphasizing the incongruity of a believer's sinful practice and a believer's saved position.

In contrast to Diotrophes the author mentions Demetrius, a positive example: "Demetrius hath good report of all *men*" [italics in KJV] (3 John 12). The NASB says, "Demetrius has received a *good* testimony from everyone" [italics in NASB]. A second witness on Demetrius's behalf is "truth" (ἀλήθεια) itself: "and from truth itself" (3 John 12 NASB). The third witness consists of multiple witnesses, John and his associates: "and we also bear record; and ye know that our record is true" (3 John 12). A witness either exonerates or condemns, upholds or denies. Multiple witnesses testified not only to the godliness of Demetrius but also to the benefit of following his godly example.

Evidence for the Identity of Jesus in the Epistle of Jude

According to Jude "salvation" (σωτηρία) was the subject he first intended to write about and then got interrupted: "Beloved, when I gave all diligence to write unto you of the common salvation, it was needful for me to write unto you, and exhort *you* that *ye* should earnestly contend for the faith which was once delivered unto the saints" [italics in KJV] (Jude 3). Whatever the author meant by "salvation" (σωτηρία), whether the initial rescue from sin when they had received eternal life or deliverance in a more general or inclusive sense, the believers were built on a doctrinal foundation referred to as "the faith" (τῇ πίστις). The biblical basis for Christianity has been built and believers are told to protect it. The reason the readers were to "earnestly contend" (ἐπαγωνίζομαι) was that the foundation of faith was under attack: "For there are certain men crept in unawares" (Jude 4).

The covert operation that was underway had a two-pronged agenda. The "ungodly" (ἀσεβής) who were attempting to undermine the "faith" (πίστις) were (1) "ungodly *men*, turning the grace of our God into lasciviousness" [italics in KJV] (Jude 4); and (2) "denying the only Lord God, and our Lord Jesus Christ" (Jude 4). The first of these led to the second. The first, the attempt to transform God's "grace" (χάρις) into "lasciviousness" (ἀσέλγεια) was what Paul anticipated when he asked the questions, "What shall we say then? Shall we continue in sin, that grace may abound?" (Romans 6:1). Paul knew that his teaching about "grace" (χάρις) would be used by some to excuse sin.

Teaching on the subject of "grace" (χάρις) that does not lead to the charge of antinomianism is not what Paul taught. In the first century and thereafter many have distorted the biblical doctrine of "grace" (χάρις), suggesting that it is a license to sin. The Greek noun Jude used that is rendered in the KJV with "lasciviousness" in the NASB is translated "licentiousness" (ἀσέλγεια). Louw and Nida define the word as "behavior completely lacking in moral restraint, usually with the implication of sexual licentiousness–'licentious behavior, extreme immorality'" (Johannes P. Louw and Eugene A. Nida, *Greek-English Lexicon of the New Testament Based on Semantic Domains*, 2nd ed. [New York: United Bible Societies, 2nd ed], 1989, 1:771).

The argument is that biblical "grace" removes all restraints. Paul's response was not to tell his readers that they had misunderstood "grace" (χάρις). They understood it quite well. His response to the contention that "grace" (χάρις) provided no restraint on evil was that as a result of their regeneration they had undergone an inner change that would restrain sin.

In Romans Paul expressed it with the words, "Knowing this, that our old man is crucified with *him*, that the body of sin might be destroyed, that henceforth we should not serve sin. For he that is dead is freed from sin" [italics in KJV] (Romans 6:6-7). The concept of "grace" (χάρις) did not require change; it was Jude's readers who needed to be transformed.

The second item that Jude mentions is a result of the first. Jude says that those who had "crept in unawares" (Jude 4) (παρεισδύω) were "denying the only Lord God, and our Lord Jesus Christ" (Jude 4). Jude considered it his duty to warn about those who were undermining Jesus' identity. The identity of Jesus as "the only Master and Lord" (NASB) of believers was being subverted by those who used "the grace of our God" as a justification for evil activity.

The readers are reminded of the judgment of evil men of the past. The Egyptians who were judged at the time of the Exodus were "them that believed not" (Jude 5). The implication is that those who were delivered had believed. These false teachers, who were contemporaries of Jude's readers, did not understand spiritual truths, and they even despised them. "But these speak evil of those *things* which they know not" [italics in KJV] (Jude 10).

The writer lets the reader know that he is referring to the false teachers in their church: "These are spots in your feasts of charity when they feast with *you*, feeding themselves without fear: clouds *they are* without water, carried about of winds; trees whose fruit withereth, without fruit, twice dead, plucked up by the roots; raging waves of the sea, foaming out their own shame" [italics in KJV] (Jude 12-13).

The NASB says, "These men are those who are hidden reefs in your love feasts when they feast with you without fear, caring for themselves; clouds without water, carried along by winds; autumn trees without fruit, doubly dead, uprooted; wild waves of the sea, casting up their own shame like foam." The description "twice dead" or "doubly dead" (Jude 12) (δὶς ἀποθανόντα) perhaps refers to their own spiritual condition and their uselessness to the church or their impending physical and spiritual demise.

The lost condition of the false teachers is confirmed by the words, "wandering stars, to whom is reserved the blackness of darkness for ever" (Jude 13). Additional evidence that they are unsaved is the author's enigmatic application of a prophecy by Enoch to them: "And Enoch also, the seventh from Adam, prophesied of these, saying, Behold, the Lord cometh with ten thousands of his saints, to execute judgment upon all, and to convince all *that are* ungodly among them of all their ungodly deeds which they have ungodly committed, and of all *their* hard *speeches* which ungodly sinners have spoken against him" [italics in KJV] (Jude 14-15). The NASB describes what God will do with the words, "to execute judgment upon all, and to convict all the ungodly of all their ungodly deeds which they have done in an ungodly way, and of all the harsh things which ungodly sinners have spoken against Him." The words, "and of all the harsh things which the ungodly sinners have spoken against Him" relate to Jesus' identity which they have rejected. The conclusive phrase, "having not the Spirit" (Jude 19) (πνεῦμα μὴ ἔχοντες) removes any doubt that the false teachers were unsaved.

Believers are not to follow the false teachers: "But ye, beloved, building up yourselves on your most holy faith, praying in the Holy Ghost, keep yourselves in the love of God, looking for the mercy of our Lord Jesus Christ unto eternal life" (Jude 20-21). Because of who Jesus is believers can keep from false teaching and live lives that show their love for God. Eternal life is the certain expectation of all who have put their trust in Jesus.

The writer commends his readers to Jesus' care: "Now unto him that is able to keep you from falling, and to present *you* faultless before the presence of his glory with exceeding joy, to the only wise God our Saviour, *be* glory and majesty, dominion and power, both now and ever. Amen" [italics in KJV] (Jude 24-25). The words, "both now and forever" ("before all time and now and forever" = NASB) (πρὸ παντὸς τοῦ αἰῶνος καὶ νῦν καὶ εἰς πάντας τοὺς αἰῶνας), identify Jesus as having existed from all eternity. Wallace uses this verse as an example of a theologically significant passage involving the preposition "before" (πρὸ) (Daniel Wallace, *Greek Grammar beyond the Basics*, [Grand Rapids: Zondervan, 1996], 379). Jude can confidently commend believers into the hands of the one to whom they have entrusted their eternal destiny because He is eternal.

Chapter 11

Evidence for the Identity of Jesus in the Apocalypse

Earth Interrupted

John is presumed by tradition to be the longest living of the original twelve disciples and was privileged to write the culminating treatise on the future unveiling of Jesus' identity. The entire world will witness the eschatological denouement of history, and the central figure through it all will be Jesus. Were it not for divine inspiration the author would have been at a loss for words to describe the terrifying events that the whole earth will experience. The lasting consequences of trusting or not trusting in Jesus for one's eternal destiny will become reality. The same apostle who provided evidence in his Gospel for the express purpose that people might have eternal life, offers the ultimate rationale for placing one's trust in Jesus in his Apocalypse.

Pretribulation Times

The book's author gives it the title "The Revelation of Jesus Christ" (Revelation 1:1) (Ἀποκάλυψις Ἰησοῦ Χριστοῦ), hence the transliterated title, "The Apocalypse." Bauer, Arndt, Gingrich and Danker, give the noun ἀποκάλυψις the definition, "revelation" or "disclosure" (*Greek-English Lexicon of the New Testament*, 91). The Greek genitive form translated "of Jesus Christ" (Ἰησοῦ Χριστοῦ) can be either a subjective ("by Jesus Christ") or objective ("about Jesus Christ") genitive, or as Wallace states, Revelation 1:1 is a possible example of a plenary genitive in which "The noun in the genitive is *both* subjective and objective" [italics Wallace's] (Daniel Wallace, *Greek Grammar beyond the Basics*, [Grand Rapids: Zondervan, 1996], 119). A plenary genitive would include the thoughts that the "revelation" or "disclosure" is both *by* Jesus and *about* Jesus. Wallace notes that:

> One of the reasons that most NT grammarians have been reticent to accept this category is simply that most NT grammarians are Protestants. And the Protestant tradition of a singular meaning for a text (which, historically, was a reaction to the fourfold meaning employed in the Middle Ages) has been fundamental in their thinking. However, current biblical research recognizes that a given author may, at times, be *intentionally* ambiguous (ibid., 120) [italics in original].

The Apostle John considered himself qualified to write what is in the book because he was an eyewitness, "who bare record of the word of God, and of the testimony of Jesus Christ, and of all things that he saw" (Revelation 1:2). The NASB says that John was one "who bore witness to the word of God and to the testimony of Jesus Christ, *even* to all that he saw" [italics in NASB] (ὃς ἐμαρτύρησεν τὸν λόγον τοῦ θεοῦ καὶ τὴν μαρτυρίαν Ἰησοῦ Χριστοῦ ὅσα εἶδεν). The author will subsequently explain in detail how he came to be an eyewitness of the events he describes.

John's greeting to his addressees, "to the seven churches which are in Asia" (Revelation 1:4), has a description of God the Father as "him which is, and which was, and which is to come" (Revelation 1:4), and speaks of "his throne" (Revelation 1:4). In the author's presentation of Jesus' identity he will include qualities and attributes that Jesus shares with God the Father as a member of the Trinity. As "the faithful witness" (Revelation 1:5) (ὁ μάρτυς, ὁ πιστός), Jesus is both the One whom the testimony is about and the One who gives evidence for His own identity.

In the Gospel of John Jesus repeatedly testifies to His divine self-identity with His words and works. Jesus is also "the begotten ["first-born" = NASB] of the dead" (Revelation 1:5) (ὁ πρωτότοκος τῶν νεκρῶν). He is superior in status to all who will be resurrected after Him. In anticipation of Jesus' direct intervention in the affairs of nations He is also referred to as "the prince ["ruler" = NASB] of the kings of the earth" (Revelation 1:5) (ὁ ἄρχων τῶν βασιλέων τῆς γῆς). Jesus' position as "the ruler" (ὁ ἄρχων) is in concert with that of God the Father whose "throne" (θρόνος) the author mentioned (Revelation 1:4).

Jesus' identity includes divine transcendence and immanence. Speaking as one of Jesus' beneficiaries the author says, "Unto him that loved us, and washed us from our sins in his own blood, and hath made us kings and priests unto God and his Father" (Revelation 1:5-6). The realm of "priests" (ἱερεύς) has existed without the physical presence of its king but that will change: "Behold, he cometh with clouds; and every eye shall see him, and they *also* which pierced him: and all kindreds of the earth shall wail because of him" [italics in KJV] (Revelation 1:7). The event will be a fulfillment of Zechariah's prophecy. "And they shall look upon me whom they have pierced, And they shall mourn for him, as one mourneth for *his* only *son*, And shall be in bitterness for him, as one that is in bitterness for *his* firstborn" [italics in KJV] (Zechariah 12:10). The author expresses his eager anticipation of that event with the words, "Even so. Amen" (Revelation 1:7) (ναί, ἀμήν).

Revelation 1:8 attributes the words in the verse to "the Lord God" (κύριος ὁ θεός). The verse says, "I am Alpha and Omega, the beginning and the ending, saith the Lord, which is, and which was, and which is to come, the Almighty" Many interpreters understand it to be Jesus' words that identify Himself. However, it is probably God the Father referring to Himself because the title "the Almighty" (ὁ παντοκράτωρ) is used exclusively for Him in the rest of the book. Swete says, "The solemn opening of the book reaches its climax here with words ascribed to the Eternal and Almighty Father" (Henry Barclay Swete, *Commentary on Revelation* [London: Macmillan, 1911; reprint, Grand Rapids: Kregel, 1977], 11). While it is debated who the speaker is in Revelation 1:8, there is a similar self-identification in Revelation 22:12-13 that is definitely that of Jesus, who says, "And, behold, I come quickly; and my reward *is* with me, to give every man according as his work shall be. I am Alpha and Omega, the beginning and the end, the first and the last" [italics in KJV].

The term "testimony" (μαρτυρία) is used by the author in the reason he gives for his exile: "I John, who also am your brother, and companion in tribulation, and in the kingdom and patience of Jesus Christ, was in the isle that is called Patmos, for the word of God, and for the testimony of Jesus Christ" (Revelation 1:9). The words, "the testimony of Jesus" (τὴν μαρτυρίαν Ἰησοῦ), should be taken as an objective genitive, "the testimony" (τὴν μαρτυρίαν) consists of information about Jesus. This parallels the phrase before it where "the words" (τὸν λόγον) are what God has spoken. The content of "the testimony of Jesus" (τὴν μαρτυρίαν Ἰησοῦ) consisted of His identity, who He is and what He has done, that caused John the Apostle to run afoul of the Roman authorities.

In Revelation 1:13-16 is the first of many descriptions of Jesus in this book. He is:

> ...in the midst of the seven candlesticks *one* like unto the Son of man, clothed with a garment down to the foot, and girt about the paps with a golden girdle. His head and *his* hairs *were* white like wool, as white as snow; and his eyes *were* as a flame of fire; and his feet like unto fine brass, as if they burned in a furnace; and his voice as the sound of many waters. And he had in his right hand seven stars: and out of his mouth went a sharp twoedged sword: and his countenance *was* as the sun shineth in his strength [italics in KJV].

In reaction to Jesus' appearance John "fell at his feet as dead" (Revelation 1:17). Jesus identifies Himself with the words, "I am the first and the last: *I am* he that liveth, and was dead; and, behold, I am alive for evermore, Amen; and have the keys of hell and of death" [italics in KJV] (Revelation 1:17-18). He is the crucified, risen, and eternal Jesus who has authority over man's physical life, death, and eternal destiny.

Jesus makes statements addressed "unto the angel of the church of Ephesus" (Revelation 2:1) about that church's performance. Among other commendations Jesus says, "and hast borne, and hast patience" (Revelation 2:3). But there are also criticisms. The church faced the unique challenge of individuals who impersonated the apostles, "those who call themselves apostles" (Revelation 2:2) (τοὺς λέγοντας ἑαυτοὺς ἀποστόλους) and that of the "Nicolaitans" (Revelation 2:6) (Νικολαΐτης). Jesus' exhortation applies to an historical church at the time of the writing of the book or it refers to one at the time of the Tribulation. Both experience persecution. Difficult circumstances call for encouragement and Jesus provides it. In Revelation 2:7 Jesus makes the statement, "To him that overcometh will I give to eat of the tree of life, which is in the midst of the paradise of God."

The enigmatic "tree of life, which is in the Paradise of God" (τοῦ ξύλου τῆς ζωῆς, ὅ ἐστιν ἐν τῷ παραδείσῳ τοῦ θεοῦ) has been taken by some to mean eternal life and the term "overcome" (νικάω) to apply to the believer's life. Frequently those who hold that view take 1 John 5:4-5, written by the same author as the book of Revelation, as support because there the term "overcome" (νικάω) refers to all believers. However, the semantic transfer employed in that interpretation is not legitimate. The context of the book of Revelation probably has the martyrdom of believers in mind. Louw and Nida give this definition for the verb "overcome" (νικάω): "to win a victory over–'to be victorious over, to be a victor, to conquer, victory'" (Johannes P. Louw and Eugene

A. Nida, *Greek-English Lexicon of the New Testament Based on Semantic Domains*, 2nd ed. [New York: United Bible Societies, 2nd ed], 1989, 1:501).

Jesus was encouraging believers in the church at Ephesus, or prophetically in the Tribulation, to hold on to their faith in the face of deadly persecution. The promise Jesus held out to them was conditioned on their "overcoming" (νικάω). It was not a promise that they would in fact "overcome" (νικάω), or much less a guarantee that every believer in every age would always do so. Unique circumstances do not necessarily have a particular universal application. "To eat of the tree of life" (Revelation 2:7) cannot be the reward of eternal life granted on the basis of "overcoming" (νικάω) because that would contradict what John wrote in his Gospel.

One of the principles of logic that many learn as a child is that when you use the words "always" and "never" you are almost always wrong. That is because "always" and "never" are universals that are invalidated by a single contrary instance. The universal proposition that all believers are "overcomers" is easily disproved by many biblical statements and examples. For example, it borders on the absurd to claim that Ananias and Sapphira were "overcomers." The apostle Paul did not share the opinion that all believers are "overcomers." He wrote this about a believer, "deliver such an one unto Satan for the destruction of the flesh, that the spirit may be saved in the day of the Lord Jesus" (1 Corinthians 5:4-5).

Paul also wrote that a believer can be subject to a negative future evaluation: "If any man's work shall be burned, he shall suffer loss: but he himself shall be saved; yet so as by fire" (1 Corinthians 3:15). Only a semantic evisceration of the term "overcome" (νικάω) can support the universal statement that all believers are "overcomers." Perhaps one reason why theological systems defend their universal assumptions at all costs is that when a universal is invalidated every instance in support of it is brought into question.

In Revelation 2:8 Jesus identifies Himself as "the first and the last, which was dead, and is alive." With the words "the first and the last" (ὁ πρῶτος καὶ ὁ ἔσχατος) Jesus identifies Himself with God the Father "which is, and which was, and which is to come" (Revelation 1:4, 8). God the Father and Jesus the Son are eternal. Furthermore the identity of Jesus as revealed in Scripture is incomplete without His death and resurrection: "which was dead, and is alive" (Revelation 2:8).

Jesus' words indicate that the church in Smyrna was undergoing persecution: "I know thy works, and tribulation, and poverty" (Revelation 2:9). Jesus' encouragement was, "Fear none of those things which thou shalt suffer: behold, the devil shall cast *some* of you into prison, that ye may be tried; and ye shall have tribulation ten days" [italics in KJV] (Revelation 2:10). The promise given to them was, "be thou faithful unto death, and I will give thee a crown of life" (Revelation 2:10). To equate "the crown of life" with salvation would make it contingent on being "faithful" (πιστός). John's Gospel was written for the express purpose of showing how to acquire eternal life, and never once did he include being "faithful" (πιστός) as a requirement. Nor did he ever refer to eternal life as "the crown of life" (τὸν στέφανον τῆς ζωῆς). Being "faithful" (πιστός) cannot be separated from works. Being "faithful" (πιστός) cannot mean merely wanting to, being willing to, or being committed to. Instead it means being "faithful" (πιστός) in word, actions, and attitude.

Jesus concludes His address to the angel of the church in Smyrna with, "he that overcometh shall not be hurt of the second death" (Revelation 2:11). Believers were to be encouraged that even though martyrdom would result in physical death (the first death), their eternal spiritual destiny (a second death) was not in jeopardy. Jesus does not say that a failure to "overcome" (νικάω) will result in "the second death" (τοῦ θανάτου τοῦ δευτέρου). Possible implications, particularly opposite ones, are not necessarily intended by a speaker. Negative implications are not always true. John, the author of both the book of Revelation and the Gospel of John recognized this, and in his Gospel he indicated when the negative of his positive statements were to be understood. For example, John 3:36 says, "He that believeth on the Son hath everlasting life: and he that believeth not the Son shall not see life; but the wrath of God abideth on him." Stating the opposite of the initial proposition is not redundant but is an affirmation of the truth of that negative implication.

Although Mark 16:16 is in the longer ending of Mark and may not have been included in the original manuscript, it illustrates a writer's exclusion of a possible negative implication. Jesus said, "He that believeth and is baptized shall be saved; but he that believeth not shall be damned." In the first part of the sentence, the inclusion of baptism is innocuous, as long as it is not considered a requirement for the acquisition of salvation in addition to "believing" (πιστεύω). But when the statement is reversed and stated negatively, being "baptized" (βαπτίζω) is omitted because only the failure to "believe" (πιστεύω) results in someone being "damned" ("condemned" = NASB) (κατακρίνω).

Jesus' address "to the angel of the church in Pergamos" (Revelation 2:12) is also given in the context of persecution. Jesus describes the environment of the church as "where Satan's seat *is*" [italics in KJV] (Revelation 2:13) and He mentions that a man named "Antipas *was* my faithful martyr, who was slain among you, where Satan dwelleth" [italics in KJV] (Revelation 2:13). Jesus commended the Pergamum church by saying, "thou holdest fast my name, and hast not denied my faith" (Revelation 2:13). The person of Jesus and faith in Him was held in high regard.

However, Jesus condemned them for two teachings that were tolerated in their midst: (1) "But I have a few things against thee, because thou hast there them that hold the doctrine of Balaam, who taught Balac to cast a stumblingblock before the children of Israel, to eat things sacrificed unto idols, and to commit fornication" (Revelation 2:14); and (2) "So hast thou also them that hold the doctrine of the Nicolaitans, which thing I hate" (Revelation 2:15). The continued failure to deal with those whose teaching promoted such activity would result in their judgment: "Repent; or else I will come unto thee quickly, and will fight against them with the sword of my mouth" (Revelation 2:16). Jesus' mention of "the sword of My mouth" (τῇ ῥομφαίᾳ τοῦ στόματός μου) places the application in the eschatological future. Doctrinal purity was to be maintained in the face of persecution.

Just as Jesus encouraged the members of the churches in Ephesus and Smyrna, He challenges those in the church in Pergamum to "overcome" (νικάω): "To him that overcometh will I give to eat of the hidden manna, and will give him a white stone, and in the stone a new name written, which no man knoweth saving he that receiveth *it*" [italics in KJV] (Revelation 2:17). Just as manna in the Old Testament provided for the Israelites when they had no human source for food, so Jesus will give "the hidden manna" to those undergoing persecution. They are to trust Him; for He will supply in their hour of need. "A white stone" (ψῆφον λευκήν) with the mysterious name written on it will encourage them in some undisclosed way. They are to trust Jesus that "the white stone" will be there if they "overcome" (νικάω). Jesus did not say what "the hidden manna" (τοῦ μάννα τοῦ κεκρυμμένου) or "a white stone" (ψῆφον λευκήν) represent. However, "overcoming" (νικάω) is not to be added to "believe" (πιστεύω) as a requirement for eternal life.

Jesus is described to "the angel of the church in Thyatira" (Revelation 2:18) as "the Son of God, who hath his eyes like unto a flame of fire, and his feet *are* like fine brass" [italics in KJV] (Revelation 2:18). Jesus is poised to execute judgment but before he condemns them He commends the church at large for five qualities (Revelation 2:19): (1) "charity" ("love") (ἀγάπη); (2) "faith" (πίστις); (3) "service" (διακονία); (4) "patience" ("perseverance") (ὑπομονή); and (5) "thy works; and the last to be more than the first." They had grown in their obedience but the entire church is rebuked for allowing one person to lead other believers astray: "Notwithstanding I have a few things against thee, because thou sufferest that woman Jezebel, which calleth herself a prophetess, to teach and to seduce my servants to commit fornication, and to eat things sacrificed unto idols" (Revelation 2:20).

Judgment will be severe for "Jezebel" (Ἰεζάβελ) because she does not take advantage of the opportunity given to her: "And I gave her space to repent of her fornication; and she repented not. Behold, I will cast her into a bed" (Revelation 2:21-22). Those following her, "them that commit adultery with her" (Revelation 2:22), referred to as "her children" (τὰ τέκνα αὐτῆς), will also be judged: "I will cast her into a bed, and them that commit adultery with her into great tribulation, except they repent of their deeds. And I will kill her children with death" (Revelation 2:22-23). The criteria for this judgment will be their "works" (ἔργα): "and all the churches shall know that I am he which searcheth the reins and hearts: and I will give unto every one of you according to your works" (Revelation 2:23).

Some, however, will not be led astray, and so Jesus' instructed them: "But unto you I say, and unto the rest in Thyatira, as many as have not this doctrine, and which have not known the depths of Satan, as they speak; I will put upon you none other burden. But that which ye have *already* hold fast till I come" [italics in KJV] (Revelation 2:24-25). Those who "hold fast" (κρατέω) are further described with the words, "he that overcometh, and keepeth my works unto the end" (Revelation 2:26). As incentives for "overcoming" (νικάω) and "keeping" (τηρέω) Jesus' "deeds" (τὰ ἔργα), that is, obeying Him, He makes a twofold promise: (1) "to him will I give power over the nations: and he shall rule them with a rod of iron; as the vessels of a potter shall they be broken to shivers: even as I received of my Father" (Revelation 2:26-27); and (2) "I will give him the morning star" (Revelation 2:28).

Jesus does not promise that all believers will in fact "overcome" (νικάω), but those who do so will be rewarded. They will rule with Jesus in His coming kingdom. Jesus does not explain it, but those faithful believers will also be given "the morning star" as a reward. Whatever it is, it will be worth it. Both of these rewards will be given in addition to eternal life that all who put their trust in Jesus will receive. The fact that Jesus can reward believers in the afterlife identifies Him as God.

Jesus tells the author to write "unto the angel of the church in Sardis" (Revelation 3:1). Jesus describes Himself as "he that hath the seven Spirits of God, and the seven stars" (Revelation 3:1). Perhaps "the seven stars" are related to "the morning star" (Revelation 2:28) that will be rewarded to those who "overcome" (νικάω). The fact that "the seven Spirits of God" (Revelation 3:1) belong to Jesus, literally "has" (ἔχω), is consistent with His deity.

Jesus criticizes "the deeds" (τὰ ἔργα) of the church: "I know thy works, that thou hast a name that thou livest, and art dead" (Revelation 3:1). Perhaps their reputation did not match reality. That Jesus "knows" (οἶδα) about each individual in this church is the exercise of a divine attribute. The solution for their "dead" (νεκρός) condition is, "Be watchful, and strengthen the things which remain, that are ready to die: for I have not found thy works perfect ["completed" = NASB] before God" (Revelation 3:2). Jesus addresses the issue not of their salvation but of their sanctification on the basis of their saved condition. He says, "Remember therefore how thou hast received and heard, and hold fast, and repent" (Revelation 3:3). Jesus does not want them to be unprepared for His return: "If therefore thou shalt not watch, I will come on thee as a thief, and thou shalt not know what hour I will come upon thee" (Revelation 3:3).

Because of Jesus' divine omniscience He knows who is faithful: "Thou hast a few names even in Sardis which have not defiled their garments" (Revelation 3:4). The implied contrast is that those who were "dead" (Revelation 3:1) (νεκρὸς) had garments that were soiled. Of those "who have not defiled their garments" (Revelation 3:4), Jesus said, "they shall walk with me in white: for they are worthy" (Revelation 3:4). They are "worthy" (ἄξιος) to "walk" (περιπατέω) with Jesus (not referring to being worthy of receiving eternal life whose only requirement is trust in Him).

Some who hold that being "worthy" (ἄξιος) is a condition for entrance into heaven seek support from the next verse that says, "He that overcometh, the same shall be clothed in white raiment; and I will not blot out his name out of the book of life, but I will confess his name before my Father, and before his angels" (Revelation 3:5). Some say the words, "I will not blot out his name out of the book of life" mean that if a believer does not "overcome" (νικάω), that is, persevere, he will not be granted admittance into heaven because his name is missing from "the roll up yonder." This would not mean that a person's name had never been written in the book of life, but that it was written and then erased. However, Jesus' words about "erasure" (ἐξαλείφω) are better understood as the attempted obliteration of a name and therefore the individual was not being remembered. In fact that was a well-known ancient practice.

Historian Sarah Bond writes that "Romans saw it as a punishment worse than execution: the fate of being forgotten. It was suffered by numerous ignominious emperors of Rome in the early empire, and, even in the later empire, it was a mark of great disgrace" ("Erasing the Face of History," http//:www.nytimes.com, accessed 4/9/2012). Bond writes about an event that the apostle John may well have been aware of when Jesus said those words to him in a vision: "According to the historian Suetonius, in the chaos that followed the assassination of the emperor Caligula in A.D. 41, 'some wanted all memory of the Caesars obliterated, and their temples destroyed.' The new emperor, Claudius, ultimately blocked the Senate's attempt to decree a formal damnation of his predecessor's memory" (ibid.).

Also the author of Revelation may have been aware of Egyptian history. Again, Bond writes:

> The Egyptian Book of the Dead directs those traveling to the underworld to confront the demons that guard the gates by telling them, "Make a way for me, for I know you, I know your name," before continuing on their journey to the afterlife. Names in Egyptian culture have an innate power, and can be a means of control. When the pharaoh Akhenaton tried to institute his own brand of monotheism, he had the name of the rival god Amon stricken from monuments throughout Egypt.
>
> Like gods, rulers were also vulnerable to such erasures. Queen Hatshepsut, a prolific builder who was a regent for her stepson, Thutmose III, was almost obliterated from history after he ascended the throne in the 15th century B.C. Thutmose, and then his son Amenhotep II, systematically removed her image from monuments, reliefs, statues, cartouches and the official list of Egyptian rulers, perhaps in an effort to underline their own legitimacy (ibid.).

Jesus, however, promises that those who "overcome" (νικάω) will not be forgotten. He will make sure that their faithfulness is communicated in heaven to God Himself and the holy angels: "I will not blot out his name out of the book of life, but I will confess his name before my Father, and before his angels" (Revelation 3:5).

Jesus identifies Himself "to the angel of the church in Philadelphia" (Revelation 3:7) as "he that is holy, he that is true, he that hath the key of David, he that openeth, and no man shutteth; and shutteth, and no man openeth" (Revelation 3:7). Jesus is "holy" (ἅγιος) and omnipotent, attributes of deity. He is also the Messiah "that hath the key of David." Jesus claims to have divine power to protect those who "have kept My word, and have not denied My name" (Revelation 3:8 NASB). Jesus then promises reward for their obedient allegiance: "Because thou hast kept the word of my patience, I also will keep thee from the hour of temptation, which shall come upon all the world, to try them that dwell upon the earth" (Revelation 3:10).

In Revelation 3:11 Jesus refers to His soon return as He urges perseverance, "Behold, I come quickly: hold that fast which thou hast, that no man take thy crown." "The crown" (τὸν στέφανόν) is not eternal life that would be lost by a failure to "hold fast" (κρατέω). Instead, the failure is the forfeiture of future reward. The thought "that no one take" (ἵνα μηδεὶς λάβῃ) is not that there is a limited supply of rewards that must be fought over. In the immediate context perhaps "the crown" (τὸν στέφανόν) can be lost by following "them of the synagogue of Satan, which say they are Jews, and are not, but do lie" (Revelation 3:9) who may have been attempting to lead believers astray. In contrast to having that happen Jesus encourages believers to "overcome" (νικάω): "Him that overcometh will I make a pillar in the temple of my God, and he shall go no more out: and I will write upon him the name of my God, and the name of the city of my God, *which is* new Jerusalem, which cometh down out of heaven from my God: and *I will write upon him* my new name" [italics in KJV] (Revelation 3:12).

The words, "a pillar in the temple" (στῦλον ἐν τῷ ναῷ) elicit thoughts of prominence and permanence. The permanence of the reward is reinforced: "and he shall not go out from it anymore." The exhortation includes a three-fold writing of names on the one who "overcomes" (νικάω). The names are of (1) God the Father, "the name of my God"; (2) God's city, "the name of the city of my God, *which is* new Jerusalem" [italics in KJV]; and (3) "my new name." God will reward those who are faithful by having Himself identified with them.

Jesus' seventh and final address is "unto the angel of the church in Laodicea" (Revelation 3:14). Jesus identifies Himself as, "the Amen, the faithful and true witness, the beginning of the creation of God" (Revelation 3:14). Jesus personifies the asseverative (to declare seriously or positively; affirm) particle "amen" (ἀμήν) that Louw and Nida define as a "strong affirmation of what is declared–'truly, indeed, it is true that'" (Johannes P. Louw and Eugene A. Nida, *Greek-English Lexicon of the New Testament Based on Semantic Domains*, 2nd ed. [New York: United Bible Societies, 2nd ed], 1989, 1:673). The reliability of Jesus' testimony is reinforced with the adjectives "faithful" (πιστός) and "true" (ἀληθινός) that modify "witness" (μάρτυς). What He says about His own identity is true and everything else He says is true. The words, "the Beginning of the creation of God" (Revelation 3:14) do not mean that Jesus is a created being. Louw and Nida define the term translated "beginning" (ἀρχὴ) as: "one who or that which constitutes an initial cause–'first cause, origin'" and, therefore, "the origin of what God has created" (ibid., 1:779). Jesus is the One who brought creation into being.

Jesus has nothing good to say about the church in Laodicea. They are not complete failures but neither are they on fire for the Lord: "I know thy works, that thou art neither cold nor hot: I would thou wert cold or hot" (Revelation 3:15). With a memorable word picture Jesus tells them, "So then because thou art lukewarm, and neither cold nor hot, I will spue thee out of my mouth" (Revelation 3:16). Jesus wanted them to feel the same revulsion He did over their condition. Spiritual complacency nauseates Him. Their satisfaction ignored their true situation: "Because thou sayest, I am rich, and increased with goods, and have need of nothing; and knowest not that thou art wretched, and miserable, and poor, and blind, and naked" (Revelation 3:17).

This is a serious accusation for which Jesus has the solution: "I counsel thee to buy of me gold tried in the fire, that thou mayest be rich; and white raiment, that thou mayest be clothed, and *that* the shame of thy nakedness do not appear; and anoint thine eyes with eyesalve, that thou mayest see" [italics in KJV] (Revelation 3:18). Jesus is referring to the spiritual poverty, nakedness and blindness of believers. Their problem is not that they need to get saved. Jesus addresses them as children of God, particularly with the use of the verb translated "I. . .chasten" ("discipline" = NASB) (παιδεύω): "As many as I love, I rebuke and chasten: be zealous therefore, and repent" (Revelation 3:19).

The author of Hebrews makes the same connection between sonship and discipline using the noun "chastisement" ("discipline" = NASB) (παιδεία). In a passage on discipline in the life of a believer he writes: "But if ye be without chastisement, whereof all are partakers, then are ye bastards, and not sons" (Hebrews 12:8). The NASB says, "But if you are without discipline, of which all have become partakers, then you are illegitimate children and not sons."

In Revelation 3:20 Jesus invites believers to hear His words and enter a life of obedient fellowship: "Behold, I stand at the door, and knock: if any man hear my voice, and open the door, I will come in to him, and will sup with him, and he with me." The condition for such fellowship with Jesus is being an obedient believer who "overcomes" (νικάω), and the offer includes the invitation to share in His role by ruling with Him: "To him that overcometh will I grant to sit with me in my throne, even as I also overcame, and am set down with my Father in his throne" (Revelation 3:21).

Tribulation Times

Heaven is a holy place. The twenty-four elders whom John saw were "clothed in white raiment" (Revelation 4:4), which were emblematic of holiness. The ceaseless praise of "the four beasts" ("the four living creatures" = NASB) (τὰ τέσσαρα ζῷα) is, "Holy, holy, holy, Lord God Almighty, which was, and is, and is to come" (Revelation 4:8). In reaction to being in God's presence; "the four and twenty elders fall down before him that sat on the throne, and worship him that liveth for ever and ever" (Revelation 4:10). In God's presence they will acknowledge their unworthiness to be attired in anything symbolizing their own authority, "and cast their crowns before the throne" (Revelation 4:10). Their words will be about the One seated on the throne: "Thou art worthy, O Lord, to receive glory and honour and power: for thou hast created all things, and for thy pleasure they are and were created" (Revelation 4:11). The unworthiness of all created creatures to stand before God is contrasted with Jesus, the only One "worthy" (ἄξιος) to do so.

In God's hand is a book and an angel asks, "Who is worthy to open the book, and to loose the seals thereof?" (Revelation 5:2). The first answer to the question is that no one qualifies: "And no man in heaven, nor in earth, neither under the earth, was able to open the book, neither to look thereon" (Revelation 5:3). The only One who can open the book is Jesus. He is identified as "the Lion of the tribe of Juda[h], the Root of David" (Revelation 5:5). Jesus is described as "a Lamb as it had been slain" (Revelation 5:6). John would have recognized Him as the One of whom he bore witness. Jesus is accompanied by "seven horns and seven eyes, which are the seven Spirits of God sent forth into all the earth" (Revelation 5:6).

In acknowledgment of who Jesus is, "the four beasts and four *and* twenty elders fell down before the Lamb" [italics in KJV] (Revelation 5:8). With reverence they recognize His relationship to the believers whose prayers they are presenting to God. "The prayers of the saints" (αἱ προσευχαὶ τῶν ἁγίων) are in "golden bowls" (φιάλας χρυσᾶς) and are pictured as "incense" (θυμίαμα). In reverent worship "the four beasts" ("the four living creatures" = NASB) (τὰ τέσσαρα ζῷα) and "the four *and* twenty elders" [italics in KJV] (οἱ εἴκοσι τέσσαρες πρεσβύτεροι) sing a song with the words, "Thou art worthy to take the book, and to open the seals thereof: for thou wast slain, and hast redeemed us to God by thy blood out of every kindred, and tongue, and people, and nation; and hast made us unto our God kings and priests: and we shall reign on the earth" (Revelation 5:9-10).

Those singing the song are joined by angels and together "the number of them was ten thousand times ten thousand, and thousands of thousands" (Revelation 5:11). As John saw the innumerable gathering, he may have thought of the prophet Daniel who similarly described a heavenly scene: "A fiery stream issued and came forth from before him: thousand thousands ministered unto him, and ten thousand times ten thousand stood before him: the judgment was set, and the books were opened" (Daniel 7:10).

In Revelation 5:12 the heavenly multitude was "saying with a loud voice, Worthy is the Lamb that was slain to receive power, and riches, and wisdom, and strength, and honour, and glory, and blessing." John heard all creation joining in: "And every creature which is in heaven, and on the earth, and under the earth, and such as are in the sea, and all that are in them, heard I saying" (Revelation 5:13). Their words apply equally to God the Father and to Jesus: "Blessing, and honour, and glory, and power, *be* unto him that sitteth upon the throne, and unto the Lamb for ever and ever" [italics in KJV] (Revelation 5:13). Simultaneously the antiphonal refrain of "the four living creatures" (τὰ τέσσαρα ζῷα) was "Amen" (ἀμήν), and the reaction of "the four *and* twenty elders" [italics in KJV] (οἱ εἴκοσι τέσσαρες πρεσβύτεροι): "And the four *and* twenty elders fell down and worshiped" [italics in KJV] (Revelation 5:14) (καὶ οἱ πρεσβύτεροι ἔπεσαν καὶ προσεκύνησαν). The scene of universal worship leaves no doubt about the deity and equality of Jesus with God the Father.

Jesus, "the Lamb," the only One qualified to open the seals, opens six of them in this chapter. The first four seals have riders on horses who unleash calamities on the earth.

From them literature, media, and even marital counseling (marital counselor Howard Lambert uses the image for four relationship destroyers) have taken the image of "The Four Horsemen of the Apocalypse" (http://www.relationshipresourcecenter.com, accessed 08/01/2012). During the Tribulation there will be those who put their trust in Jesus and will pay for it with their lives. John refers to them: "I saw under the altar the souls of them that were slain for the word of God, and for the testimony which they held" (Revelation 6:9). The NASB says, "I saw underneath the altar the souls of those who had been slain because of the word of God, and because of the testimony which they maintained." Their "testimony" (μαρτυρία) will be about who Jesus is and what He has done. In heaven they will cry out to God for vindication: "And they cried with a loud voice, saying, How long, O Lord, holy and true, dost thou not judge and avenge our blood on them that dwell on the earth?" (Revelation 6:10).

God's response is that more witnesses will be killed and then they will be avenged: "and it was said unto them, that they should rest yet for a little season, until their fellowservants also and their brethren, that should be killed as they *were*, should be fulfilled" [italics in KJV] (Revelation 6:11). The objects of God's wrath will identify the source as God the Father and Jesus: "And [they] said to the mountains and rocks, Fall on us, and hide us from the face of him that sitteth on the throne, and from the wrath of the Lamb: for the great day of his wrath is come; and who shall be able to stand?" (Revelation 6:16-17). In their anguish they will acknowledge who Jesus is and unwittingly begin to fulfill God's purpose that Paul wrote about in Philippians 2:9-11: "Wherefore God also hath highly exalted him, and given him a name which is above every name: that at the name of Jesus every knee should bow, of *things* in heaven, and *things* in earth, and *things* under the earth; and *that* every tongue should confess that Jesus Christ *is* Lord, to the glory of God the Father" [italics in KJV]. Jesus' identity is indisputable.

Salvation is attributed to God the Father and Jesus the Son. The saved before God's throne say, "Salvation to our God which sitteth upon the throne, and unto the Lamb" (Revelation 7:10). One of the elders engages John in a conversation to get him to ask how the saved multitude came to be there. The elder asks John, "What are these which are arrayed in white robes? and whence came they?" (Revelation 7:13). Perhaps John knew but wanted confirmation from the elder, or in deference to him, he replied, "Sir, thou knowest" (Revelation 7:14) (κύριέ μου, σὺ οἶδας). The heavenly elder's response is, "These are they which came out of great tribulation, and have washed their robes, and made them white in the blood of the Lamb" (Revelation 7:14). "The blood of the Lamb" (τῷ αἵματι τοῦ ἀρνίου) refers to Jesus' death on the cross for their sin. They put their trust in Jesus who died on their behalf. According to the elder that is why they are qualified to be in heaven and serve in God's presence: "Therefore are they before the throne of God, and serve him day and night in his temple" (Revelation 7:15). The NASB says, "For this reason, they are before the throne of God; and they serve Him day and night in His temple."

Since these saints suffered severe persecution on earth during the Tribulation God the Father and Jesus provide for them in heaven. God the Father "shall dwell among them"

(Revelation 7:15). The NASB says that God "shall spread His tabernacle over them" (σκηνώσει ἐπ᾽ αὐτούς), a metaphor that connotes protection and provision that is explained in these words: "They shall hunger no more, neither thirst any more; neither shall the sun light on them, nor any heat" (Revelation 7:16). What they had been exposed to on earth would no longer be a problem for them in heaven.

In addition to God the Father protecting them and providing for them, they will be cared for by Jesus, "For the Lamb which is in the midst of the throne shall feed them, and shall lead them unto living fountains of waters: and God shall wipe away all tears from their eyes" (Revelation 7:17). Perhaps even the memory of their time of distress will disappear. Nowhere in the description of these prophetic events is there any hint that Jesus is any less God than God the Father. The coordination of their actions reflects the deity that they share.

Jesus, the only one qualified to do so, breaks the seventh seal. The sounds accompanying the prior seals contrast with the silence surrounding the unveiling of this seal: "And when he had opened the seventh seal, there was silence in heaven about the space of half an hour" (Revelation 8:1). Even those praising God stop, signaling the significance of the seventh seal. Whether the apocalyptic events announced by the seven trumpets will occur during or after the seals, the war being waged is between Jesus and the devil. "The bottomless pit" (Revelation 9:1, 2) (τὸ φρέαρ τῆς ἀβύσσου) is opened by the angel of the fifth trumpet and those let loose are described as having the devil as their leader: "And they had a king over them, *which is* the angel of the bottomless pit, whose name in the Hebrew tongue *is* Abaddon, but in the Greek tongue hath *his* name Apollyon" [italics in KJV] (Revelation 9:11).

Two special witnesses in the Tribulation will be supernaturally empowered for three and one-half years in order to continue their work in spite of attempts to silence them:

> And if any man will hurt them, fire proceedeth out of their mouth, and devoureth their enemies: and if any man will hurt them, he must in this manner be killed. These have power to shut heaven, that it rain not in the days of their prophecy: and have power over waters to turn them to blood, and to smite the earth with all plagues, as often as they will (Revelation 11:5-6).

Throughout church history witnesses to Jesus' identity, his person, and his work, have individually been silenced and God has usually not intervened. But in the last half of the Tribulation it will be impossible to stop the testimony of these two witnesses until their work is complete: "And when they shall have finished their testimony, the beast that ascendeth out of the bottomless pit shall make war against them, and shall overcome them, and kill them" (Revelation 11:7).

The testimony of the two witnesses was about Jesus, and their apparent defeat would mirror the death of the One about whom they testified. The text mentions four parallels: (1) the location where their bodies will be on display, "And their dead bodies *shall lie* in the street of the great city, which spiritually is called Sodom and Egypt, where also our Lord was crucified" [italics in KJV] (Revelation 11:8); (2) the time interval between their death and being brought back to life, "And after three days and an half the Spirit of life from God entered into them" (Revelation 11:11); (3) their being taken up into heaven, "and they ascended up to heaven in a cloud" (Revelation 11:12); and (4) an earthquake will accompany those events, "And the same hour was there a great earthquake, and the tenth part of the city fell, and in the earthquake were slain of men seven thousand: and the remnant were affrighted, and gave glory to the God of heaven" (Revelation 11:13).

God will be universally recognized as the source of the calamities that earth will experience. The seventh trumpet will elicit a heavenly response: "And the seventh angel sounded; and there were great voices in heaven, saying, The kingdoms of this world are become *the kingdoms* of our Lord, and of his Christ; and he shall reign for ever and ever" [italics in KJV] (Revelation 11:15). "The kingdom" (ἡ βασιλεία) belongs to God the Father and to Jesus. After the battle when the archangel Michael's army defeats the devil these words are heard in heaven, "now is come salvation, and strength, and the kingdom of our God, and the power of his Christ" (Revelation 12:10).

Jesus is the means by which victory over the devil will be achieved: "And they overcame him by the blood of the Lamb, and by the word of their testimony" (Revelation 12:11). Believers will overcome the devil by invoking Jesus' substitutionary death on their behalf. In the account of the dragon (the devil) setting out to destroy the woman (probably a symbolic reference to Israel) and her children, the latter are described as those "which keep the commandments of God, and have the testimony of Jesus Christ" (Revelation 12:17). The message that the devil will seek to silence is about Jesus, that is, the gospel. If the devil can keep people from hearing about who Jesus is and what He has done, they will not be able to put their trust in Him and be saved.

The devil will be allowed by God to attempt to persuade men to reject the true God and Jesus and instead to worship him (the devil) through surrogates, one of which is the beast out of the sea: "And they worshipped the dragon which gave power unto the beast: and they worshipped the beast, saying, Who *is* like unto the beast? who is able to make war with him?" [italics in KJV] (Revelation 13:4). The devil will succeed with the exception of the saved: "And all who dwell on the earth will worship him, *everyone* whose name has not been written from the foundation of the world in the book of life of the Lamb who had been slain" [italics in NASB] (Revelation 13:8 NASB). Those who trust in the crucified Jesus consequently have their names written in the book of life that will determine their eternal destiny.

Descriptive details of the devil's surrogates reveal his deception. In Revelation 5:5 Jesus is referred to as "the Lion of the tribe of Juda[h]" (ὁ λέων ὁ ἐκ τῆς φυλῆς Ἰούδα), and in Revelation 13:2 the beast from the sea has "his mouth as the mouth of a lion" (τὸ στόμα αὐτοῦ ὡς στόμα λέοντος). Jesus' death is mentioned repeatedly. Revelation 5:6 refers to Jesus as "a Lamb as it had been slain" (ἀρνίον ἑστηκὸς ὡς ἐσφαγμένον). In Revelation 5:9 the new song says, "thou wast slain" (ἐσφάγης) and verse 12 has "the

Lamb that was slain" (τὸ ἀρνίον τὸ ἐσφαγμένον). The beast in Revelation 13:3 has seven heads and it describes, "one of his heads as it were wounded to death." Revelation 13:8 also refers to Jesus as "the Lamb slain from the foundation of the world" (τοῦ ἀρνίου τοῦ ἐσφαγμένου ἀπὸ καταβολῆς κόσμου). The beast out of the earth also deceives: "and deceiveth them that dwell on the earth by *the means of* those miracles which he had power to do in the sight of the beast; saying to them that dwell on the earth, that they should make an image to the beast, which had the wound by a sword, and did live" [italics in KJV] (Revelation 13:14).

Jesus' equality with God the Father is seen in their relationship with the one hundred and forty-four thousand who are saved during the Tribulation. Jesus' name, and that of God the Father, will be written on their foreheads: "And I looked, and, lo, a Lamb stood on the mount Sion, and with him an hundred forty *and* four thousand, having his Father's name written in their foreheads" [italics in KJV] (Revelation 14:1). The NASB says, "And I looked, and behold, the Lamb *was* standing on Mount Zion, and with Him one hundred and forty-four thousand, having His name and the name of His Father written on their foreheads" [italics in NASB]. They belong to both Jesus and to God the Father: "These were redeemed from among men, *being* the firstfruits unto God and to the Lamb" [italics in KJV] (Revelation 14:4).

In Revelation 14:6 the author sees an angel flying through the air: "And I saw another angel fly in the midst of heaven, having the everlasting gospel to preach unto them that dwell on the earth, and to every nation, and kindred, and tongue, and people." There has been debate whether the "everlasting gospel" (εὐαγγέλιον αἰώνιον) is the message of salvation or news about the kingdom or judgment. Some hesitate to conclude that it refers to salvation because of the adjective "eternal" (αἰώνιος). However, "everlasting" ("eternal" = NASB) (αἰώνιος) can qualify the "good news" (εὐαγγέλιον) of salvation because it concerns eternal matters. Alternatively, given the fact of biblical Trinitarianism, referring to the "gospel" (εὐαγγέλιον) as "eternal" (αἰώνιος) is appropriate because salvation is always trust in God (whether God the Father or Jesus, with varying degrees of knowledge about Jesus) for one's eternal destiny.

The great majority of mankind in the Tribulation are those who "worship the beast and his image" (Revelation 14:9, 11) and accept "*his* mark in his forehead, or in his hand" [italics in KJV] (Revelation 14:9). In contrast to those who worship the beast, the saved are introduced with the words, "Here is the patience of the saints" (Revelation 14:12). Believers who persevere are "they that keep the commandments of God, and the faith of Jesus" (Revelation 14:12). The NASB says, "who keep the commandments of God and their faith in Jesus" (οἱ τηροῦντες τὰς ἐντολὰς τοῦ θεοῦ καὶ τὴν πίστιν Ἰησοῦ). "Faith in Jesus" (τὴν πίστιν Ἰησοῦ) could refer to truths or doctrine related to Jesus, paralleling "the commandments of God" (τὰς ἐντολὰς τοῦ θεοῦ), or it could be a reference to their maintaining the reliance on Jesus that they exercised at conversion, the latter being taken as an objective genitive.

Tribulation saints can take heart from the words the author heard from heaven. John, the writer, heard, "Write, Blessed *are* the dead which die in the Lord from henceforth:

Yea, saith the Spirit, that they may rest from their labours; and their works do follow them" [italics in KJV] (Revelation 14:13). The believer's eternal hope will more than compensate for a martyr's death, and eternal rewards will insure that their works will be remembered and have lasting value.

In Revelation 17 "the great whore" (Revelation 17:1) (τῆς πόρνης τῆς μεγάλη), also known as "the great harlot," is out to kill believers and especially "the witnesses" (τῶν μαρτύρων): "And I saw the woman drunken with the blood of the saints, and with the blood of the martyrs [or "witnesses" = NASB = μάρτυς = "one who testifies" or "a person who has been deprived of life as the result of bearing witness to his beliefs" Johannes P. Louw and Eugene A. Nida, *Greek-English Lexicon of the New Testament Based on Semantic Domains*, 2nd ed. [New York: United Bible Societies, 2nd ed, 1989, 1:235] of Jesus" (Revelation 17:6). The "martyrs" or "witnesses" belong to Jesus, and their testimony is about who He is. The harlot's mission is to prevent them from proclaiming their message. "The beast" (τὸ θηρίον) and the "ten kings" (δέκα βασιλεῖς) will confront Jesus Himself in battle and will be conquered: "These shall make war with the Lamb, and the Lamb shall overcome them" (Revelation 17:14). Jesus can defeat them "for [because] he is Lord of lords, and King of kings" (Revelation 17:14).

"The beast" (τὸ θηρίον) and the "ten kings" (δέκα βασιλεύς) will turn against "the harlot" (ἡ πόρνη), perhaps because she will not join them in fighting "the Lamb" (τό ἀρνίον): "And the ten horns which thou sawest upon the beast, these shall hate the whore, and shall make her desolate and naked, and shall eat her flesh, and burn her with fire" (Revelation 17:16). The betrayal and intrigue will be orchestrated by God: "For God hath put in their hearts to fulfil his will, and to agree, and give their kingdom unto the beast, until the words of God shall be fulfilled" (Revelation 17:17). Their victory will be short-lived, lasting only until they are in turn defeated by God.

Posttribulation Times

At His second coming Jesus will execute judgment: "And I saw heaven opened, and behold a white horse; and he that sat upon him *was* called Faithful and True, and in righteousness he doth judge and make war" [italics in KJV] (Revelation 19:11). What was veiled in His first coming is visible in His second coming. His royal identity will be revealed: "His eyes *were* as a flame of fire, and on his head *were* many crowns" [italics in KJV] (Revelation 19:12). Being God, there will be identifying features that will remain a mystery: "and he had a name written, that no man knew, but he himself" (Revelation 19:12). But there will be no doubt who Jesus is. Characteristics unique to Jesus will be present so that He can be identified: "And he *was* clothed with a vesture dipped in blood: and his name is called The Word of God" [italics in KJV] (Revelation 19:13). In John 1:1 the author had identified "the Word" (ὁ λόγος) as Jesus: "In the beginning was the Word, and the Word was with God, and the Word was God."

Jesus is equipped to execute judgment: "And out of his mouth goeth a sharp sword" (Revelation 19:15). Revelation 19:15 says that Jesus "shall rule them ["the nations"] with a rod of iron." The author uses the verb "shepherd" (ποιμαίνω), translated "rule."

Jesus' identity as His people's shepherd and His righteous rule in His autocratic theocracy continues even as He unleashes terrifying judgment. What Jesus does is the work of God Himself: "and he treadeth the winepress of the fierceness and wrath of Almighty God" (Revelation 19:15). Jesus' royal robe and His person are emblazoned with His identity: "And he hath on *his* vesture and on his thigh a name written, KING OF KINGS, AND LORD OF LORDS" [italics in KJV] (Revelation 19:16).

The rulers of the earth will mobilize to take on the army of heaven led by Jesus: "And I saw the beast, and the kings of the earth, and their armies, gathered together to make war against him that sat on the horse, and against his army" (Revelation 19:19). In John's Gospel he displayed seven signs that identified Jesus. In the book of Revelation the mark that world leaders will require for any commercial transaction will identify them as the target of Jesus and His army: "And the beast was taken, and with him the false prophet that wrought miracles before him, with which he deceived them that had received the mark of the beast, and them that worshipped his image" (Revelation 19:20). Jesus will be personally involved in executing judgment at the end of the Tribulation: "And the remnant were slain with the sword of him that sat upon the horse" (Revelation 19:21).

God the Father and Jesus are the focal points of antagonism during the Tribulation. The author describes the martyrs: "and *I saw* the souls of them that were beheaded for the witness of Jesus, and for the word of God" [italics in KJV] (Revelation 20:4). Truth about Jesus (witness or testimony about Him) cannot be separated from truth about God the Father. The horrific martyrdom endured by Tribulation believers is a physical death that will be eclipsed by the prospect of immunity from spiritual death: "Blessed and holy *is* he that hath part in the first resurrection: on such the second death hath no power, but they shall be priests of God and of Christ, and shall reign with him a thousand years" [italics in KJV] (Revelation 20:6). Eternity will begin for them with privileged positions in the Millennium: "but they shall be priests of God and of Christ, and shall reign with him a thousand years" (Revelation 20:6). Their position as "priests of God and of Christ" (ἱερεῖς τοῦ θεοῦ καὶ τοῦ Χριστοῦ) point to the equality of God the Father and Jesus the Son.

At the "great white throne" (Revelation 20:11) (θρόνον μέγαν λευκὸν) judgment at the end of the Millennium several "books were opened" (Revelation 20:12) (βιβλία ἠνοίχθησαν). "Books" (βιβλία), plural, have "deeds" (ἔργα) or "works" in them and "the book of life" (ἡ βιβλίον τῆς ζωῆς), singular, lists the names of the saved. "The book of life" (ἡ βιβλίον τῆς ζωῆς) determines entrance or exclusion from heaven: "And whosoever was not found written in the book of life was cast into the lake of fire" (Revelation 20:15).

In Revelation 21 the author is given a glimpse of "a new heaven and a new earth" (Revelation 21:1) and within it the "new Jerusalem" (Revelation 21:2). Persecuted believers could look forward to that future place where "the tabernacle of God *is* with men, and he will dwell with them, and they shall be his people, and God himself shall be with them, *and be* their God" [italics in NASB] (Revelation 21:3). During desolate times they can take comfort in the prospect of God's future presence. Physical and emotional pain will be gone: "and God shall wipe away all tears from their eyes; and there shall be no more death, neither sorrow, nor crying, neither shall there be any more pain: for the former things are passed away" (Revelation 21:4). Pain will be a thing of the past: "Behold, I make all things new" (Revelation 21:5). God's power insures that what He promises He will perform: "It is done. I am Alpha and Omega, the beginning and the end" (Revelation 21:6).

God sovereignly sets the terms for the acquisition of eternal life and He says, "I will give unto him that is athirst of the fountain of the water of life freely" (Revelation 21:6). Suffering Tribulation saints can rest assured that their eternal destiny will not depend on anything that they will or will not do. Incidentally, but equally important, everyone who trusts in Jesus for his or her salvation can receive comfort from that reality. Salvation is freely bestowed on the basis of faith alone.

The encouragement to persevere under severe persecution looks forward to that future day when "He that overcometh shall inherit all things; and I will be his God, and he shall be my son" (Revelation 21:7). These words were intended to be of personal comfort. It was not the author's intention to imply that the opposite possibility was true, namely, that failure to stand up under persecution would undermine or undo their eternal salvation. Every possible implication of an author's words is not necessarily intended.

In contrast to believers who can confidently look forward to a future with God, are unbelievers whose future is not something to be envied: "But the fearful, and unbelieving, and the abominable, and murderers, and whoremongers, and sorcerers, and idolaters, and all liars, shall have their part in the lake which burneth with fire and brimstone: which is the second death" (Revelation 21:8). The reader is invited to remember the descriptions earlier in the book of Revelation of those in the Tribulation who could be thus characterized. In contrast to their future suffering, the prospect of present martyrdom and future blessedness would be a source of encouragement for believers. As believers faced the imminent possibility and reality of the first death that was physical, they would be exempt from the second spiritual death.

In the Jerusalem of the future, the absence of a temple is explained: "And I saw no temple therein: for the Lord God Almighty and the Lamb are the temple of it" (Revelation 21:22). For Jesus to have a coordinate position with God the Father, He must also be God. Another parallel is the city's source of light: "And the city had no need of the sun, neither of the moon, to shine in it: for the glory of God did lighten it, and the Lamb *is* the light thereof" [italics in KJV] (Revelation 21:23). In Isaiah 42:8 God says, "I *am* the Lord: that *is* my name: And my glory will I not give to another" [italics in KJV]. Throughout the book of Revelation God the Father shares glory with Jesus.

Jesus is the gatekeeper of heaven and one's name must appear in His book in order for him to be granted entrance: "And there shall in no wise enter into it any thing that defileth, neither *whatsoever* worketh abomination, or *maketh* a lie: but they which are written in the Lamb's book of life" [italics in KJV] (Revelation 21:27). God and Jesus are the source of eternal life: "And he shewed me a pure river of water of life, clear as crystal, proceeding out of the throne of God and of the Lamb" (Revelation 22:1). The description of eternity treats God the Father and Jesus equally: "And there shall be no more curse: but the throne of God and of the Lamb shall be in it; and his servants shall serve him: and they shall see his face; and his name *shall be* in their foreheads" [italics in KJV] (Revelation 22:3-4). The curse will be reversed, and believers will be identified as belonging to Him in whom they have placed their trust. The contrast with the preceding horrors of the Great Tribulation will be fitting.

Blessings are promised to believers who follow the instructions found in the book of Revelation. Jesus says, "Behold, I come quickly: blessed *is* he that keepeth the sayings of the prophecy of this book" [italics in KJV] (Revelation 22:7). Jesus and the Holy Spirit will communicate the offer of salvation along with anyone hearing their words: "And the Spirit and the bride say, Come. And let him that heareth say, Come. And let him that is athirst come. And whosoever will, let him take the water of life freely" (Revelation 22:17). Louw and Nida define the adverb translated "freely" ("without cost" = NASB) (δωρεάν) as "pertaining to being freely given–'without cost, as a free gift, without paying'" (Johannes P. Louw and Eugene A. Nida, *Greek-English Lexicon of the New Testament Based on Semantic Domains*, 2nd ed. [New York: United Bible Societies, 2nd ed], 1989, 1:567).

Those who add to "without cost" (δωρεάν) would do well to heed the biblical words that immediately follow: "For I testify unto every man that heareth the words of the prophecy of this book, if any man shall add unto these things, God shall add unto him the plagues that are written in this book" (Revelation 22:18). Adding to the gospel does not improve it; instead it destroys it and anyone doing so is subject to divine judgment.

Removing from the book also has consequences: "And if any man shall take away from the words of the book of this prophecy, God shall take away his part out of the book of life, and out of the holy city, and *from* the things which are written in this book" [italics in KJV] (Revelation 22:19). The book of Revelation highlights the identity of Jesus. The "part" (μέρος) that would have been theirs had they trusted in Christ would not be theirs. God desires that all men be saved but their rejection of His Son results in their not experiencing eternal life and its blessings.

God is the only One who can right the wrongs of human history. Jesus is God and He "testifies" (μαρτυρέω) that He will do it: "He which testifieth these things" (Revelation 22:20) (ὁ μαρτυρῶν ταῦτα). Jesus affirms, "Surely I come quickly" (Revelation 22:20) (ναί, ἔρχομαι ταχύ). John the apostle adds, "Amen. Even so, come, Lord Jesus" (Revelation 22:20) (Ἀμήν, ἔρχου κύριε Ἰησοῦ). The precursor to Jesus' return, the Great Tribulation, will bring unprecedented trouble on the earth. But the second coming of Christ is ultimately something to look forward to. Believers who presently await Jesus' return and the rapture of His church concur with John, the author of Revelation, "Even so, come, Lord Jesus."

Chapter 12

The Biblical Gospel

One of the characteristics that man, made in the image of his Creator, was given to employ and enjoy is creativity. Jonah Lehrer, in the science blog *The Frontal Cortex*, has an article with the title, "Need to Create? Get a constraint," in which he says,

> One of the many paradoxes of human creativity is that it seems to benefit from constraints. Although we imagine the imagination as requiring total freedom, the reality of the creative process is that it's often entangled with strict conventions and formal requirements. . . .It's not until we encounter hindrance–a challenge we can't easily resolve–that the chains of cognition are loosened (http://www.wired.com, accessed 6/29/2012).

The gospel was not delivered to us in the Bible as a cookie-cutter pattern. Creativity in evangelism can be used to get the attention of the unsaved; however, there are constraints and parameters within which the gospel must remain in order to be biblical. Winsomeness in winning the lost is never appropriate if it comes at the expense of scriptural accuracy.

Lexical Limitations

The meaning/s of words are not limitless; otherwise communication would be extremely difficult at best and impossible at worst. Semantic ranges can be illustrated using Venn diagrams that are usually circles that overlap or intersect. They are used to graphically depict the relationship of a finite set of elements or aggregation of items with that of another set or aggregation. Venn diagrams can be used to show what meanings two or more lexical terms may share and also visualize those meanings that are not shared. No two terms are completely synonymous either semantically or functionally.

The word "believe" in the Old Testament (Hiphil form of אָמַן) and the New Testament (πιστεύω) have definite boundaries. The two meanings they share are belief in statements or propositions to be true, and trust in something or someone. Venturing beyond those semantic parameters soteriologically creates a construct unintended by the biblical authors. Semantics should not be thought of as a chain where what is shared with another term initially is also shared with a term at the other end of the chain.

For example, some Bible teachers take the word "receive" (λαμβάνω) in John 1:12, "But as many as received Him" (ὅσοι δὲ ἔλαβον αὐτόν), whose meaning is contextually restricted later in the sentence with the words, "*even* to them that believe on his name" [italics in KJV] (τοῖς πιστεύουσιν εἰς τὸ ὄνομα αὐτοῦ), and expand the meaning of "believe" (πιστεύω) to include everything that "receive" (λαμβάνω) can refer to. They hold that one must "receive" (λαμβάνω) the complete Jesus and take the identifying feature "Lord" (κύριος), to introduce works or a willingness to work through an illegitimate linguistic back door. This unacceptable linguistic methodology has been referred to as illegitimate totality transfer. A specific meaning in a particular context cannot be expanded to include whatever it may mean somewhere or everywhere else in a text. The soteriological result with the term "Lord" (κύριος) has transformed a term identifying Jesus into an imperative and has added an extrabiblical requirement for the acquisition of eternal life. Employing the term "Lord" (κύριος) in a manner unintended by the biblical author is tantamount to tampering with the evidence of Jesus' identity.

The addition is not innocuous but deleterious. Altering the biblical requirement for salvation produces a different result. Salvation by grace is changed into condemnation by works. Jesus Himself anticipated that that would happen. On judgment day more than a few individuals will appeal their case: "Many will say to me in that day, Lord, Lord, have we not prophesied in thy name? and in thy name have cast out devils? and in thy name done many wonderful works?" (Matthew 7:22). Even supernatural deeds cannot substitute for trust in the Savior for eternal salvation.

A similar exercise is engaged in when the term "follow" (ἀκολουθέω) is equated with "believe" (πιστεύω) and then the meaning of the latter is expanded by incorporating meanings such as obedience that can be present in the semantic range of the former. In many churches today it is in vogue to include producing "fully devoted followers of Christ" in their vision statement. Usually what is meant is that individuals are obedient to Christ's commands. There is nothing wrong with that goal. Tragically, however, some churches have replaced "believing" (πιστεύω) with "following" (ἀκολουθέω). The frustration of trying to get unbelievers to follow Christ's commands is understandable. Transformation cannot be expected of those who have not put their trust in Jesus alone for eternal life and undergone a new birth experience. There will be followers who are not in God's family. Tragically, many who think that they are God's children because of their behavior, will find out to their eternal sorrow that they never were saved, not because their behavior did not match their belief, but because they never put their trust in Jesus and Him alone for their eternal salvation.

Driving through any city or town, one may see a sign saying, "Under New Management." The expectation is that things have changed, hopefully for the better. When the sign on an establishment says "Under New Ownership," it is understood that the new owners will change the management and the expectation is even higher that things will improve. Becoming a child of God is not about new management, but new ownership. Trying to act like a believer will never result in a spiritual new birth; only trusting in Jesus alone for one's eternal destiny will do so.

The Wiles of Works

Not all highways lead to heaven. Jesus said, "Enter ye in at the strait gate: for wide *is* the gate, and broad *is* the way, that leadeth to destruction, and many there be which go in thereat: because strait *is* the gate, and narrow *is* the way, which leadeth unto life, and few there be that find it" [italics in KJV] (Matthew 7:13-14). An infinite number of heretical interpretations of the gospel are possible, limited only by the ingenuity and imagination of man. But the broad path does not lead to biblical paradise. The scriptural requirement for eternal salvation is restrictive.

Many spiritually lost people are like a homeless person standing on a street corner holding a sign that says, "Willing to work for heaven." While euphemisms for "work" abound, the biblical parameters of the gospel allow no "wiggle room" for works. Nothing can be given in exchange for eternal life. If a payment of any kind is made, what is given is worthless for obtaining eternal salvation. And the payment cannot be hidden in the fine print, to be paid at a later date. The homeless person might promise, "I'll pay you back when I get back on my feet." However unlikely a repayment might be, anyone entering into such an arrangement has in fact effected a *quid pro quo* (Latin for an arrangement in which something is given or received for something else) transaction.

Those who articulate the gospel as a *quid pro quo* exchange, overtly or covertly, are rightfully under divine condemnation and the words of the apostle Paul apply personally to them when he said, "But though we, or an angel from heaven, preach any other gospel unto you than that which we have preached unto you, let him be accursed. As we said before, so say I now again, If any *man* preach any other gospel unto you than that ye have received, let him be accursed" [italics in KJV] (Galatians 1:8-9). Their pedigree notwithstanding their gospel is not to be promoted. The Greek third person imperative translated as a concession "let him be" (ἔστω) has the force of a command. Those who preach an aberrant gospel are to be condemned, not commended.

Paul's position on the gospel was no more popular in his day than it is today. Paul followed his statement of condemnation with the questions, "For do I now persuade men, or God?" (Galatians 1:10) The word translated "persuade" is the Greek verb πείθω that means "persuade" or "convince." Distorting the gospel is the same as attempting to convince God that His requirement for the acquisition of eternal life is mistaken. If Paul had altered the gospel, he may have gained man's approval, but he would have been subject to divine disapproval. Paul answered to God; he was not accountable to man. Paul said, "for if I yet pleased men, I should not be the servant of Christ" (Galatians 1:10). Paul recognized Christ's lordship and his submission to Christ precluded him (Paul) from proclaiming a gospel other than that of his master, the Lord Jesus Christ.

Perhaps for some who are homeless, offering to do something preserves a measure of dignity. They do not want to be the object of pity or the recipient of charity. But when it comes to salvation that mindset must be rejected. Hell-bound sinners, which we all were or are, have absolutely nothing to offer in order to be headed for heaven. Works cannot be finessed into the soteriological formula. There is no biblical way to nuance works into the requirement for the new birth.

The Person and the Provision

Christ who is revealed in Scripture cannot be compromised. If He is, He is not the one in whom trust is to be placed for eternal life. Jesus is no longer the Jesus of the Bible if He is added to, subtracted from, or replaced with anything or anyone else. Jesus said, "I and *my* Father are one" [italics in KJV] (John 10:30). The NASB says, "I and the Father are one" (ἐγὼ καὶ ὁ πατὴρ ἕν ἐσμεν). Theologians may argue over whether Jesus was claiming ontological equality with God the Father, but Jesus' contemporaries exhibited no such hesitation. And it was not the first time Jesus' words were taken as blasphemy. The apostle John recorded the Jewish response to Jesus' words. "Then the Jews took up stones again to stone him" (John 10:31). If the Savior identified in one's presentation of the gospel is not subject to the charge of blasphemy in relation to God the Father, He is not the Jesus revealed in Scripture. A Christ of one's own creation is not the one crucified for the sins of man.

The Old Testament revelation of God and trust in Him is presented in terms of exclusivity. Exclusivity extends to Jesus in the New Testament. The exclusion of works as a requirement for salvation flows from Jesus' unique identity. Nothing and no one is to be added to trust in the person of Jesus for eternal life. Jesus associated His person with His provision, saying, "I am the way, the truth, and the life: no man cometh unto the Father, but by me" (John 14:6). Because of Jesus' unique identity, trust in Him is the only instrumentality through which God the Father and eternal life can be accessed. Peter confidently asserted, "Neither is there salvation in any other: for there is none other name under heaven given among men, whereby we must be saved" (Acts 4:12).

The Christ of the gospel is identified with reference to His crucifixion. Paul told the Corinthians the basics in the words, "For I determined not to know any thing among you, save Jesus Christ, and him crucified" (1 Corinthians 2:2). The goal in evangelism is to present to people as much evidence for Jesus' identity as time and circumstances permit and invite them to put their trust in Him for their eternal destiny. God, in His sovereignty determines when an individual has put their trust in Jesus whom He has revealed. Knowing about the person of Christ and the means of His provision, one is able to put his or her trust in Him. The believer's mission is to proclaim to the lost the identity of Jesus who died in their place and invite the lost to trust in Him.

Evangelism and Evidence

The present writer recently sat on a jury in which we, the twelve jurors, unanimously acquitted the accused defendant. After the verdict was read, the judge dismissed the jury. The prosecutor sought me out and asked me, among other things, what had been the key evidence to our coming to our conclusion. The young prosecutor was not just driven by curiosity but wanted to learn from his losing experience. Perhaps in evangelism, one could learn from those who reject the claims of Christ. Learning about the value and relative weight placed on our testimony could be instructive.

Some Bible teachers may object that persuasive evangelism does violence to the sovereignty of God. Paul expressed no such qualms when he said, "Now then we are ambassadors for Christ, as though God did beseech *you* by us: we pray *you* in Christ's stead, be ye reconciled to God" [italics in KJV] (2 Corinthians 5:20). The NASB says, "Therefore, we are ambassadors for Christ, as though God were entreating through us; we beg you on behalf of Christ, be reconciled to God." Louw and Nida define the word translated "we beg" (δέομαι) "to ask for with urgency, with the implication of presumed need–'to plead, to beg'" (Johannes P. Louw and Eugene A. Nida, *Greek-English lexicon of the New Testament based on Semantic Domains*, 1:408). The writers of the New Testament saw themselves as witnesses who presented evidence. May we follow their example. The task of evangelism is to present evidence about the person of Jesus and His provision of salvation to the lost and to invite them, even implore them, to put their trust in Him.

Scripture Index

Genesis
1:28, *45*
2:16, *45*
2:17, *45*
3:8, *45*
3:15, *45, 46*
3:17, *46*
4:10, *46*
4:11, *46*
4:12, *46*
5:3-32, *47*
6:1-4, *46, 369*
6:6, *46*
6:7, *47*
6:9, *47*
9:8, *47*
9:9, *47*
9:10, *47*
11, *47*
11:31, *48*
12, *48*
12:1, *48*
12:3, *47, 67, 269, 273*
12:4, *48*
15, *268, 357*
15:6, *21, 47, 48, 49, 56, 267, 269, 270*
15:7, *49*
17, *357*
17:4, *295*
17:6, *295*
22, *357*
24:12, *50*
26:24, *50*
28:13, *50*
29:31, *146*
31:5, *50*
31:29, *50*
31:30, *50*
31:42, *50*
31:53, *48, 50*
32:9, *50*
32:28, *50*
33:20, *50*
43:23, *50*
45:26, *56*
46:1, *50*
46:3, *50*
49:24, *51, 69*
49:25, *51*
50:17, *51*

Exodus
3:6, *51*
3:13, *51*
3:14, *51, 87, 110, 186*
3:15, *51*
4:1, *56*
4:5, *56*
4:8, *56*
4:9, *56*
4:30, *56*
4:31, *56*
5:1, *51*
6:7, *55*
7:5, *55*
7:17, *55*
8:22, *55*
10:2, *55*
14:4, *55*
14:18, *55*
14:31, *21, 57*
16:12, *55*
19:9, *21, 57*
20:3, *52, 53*
20:4, *53*
20:5, *53*
20:14, *151*
20:16, *99*
23:32, *52*
24:10, *52*
29:46, *55*
31:13, *55*
33:20, *171, 188*

Leviticus
19:18, *146, 374*
24:16, *214*

Numbers
14:11, *21, 57*
20, *57*
20:12, *21, 57*
25:11, *53*

Deuteronomy
1, *55*
1:32, *21, 57*
5:7, *53*
6:13, *73*
6:14, *53*
6:16, *73, 124*
7:4, *53*
8:3, *72*
8:19, *53*

9:23, *57*
11:16, *53*
11:28, *53*
13:2, *53*
13:6, *53*
17:3, *53*
17:6, *68, 71, 192*
18:15-19, *226*
18:20, *53*
19:15, *91, 192*
28:14, *53*
28:36, *53*
28:52, *55*
28:64, *53*
28:66, *21, 57*
29:26, *53*
29:28, *53*
30:6, *39*
30:14, *39*
30:17, *53*
31:18, *53*
31:20, *53*
32:37, *54*

Joshua
2:9, *56*
7:13, *52*
7:19, *52*
7:20, *52*
8:30, *52*
9:18, *52*
9:19, *52*
10:40, *52*
10:42, *52*
13:14, *52*
13:33, *52*
14:14, *52*
22:16, *52*
22:24, *52*
23:13, *56*
23:16, *53*
24:2, *52, 53*
24:15, *345*
24:16, *53*

Judges
2:12, *53*
2:17, *53*
2:19, *53*
4:6, *52*
5:5, *52*
6:8, *52*
9:15, *54*
9:26, *54*

10:13, *53*
11:19, *58*
11:20, *58*
11:21, *52*
11:23, *52*
21:3, *52*

Ruth
2, *54*
2:12, *54*

1 Samuel
15:29, *14*
27:12, *21*

2 Samuel
1, *69*
5:2, *69*
7, *120*
7:19, *120*
22:3, *54*
22:31, *54*

1 Kings
10:6, *58*
10:7, *58*

2 Kings
17:14, *21, 58*
18:21, *55*

1 Chronicles
5:20, *55*
11:2, *69*

2 Chronicles
9:6, *58*
15:3, *53*
20:20, *21, 58*
32:13, *58—59*
32:15, *59*

Nehemiah
9:6, *53*

Job
1:1, *318*
1:12, *318*
2:6, *318*
4:17, *59*
4:18, *21, 59*
6:20, *55*
8:14, *55*
9:16, *59*

15, *59*
15:15, *21, 59*
15:22, *59*
15:31, *21, 59*
18:14, *55*
19:25, *55*
24:8, *54*
24:22, *21, 59*
29:21, *59*
29:24, *59*
31:24, *55*
39, *60*
39:10, *59*
39:11, *60*
39:12, *21, 60*
41:11, *274*

Psalms
2:2, *227*
2:6-7, *172*
2:12, *54*
5:11, *54*
6, *145*
6:8, *145*
7:1, *8, 54,*
80, 94, 336
8:2, *94*
8:4-6, *80*
8:6, *287*
11:1, *54*
13:5, *55*
14:6, *54*
16, *223, 240*
16:1, *54*
16:8, *223*
16:10, *216, 223*
17:7, *54*
18:2, *54*
18:30, *54*
19:1, *20*
21:23, *337*
22, *100, 337*
22:4, *55*
22:8, *100*
22:15, *215*
22:18, *215*
25:2, *55*
25:20, *54*
26:1, *55*
27:13, *60*
28:7, *55*
31:1, *54*
31:6, *55*
31:14, *55*
31:19, *54*
34:20, *215*
40:4, *55*

46:1, *54*
61:3, *54*
62:7, *54*
62:8, *54*
65:5, *55*
69:21, *215*
71:5, *55*
71:7, *54*
73:28, *54*
73:28, *54*
77:32, *21*
78:22, *21*
78:32, *60, 64*
91, *73*
91:2, *54*
91:9, *54*
94:22, *54*
104:18, *54*
106, *60*
106:12, *21, 60*
106:13, *60*
106:14, *60*
106:19, *61*
106:20, *61*
106:21, *61*
106:24, *61*
110, *159*
110:1, *95, 114,*
116
110:4, *339*
116, *61*
116:8, *288*
116:9, *288*
116:10, *61, 288*
116:12, *61*
116:13, *61*
118, *226*
118:22-23, *114*
118:22, *226*
118:26, *96, 113*
119:66, *21, 61*
119:81, *61*
119:101, *61*
135:14, *345*
142:5, *54*

Proverbs
14:15, *15, 61*
14:26, *54, 55*
14:32, *54*
20:25, *15*
21:22, *55*
22:19, *55*
25:19, *55*
26:24, *61*
26:25, *61*
30:4, *65*

30:5, *54*
31:11, *55*

Isaiah
4:6, *54*
6:9-10, *108*
6:9, *108*
6:9-10, *260*
6:10, *108*
7, *61*
7:2, *62*
7:4, *62*
7:6, *62*
7:7, *62, 64*
7:9, *62*
7:14, *61, 68*
8:17, *337*
8:18, *337*
9:1, *73*
9:1-2, *73*
9:6, *73*
11:1-2, *172*
14:32, *54*
25:4, *54*
26:25, *21*
28:15, *54, 62*
28:16, *62, 273,*
363
28:17, *54*
30:2, *54*
32:18, *55*
35:6, *83*
36:4, *55*
36:5, *55*
36:6, *55*
36:7, *55*
40:3, *71, 171*
40:6-8, *363*
40:13, *274*
41:4, *110, 186*
42:1-4, *85*
42:8, *406*
43, *62*
43:9, *63*
43:10, *63, 110*
43:12, *63*
43:13, *63*
43:15, *63*
45:23, *275*
49:8, *289*
49:18, *275*
51:12, *110*
52:6, *110*
52:15, *276*
53, *63*
53:1, *16, 63*
53:4-5, *79*

53:7-8, *232*
53:9, *216*
53:12, *160*
54:5, *63*
55:3, *240*
56:7, *94, 113*
57:13, *54*
58:11, *191*
61:1, *83, 124*

Jeremiah
2:37, *55*
4:28, *14*
7:11, *94, 113*
10:6, *54*
10:8, *54*
10:10, *54*
12:6, *21, 63*
17:7, *55*
17:17, *54*
18:8, *14*
18:10, *14*
31:15, *70*
39:18, *55*
40, *63*
40:14, *63*
40:16, *63*
48:13, *55*

Lamentations
4:12, *64*

Ezekiel
29:16, *55*

Daniel
7:10, *399*
7:13-14, *80*
7:13, *116*

Hosea
6:1, *81*
6:6, *81, 84*
11:1, *70*

Joel
2:13, *14*
2:14, *14*
2:31, *41*
2:32, *41*
3:16, *54*

Amos
7:3, *14*
7:6, *14*
9:11-12, *244*

Author Index